MASTERPIECES OF RELIGIOUS VERSE

✠

MASTERPIECES OF RELIGIOUS VERSE

EDITED BY

JAMES DALTON MORRISON

HARPER & ROW, PUBLISHERS
NEW YORK AND EVANSTON

Acknowledgment is made to the following, who have granted permission for the reprinting of copyrighted material (see also pp. 699-701):
ABINGDON-COKESBURY PRESS for "Christmas Prayer," "I Will Not Hurry" from *I Have A Stewardship* by Ralph S. Cushman, copyright, 1939, by Abingdon-Cokesbury Press; "The Secret" from *Spiritual Hilltops* by Ralph S. Cushman, copyright, 1932, by Abingdon-Cokesbury Press; "The Parson's Prayer" from *Practicing the Presence* by Ralph S. Cushman, copyright, 1936, by Abingdon-Cokesbury Press; "The Agony of God," "Swinging toward the Light" from *The Glory of God* by Georgia Harkness, copyright, 1943, by Abingdon-Cokesbury Press; "The Understanding Heart" from *Be Still and Know* by Georgia Harkness, copyright, 1953, by Pierce & Washabaugh; "Only a Flower," "Penniless," "Day's End," "Sculptor of the Soul," "The Burden" from *Songs from the Slums* by Toyohiko Kagawa, copyright, 1935, by Abingdon-Cokesbury Press; "The Challenge" from *Poems for the Great Days* by Thomas Curtis Clark, copyright, 1948, by Stone & Pierce. Used by permission of the publisher, Abingdon-Cokesbury Press.
ASSOCIATION PRESS for "A Prayer for Peace" from *The Quiet Hour* by William Adams Brown, copyright, 1926, by Association Press; "O God Of Light," "Prayer at Eventide" by R. B. Y. Scott.
THOMAS ALLEN, LTD. for "In Flanders Now" from *Beside Still Waters* by Edna Jaques, copyright, 1939, by Thomas Allen, Ltd.
WALTER H. BAKER CO. for "The Christ of the World's Highway," "God's Way" by Dorothy Clarke Wilson from *Twelve Months of Drama* by Dorothy Clarke Wilson, copyright, 1933, by Walter H. Baker Co.
A. S. BARNES & COMPANY, INC. for "Ecce Homo" by John Ackerson from *Reveille*, copyright, 1943, by A. S. Barnes & Company, Inc.
THE BEACON PRESS for "O Beautiful My Country!" by Frederick Lucian from *Hymns of the Spirit;* "All Beautiful the March of Days" by Frances Whitemarsh Wile from *Hymns of the Spirit;* "Almighty Builder; Bless We Pray" by Edward A. Church from *Hymn and Tune Book;* "O Lord of Life, Thy Kingdom Is at Hand" by Marion Franklin Ham from *Hymns of the Spirit* and *Songs of Faith and Hope.*
THE BOBBS-MERRILL COMPANY for "Childhood," "The Shepherd Speaks" from *Collected Poems 1907-1922* by John Erskine, copyright, 1922, 1934, used by special permission of the publisher and author; selections by James Whitcomb Riley from *Complete Works of James Whitcomb Riley*, published by Bobbs-Merrill Company.
BOOSEY AND HAWKES INC. for excerpt from "Lincoln Portrait" by Aaron Copland, copyright, 1943, in U.S.A. by Hawkes and Son, Inc., London, Ltd.
BRANDT & BRANDT for "To Jesus on His Birthday" from *The Buck in the Snow & Other Poems* by Edna St. Vincent Millay, published by Harper & Brothers, copyright, 1928, by Edna St. Vincent Millay; selection from "Renascence" from *Renascence and Other Poems* by Edna St. Vincent Millay, published by Harper & Brothers, copyright, 1912, 1940, by Edna St. Vincent Millay.
BRETHREN PUBLISHING HOUSE for "The Greater Glory" from *The Touch of the Master's Hand* by Myra Brooks Welch.
BURNS, OATES & WASHBOURNE, LTD., for "Lo, I Am with You Always," "Onward and Upward," "Seeking and Finding God" by John Charles Earle; "The Newer Vainglory," "Via, Et Veritas, Et Vita," "Mother," "I Am the Way," "A Song of Derivations" by Alice Meynell; for selections by Francis Thompson (selections of Alice Meynell and Francis Thompson also by permission of Mr. Wilfred Meynell executor).
CHATTO & WINDUS for "Anthem for Doomed Youth" by Wilfred Owen.
CHRISTY & MOORE, LTD. for selection from "The Gate of the Year" by M. Louise Haskins.
THE CLARENDON PRESS for selections from *The Testament of Beauty* by Robert Bridges; "At Eventide" from *The Yattendon Hymnal* edited by Robert Bridges and H. Ellis Woolridge; "Thanksgiving Day" by Robert Bridges.
CLARK & STUART CO. LTD. for "Crucifixion," "Dawn," and selection from "Ad Majorem Dei Gloriam" by Frederick George Scott.
W. B. CONKEY COMPANY for "Love Thyself Last," "Leaners or Lifters," "A Morning Prayer" from *Poems of Power* by Ella Wheeler Wilcox; "The Beyond," "The Goal," "Faith," "Gethsemane," "The Winds of Fate" by Ella Wheeler Wilcox.
COWARD-MCCANN INC. for selection from "The White Cliffs" by Alice Duer Miller, copyright, 1940, by Alice Duer Miller.
CURTIS BROWN LTD. for "A Prayer" from *Poems 1902-1919* by John Drinkwater, copyright, 1919, by John Drinkwater, published by Houghton Mifflin Company; "To and Fro about the City" from *Seeds of Time* by John Drinkwater, copyright, 1922, by John Drinkwater, published by Houghton Mifflin Company. Reprinted by permission of the author's estate.
D. APPLETON-CENTURY COMPANY, INC. for "Create Great Peace" from *War and Laughter* by James Oppenheim.
THE JOHN DAY COMPANY for "Prologue to Morning," "Starry Night" from *Combat at Midnight* by Hermann Hagedorn.
PURD E. DEITZ for "We Would Be Building," copyright, 1936, by Purd E. Deitz.
DODD, MEAD & COMPANY INC. Reprinted by permission of Dodd, Mead & Company, Inc. "Daisies," "Hem and Haw," "Lord of the Far Horizons," "Veni Creator," "Vestigia," "Where Is Heaven" from *Bliss Carman Poems* (also permission McClelland & Stewart Ltd., Toronto, Canada); "A Hymn," "A Warrior's Prayer," "He Had His Dream," "The Debt," "Conscience and Remorse," "When All Is Done," "The Master Player" from *The Complete Poems of Paul Laurence Dunbar;* "Communion," "Evolution," "Holy Saturday," "Out of Bounds," "The Light of Bethlehem," "The Sisters" from *The Poetry of Father Tabb;* "The House of Christmas" from *Collected Poems of G. K. Chesterton;* "For a Materialist" from *The Slender Singing Tree* by Adelaide Love, copyright, 1933, by Adelaide Love; "Soldier, What Did You See," "A Journey Ends" from

Pilot Bails Out by Don Blanding, copyright, 1943, by Don Blanding; "Carry On" from *The Complete Poems of Robert Service*, copyright, 1916, 1944, by Robert Service (also permission of the Ryerson Press, Toronto, Canada); "The Second Crucifixion," "War," by Richard Le Gallienne (also permission of The Society of Authors, London, Literary Representative of the Estate of the late Richard Le Gallienne).
Dorrance and Company for "Intolerance" from *Heritage and Other Poems* by Molly Anderson Haley.
Doubleday & Company, Inc. for "Trees," "Memorial Day" from *Trees and Other Poems* by Joyce Kilmer, copyright, 1914, by Doubleday & Company, Inc.; "The Peacemaker" from *Poems, Essays and Letters* by Joyce Kilmer, copyright, 1914, 1917, 1918, by Doubleday & Company, Inc.; "Thanksgiving" from *Main Street and Other Poems* by Joyce Kilmer, copyright 1917, by Doubleday & Company, Inc.; selection from "The God-Maker, Man," "Unrest," "The Wages" from *Dreams and Dust* by Don Marquis, copyright, 1915, by Don Marquis; "Mother O'Mine" from *The Light That Failed* by Rudyard Kipling, copyright, 1897, 1899, 1903, by Rudyard Kipling; "If" from *Rewards and Fairies* by Rudyard Kipling, copyright 1910 by Rudyard Kipling; "L'Envoi" from *The Seven Seas* by Rudyard Kipling, copyright, 1892, 1893, 1894, 1896, 1905, 1933, by Rudyard Kipling; "A Dedication" from *Life's Handicap* by Rudyard Kipling, copyright, 1891, 1918, by Rudyard Kipling; "Recessional" from *The Five Nations* by Rudyard Kipling, copyright, 1903, 1931, by Rudyard Kipling; "Ballad of East and West" from *Departmental Ditties and Barrack-Room Ballads* by Rudyard Kipling, copyright, 1892, 1893, 1899, 1927, by Rudyard Kipling; "The Children's Song" from *Puck of Pook's Hill* by Rudyard Kipling, copyright, 1905, 1906, by Rudyard Kipling. The selections by Rudyard Kipling are reprinted by permission also of Mr. Kipling's daughter, Mrs. George Bambridge, and the Macmillan Company of Canada Ltd. Arrangements made through A. P. Watt and Son Ltd., authorized representatives.
E. P. Dutton & Co., Inc. for "That Holy Thing," "Obedience," "Lost and Found" from *Poems* by George Macdonald; "Creeds" from *Lanterns In Gethsemane* by Willard Wattles, copyright, 1918, by E. P. Dutton & Co., Inc.; "America the Beautiful" from *Poems* by Katharine Lee Bates; "Broken Bodies" from *Prophet and Fool* by Louis Golding, copyright, 1923, by E. P. Dutton & Co., Inc.; "The Spires of Oxford" from *The Spires of Oxford* by Winifred Letts, copyright, 1917, by E. P. Dutton & Co., Inc., renewed, 1945; "Hills," "House Blessing," "Education," "In the Hospital" from *Death and General Putnam and 101 Other Poems* by Arthur Guiterman, copyright, 1935, by E. P. Dutton & Co., Inc.; "Theophanies," "Immanence" by Evelyn Underhill, published in the United States by E. P. Dutton & Co., Inc.; "The Donkey," selection from "The Wild Knight," "A Christmas Carol" from *The Wild Knight and Other Poems* by Gilbert K. Chesterton, published in the United States by E. P. Dutton & Co., Inc., published in England by J. M. Dent & Co. Ltd.; selection from *The Church and the Hour* by Vida D. Scudder, copyright, 1917, 1945, by E. P. Dutton & Co., Inc.
The Epworth Press for "The Cup of Happiness" by Gilbert Thomas.
Evangelical Publishers for "Christ and We," "What God Hath Promised" by Annie Johnson Flint.
Farrar, Straus and Company, Inc. for "Easter Eve" by James Branch Cabell, copyright, 1916, 1943, by James Branch Cabell.
A. Flanagan Company for "A Christmas Song" by Florence Evelyn Dratt from *The Golden Christmas Book*.
The Fortune Press for "Poem for Combatants" by Alan White from *Poets in Battledress*.
Forward and the author for "Progression" by Inez Clark Thorson. Reprinted from *Forward*. Published and copyright, 1947, W. L. Jenkins.
Ethel Romig Fuller for "Proof" from *Kitchen Sonnets*, copyright, 1931, by Ethel Romig Fuller.
Funk and Wagnalls Company for "Life and Death" from *Swords and Plowshares* by Ernest Crosby.
Garden City Publishing Co. for "Prayer of an Unemployed Man" by W. C. Ackerly, "Together" by Ludwig Lewisohn from *Poems That Touch the Heart* compiled by A. L. Alexander, copyright, 1941, by Garden City Publishing Co.
The Gift Loft for "Overheard in an Orchard" by Elizabeth Cheney (also permission of Mrs. Elizabeth Cheney).
The H. W. Gray Company, Inc. for "How Burn the Stars Unchanging" by John J. Moment.
Harcourt, Brace and Company, Inc. for "Prayer," "Caliban in the Coal Mines" from *Challenge* by Louis Untermeyer, copyright, 1914, by Harcourt, Brace and Company, Inc.; "Prayer for This House" by Louis Untermeyer from *This Singing World*, edited by Louis Untermeyer, copyright, 1923, by Harcourt, Brace and Company, Inc.; "The Factories," "Search," "The Watcher" from *Collected Poems of Margaret Widdemer*, copyright, 1928, by Harcourt, Brace and Company, Inc.; selection from "Ode—Written during the Battle of Dunkirk" from *A World within a War* by Herbert Read, copyright, 1945, by Harcourt, Brace and Company, Inc. (also permission of Faber and Faber, Ltd.); "When the Church Is No Longer Regarded," "Men Who Turn from God," "Knowledge without Wisdom" from *The Rock* by T. S. Eliot, copyright, 1934, by Harcourt, Brace and Company, Inc.; "There Shall Always Be the Church" by T. S. Eliot; "A Song for Simeon" from *Collected Poems 1909-1935* by T. S. Eliot, copyright, 1934, 1936, by Harcourt, Brace and Company, Inc. (also permission of Faber and Faber Ltd.); "From the People, Yes," "The Best Preacher Is the Heart" from *The People, Yes*, by Carl Sandburg, copyright, 1936, by Harcourt, Brace and Company, Inc.
Harper & Brothers for "So Long As There Are Homes" from *Light of the Years* by Grace Noll Crowell, Copyright, 1936, by Harper & Brothers; selection from "Tibetan Comforter" from *Tibetan Voices* by Robert K. Ekvall, copyright, 1946, by Robert K. Ekvall; "We Met Them on the Common Way" by Elizabeth C. Cardozo; "I Thank Thee, Lord, for Strength of Arms" by Robert Davis; "God of the Nations" by W. Russell Bowie from *Social Hymns of Brotherhood and Aspiration* edited by Mabel Hay Barrows Mussey, copyright, 1914, 1942, by Harper & Brothers; "The Holy City" by W. Russell Bowie, "The Master's Man" by William G. Tarrant from *Hymns of the Kingdom of God*, copyright, 1916, 1923, by Harper & Brothers; "And with No Language but a Cry," "Alive for Evermore," "Thanksgiving," "To Pulpit and Tribune" from *The Healing of the Waters* by Amos Niven Wilder, copyright, 1943, by Harper & Brothers; "Litany of the Dark People" from *Copper Sun* by Countee Cullen, copyright, 1927 by Harper & Brothers; "Simon the Cyrenian Speaks," "For a Lady I Know," "I Have a Rendezvous with Life," from *Color* by Countee Cullen, copyright, 1925, by Harper & Brothers; "The Greatness of Love" from *The New Testament, A New Translation* by James Moffatt; Psalm 62: 1–8 from *The Old Testament, A New Translation* by James Moffatt; "Miracles" from *Come Back To Earth* by Roy Helton, copyright, 1946, by Roy Helton; "Civitas Dei" from *In This Our Day* by Edith Lovejoy Pierce, copyright, 1944, by Harper & Brothers; "O Christ Thou Art within Me Like a Sea" from *Therefore Choose Life* by Edith Lovejoy Pierce, copyright, 1947, by Harper & Brothers; "Incarnation" by Edith Lovejoy Pierce; "Barabbas Speaks," "Casualty," "Eternal God Whose Searching Eye Doth Scan,"

"Palm Sunday and Monday," "The Jericho Road," "Faith" from *Over the Sea, the Sky* by Edwin McNeill Poteat, copyright, 1945, by Harper & Brothers; "If My Bark Sink," "One Crown Not Any Seek," "I Thought That Nature Was Enough" by Emily Dickinson from *Bolts of Melody, New Poems of Emily Dickinson* edited by Mabel Loomis Todd and Millicent Todd Bingham, copyright, 1945, by Millicent Todd Bingham; "The Sin of Omission" from *On the Road Home* by Margaret Sangster; "My Peace I Give unto You," "Indifference," "Faith," "Peace and Joy," "The Suffering God" from *The Sorrows of God* by G. A. Studdert-Kennedy, copyright, 1924, by Harper & Brothers; "Gambler," "The Christian Soldier," "The Rose," "When Through the Whirl of Wheels," by G. A. Studdert-Kennedy; "We Shall Build On" by G. A. Studdert-Kennedy from *Quotable Poems*, Volume II, copyright, 1928, by Harper & Brothers; "Thy Will Be Done" from *The Wicket Gate* by G. A. Studdert-Kennedy; "The Kingdom," "To Poets All," "In an Age of Science" from *Home Roads and Far Horizons* by Thomas Curtis Clark, copyright, 1936, by Harper & Brothers; "The Journey" from *Poems for Life* by Thomas Curtis Clark, copyright, 1942, by Harper & Brothers; "Evidence" from *Master of Men* by Thomas Curtis Clark, copyright, 1930, by Harper & Brothers; for "Apparitions" by Thomas Curtis Clark from *Quotable Poems*, Volume I, copyright, 1928, by Harper & Brothers.

HENRY HARRISON, POETRY PUBLISHER for "December the Twenty-fourth," "Bigot," "Cradle Carol," "A Ballad of Wonder" from *Why Hold the Hound?* by Eleanor Slater, copyright, 1941, by Henry Harrison, Poetry Publisher.

GEORGE G. HARRAP & CO., LTD., London and Lady Watson for "The Church Today" and "At a Burial" from *The Poems of Sir William Watson 1878-1935*.

WILLIAM HEINEMANN, LTD. for "The Soul's Prayer" by Sarojini Naidu; "The Peace Giver," and selection from "Super Flumina Babylonis" by A. C. Swinburne; "Pax" by D. H. Lawrence (also permission of Mrs. Frieda Lawrence).

HENRY HOLT AND COMPANY, INC. for "The Listeners" from *Collected Poems* by Walter de la Mare, copyright, 1941, by Walter de la Mare; "Mending Wall" from *Mending Wall* by Robert Frost, "Home" from *The Death of the Hired Man* by Robert Frost, included in *Collected Poems of Robert Frost*, copyright, 1930, 1939, by Henry Holt and Company, Inc., copyright, 1936, by Robert Frost; "Grass" from *Cornhuskers* by Carl Sandburg, copyright, 1918, by Henry Holt and Company, Inc., copyright, 1945, by Carl Sandburg; "Wind in the Pine," "Requiem for a Modern Croesus," "God Is at the Anvil," "Hang Me among Your Winds" from *The Collected Poems of Lew Sarett*, copyright 1941 by Henry Holt and Company, Inc.; "Refuge" from *Many, Many Moons* by Lew Sarett, copyright, 1920, by Henry Holt and Company, Inc.; "After Sunset" from *Wilderness Songs* by Grace Hazard Conkling, copyright, 1920, by Henry Holt and Company, Inc.; "Yonder See the Morning Blink" from *Last Poems* by A. E. Housman, copyright, 1922, by Henry Holt and Company, Inc.; "A Prayer in Spring" from *Collected Poems of Robert Frost*, copyright, 1930, 1939, by Henry Holt and Company, Inc., copyright, 1936, by Robert Frost.

HOPE PUBLISHING COMPANY for "Thy Will be Done in Me," "Blind but Happy" from *Bells at Evening* by Fanny Crosby, copyright, 1897, 1898, by Hope Publishing Company.

HOUGHTON MIFFLIN COMPANY for "Still, Still with Thee" by Harriet Beecher Stowe; "Io Victus" by William Wetmore Story; "Heroism" from *A Handful of Lavender* by Lizette Woodworth Reese; selection from the play *Abraham Lincoln* by John Drinkwater; "The Butterfly," "Communion Hymn," "On a Gloomy Easter" by Alice Freeman Palmer; selection from "The Monk in the Kitchen," "An Unbeliever" by Anne Hempstead Branch; "The Undiscovered Country," "Faith" by William Dean Howells; "The Lamp of Life" from *A Dome of Many Colored Glass* by Amy Lowell, copyright, 1912, by Houghton Mifflin Company; "The Fool's Prayer," "Opportunity," "Life" by Edward Roland Sill; "Lines for an Interment" by Archibald MacLeish; "Work" by Abbie Farwell Brown; "The Two Ships" from *Bret Harte's Complete Poetical Works*, copyright, 1902, by Houghton Mifflin Company; "Our Christ," selection from "A Strip of Blue" from *The Poetical Works of Lucy Larcom;* "The Quest," "Thou Life within My Life" by Eliza Scudder.

THE HYMN SOCIETY OF AMERICA for "God of a Universe Within Whose Bounds" by Katharine L. Aller, copyright, 1945, by The Hymn Society of America; "Come, Thou My Light," by Hugh Thomson Kerr.

JONATHAN CAPE LTD. for extracts from *The Collected Poems* by Laurence Housman and *Little Plays of St. Francis* (also permission of Mr. Housman, and Sidgwick & Jackson Ltd.); "Christ the Man," "The Little Ones" from *The Collected Poems of W. H. Davies* (also permission of Mrs. W. H. Davies); selection from "Nicodemus" by Andrew Young.

KALEIDOGRAPH PRESS for "Prayer for Strength," "Christmas Eve Meditation" from *Be Slow to Falter* by Margaret E. Bruner; "Selfishness" from *The Hill Road* by Margaret E. Bruner; "Atonement" from *In Thoughtful Mood* by Margaret E. Bruner (also permission of Margaret E. Bruner).

PATRICK F. KIRBY for "Sequel to Finality" from *Poet on Mule*, copyright, 1940, by Patrick F. Kirby.

ALFRED A. KNOPF, INC. for "Warning" from *This, My Letter* by Sara Henderson Hay, copyright, 1939, by Alfred A. Knopf, Inc.; "Christmas Eve" from *Poems for Music* by Robert Hillyer, copyright, 1947, by Robert Hillyer; "Thermopylae and Golgotha," "Christmas Pastoral" from *Collected Verse of Robert Hillyer*, copyright, 1933, by Robert Hillyer; "The House," "Christ Child," "Love Song," "War Poem" from *Collected Poems of Henry Treece*, copyright, 1946, by Henry Treece; "On Giving" from *The Prophet* by Kahlil Gibran, copyright, 1923, by Alfred A. Knopf, Inc.; "Why" from *Verse* by Adelaide Crapsey, copyright, 1922, by Algernon S. Crapsey; "Overtone," "Farmers" from *Collected Poems of William Alexander Percy*, copyright, 1920, 1943, by LeRoy Pratt Percy; selection from "Arraignment" from *Day of Deliverence* by William Rose Benét, copyright, 1944, by Alfred A. Knopf, Inc.; "To an Enemy" from *Collected Poems* by Edward J. Pratt, copyright, 1945, by Edward J. Pratt; "Epistle," "There Are Four Doors Which Open on the Skies," "Now from the World the Light of God Is Gone" from *A Winter Tide* by Robert Nathan, copyright, 1940, by Robert Nathan.

LADIES' HOME JOURNAL and the poets indicated for "The Dead" by R. J. Crot, copyright, 1947, by The Curtis Publishing Company; "He Is Risen" by Joseph Auslander.

EDWARD D. LANDELS for "Pilate Remembers," "Immanence," and selection from "At Eighty-three" from *Things New and Old* by Thomas Durley Landels, copyright, 1946, by Edward D. Landels.

JOHN LANE THE BODLEY HEAD LTD. for "John The Pilgrim" from *The Coming of Love* by Theodore Watts-Dunton; "Marching Song" from *Letters from Prison* by Ernst Toller; "In Whom We Live and Have Our Being" from *Out of the Silence* by James Rhoades.

J. B. LIPPINCOTT COMPANY for selection from "Watchers of the Sky" from *Collected Poems in One Volume* by Alfred Noyes, copyright, 1922, by J. B. Lippincott Company; "The Dawn of Peace," "The Diplomats" from "The Winepress" in *Collected Poems in One Volume*, copyright, 1913, 1941, by Alfred Noyes:

selection from "The Loom of the Years" from *Collected Poems, Volume I* by Alfred Noyes, copyright, 1906, 1934, by Alfred Noyes; selection from "The Pact" from *Collected Poems in One Volume* by Alfred Noyes, copyright, 1941, by Alfred Noyes; "Memorial Day" from *For Days and Days* by Annette Wynne, copyright, 1919, by J. B. Lippincott Company; "The Power-House" by Christopher Morley.

LITTLE, BROWN & COMPANY for "Dost Thou Remember Me" by Emily Dickinson from *Poems of Emily Dickinson* edited by Martha Dickinson Bianchi and Alfred L. Hampson; for "Yes and No" from *I'm a Stranger Here Myself* by Ogden Nash, copyright, 1936, by Ogden Nash; selection from "Heil, Heilige Nacht!" from *Good Intentions* by Ogden Nash, copyright, 1942, by Ogden Nash.

LONGMANS, GREEN AND COMPANY, INC. for "Crucifixion," "The Quest," "Form," "The Cross" by Eva Gore-Booth (also permission of the executors of Eva Gore-Booth).

LOTHROP, LEE AND SHEPARD CO. for "The House By the Side of the Road," "Two Gods" from *Songs of the Average Man* by Sam Walter Foss, copyright, 1897, by Lothrop, Lee and Shepard Co.; "From the Coming American" from *Whiffs from Wild Meadows* by Sam Walter Foss; "Factory Children" by Richard Burton; "Strength in Weakness" from *Message and Melody* by Richard Burton; "The Larger Prayer" by Edna D. Cheney.

WILSON MACDONALD for "Nineteen Twenty-six," "The Masked Ball," selection from "The Last Portage" from *Out of the Wilderness*, 1926, copyright by the author; "The Battle of Peace," copyright, 1947, by Kappa Delta Pi, Heidelberg College, Tiffin, Ohio.

THE MACMILLAN COMPANY for "For the Fallen," "Woe to Him," "Little Hands" from *Collected Poems of Laurence Binyon;* selections from *The Modern Reader's Bible* translated by Moulton, copyright, 1895, by The Macmillan Company; "When You Are Old" from *Collected Poems* by W. B. Yeats (also permission of A. P. Watt & Son, and Mrs. W. B. Yeats); "Back," "The Conscript" from *Collected Poems* by Wilfrid Wilson Gibson; "The Unpardonable Sin," "The Leaden-Eyed," "Abraham Lincoln Walks at Midnight," "Foreign Missions," "General Booth Enters Heaven" by Vachel Lindsay; "The Word," "The Seekers," selection from "The Everlasting Mercy" from *Poems* by John Masefield; "The Man of Science Speaks" from *Chosen Poems* by Harriet Monroe; "Oversoul" from *Collected Poems* by AE (George W. Russell); "The Paradox" from *Trophy of Arms* by Ruth Pitter; "The Mystery" from *Poems* by Ralph Hodgson, copyright, 1917, by The Macmillan Company; "The Old Enemy" from *Collected Poems* by Sara Teasdale, copyright, 1907, 1911, by Sara Teasdale, 1930 by Sara Teasdale Filsinger, 1915, 1917, 1920, 1922, 1926, 1933, 1937, by The Macmillan Company; "Again the Story Is Told" from *Against the Sky* by Ada Jackson, copyright, 1940, by Ada Jackson; "The Ass Speaks" from *Collected Poems* by Katharine Tynan Hinkson; "L'Envoi," "Let Me Live Out My Years" from *Collected Poems* by John Neihardt; "A Prayer" from *Sonnets* by Mary Dixon Thayer, copyright, 1933, by The Macmillan Company; "A Christmas Sonnet" from *Collected Poems* by Edward Arlington Robinson; "Prayer for Strength" from *Gitanjali* by Rabindranath Tagore; selection from "Gitanjali," "Prayer for Courage" from *Fruit Gathering* by Rabindranath Tagore; selection from "The Oarsmen" by Rabindranath Tagore; "Resurrection" by John Gilland Brunini; "Country Church" from *Strange Holiness* by Robert P. T. Coffin, copyright, 1935, by The Macmillan Company; "The Impercipient" from *Wessex Poems* by Thomas Hardy, copyright, 1898, by Harper & Brothers, 1926 by Thomas Hardy; "The Oxen" from *Collected Poems* by Thomas Hardy, copyright, 1925, by The Macmillan Company.

THE MASTER LIBRARY COMPANY for "The Boat" by George Macdonald from *The Master Library, Volume III*, copyright, 1927, by The Master Library Company, formerly The Foundation Press.

HAROLD MATSON for "Come Live with Me and Be My Love" by Cecil Day Lewis.

M. C. A. MANAGEMENT, LTD. for "Easter Hymn" by A. E. Housman (also permission of The Estate of A. E. Housman).

MCCLELLAND AND STEWART for "Legacies," "My Orders" by Ethelwyn Wetherald; "Altars," "The Songs We Need," "Ici Repose" from *A Canadian Twilight and Other Poems* by Bernard Freeman Trotter, "The Soldier," "Peace" from *Complete Poems*, by Rupert Brooke.

DAVID MCKAY COMPANY for selections from *Leaves of Grass* by Walt Whitman, copyright, 1900, by David McKay Company.

MEIGS PUBLISHING COMPANY for "Others" by Charles D. Meigs, copyright, 1907, by Meigs Publishing Company.

METHODIST PUBLISHING HOUSE, LONDON for "Wise Men Seeking Jesus" by James T. East.

JUANITA JOAQUINA MILLER for "For Those Who Fail," "Christmas Morning," "Byron," "The Greatest Battle That Ever Was Fought" by Joaquin Miller, copyright, 1936, by Juanita Joaquina Miller.

THE MODERN PRINTING COMPANY for "Easter Must Be Reclaimed" by George W. Wiseman.

MORAY PRESS for "Christmas Night" from *Feast of Candlemas* by Marion Lochhead (also permission of Marion Lochhead).

BELLE C. MORRILL for selections from *The Blue Platter*, copyright, 1945, by Belle C. Morrill.

A. R. MOWBRAY AND COMPANY, LTD. for "I Took Love to Task" from *Love's Argument* by Father Andrew; "O Love That Maketh Heavy Burdens Light" from *The Birth Mystical* by Father Andrew.

THE MUSSON BOOK COMPANY for "Brier" from *Flint and Feather*, The Complete Poems of E. Pauline Johnson, published and copyrighted by The Musson Book Company, Ltd., Toronto, Canada.

NEW DIRECTIONS for "Put out My Eyes and I Can See You Still," "You Are the Future" from *Poems from the Book of Hours* by Rainer Maria Rilke, translated by Babette Deutsch, copyright, 1941, by New Directions.

NOVELLO AND COMPANY, LTD., LONDON for "Hush All Ye Sounds of War" by William Draper.

OXFORD UNIVERSITY PRESS for "O Son of Man, Our Hero Strong and Tender" by Frank Fletcher from *Enlarged Songs of Praise* (also permission of Sir Frank Fletcher); "Servants of the Great Adventure" by Percy Dearmer from *Enlarged Songs of Praise* (also permission of Percy Dearmer); selection from "In After Days" by Austin Dobson; "O God of Earth and Altar" by Gilbert K. Chesterton from *Revised Church Hymnary;* "O Love That Triumphs over Loss" by W. Russell Bowie from *The Hymnal.*

THE PILGRIM PRESS for "The Ways" from *Gentlemen The King!* by John Oxenham; "The Greatest" by Marion Brown Shelton; "The Patient Scientists" by Bertha Gerneaux Woods from *The Congregationalist;* "O Master-Workman of the Race" by J. T. Stocking.

MRS. HAROLD T. PULSIFER for "Immortal Living" from *First Symphony*, copyright, 1935, by Harold T. Pulsifer; "The Riderless Horse" by Harold Pulsifer.

G. P. PUTNAM'S SONS for "Courage" by Amelia Earhart.

RANDOM HOUSE, INC. for "Munitions Expert," "Truth," "He Is the Way" by W. H. Auden, copyright, 1945, by W. H. Auden; "I Think Continually of Those" by Stephen Spender, copyright, 1934, by Modern Library Inc.; "Ultima Ratio Regum" by Stephen Spender, copyright, 1942, by Stephen Spender;

'Weapons of Evil" by Lin Yutang, copyright, 1942, by Random House, Inc.; "The Excesses of God" from *Be Angry at the Sun* by Robinson Jeffers, copyright, 1941, by Robinson Jeffers.

THE REILLY & LEE CO. for "The Kindly Neighbor" from *All That Matters* by Edgar A. Guest, copyright, 1922, by The Reilly & Lee Co.; "When Life Is Done," "My Creed," "My Bible," "Prayer for the Home," "Sermons We See," "Myself" from *Collected Verse of Edgar A. Guest*, copyright, 1934, by The Reilly & Lee Co.

FLEMING H. REVELL COMPANY for "Now, Lord, upon Thy Sea of Air" by Mary Louise Anderson from *The New Church Hymnal*, copyright, 1937, by Fleming H. Revell Company; "Voyagers" by Henry van Dyke, copyright, 1922, by Fleming H. Revell Company.

RHODEHEAVER–HALL–MACK for "Judean Hills," "I Saw God Wash the World" from *I Saw God Wash the World* by William L. Stidger (also permission of William L. Stidger).

THE RICHARDS PRESS, LTD. for "The Question" by Rachel Annand Taylor.

RINEHART AND COMPANY INC. for "Vigil" from *Sign Posts* by Faith Baldwin, copyright, 1924, by Rinehart and Company Inc., (reprinted by permission of author and publisher); "Tears," "Heroism" from *The Selected Poems of Lizette Woodworth Reese*, copyright, 1926, by Lizette Woodworth Reese; "Sometimes," "The Cathedral" from *Shadow of the Perfect Rose* by Thomas S. Jones, Jr., copyright, 1937, by John L. Foley; "Advent" from *Selected Poems* by John Gould Fletcher, copyright, 1938, by John Gould Fletcher, (reprinted by permission of author and publisher).

E. MERRILL ROOT for "Still the Cross" from *Lost Eden*, copyright, 1928, by E. Merrill Root, published by The Unicorn Press.

ROUTLEDGE AND KEGAN PAUL, LTD. for "God within Yet Above," "A Heathen Hymn" by Sir Lewis Morris.

THE RYERSON PRESS for "There Is a Beauty" from *Selected Poems of Archibald Lampman;* "Peccavi, Domine" from *Lampman's Poems;* "The Aim" from *The Collected Poems of Sir Charles G. D. Roberts;* "April" from *Reward and Other Poems* by Isobel McFadden; "In Flanders Fields" by John McCrae.

SATURDAY EVENING POST and the poets indicated for "Golden Wedding" by William W. Pratt, copyright, 1945, by Saturday Evening Post; "Stranger at the Peace Table" by Esther Baldwin York.

CHARLES SCRIBNER'S SONS for selection from "Be Strong," "No Distant Lord," "School Days" by Maltbie D. Babcock; "Give Us This Day Our Daily Bread," "Death," "This Is My Father's World" from *Thoughts for Everyday Living* by Maltbie D. Babcock, copyright, 1901, by Charles Scribner's Sons, 1929, by Katherine T. Babcock; for "Peace in the World" from *The Collected Poems of John Galsworthy*, copyright, 1934, by Charles Scribner's Sons; "Valley of the Shadow" from *A Sheaf* by John Galsworthy, copyright, 1916, by Charles Scribner's Sons, 1944 by Ada Galsworthy; "Lincoln" from *The Call of Brotherhood* by Corinne Roosevelt Robinson, copyright, 1912, by Charles Scribner's Sons, 1940, by Corinne Roosevelt Alsop; "I Have a Rendezvous with Death" from *Poems* by Alan Seeger, copyright, 1916, by Charles Scribner's Sons, 1944, by Elsie Adams Seeger; selection from "To the Child Jesus," "America for Me" by Henry van Dyke; "Four Things," "Hymn of Joy," "The Child in the Garden," "Jesus, Thou Divine Companion," "Life," "Work," "A Mother's Birthday," "The Way," "Martins," "Peace," from *The Poems of Henry van Dyke*, copyright, 1911, by Charles Scribner's Sons, 1939, by Tertius van Dyke; "I Lift up My Gaze" from *The Black Panther* by John Hall Wheelock, copyright, 1922, by Charles Scribner's Sons; "The Hub" from *Selected Poems by Oscar Williams*, copyright, 1947, by Oscar Williams; "Laughter and Tears" from *Songs of Seeking and Finding* by Tertius van Dyke, copyright, 1920, by Charles Scribner's Sons, 1948, by Tertius van Dyke; "The Resurrection and the Life" from *Issa* by Robert Norwood, copyright, 1931, by Charles Scribner's Sons; "O World" from *Poems* by George Santayana, copyright, 1921, by George Santayana.

ANDERSON M. SCRUGGS for "Glory to Them," "Christmas Today" from *Glory of Earth*, copyright, 1933, 1937, by Oglethorpe University Press, 1948, by Anderson M. Scruggs.

SOCIETY FOR PROMOTING CHRISTIAN KNOWLEDGE for "A Prayer for Family Love," "A Prayer for Our Home," "A Prayer for Brotherhood" from *A Book of Prayers for Use in an Indian College* by J. S. Hoyland.

SPIRIT and the poets indicated for "Man" by Marvin Stevens; "Psalm against the Darkness" by A. M. Sullivan, copyright, 1944, by The Catholic Poetry Society of America, Inc.; "Dies Irae" by James L. Duff; "The Prophecy" by Lon Woodrum; "To a Baffled Idealist" by J. G. E. Hopkins.

TALARIA and Mrs. B. Y. Williams for "A Prayer," "Who Are the Wise Men," "A Prayer for Busy Hands," "Your House of Happiness" from *House of Happiness* by B. Y. Williams, copyright, 1928, by Sully & Co.

THE TALBOT PRESS LTD., DUBLIN for "I See His Blood upon the Rose" by Joseph Mary Plunkett.

THOMAS TIPLADY for "A Prayer for the Presence of Christ," "A Wedding Hymn" selection from "A Wedding Hymn," "Above the Hills of Time," "When Life's Day Closes," from *Hymns of Praise*, copyright, 1944, by Thomas Tiplady; "Hymn of the Unemployed," "When the Daylight Wanes" from *Hymns for the Times*, copyright, 1918, by Epworth Press.

TOC H for "Chapel" by Donald Cox, reprinted from *Tales of Talbot House*.

THE TURNER COMPANY for "Courage" from *Dreamers on Horseback* by Karle Wilson Baker.

THE UNIVERSITY OF CHICAGO PRESS for "Psalm 148," "Psalm 150" from *The Bible: An American Translation* translated by Smith and Goodspeed.

THE UNIVERSITY PRESS, CAMBRIDGE, ENGLAND for "Expectans Expectavi" from *Marlborough and Other Poems* by Charles Hamilton Sorley.

THE VIKING PRESS, INC. for "The Creation," "Go Down, Death" from *God's Trombones* by James Weldon Johnson, copyright, 1927, by The Viking Press, Inc.; "The Passionate Sword" from *Love and Need* by Jean Starr Untermeyer, copyright, 1921, by B. W. Huebsch, Inc., 1940, by Jean Starr Untermeyer; "Gesture" from *The Hesitant Heart* by Winifred Welles, copyright, 1919, by B. W. Huebsch, Inc., 1947 by James Welles Shearer; "Christmas Morning" from *Under the Tree* by Elizabeth Roberts, copyright, 1922, by B. W. Huebsch, Inc.; "Pax" from *Last Poems of D. H. Lawrence*, copyright, 1933, by Mrs. Frieda Lawrence (permission also of Mrs. Frieda Lawrence and Messrs. William Heinemann Ltd.).

ANN WATKINS, INC. for "Hymn for the Day," "The Teacher's Prayer" by Gabriela Mistral, translated by Dr. James H. McLean, by courtesy of Gabriela Mistral; for "The Choice of the Cross," "Judgment and Mercy" from *The Devil to Pay* by Dorothy L. Sayers.

THE WINGS PRESS for "Omnipresence" from *The Mountain of the Sleeping Maiden* by Stanton A. Coblentz, copyright, 1946, by The Wings Press; "Patient Is Time" from *The Pageant of Man* by Stanton A. Coblentz, copyright, 1936, by The Wings Press; "The Nightingales of Surrey" by Jessie B. Rittenhouse.

WORLD CALL for "The Silent Stars Go By" by Harriet Hartridge Tompkins, copyright, 1934, by World Call.

YALE UNIVERSITY PRESS for "Prayer" from *Sea Moods* by Edward Bliss Reed; "Exit God," "God" from *Shadow Verses* by Gamaliel Bradford; "The Falconer of God" from *The Falconer of God & Other Poems* by William Rose Benét.

FOR

Marion My Wife

AND ALL OTHERS WHO SHARE

THE POET'S FAITH AND VISION

I believed the poets; it is they
Who utter wisdom from the central deep,
And, listening to the inner flow of things,
Speak to the age out of eternity.

from COLUMBUS
by James Russell Lowell

CONTENTS

The Index of Authors, the Title Index, the First Line Index, the Topical Index and the Acknowledgments will be found at the back of the book.

BOOK I. GOD

BOOK II. JESUS

BOOK III. MAN

BOOK IV. THE CHRISTIAN LIFE

BOOK V. THE KINGDOM OF GOD

BOOK VI. THE NATION AND THE NATIONS

BOOK VII. DEATH AND IMMORTALITY

FOREWORD

The compilation of this anthology began in a dugout in France during the closing days of World War I. In the darkness, in the strained silence between guns, the voice of the captain rose and fell reciting Colonel McCrae's now famous lyric. I can still recall the emotion with which he spoke the lines

We are the Dead. Short days ago
We lived, *felt* dawn, saw sunset's glow,
Loved and were loved. . . .

We were not so far from the place where Colonel McCrae had died and where his body lay under the white crosses and the poppies. I was strangely moved. I realized then the power of poetry to capture a mood and immortalize it in language that not only expresses but deepens emotion. My interest in poetry was reawakened and I began to tuck away in my tunic pocket odd bits of verse that made a special appeal.

When I returned to the Divinity School and had access to books and periodicals, the collection began to grow more rapidly. Later, in the pastorate, I found the selections—now arranged in loose-leaf notebooks—so helpful, not only as a source of refreshment and renewal, but as a practical aid in teaching and preaching, that although I had no thought of publishing an anthology I continued with increasing interest to seek out the best religious verse of our own and other times. During more recent years, as a teacher of homiletics whose privilege it is to listen to the preachers of tomorrow, I have had occasion to observe the contribution poetry can make to effective public speaking; I have also come to a fuller appreciation of the work of some of the younger poets.

No one can pursue such a study as this without being impressed with the close affinity of religion and poetry. As George Santayana and many others have pointed out, both spring from the same source. Indeed, poetry seems to have had its beginning as the handmaiden of religion. Certainly much of the world's greatest poetry is religious poetry. This is not surprising. True religion and great poetry both deal with reality and touch life on its highest and its deepest levels. The poets who have stood the test of time have, as a rule, been men of faith and vision.

The criticism is frequently heard that modern poetry is entirely secular and lacking in spiritual emphasis. While much modern verse *is* secular and even pagan in outlook and spirit, there is much also that is deeply religious. As a matter of fact, some of the best poetry written in the present century is religious poetry and many poets who are not generally regarded as religious are nevertheless profoundly religious in their implications.

❖

In this volume I have tried to bring together in convenient form the best religious verse I have come upon. While I have sought far and wide and have endeavored to cover the field in a comprehensive manner, my aim has been selective rather than inclusive. Literary qualities have not been ignored but my chief interest has been in the religious message. Some selections have been included not because they are great poems but because of their historic significance and the contribution they have made to religious thought. Most of the world's great poets are represented but the emphasis is on poems not poets. Some of the finest selections in this volume are by writers comparatively unknown. Old favorites are here and many new poems which, I hope, will become favorites. As the Index of Authors reveals, a goodly portion of the anthology is the work of poets who are our contemporaries.

It is hoped that in an age when the old order is changing and men feel separated from the past such a compilation will provide perspective and a sense of the spiritual continuity and ultimate triumph of civilization.

❖

The selections have been arranged in seven books according to their dominant ideas. The plan is simple and follows a familiar and logical pattern. As readers will recognize, it is an adaptation of the traditional order used in most hymnals. An effort has been made to follow the text of the authorized versions. This will account for variations in punctuation and spelling. In certain instances where it seemed advantageous to suggest the atmosphere of an earlier day the older spelling has been retained. Most lyrics are reprinted in their entirety but, in order that as wide a field as possible might be covered in a single volume, I have not hesitated to lift selections out of longer poems, when so to do did not impair the unity of the thought. To enable readers to place the poems in their historical settings I have, whenever the information was available, indicated at the end of the selection the writer's birth year or life span. While the term "contemporary" usually refers to a poet still living, the purpose of the term here is to signify that the selection is by a writer of the present generation.

So interesting and dramatic are the stories back of some of the poems that time and again I was tempted to insert voluminous footnotes. In the Index of Authors is summed up the result of considerable research which may assist the reader to a fuller appreciation of the poems.

❖

To the many friends who have coöperated in the making of this book I wish to express sincere appreciation. It is impossible to name all to whom I am indebted but special mention is due:

The members of the staff of Harper & Brothers for their helpful counsel and patient assistance;

The libraries whose services have been so generously made available, especially the Library of Congress, the Canadian Parliamentary Library, the New York Public Library, the Harvard University Library and the Toronto Public Library. I am particularly under obligation to the Colgate-Rochester Divinity School Library and to the Rochester Public Library, the staff of whose Literature Division has been unfailing in its courtesy and in its practical helpfulness.

I am also grateful to poets and ministers in England who have sent me from their own libraries, and who have secured from the libraries of others, books not readily available in America. To Professor Charles Wallis I owe a special debt of gratitude for many helpful suggestions and invaluable assistance in classifying the poems and in preparing the Topical Index.

Above all I wish to express appreciation to my wife, Marion Wilder Morrison, for her cheerful and generous coöperation in every phase of the project, and for her supervision of the research workers, typists and proofreaders who helped to prepare the book for the press.

Earnest efforts have been made to communicate with all copyright owners and to respect their rights. If any have been infringed upon, it is hoped that I may be informed of my unintentional oversight that proper credit may be given on the copyright pages of future editions.

The compilation of this volume has been a labor of love and it is not without a sense of regret that I write *finis* to a task which has been so enjoyable and inspiring. I hope that others may find a like reward in reading and rereading these selections.

Rochester, N. Y. J. D. M.
July 1948.

Book I: GOD

1. THE HEAVENS DECLARE THE GLORY OF GOD

Psalm 19: 1–6

The heavens declare the glory of God;
and the firmament sheweth his handywork,
Day unto day uttereth speech,
and night unto night sheweth knowledge.
There is no speech nor language,
where their voice is not heard.
Their line is gone out through all the earth,
and their words to the end of the world.

In them hath he set a tabernacle for the sun,
Which is as a bridegroom coming out of his chamber,
and rejoiceth as a strong man to run a race.
His going forth is from the end of the heaven,
and his circuit unto the ends of it:
And there is nothing hid from the heat thereof.

King James Version, 1611

2. ODE

The spacious firmament on high,
With all the blue ethereal sky,
And spangled heavens, a shining frame,
Their great Original proclaim.
The unwearied sun, from day to day,
Does his Creator's power display,
And publishes to every land
The work of an Almighty hand.

Soon as the evening shades prevail,
The moon takes up the wondrous tale,
And nightly to the listening earth
Repeats the story of her birth;
Whilst all the stars that round her burn,
And all the planets in their turn,
Confirm the tidings as they roll,
And spread the truth from pole to pole.

What though in solemn silence all
Move round the dark terrestrial ball;
What though no real voice or sound
Amidst their radiant orbs be found:
In reason's ear they all rejoice,
And utter forth a glorious voice,
Forever singing as they shine,
"The hand that made us is divine."

Joseph Addison, 1672–1719

3. THIS IS MY FATHER'S WORLD

This is my Father's world,
And to my listening ears,
All nature sings, and round me rings
The music of the spheres.
This is my Father's world:
I rest me in the thought
Of rocks and trees, of skies and seas;
His hand the wonders wrought.

This is my Father's world,
The birds their carols raise,
The morning light, the lily white,
Declare their Maker's praise.
This is my Father's world:
He shines in all that's fair;
In the rustling grass I hear Him pass,
He speaks to me everywhere.

This is my Father's world,
O! let me ne'er forget
That though the wrong seems oft so strong,
God is the Ruler yet.
This is my Father's world:
The battle is not done;
Jesus who died shall be satisfied,
And earth and heaven be one.

Maltbie D. Babcock, 1858–1901

4. OMNIPRESENCE

The heavens are the mind of God, the systems are His word,
The message of the All-in-One, the Ever-Seen and Heard.
In planets He has marked His name, in galaxies His thought,
And the shapes of constellations are the dreams that He has wrought.

The star-swarms are His mirrors, and His glass the atom's heart,
And earth's a bright reflection of His never-resting art.
He thinks in woods and mountains, and the storm-wind is His sigh,
And He smiles in every daisy-face, and every violet's eye.

In lakes and hills and rivers, in a bluejay's twinkling wing,
In pattern of a maple leaf, and hawthorns white with spring,
In the green sculpture of a fern, a palm, a redwood tree,
His spirit moves to an old design the simple and pure may see.

The heavens are the mind of God, the systems are His word,
And He has left His signature on every bush and bird.
And deep within your breast and mine, though earth-clouds interfere,
The light of that which fires the stars is shining warm and clear.

Stanton A. Coblentz, contemporary American

5. THESE ARE THY GLORIOUS WORKS

From "Paradise Lost," Book V

These are thy glorious works, Parent of good,
Almighty! thine this universal frame,
Thus wondrous fair! Thyself how wondrous then!
Unspeakable! who sitt'st above these Heavens
To us invisible, or dimly seen
In these thy lowest works; yet these declare
Thy goodness beyond thought and power divine.

John Milton, 1608–1674

6. THE UNKNOWN GOD

The Lord hath builded for Himself
He needs no earthly dome;
The universe His dwelling is,
Eternity His home.

Yon glorious sky His temple stands,
So lofty, bright, and blue,
All lamped with stars, and curtained round
With clouds of every hue.

Earth is His altar: Nature there
Her daily tribute pays;
The elements upon Him wait;
The seasons roll His praise.

Where shall I see Him? How describe
The Dread, Eternal One?
His foot-prints are in every place,
Himself is found in none.

He called the world, and it arose;
The heavens, and they appeared:
His hand poured forth the mighty deep;
His arm the mountains reared.

He sets His foot upon the hills,
And earth beneath Him quakes;
He walks upon the hurricane,
And in the thunder speaks.

I search the rounds of space and time,
Nor find His semblance there:
Grandeur has nothing so sublime,
Nor Beauty half so fair.

Henry Francis Lyte, 1793–1847

7. ONE WORLD

From "The Divine Comedy"

I raised my eyes aloft, and I beheld
The scattered chapters of the Universe
Gathered and bound into a single book
By the austere and tender hand of God.

Dante Alighieri, 1265–1321

8. THE GLORY OF GOD IN CREATION

Thou art, O God, the life and light
Of all this wondrous world we see;
Its glow by day, its smile by night,
Are but reflections caught from Thee.
Where'er we turn, Thy glories shine,
And all things fair and bright are Thine!

When day, with farewell beam, delays
Among the opening clouds of even,
And we can almost think we gaze
Through golden vistas into heaven—
Those hues that make the sun's decline
So soft, so radiant, Lord! are Thine.

When night, with wings of starry gloom,
O'ershadows all the earth and skies,
Like some dark, beauteous bird, whose plume
Is sparkling with unnumber'd eyes—
That sacred gloom, those fires divine,
So grand, so countless, Lord! are Thine.

When youthful Spring around us breathes,
Thy Spirit warms her fragrant sigh;
And every flower the Summer wreathes
Is born beneath Thy kindling eye:
Where'er we turn, Thy glories shine,
And all things fair and bright are Thine!

Thomas Moore, 1779–1852

9. GOD OF THE EARTH, THE SKY, THE SEA

God of the earth, the sky, the sea,
Maker of all above, below,
Creation lives and moves in Thee;
Thy present life through all doth flow.

Thy love is in the sun-shine's glow,
Thy life is in the quickening air;
When lightnings flash and storm winds blow,
There is Thy power, Thy law is there.

We feel Thy calm at evening's hour,
Thy grandeur in the march of night,
And when the morning breaks in power,
We hear Thy word, "Let there be light."

But higher far, and far more clear,
Thee in man's spirit we behold,
Thine image and Thyself are there,—
Th' in-dwelling God, proclaimed of old.

Samuel Longfellow, 1819–1892

10. THE MANUSCRIPTS OF GOD[1]

And nature, the old nurse, took
The child upon her knee,
Saying, "Here is a story book
My father hath writ for thee.
Come, wander with me," she said,
"In regions yet untrod
And read what is still unread
In the manuscripts of God."

Henry W. Longfellow, 1807–1882

11. NATURE'S CREED

I believe in the brook as it wanders
From hillside into glade;
I believe in the breeze as it whispers
When evening's shadows fade.
I believe in the roar of the river
As it dashes from high cascade;

[1] On the naturalist, Agassiz.

I believe in the cry of the tempest
  'Mid the thunder's cannonade.
I believe in the light of shining stars,
  I believe in the sun and the moon;
I believe in the flash of lightning,
  I believe in the night-bird's croon.
I believe in the faith of the flowers,
  I believe in the rock and sod,
For in all of these appeareth clear
  The handiwork of God.

Author unknown

12. THE WORLD

O Earth! thou hast not any wind that blows
Which is not music; every weed of thine
Pressed rightly flows in aromatic wine;
And every humble hedgerow flower that
  grows,
And every little brown bird that doth sing,
Hath something greater than itself, and bears
A living Word to every living thing,
Albeit it hold the Message unawares.
All shapes and sounds have something which
  is not
Of them: a Spirit broods amid the grass;
Vague outlines of the Everlasting Thought
Lie in the melting shadows as they pass;
The touch of an Eternal Presence thrills
The fringes of the sunsets and the hills.

Richard Realf, 1834–1878

13. VOICE OUT OF THE WHIRLWIND

Job 38:2–40:2

Who is this that darkeneth counsel by words without knowledge?
Gird up now thy loins like a man;
For I will demand of thee, and declare thou unto me.

Where wast thou when I laid the foundations of the earth?
  — Declare, if thou hast understanding —
Who determined the measures thereof, if thou knowest?
Or who stretched the line upon it?
Whereupon were the foundations thereof fastened?
Or who laid the corner stone thereof;
  When the morning stars sang together,
  And all the sons of God shouted for joy?
Or who shut up the sea with doors,
When it brake forth, and issued out of the womb;
  When I made the cloud the garment thereof,
  And thick darkness a swaddling band for it,
  And prescribed for it my decree,
  And set bars and doors,
  And said, "Hitherto shalt thou come, but no further;
  And here shall thy proud waves be stayed?"
Hast thou commanded the morning since thy days began,
And caused the dayspring to know its place;
  That it might take hold of the ends of the earth,
  And the wicked be shaken out of it?
  It is changed as clay under the seal;
  And all things stand forth as a garment:
  And from the wicked their light is withholden,
  And the high arm is broken.
Hast thou entered into the springs of the sea?
Or hast thou walked in the recesses of the deep?
Have the gates of death been revealed unto thee?
Or hast thou seen the gates of the shadow of death?

Hast thou comprehended the breadth of the earth?
— Declare, if thou knowest it all —
Where is the way to the dwelling of light,
And as for darkness, where is the place thereof;
That thou shouldest take it to the bound thereof,
And that thou shouldest discern the paths to the house thereof?
— Doubtless, thou knowest, for thou wast then born,
And the number of thy days is great! —
Hast thou entered the treasuries of the snow,
Or hast thou seen the treasuries of the hail,
Which I have reserved against the time of trouble,
Against the day of battle and war?
By what way is the light parted,
Or the east wind scattered upon the earth?
Who hath cleft a channel for the waterflood,
Or a way for the lightning of the thunder;
To cause it to rain on a land where no man is;
On the wilderness, wherein there is no man;
To satisfy the waste and desolate ground;
And to cause the tender grass to spring forth?
Hath the rain a father?
Or who hath begotten the drops of dew?
Out of whose womb came the ice?
And the hoary frost of heaven, who hath gendered it?
The waters are hidden as with stone,
And the face of the deep is frozen.
Canst thou bind the cluster of the Pleiades,
Or loose the bands of Orion?
Canst thou lead forth the signs of the Zodiac in their season?
Or canst thou guide the Bear with her train?
Knowest thou the ordinances of the heavens?
Canst thou establish the dominion thereof in the earth?
Canst thou lift up thy voice to the clouds,
That abundance of waters may cover thee?
Canst thou send forth lightnings, that they may go,
And say unto thee, Here we are?
Who hath put wisdom in the inward parts?
Or who hath given understanding to the mind?
Who can number the clouds by wisdom?
Or who can pour out the bottles of heaven,
When the dust runneth into a mass,
And the clods cleave fast together?
Wilt thou hunt the prey for the lioness?
Or satisfy the appetite of the young lions,
When they couch in their dens,
And abide in the covert to lie in wait?
Who provideth for the raven his food,
When his young ones cry unto God,
And wander for lack of meat?
Knowest thou the time when the wild goats of the rock bring forth?
Or canst thou mark when the hinds do calve?
Canst thou number the months that they fulfil?
Or knowest thou the time when they bring forth?
They bow themselves, they bring forth their young,

They cast out their sorrows.
Their young ones are in good liking,
They grow up in the open field;
They go forth, and return not again.
Who hath sent out the wild ass free?
Or who hath loosed the bands of the wild ass?
Whose house I have made the wilderness,
And the salt land his dwelling place;
He scorneth the tumult of the city,
Neither heareth he the shoutings of the driver.
The range of the mountains is his pasture,
And he searcheth after every green thing.
Will the wild-ox be content to serve thee?
Or will he abide by thy crib?
Canst thou bind the wild-ox with his band in the furrow?
Or will he harrow the valleys after thee?
Wilt thou trust him, because his strength is great?
Or wilt thou leave to him thy labour?
Wilt thou confide in him, that he will bring home thy seed,
And gather the corn of thy threshing-floor?
The wing of the ostrich rejoiceth;
But are her pinions and feathers kindly?
For she leaveth her eggs on the earth,
And warmeth them in the dust,
And forgetteth that the foot may crush them,
Or that the wild beast may trample them.
She is hardened against her young ones, as if they were not hers:
Though her labour be in vain, she is without fear;
Because God hath deprived her of wisdom,
Neither hath he imparted to her understanding.
What time she lifteth up herself on high,
She scorneth the horse and his rider.
Hast thou given the horse his might?
Hast thou clothed his neck with the quivering mane?
Hast thou made him to leap as a locust?
The glory of his snorting is terrible.
He paweth in the valley, and rejoiceth in his strength:
He goeth out to meet the armed men.
He mocketh at fear and is not dismayed;
Neither turneth he back from the sword.
The quiver rattleth against him,
The flashing spear and the javelin.
He swalloweth the ground with fierceness and rage;
Neither standeth he still at the voice of the trumpet.
As oft as the trumpet soundeth he saith, Aha!
And he smelleth the battle afar off,
The thunder of the captains, and the shouting.
Doth the hawk soar by thy wisdom,
And stretch her wings toward the south?
Doth the eagle mount up at thy command,
And make her nest on high?
She dwelleth on the rock, and hath her lodging there,
Upon the crag of the rock and the strong hold.
From thence she spieth out the prey;

Her eyes behold it afar off.
Her young ones also suck up blood:
And where the slain are, there is she.

Shall he that cavilleth contend with the Almighty?
He that argueth with God, let him answer it.

Moulton: The Modern Reader's Bible, 1895

14. LIFE

By one great Heart the Universe is stirred:
By Its strong pulse, stars climb the darkening blue;
It throbs in each fresh sunset's changing hue,
And thrills through low sweet song of every bird:

By It, the plunging blood reds all men's veins;
Joy feels that heart against his rapturous own,
And on It, Sorrow breathes her sharpest groan;
And bounds through gladnesses and deepest pains.

Passionless beating through all Time and Space,
Relentless, calm, majestic in Its march,
Alike, though Nature shake heaven's endless arch,
Or man's heart break, because of some dead face!

'Tis felt in sunshine greening the soft sod,
In children's smiling, as in mother's tears;
And, for strange comfort, through the aching years,
Men's hungry souls have named that great Heart, God!

Margaret Deland, 1857–1945

15. DESIGN

This is a piece too fair
To be the child of Chance, and not of Care.
No Atoms casually together hurl'd
Could e'er produce so beautifull a world.

John Dryden, 1631–1700

16. GOD IS AT THE ORGAN

God is at the organ;
I can hear
A mighty music echoing,
Far and near.

God is at the organ
And the keys
Are storm-strewn billows,
Moorlands, trees.

God is at the organ,
I can hear
A mighty music, echoing
Far and near.

Egbert Sandford, contemporary English

17. REFLECTIONS

In a puddle by the roadside
Left by the warm, spring rain,
Its waters dark and muddy
With the brown earth stain,
I saw a glorious mountain
That stood up bold and high
Reflected in the water,
With a patch of cloud-decked sky.

Sometimes in folk around me
With burdens, hurts and fears:
Through joyful, happy hours
And often through their tears:

In some loving acts of kindness
As they show how much they care—
In the lives of folk around me
I find God reflected there.

Cyrus E. Albertson

18. ALL BEAUTIFUL THE MARCH OF DAYS

All beautiful the march of days,
As seasons come and go;
The hand that shaped the rose hath wrought
The crystal of the snow;
Hath sent the hoary frost of heaven,
The flowing waters sealed,
And laid a silent loveliness
On hill, and wood, and field.

O'er white expanses sparkling pure
The radiant morns unfold;
The solemn splendours of the night
Burn brighter through the cold:
Life mounts in every throbbing vein,
Love deepens round the hearth,
And clearer sounds the angel-hymn,
"Good will to men on earth."

O Thou from whose unfathomed law
The year in beauty flows,
Thyself the vision passing by
In crystal and in rose:
Day unto day doth utter speech,
And night to night proclaim,
In everlasting words of light,
The wonder of Thy Name.

Frances Whitmarsh Wile, 1878–1939

19. INDIRECTION

Fair are the flowers and the children, but their subtle suggestion is fairer;
Rare is the roseburst of dawn, but the secret that clasps it is rarer;
Sweet the exultance of song, but the strain that precedes it is sweeter;
And never was poem yet writ, but the meaning outmastered the meter.

Never a daisy that grows, but a mystery guideth the growing;
Never a river that flows, but a majesty scepters the flowing;
Never a Shakespeare that soared, but a stronger than he did enfold him,
Nor ever a prophet foretells, but a mightier seer hath foretold him.

Back of the canvas that throbs, the painter is hinted and hidden;
Into the statue that breathes, the soul of the sculptor is bidden;
Under the joy that is felt, lie the infinite issues of feeling;
Crowning the glory revealed is the glory that crowns the revealing.

Great are the symbols of being, but that which is symboled is greater;
Vast the create and beheld, but vaster the inward creator;
Back of the sound broods the silence, back of the gift stands the giving;
Back of the hand that received thrill the sensitive nerves of receiving.

Space is as nothing to spirit, the deed is outdone by the doing;
The heart of the wooer is warm, but warmer the heart of the wooing;
And up from the pits where these shiver and up from the heights where those shine
Twin voices and shadows swim starward, and the essence of life is divine.

Richard Realf, 1834–1878

20. LIGHT SHINING OUT OF DARKNESS

God moves in a mysterious way
His wonders to perform;
He plants His footsteps in the sea,
And rides upon the storm.

Deep in unfathomable mines
Of never-failing skill

He treasures up His bright designs,
And works His sovereign will.

Ye fearful saints, fresh courage take;
The clouds ye so much dread
Are big with mercy, and shall break
In blessings on your head.

Judge not the Lord by feeble sense,
But trust Him for His grace;
Behind a frowning providence
He hides a smiling face.

His purposes will ripen fast,
Unfolding every hour;
The bud may have a bitter taste,
But sweet will be the flower.

Blind unbelief is sure to err,
And scan His work in vain;
God is His own interpreter,
And He will make it plain.

William Cowper, 1731–1800

21. OUT OF THE VAST

There's a part of the sun in the apple,
There's a part of the moon in a rose;
There's a part of the flaming Pleiades
In every leaf that grows.

Out of the vast comes nearness;
For the God whose love we sing
Lends a little of His heaven
To every living thing.

Augustus Wright Bamberger

22. THE HIGHER PANTHEISM

The sun, the moon, the stars, the seas, the hills and the plains,—
Are not these, O Soul, the Vision of Him who reigns?

Is not the Vision He, tho' He be not that which He seems?
Dreams are true while they last, and do we not live in dreams?

Earth, these solid stars, this weight of body and limb,
Are they not sign and symbol of thy division from Him?

Dark is the world to thee; thyself art the reason why,
For is He not all but thou, that hast power to feel "I am I"?

Glory about thee, without thee; and thou fulfillest thy doom,
Making Him broken gleams and a stifled splendor and gloom.

Speak to Him, thou, for He hears, and Spirit with Spirit can meet—
Closer is He than breathing, and nearer than hands and feet.

God is law, say the wise; O Soul, and let us rejoice,
For if He thunder by law the thunder is yet His voice.

Law is God, say some; no God at all, says the fool,
For all we have power to see is a straight staff bent in a pool;

And the ear of man cannot hear, and the eye of man cannot see;
But if we could see and hear, this Vision—were it not He?

Alfred Tennyson, 1809–1892

23. MUSIC

Let me go where'er I will
I hear a sky-born music still;
It sounds from all things old,
It sounds from all things young,
From all that's fair, from all that's foul,
Peals out a cheerful song.

It is not only in the rose,
It is not only in the bird,
Not only when the rainbow glows,
Nor in the song of woman heard,
But in the darkest, meanest things
There alway, alway, something sings.

'Tis not in the high stars alone,
Nor in the cup of budding flowers,
Nor in the redbreast's mellow tones,
Nor in the bow that smiles in showers,
But in the mud and scum of things
There alway, alway, something sings.

Ralph Waldo Emerson, 1803–1882

24. TWO GODS

I

A boy was born 'mid little things,
Between a little world and sky—
And dreamed not of the cosmic rings
Round which the circling planets fly.

He lived in little works and thoughts,
Where little ventures grow and plod,
And paced and ploughed his little plots,
And prayed unto his little God.

But as the mighty system grew,
His faith grew faint with many scars;
The Cosmos widened in his view—
But God was lost among His stars.

II

Another boy in lowly days,
As he, to little things was born,
But gathered lore in woodland ways,
And from the glory of the morn.

As wider skies broke on his view,
God greatened in his growing mind;
Each year he dreamed his God anew,
And left his older God behind.

He saw the boundless scheme dilate,
In star and blossom, sky and clod;
And as the universe grew great,
He dreamed for it a greater God.

Sam Walter Foss, 1858–1911

25. RIGHT MUST WIN

From "On the Field"

O it is hard to work for God,
To rise and take His part
Upon this battle-field of earth,
And not sometimes lose heart!

He hides Himself so wondrously,
As though there were no God;
He is least seen when all the powers
Of ill are most abroad.

Or He deserts us at the hour
The fight is all but lost;
And seems to leave us to ourselves
Just when we need Him most.

Ill masters good, good seems to change
To ill with greatest ease;
And, worst of all, the good with good
Is at cross purposes.

It is not so, but so it looks,
And we lose courage then;
And doubts will come if God hath kept
His promises to men.

Workman of God! oh, lose not heart,
But learn what God is like,
And in the darkest battle-field,
Thou shalt know where to strike.

Thrice blest is he to whom is given
The instinct that can tell
That God is on the field when He
Is most invisible.

Blest too is he who can divine
Where real right doth lie,
And dares to take the side that seems
Wrong to man's blindfold eye.

Muse on His justice, downcast soul,
  Muse, and take better heart;
Back with thine angel to the field,
  And bravely do thy part.

For right is right, since God is God,
  And right the day must win;
To doubt would be disloyalty,
  To falter would be sin.

Frederick William Faber, 1814–1863

26. THE GREAT VOICE

I who have heard solemnities of sound—
The throbbing pulse of cities, the loud roar
Of ocean on sheer ledges of gaunt rock,
The chanting of innumerable winds
Around white peaks, the plunge of cataracts,
The whelm of avalanches, and, by night,
The thunder's panic breath—have come to
  know
What is earth's mightiest voice—the desert's
  voice—
Silence, that speaks with deafening tones of
  God.

Clinton Scollard, 1860–1932

27. PRIVATE ENTERPRISE

Quiet is what we need. By telephone,
The press, the mail, the doorbell, radio,
AP or NAM or CIO,
We're micro-organized and overgrown
With everybody's business but our own;
Pipe it down, chain talkers. Muffle and slow
The rapid pulse. I wonder if you know
How good it feels, sometimes to be alone?

Incessantly loquacious generation,
Let yeah and nyah be your communication.
Before the world comes open at the seams
Invest some private enterprise in dreams.
In unimpassioned silence we might find
(If ever) What the Author Had In Mind.

Christopher Morley, 1890–

28. MIRACLES

From "Song of Myself"

I believe a leaf of grass is no less than the journey-work of the stars,
And the pismire is equally perfect, and a grain of sand, and the egg of the wren,
And the tree-toad is a chef-d'oeuvre for the highest,
And the running blackberry would adorn the parlors of heaven,
And the narrowest hinge in my hand puts to scorn all machinery,
And the cow crunching with depress'd head surpasses any statue,
And a mouse is miracle enough to stagger sextillions of infidels.

Walt Whitman, 1819–1892

29. MIRACLES

On these electric branches
  The lightnings of the sun
Shall smite as Moses smote the rock
  And tides of life shall run.

The miracles of April
  God's first and fairest were.
The wonders of the earth are things
  Which constantly occur.

Roy Helton, 1886–

30. PARADOX

If the good God were suddenly
To make a solitary Blind to see
We would stand wondering all
And call it miracle;
But that He gives with lavish hand
Sight to a million souls we stand
And say, with little awe,
He but fulfils a natural law!

Huw Menai, contemporary
Welsh miner-poet

31. THEOPHANY

Deep cradled in the fringed mow to lie
And feel the rhythmic flux of life sweep by,
This is to know the easy heaven that waits
Before our timidly-embattled gates:
To show the exultant leap and thrust of things
Outward toward perfection, in the heart
Of every bud to see the folded wings,
Discern the patient whole in every part.

Evelyn Underhill, 1875–1941

32. "GIVE US THIS DAY OUR DAILY BREAD"

Back of the loaf is the snowy flour,
And back of the flour the mill,
And back of the mill is the wheat and the shower,
And the sun and the Father's will.

Maltbie D. Babcock, 1858–1901

33. I SAW GOD WASH THE WORLD

I saw God wash the world last night
With his sweet showers on high,
And then, when morning came, I saw
Him hang it out to dry.

He washed each tiny blade of grass
And every trembling tree;
He flung his showers against the hill,
And swept the billowing sea.

The white rose is a cleaner white,
The red rose is more red,
Since God washed every fragrant face
And put them all to bed.

There's not a bird, there's not a bee
That wings along the way
But is a cleaner bird and bee
Than it was yesterday.

I saw God wash the world last night.
Ah, would He had washed me
As clean of all my dust and dirt
As that old white birch tree.

William L. Stidger, 1885–

34. SCIENCE

Nature and nature's laws
Lay hid in night;
God said, "Let Newton be,"
And all was light.

Alexander Pope, 1688–1744

35. IN AN AGE OF SCIENCE

The little world of olden days is gone,
A thousand universes come to light;
The eyes of science penetrate the night,
And bring good tidings of eternal dawn;
There is no night, they find; there is no death,
But life begetting ever fuller life;
They look still deeper and amid the strife
They note pervading harmony. The breath
Of morning sweeps the wastes of earth,
And we who talked of age become as gods,
Scanning the spheres, discoursing of the birth
Of countless suns. No longer human clods,
We stand alert and speak direct to Him
Who hides no more behind dumb Seraphim.

Thomas Curtis Clark, 1877–

36. THE MAN OF SCIENCE SPEAKS

Throw your little dreams away,
Scrap philosophies and creeds.
Can your vision of truth climb higher
Than our calculation leads?

While you speculate in vain,
Making little gods, forsooth,
We fathom infinities—
Mathematics *is* the truth.

You put limits of your own
On the illimitable power—
We explore immensities
Beyond our little place and hour.

With small beliefs or coward doubts
You lean upon the rotted past.
We neither believe nor doubt—we know;
Our rock of faith is anchored fast.

Yesterday's failure is today
The take-off for tomorrow's goal.
We watch you trembling while we win
New spaces for the searching soul.

You dream the same old idle dreams,
You move not in the drift of years.

We count the paces of the stars,
We hear the singing of the spheres.

Harriet Monroe, 1861?–1936

37. EACH IN HIS OWN TONGUE

A fire-mist and a planet—
A crystal and a cell,
A jelly-fish and a saurian,
And caves where the cave-men dwell:
Then a sense of law and beauty
And a face turned from the clod,—
Some call it Evolution,
And others call it God.

A haze on the far horizon,
The infinite, tender sky,
The ripe, rich tint of the cornfields,
And the wild geese sailing high;
And all over upland and lowland
The charm of the golden-rod,—
Some of us call it Autumn,
And others call it God.

Like tides on a crescent sea-beach,
When the moon is new and thin,
Into our hearts high yearnings
Come welling and surging in;
Come from the mystic ocean
Whose rim no foot has trod,—
Some of us call it Longing,
And others call it God.

A picket frozen on duty,
A mother starved for her brood,
Socrates drinking the hemlock,
And Jesus on the rood;
And millions who, humble and nameless,
The straight, hard pathway plod,—
Some call it Consecration,
And others call it God.

William Herbert Carruth, 1859–1924

38. LET NATURE BE YOUR TEACHER

From "The Tables Turned"

And hark! how blithe the throstle sings!
He, too, is no mean preacher:
Come forth into the light of things,
Let Nature be your teacher.

She has a world of ready wealth,
Our minds and hearts to bless—
Spontaneous wisdom breathed by health,
Truth breathed by cheerfulness.

One impulse from a vernal wood
May teach you more of man,
Of moral evil and of good,
Than all the sages can.

Sweet is the lore which Nature brings;
Our meddling intellect
Mis-shapes the beauteous forms of things:—
We murder to dissect.

Enough of Science and of Art;
Close up those barren leaves;
Come forth, and bring with you a heart
That watches and receives.

William Wordsworth, 1770–1850

39. A SONG OF THE ROAD

I lift my cap to Beauty,
I lift my cap to Love;
I bow before my Duty,
And know that God's above!
My heart through shining arches
Of leaf and blossom goes;
My soul, triumphant, marches
Through life to life's repose.
And I, through all this glory,
Nor know, nor fear my fate—
The great things are so simple,
The simple are so great!

Fred G. Bowles

40. OVERSOUL

I am Beauty itself among beautiful things.
Bhagavad-Gitâ

The East was crowned with snow-cold bloom
And hung with veils of pearly fleece:
They died away into the gloom,
Vistas of peace—and deeper peace.

And earth and air and wave and fire
In awe and breathless silence stood;
For One who passed into their choir
Linked them in mystic brotherhood.

Twilight of amethyst, amid
Thy few strange stars that lit the heights,
Where was the secret spirit hid?
Where was Thy place, O Light of Lights?

The flame of Beauty far in space—
Where rose the fire: in Thee? in Me?
Which bowed the elemental race
To adoration silently?

G. W. Russell (A.E.), 1867–1935

A THING OF BEAUTY

From "Endymion"

A thing of beauty is a joy for ever:
Its loveliness increases; it will never
Pass into nothingness; but still will keep
A bower quiet for us, and a sleep
Full of sweet dreams, and health, and quiet
breathing.
Therefore, on every morrow, are we wreath-
ing
A flowery band to bind us to the earth,
Spite of despondence, of the inhuman dearth
Of noble natures, of the gloomy days,
Of all the unhealthy and o'er-darkened ways
Made for our searching: yes, in spite of all,
Some shape of beauty moves away the pall
From our dark spirits. Such the sun, the
moon,
Trees old and young, sprouting a shady boon
For simple sheep; and such are daffodils
With the green world they live in; and clear
rills
That for themselves a cooling covert make
'Gainst the hot season; the mid-forest brake,
Rich with a sprinkling of fair musk-rose
blooms:
And such too is the grandeur of the dooms
We have imagined for the mighty dead;
All lovely tales that we have heard or read:
An endless fountain of immortal drink,
Pouring unto us from the heaven's brink.

John Keats, 1795–1821

42. GLORY IN THE COMMONPLACE

From "Aurora Leigh"

Earth's crammed with heaven,
And every common bush afire with God;
But only he who sees, takes off his shoes,
The rest sit round it and pluck blackberries,
And daub their natural faces unaware
More and more from the first similitude.

Elizabeth Barrett Browning, 1806–1861

43. EARTH'S COMMON THINGS

Seek not afar for beauty. Lo! it glows
In dew-wet grasses all about thy feet;
In birds, in sunshine, childish faces sweet,
In stars and mountain summits topped with
snows.

Go not abroad for happiness. For see,
It is a flower that blooms at thy door.
Bring love and justice home, and then no
more
Thou'lt wonder in what dwelling joy may be.

Dream not of noble service elsewhere
wrought;
The simple duty that awaits thy hand
Is God's voice uttering a divine command,
Life's common deeds build all that saints
have thought.

In wonder-workings, or some bush aflame,
Men look for God and fancy him concealed;
But in earth's common things he stands
revealed
While grass and flowers and stars spell out
his name.

Minot J. Savage, 1841–1918

44. THE EXCESSES OF GOD

Is it not by his high superfluousness we know
Our God? For to equal a need
Is natural, animal, mineral: but to fling
Rainbows over the rain
And beauty above the moon, and secret
rainbows
On the domes of deep sea-shells,
And make the necessary embrace of breeding
Beautiful also as fire,
Not even the weeds to multiply without
blossom
Nor the birds without music:
There is the great humaneness at the heart of
things,
The extravagant kindness, the fountain

Humanity can understand, and would flow
likewise
If power and desire were perch-mates.

Robinson Jeffers, 1887–

45. ADORATION

Now the last light of amber day is dying,
Over the levels of this field in flower,
And in my heart a voice of worship crying:
O lovely, lovely is the earth, this hour—
Never so dearly held, so deep adored,
As now when I alone of weary men
Am witness how the fragrant-vestured Lord,
In the cool evening, walks His earth again.

David Morton, 1886–

46. ON THE SETTING SUN

Those evening clouds, that setting ray,
And beauteous tints, serve to display
Their great Creator's praise;
Then let the short-lived thing call'd man,
Whose life's comprised within a span,
To him his homage raise.

We often praise the evening clouds,
And tints so gay and bold,
But seldom think upon our God,
Who tinged these clouds with gold.

Sir Walter Scott, 1771–1832

47. COMMUNION

Once when my heart was passion-free
To learn of things divine,
The soul of nature suddenly
Outpoured itself in mine.

I held the secrets of the deep,
And of the heavens above;
I knew the harmonies of sleep
The mysteries of love.

And for a moment's interval
The earth, the sky, the sea—
My soul encompassed, each and all,
As now they compass me.

To one in all, to all in one—
Since Love the work began—
Life's ever widening circles run,
Revealing God and man.

John Banister Tabb, 1845–1909

48. ALL THINGS BRIGHT AND BEAUTIFUL

All things bright and beautiful,
All creatures great and small,
All things wise and wonderful,
The Lord God made them all.

Each little flower that opens,
Each little bird that sings,
He made their glowing colours,
He made their tiny wings.

The purple-headed mountain,
The river running by,
The sunset, and the morning
That brightens up the sky,

The cold wind in the winter,
The pleasant summer sun,
The ripe fruits in the garden,
He made them every one.

The tall trees in the greenwood,
The meadows where we play,
The rushes by the water,
We gather every day.

He gave us eyes to see them,
And lips that we might tell
How great is God Almighty,
Who has made all things well.

Cecil Frances Alexander, 1818–1895

49. THE WIND

"The wind bloweth where it listeth, but thou canst not tell"...

Who has seen the wind?
Neither I nor you.
But when the leaves hang trembling,
The wind is passing through.
Who has seen the wind?
Neither you nor I.
But when the trees bow down their heads,
The wind is passing by.

Christina Georgina Rossetti, 1830–1894

50. HANG ME AMONG YOUR WINDS

Hang me among your winds, O God,
Above the tremulous stars,
Like a harp of quivering silver strings,
Showering, as it swings,
Its tuneful bars
Of eerie music on the earth.

Play over me, God,
Your cosmic melodies:
The gusty overture for Spring's
Caprice and wayward April's mirth;
The sensuous serenade
Of Summer, languid in the alder glade;
The wistful symphonies
Of Autumn; and Winter's rhapsodies
Among the drifted dunes—
Her lullabies and her torrential tunes
Moody with wild cadenzas, with fitful stress
And poignant soundlessness.

Touch me, O God, with but a gesture—
And let each finger sweep
Over my strings until they leap
With life, and rain
Their silver chimes upon the plain,
In harmonies of far celestial spaces,
Of high and holy places.

Lew Sarett, 1888–

51. WHAT MAN HAS MADE OF MAN

From "Written in Early Spring"

I heard a thousand blended notes
While in a grove I sat reclined,
In that sweet mood when pleasant thoughts
Bring sad thoughts to the mind.

To her fair works did Nature link
The human soul that through me ran;
And much it grieved my heart to think
What Man has made of Man.

Through primrose tufts, in that green bower,
The periwinkle trail'd its wreaths;
And 'tis my faith that every flower
Enjoys the air it breathes.

The birds around me hopp'd and play'd,
Their thoughts I cannot measure,—
But the least motion which they made
It seem'd a thrill of pleasure.

The budding twigs spread out their fan
To catch the breezy air;
And I must think, do all I can,
That there was pleasure there.

If this belief from heaven be sent,
If such be Nature's holy plan,
Have I not reason to lament
What Man has made of Man?

William Wordsworth, 1770–1850

52. THE TIDE WILL WIN

On the far reef the breakers
Recoil in shattered foam,
While still the sea behind them
Urges its forces home;
Its song of triumph surges
O'er all the thunderous din,
The wave may break in failure,
But the tide is sure to win!

The reef is strong and cruel;
Upon its jagged wall
One wave, a score, a hundred,
Broken and beaten fall;
Yet in defeat they conquer,
The sea comes flooding in,
Wave upon wave is routed,
But the tide is sure to win.

O mighty sea! thy message
In clanging spray is cast;
Within God's plan of progress
It matters not at last
How wide the shores of evil,
How strong the reefs of sin,
The wave may be defeated,
But the tide is sure to win!

Priscilla Leonard, 1852–

53. THE SNOWDROP

Close to the sod
There can be seen
A thought of God
In white and green.

Unmarred, unsoiled,
It cleft the clay,
Serene, unspoiled
It views the day.

It is so holy
  And yet so lowly.
Would you enjoy
  Its grace and dower

And not destroy
  The living flower?
Then you must, please,
  Fall on your knees.

Anna Bunston de Bary, contemporary English

54. FLOWER IN THE CRANNIED WALL

Flower in the crannied wall,
I pluck you out of the crannies,
I hold you here, root and all, in my hand,
Little flower—but *if* I could understand
What you are, root and all, and all in all,
I should know what God and man is.

Alfred Tennyson, 1809–1892

55. ONLY A FLOWER

Strange that the spring has come
On meadow and vale and hill,
For here in the sunless slum
My bosom is frozen still.
And I wear the wadded things
Of the dreary winter days,
But out of the heart of this little flower
God gazes into my face!

Toyohiko Kagawa, 1888–

56. GOD

I see Thee in the distant blue;
But in the violet's dell of dew,
Behold, I *breathe* and *touch* Thee too.

John Banister Tabb, 1845–1909

57. GOD IS HERE

God is here! I hear His voice
While thrushes make the woods rejoice.

I touch His robe each time I place
My hand against a pansy's face.

I breathe His breath if I but pass
Verbenas trailing through the grass.

God is here! From every tree
His leafy fingers beckon me.

Madeleine Aaron, 1895–

58. DAISIES

Over the shoulders and slopes of the dune
I saw the white daisies go down to the sea,
A host in the sunshine, an army in June,
The people God sends us to set our hearts free.

The bobolinks rallied them up from the dell,
The orioles whistled them out of the wood;
And all of their singing was, "Earth, it is well!"
And all of their dancing was, "Life, thou art good!"

Bliss Carman, 1861–1929

59. CONSIDER THE LILIES

He hides within the lily
  A strong and tender Care,
That wins the earth-born atoms
  To glory of the air;
He weaves the shining garments
  Unceasingly and still,
Along the quiet waters,
  In niches of the hill.

We linger at the vigil
  With him who bent the knee,
To watch the old-time lilies
  In distant Galilee;
And still the worship deepens
  And quickens into new,
As brightening down the ages
  God's secret thrilleth through.

O Toiler of the lily,
  Thy touch is in the man!
No leaf that dawns to petal
  But hints the angel-plan:
The flower-horizons open,
  The blossom vaster shows;
We hear thy wide world's echo,—
  "See how the lily grows!"

Shy yearnings of the savage,
  Unfolding, thought by thought,
To holy lives are lifted,
  To visions fair are wrought:

The races rise and cluster,
  And evils fade and fall,
Till chaos blooms to beauty,
  Thy purpose crowning all!

William Channing Gannett, 1840–1923

60. THE DAFFODILS

I wandered lonely as a cloud
  That floats on high o'er vales and hills,
When all at once I saw a crowd,
  A host, of golden daffodils,
Beside the lake, beneath the trees,
Fluttering and dancing in the breeze.

Continuous as the stars that shine
  And twinkle on the Milky Way,
They stretched in never-ending line
  Along the margin of a bay:
Ten thousand saw I at a glance,
Tossing their heads in sprightly dance.

The waves beside them danced, but they
  Outdid the sparkling waves in glee;
A poet could not but be gay
  In such a jocund company.
I gazed, and gazed, but little thought
What wealth the show to me had brought:

For oft, when on my couch I lie
  In vacant or in pensive mood,
They flash upon that inward eye
  Which is the bliss of solitude;
And then my heart with pleasure fills,
And dances with the daffodils.

William Wordsworth, 1770–1850

61. APRIL RAIN

It is not raining rain to me,
  It's raining daffodils;
In every dimpled drop I see
  Wild flowers on the hills.

The clouds of gray engulf the day
  And overwhelm the town;
It is not raining rain to me,
  It's raining roses down.

It is not raining rain to me,
  But fields of clover bloom,
Where any buccaneering bee
  May find a bed and room.

A health unto the happy!
  A fig for him who frets!—
It is not raining rain to me,
  It's raining violets.

Robert Loveman, 1864–1923

62. MIRACLE

We muse on miracles who look
  But lightly on a rose!
Who gives it fragrance or the glint
  Of glory that it shows?

Who holds it here between the sky
  And earth's rain-softened sod?
The miracle of one pale rose
  Is proof enough of God!

Edith Daley

63. THE MYSTERY

He came and took me by the hand
  Up to a red rose tree,
He kept His meaning to Himself
  But gave a rose to me.

I did not pray Him to lay bare
  The mystery to me.
Enough the rose was Heaven to smell,
  And His own face to see.

Ralph Hodgson, 1871–

64. THE ROSE

There is a world of wonder in this rose;
God made it, and His whole creation grows
To a point of perfect beauty
In this garden plot. He knows
The poet's thrill
On this June morning, as He sees
His Will
To beauty taking form, His word
Made flesh, and dwelling among men.
All mysteries
In this one flower meet
And intertwine,
The universal is concrete
The human and divine,
In one unique and perfect thing, are fused
Into a unity of Love,
This rose as I behold it;
For all things gave it me,

The stars have helped to mould it,
The air, soft moonshine, and the rain,
The meekness of old mother earth,
The many-billowed sea.
The evolution of ten million years,
And all the pain
Of ages, brought it to its birth
And gave it me.
The tears
Of Christ are in it
And His Blood
Has dyed it red,
I could not see it but for Him
Because He led
Me to the Love of God,
From which all Beauty springs.
I and my rose
Are one.

G. A. Studdert-Kennedy, 1883–1929

65. INFLUENCE

A Persian fable says; One day
A wanderer found a piece of clay
So redolent of sweet perfume
Its odor scented all the room.

"What art thou?" was the quick demand
"Art thou some gem from Samarcand
Or spikenard rare in rich disguise?
Or other costly merchandise?"

"Nay, I am but a piece of clay."
"Then whence this wondrous sweetness,
pray?"

"Friend, if the secret I disclose,
I have been dwelling with a rose."

Author unknown

66. A PRIMROSE BY THE WAYSIDE

Close to the road's impurity
It knows of nothing base
So meekly and so trustfully
It lifts its lovely face.

So innocent, and yet with art
Incomparably sweet
It leaned up and caressed my heart
While lying at my feet.

Can anything so fair and free
Be fashioned out of clay?
Then God may yet cull flowers from me
Some holy summer day.

Anna Bunston de Bary,
contemporary English

67. A PRAYER IN SPRING

Oh, give us pleasure in the flowers to-day;
And give us not to think so far away
As the uncertain harvest; keep us here
All simply in the springing of the year.

Oh, give us pleasure in the orchard white,
Like nothing else by day, like ghosts by night;
And make us happy in the happy bees,
The swarm dilating round the perfect trees.

And make us happy in the darting bird
That suddenly above the bees is heard,
The meteor that thrusts in with needle bill,
And off a blossom in mid air stands still.

For this is love and nothing else is love,
The which it is reserved for God above
To sanctify to what far ends He will,
But which it only needs that we fulfil.

Robert Frost, 1875–

68. HYACINTHS TO FEED THY SOUL

If of thy mortal goods thou art bereft,
And from thy slender store two loaves alone
to thee are left,
Sell one, and with the dole
Buy hyacinths to feed thy soul.

Gulistan of Moslih Eddin Saadi,
(Persia), c. 1184–1291

69. TO NATURE

It may indeed be phantasy when I
Essay to draw from all created things
Deep, heartfelt, inward joy that closely
clings;
And trace in leaves and flowers that round
me lie
Lessons of love and earnest piety.
So let it be; and if the wide world rings
In mock of this belief, it brings

Nor fear, nor grief, nor vain perplexity.
So will I build my altar in the fields,
And the blue sky my fretted dome shall be,
And the sweet fragrance that the wild flower
yields
Shall be the incense I will yield to Thee,
The only God! and thou shalt not despise
Even me, the priest of this poor sacrifice.

Samuel Taylor Coleridge, 1772–1834

70. TREES

I think that I shall never see
A poem lovely as a tree.

A tree whose hungry mouth is pressed
Against the earth's sweet-flowing breast;

A tree that looks at God all day,
And lifts her leafy arms to pray;

A tree that may in summer wear
A nest of robins in her hair;

Upon whose bosom snow has lain;
Who intimately lives with rain.

Poems are made by fools like me,
But only God can make a tree.

Joyce Kilmer, 1886–1918

71. SHADE

The kindliest thing God ever made,
His hand of very healing laid
Upon a fevered world, is shade.

His glorious company of trees
Throw out their mantles, and on these
The dust-stained wanderer finds ease.

Green temples, closed against the beat
Of noontime's blinding glare and heat,
Open to any pilgrim's feet.

The white road blisters in the sun;
Now half the weary journey done,
Enter and rest, O weary one!

And feel the dew of dawn still wet
Beneath thy feet, and so forget
The burning highway's ache and fret.

This is God's hospitality,
And whoso rests beneath a tree
Hath cause to thank Him gratefully.

Theodosia Garrison, 1874–1944

72. LEADING

Forests are made for weary men,
That they may find their soul again.
And little leaves are hung on trees
To whisper of old memories.
And trails with cedar shadows black
Are placed there just to lead men back
Past all the pitfalls of success
To boyhood's faith and happiness.
Far from the city's craft and fraud,
O Forest, lead me back to God

Mary Carolyn Davies,
contemporary American

73. SYMBOL

My faith is all a doubtful thing,
Wove on a doubtful loom,
Until there comes, each showery spring,
A cherry tree in bloom;

And Christ, who died upon a tree
That death had stricken bare,
Comes beautifully back to me,
In blossoms everywhere.

David Morton, 1886–

74. SILENCE

I need not shout my faith. Thrice eloquent
Are quiet trees and the green listening sod;
Hushed are the stars, whose power is never
spent;
The hills are mute: yet how they speak of
God!

Charles Hanson Towne, 1877–

75. IMMANENCE

Earth is instinct with spirit everywhere;
Each tree an aspiration; every clod,
A lowly lyric; every star, a prayer;
Each mountain-top, a stepping stone of
God.

Thomas Durley Landels,
contemporary American

76. THE WOODLAND SINGER

There runs a rhythm thro' the woods and seas;
In the dark pines and from the wayside rose
  A mystic soul of hidden motion blows,
A breath of life, a pulse within the breeze,
Weaving all discords to its harmonies;
  And, as its wave alternate comes and goes,
  A living power, a deathless essence flows
And moves all things and all things bounden frees.

Within this woodland lodge, remote, apart—
He heard Spring's footfall on the circling hills,
The rain's soft whisper, the young violet's stir;
Yea, and he heard Humanity's great heart
Throbbing afar amid its joys and ills,
And he their herald and interpreter!

John Jerome Rooney, 1866–1934

77. A CREED IN A GARDEN

I believe in the God of my garden, the God of the trees,
The God with the feet of the fairy who treads on the breeze
And makes of the rose-leaves a carpet. The God of the Light,
The God of the dusk and the sunset; the God of the Night
Who freshens the scents in my garden with breaths of the earth,
And juggles and frets with the tulip and brings it to birth.
I believe in the God of the thorn-bud, the God of the bird
Who fashions a song from an egg-shell; of the new world stirr'd
By the sudden comfort of April; the God of all grief
In the whimpering pain and the death of the leaf.
I believe in the God of the sky-paths, whose cumbersome cloud
Shakes warm, laughing rain o'er my garden and whispers aloud
To the slumbering ant and the earthworm, to the uttermost weed
His challenge of Life and Achievement—*That is my creed.*

Newman Flower, contemporary English

78. MY GARDEN

A garden is a lovesome thing, God wot!
  Rose plot,
  Fringed pool,
Fern'd grot—
  The veriest school
  Of peace; and yet the fool
Contends that God is not—
Not God! in gardens! when the eve is cool?
  Nay, but I have a sign;
  'Tis very sure God walks in mine.

Thomas Edward Brown, 1830–1897

79. IN THE GARDEN

Men go to their garden for pleasure;
  Go, thou, to thy garden for prayer;
The Lord walks in the cool of the evening
  With those who seek sanctuary there.

Inscription on a plaque in an old garden wall in England

80. IN THE GARDEN OF THE LORD

The word of God came unto me,
Sitting alone among the multitudes;
And my blind eyes were touched with light.
And there was laid upon my lips a flame of fire.

I laugh and shout for life is good,
Though my feet are set in silent ways.
In merry mood I leave the crowd
To walk in my garden. Ever as I walk

I gather fruits and flowers in my hands.
And with joyful heart I bless the sun
That kindles all the place with radiant life.

I run with playful winds that blow the scent
Of rose and jessamine in eddying whirls.
At last I come where tall lilies grow,
Lifting their faces like white saints to God.
While the lilies pray, I kneel upon the ground;
I have strayed into the holy temple of the
Lord.

Helen Keller,[1] *1880–*

81. EVENTIDE

At cool of day, with God I walk
My garden's grateful shade;
I hear His voice among the trees,
And I am not afraid.

He speaks to me in every wind,
He smiles from every star;
He is not deaf to me, nor blind,
Nor absent, nor afar.

His hand that shuts the flowers to sleep,
Each in its dewy fold,
Is strong my feeble life to keep,
And competent to hold.

The powers below and powers above,
Are subject to His care—
I cannot wander from His love
Who loves me everywhere.

Thus dowered, and guarded thus, with Him
I walk this peaceful shade;
I hear His voice among the trees,
And I am not afraid.

Caroline Atherton Mason, 1823–1890

82. GOOD-BYE

Good-bye, proud world! I'm going home:
Thou art not my friend, and I'm not thine.
Long through thy weary crowds I roam;
A river-ark on the ocean brine,
Long I've been tossed like the driven foam;
But now, proud world! I'm going home.

Good-bye to Flattery's fawning face;
To Grandeur with his wise grimace;
To upstart Wealth's averted eye;
To supple Office, low and high;
To crowded halls, to court and street;
To frozen hearts and hasting feet;
To those who go and those who come;
Good-bye, proud world! I'm going home.

I am going to my own hearth-stone,
Bosomed in yon green hills alone,—
A secret nook in a pleasant land,
Whose groves the frolic fairies planned;
Where arches green, the livelong day,
Echo the blackbird's roundelay,
And vulgar feet have never trod
A spot that is sacred to thought and God.

Oh, when I am safe in my sylvan home,
I tread on the pride of Greece and Rome;
And when I am stretched beneath the pines,
Where the evening star so holy shines,
I laugh at the lore and the pride of man,
At the sophist schools and the learned clan;
For what are they all in their high conceit,
When man in the bush with God may meet?

Ralph Waldo Emerson, 1803–1882

83. OUT IN THE FIELDS WITH GOD

The little cares that fretted me,
I lost them yesterday,
Among the fields above the sea,
Among the winds at play,
Among the lowing of the herds,
The rustling of the trees,
Among the singing of the birds,
The humming of the bees.

The foolish fears of what might pass
I cast them all away
Among the clover-scented grass
Among the new-mown hay,
Among the rustling of the corn
Where drowsy poppies nod,
Where ill thoughts die and good are born—
Out in the fields with God!

Author unknown[2]

[1] Miss Keller has been blind and deaf because of illness since she was nineteen months of age.
[2] Frequently attributed to Elizabeth Barrett Browning; sometimes to Louise Imogen Guiney.

84. OVERTONES

I heard a bird at break of day
Sing from the autumn trees
A song so mystical and calm
So full of certainties,
No man, I think, could listen long
Except upon his knees.
Yet this was but a simple bird,
Alone, among the trees.

William Alexander Percy, 1885–1942

85. A BLACKBIRD SUDDENLY

Heaven is in my hand, and I
Touch a heart-beat of the sky,
Hearing a blackbird's cry.

Strange, beautiful, unquiet thing,
Lone flute of God, how can you sing
Winter to spring?

You have outdistanced every voice and word,
And given my spirit wings until it stirred
Like you—a bird!

Joseph Auslander, 1897–

86. IN THE HEART

A Basque peasant returning from church speaks:

O little lark, you need not fly
To seek your Master in the sky,
He treads our native sod;
Why should you sing aloft, apart?
Sing to the heaven of my heart;
In me, in me, in me is God!

O strangers passing in your car,
You pity me who come so far
On dusty feet, ill shod;
You cannot guess, you cannot know
Upon what wings of joy I go
Who travel home with God.

From far-off lands they bring your fare,
Earth's choicest morsels are your share,
And prize of gun and rod;
At richer boards I take my seat,
Have dainties angels may not eat:
In me, in me, in me is God!

O little lark, sing loud and long
To Him who gave you flight and song,
And me a heart aflame.
He loveth them of low degree,
And He hath magnified me,
And holy, holy, holy is His Name!

Anna Bunston de Bary, contemporary English

87. TIGER

Tiger! Tiger! burning bright
In the forests of the night,
What immortal hand or eye
Could frame thy fearful symmetry?

In what distant deeps or skies
Burnt the fire of thine eyes?
On what wings dare he aspire?
What the hand dare seize the fire?

And what shoulder, and what art,
Could twist the sinews of thy heart?
And when thy heart began to beat,
What dread hand? and what dread feet?

What the hammer? what the chain?
In what furnace was thy brain?
What the anvil? what dread grasp
Dare its deadly terrors clasp?

When the stars threw down their spears,
And watered heaven with their tears,
Did He smile His work to see?
Did He who made the Lamb make thee?

Tiger! Tiger! burning bright
In the forests of the night,
What immortal hand or eye
Dare frame thy fearful symmetry?

William Blake, 1757–1827

88. THE ASS SPEAKS

I am the little ass of Christ,
I carried Him ere He was born,
And bore Him to His bitter Tryst
Unwilling, that Palm Sunday morn.

I was His mother's servant, I,
I carried her from Nazareth,

Up to the shining hill-country,
  To see the Lady Elizabeth.

The stones were many in my road,
  By valleys steeper than a cup,
I, trembling for my heavenly Load,
  Went cat-foot since I held It up.

To me the wonderful charge was given,
  I, even the little ass, did go,
Bearing the very weight of Heaven;
  So I crept cat-foot, sure and slow.

Again that night when He was born,
  I carried my dear burdens twain,
And heard dull people's insolent scorn
  Bidding Them to the night and rain.

I knelt beside my Brother Ox,
  And saw the very Birth! Oh, Love!
And awe and wonder! Little folks
  May see such sights nor die thereof.

The chilly Babe we breathed upon,
  Warmed with our breath the frozen air,
Kneeling beside Our Lady's gown,
  His only comfort, saving her.

I am beaten, weary-foot, ill-fed;
  Men curse me: yet I bear withal
Christ's Cross betwixt my shoulders laid.
  So I am honoured, though I'm small.

I served Christ Jesus and I bear
  His Cross upon my rough grey back.
Dear Christian people, pray you, spare
  The whip, for Jesus Christ His sake.

Katharine Tynan Hinkson, 1861–1931

89. THE HILLS KEEP HOLY GROUND

When morning moves in slow processional
To worship day, the hills keep holy ground,
Where spirit meets in high confessional
The presence of Infinity, and sound
Of an eternal power stirs the air.
From silence unto silence echoes roll
The deep acclaim of consciousness aware
Of oneness with the universal soul.

No prophet blessed the quiet of these hills,
Nor stood at prayer before their solitude.
But in their boundless peace the mind fulfills
Diameters of vision that include
Eternity, the instant of God's hand—
Who worships here has found the Holy Land

Hellene Seaman, contemporary American

90. HILLS

I never loved your plains,
  Your gentle valleys,
Your drowsy country lanes
  And pleachèd alleys.

I want my hills!—the trail
  That scorns the hollow.
Up, up the ragged shale
  Where few will follow.

Up, over wooded crest
  And mossy boulder
With strong thigh, heaving chest
  And swinging shoulder,

So let me hold my way,
  By nothing halted,
Until, at close of day
  I stand exalted

High on my hills of dream,
  Dear hills that know me.
And then, how fair will seem
  The lands below me,

How pure at vesper-time
  The far bells chiming!
God, give me hills to climb
  And strength for climbing!

Arthur Guiterman, 1871–1943

91. From A STRIP OF BLUE

I do not own an inch of land,
  But all I see is mine,—
The orchard and the mowing-fields,
  The lawns and gardens fine.
The winds my tax-collectors are,
  They bring me tithes divine,—
Wild scents and subtle essences,
  A tribute rare and free;
And, more magnificent than all,
  My window keeps for me
A glimpse of blue immensity,—
  A little strip of sea.

❖

Here sit I, as a little child;
  The threshold of God's door
Is that clear band of chrysoprase
  Now the vast temple floor,
The blinding glory of the dome
  I bow my head before.
Thy universe, O God, is home,
  In height or depth, to me;
Yet here upon thy footstool green
  Content am I to be;
Glad when is oped unto my need
  Some sea-like glimpse of Thee.

Lucy Larcom, 1824–1893

92. CLEON AND I

Cleon hath a million acres,—
  Ne'er a one have I;
Cleon dwelleth in a palace,—
  In a cottage I.
Cleon hath a dozen fortunes,—
  Not a penny I;
Yet the poorer of the twain is
  Cleon, and not I.

Cleon, true, possesseth acres,—
  But the landscape I;
Half the charms to me it yieldeth,
  Money cannot buy.
Cleon harbors sloth and dullness,—
  Freshening vigor I;
He in velvet, I in fustian,
  Richer man am I.

Cleon is a slave to grandeur,—
  Free as thought am I;
Cleon fees a score of doctors,
  Need of none have I.
Wealth-surrounded, care-environed,—
  Cleon fears to die.
Death may come, he'll find me ready,—
  Happier man am I.

Cleon sees no charm in nature,—
  In a daisy I;
Cleon hears no anthem ringing
  In the sea and sky;
Nature sings to me forever,—
  Earnest listener I!
State for state, with all attendants,
  Who would change? Not I.

Charles Mackay, 1814–1889

93. THE HILL-BORN

You who are born of the hills,
Hill-bred, lover of hills,
Though the world may not treat you aright,
Though your soul be aweary with ills:
This will you know above other men,
In the hills you will find your peace again.

You who were nursed on the heights,
Hill-bred, lover of skies,
Though your love and your hope and your
  heart,
Though your trust be hurt till it dies:
This will you know above other men,
In the hills you will find your faith again.

You who are brave from the winds,
Hill-bred, lover of winds,
Though the God whom you know seems dim,
Seems lost in a mist that blinds:
This will you know above other men,
In the hills you will find your God again.

Maxwell Struthers Burt, 1882–

94. THE POEM I SHOULD LIKE TO WRITE

The poem I should like to write was written long ago,
In vast primeval valleys and on mountains clad in snow;
It was written where no foot of man or beast had ever trod,
And where the first wild flower turned its smiling face to God;
Where mighty winds swept far and wide o'er dark and sullen seas,
And where the first earth-mother sat, a child upon her knees.

The poem I should like to write is written in the stars,
Where Venus holds her glowing torch behind her gleaming bars;
Where old Arcturus swings his lamp across the fields of space,

And all his brilliant retinue is wheeling into place;
Where unknown suns must rise and set, as ages onward fare—
The poem I should like to write is surely written there.
No human hand can write it, for with a pen divine,
The Master Poet wrote it—each burning word and line.

Margaret A. Windes, contemporary American

95. WHEN I HEARD THE LEARN'D ASTRONOMER

When I heard the learn'd astronomer;
When the proofs, the figures, were ranged in columns before me;
When I was shown the charts and diagrams, to add, divide, and measure them;
When I, sitting, heard the astronomer, where he lectured with much applause in
the lecture-room,
How soon, unaccountable, I became tired and sick;
Till rising and gliding out, I wander'd off by myself,
In the mystical moist night-air, and from time to time,
Look'd up in perfect silence at the stars.

Walt Whitman, 1819–1892

96. GOD IS AT THE ANVIL

God is at the anvil, beating out the sun;
Where the molten metal spills,
At His forge among the hills
He has hammered out the glory of a day that's done.

God is at the anvil, welding golden bars;
In the scarlet-streaming flame
He is fashioning a frame
For the shimmering silver beauty of the evening stars.

Lew Sarett, 1888–

97. STARRY NIGHT

We are such little men when the stars come out,
So small under the open maw of the night,
That we must shout and pound the table and drive wild,
And gather dollars and madly dance and drink deep,
And send the great birds flying, and drop death.
When the stars come out we are such little men
That we must arm ourselves in glare and thunder,
Or cave in on our own dry littleness.

We are such little men when the stars come out!
Ah, God behind the stars, touch with your finger
This mite of meaningless dust and give it substance.
I am so little, under the frown of the night!
Be you my body, you my eyes, my lips,
My hands, my feet, my heart-beat and my hunger,
That I may face the infinite spaces, and live;
And stand in quietness, when the stars come out.

Hermann Hagedorn, 1882–

98. THE STARS ARE TRUE

We do not know the ports from which we sail,
  Nor in what harbors our frail barques are due;
The waters that we sail are strange as sleep,
  The winds are fickle, but the stars are true.

Author unknown

99. REFUGE

When stars ride in on the wings of dusk,
  Out on the silent plain,
After the fevered fret of day,
  I find my strength again.

Under the million friendly eyes
  That smile in the lonely night,
Close to the rolling prairie's heart,
  I find my heart for the fight.

Out where the cool long winds blow free
  I fling myself on the sod;
And there in the tranquil solitude
  I find my soul,—and God.

Lew Sarett, 1888–

100. O GOD, WHOSE SMILE IS IN THE SKY

O God, whose smile is in the sky,
Whose path is in the sea,
Once more from earth's tumultuous strife,
We gladly turn to Thee.

Now all the myriad sounds of earth
In solemn stillness die;
While wind and wave unite to chant
Their anthems to the sky.

We come as those with toil far spent
Who crave Thy rest and peace,
And from the care and fret of life
Would find in Thee release.

O Father, soothe all troubled thought,
Dispel all idle fear,
Purge Thou each heart of secret sin,
And banish every care;

Until, as shine upon the sea
The silent stars above,
There shines upon our trusting souls
The light of Thine own love.

John Haynes Holmes, 1879–

101. THE ONE GOD

God is One and Alone, and there is none other with him.
God is the One, the One who has made all things.
God is a Spirit, a hidden Spirit, the Spirit of Spirits, the great Spirit of Egypt, the divine Spirit.
God is from the beginning, and has existed from the beginning.
He is the primeval One, and existed when as yet nothing existed:
  He existed when as yet there was nothing, and whatever is,
  He made it after He was. He is the Father of Beginnings. . . .
God is hidden, and no one hath perceived his form, no one hath fathomed his likeness, He is hidden in respect of Gods and men, and is a mystery to his creatures.
God is the Truth . . . He is the King of Truth.
God is Life and man lives through him alone. . . .
God is Father and Mother: the Father of fathers, and the Mother of mothers.
God begets, but He is not begotten. . . .
He begets Himself, and gives birth to Himself: He makes, but is not made. . . .
That which emanates from his heart is performed immediately, and when He has once spoken, it actually comes to pass, and endures for ever and ever.

Ancient Egyptian hymn; tr. by E. A. Wallis Budge

102. GOD IS ONE

Into the bosom of the one great sea
Flow streams that come from hills on every side.
Their names are various as their springs.
And thus in every land do men bow down
To one great God, though known by many names.
This mighty Being we would worship now.

What though the six religions loudly shout
That each alone is true, all else are false?
Yet when in each the wise man worships God,
The great almighty *One* receives the prayer.

Oh Lord, when may I hope
To find the clue that leads
From out the labyrinth
Of brawling erring sects?

Six blind men once described an elephant
That stood before them all. One felt the back.
The second noticed pendent ears. The third
Could only find the tail. The beauteous tusks
Absorbed the admiration of the fourth.
While of the other two, one grasped the trunk.
The last sought for small things and found
Four thick and clumsy feet. From what each learned,
He drew the beast. Six monsters stood revealed.

Just so the six religions learned of God,
And tell their wondrous tales. Our God is one.

Panatattu (E. India), 10th century A.D.

103. SO MANY!

So many stars in the infinite space—
So many worlds in the light of God's face.

So many storms ere the thunders shall cease—
So many paths to the portals of Peace.

So many years, so many tears—
Sighs and sorrows and pangs and prayers.

So many ships in the desolate night—
So many harbors, and only one Light.

So many creeds like the weeds in the sod—
So many temples, and only one God.

Frank L. Stanton, 1857–1927

104. IMMANENCE

I come in the little things,
Saith the Lord:
Not borne on morning wings
Of majesty, but I have set My Feet
Amidst the delicate and bladed wheat
That springs triumphant in the furrowed sod.
There do I dwell, in weakness and in power;
Not broken or divided, saith our God!
In your strait garden plot I come to flower:
About your porch My Vine
Meek, fruitful, doth entwine;
Waits, at the threshold, Love's appointed hour.

I come in the little things,
Saith the Lord:
Yea! on the glancing wings
Of eager birds, the softly pattering feet
Of furred and gentle beasts, I come to meet
Your hard and wayward heart. In brown bright eyes
That peep from out the brake, I stand confest.
On every nest
Where feathery patience is content to brood

And leaves her pleasure for the high emprise
Of motherhood—
There doth My Godhead rest.

I come in the little things,
Saith the Lord:
My starry wings
I do forsake,
Love's highway of humility to take:
Meekly I fit My Stature to your need.
In beggar's part
About your gates I shall not cease to plead—
As man, to speak with man—
Till by such art
I shall achieve My Immemorial Plan,
Pass the low lintel of the human heart.

Evelyn Underhill, 1875–1941

105. THE IMMANENT GOD

From "Woodnotes"

Ever fresh the broad creation,
A divine improvisation,
From the heart of God proceeds,
A single Will, a million deeds. . . .
Alike to Him the better, the worse—
The glowing angel, the outcast corse.
Thou meetest Him by centuries,
And lo! He passes like the breeze;
Thou seek'st in globe the galaxy,
He hides in true transparency;
Thou askest in fountain and in fires,
He is the essence that inquires,
He is the axis of the star;
He is the sparkle of the spar;
He is the heart of every creature;
He is the meaning of each feature;
And His mind is the sky,
Than all it holds, more deep, more high.

Ralph Waldo Emerson, 1803–1882

106. IMMANENCE

Could my heart but see Creation as God sees it,—from within;
See His grace behind its beauty, see His will behind its force;
See the flame of life shoot upward when the April days begin;
See the wave of life rush outward from its pure eternal source;

Could I see the summer sunrise glow with God's transcendent hope;
See His peace upon the waters in the moonlight summer night;
See Him nearer still when, blinded, in the depths of gloom I grope,—
See the darkness flash and quiver with the gladness of His light;

Could I see the red-hot passion of His love resistless burn
Through the dumb despair of winter, through the frozen lifeless clod;—
Could I see what lies around me as God sees it, I should learn
That its outward life is nothing, that its inward life is God.

Edmond G. A. Holmes, 1850–1906

107. THE INDWELLING GOD

Go not, my soul, in search of Him;
  Thou wilt not find Him there,—
Or in the depths of shadow dim,
  Or heights of upper air.

For not in far-off realms of space
  The Spirit hath its throne;
In every heart it findeth place
  And waiteth to be known.

Thought answereth alone to thought
  And Soul with soul hath kin;
The outward God he findeth not,
  Who finds not God within.

And if the vision come to thee
  Revealed by inward sign,
Earth will be full of Deity
  And with His glory shine!

Thou shalt not want for company,
  Nor pitch thy tent alone;
The Indwelling God will go with thee,
  And show thee of His own.

O gift of gifts, O grace of grace,
  That God should condescend
To make thy heart His dwelling-place,
  And be thy daily Friend!

Then go not thou in search of Him,
  But to thyself repair;
Wait thou within the silence dim
  And thou shalt find Him there.

Frederick Lucian Hosmer, 1840–1929

108. THOU LIFE WITHIN MY LIFE

Thou Life within my life, than self more near,
Thou veiléd Presence infinitely clear,
From all illusive shows of sense I flee,
To find my center and my rest in Thee.

Below all depths Thy saving mercy lies,
Through thickest glooms I see Thy light arise;
Above the highest heavens Thou art not found
More surely than within this earthly round.

Take part with me against these doubts that rise,
And seek to throne Thee far in distant skies;
Take part with me against this self that dares
Assume the burden of these sins and cares.

How shall I call Thee who art always here?
How shall I praise Thee who art still most dear?
What may I give Thee save what Thou hast given,
And whom but Thee have I in earth or heaven?

Eliza Scudder, 1821–1896

109. GOD WITHIN YET ABOVE

The peaks, and the starlit skies, the deeps of the fathomless seas,
Immanent is He in all, yet higher and deeper than these.

The heart, and the mind, and the soul, the thoughts and the yearnings of Man,
Of His essence are one and all, and yet define it who can?

The love of the Right, tho' cast down, the hate of victorious ill,
All are sparks from the central fire of a boundless beneficent Will.

Oh, mystical secrets of Nature, great Universe undefined,
Ye are parts of the infinite work of a mighty ineffable Mind.

Beyond your limitless Space, before your measureless Time,
Ere Life or Death began was this changeless Essence sublime.

In the core of eternal calm He dwelleth unmoved and alone
Mid the Universe He has made, as a monarch upon his throne.

And the self-same inscrutable Power which fashioned the sun and the star
Is Lord of the feeble strength of the humblest creatures that are.

The weak things that float or creep for their little life of a day,
The weak souls that falter and faint, as feeble and futile as they;

The malefic invisible atoms unmarked by man's purblind eye
That beleaguer our House of Life, and compass us till we die;

All these are parts of Him, the indivisible One,
Who supports and illumines the many, Creation's Pillar and Sun!

Yea, and far in the depths of Being, too dark for a mortal brain,
Lurk His secrets of Evil and Wrong, His creatures of Death and Pain.

A viewless Necessity binds, a determinate Impetus drives
To a hidden invisible goal the freightage of numberless lives.

The waste, and the pain, and the wrong, the abysmal mysteries dim,
Come not of themselves alone, but are seed and issue of Him.

And Man's spirit that spends and is spent in mystical questionings,
Oh, the depths of the fathomless deep, oh, the riddle and secret of things,
And the voice through the darkness heard, and the rush of winnowing wings!

Lewis Morris, 1833–1907

110. WITHOUT AND WITHIN

"If I ascend to heaven, thou art there;
There too, thou, if I make my bed in hell;
And if I take the wings of morning, there
Within the sea's most utmost parts to dwell,
Thy hand shall lead and hold me, even there."
Of old, thy singer thus; and in my heart
I hid myself from thee, long years apart.

"Raise but the stone, and thou shalt find me
there;
Or cleave the wood, and there am I. I say
Wherever there is one alone, yea, there
Am I in him." These thy new words, to-day
I heard, still darkly hid, and looked, and
there—
Where I so long had thought thou hadst my
part,—
I found thee hiding with me in my heart.

Norman Ault, 1880–

111. SO FAR, SO NEAR

Thou, so far, we grope to grasp thee—
Thou, so near, we cannot clasp thee—
Thou, so wise, our prayers grow heedless—
Thou, so loving, they are needless!
In each human soul thou shinest,
Human-best is thy divinest.
In each deed of love thou warmest;

Evil into good transformest.
Soul of all, and moving centre
Of each moment's life we enter.
Breath of breathing—light of gladness—
Infinite antidote of sadness;—
All-preserving ether flowing
Through the worlds, yet past our knowing.
Never past our trust and loving,
Nor from thine our life removing.
Still creating, still inspiring,
Never of thy creatures tiring;
Artist of thy solar spaces;
And thy humble human faces;
Mighty glooms and splendours voicing;
In thy plastic work rejoicing;
Through benignant law connecting
Best with best—and all perfecting,
Though all human races claim thee,
Thought and language fail to name thee,
Mortal lips be dumb before thee,
Silence only may adore thee!

Christopher Pearse Cranch, 1813–1892

112. THE DWELLING PLACE

What happy secret fountain,
Fair shade or mountain,
Whose undiscovered virgin glory
Boasts it this day, though not in story,
Was then thy dwelling? did some cloud
Fix'd to a tent, descend and shroud
My distrest Lord? or did a star,
Beckoned by thee, though high and far,
In sparkling smiles haste gladly down
To lodge light and increase her own?
My dear, dear God! I do not know
What lodged thee then, nor where, nor how;
But I am sure thou now dost come
Oft to a narrow, homely room,
Where thou too hast but the least part,
My God, I mean *my sinful heart.*

Henry Vaughan, 1622–1695

113. LOST AND FOUND

I missed him when the sun began to bend;
I found him not when I had lost his rim;
With many tears I went in search of him,
Climbing high mountains which did still
ascend,
And gave me echoes when I called my friend;
Through cities vast and charnel-houses grim,
And high cathedrals where the light was dim,
Through books and arts and works without
an end,
But found him not—the friend whom I had
lost.
And yet I found him—as I found the lark,
A sound in fields I heard but could not mark;
I found him nearest when I missed him most;
I found him in my heart, a life in frost,
A light I knew not till my soul was dark.

George Macdonald, 1824–1905

114. LIFE OF OUR LIFE

Not in the cosmic vast alone
Hast Thou Thine awesome dwelling-place;
Thou in the midst of life art known,
Here may Thy servants see Thy face.

Life of our Life, Immortal Love,
Thou art our quest in this glad hour!
Thee would we worship! From above,
Send Thou, we pray, Thy Spirit's power!

Faith, on this height, her fane doth rear,
Buildeth her altar unto Thee
Above the vale. Oh draw Thou near!
Thyself transfigured let us see!

Spirit of God, this very hour,
As we Thy hallowing presence seek,
Breathe Thou on us Thy girding power,
And to our inmost spirits speak!

Take Thou the gift, Thou whom we name,
Unto Thy uses dedicate!
Kindle the altar with Thy flame
Which with our vows we consecrate!

May chastened glories of the years
Upon these halls their halo shed,
As when an Inner Light appears
To him who walks with softer tread.

May Life, illumined Life, be laid
Over against earth's pain and loss!
May serving Love march unafraid,
Living its faith, bearing its cross!

Life of our Life, Immortal Love,
Thine is the altar, Thine the flame.
Kindle the altar from above!
Take Thou the gift, Thou whom we name!

Henry Burke Robins, 1874–

115. GOD BE IN MY HEAD

God be in my head,
And in my understanding;

God be in my eyes,
And in my looking;

God be in my mouth,
And in my speaking;

God be in my heart,
And in my thinking;

God be at my end,
And at my departing.

Sarum Primer, 1558

116. THE HIGHER COMMAND

From "Antigone"

Antigone, a young girl, standing alone before Creon, tyrant of Thebes, defies the cruel decree of the tyrant. Basing her defense on "the unwritten laws of God that know not change" she anticipates the fundamental principle of the American Declaration of Independence (1776), and the International war crimes trial at Nuremberg (1946).

Creon. [*To* ANTIGONE] Knew'st thou the edicts which forbade these things?
Antigone. I knew them. Could I fail? Full clear were they.
Creon. And thou did'st dare to disobey these laws?
Antigone. Yes, for it was not Zeus who gave them forth,
Nor Justice, dwelling with the Gods below,
Who traced these laws for all the sons of men;
Nor did I deem thy edicts strong enough,
That thou, a mortal man, should'st over-pass
The unwritten laws of God that know not change.
They are not of to-day nor yesterday,
But live for ever, nor can man assign
When first they sprang to being.

Sophocles, 495–406 B.C.

117. JUDGMENT AND MERCY

From "The Devil to Pay"

All things God can do, but this thing He will not:
Unbind the chain of cause and consequence,
Or speed time's arrow backward. When man chose
To know like God, he also chose to be
Judged by God's values. Adam sinned, indeed,
And with him all mankind; and from that sin
God wrought a nobler virtue out for Adam,
And with him, all mankind. No soul can 'scape
That universal kinship and remain
Human—no man; not even God made man.
He, when He hung upon the fatal tree,
Felt all the passion of the world pierce through Him,
Nor shirked one moment of the ineluctable
Load of the years; but from the griefs of time
Wrought out the splendour of His eternity.
There is no waste with God; He cancels nothing
But redeems all.

Dorothy L. Sayers, 1893–

118. RETRIBUTION

The mills of the gods grind late, but they grind fine.
Greek poet

Though the mills of God grind slowly,
Yet they grind exceeding small;
Though with patience he stands waiting,
With exactness grinds he all.

Henry Wadsworth Longfellow, 1807–1882

119. GOD'S MERCY

There's a wideness in God's mercy,
Like the wideness of the sea;
There's a kindness in His justice
Which is more than liberty.

There is no place where earth's sorrows
Are more felt than up in heaven;
There is no place where earth's failings
Have such kindly judgment given.

For the love of God is broader
Than the measure of man's mind,
And the heart of the Eternal
Is most wonderfully kind.

If our love were but more simple,
We should take Him at His word,
And our lives would be all sunshine
In the sweetness of our Lord.

Frederick William Faber, 1814–1863

120. LORD, WHO ART MERCIFUL

Lord, who art merciful as well as just,
Incline Thine ear, to me, a child of dust.
Not what I would, O Lord, I offer Thee,
Alas! but what I can.
Father Almighty, who hast made me man,
And bade me look to heav'n, for Thou art there,
Accept my sacrifice and humble prayer:
Four things, which are in Thy treasury,
I lay before Thee, Lord, with this petition:
My nothingness, my wants, my sin, and my contrition.

From the Persian; tr. by
Robert Southey, 1774–1843

121. From SUPPLICATION

Dost Thou not see about our feet
The tangles of our erring thought?
Thou knowest that we run to greet
High hopes that vanish into naught.
We bleed, we fall, we rise again;
How can we be of Thee abhorred?
We are Thy breed, we little men—
Have mercy, Lord!

Edgar Lee Masters, 1869–

122. GOD IS LOVE

God is love; His mercy brightens
All the path in which we rove;
Bliss He wakes and woe He lightens:
God is wisdom, God is love.

Chance and change are busy ever;
Man decays and ages move;
But His mercy waneth never:
God is wisdom, God is love.

Even the hour that darkest seemeth
Will His changeless goodness prove;
From the mist His brightness streameth:
God is wisdom, God is love.

He with earthly cares entwineth
Hope and comfort from above:
Everywhere His glory shineth:
God is wisdom, God is love.

John Bowring, 1792–1872

123. LOVE IS OF GOD

Beloved, let us love: love is of God;
In God alone hath love its true abode.

Beloved, let us love: for they who love,
They only, are His sons, born from above.

Beloved, let us love: for love is rest,
And he who loveth not abides unblest.

Beloved, let us love: for love is light,
And he who loveth not dwelleth in night.

Beloved, let us love: for only thus
Shall we behold that God Who loveth us.

Horatius Bonar, 1808–1889

124. GOD, OUR DWELLING PLACE

Psalm 90

LORD, thou hast been our dwelling place
In all generations.

Before the mountains were brought forth,
Or ever thou hadst formed the earth and the world,
  Even from everlasting to everlasting, thou art God.
Thou turnest man to dust;
  And sayest, Return, ye children of men.
For a thousand years in thy sight
  Are but as yesterday when it passeth,
  And as a watch in the night.
Thou carriest them away as with a flood;
  They are as a sleep.
In the morning they are like grass which groweth up.
  In the morning it flourisheth, and groweth up;
  In the evening it is cut down, and withereth.

For we are consumed in thine anger,
And in thy wrath are we troubled.

Thou hast set our iniquities before thee,
  Our secret sins in the light of thy countenance.
For all our days are passed away in thy wrath:
  We bring our years to an end as a tale that is told.
The days of our years are threescore years and ten,
  Or even by reason of strength fourscore years;
Yet is their pride but labour and sorrow;
  For it is soon gone, and we fly away.
Who knoweth the power of thine anger,
  And thy wrath according to the fear that is due unto thee?

So teach us to number our days,
That we may get us an heart of wisdom.

Return, O LORD; how long?
  And let it repent thee concerning thy servants.
O satisfy us in the morning with thy mercy;
  That we may rejoice and be glad all our days.
Make us glad according to the days wherein thou hast afflicted us,
  And the years wherein we have seen evil.
Let thy work appear unto thy servants,
  And thy glory upon their children.
And let the beauty of the LORD our God be upon us:
  And establish thou the work of our hands upon us;
  Yea, the work of our hands establish thou it.

Moulton: The Modern Reader's Bible, 1895

125. IN WHOM IS NO VARIABLENESS

God will not change; the restless years may bring
Sunlight and shade—the glories of the spring,

And silent gloom of winter hours—
Joy mixed with grief—sharp thorns with fragrant flowers.
Earth's lights may shine awhile, and then grow dim,
But God is true; there is no change in Him.

Edith Hickman Divall

126. From EVERLASTING TO EVERLASTING

Before all Time, before all worlds,
Before the dawn of every age, the dawn of every world,
Is God! And He remains
Beyond all coming ages, and beyond
All unthought worlds that yet may be!

He is, in all that is, in all that not yet is:
Even to-day He dwells in the tone of the chord
That to-morrow will draw from the strings of my harp.

Namdev, 1270; tr. by R. T. Gribble

127. From ABT VOGLER

IX

Therefore to whom turn I but to thee, the ineffable Name?
Builder and maker, thou, of houses not made with hands!
What, have fear of change from thee who art ever the same?
Doubt that thy power can fill the heart that thy power expands?
There shall never be one lost good! What was, shall live as before;
The evil is null, is naught, is silence implying sound;
What was good shall be good, with, for evil, so much good more;
On the earth the broken arcs; in the heaven a perfect round.

X

All we have willed or hoped or dreamed of good shall exist;
Not its semblance, but itself; no beauty, nor good, nor power
Whose voice has gone forth, but each survives for the melodist
When eternity affirms the conception of an hour.
The high that proved too high, the heroic for earth too hard,
The passion that left the ground to lose itself in the sky,
Are music sent up to God by the lover and the bard;
Enough that he heard it once: we shall hear it by and by.

Robert Browning, 1812–1889

128. WE ARE NOT CAST AWAY

We are not cast away, not separate;
What though the body-nature press us close?—
We breathe and hold our ground,
For the Supreme does not give and pass,
But abides forever.
Our being is the fuller for our turning toward God;

This is our peace, escape from evil, refuge from the wrong;
To hold aloof is loneliness and loss.
Here is living, since apart from God,
All life is but a shadow and a mimicry.
Life, in the consciousness of the Supreme,
In virtue of that converse, brings forth beauty, richness,—
Brings forth moral good.
The soul is pregnant that is filled with God.
From God the soul proceeds, its good lies there.
Life here, with things of earth, is but defeat—
A sinking, a failing of the wing.
Love for God is native to the soul;
We long to be at one with Him.
Even as a child, lured by a lower love, forgets a time
The ties that bind her to a noble sire,
But comes at length to hate her shame,
Returns at last to seek his face,
And in his presence finds her peace.

Plotinus, 3rd century, B.C.

129. "WITH WHOM IS NO VARIABLENESS, NEITHER SHADOW OF TURNING"

It fortifies my soul to know
That, though I perish, truth is so:
That, howsoe'er I stray and range,
Whate'er I do, Thou dost not change.
I steadier step when I recall
That, if I slip, Thou dost not fall.

Arthur Hugh Clough, 1819–1861

130. LINES WRITTEN IN HER BREVIARY

Let nothing disturb thee,
Nothing affright thee;
All things are passing;
God never changeth;
Patient endurance
Attaineth to all things;
Who God possesseth
In nothing is wanting;
Alone God sufficeth.

Ste. Theresa, 1515-1582; tr. by
Henry Wadsworth Longfellow, 1807–1882

131. THE SILENT STARS

Thoughts while on guard before Ypres, October 1917

The bark and boom of guns and shrieking flight
  Of shells;—then silence. Torn and half-decayed
  Lie scattered fragments; all is overlaid
With nauseous mire. Some flick'ring fire leaps bright
In sudden majesty, its very might
  In thund'rous self-extinguishment displayed.
  The lonely sentry, restless, half-afraid,
Finds comfort in the stars' unchanging light.

Ye strugglers mid the sordid things of life:—
Degrading poverty's unequal strife,

Triumphant evil's smug complacency,
  Thoughtless impurity, cold unbelief,
  Avarice, war, and death, and blinding grief—
Look up, and see God's loving constancy.

Eric H. Daniell, contemporary English

132. GOD IS NOT DUMB

From "Bibliolatres"

God is not dumb, that he should speak no more;
  If thou hast wanderings in the wilderness
And findest not Sinai, 'tis thy soul is poor;
  There towers the mountain of the Voice no less,
Which whoso seeks shall find; but he who bends,
Intent on manna still and mortal ends,
  Sees it not, neither hears its thundered lore.

Slowly the Bible of the race is writ,
  And not on paper leaves nor leaves of stone;
Each age, each kindred, adds a verse to it,
  Texts of despair or hope, of joy or moan.
While swings the sea, while mists the mountains shroud,
  While thunder's surges burst on cliffs of cloud,
Still at the prophets' feet the nations sit.

James Russell Lowell, 1819–1891

133. THE PRAYER

  Wilt thou not visit me?
The plant beside me feels thy gentle dew;
  And every blade of grass I see
From thy deep earth its moisture drew.

  Wilt thou not visit me?
Thy morning calls on me with cheering tone;
  And every hill and tree
Lend but one voice, the voice of Thee Alone.

  Come, for I need thy love,
More than the flower the dew, or grass the
    rain.
  Come gentle as thy holy dove,
And let me in thy sight rejoice to live again.

  I will not hide from them,
When thy storms come, though fierce may be
    their wrath;
  But bow with leafy stem
And strengthened follow on thy chosen path.

  Yes, Thou wilt visit me;
Nor plant nor tree thy eye delight so well,
  As when from sin set free
My spirit loves with thine in peace to dwell.

Jones Very, 1813–1880

134. RECOGNITION

Out of my need you come to me, O Father,
  Not as a spirit, gazing from on high,
Not as a wraith, gigantic in its outlines,
  Waiting against the tumult of the sky!
Father, you come to me in threads of music,
  And in the blessedness of whispered mirth,
And in the fragrance of frail garden flowers,
  When summer lies across the drowsy earth!

Out of my need you come to me, O Father,
  When I can scarcely see the path ahead—
It is your Hand that turns the sky, at evening,
  Into a sea of throbbing, pulsing red—
It is your call that sounds across the marshes,
  It is your smile that touches fields of grain,
Painting them with pale gold—it is your
    nearness
  That makes me see new beauty, after pain!

Out of my need you come to me, O Father—
Not as a presence vast and great and still,
But as the purple mist that clings, each
morning
To the slim summit of a pine-crowned hill.
Not as a vague and awful power that urges,
Urges and prods and hurries me along—
But as a hand that paints a lovely picture,
But as a voice that sings a tender song!

Margaret E. Sangster,
contemporary American

135. From THE CRY OF THE HUMAN

I

"There is no God," the foolish saith,
But none "There is no sorrow,"
And nature oft the cry of faith
In bitter need will borrow:
Eyes, which the preacher could not school,
By wayside graves are raiséd,
And lips say, "God be pitiful,"
Who ne'er said, "God be praiséd."

Elizabeth Barrett Browning, 1806–1861

136. EXIT GOD

Of old our fathers' God was real,
Something they almost saw,
Which kept them to a stern ideal
And scourged them into awe.

They walked the narrow path of right,
Most vigilantly well,
Because they feared eternal night
And boiling depths of Hell.

Now Hell has wholly boiled away
And God become a shade.
There is no place for him to stay
In all the world he made.

The followers of William James
Still let the Lord exist,
And call him by imposing names,
A venerable list.

But nerve and muscle only count,
Gray matter of the brain,
And an astonishing amount
Of inconvenient pain.

I sometimes wish that God were back
In this dark world and wide;
For though some virtues he might lack,
He had his pleasant side.

Gamaliel Bradford, 1863–1932

137. ROUND OUR RESTLESSNESS

Oh, the little birds sang east, and the little birds sang west,
And I smiled to think God's greatness flowed around our incompleteness,—
Round our restlessness, his rest.

Elizabeth Barrett Browning, 1806–1861

138. THE IMPERCIPIENT

(AT A CATHEDRAL SERVICE)

That with this bright believing band
I have no claim to be,
That faiths by which my comrades stand
Seem fantasies to me,
And mirage-mists their Shining Land,
Is a strange destiny.

Why thus my soul should be consigned
To infelicity,
Why always I must feel as blind
To sights my brethren see,
Why joys they've found I cannot find,
Abides a mystery.

Since heart of mine knows not that ease
Which they know; since it be
That He who breathes All's Well to these
Breathes no All's-Well to me,
My lack might move their sympathies
And Christian charity!

I am like a gazer who should mark
  An inland company
Standing upfingered, with, "Hark! hark!
  The glorious distant sea!"
And feel, "Alas, 'tis but yon dark
  And wind-swept pine to me!"

Yet I would bear my shortcomings
  With meet tranquillity,
But for the charge that blessed things
  I'd liefer not have be.
O doth a bird deprived of wings
  Go earth-bound wilfully!

❖

Enough. As yet disquiet clings
  About us. Rest shall we.

Thomas Hardy, 1840–1928

139. OH THAT I KNEW WHERE I MIGHT FIND HIM

Job 23: 3, 8–10

Oh that I knew where I might find him!
  that I might come even to his seat!

  Behold, I go forward,
    but he is not there;
    and backward,
    but I cannot perceive him:
  On the left hand, where he doth work,
    but I cannot behold him:
    he hideth himself on the right hand,
    that I cannot see him:

But he knoweth the way that I take:
  when he hath tried me, I shall come forth
    as gold.

King James Version, 1611

140. THE GOD WHO HIDES

"Wherefore hidest thou thy face,
  And holdest me for thy enemy?"
Job 13: 24

Why dost thou shade thy lovely face? O why
Does that eclipsing hand so long deny
The sunshine of thy soul enliv'ning eye?

Without that light, what light remains in me?
Thou art my life, my way, my light; in thee
I live, I move, and by thy beams I see.

Thou art my life; if thou but turn away,
My life's a thousand deaths: thou art my way;
Without thee, Lord, I travel not, but stray.

My light thou art; without thy glorious sight,
Mine eyes are dark'ned with perpetual night:
My God, thou art my way, my life, my light.

Thou art my way; I wander, if thou fly:
Thou art my light; if hid, how blind am I!
Thou art my life; if thou withdraw, I die.

Mine eyes are blind and dark, I cannot see;
To whom, or whither, should my darkness flee,
But to the light? and who's that light but thee?

My path is lost; my wand'ring steps do stray;
I cannot safely go, nor safely stay;
Whom should I seek but thee, my path, my way?

O, I am dead: to whom shall I, poor I,
Repair? To whom shall my sad ashes fly
But life? And where is life but in thine eye?

And yet thou turn'st away thy face, and fly'st me;
And yet I sue for grace, and thou deny'st me;
Speak, art thou angry, Lord, or only try'st me?

Unscreen those heavenly lamps, or tell me why
Thou shad'st thy face; perhaps, thou think'st no eye
Can view those flames, and not drop down and die.

If that be all, shine forth, and draw thee nigher;
Let me behold and die; for my desire
Is, phoenix-like, to perish in that fire.

❖

If I have lost my path, great Shepherd, say,
Shall I still wander in a doubtful way?
Lord, shall a lamb of Isr'el's sheepfold stray?

Thou art the pilgrim's path; the blind man's eye;
The dead man's life; on thee my hopes rely;
If thou remove, I err; I grope; I die.

Disclose thy sun-beams, close thy wings and stay;
See, see, how I am blind, and deaf, and stray,
O thou, that art my Light, my Life, my Way.

Francis Quarles, 1592–1644

141. WHERE IS THY GOD?

Psalm 42

Like as the hart, athirst in desert dreary,
Pants for the brooklet and the soft green sod,
So doth my soul, with toil and sorrow weary,
Yearn for the presence of the living God.

By day and night my inmost heart is shaken
With grief and fearing, while the scoffers say:
"Where is thy God, that thou art thus forsaken?"
And in my shame I turn my face away.

There was a time, when Sabbath bells were ringing,
I went rejoicing to the House of Prayer,
Joining with rapture in the reverent singing,
Soaring on wings of faith to mansions fair.

And now, with downcast eyes and ever grieving,
  I go reluctant and with heavy tread,—
Why, O my soul, art thou so unbelieving?
  Trust thou in God, He shall lift up thy head.

The Lord will yet command His loving-kindness,
  Even when the day of toil is hard and long;
And when the night enshrouds my soul with blindness,
  His presence shall rise in me like a song.

J. Lewis Milligan, contemporary Canadian

142. From "LIKE TO THE ARCTIC NEEDLE"

Eternal God! O Thou that only art
  The sacred fountain of eternal light,
And blessed loadstone of my better part,
  O Thou, my heart's desire, my soul's delight!
Reflect upon my soul, and touch my heart,
  And then my heart shall prize no good above Thee;
  And then my soul shall know Thee; knowing, love Thee;
And then my trembling thoughts shall never start
  From Thy commands, or swerve the least degree,
Or once presume to move, but as they move in Thee.

Francis Quarles, 1592–1644

143. DEPENDENCE ON GOD

Even as the needle, that directs the hour,
Touched with the loadstone, by the secret power
Of hidden nature, points unto the Pole;
Even so the wavering powers of my soul,
Touched by the virtue of Thy Spirit, flee
From what is earth, and point alone to Thee.

When I have faith to hold Thee by the hand,
I walk securely, and methinks I stand
More firm than Atlas; but when I forsake
The safe protection of Thine arm, I quake
Like wind-shaked reeds, and have no strength at all,
But like a vine, the prop cut down, I fall.

Francis Quarles, 1592–1644

144. MY LODE-STAR

From "Pauline"

I have always had one lode-star; now,
As I look back, I see that I have halted
Or hastened as I looked towards that star—
A need, a trust, a yearning after God.

❖

My God, my God, let me for once look on thee
As though naught else existed, we alone!
And as creation crumbles, my soul's spark
Expands till I can say,—"Even from myself
I need thee and I feel thee and I love thee.
I do not plead my rapture in thy works
For love of thee, nor that I feel as one
Who cannot die: but there is that in me
Which turns to thee, which loves or which should love."

Robert Browning, 1812–1889

145. GOD

Day and night I wander widely through the wilderness of thought,
Catching dainty things of fancy most reluctant to be caught.
Shining tangles leading nowhere persistently unravel,
Tread strange paths of meditation very intricate to travel.

Gleaming bits of quaint desire tempt my steps beyond the decent.
I confound old solid glory with publicity too recent.
But my one unchanged obsession, wheresoe'er my feet have trod,
Is a keen, enormous, haunting, never-sated thirst for God.

Gamaliel Bradford, 1863–1932

146. INTUITION

From "In Memoriam"

CXXIV

That which we dare invoke to bless;
Our dearest faith; our ghastliest doubt;
He, They, One, All; within, without;
The Power in darkness whom we guess,—

I found Him not in world or sun,
Or eagle's wings, or insect's eye,
Nor thro' the questions men may try,
The petty cobwebs we have spun.

If e'er when faith had fall'n asleep,
I heard a voice "Believe no more;"
And heard an ever-breaking shore
That tumbled in the Godless deep,

A warmth within the breast would melt
The freezing reason's colder part,
And like a man in wrath the heart
Stood up and answer'd, "I have felt."

No, like a child in doubt and fear:
But that blind clamor made me wise;
Then was I as a child that cries,
But, crying, knows his father near;

And what I am beheld again
What is, and no man understands;
And out of darkness came the hands
That reach thro' nature, moulding men.

Alfred Tennyson, 1809–1892

147. From THE WILD KNIGHT

So, with the wan waste grasses on my spear,
I ride forever, seeking after God.
My hair grows whiter than my thistle plume,
And all my limbs are loose; but in my eyes
The star of an unconquerable praise:
For in my soul one hope forever sings,
That at the next white corner of a road
My eyes may look on Him. . . .

Gilbert K. Chesterton, 1874–1936

148. THE FALCONER OF GOD

I flung my soul to the air like a falcon flying.
I said, "Wait on, wait on, while I ride below!
I shall start a heron soon
In the marsh beneath the moon—
A strange white heron rising with silver on its wings,
Rising and crying
Wordless, wondrous things;
The secret of the stars, of the world's heart-strings
The answer to their woe.
Then stoop thou upon him, and grip and hold him so!"

My wild soul waited on as falcons hover.
I beat the reedy fens as I trampled past.
I heard the mournful loon
In the marsh beneath the moon.
And then, with feathery thunder, the bird of my desire
Broke from the cover
Flashing silver fire.
High up among the stars I saw his pinions spire.
The pale clouds gazed aghast
As my falcon stooped upon him, and gripped and held him fast.

My soul dropped through the air—with heavenly plunder?—
Gripping the dazzling bird my dreaming knew?
Nay! but a piteous freight,
A dark and heavy weight
Despoiled of silver plumage, its voice forever stilled,—
All of the wonder
Gone that ever filled
Its guise with glory. O bird that I have killed,
How brilliantly you flew
Across my rapturous vision when first I dreamed of you!

Yet I fling my soul on high with new endeavor,
And I ride the world below with a joyful mind.
I shall start a heron soon
In the marsh beneath the moon—
A wondrous silver heron its inner darkness fledges!
I beat forever
The fens and the sedges.
The pledge is still the same—for all disastrous pledges,
All hopes resigned!
My soul still flies above me for the quarry it shall find!

William Rose Benét, 1886–

149. GOD THE ARCHITECT

Who Thou art I know not,
But this much I know:
Thou hast set the Pleiades
In a silver row;

Thou hast sent the trackless winds
Loose upon their way;
Thou hast reared a colored wall
'Twixt the night and day;

Thou hast made the flowers to bloom
  And the stars to shine;
Hid rare gems of richest ore
  In the tunneled mine;

But chief of all Thy wondrous works,
  Supreme of all Thy plan,
Thou hast put an upward reach
  In the heart of Man.

Harry Kemp, 1883–

150. THE OCEAN

From "Childe Harold," Canto IV

There is a pleasure in the pathless woods,
There is a rapture on the lonely shore,
There is society where none intrudes,
By the deep Sea, and music in its roar:
I love not Man the less, but Nature more,
From these our interviews, in which I steal
From all I may be, or have been before,
To mingle with the Universe, and feel
What I can ne'er express, yet cannot all
    conceal.

George Gordon, Lord Byron, 1788–1824

151. MEDITATION

Holding a beggar's child
  Against my heart,
Through blinding tears I see
  That as I love the tiny, piteous thing,
So God loves me!

Toyohiko Kagawa, 1888–

152. REQUESTS

I asked for Peace—
  My sins arose,
  And bound me close,
I could not find release.

I asked for Truth—
  My doubts came in,
  And with their din
They wearied all my youth.

I asked for Love—
  My lovers failed,
  And griefs assailed
Around, beneath, above.

I asked for Thee—
  And Thou didst come
  To take me home
Within Thy Heart to be.

Digby M. Dolben, 1848–1867

153. LIFE

O Love triumphant over guilt and sin,
My Soul is soiled, but Thou shalt enter in;
My feet must stumble if I walk alone,
Lonely my heart, till beating by Thine own,
My will is weakness till it rest in Thine,
Cut off, I wither, thirsting for the Vine,
My deeds are dry leaves on a sapless tree,
My live is lifeless till it live in Thee!

Frederick Lawrence Knowles, 1869–1905

154. THE ALL-LOVING

From "An Epistle"

So, the All-Great, were the All-Loving too—
So, through the thunder comes a human voice
Saying, "O heart I made, a heart beats here!
Face, my hands fashioned, see it in myself!
Thou hast no power nor mayst conceive of mine,
But love I gave thee, with myself to love,
And thou must love me who have died for thee!"

Robert Browning, 1812–1889

155. LOVE IS STRONG AS DEATH

"I have not sought Thee, I have not found Thee,
  I have not thirsted for Thee:
And now cold billows of death surround me,
Buffeting billows of death astound me,—
 Wilt Thou look upon, wilt Thou see
 Thy perishing me?"

"Yea, I have sought thee, yea, I have found thee,
  Yea, I have thirsted for thee,
Yea, long ago with love's bands I bound thee:
Now the Everlasting Arms surround thee,—
 Through death's darkness I look and see
 And clasp thee to Me."

Christina G. Rossetti, 1830–1894

156. O VOICE THAT CALLS TO ME

O Voice that calls to me from distant places
I have not seen, but visioned in a dream
Thy sound compelling startles my contentment
In this safe harbour from the tossing stream.

O Voice—I know Thee who Thou art: Strong Captain,
Master of ships and men and of the sea,
There is no night can 'fright Thee, nor a tempest
Can cast away the soul embarked with Thee.

Thine eyes have searched the ancient farthest ocean,
Full-sailed Thy ship drives onward toward the day;
I hear Thy summons to that distant voyage;
It is a cry no wind can hurl away.

I hear Thee and I answer, O my Captain,
I will aboard and quickly put to sea,
For where Thou art 'tis better than in harbour,
And in the breeze beside Thee I am free.

R. B. Y. Scott, contemporary Canadian

157. THE PRIEST

Man of Song and Man of Science,
Truly you are as people on the outside of a house,
And one of you only sees that it is made of stone, and its windows of glass, and that fire burns in the hearth,
And the other of you sees that the house is beautiful and very human,

But I have gone inside the house,
And I live with the host in that house
And have broken bread with him, and drunk his wine,
And seen the transfiguration that love and awe make in the brain . . .

For the house is the world, and the Lord is my host and my Father:
It is my Father's house.

❖

Enough? I see what is enough!
Machinery is enough for a Scientist,
And Beauty is enough for a Poet;
But in the hearts of men and women, and in the thirsty hearts of little children
There is a hunger, and there is an unappeasable longing,
For a Father and for the love of a Father . . .
For the root of a soul is mystery,
And the Night is mystery,
And in that mystery men would open inward into Eternity,
And know love, the Lord.
Blessed be his works, and his angels, and his sons crowned with his glory!

James Oppenheim, 1882–1932

158. AND WITH NO LANGUAGE BUT A CRY

I have a heart that cries to God
Abandonedly across the blind
Imperfect avenue of mind,
I have a heart that cries to God.

I have a heart that cries to God
Across the quarried stones of thought,
The labored temple slowly wrought,
A heart, a heart that cries to God.

I have a heart that cries to God
Immediately and must dispense
With faltering through the world of sense,
And calls across the mind to God;

That calls across the worlds to God,
Nor stays to elaborate the tongue
Of sacrament too slowly wrung,
I have a heart that cries to God.

Amos Niven Wilder, 1895–

159. A LAST APPEAL

O somewhere, somewhere, God unknown,
  Exist and be!
I am dying; I am all alone;
  I must have Thee!
God! God! my sense, my soul, my all,
  Dies in the cry:—
Saw'st thou the faint star flame and fall?
  Ah! it was I.

Frederick W. H. Myers, 1843–1901

160. THROUGH A FOG OF STARS

Once in a simple quest,
  Once when a lad of seven,
I stood on a kind world's breast
  And touched the cheek of heaven.

Now, in a taller hour,
  Where is that lofty place?
Where is the peak, the tower
  Where I may touch that face?

John Nixon, Jr., contemporary American

161. THE ETERNAL QUEST

Job 11: 7–8

Canst thou by searching find out God?
Canst thou find out the Almighty unto
    perfection?
  It is high as heaven;
  What canst thou do?
  Deeper than Sheol;
  What canst thou know?
  The measure thereof is longer than the
    earth,
  And broader than the sea.
  If he pass through, and shut up,
  And call unto judgement, then who can
    hinder him?

Moulton: The Modern Reader's Bible, 1895

162. PILGRIMAGE

For each of us a different path to God,
The poet by the stairway of his dreams
Or yet perhaps the sound of singing streams
May lead to hidden pinnacles untrod.
The lover finds in love the magic rod
Which wafts him upward. And a beauty gleams
Sometimes in strange and unseen ways. It seems
We go our way upon the flowering sod.

Seeking forever an invisible goal,
For deeper beauty always hungering,
Yet never nearing the desired height,
For hidden it waits beyond us, and the whole
Of life is but a pilgrimage, to wring
From chaos one star burning in the night.

Blanche Shoemaker Wagstaff, 1888–

163. THE HUB

The lights along the shore at night
Make spokes of flame upon the sea;
These twinkling shafts radiate
From where I stand, the hub of me.

Imagination the long rim
So swiftly treads a road of stars
The wheel kicks up the years in hills,
The dust of peace, the drift of wars.

The spokes now probe around for God
And in that nest of search I lie
Close to the miracle of the man
Who walked the waters and the sky.

Oscar Williams, 1900–

164. REVELATION

I made a pilgrimage to find the God:
I listened for His voice at holy tombs,
Searched for the print of His immortal feet
In dust of broken altars: yet turned back
With empty heart. But on the homeward road
A great light came upon me, and I heard
The God's voice singing in a nestling lark;
Felt His sweet wonder in a swaying rose;
Received His blessing from a wayside well;
Looked on His beauty in a lover's face;
Saw His bright hand send signals from the suns.

Edwin Markham, 1852-1940

165. VESTIGIA

I took a day to search for God,
And found Him not. But as I trod
By rocky ledge, through woods untamed,
Just where one scarlet lily flamed,
I saw His footprint in the sod.

Then suddenly, all unaware,
Far off in the deep shadows, where
A solitary hermit thrush
Sang through the holy twilight hush—
I heard His voice upon the air.

And even as I marveled how
God gives us Heaven here and now,
In a stir of wind that hardly shook
The poplar leaves beside the brook—
His hand was light upon my brow.

At last with evening as I turned
Homeward, and thought what I had learned
And all that there was still to probe—
I caught the glory of His robe
Where the last fires of sunset burned.

Back to the world with quickening start
I looked and longed for any part
In making saving Beauty be . . .
And from that kindling ecstasy
I knew God dwelt within my heart.

Bliss Carman, 1861–1929

166. THE SEARCH FOR GOD

I sought Thee round about, O Thou my God,
  To find Thy abode:
I said unto the Earth, "Speak, art thou He?"
  She answered me,
"I am not." I enquired of creatures all,
  In general,
Contained therein: they with one voice proclaim
That none amongst them challenged such a name.

I asked the seas, and all the deeps below,
  My God to know:
I asked the reptiles, and whatever is
  In the abyss:
Even from the shrimp to the leviathan
  My enquiry ran:
But in those deserts, which no line can sound,
The God I sought for was not to be found.

I asked the Air, if that were He, but know
  It told me, "No":
I from the towering eagle to the wren
  Demanded then,
If any feathered fowl 'mong them were such:
  But they, all much
Offended at my question, in full quire
Answered, to find my God I must look higher.

And now, my God, by Thy illumining grace,
  Thy glorious face
(So far forth as Thou wilt discovered be)
  Methinks I see:
And though invisible and infinite,
  To human sight
Thou in Thy Mercy, Justice, Truth, appearest,
In which to our frail senses Thou com'st nearest.

O, make us apt to seek and quick to find,
  Thou God most kind:
Give us Love, Hope, and Faith in Thee to trust,
  Thou God most just:
Remit all our offenses, we entreat,
  Most Good, most Great:
Grant that our willing though unworthy quest
May, through Thy grace, admit us 'mongst the blest.

Thomas Heywood, 1574?–1641

167. THE QUEST

For years I sought the Many in the One,
I thought to find lost waves and broken
    rays,
The rainbow's faded colours in the sun—
The dawns and twilights of forgotten days.

But now I seek the One in every form,
Scorning no vision that a dewdrop holds,
The gentle Light that shines behind the storm,
The Dream that many a twilight hour
    enfolds.

Eva Gore-Booth, 1872–1926

168. I'VE TRAVELLED FAR IN MANY LANDS

I've travelled far in many lands,
The open road I've trod;
And through the devious ways of men
I've searched with them for God.

The Ancients found Him in their groves,
The Wise Men saw the Star.
God comes to some in paths of peace,
To some in flaming war.

Before the Buddha some men bow;
Some love the Nazarene.
The mystic feels a presence near,
Although no form is seen.

On desert sands the vision comes,
As men turn toward the East,
And while some fasting see His face,
Some find Him at the feast.

In temple, mosque, cathedral dim,
Through vigil, chant, and prayer,
Wherever man cries out to God
The living God is there.

Wherever man has fought for right,
Where man for man has died;
Beside him stands, could we but see,
One that was crucified.

Alone I have communed with Him
Beneath a starlit sky,
And I have touched His garment hem
Where crowds go thronging by.

And this is clear in all my search,
As clear as noonday sun;
The name and form are nought to God,
To Him all shrines are one.

Hinton White, c. 1900

169. THE CATHEDRAL

Each lonely haunt where vanished tribes have dwelt
Still holds a time-worn god long overthrown,
Or ruined temple where dark woods have grown,
With whose cold shrines warm earth has kindly dealt;
For through all passing ages man has felt
He has not wandered aimless or alone,
And here within these walls of hallowed stone
At last before Love's very Presence knelt.

No blood of victims round the altar clings,
Where he whose guerdon was a thorny crown
Is sacrificed for men perpetually;
And gifts of gold are dimmed by greater things—
The Bread in pity shared, the Life laid down
That they who sit in darkness may be free.

Thomas S. Jones, Jr., 1882–1932

170. THE HIGH HILL

I went up to a high hill
To seek a spirit leaven;
I went up to a high hill
To get me nearer Heaven.

I went up to a high hill
In blue serener air;
I went up to a high hill
To see if God were there.

But God was not on the high hill,
On the high hill apart;
God was not on the high hill,
Not being in my heart.

I went down to a deep vale,
And there I made my prayer;
I went down to a deep vale,
And lo, my God was there!

One need not go to a high hill
Be he with faith unshod;
One need not go to a high hill
If he would find out God.

Clinton Scollard, 1860–1932

171. THE SEEKERS

One asked a sign from God; and day by day
The sun arose in pearl, in scarlet set,
Each night the stars appeared in bright array,
Each morn the thirsting grass with dew was wet.
The corn failed not its harvest, nor the vine.
And yet he saw no sign.

One longed to hear a prophet; and he strayed
Through crowded streets, and by the open sea.
He saw men send their ships for distant trade,
And build for generations yet to be.
He saw the farmer sow his acres wide,
But went unsatisfied.

One prayed a sight of heaven; and erewhile
He saw a workman at his noontime rest.
He saw one dare for honor, and the smile
Of one who held a babe upon her breast;
At dusk two lovers walking hand in hand;
But did not understand.

Victor Starbuck, 1887–1935

172. THIS IS THE TRAGEDY

God pity eyes that have not seen the dawn,
Twilight, or shadow, or a wind-blown tree,
But pity more the eyes that look upon
All loveliness, and yet can never see;
God pity ears that have not caught the notes
Of wind or wave, of violin or bird,
But pity more that, daily, music floats
To ears that hear and yet have never heard.

God pity hearts that have not known the gift
Of love requited, comfort and caress,
But, O God, pity more the hearts that drift
From love's high moment to forgetfulness.
This is the tragedy of common sense:
To dim all wonder by indifference.

Helen Frazee-Bower, contemporary American

173. UNFAITH

"There is no sun!" the blind man said.
And so I asked him: "What
Pours down its warmth upon your head,
If there is not?"

I asked him why the nights were cool
If sunset there were none;
But answered this pathetic fool,
"There is no sun!"

"'Tis no illusion of the mind,"
Said I, "that I can see—
The fact that all men call you blind
Proves light to be.

"Winter and summer, what are they,
And odor of the flowers?
And what the meaning of the day,
And night's long hours?"

"God," said this simple-minded child,
"Calls life from out the sod."
"God pity you, blind fool!" I smiled—
"There is no God."

And so we parted, he and I,
Each skeptically proud . . .
But as I went, I wondered why
He laughed so loud.

Ted Robinson, contemporary American

174. BLIND

"Show me your God!" the doubter cries.
I point him to the smiling skies;
I show him all the woodland greens;
I show him peaceful sylvan scenes;
I show him winter snows and frost;
I show him waters tempest-tossed;
I show him hills rock-ribbed and strong;
I bid him hear the thrush's song;
I show him flowers in the close—
The lily, violet and rose;
I show him rivers, babbling streams;
I show him youthful hopes and dreams;
I show him maids with eager hearts;

I show him toilers in the marts;
I show him stars, the moon, the sun;
I show him deeds of kindness done;
I show him joy; I show him care,
And still he holds his doubting air,
And faithless goes his way, for he
Is blind of soul, and cannot see!

John Kendrick Bangs, 1862–1922

175. THE POET CONSIDERS PERFECTION

I sat, and held the book upon my knees,
And turned the pages idly, one by one,
Musing on many a splendid sonnet, done
With greater skill than mine. And thought: now these—
Seemingly perfected with careless ease—
Have been with utmost care and effort spun;
From inspiration's thread of gold begun,
And brought to matchless beauty by degrees.

Perfection thus emerges from the sod:
This stately tree, which shelters us today,
Came from how small a seed; this lovely rose
Was once a tight-closed bud. So each thing grows
By gradual steps to loveliness. That way
The soul has come on its long search for God.

Elizabeth Virginia Raplee, contemporary American

176. SEEKING GOD

I said, "I will find God," and forth I went
To seek Him in the clearness of the sky,
But He, over me, stood unendurably
Only a pitiless sapphire firmament
Ringing the world—blank splendor; yet intent
Still to find God, "I will go seek," said I,
"His way upon the waters," and drew nigh
An ocean marge weed-strewn and foam-besprent;
And the waves dashed on idle sand and stone,
And very vacant was the long, blue sea;
But in the evening as I sat alone,
My window open to the vanishing day,
Dear God! I could not choose but kneel and pray,
And it sufficed that I was found of Thee.

Edward Dowden, 1843–1913

177. THE REWARD

If I can lead a man who has been blind
To see the beauty in a blade of grass;
If I can aid my fellow-men to find
The friendliness of trees they daily pass;

If I can stir a soul to view the dawn
With seeing eyes and hold the vision clear
So he may drink the rapture when 'tis gone,
To purify some sordid atmosphere;

If I can help the human ear to hear
The gladness in the waterfall's refrain;
The tenderness of robins piping clear;
The healing in the sound of falling rain;

If I can rouse but one to that rebirth
Which sees God mirrored in each flower and tree—
To feel his oneness with the whole of earth—
Why, that will be a priceless joy to me!

Grace G. Bostwick, contemporary American

178. THE QUEST

I cannot find Thee. Still on restless pinion
My spirit beats the void where Thou dost dwell;
I wander lost through all Thy vast dominion,
And shrink beneath Thy light ineffable.

I cannot find Thee. E'en when most adoring,
Before Thy throne I bend in lowliest prayer;
Beyond these bounds of thought my thought upsoaring
From farthest quest comes back: Thou art not there.

Yet high above the limits of my seeing,
And folded far within the inmost heart,
And deep below the deeps of conscious being,
Thy splendor shineth; there, O God, Thou art.

I cannot lose Thee! Still in Thee abiding,
The end is clear, how wide soe'er I roam;
The Hand that holds the worlds my steps is guiding,
And I must rest at last in Thee, my home.

Eliza Scudder, 1821–1896

179. THE MYSTIC

There is a quest that calls me
  In nights when I am lone,
The need to ride where the ways divide
  The Known from the Unknown.
I mount what thought is near me
  And soon I reach the place,
The tenuous rim where the Seen grows dim
  And the Sightless hides its face.

I have ridden the wind,
I have ridden the sea,
I have ridden the moon and stars,
I have set my feet in the stirrup seat
Of a comet coursing Mars.
And everywhere,
Thro' earth and air
My thought speeds, lightning-shod,
It comes to a place where checking pace
It cries, "Beyond lies God."

It calls me out of the darkness,
  It calls me out of sleep,
"Ride, ride! for you must, to the end of Dust!"
  It bids—and on I sweep
To the wide outposts of Being
  Where there is Gulf alone—
And thro' a vast that was never passed
  I listen for Life's tone.

I have ridden the wind
I have ridden the night,
I have ridden the ghosts that flee
From the vaults of death like a chilling breath
Over eternity.
And everywhere
Is the world laid bare—
Ether and star and clod—
Until I wind to its brink and find
But the cry, "Beyond lies God!"

It calls and ever calls me!
  And vainly I reply,
"Fools only ride where the ways divide
  What Is from the Whence and Why!"
I'm lifted into the saddle
  Of thoughts too strong to tame
And down the deeps and over the steeps
  I find—ever the same.

I have ridden the wind,
I have ridden the stars
I have ridden the force that flies
With far intent through the firmament
And each to each allies.
And everywhere
That a thought may dare
To gallop, mine has trod—
Only to stand at last on the strand
Where just beyond lies God.

Cale Young Rice, 1872-1943

180. THE DIVINE PRESENCE

All but unutterable Name!
  Adorable, yet awful sound!
Thee can the sinful nations frame
  Save with their foreheads on the ground?

Soul-searching and all-cleansing Fire;
  To see Thy countenance were to die:
Yet how beyond the bound retire
  Of Thy serene immensity?

Thou mov'st beside us, if the spot
  We change—a noteless, wandering tribe;
The orbits of our life and thought
  In Thee their little arcs describe.

In their dead calm, at cool of day,
  We hear Thy voice, and turn, and flee:
Thy love outstrips us on our way!
  From Thee, O God, we fly—to Thee.

Aubrey Thomas de Vere, 1814–1902

181. From NIGHT THOUGHTS

On nature's Alps I stand,
And see a thousand firmaments beneath:
A thousand systems, as a thousand grains!
Here human effort ends;
And leaves me still a stranger to his throne.
Full well it might. I quite mistook my road,—
Born in an age more curious than devout,
More fond to fix the place of heaven or hell
Than studious this to shun, or that secure.
'Tis not the curious, but the pious, path
That leads me to my point, Lorenzo. Know,
Without or star or angel for their guide,
Who worship God shall find him. Humble love,
And not proud reason, keeps the door of heaven;
Love finds admission where proud science fails.

Edward Young, 1683–1765

182. HO, EVERYONE THAT THIRSTETH

Isaiah 55: 1–3; 6–7

Ho, every one that thirsteth, come ye to the waters,
And he that hath no money, come ye, buy and eat;
Yea, come, buy wine and milk,
Without money and without price.

Wherefore do ye spend money for that which is not bread?
And your labour for that which satisfieth not? . . .
Incline your ear, and come unto me;
Hear, and your soul shall live:
And I will make an everlasting covenant with you. . . .

Seek ye the LORD *while he may be found,*
Call ye upon him while he is near:
Let the wicked forsake his way,
And the unrighteous man his thoughts;

And let him return unto the LORD,
And he will have mercy upon him;
And to our God,
For he will abundantly pardon.

English Revised Version, 1884

183. IN WHOM WE LIVE AND HAVE OUR BEING

Lo! in the vigils of the night, ere sped
The first bright arrows from the Orient shed,
The heart of Silence trembled into sound,
And out of Vastness came a Voice, which said:

I AM alone; thou only art in Me:
I am the stream of Life that flows through thee:
I comprehend all substance, fill all space:
I am pure Being, by whom all things be.

I am thy Dawn, from darkness to release:
I am the Deep, wherein thy sorrows cease:
Be still! be still! and know that I am God:
Acquaint thyself with Me, and be at peace!

I am the Silence that is more than sound:
If there within thou lose thee, thou art found:
The stormless, shoreless Ocean, which is I—
Thou canst not breathe, but in its bosom drowned.

I am all Love: there is naught else but I:
I am all Power: the rest is phantasy:
Evil, and anguish, sorrow, death and hell—
These are the fear-flung shadows of a lie.

Arraign not Mine Omnipotence, to say
  That aught beside in earth or heaven hath sway!
The powers of darkness are not: that which is
  Abideth: these but vaunt them for a day.

I, God, enfold thee like an atmosphere:
  Thou to thyself wert never yet more near;
Think not to shun Me; whither would'st thou fly?
  Nor go not hence to seek Me: I am here.

James Rhoades, 1841–1923

184. I SOUGHT THE LORD

I sought the Lord, and afterward I knew
He moved my soul to seek Him, seeking me;
It was not I that found, O Saviour true,
No, I was found of Thee.

Thou didst reach forth Thy hand and mine
  enfold;
I walked and sank not on the storm-vexed
  sea,—
'Twas not so much that I on Thee took hold,
As Thou, dear Lord, on me.

I find, I walk, I love, but, O the whole
Of love is but my answer, Lord, to Thee;
For Thou wert long before-hand with my
  soul,
Always Thou lovedst me.

Author unknown

185. WHOSO DRAWS NIGH TO GOD

Whoso draws nigh to God one step
  through doubtings dim,
God will advance a mile
  in blazing light to him.

Author unknown

186. THE HOUND OF HEAVEN

I fled Him, down the nights and down the days;
  I fled Him down the arches of the years;
I fled Him down the labyrinthine ways
  Of my own mind; and in the mist of tears
I hid from Him, and under running laughter.
      Up vistaed hopes I sped;
      And shot, precipitated,
  Adown titanic glooms of chasmèd fears,
From those strong Feet that followed, followed after.
      But with unhurrying chase
      And unperturbèd pace,
  Deliberate speed, majestic instancy,
      They beat—and a Voice beat
      More instant than the Feet—
"All things betray thee, who betrayest Me."

    I pleaded, outlaw-wise,
By many a hearted casement, curtained red,
  Trellised with intertwining charities;
(For, though I knew His love Who followèd,
      Yet I was sore adread
Lest, having Him, I must have naught beside;)

But, if one little casement parted wide,
The gust of His approach would clash it to.
Fear wist not to evade, as Love wist to pursue.
Across the margent of the world I fled,
And troubled the gold gateways of the stars,
Smiting for shelter on their clangèd bars;
Fretted to dulcet jars
And silvern chatter the pale ports o' the moon.
I said to dawn, Be sudden; to eve, Be soon;
With thy young skyey blossoms heap me over
From this tremendous Lover!
Float thy vague veil about me, lest He see!
I tempted all His servitors, but to find
My own betrayal in their constancy,
In faith to Him their fickleness to me,
Their traitorous trueness, and their loyal deceit.
To all swift things for swiftness did I sue;
Clung to the whistling mane of every wind.
But whether they swept, smoothly fleet,
The long savannahs of the blue;
Or whether, Thunder-driven,
They clanged His chariot 'thwart a heaven
Plashy with flying lightnings round the spurn o' their feet:—
Fear wist not to evade as Love wist to pursue.
Still with unhurrying chase
And unperturbèd pace,
Deliberate speed, majestic instancy,
Came on the following Feet,
And a Voice above their beat—
"Naught shelters thee, who wilt not shelter Me."

I sought no more that after which I strayed
In face of man or maid;
But still within the little children's eyes
Seems something, something that replies,
They at least are for me, surely for me!
I turned me to them very wistfully;
But just as their young eyes grew sudden fair
With dawning answers there,
Their angel plucked them from me by the hair.
"Come then, ye other children, Nature's—share
With me" (said I) "your delicate fellowship;
Let me greet you, lip to lip,
Let me twine with you caresses,
Wantoning
With our Lady Mother's vagrant tresses,
Banqueting
With her in her wind-walled palace,
Underneath her azure daïs,
Quaffing, as your taintless way is,
From a chalice
Lucent-weeping out of the dayspring."
So it was done:
I in their delicate fellowship was one—

Drew the bolt of Nature's secrecies.
I knew all the swift importings
On the wilful face of skies;
I knew how the clouds arise
Spumèd of the wild sea-snortings;
All that's born or dies
Rose and drooped with; made them shapers
Of mine own moods, or wailful or divine—
With them joyed and was bereaven.
I was heavy with the even
When she lit her glimmering tapers
Round the day's dead sanctities.
I laughed in the morning's eyes.
I triumphed and I saddened with all weather,
Heaven and I wept together,
And its sweet tears were salt with mortal mine;
Against the red throb of its sunset-heart
I laid my own to beat,
And share commingling heat;
But not by that, by that, was eased my human smart.
In vain my tears were wet on Heaven's grey cheek.
For ah! we know not what each other says,
These things and I; in sound *I* speak—
Their sound is but their stir, they speak by silences.
Nature, poor stepdame, cannot slake my drouth;
Let her, if she would owe me,
Drop yon blue bosom-veil of sky, and show me
The breasts o' her tenderness:
Never did any milk of hers once bless
My thirsting mouth.
Nigh and nigh draws the chase
With unperturbèd pace,
Deliberate speed, majestic instancy;
And past those noisèd Feet
A voice comes yet more fleet—
"Lo, naught contents thee, who content'st not Me."

Naked I wait Thy love's uplifted stroke!
My harness, piece by piece, Thou hast hewn from me,
And smitten me to my knee;
I am defenseless utterly.
I slept, methinks, and woke,
And, slowly gazing, find me stripped in sleep.
In the rash lustihead of my young powers,
I shook the pillaring hours
And pulled my life upon me; grimed with smears
I stand amid the dust o' the mounded years—
My mangled youth lies dead beneath the heap.
My days have crackled and gone up in smoke,
Have puffed and burst as sun-starts on a stream.
Yea, faileth now even dream
The dreamer, and the lute the lutanist;
Even the linked fantasies in whose blossomy twist
I swung the earth a trinket at my wrist,

Are yielding; cords of all too weak account
For earth with heavy griefs so overplussed.
  Ah! is Thy love indeed
A weed, albeit an amaranthine weed,
Suffering no flowers except its own to mount?
  Ah! must—
  Designer Infinite!—
Ah, must Thou char the wood ere Thou canst limn with it?
My freshness spent its wavering shower i' the dust;
And now my heart is as a broken fount,
Wherein tear-drippings stagnate, spilt down ever
  From the dank thoughts that shiver
Upon the sighful branches of my mind.
  Such is; what is to be?
The pulp so bitter, how shall taste the rind?
I dimly guess what Time in mists confounds;
Yet ever and anon a trumpet sounds
From the hid battlements of Eternity;
Those shaken mists a space unsettle, then
Round the half-glimpsèd turrets slowly wash again.
  But not ere him who summoneth
  I first have seen, enwound
With glooming robes purpureal, cypress-crowned;
His name I know, and what his trumpet saith.
Whether man's heart or life it be which yields
  Thee harvest, must Thy harvest fields
  Be dunged with rotten death?

    Now of that long pursuit
    Comes on at hand the bruit;
  That Voice is round me like a bursting sea:
    "And is thy earth so marred,
    Shattered in shard on shard?
  Lo, all things fly thee, for thou flyest Me!
  Strange, piteous, futile thing,
Wherefore should any set thee love apart?
Seeing none but I makes much of naught" (He said),
"And human love needs human meriting:
  How hast thou merited—
Of all man's clotted clay the dingiest clot?
  Alack, thou knowest not
How little worthy of any love thou art!
Whom wilt thou find to love ignoble thee
  Save Me, save only Me?
All which I took from thee I did but take,
  Not for thy harms,
But just that thou might'st seek it in My arms.
  All which thy child's mistake
Fancies as lost, I have stored for thee at home:
  Rise, clasp My hand, and come!"

  Halts by me that footfall:
  Is my gloom, after all,
Shade of His hand, outstretched caressingly?

"Ah, fondest, blindest, weakest,
I am He Whom thou seekest!
Thou dravest love from thee, who dravest Me."

Francis Thompson, 1859–1907

187. THE TESTING

When in the dim beginning of the years,
God mixed in man the raptures and the tears
And scattered through his brain the starry
stuff,
He said, "Behold! yet this is not enough,
For I must test his spirit to make sure
That he can dare the Vision and endure.

"I will withdraw my Face,
Vail me in shadow for a certain space,
Leaving behind Me only a broken clue—
A crevice where the glory glimmers through,
Some whisper from the sky,
Some footprint in the road to track Me by.

"I will leave man to make the fateful guess,
Will leave him torn between the No and Yes,
Leave him unresting till he rests in Me,
Drawn upward by the choice that makes him
free—
Leave him in tragic loneliness to choose,
With all in life to win or all to lose."

Edwin Markham, 1852–1940

188. THE SOUL'S PRAYER

In childhood's pride I said to Thee:
"O Thou, who mad'st me of Thy breath,
Speak, Master, and reveal to me
Thine inmost laws of life and death.

"Give me to drink each joy and pain
Which Thine eternal hand can mete,
For my insatiate soul would drain
Earth's utmost bitter, utmost sweet.

"Spare me no bliss, no pang of strife,
Withhold no gift or grief I crave,
The intricate lore of love and life
And mystic knowledge of the grave."

Lord, Thou didst answer stern and low:
"Child, I will hearken to thy prayer,
And thy unconquered soul shall know
All passionate rapture and despair.

"Thou shalt drink deep of joy and fame,
And love shall burn thee like a fire,
And pain shall cleanse thee like a flame,
To purge the dross from thy desire.

"So shall thy chastened spirit yearn
To seek from its blind prayer release,
And spent and pardoned, sue to learn
The simple secret of My peace.

"I, bending from my sevenfold height,
Will teach thee of My quickening grace,
Life is a prism of My light,
And death the shadow of My face."

Sarojini Naidu, 1879–

189. GOD'S PLAN

From "Commonplace"

One small life in God's great plan,
How futile it seems as the ages roll,
Do what it may, or strive how it can,
To alter the sweep of the infinite whole!
A single stitch in an endless web,
A drop in the ocean's flow and ebb!
But the pattern is rent where the stitch is lost,
Or marred where the tangled threads have
crossed;
And each life that fails of its true intent
Mars the perfect plan that its Maker meant.

Susan Coolidge, 1845–1905

190. THE LISTENERS

"Is there anybody there?" said the Traveller,
Knocking on the moonlit door;
And his horse in the silence champed the
grasses
Of the forest's ferny floor:
And a bird flew up out of the turret,
Above the Traveller's head:
And he smote upon the door again a second
time;

"Is there anybody there?" he said.
But no one descended to the Traveller;
No head from the leaf-fringed sill
Leaned over and looked into his gray eyes,
Where he stood perplexed and still.
But only a host of phantom listeners
That dwelt in the lone house then
Stood listening in the quiet of the moonlight
To that voice from the world of men:
Stood thronging the faint moon-beams on the dark stair,
That goes down to the empty hall,
Hearkening in an air stirred and shaken
By the lone Traveller's call.

And he felt in his heart their strangeness,
Their stillness answering his cry,
While his horse moved, cropping the dark turf,
'Neath the starred and leafy sky;
For he suddenly smote on the door, even
Louder, and lifted his head:—
"Tell them that I came, and no one answered,
That I kept my word," he said.
Never the least stir made the listeners,
Though every word he spake
Fell echoing through the shadowiness of the still house
From the one man left awake:
Ay, they heard his foot upon the stirrup,
And the sound of iron on stone
And how the silence surged softly backward
When the plunging hoofs were gone.

Walter de la Mare, 1873–

191. CONSCIENCE

Yet still there whispers the small voice within,
Heard through gain's silence, and o'er glory's din:
Whatever creed be taught or land be trod,
Man's conscience is the oracle of God.

George Gordon, Lord Byron, 1788–1824

192. CONSCIENCE

Macbeth, Act II, sc. 2

Methought I heard a voice cry, "Sleep no more!
Macbeth doth murder sleep!" the innocent sleep,
Sleep that knits up the ravell'd sleave of care,
The death of each day's life, sore labour's bath,
Balm of hurt minds, great nature's second course,
Chief nourisher of life's feast.

William Shakespeare, 1564–1616

193. LOST DAYS

The lost days of my life until today,
What were they, could I see them on the street
Lie as they fell? Would they be ears of wheat
Sown once for food but trodden into clay?
Or golden coins squandered and still to pay?
Or drops of blood dabbling the guilty feet?
Or such spilt water as in dreams must cheat
The undying throats of Hell, athirst alway?

I do not see them here; but after death
God knows I know the faces I shall see,
Each one a murdered self, with low last breath,
"I am thyself,—what hast thou done to me?"
"And I—and I—thyself," (lo! each one saith,)
"And thou thyself to all eternity!"

Dante Gabriel Rossetti, 1828–1882

194. CONSCIENCE and FUTURE JUDGMENT

I sat alone with my conscience
  In a place where time had ceased,
And we talked of my former living
  In the land where the years increased,
And I felt I should have to answer
  The question it put to me,
And to face the answer and question
  Through all eternity.

The ghost of forgotten actions
  Came floating before my sight,
And things that I thought were dead things
  Were alive with a terrible might;
And the vision of all my past life
  Was an awful thing to face,
Alone with my conscience sitting
  In that solemn silent place.

❖

And I know of the future Judgment,
  How dreadful soe'er it be,
To sit alone with my conscience
  Will be judgment enough for me.

Charles William Stubbs, 1845–1912

195. THE DESTRUCTION OF SENNACHERIB

The Assyrian came down like the wolf on the fold,
And his cohorts were gleaming with purple and gold;
And the sheen of their spears was like stars on the sea,
When the blue wave rolls nightly on deep Galilee.

Like the leaves of the forest when Summer is green,
That host with their banners at sunset were seen;
Like the leaves of the forest when Autumn hath blown,
That host on the morrow lay withered and strown.

For the Angel of Death spread his wings on the blast,
And breathed in the face of the foe as he passed;
And the eyes of the sleepers waxed deadly and chill,
And their hearts but once heaved, and for ever grew still!

And there lay the steed with his nostrils all wide,
But through them there rolled not the breath of his pride;
And the foam of his gasping lay white on the turf,
And cold as the spray of the rock-beating surf.

And there lay the rider, distorted and pale,
With the dew on his brow, and the rust on his mail;
And the tents were all silent, the banners alone,
The lances unlifted, the trumpet unblown.

And the widows of Ashur are loud in their wail,
And the idols are broken in the temple of Baal;
And the might of the Gentile, unsmote by the sword,
Hath melted like snow in the glance of the Lord.

George Gordon, Lord Byron, 1788–1824

196. SOUND THE LOUD TIMBREL

"And Miriam the prophetess, the sister of Aaron, took a timbrel in her hand; and all the women went out after her with timbrels and with dances."

Exod. xv, 20

"And it came to pass, that in the morning watch the Lord looked unto the host of the Egyptians through the pillar of fire and of cloud, and troubled the host of the Egyptians."

Exod. xiv, 24

Sound the loud Timbrel o'er Egypt's dark sea!
Jehovah has triumphed—his people are free.
Sing—for the pride of the Tyrant is broken,
His chariots, his horsemen, all splendid and brave—
How vain was their boast, for the Lord hath but spoken,
And chariots and horsemen are sunk in the wave.
Sound the loud Timbrel o'er Egypt's dark sea;
Jehovah has triumphed—his people are free!

Praise to the Conqueror, praise to the Lord!
His word was our arrow, his breath was our sword.—
Who shall return to tell Egypt the story
Of those she sent forth in the hour of her pride?
For the Lord hath looked out from his pillar of glory,
And all her brave thousands are dashed in the tide.
Sound the loud Timbrel o'er Egypt's dark sea;
Jehovah has triumphed—his people are free!

Thomas Moore, 1779–1852

197. GOD OUR REFUGE

Psalm 91

He that dwelleth in the secret place of the Most High
Shall abide under the shadow of the Almighty.
I will say of the LORD, "He is my refuge and my fortress;
"My God, in whom I trust."
For he shall deliver thee from the snare of the fowler,
And from the noisome pestilence.
He shall cover thee with his pinions,
And under his wings shall thou take refuge:
His truth is a shield and a buckler.
Thou shalt not be afraid for the terror by night,
Nor for the arrow that flieth by day;
For the pestilence that walketh in darkness,
Nor for the destruction that wasteth at noonday.
A thousand shall fall at thy side,
And ten thousand at thy right hand;
But it shall not come nigh thee.
Only with thine eyes shalt thou behold,
And see the reward of the wicked.

"For thou, O LORD, art my refuge!"
  Thou hast made the Most High thy habitation:
There shall no evil befall thee,
  Neither shall any plague come nigh thy tent.
For he shall give his angels charge over thee,
  To keep thee in all thy ways.
They shall bear thee up in their hands,
  Lest thou dash thy foot against a stone.
Thou shalt tread upon the lion and adder:
  The young lion and the serpent shalt thou trample under feet.
"Because he hath set his love upon me, therefore will I deliver him:
  "I will set him on high, because he hath known my name.
"He shall call upon me, and I will answer him;
  "I will be with him in trouble:
  "I will deliver him, and honour him,
"With long life will I satisfy him,
  "And shew him my salvation."

Moulton: The Modern Reader's Bible, 1895

198. GREAT ART THOU, O LORD

Great art Thou, O Lord, and greatly to be praised;
Great is Thy power, and of Thy wisdom there is no end.
And man, being a part of Thy creation, desires to praise Thee,—
Man, who bears about with him his mortality,
The witness of his sin, even the witness that Thou "resistest the proud,"—
Yet man, this part of Thy creation, desires to praise Thee.
Thou movest us to delight in praising Thee;
For Thou hast formed us for Thyself,
And our hearts are restless till they find rest in Thee.

St. Augustine, 354–430 A.D.

199. GIVE ME YOUR WHOLE HEART

From "The Bhagavad Gîtâ"

Give me your whole heart,
Love and adore me,
Worship me always,
Bow to me only,
And you shall find me:
This is my promise
Who love you dearly.
Lay down all duties
In me, your refuge.
Fear no longer,
For I will save you
From sin and from bondage.

From the Sanskrit, 5th to 2nd centuries B.C., tr. by Swami Prabhavananda and Christopher Isherwood

200. "I HAVE FELT A PRESENCE"

From "Tintern Abbey"

For I have learned
To look on Nature, not as in the hour
Of thoughtless youth; but hearing oftentimes
The still, sad music of humanity,
Nor harsh nor grating, though of ample power
To chasten and subdue. And I have felt
A presence that disturbs me with the joy
Of elevated thoughts; a sense sublime,
Of something far more deeply interfused,
Whose dwelling is the light of setting suns,
And the round ocean and the living air,
And the blue sky, and in the mind of man;
A motion and a spirit, that impels
All thinking things, all objects of all thought,
And rolls through all things. Therefore am I still

A lover of the meadows and the woods,
And mountains; and of all that we behold
From this green earth; of all the mighty world
Of eye and ear,—both what they half create,
And what perceive; well pleased to recognize
In nature and the language of the sense,
The anchor of my purest thoughts, the nurse,
The guide, the guardian of my heart, and soul
Of all my moral being. . . .
Nature never did betray
The heart that loved her; 'tis her privilege,
Through all the years of this our life, to lead
From joy to joy: for she can so inform
The mind that is within us, so impress
With quietness and beauty, and so feed
With lofty thoughts, that neither evil tongues,
Rash judgments, nor the sneers of selfish men,
Nor greetings where no kindness is, nor all
The dreary intercourse of daily life,
Shall e'er prevail against us or disturb
Our cheerful faith, that all which we behold
Is full of blessings.

William Wordsworth, 1770–1850

201. THE END OF BEING

The end of being is to find out God!
And what is God? A vast almighty Power
Great and unlimited, whose potent will
Brings to achievement whatsoe'er He please.
He is all mind. His being infinite—
All that we see and all that we do not see.
The Lord of heaven and earth, the God of Gods.
Without Him nothing is. Yet what He is
We know not! When we strive to comprehend
Our feeble guesses leave the most concealed.
To Him we owe all good we call our own.
To Him we live, to Him ourselves approve.
He is a friend forever at our side.
What cares He for the bleeding sacrifice?
O purge your hearts and lead the life of good!
Not in the pride of temples made with stone
His pleasure lies, but in the piety
Of consecrated hearts and lives devout.

Seneca, 8 B.C.–65 A.D.,
tr. by H. C. Leonard

202. From THRENODY

Wilt thou not ope thy heart to know
What rainbows teach, and sunsets show?
Verdict which accumulates
From lengthening scroll of human fates,
Voice of earth to earth returned,
Prayers of saints that inly burned,—
Saying, *What is excellent,*
As God lives, is permanent;
Hearts are dust, hearts' loves remain;
Hearts' love will meet thee again.
Revere the Maker; fetch thine eye
Up to His style, and manners of the sky.
Not of adamant and gold
Built He heaven stark and cold;
No, but a nest of bending reeds,
Flowering grass and scented weeds;
Or like a traveler's fleeing tent,
Or bow above the tempest bent;
Built of tears and sacred flames,
And virtue reaching to its aims;
Built of furtherance and pursuing,
Not of spent deeds, but of doing.
Silent rushes the swift Lord
Through ruined systems still restored,
Broadsowing, bleak and void to bless,
Plants with worlds the wilderness;
Waters with tears of ancient sorrow
Apples of Eden ripe to-morrow.
House and tenant go to ground,
Lost in God, in Godhead found.

Ralph Waldo Emerson, 1803–1882

203. WHERE IS THY GOD, MY SOUL?

Where is thy God, my soul?
Is He within thy heart,
Or ruler of a distant realm
In which thou hast no part?

Where is thy God, my soul?
Only in stars and sun,
Or have the holy words of truth,
His light in ev'ry one?

Where is thy God, my soul?
Confined to Scripture's page,
Or does His Spirit check and guide
The spirit of each age?

O Ruler of the sky,
Rule Thou within my heart;
O great Adorner of the world,
Thy light of life impart.

Giver of holy words,
Bestow Thy sacred power,
And aid me, whether work or thought
Engage the varying hour.

Thomas T. Lynch, 1818–1871

204. SEEKING AND FINDING GOD

I will arise and to my Father go;
  This very hour the journey is begun.
I start to reach the blissful goal, and, lo,
  My spirit at one bound her race has run.
For seeking God and finding Him are one.
  He feeds the rillets that towards Him flow.
It is the Father who first seeks the son,
  And moves all heavenward movement, swift or slow.
I dare not pride myself on finding Him.
  I dare not dream a single step was mine.
His was the vigour in the palsied limb—
  His the electric fire along the line—
When drowning, His the untaught power to swim
  Float o'er the surge, and grasp the rock divine.

John C. Earle, 1824–1903

205. A SUN-DAY HYMN

Lord of all being, throned afar,
Thy glory flames from sun and star;
Center and soul of every sphere,
Yet to each loving heart how near!

Sun of our life, thy quickening ray
Sheds on our path the glow of day:
Star of our hope, thy softened light
Cheers the long watches of the night.

Our midnight is thy smile withdrawn;
Our noontide is thy gracious dawn;
Our rainbow arch, thy mercy's sign:
All, save the clouds of sin, are thine.

Lord of all life, below, above,
Whose light is truth, whose warmth is love,
Before thy ever-blazing throne
We ask no luster of our own.

Grant us thy truth to make us free,
And kindling hearts that burn for thee,
Till all thy living altars claim
One holy light, one heavenly flame.

Oliver Wendell Holmes, 1809–1894

206. QUO VADIS?

Fare not abroad, O Soul, to win
  Man's friendly smile or favoring nod;
Be still, be strong, and seek within
  The Comradeship of God.

Beyond is not the journey's end,
  The fool goes wayfaring apart,
And even as he goes, his Friend
  Is knocking at his heart.

Myles E. Connolly,
contemporary American

207. I WILL NOT HURRY

I will not hurry through this day!
Lord, I will listen by the way,
To humming bees and singing birds,
To speaking trees and friendly words;
And for the moments in between
Seek glimpses of Thy great Unseen.

I will not hurry through this day;
I will take time to think and pray;
I will look up into the sky,
Where fleecy clouds and swallows fly;
And somewhere in the day, maybe
I will catch whispers, Lord, from Thee!

Ralph Spaulding Cushman, 1879–

208. WAIT ON

To talk with God,
No breath is lost—
  Talk on!

To walk with God,
No strength is lost—
  Walk on!

To wait on God,
No time is lost—
  Wait on!

Dnyanodaya (Indian Poet)

209. HYMN OF AT-ONE-MENT

Thou God of all, whose spirit moves
  From pole to silent pole;
Whose purpose binds the starry spheres
  In one stupendous whole;

Whose life, like light, is freely poured
  On all men 'neath the sun;
To Thee we lift our hearts, and pray
  That Thou wilt make us one.

One in the patient company
  Of those who heed Thy will,
And stedfastly pursue the way
  Of Thy commandments still;
One in the holy fellowship
  Of those who challenge wrong,
And lift the spirit's sword to shield
  The weak against the strong.

One in the truth that makes men free,
  The faith that makes men brave;
One in the love that suffers long
  To seek, and serve, and save;

One in the vision of Thy peace,
  The kingdom yet to be—
When Thou shalt be the God of all,
  And all be one in Thee.

John Haynes Holmes, 1879–

210. FARMERS

I watch the farmers in their fields
  And marvel secretly.
They are so very calm and sure,
  They have such dignity.

They know such simple things so well,
  Although their learning's small,
They find a steady, brown content
  Where some find none at all.

And all their quarrelings with God
  Are soon made up again;
They grant forgiveness when He sends
  His silver, tardy rain.

Their pleasure is so grave and full
  When gathered crops are trim,
You know they think their work was done
  In partnership with Him.

William Alexander Percy, 1885–

211. INSPIRATIONS

Sometimes, I know not why, nor how, nor whence,
  A change comes over me, and then the task
  Of common life slips from me. Would you ask
What power is this which bids the world go hence?
  Who knows? I only feel a faint perfume
Steal through the rooms of life; a saddened sense
Of something lost; a music as of brooks
That babble to the sea; pathetic looks
  Of closing eyes that in a darkened room
  Once dwelt on mine: I feel the general doom
Creep nearer, and with God I stand alone.
  O mystic sense of sudden quickening!
Hope's lark-song rings, or life's deep undertone
  Wails through my heart—and then I needs must sing.

William James Dawson, 1854–1928

212. MUSIC

How many of us ever stop to think
Of music as a wondrous magic link
With God; taking sometimes the place of prayer,
When words have failed us 'neath the weight of care?
Music, that knows no country, race or creed;
But gives to each according to his need.

Author unknown

213. THE BEST

From "The People, Yes"

The best preacher is the heart,
 say the Jews of faith.
The best teacher is time.
The best book is the world.
The best friend is God.

Carl Sandburg, 1878–

214. WORKING WITH GOD

From "Stradivarius"

God be praised,
Antonio Stradivari has an eye
That winces at false work and loves the
 true . . .
And for my fame—when any master holds
'Twixt chin and hand a violin of mine,
He will be glad that Stradivari lived,
Made violins, and made them of the best . . .

I say not God Himself can make man's best
Without best men to help Him . . .
 'Tis God gives skill,
But not without men's hands: He could not
 make
Antonio Stradivari's violins
Without Antonio.

George Eliot, 1819–1880

215. COUNTRYMAN'S GOD

Who reaps the grain and plows the sod
Must feel a kinship with his God:

For there's so much on earth to see
That marks the hand of Deity.

When blossom springs from tiny shoot:
When orchard yields its luscious fruit:

When sap is running from great trees—
On all occasions such as these

The man who breathes fresh country air
Must know full well that God is there.

Roger Winship Stuart

216. THE ETERNAL GOODNESS

O Friends! with whom my feet have trod
 The quiet aisles of prayer,
Glad witness to your zeal for God
 And love of man I bear.

I trace your lines of argument,
 Your logic linked and strong
I weigh as one who dreads dissent,
 And fears a doubt as wrong.

But still my human hands are weak
 To hold your iron creeds:
Against the words ye bid me speak
 My heart within me pleads.

Who fathoms the Eternal Thought?
 Who talks of scheme and plan?
The Lord is God! He needeth not
 The poor device of man.

I walk with bare, hushed feet the ground
 Ye tread with boldness shod;
I dare not fix with mete and bound
 The love and power of God.

Ye praise His justice; even such
 His pitying love I deem:
Ye seek a king; I fain would touch
 The robe that hath no seam.

Ye see the curse which overbroods
 A world of pain and loss;
I hear our Lord's beatitudes
 And prayer upon the cross.

More than your schoolmen teach, within
 Myself, alas! I know:
Too dark ye cannot paint the sin,
 Too small the merit show.

I bow my forehead to the dust,
 I veil mine eyes for shame,
And urge, in trembling self-distrust,
 A prayer without a claim.

I see the wrong that round me lies,
 I feel the guilt within;
I hear, with groan and travail-cries,
 The world confess its sin.

Yet, in the maddening maze of things,
 And tossed by storm and flood,

To one fixed trust my spirit clings;
  I know that God is good!

Not mine to look where cherubim
  And seraphs may not see,
But nothing can be good in Him
  Which evil is in me.

The wrong that pains my soul below
  I dare not throne above,
I know not of His hate,—I know
  His goodness and His love.

I dimly guess from blessings known
  Of greater out of sight,
And, with the chastened Psalmist, own
  His judgments too are right.

I long for household voices gone,
  For vanished smiles I long,
But God hath led my dear ones on,
  And He can do no wrong.

I know not what the future hath
  Of marvel or surprise,
Assured alone that life and death
  His mercy underlies.

And if my heart and flesh are weak
  To bear an untried pain,
The bruisèd reed He will not break,
  But strengthen and sustain.

No offering of my own I have,
  Nor works my faith to prove;
I can but give the gifts He gave,
  And plead His love for love.

And so beside the Silent Sea
  I wait the muffled oar;
No harm from Him can come to me
  On ocean or on shore.

I know not where His islands lift
  Their fronded palms in air;
I only know I cannot drift
  Beyond His love and care.

O brothers! if my faith is vain,
  If hopes like these betray,
Pray for me that my feet may gain
  The sure and safer way.

And Thou, O Lord! by whom are seen
  Thy creatures as they be,
Forgive me if too close I lean
  My human heart on Thee!

John Greenleaf Whittier, 1807–1892

217. WALKING WITH GOD

O for a closer walk with God,
  A calm and heavenly frame,
A light to shine upon the road
  That leads me to the Lamb!

Where is the blessedness I knew
  When first I saw the Lord?
Where is the soul-refreshing view
  Of Jesus and His word?

What peaceful hours I once enjoy'd!
  How sweet their memory still!
But they have left an aching void,
  The world can never fill.

Return, O holy Dove, return,
  Sweet messenger of rest:
I hate the sins that made Thee mourn,
  And drove Thee from my breast.

The dearest idol I have known,
  Whate'er that idol be,
Help me to tear it from Thy throne,
  And worship only Thee.

So shall my walk be close with God,
  Calm and serene my frame;
So purer light shall mark the road
  That leads me to the Lamb.

William Cowper, 1731–1800

218. JUST FOR TODAY

Lord, for to-morrow and its needs,
  I do not pray:
Keep me, my God, from stain of sin,
  Just for to-day;
Let me no wrong or idle word
  Unthinking say:
Set Thou a seal upon my lips,
  Just for to-day.

Let me both diligently work,
  And duly pray;

Let me be kind in word and deed,
  Just for to-day;
Let me in season, Lord, be grave,
  In season, gay;
Let me be faithful to Thy grace.
  Just for to-day.

In pain and sorrow's cleansing fires,
  Brief be my stay;
Oh, bid me if to-day I die,
  Come home to-day;
So, for to-morrow and its needs,
  I do not pray;
But keep me, guide me, love me, Lord,
  Just for to-day.

Sybil F. Partridge, 19th century

219. DELIGHT IN GOD ONLY

In having all things, and not Thee, what
    have I?
Not having Thee what have my labours got?
Let me enjoy but Thee, what further crave I?
And having Thee alone, what have I not?
  I wish nor sea nor land; nor would I be
  Possess'd of heaven, heaven unpossess'd of
    Thee.

Francis Quarles, 1592–1644

220. O GOD, WHOSE LOVE IS OVER ALL

O God, whose love is over all
  The children of Thy grace,
Whose rich and tender blessings fall
  On every age and place,
Hear Thou the songs and prayers we raise
  In eager joy to Thee,
And teach us, as we sound Thy praise,
  In all things Thee to see.

To see Thee in the sun by day,
  And in the stars by night,
In waving grass and ocean spray,
  And leaves and flowers bright;
To hear Thy voice, like spoken word,
  In every breeze that blows,
In every song of every bird,
  And every brook that flows.

To see Thee in each quiet home
  Where faith and love abide,
In school and church, where all may come
  To seek Thee side by side;
To see Thee in each human life,
  Each struggling human heart,
Each path by which, in eager strife,
  Men seek the better part.

John Haynes Holmes, 1879–

221. THE INNER LIGHT

From "Saint Paul"

Lo, as some bard on isles of the Aegean
  Lovely and eager when the earth was young,
Burning to hurl his heart into a paean,
  Praise of the hero from whose loins he sprung;—

He, I suppose, with such a care to carry,
  Wandered disconsolate and waited long,
Smiting his breast, wherein the notes would tarry,
  Chiding the slumber of the seed of song:

Then in the sudden glory of a minute
  Airy and excellent the proem came,
Rending his bosom, for a god was in it,
  Waking the seed, for it had burst in flame.

So even I athirst for his inspiring,
  I who have talked with Him forget again,

Yes, many days with sobs and with desiring
  Offer to God a patience and a pain;

Then thro' the mid complaint of my confession,
  Then thro' the pang and passion of my prayer,
Leaps with a start the shock of his possession,
  Thrills me and touches, and the Lord is there.

Lo, if some pen should write upon your rafter
  MENE and MENE in the folds of flame,
Think you could any memories thereafter
  Wholly retrace the couplet as it came?

Lo, if some strange intelligible thunder
  Sang to the earth the secret of a star,
Scarce could ye catch, for terror and for wonder,
  Shreds of the story that was pealed so far:—

Scarcely I catch the words of his revealing,
  Hardly I hear Him, dimly understand,
Only the Power that is within me pealing
  Lives on my lips and beckons to my hand.

Whoso has felt the Spirit of the Highest
  Cannot confound nor doubt Him nor deny:
Yea with one voice, O world, tho' thou deniest,
  Stand thou on that side, for on this am I.

Rather the earth shall doubt when her retrieving
  Pours in the rain and rushes from the sod,
Rather than he for whom the great conceiving
  Stirs in his soul to quicken into God.

Aye, tho' thou then shouldst strike him from his glory
  Blind and tormented, maddened and alone,
Even on the cross would he maintain his story,
  Yes and in hell would whisper, I have known.

Frederick William Henry Myers, 1843–1901

222. THE LITTLE GATE TO GOD

In the castle of my soul
Is a little postern gate,
Whereat, when I enter,
I am in the presence of God.
In a moment, in the turning of a thought,
I am where God is,
This is a fact.

❖

When I enter into God,
All life has a meaning,
Without asking I know;
My desires are even now fulfilled,
My fever is gone
In the great quiet of God.
My troubles are but pebbles on the road,
My joys are like the everlasting hills.

❖

So it is when my soul steps through the
    postern gate
Into the presence of God.
Big things become small, and small things
    become great.
The near becomes far, and the future is near.

The lowly and despised is shot through with
glory. . . .
God is the substance of all revolutions;
When I am in Him, I am in the Kingdom of
God.
And in the Fatherland of my Soul.

Walter Rauschenbusch, 1861–1918

223. PRESENCE

God is very near to me
In the whispering of a tree;
And His voice I've often heard
In the singing of a bird.

I have often walked with Him
In the twilight warm and dim;
Sure and tender, He is there
In the clover-scented air.

I have waited in the wood,
Where the mystic asters brood,
Where the maples' altars flame—
Even there His splendour came.

I have watched for God at night
In the silent silver light,
I have seen His footsteps go
Softly over fallen snow.

God is near, for He is found
In all lovely things around,
Hill, or cloud, or leaf, or star—
He is never very far.

Mary E. McCullough, 1915–1942

224. HOLY PLACES

Wherever souls of men have worshiped, there
Is God: where old cathedrals climb the sky,
Or shining hillsides lift their heads on high,
Or silent woodland spaces challenge prayer,
Or inner chambers shut the heart from care;
Where broken temples of old faiths now lie
Forgotten in the sun, or swallows cry
At dusk about some crossroads chapel, bare
Alike of bells and beauty; where saints walked
Of old with speaking presences unseen,
Or dreaming boys with quiet voices talked
In pairs last night on some still college green;
Where Moses' Sinai flamed, or Jesus trod
The upward way apart: there, *here*, is God!

Herbert D. Gallaudet, 1876–

225. HIGH FLIGHT[1]

Oh! I have slipped the surly bonds of earth
And danced the skies on laughter-silvered wings;
Sunward I've climbed, and joined the tumbling mirth
Of sun-split clouds—and done a hundred things
You have not dreamed of—wheeled and soared and swung
High in the sunlit silence. Hov'ring there,
I've chased the shouting wind along, and flung
My eager craft through footless halls of air.

Up, up the long, delirious, burning blue
I've topped the wind-swept heights with easy grace

[1] Composed by Flight-Lieutenant Magee (son of American Missionaries to China) while flying at an altitude of thirty thousand feet above England. Shortly afterwards the author, at the age of nineteen, was killed, serving with the R. C. A. F.

Where never lark, or even eagle flew—
And, while with silent lifting mind I've trod
The high untrespassed sanctity of space,
Put out my hand and touched the face of God.

John Gillespie Magee, Jr., 1922–1941

226. APRIL

Always the month of April fills
All of our world with coloured thrills
Leaves on a tree on a low green hill
And crocus blooms where the sun lies still.
Always with eager hands she spills
Poems of gold on the daffodils,
And back of the miracles we see
Is the caring of God for you and me.

Even the rain in April sings,
Even the blue in a pair of wings,
And oh, the beauty of song that's heard
In the magical singing of a bird.
Even the bell in a snowdrop rings
Of tiny dreams of lovely things.
Even the chords in a weary heart
Sing with the wonder flowers impart!

Isobel McFadden,
contemporary Canadian

227. SINCE GOD IS THERE

My Lord, how full of sweet content,
I pass my years of banishment!
Where'er I dwell, I dwell with thee,
In Heaven, in earth, or on the sea.

To me remains nor place nor time;
My country is in every clime:
I can be calm and free from care
On any shore, since God is there.

Madame Guyon,[1] *1648–1717;*
tr. from the French by
William Cowper, 1731–1800

228. PAX

All that matters is to be at one with the living God
To be a creature in the house of the God of Life.

Like a cat asleep on a chair
At peace, in peace
And at one with the master of the house, with the mistress,
At home, at home in the house of the living,
Sleeping on the hearth, and yawning before the fire.

Sleeping on the hearth of the living world
Yawning at home before the fire of life
Feeling the presence of the living God
Like a great reassurance
A deep calm in the heart
A presence
As of the master sitting at the board
In his own and greater being,
In the house of life.

David Herbert Lawrence, 1885–1930

229. COMMUNION WITH NATURE

From "Expostulation and Reply"

Think you 'mid all this mighty sum
Of things for ever speaking
That nothing of itself will come,
But we must still be seeking?
Nor less I deem that there are powers,
Which of themselves our minds impress,
And we can feed this mind of ours,
In a wise passiveness.

William Wordsworth, 1770–1850

230. LORD! IT IS NOT LIFE TO LIVE

Lord! it is not life to live,
If Thy presence Thou deny;
Lord! if Thou Thy presence give,
'Tis no longer death—to die.

Source and Giver of repose,
Singly from Thy smile it flows;
Peace and happiness are Thine,—
Mine they are, if Thou art mine.

Augustus Montague Toplady, 1740–1778

[1] Madame Guyon was imprisoned in 1695 and later banished from Paris to Blois.

231. STILL, STILL WITH THEE

Still, still with Thee, when purple morning breaketh,
When the bird waketh and the shadows flee;
Fairer than morning, lovelier than the daylight,
Dawns the sweet consciousness, I am with Thee!

Alone with Thee, amid the mystic shadows,
The solemn hush of nature newly born;
Alone with Thee, in breathless adoration,
In the calm dew and freshness of the morn.

❖

Still, still with Thee, as to each new-born morning
A fresh and solemn splendor still is given,
So doth this blessed consciousness awakening,
Breathe, each day, nearness unto Thee and heaven.

When sinks the soul, subdued by toil, to slumber,
Its closing eye looks up to Thee in prayer;
Sweet the repose beneath Thy wings o'ershading,
But sweeter still to wake and find Thee there.

So shall it be at last, in that bright morning
When the soul waketh and life's shadows flee;
Oh, in that hour fairer than daylight dawning,
Shall rise the glorious thought, I am with Thee!

Harriet Beecher Stowe, 1811–1896

232. HOLY SPIRIT, DWELL WITH ME

Gracious Spirit, dwell with me!
I myself would gracious be;
And, with words that help and heal,
Would Thy life in mine reveal;
And, with actions bold and meek,
Would for Christ, my Saviour, speak.

Truthful Spirit, dwell with me!
I myself would truthful be;
And, with wisdom kind and clear,
Let Thy life in mine appear;
And, with actions brotherly,
Speak my Lord's sincerity.

Tender Spirit, dwell with me!
I myself would tender be;
Shut my heart up like a flower
In temptation's darksome hour;
Open it when shines the sun,
And His love by fragrance own.

Holy Spirit, dwell with me!
I myself would holy be;
Separate from sin, I would
Choose and cherish all things good,
And whatever I can be
Give to Him who gave me Thee.

Thomas Toke Lynch, 1818–1871

233. PUT OUT MY EYES, AND I CAN SEE YOU STILL

Put out my eyes, and I can see you still;
slam my ears to, and I can hear you yet;
and without any feet can go to you;
and tongueless, I can conjure you at will.
Break off my arms, I shall take hold of you
and grasp you with my heart as with a hand;
arrest my heart, my brain will beat as true;
and if you set this brain of mine afire,
then on my blood-stream I will carry you.

Rainer Maria Rilke, 1875–1926; tr. from the German by Babette Deutsch, 1895–

234. FOR ALL WHO NEED

For all who watch tonight—by land or sea or air—
O Father, may they know that Thou art with them there.

For all who weep tonight, the hearts that cannot rest,
Reveal Thy love, that wondrous love which gave for us Thy best.

For all who wake tonight, love's tender watch to keep,
Watcher Divine, Thyself draw nigh, Thou who dost never sleep.

For all who fear tonight, whate'er the dread may be,
We ask for them the perfect peace of hearts that rest in Thee.

Our own belov'd tonight, O Father, keep, and where
Our love and succor cannot reach, now bless them through our prayer.

And all who pray tonight, Thy wrestling hosts, O Lord,
Make weakness strong, let them prevail according to Thy word.

Author unknown

235. ONENESS WITH HIM

I take a comfort from my very badness:
It is for lack of Thee that I am bad.
How close, how infinitely closer yet
Must I come to Thee, ere I can pay one debt
Which mere humanity has on me set!
"How close to Thee!"—no wonder, soul,
thou art glad!
Oneness with Him is the eternal gladness.

George Macdonald, 1824–1905

236. TRUE RICHES

Of all the prizes
That earth can give,
This is the best:
To find Thee, Lord,
A living Presence near
And in Thee rest!

Friends, fortune, fame,
Or what might come to me—
I count all loss
If I find not
Companionship
With Thee!

Author unknown

237. THY PRESENCE

Thou layest thy hand on the fluttering heart
And sayest, "Be still!"
The shadow and silence are only a part
Of Thy sweet will.
Thy Presence is with me, and where Thou art
I fear no ill.

Frances Ridley Havergal, 1836–1879

238. MY LIGHT AND MY SALVATION

Psalm 27

The LORD is my light and my salvation;
Whom shall I fear?
The LORD is the strength of my life;
Of whom shall I be afraid?
When evil-doers came upon me
To eat up my flesh,

Even mine adversaries and my foes,
 They stumbled and fell.
Though an host should encamp against me,
 My heart shall not fear:
Though war should rise against me,
 Even then will I be confident.

One thing have I asked of the LORD,
 That will I seek after;
That I may dwell in the house of the LORD
 All the days of my life,
To behold the beauty of the LORD,
 And to inquire in his temple.
For in the day of trouble he shall keep me secretly in his pavilion:
 In the covert of his tabernacle shall he hide me;
He shall lift me up upon a rock,
 And now shall mine head be lifted up above mine enemies round about me;
And I will offer in his tabernacle sacrifices of joy;
 I will sing, yea, I will sing praises unto the LORD.

'Hear, O LORD, when I cry with my voice:
'Have mercy also upon me, and answer me.
'"Seek ye my face"—
'My heart said unto thee, Thy face, LORD, will I seek.
'Hide not thy face from me;
'Put not thy servant away in anger.

'Thou hast been my help, cast me not off:
'Neither forsake me, O God of my salvation.
'When my father and my mother forsake me,
'The LORD will take me up.

'Teach me thy way, O LORD,
'And lead me in a plain path because of mine enemies;
'Deliver me not over unto the will of mine adversaries:
'For false witnesses are risen up against me, and such as breathe out
 cruelty.'—

I had fainted, unless I had believed to see the goodness of the LORD
 In the land of the living.
Wait on the LORD: be strong, and let thine heart take courage;
 Yea, wait thou on the LORD.

Moulton: The Modern Reader's Bible, 1895

239. RABBI BEN EZRA

Grow old along with me!
The best is yet to be,
The last of life, for which the first was made:
Our times are in his hand
Who saith "A whole I planned,
Youth shows but half; trust God: see all, nor
 be afraid!"

Not that, amassing flowers,
Youth sighed, "Which rose make ours,
Which lily leave and then as best recall?"
Not that, admiring stars,
It yearned, "Nor Jove, nor Mars;
Mine be some figured flame which blends,
 transcends them all!"

Not for such hopes and fears
Annulling youth's brief years,
Do I remonstrate: folly wide the mark!
Rather I prize the doubt
Low kinds exist without,
Finished and finite clods, untroubled by a
spark.

Poor vaunt of life indeed,
Were man but formed to feed
On joy, to solely seek and find and feast:
Such feasting ended, then
As sure an end to men;
Irks care the crop full bird? Frets doubt the
maw-crammed beast?

Rejoice we are allied
To that which doth provide
And not partake, effect and not receive!
A spark disturbs our clod;
Nearer we hold of God
Who gives, than of his tribes that take, I
must believe.

Then, welcome each rebuff
That turns earth's smoothness rough,
Each sting that bids nor sit nor stand but go!
Be our joys three-parts pain!
Strive, and hold cheap the strain;
Learn, nor account the pang; dare, never
grudge the throe!

For thence,—a paradox
Which comforts while it mocks,—
Shall life succeed in that it seems to fail:
What I aspired to be,
And was not, comforts me:
A brute I might have been, but would not
sink i' the scale.

What is he but a brute
Whose flesh has soul to suit,
Whose spirit works lest arms and legs want
play?
To man, propose this test—
Thy body at its best,
How far can that project thy soul on its lone
way?

Yet gifts should prove their use:
I own the Past profuse
Of power each side, perfection every turn:
Eyes, ears took in their dole,
Brain treasured up the whole;
Should not the heart beat once "How good to
live and learn"?

Not once beat "Praise be thine!
I see the whole design,
I, who saw power, see now Love perfect too:
Perfect I call thy plan:
Thanks that I was a man!
Maker, remake, complete,—I trust what
thou shalt do!"

For pleasant is this flesh;
Our soul, in its rose-mesh
Pulled ever to the earth, still yearns for rest:
Would we some prize might hold
To match those manifold
Possessions of the brute,—gain most, as we
did best!

Let us not always say,
"Spite of this flesh to-day
I strove, made head, gained ground upon the
whole!"
As the bird wings and sings.
Let us cry, "All good things
Are ours, nor soul helps flesh more, now, than
flesh helps soul!"

Therefore I summon age
To grant youth's heritage,
Life's struggle having so far reached its term:
Thence shall I pass, approved
A man, for aye removed
From the developed brute; a God though in
the germ.

And I shall thereupon
Take rest, ere I be gone
Once more on my adventure brave and new:
Fearless and unperplexed,
When I wage battle next,
What weapons to select, what armor to indue.

Youth ended, I shall try
My gain or loss thereby;
Leave the fire ashes, what survives is gold:
And I shall weigh the same,
Give life its praise or blame:
Young, all lay in dispute; I shall know, being
old.

For note, when evening shuts,
A certain moment cuts
The deed off, calls the glory from the gray:

A whisper from the west
Shoots—"Add this to the rest,
Take it and try its worth: here dies another
day."

So, still within this life,
Though lifted o'er its strife,
Let me discern, compare, pronounce at last,
"This rage was right i' the main,
That acquiescence vain:
The Future I may face now I have proved
the Past."

For more is not reserved
To man, with soul just nerved
To act to-morrow what he learns to-day:
Here, work enough to watch
The Master work, and catch
Hints of the proper craft, tricks of the tool's
true play.

As it was better, youth
Should strive, through acts uncouth,
Toward making, than repose on aught
found made:
So, better, age, exempt
From strife, should know, than tempt
Further. Thou waitedst age: wait death nor
be afraid!

Enough now, if the Right
And Good and Infinite
Be named here, as thou callest thy hand
thine own,
With knowledge absolute,
Subject to no dispute
From fools that crowded youth, nor let thee
feel alone.

Be there, for once and all,
Severed great minds from small,
Announced to each his station in the Past!
Was I, the world arraigned,
Were they, my soul disdained,
Right? Let age speak the truth and give us
peace at last!

Now, who shall arbitrate?
Ten men love what I hate,
Shun what I follow, slight what I receive;
Ten, who in ears and eyes
Match me: we all surmise,
They this thing, and I that: whom shall my
soul believe?

Not on the vulgar mass
Called "work," must sentence pass,
Things done, that took the eye and had the
price;
O'er which, from level stand,
The low world laid its hand,
Found straightway to its mind, could value
in a trice:

But all, the world's coarse thumb
And finger failed to plumb,
So passed in making up the main account;
All instincts immature,
All purposes unsure,
That weighed not as his work, yet swelled the
man's amount:

Thoughts hardly to be packed
Into a narrow act,
Fancies that broke through language and
escaped;
All I could never be,
All, men ignored in me,
This, I was worth to God, whose wheel the
pitcher shaped.

Ay, note that Potter's wheel,
That metaphor! and feel
Why time spins fast, why passive lies our
clay,—
Thou, to whom fools propound,
When the wine makes its round,
"Since life fleets, all is change; the Past gone,
seize to-day!"

Fool! All that is, at all,
Lasts ever, past recall;
Earth changes, but thy soul and God stand
sure:
What entered into thee,
That was, is, and shall be:
Time's wheel runs back or stops: Potter and
clay endure.

He fixed thee 'mid this dance
Of plastic circumstance,
This Present, thou, forsooth, would fain
arrest:
Machinery just meant
To give thy soul its bent,
Try thee and turn thee forth, sufficiently
impressed.

What though the earlier grooves,
Which ran the laughing loves

Around thy base, no longer pause and press?
What though, about thy rim,
Skull-things in order grim
Grow out, in graver mood, obey the sterner stress?

Look not thou down but up!
To uses of a cup,
The festal board, lamp's flash and trumpet's peal,
The new wine's foaming flow,
The Master's lips a-glow!
Thou, heaven's consummate cup, what needst thou with earth's wheel?

But I need, now as then,
Thee, God, who mouldest men;
And since, not even while the whirl was worst,
Did I—to the wheel of life
With shapes and colors rife,
Bound dizzily—mistake my end, to slake thy thirst:

So, take and use thy work:
Amend what flaws may lurk,
What strain o' the stuff, what warpings past the aim!
My times be in thy hand!
Perfect the cup as planned!
Let age approve of youth, and death complete the same!

Robert Browning, 1812–1889

240. THE LOOM OF TIME

Man's life is laid in the loom of time
To a pattern he does not see,
While the weavers work and the shuttles fly
Till the dawn of eternity.

Some shuttles are filled with silver threads
And some with threads of gold,
While often but the darker hues
Are all that they may hold.

But the weaver watches with skillful eye
Each shuttle fly to and fro,
And sees the pattern so deftly wrought
As the loom moves sure and slow.

God surely planned the pattern:
Each thread, the dark and fair,
Is chosen by His master skill
And placed in the web with care.

He only knows its beauty,
And guides the shuttles which hold
The threads so unattractive,
As well as the threads of gold.

Not till each loom is silent
And the shuttles cease to fly,
Shall God reveal the pattern
And explain the reason why

The dark threads were as needful
In the weaver's skillful hand
As the threads of gold and silver
For the pattern which He planned.

Author unknown

241. GOD MAKES A PATH

God makes a path, provides a guide,
And feeds a wilderness;
His glorious name, while breath remains,
O that I may confess.

Lost many a time, I have had no guide,
No house but a hollow tree!
In stormy winter night no fire,
No food, no company;

In Him I found a house, a bed,
A table, company;
No cup so bitter but's made sweet,
Where God shall sweetening be.

Roger Williams, 1603?–1683

242. GOD KNOWS BEST

Whichever way the wind doth blow,
Some heart is glad to have it so;
Then blow it east or blow it west,
The wind that blows, that wind is best.

My little craft sails not alone;
A thousand fleets from every zone
Are out upon a thousand seas;
What blows for one a favorite breeze
Might dash another, with the shock
Of doom, upon some hidden rock,
And so I do not dare to pray
For winds to waft me on my way,

But leave it to a Higher Will
To stay or speed me, trusting still
That all is well, and sure that He
Who launched my bark will sail with me
Through storm and calm, and will not fail,
Whatever breezes may prevail,
To land me, every peril past,
Within His sheltering heaven at last.

Then, whatsoever wind doth blow,
My heart is glad to have it so;
And blow it east or blow it west,
The wind that blows, that wind is best.

Caroline Atherton Mason, 1823–1890

243. THE ARROW

The life of men
  Is an arrow's flight,
Out of darkness
  Into light,
And out of light
  Into darkness again;
Perhaps to pleasure,
  Perhaps to pain.

There must be Something,
  Above, or below;
Something unseen
  A mighty Bow,
A Hand that tires not,
  A sleepless Eye
That sees the arrow
  Fly, and fly;
One who knows
  Why we live—and die.

Richard Henry Stoddard, 1825–1903

244. NOW FROM THE WORLD THE LIGHT OF GOD IS GONE

Now from the world the light of God is gone,
And men in darkness move and are afraid,
Some blaming heaven for the evil done,
And some each other for the part they played;
And all their woes on Him are strictly laid,
For being absent from these earthly ills,
Who set the trees to be the noonday shade,
And placed the stars in beauty on the hills.
Turn not away, and cry that all is lost;
It is not so, the world is in His hands
As once it was when Egypt's mighty host
Rode to the sea and vanished in the sands.
For still the heart, by love and pity wrung,
Finds the same God as when the world was young.

Robert Nathan, 1894–

245. UNTO THE HILLS

Psalm 121

Unto the hills around do I lift up
  My longing eyes;
O whence for me shall my salvation come,
  From whence arise?
From God the Lord doth come my certain aid,
From God the Lord who heaven and earth
    hath made.

He will not suffer that thy foot be moved;
  Safe shalt thou be:
No careless slumber shall His eyelids close,
  Who keepeth thee.
Behold, He sleepeth not, He slumbereth ne'er,
Who keepeth Israel in His holy care.

Jehovah is Himself thy keeper true,
  Thy changeless shade;
Jehovah thy defense on thy right hand
  Himself hath made.
And thee no sun by day shall ever smite;
No moon shall harm thee in the silent night.

From every evil shall He keep thy soul,
  From every sin;

Jehovah shall preserve thy going out,
  Thy coming in.
Above thee watching, He whom we adore
Shall keep thee hence-forth, yea, for
  evermore.

Paraphrase by John Campbell,
Duke of Argyle, 1845–1914

246. ON A FLY-LEAF OF SCHOPENHAUER'S *Immortality*

There is nothing new to be written of tears and man's shuddering breath;
Nothing new to be said of his loving, or sinning, or death;
Nothing new to be thought of his loneliness under the sky—
But something is new in the knowledge that soon it will have to be I
Who will give over weeping and breathing, relinquish my love and my load,
And lie in the dark and the quiet that waits at the end of the road.

❖

There is nothing new to be whispered of blossoms breaking the sod,
But something is new in my asking—"*Take care of me, God!*"

Ruth Guthrie Harding, 1882–

247. HE CARES

Why so impatient, my heart?
He who watches over birds, beasts and insects,
He who cared for you while you were yet unborn,
Think you he will not care for you now that you have come forth?
O my heart, how could you turn away from the smile of your Lord
  and wander so far from him?

Kabir (India), 1450–1518

248. HEAVENLY AID

From "The Faery Queen"

And is there care in heaven? and is there love
In heavenly spirits to these creatures base,
That may compassion of their evils move?
There is: else much more wretched were the case
Of men than beasts. But oh! th' exceeding grace
Of highest God that loves His creatures so,
And all His works with mercy doth embrace,
That blessèd angels He sends to and fro,
To serve to wicked men, to serve His wicked foe.

How oft do they their silver bowers leave,
To come to succour us that succour want!
How oft do they with golden pinions cleave
The flitting skies, like flying pursuivant,
Against foul fiends to aid us militant!
They for us fight, they watch and duly ward,
And their bright squadrons round about us plant;
And all for love, and nothing for reward.
O! why should heavenly God to men have such regard?

Edmund Spenser, 1552?–1599

249. OUR BURDEN BEARER

The little sharp vexations
And the briars that cut the feet,
Why not take all to the Helper
Who has never failed us yet?
Tell Him about the heartache,
And tell Him the longings too,
Tell Him the baffled purpose
When we scarce know what to do.
Then, leaving all our weakness
With the One divinely strong,
Forget that we bore the burden
And carry away the song.

Phillips Brooks, 1835–1893

250. WHAT GOD HATH PROMISED

God hath not promised
Skies always blue,
Flower-strewn pathways
All our lives through;
God hath not promised
Sun without rain,
Joy without sorrow,
Peace without pain.

But God hath promised
Strength for the day,
Rest for the labor,
Light for the way,
Grace for the trials,
Help from above,
Unfailing sympathy,
Undying love.

Annie Johnson Flint, 1862–1932

251. HE CARES

Oh, wonderful story of deathless love;
Each child is dear to that Heart above.
He fights for me when I cannot fight,
He comforts me in the gloom of night,
He lifts the burden, for he is strong,
He stills the sigh and awakes the song;
The sorrow that bows me down he bears,
And loves and pardons, because he cares.

Let all who are sad take heart again;
We are not alone in our hours of pain;
Our Father stoops from his throne above
To soothe and quiet us with his love.
He leaves us not when the storm is high,
And we have safety, for he is nigh.
Can it be trouble that he doth share?
Oh, rest in peace, for the Lord doth care!

Susan Coolidge, 1845–1905

252. DIVINE CARE

Even as a nurse, whose child's imperfect pace
Can hardly lead his foot from place to place,
Leaves her fond kissing, sets him down, to go,
Nor does uphold him for a step or two;
But when she finds that he begins to fall,
She holds him up, and kisses him withal:
So God from man sometimes withdraws His hand
A while, to teach his infant faith to stand;
But when He sees his feeble strength begin
To fail, He gently takes him up again:

Lord, I'm a child; so guide my paces, then,
That I may learn to walk an upright man:
So shield my faith, that I may never doubt Thee,
For I must fall, if e'er I walk without Thee.

Francis Quarles, 1592–1644

253. CAST YOUR CARES ON GOD

From "Enoch Arden" (L. 222)

Cast all your cares on God; that anchor holds.
Is He not yonder in those uttermost
Parts of the morning? If I flee to these,
Can I go from Him? And the sea is His,
The sea is His; He made it.

Alfred Tennyson, 1809–1892

254. OUR FATHER'S WORLD

The ships glide in at the harbor's mouth,
And the ships sail out to sea,
And the wind that sweeps from the sunny south
Is sweet as sweet can be.
There's a world of toil, and a world of pains,
And a world of trouble and care,
But O, in a world where our Father reigns,
There is gladness everywhere.

The harvest waves in the breezy morn,
And the men go forth to reap;

The fullness comes to the tasselled corn,
  Whether we wake or sleep.
And far on the hills by feet untrod
  There are blossoms that scent the air,
For O, in this world of our Father God,
  There is beauty everywhere.

Margaret Sangster, 1838–1912

255. IN THE HOUR OF MY DISTRESS

In the hour of my distress,
When temptations me oppress,
And when I my sins confess,
  Sweet Spirit comfort me!

When the house doth sigh and weep,
And the world is drowned in sleep,
Yet mine eyes the watch do keep;
  Sweet Spirit comfort me!

When (God knows) I'm tost about,
Either with despair or doubt;
Yet before the glass be out,
  Sweet Spirit comfort me!

When the Judgment is revealed,
And that opened which was sealed,
When to Thee I have appealed;
  Sweet Spirit comfort me!

Robert Herrick, 1591–1674

256. ON ANOTHER'S SORROW

Can I see another's woe,
And not be in sorrow too?
Can I see another's grief,
And not seek for kind relief?

Can I see a falling tear,
And not feel my sorrow's share?
Can a father see his child
Weep, nor be with sorrow filled?

Can a mother sit and hear
An infant groan, an infant fear?
No, no! never can it be!
Never, never can it be!

And can He who smiles on all
Hear the wren with sorrows small,
Hear the small bird's grief and care,
Hear the woes that infants bear—

And not sit beside the nest,
Pouring pity in their breast,
And not sit the cradle near;
Weeping tear on infant's tear?

And not sit both night and day,
Wiping all our tears away?
Oh no! never can it be!
Never, never can it be!

He doth give His joy to all:
He becomes an Infant small,
He becomes a Man of Woe,
He doth feel the sorrow too.

Think not thou canst sigh a sigh,
And thy Maker is not by:
Think not thou canst weep a tear,
And thy Maker is not near.

Oh, He gives to us His joy,
That our grief He may destroy.
Till our grief is fled and gone
He doth sit by us and moan.

William Blake, 1757–1827

257. AN EVENING PRAYER

Now I lay me down to sleep,
I pray Thee, Lord, Thy child to keep;
Thy love go with me all the night
And wake me with the morning light.

Author unknown

258. SLEEP SWEET

Sleep sweet within thy quiet room,
  O thou, whoe'er thou art,
And let no mournful yesterday
  Disturb thy peaceful heart;
Nor let tomorrow scare thy rest
  With dreams of coming ill;
Thy Maker is thy changeless friend,
  Whose love surrounds thee still.
Forget thyself and all the world,
  Put out each feverish light;
The stars are watching overhead.
  Sleep sweet; good night, good night.

Ellen M. Gates, 1835–1920

259. COME, YE DISCONSOLATE

Come, ye disconsolate, where'er you languish,
Come, at God's altar fervently kneel;
Here bring your wounded hearts, here tell your anguish—
Earth has no sorrow that Heaven cannot heal.

Joy of the desolate, Light of the straying,
Hope, when all others die, fadeless and pure,
Here speaks the Comforter, in God's name saying—
"Earth has no sorrow that Heaven cannot cure."

Go, ask the infidel, what boon he brings us
What charm for aching hearts he can reveal,
Sweet as that heavenly promise Hope sings us—
"Earth has no sorrow that God cannot heal."

Thomas Moore, 1779–1852

260. THE SHADOWS OF THE EVENING HOURS

The shadows of the evening hours
Fall from the darkening sky;
Upon the fragrance of the flowers
The dews of evening lie:
Before Thy throne, O Lord of heaven,
We kneel at close of day;
Look on Thy children from on high,
And hear us while we pray.

Slowly the rays of daylight fade:
So fade within our heart
The hopes in earthly love and joy,
That one by one depart.
Slowly the bright stars, one by one
Within the heavens shine:
Give us, O Lord, fresh hopes in heav'n,
And trust in things divine.

Let peace, O Lord, Thy peace, O God,
Upon our souls descend;
From midnight fears and perils, Thou
Our trembling hearts defend.
Give us a respite from our toil,
Calm and subdue our woes;
Through the long day we labor, Lord,
O give us now repose.

Adelaide A. Procter, 1825–1864

261. FAITH

When the night kneels down by your bed
In the time of your sadness,
Remember O child of the mountains
This word of the law:
The night is the shadow of God
Who made you for gladness,
And your sorrows are less than your strength
Which He foresaw.

Preston Clark, 1893–

262. ALL'S WELL

My heart,
The sun hath set.
Night's paths
With dews are wet.

Sleep comes
Without regret;
Stars rise
When sun is set.

All's well.
God loves thee yet,
Heart, smile,
Sleep sweet, nor fret.

William A. Quayle, 1860–1925

263. GOD'S DARK

The Dark is kind and cozy,
The Dark is soft and deep;
The Dark will pat my pillow
And love me as I sleep.

The Dark is smooth as velvet,
  And gentle as the air,
And he is *good* to children
  And people everywhere.

The Dark can see and love me
  Without a bit of light.
He gives me dreams and resting;
  He brings the gentle Night.

God made the Dark, so Daytime
  Could close its tired eyes
And sleep a while in comfort
  Beneath the starry skies.

The Daytime, just like children,
  Needs rest from work and play,
So it can give us children
  Another happy day.

God made the Dark for children
  And birdies in their nest.
All in the Dark *He* watches
  And guards us while we rest.

John Martin, 1865–1947

264. OVERHEARD IN AN ORCHARD

Said the Robin to the Sparrow:
  "I should really like to know
Why these anxious human beings
  Rush about and worry so."

Said the Sparrow to the Robin:
  "Friend, I think that it must be
That they have no heavenly Father
  Such as cares for you and me."

Elizabeth Cheney, 1859—

265. GOD'S PITY

God pity all the brave who go
  The common way, and wear
No ribboned medals on their breasts,
  No laurels in their hair.

God pity all the lonely Folk
  With Griefs they do not tell
Women waking in the night
  And men dissembling well.

In common courage of the street
  The crushed grape is the wine,
Wheat in the mill is daily bread
  And given for a sign.

And who but God shall pity those
  Who go so quietly
And smile upon us when we meet
  And greet so pleasantly.

Louise Driscoll, 1875–

266. ETERNAL FATHER, STRONG TO SAVE

Eternal Father, strong to save,
Whose arm hath bound the restless wave
Who bidd'st the mighty ocean deep
Its own appointed limits keep:
  O hear us when we cry to Thee
  For those in peril on the sea.

O Christ, whose voice the waters heard,
And hushed their raging at Thy word,
Who walkedst on the foaming deep,
And calm amid the storm didst sleep:
  O hear us when we cry to Thee
  For those in peril on the sea.

O Holy Spirit, who didst brood
Upon the waters dark and rude,
And bid their angry tumult cease,
And give, for wild confusion, peace:
  O hear us when we cry to Thee
  For those in peril on the sea.

O Trinity of love and power,
Our brethren shield in danger's hour;
From rock and tempest, fire and foe,
Protect them wheresoe'er they go:
  Thus evermore shall rise to Thee
  Glad hymns of praise from land and sea.

William Whiting, 1825–1878

267. THE CRADLE OF THE DEEP

Rocked in the cradle of the deep,
I lay me down in peace to sleep;
Secure I rest upon the wave,
For Thou, O Lord, hast power to save.
I know Thou wilt not slight my call,
For Thou dost mark the sparrow's fall;
And calm and peaceful shall I sleep,
Rocked in the cradle of the deep.

When in the dead of night I lie
And gaze upon the trackless sky,
The star-bespangled heavenly scroll,
The boundless waters as they roll,—
I feel Thy wondrous power to save
From perils of the stormy wave:
Rocked in the cradle of the deep
I calmly rest and soundly sleep.

And such the trust that still were mine,
Though stormy winds swept o'er the brine,
Or though the tempest's fiery breath
Roused me from sleep to wreck and death.
In ocean cave still safe with Thee,
The germ of immortality;
And calm and peaceful shall I sleep,
Rocked in the cradle of the deep.

Emma Willard, 1787–1870

268. THE AIRMEN'S HYMN

O God creator, in whose hand
The rolling planets lie,
Give skill to those who now command
The ships that brave the sky.

Strong spirit, burning with mankind
On missions high to dare,
Safe pilot all who seek to find
Their haven through the air.

Enfolding Life, bear on Thy wing
Through storm, and dark, and sun
The men in air who closer bring
The nations into one.

Harry Webb Farrington, 1880–1931

269. NOW, LORD, UPON THY SEA OF AIR

Now, Lord, upon Thy sea of air
We trust the strength of new-found wings,
And seem toward nothingness to dare,
Adrift from dear and anchored things.

Grant us we pray, who thus explore
This latest world Thy will has given,
To learn the lanes of spirit more
And seek where we before have striven.

Grant them who watch the gleam of wings
Vanish beyond the sight of men
To touch unseen, eternal things
By love that leads beyond their ken.

So having in each heart Thy word,
Through trackless night, through trackless day,
We know as surely as the bird
The safety of the unseen way;

Till we unerring move at length
On earth and air, by day or night,
As spirits go, from strength to strength,
To join the one Unhindered Flight.

Mary Louisa Anderson,
contemporary American

270. A PRAYER FOR AVIATORS

God of the sky, enthroned in azure blue,
  Lord of the air, who guides the wings at will,
Guide Thou the pilot as he journeys through
  High altitudes, o'er valley, plain, and hill.

God of the storm, whose majesty and power
  Are manifested in driving hail and rain,
Guard Thou the pilot in his crisis hour,
  Oh, bring him safely to a port again.

God of the night, whose darkness all enfolds,
  Hiding from view both landing field and course,
Give Thou safe guidance, as each beacon holds
  High shafts of light, with never-failing source.

God of our lives, we journey through the years,
In joy and pain, teach us to trust Thy care!
In heights of bliss, in storms of doubts and fears,
Show us our course and Thou wilt find us there.

Norman E. Richardson, 1878–

271. NEW YEAR

How burn the stars unchanging in the midnight skies,
As on the earth the old year dies!
Like leaves before the storm, so haste our lives away;
Eternal God, to Thee we pray.

For all Thy mercies past we lift our hearts in praise,
Thy care that crowned our fleeting days;
Our follies and our sins, O Lord, remember not,
Lost hours when we Thy love forgot.

From age to age Thy love endures; Thou art our God.
Send now Thy flaming truth abroad,
That with the New Year's dawning right may conquer wrong,
Grief yield to joy, and tears to song!

John J. Moment, 1875–

272. THE LORD IS MY SHEPHERD

Psalm 23[1]

The LORD is my shepherd;
I shall not want.

He maketh me to lie down in green pastures:
he leadeth me beside the still waters.
He restoreth my soul:
he leadeth me in the paths of righteousness for his name's sake.

Yea, though I walk through the valley of the shadow of death,
I will fear no evil:
for thou art with me;
thy rod and thy staff they comfort me.

Thou preparest a table before me
in the presence of mine enemies:
thou anointest my head with oil;
my cup runneth over.

Surely goodness and mercy shall follow me all the days of my life:
and I will dwell in the house of the LORD for ever.

King James Version, 1611

[1] "The poem, as it is rendered in the King James version, . . . translation as it is, unmetrical as it is, is yet perhaps the single most popular English poem."—Professor J. B. Reeves.

273. ON THE TWENTY-THIRD PSALM

In "pastures green"? Not always; sometimes He
Who knoweth best, in kindness leadeth me
In weary ways, where heavy shadows be.

And by "still waters"? No, not always so;
Oft times the heavy tempests round me blow,
And o'er my soul the waves and billows go.

But when the storm beats loudest, and I cry
Aloud for help, the Master standeth by,
And whispers to my soul, "Lo, it is I."

So, where He leads me, I can safely go,
And in the blest hereafter I shall know,
Why, in His wisdom, He hath led me so.

Author unknown

274. THE PILLAR OF THE CLOUD

Lead, kindly Light, amid the encircling gloom;
  Lead thou me on!
The night is dark, and I am far from home;
  Lead thou me on!
Keep thou my feet: I do not ask to see
The distant scene; one step enough for me.

I was not ever thus, nor prayed that thou
  Shouldst lead me on;
I loved to choose and see my path; but now
  Lead thou me on!
I loved the garish day, and, spite of fears,
Pride ruled my will: remember not past years.

So long thy power hath blest me, sure it still
  Will lead me on,
O'er moor and fen, o'er crag and torrent, till
  The night is gone;
And with the morn, those angel faces smile
Which I have loved long since, and lost awhile.

John Henry Newman, 1801–1890

275. HE LEADETH ME

He leadeth me! Oh, blessèd thought!
Oh words with heavenly comfort fraught!
Whate'er I do, where'er I be,
Still 'tis God's hand that leadeth me.

He leadeth me! He leadeth me!
By His own hand He leadeth me;
His faithful follower I would be,
For by His hand He leadeth me.

Sometimes 'mid scenes of deepest gloom,
Sometimes where Eden's bowers bloom,
By waters calm, o'er troubled sea,
Still 'tis God's hand that leadeth me.

Lord, I would clasp Thy hand in mine;
Nor ever murmur nor repine;
Content, whatever lot I see,
Since 'tis God's hand that leadeth me.

And when my task on earth is done,
When, by Thy grace, the victory's won,
E'en death's cold wave I will not flee,
Since Thou through Jordan leadest me.

Joseph H. Gilmore, 1834–1918

276. A HYMN

After reading "Lead, Kindly Light"

Lead gently, Lord, and slow,
For oh, my steps are weak,
And ever as I go,
Some soothing sentence speak;

That I may turn my face
Through doubt's obscurity
Toward thine abiding-place,
E'en tho' I cannot see.

For lo, the way is dark;
Through mist and cloud I grope,
Save for that fitful spark,
The little flame of hope.

Lead gently, Lord, and slow,
For fear that I may fall;
I know not where to go
Unless I hear thy call.

My fainting soul doth yearn
For thy green hills afar;
So let thy mercy burn—
My greater, guiding star!

Paul Laurence Dunbar, 1872–1906

277. From AN INVOCATION

O God, unknown, invisible, secure,
Whose being by dim resemblances we guess,
Who in man's fear and love abidest sure,
Whose power we feel in darkness and confess!

Without Thee nothing is, and Thou art nought
When on Thy substance we gaze curiously:
By Thee impalpable, named Force and Thought,
The solid world still ceases not to be.

Lead Thou me God, Law, Reason, Duty, Life!
All names for Thee alike are vain and hollow—
Lead me, for I will follow without strife;
Or, if I strive, still must I blindly follow.

John Addington Symonds, 1840–1893

278. NOT SO IN HASTE, MY HEART

Not so in haste, my heart!
Have faith in God and wait;
Although He linger long,
He never comes too late.

He never cometh late;
He knoweth what is best;
Vex not thyself in vain;
Until He cometh, rest.

Until He cometh, rest,
Nor grudge the hours that roll;
The feet that wait for God
Are soonest at the goal;

Are soonest at the goal
That is not gained by speed;
Then hold Thee still, my heart,
For I shall wait His lead.

Bradford Torrey, 1843–1912

279. PER PACEM AD LUCEM

I do not ask, O Lord, that life may be
A pleasant road;
I do not ask that Thou wouldst take from me
Aught of its load;

I do not ask that flowers should always spring
Beneath my feet;
I know too well the poison and the sting
Of things too sweet.

For one thing only, Lord, dear Lord, I plead,
Lead me aright—
Though strength should falter, and though heart should bleed—
Through Peace to Light.

I do not ask, O Lord, that Thou shouldst shed
Full radiance here;
Give but a ray of peace, that I may tread
Without a fear.

I do not ask my cross to understand,
My way to see;
Better in darkness just to feel Thy Hand
And follow Thee.

Joy is like restless day; but peace divine
Like quiet night:
Lead me, O Lord,—till perfect Day shall
shine,
Through Peace to Light.

Adelaide A. Procter, 1825–1864

280. MY DAILY PRAYER

If I can do some good today,
If I can serve along life's way,
If I can something helpful say,
Lord, show me how.

If I can right a human wrong,
If I can help to make one strong,
If I can cheer with smile or song,
Lord, show me how.

If I can aid one in distress,
If I can make a burden less,
If I can spread more happiness,
Lord, show me how.

Grenville Kleiser, 1868–

281. WORRY

The world is wide
In time and tide,
And—God is guide;
Then do not hurry.

That man is blest
Who does his best
And leaves the rest;
Then do not worry.

Charles F. Deems, 1820–1893

282. THE BURDEN

Take Thou the burden, Lord;
I am exhausted with this heavy load.
My tired hands tremble,
And I stumble, stumble
Along the way.
Oh, lead with Thine unfailing arm
Again today.

Unless Thou lead me, Lord
The road I journey on is all too hard.
Through trust in Thee alone
Can I go on.

Yet not for self alone
Thus do I groan;
My people's sorrows are the load I bear.
Lord, hear my prayer—
May Thy strong hand
Strike off all chains
That load my well-loved land.
God, draw her close to Thee!

Toyohiko Kagawa, 1888–

283. I GO TO PROVE MY SOUL

From "Paracelsus," Part I

I go to prove my soul!
I see my way as birds their trackless way.
I shall arrive! What time, what circuit
first,
I ask not: but unless God send his hail
Or blinding fireballs, sleet or stifling snow,
In some time, his good time, I shall arrive:
He guides me and the bird. In his good
time.

Robert Browning, 1812–1889

284. MY BIBLE

From "My Books and I"

And should my soul be torn with grief
Upon my shelf I find
A little volume, torn and thumbed,
For comfort just designed.
I take my little Bible down
And read its pages o'er,
And when I part from it I find
I'm stronger than before.

Edgar A. Guest, 1881–

285. TO A WATERFOWL

Whither, midst falling dew,
While glow the heavens with the last steps of day,
Far, through their rosy depths, dost thou pursue
Thy solitary way?

Vainly the fowler's eye
Might mark thy distant flight to do thee wrong,
As, darkly painted on the crimson sky,
Thy figure floats along.

Seek'st thou the plashy brink
Of weedy lake, or marge of river wide,
Or where the rocking billows rise and sink
On the chafed ocean-side?

There is a Power whose care
Teaches thy way along that pathless coast—
The desert and illimitable air—
Lone wandering, but not lost.

All day thy wings have fanned,
At that far height, the cold, thin atmosphere,
Yet stoop not, weary, to the welcome land,
Though the dark night is near.

And soon that toil shall end;
Soon shalt thou find a summer home, and rest,
And scream among thy fellows; reeds shall bend,
Soon, o'er thy sheltered nest.

Thou'rt gone, the abyss of heaven
Hath swallowed up thy form; yet, on my heart
Deeply hath sunk the lesson thou hast given,
And shall not soon depart.

He who, from zone to zone,
Guides through the boundless sky thy certain flight,
In the long way that I must tread alone,
Will lead my steps aright.

William Cullen Bryant, 1794–1878

286. BENEDICTION

From "Herod"

Now unto Him who brought His people forth
Out of the wilderness, by day a cloud,
By night a pillar of fire; to Him alone,
Look we at last and to no other look we.

Stephen Phillips, 1868–1915

287. From THE GATE OF THE YEAR[1]

And I said to the man who stood at the gate of the year:
"Give me a light, that I may tread safely into the unknown!"
And he replied:
"Go out into the darkness and put your hand into the Hand of God.
That shall be to you better than light and safer than a known way."
So, I went forth, and finding the Hand of God, trod gladly into the night.
And He led me toward the hills and the breaking of day in the lone East.
So, heart, be still!
What need our little life,
Our human life, to know,
If God hath comprehension?
In all the dizzy strife
Of things both high and low
God hideth His intention.

M. Louise Haskins, contemporary English

[1] King George VI, of Great Britain, quoted the first five lines in his Christmas Broadcast to the World at the beginning of the second world war, 1939.

288. DE PROFUNDIS

Psalm 130

Out of the depths have I cried unto thee, O LORD.
Lord, hear my voice: let thine ears be attentive to the voice of my supplications.
If thou, LORD, shouldest mark iniquities, O Lord, who shall stand?
But there is forgiveness with thee, that thou mayest be feared.
I wait for the LORD, my soul doth wait, and in his word do I hope.
My soul waiteth for the Lord more than they that watch for the morning: I say, more than they that watch for the morning.
Let Israel hope in the LORD: for with the LORD there is mercy, and with him is plenteous redemption.
And he shall redeem Israel from all his iniquities.

King James Version, 1611

289. TIMES WITHOUT NUMBER HAVE I PRAY'D

Times without number have I pray'd,
"This only once forgive";
Relapsing, when Thy hand was stay'd,
And suffer'd me to live:—

Yet now the kingdom of Thy peace,
Lord, to my heart restore;
Forgive my vain repentances,
And bid me sin no more.

Charles Wesley, 1707–1788

290. A HYMN TO GOD THE FATHER

Hear me, O God!
A broken heart
Is my best part:
Use still Thy rod,
That I may prove,
Therein, Thy love.

If Thou hadst not
Been stern to me,
But left me free,
I had forgot
Myself and Thee.

For, sin's so sweet,
As minds ill-bent
Rarely repent,
Unless they meet
Their punishment.

Who more can crave
Than Thou hast done?
Thou gav'st a Son
To free a slave,
First made of naught,
With all since bought.

Sin, death, and hell
His glorious Name
Quite overcame;
Yet I rebel,
And slight the same.

But, I'll come in
Before my loss
Me farther toss;
As sure to win
Under His cross.

Ben Jonson, 1573?–1637

291. THE NEW LEAF

He came to my desk with quivering lip—
The lesson was done.
"Dear Teacher, I want a new leaf," he said,
"I have spoiled this one."
I took the old leaf, stained and blotted,
And gave him a new one, all unspotted,
And into his sad eyes smiled:
"Do better now, my child!"

I went to the Throne with a quivering soul—
The old year was done.
"Dear Father, hast Thou a new leaf for me?
"I have spoiled this one."
He took the old leaf, stained and blotted,
And gave me a new one, all unspotted,
And into my sad heart smiled:
"Do better now, my child!"

Helen Field Fisher

292. PRODIGAL

Like a bird that trails a broken wing,
  I have come home to Thee;
Home from a flight and freedom
  That was never meant for me.

And I, who have known far spaces,
  And the fierce heat of the sun,
Ask only the shelter of Thy wings,
  Now that the day is done.

Like a bird that trails a broken wing,
  I have come home, at last. . . .
O hold me to Thy Heart once more,
  And hide me from the past.

Ellen Gilbert, contemporary American

293. THE WORLD IS TOO MUCH WITH US

The World is too much with us: late and soon,
Getting and spending, we lay waste our
    powers:
Little we see in Nature that is ours;
We have given our hearts away, a sordid
    boon!
This Sea that bares her bosom to the moon,
The winds that will be howling at all hours,
And are up-gather'd now like sleeping flowers;
For this, for every thing, we are out of tune;
It moves us not.—Great God! I'd rather be
A Pagan suckled in a creed outworn,—
So might I, standing on this pleasant lea,
Have glimpses that would make me less
    forlorn;
Have sight of Proteus rising from the sea;
Or hear old Triton blow his wreathèd horn.

William Wordsworth, 1770–1850

294. HIS PRAYER FOR ABSOLUTION

For those my unbaptizèd rhymes,
Writ in my wild unhallowed times;
For every sentence, clause, and word,
That's not inlaid with Thee, (my Lord,)
Forgive me, God, and blot each line
Out of my book, that is not Thine.
But if, 'mongst all, Thou find'st here one
Worthy Thy benediction;
That one of all the rest shall be
The glory of my work and me.

Robert Herrick, 1591–1674

295. PRAYER AT EVENTIDE

Night comes again to bring us rest,
  So give us, Lord, thy peace,
To wearied bodies boon of sleep,
  To troubl'd hearts release.

Forgive us, Lord, for hasty word,
  For spirits vex'd and toss'd,
For anxious care, for heedless haste
  And precious moments lost.

Forgive our want of faith in men,
  Our mean ingratitude,
Our selfishness and careless ease,
  Our falseness to the good.

Lord, give us rest, and be to all
  Who work or watch tonight
Companion of the darkened hours
  And herald of the light.

R. B. Y. Scott, contemporary Canadian

296. THE AIM

O Thou who lovest not alone
  The swift success, the instant goal,
But hast a lenient eye to mark
  The failures of the inconstant soul,

Consider not my little worth—
  The mean achievement, scamped in act—
The high resolve and low result,
  The dream that durst not face the fact.

But count the reach of my desire—
  Let this be something in thy sight;
I have not, in the slothful dark,
  Forgot the vision and the height.

Neither my body nor my soul
  To earth's low ease will yield consent.
I praise thee for the will to strive;
  I bless thy goad and discontent.

Charles G. D. Roberts, 1860–1943

297. "THOU SHALT PURGE ME WITH HYSSOP AND I SHALL BE CLEAN"

With whom shall I find perfect ease
To whom draw near
Unhaunted by the shadow of offense,
The shade of fear?

The dearest eyes that beam down into mine
In love and trust
Light up the motes of infidelities,
My heart's rank dust.

Did those eyes penetrate, they could at best
Be sadly kind,
Might tolerate but never purge away
What they must find.

But God who sees it all can cleanse it all,
So my heart shows
To men a stagnant pool, to Him a stream
Still clearing as it flows.

Anna Bunston de Bary,
contemporary English

298. WIND IN THE PINE

Oh, I can hear you, God, above the cry
Of the tossing trees—
Rolling your windy tides across the sky,
And splashing your silver seas
Over the pine,
To the water-line
Of the moon.
Oh, I can hear you, God,
Above the wail of the lonely loon—
When the pine-tops pitch and nod—
Chanting your melodies
Of ghostly waterfalls and avalanches,
Washing your wind among the branches
To make them pure and white.

Wash over me, God, with your piney breeze,
And your moon's wet-silver pool;
Wash over me, God, with your wind and night,
And leave me clean and cool.

Lew Sarett, 1888-

299. LOVE

Love bade me welcome; yet my soul drew back,
Guilty of dust and sin,
But quick-eyed Love, observing me grow slack
From my first entrance in,
Drew nearer to me, sweetly questioning,
If I lack'd anything.
"A guest," I answer'd, "worthy to be here":
Love said, "You shall be he."
"I, the unkind, ungrateful? Ah, my dear
I cannot look on Thee."
Love took my hand, and smiling did reply,
"Who made the eyes but I?"
"Truth, Lord, but I have marr'd them; let my shame
Go where it doth deserve."
"And know you not," says Love, "Who bore the blame?"
"My dear, then I will serve."
"You must sit down," says Love, "and taste My meat."
So I did sit and eat.

George Herbert, 1593–1632

300. THE LAW WITHIN

Psalm 19 : 7–14

The law of the LORD is perfect, restoring the soul:
The testimony of the LORD is sure, making wise the simple.
The precepts of the LORD are right, rejoicing the heart:
The commandment of the LORD is pure, enlightening the eyes.
The fear of the LORD is clean, enduring for ever:
The judgements of the LORD are true, and righteous altogether.
More to be desired are they than gold, yea, than much fine gold:
Sweeter also than honey and the honeycomb.
Moreover by them is thy servant warned:
In keeping of them there is great reward.
Who can discern his errors? Clear thou me from hidden faults.
Keep back thy servant also from presumptuous sins; let them not have dominion over me:

Then shall I be perfect,
And I shall be clear from great transgression.

Let the words of my mouth and the meditation of my heart be acceptable in thy sight,
O Lord, my rock, and my redeemer.

Moulton: The Modern Reader's Bible, 1895

301. VOYAGERS

O Maker of the Mighty Deep
  Whereon our vessels fare,
Above our life's adventure keep
  Thy faithful watch and care.
In Thee we trust, whate'er befall;
Thy sea is great, our boats are small.

We know not where the secret tides
  Will help us or delay,
Nor where the lurking tempest hides,
  Nor where the fogs are gray.
We trust in Thee, whate'er befall;
Thy sea is great, our boats are small.

When outward bound we boldly sail
  And leave the friendly shore,
Let not our hearts of courage fail
  Before the voyage is o'er.
We trust in Thee, whate'er befall;
Thy sea is great, our boats are small.

When homeward bound we gladly turn,
  O bring us safely there,
Where harbour-lights of friendship burn
  And peace is in the air.
We trust in Thee, whate'er befall;
Thy sea is great, our boats are small.

Beyond the circle of the sea,
  When voyaging is past,
We seek our final port in Thee;
  O bring us home at last.
In Thee we trust, whate'er befall;
Thy sea is great, our boats are small.

Henry van Dyke, 1852–1933

302. SONG

From "Pippa Passes"

The year's at the spring
And day's at the morn;
Morning's at seven:
The hillside's dew-pearled;
The lark's on the wing;
The snail's on the thorn;
God's in his heaven—
All's right with the world!

Robert Browning, 1812–1889

303. ESCAPE

The daily work in narrow space is bound
Which each moment brings within our prison
  yard,
As one by one we circle round the guard
But skyward ever hearts and eyes we lift,
That wander far into God's realm of light,
That rise untrammeled as the bird so swift,
That bear to God our praises and our trust.

By a prisoner in a Nazi concentration camp, 1940

304. IN HIM CONFIDING

Sometimes a light surprises
  The Christian while he sings;
It is the Lord who rises
  With healing on His wings.
When comforts are declining
  He grants the soul again
A season of clear shining,
  To cheer it after rain.

In holy contemplation
  We sweetly then pursue
The theme of God's salvation,
  And find it ever new.
Set free from present sorrow,
  We cheerfully can say,
Let the unknown to-morrow
  Bring with it what it may.

It can bring with it nothing
  But He will bear us through;
Who gives the lilies clothing,
  Will clothe His people too.
Beneath the spreading heavens
  No creature but is fed;
And He who feeds the ravens
  Will give His children bread.

Though vine nor fig tree neither
  Their wonted fruit should bear,
Though all the fields should wither,
  Nor flocks nor herds be there;
Yet God the same abiding,
  His praise shall tune my voice;
For while in Him confiding,
  I cannot but rejoice.

William Cowper, 1731–1800

305. HYMN OF TRUST

O Love Divine, that stooped to share
  Our sharpest pang, our bitterest tear,
On Thee we cast each earth-born care,
  We smile at pain while Thou art near!

Though long the weary way we tread,
  And sorrow crown each lingering year,
No path we shun, no darkness dread,
  Our hearts still whispering, Thou art near!

When drooping pleasure turns to grief,
  And trembling faith is changed to fear,
The murmuring wind, the quivering leaf,
  Shall softly tell us, Thou art near!

On Thee we fling our burdening woe,
  O Love Divine, forever dear,
Content to suffer while we know,
  Living and dying, Thou art near!

Oliver Wendell Holmes, 1809–1894

306. VIEW ME, LORD, A WORK OF THINE

View me, Lord, a work of thine:
Shall I then lie drown'd in night?
Might thy grace in me but shine,
I should seem made all of light.

But my soul still surfeits so
On the poisoned baits of sin,
That I strange and ugly grow,
All is dark and foul within.

Cleanse me, Lord, that I may kneel
At thine altar, pure and white:
They that once thy mercies feel,
Gaze no more on earth's delight.

Worldly joys like shadows fade,
When the heav'nly light appears;
But the cov'nants thou hast made,
Endless, know nor days, nor years.

In thy word, Lord, is my trust,
To thy mercies fast I fly;
Though I am but clay and dust,
Yet thy grace can lift me high.

Thomas Campion, 1567–1620

307. GOD'S WAYS

I asked for grace to lift me high
  Above the world's depressing cares;
God sent me sorrows,—with a sigh
  I said, "He has not heard my prayers."

I asked for light, that I might see
  My path along life's thorny road;
But clouds and darkness shadowed me
  When I expected light from God.

I asked for peace, that I might rest
  To think my sacred duties o'er,
When, lo! such horrors filled my breast
  As I had never felt before.

"And, oh," I cried, "can this be prayer
  Whose plaints the steadfast mountains
    move?
Can this be Heaven's prevailing care?
  And, O my God, is this Thy love?"

But soon I found that sorrow, worn
  As Duty's garment, strength supplies,
And out of darkness meekly borne
  Unto the righteous light doth rise.

And soon I found that fears which stirred
  My startled soul God's will to do,
On me more lasting peace conferred
  Than in life's calm I ever knew. . . .

Author unknown

308. THE KINDLY SCREEN

"Today is hard. Tomorrow will
  Be harder still" . . .
Yet God has kindly placed between,
  A three-fold screen
Of sunset sky, sleep's downy wings,
  And dawn that sings,
That I may face with tranquil heart
  Each day apart.

Belle Chapman Morrill,
contemporary American

309. A ONE HUNDRED FIFTY-FIRST PSALM

The Lord is my friend, so I shall not be lonely
even in a strange land;
He is the Good Angel above my bed, so I
shall see the dawn.

Even though I wandered far from His counsel,
He did not desert me;
When I arose to return, it was His voice
that I heard.

When I beheld the glory of the West at eve,
I remembered Him;
The moonrise over the mountains was
the trailing of His mantle.

When the storm crashed against the mountain,
His almightiness pealed forth,
And the gray face of the desert whispered
His holy austerity.

As I entered the place of prayer,
I was strangely moved;
When I came away, I had said
not a word.

Yet, as I kept silence before Him,
He understood:
My soul was lifted as though
I had seen His face.

When I awoke in the night,
He possessed my thought;
And in the morning I turned a moment from my task
to speak of Him.

He has traveled further for me than any one;
He has done more;
Yet there is no price upon Love,
and I cannot repay Him.

When I was at Death's door,
He closed it and led me away.
Surely He will be there
when I must pass through.

Henry B. Robins, 1874–

310. NEW YEAR

Upon the threshold of another year
We stand again.
We know not what of gladness and good cheer,

Of grief or pain
May visit us while journeying to its close.
In this we rest,
God dealeth out in wisdom what He knows
For us is best.

Thomas Wearing, 1881–

311. GOD OF OUR LIFE

God of our life, through all the circling years,
We trust in Thee;
In all the past, through all our hopes and fears,
Thy hand we see.
With each new day, when morning lifts the veil,
We own Thy mercies, Lord, which never fail.

God of the past, our times are in Thy hand;
With us abide.
Lead us by faith to hope's true Promised Land;
Be Thou our guide.
With Thee to bless, the darkness shines as light,
And faith's fair vision changes into sight.

God of the coming years, through paths unknown
We follow Thee;
When we are strong, Lord, leave us not alone;
Our refuge be.
Be Thou for us in life our Daily Bread,
Our heart's true Home when all our years have sped.

Hugh Thomson Kerr, 1871–

312. SOMETIME

Sometime, when all life's lessons have been learned,
And sun and stars forevermore have set,
The things which our weak judgments here have spurned,
The things o'er which we grieved with lashes wet,
Will flash before us out of life's dark night,
As stars shine most in deeper tints of blue;
And we shall see how all God's plans are right,
And how what seemed reproof was love most true.

And we shall see how, while we frown and sigh,
God's plans go on as best for you and me;
How, when we called, He heeded not our cry,
Because His wisdom to the end could see.
And e'en as prudent parents disallow
Too much of sweet to craving babyhood,
So God, perhaps, is keeping from us now
Life's sweetest things, because it seemeth good.

❖

Then be content, poor heart;
God's plans, like lilies pure and white, unfold;
We must not tear the close-shut leaves apart,—
Time will reveal the chalices of gold.
And if, through patient toil, we reach the land
Where tired feet, with sandals loosed, may rest,
When we shall clearly see and understand,
I think that we will say, "God knew the best!"

May Riley Smith, 1842–1927

313. AFTER ST. AUGUSTINE

Sunshine let it be or frost,
Storm or calm, as Thou shalt choose;
Though Thine every gift were lost,
Thee Thyself we could not lose.

Mary Elizabeth Coleridge, 1861–1907

314. BY THY LIFE I LIVE

I love, my God, but with no love of mine,
For I have none to give;
I love Thee, Lord, but all the love is Thine,
For by Thy life I live.
I am as nothing, and rejoice to be
Emptied and lost and swallowed up in Thee.

Thou, Lord, alone art all Thy children need,
And there is none beside;
From Thee the streams of blessedness
proceed;
In Thee the blest abide,
Fountain of life, and all-abounding grace,
Our source, our center, and our dwelling-
place!

Madame Jeanne Marie Guyon, 1648–1717

315. IN HEAVENLY LOVE ABIDING

In heavenly love abiding,
No change my heart shall fear;
And safe is such confiding,
For nothing changes here.
The storm may roar without me,
My heart may low be laid;
But God is round about me,
And can I be dismayed?

Wherever He may guide me,
No want shall turn me back;
My Shepherd is beside me,
And nothing can I lack.
His wisdom ever waketh,
His sight is never dim;
He knows the way He taketh,
And I will walk with Him.

Green pastures are before me,
Which yet I have not seen;
Bright skies will soon be o'er me,
Where darkest clouds have been.
My hope I cannot measure,
My path to life is free;
My Saviour has my treasure,
And He will walk with me.

Anna L. Waring, 1820–1910

316. LEAVE IT ALL QUIETLY TO GOD

Psalm 62: 1–8

Leave it all quietly to God, my soul,
my rescue comes from him alone;
rock, rescue, refuge, he is all to me,
never shall I be overthrown.

How long will you be threatening a man,
you murderers all,
as if he were a shaky fence,
a tottering wall?

They plan to push me from my place,
delighting in a crafty part;
blessings are on their lips,
and curses in their heart.

Leave it all quietly to God, my soul,
my rescue comes from him alone;
rock, rescue, refuge, he is all to me,
never shall I be overthrown.

My safety and my honour rest on God;
God is my strong rock and refuge.
Always rely on him, my followers,
pour out your prayers to him;
God is a refuge for us.

The Old Testament, A New Translation by James Moffatt, 1925

317. MILTON'S PRAYER

I am old and blind!
Men point at me as smitten by God's frown:
Afflicted and deserted of my kind,
Yet am I not cast down.

I am weak, yet strong;
I murmur not that I no longer see;
Poor, old, and helpless, I the more belong,
Father supreme, to thee!

All-merciful One!
When men are furthest, then art thou most near;
When friends pass by, my weaknesses to shun,
Thy chariot I hear.

Thy glorious face
Is leaning toward me; and its holy light
Shines in upon my lonely dwelling place,
And there is no more night.

❖

I have naught to fear;
This darkness is the shadow of thy wing;
Beneath it I am almost sacred; here
Can come no evil thing.

Oh, I seem to stand
Trembling, where foot of mortal ne'er hath been,
Wrapt in that radiance from the sinless land,
Which eye hath never seen!

Visions come and go:
Shapes of resplendent beauty around me throng;
From angel lips I seem to hear the flow
Of soft and holy song.

❖

Give me now my lyre!
I feel the stirrings of a gift divine:
Within my bosom glows unearthly fire,
Lit by no skill of mine.

Elizabeth Lloyd Howell, 1811–1896

318. From PRAYER

O God, thy ways are dark.
Man cannot mark
Thy path upon the mountain or the sea.
We cannot read thy will or know thy mind,
Baffled by one small world thou hast designed.
Awed by the grandeur of infinity.
He who can trace
The marching stars through space,
Measure the oceans, lift the mountains up,
Scatter the perfume in the lily's cup,
Planning for aeons, measuring each year,
Will this God hear?
Yes; if we call to Him in joy, dismay,
(For that is prayer) He cannot turn away,
A Father dwelling with us, not apart.
When my child's call I hear, I catch her to my heart.

Edward Bliss Reed, 1872–1940

319. LONG DID I TOIL

Long did I toil, and knew no earthly rest,
Far did I rove, and found no certain home;
At last I sought them in His sheltering breast,
Who opes His arms, and bids the weary come:
With Him I found a home, a rest divine,
And I since then am His, and He is mine.

The good I have is from His stores supplied,
The ill is only what He deems the best;
He for my Friend, I'm rich with nought beside,
And poor without Him, though of all possessed:
Changes may come—I take, or I resign,
Content, while I am His, while He is mine.

John Quarles, 1624–1665 and Henry F. Lyte, 1793–1847

320. HE DOETH ALL THINGS WELL

I hoped that with the brave and strong,
My portioned task might lie;
To toil amid the busy throng,
With purpose pure and high;
But God has fixed another part,
And he has fixed it well,
I said so with my breaking heart,
When first this trouble fell.

These weary hours will not be lost,
These days of misery,
These nights of darkness, anguish-tossed,
Can I but turn to Thee:
With secret labour to sustain
In patience every blow
To gather fortitude from pain,
And holiness from woe.

If Thou shouldst bring me back to life,
More humble I should be,
More wise, more strengthened for the strife,
More apt to lean on Thee;
Should death be standing at the gate,
Thus should I keep my vow;
But, Lord, whatever be my fate,
O let me serve Thee now!

Anne Brontë, 1820–1849

321. BATTER MY HEART

From "Holy Sonnets," XIX

Batter my heart, three-personed God: for you
As yet but knock; breathe, shine, and seek to mend;
That I may rise and stand, o'erthrow me, and bend
Your force, to break, blow, burn, and make me new.
I, like an usurped town, to another due,
Labour to admit you, but oh, to no end;
Reason, your viceroy in me, me should defend,
But is captived, and proves weak or untrue.
Yet dearly I love you, and would be lovèd fain,
But am betrothed unto your enemy;
Divorce me, untie, or break that knot again,
Take me to you, imprison me, for I,
Except you enthrall me, never shall be free;
Nor ever chaste, except you ravish me.

John Donne, 1573–1631

322. VENI CREATOR

Lord of my heart's elation,
Spirit of things unseen,
Be thou my aspiration
Consuming and serene!

Bear up, bear out, bear onward
This mortal soul alone,
To selfhood or oblivion,
Incredibly thine own,—

As the foam heads are loosened
And blown along the sea,
Or sink and merge forever
In that which bids them be.

I, too, must climb in wonder,
Uplift at thy command,—
Be one with my frail fellows
Beneath the wind's strong hand,

A fleet and shadowy column
Of dust or mountain rain,
To walk the earth a moment
And be dissolved again.

Be thou my exaltation
Or fortitude of mien,
Lord of the world's elation
Thou breath of things unseen!

Bliss Carman, 1861–1929

323. PECCAVI, DOMINE

O Power to whom this earthly clime
Is but an atom in the whole,
O Poet-heart of Space and Time,
O Maker and immortal Soul,
Within whose glowing rings are bound,

Out of whose sleepless heart had birth
The cloudy blue, the starry round,
And this small miracle of earth:

Who liv'st in every living thing,
And all things are thy script and chart,
Who rid'st upon the eagle's wing,
And yearnest in the human heart;
O Riddle with a single clue,
Love, deathless, protean, secure,
The ever old, the ever new,
O Energy, serene and pure.

Thou, who art also part of me,
Whose glory I have sometime seen,
O Vision of the Ought-to-be,
O Memory of the Might-have-been,
I have had glimpses of thy way,
And moved with winds and walked with stars,
But, weary, I have fallen astray,
And, wounded, who shall count my scars?

O Master, all my strength is gone;
Unto the very earth I bow;
I have no light to lead me on;
With aching heart and burning brow,
I lie as one that travaileth
In sorrow more than he can bear;
I sit in darkness as of death,
And scatter dust upon my hair.

The God within my soul hath slept,
And I have shamed the nobler rule;
O Master, I have whined and crept;
O Spirit, I have played the fool.
Like him of old upon whose head
His follies hung in dark arrears,
I groan and travail in my bed,
And water it with bitter tears.

I stand upon thy mountain-heads,
And gaze until mine eyes are dim;
The golden morning glows and spreads;
The hoary vapours break and swim.
I see thy blossoming fields, divine,
Thy shining clouds, thy blessed trees—
And then that broken soul of mine—
How much less beautiful than these!

O Spirit, passionless, but kind,
Is there in all the world, I cry,
Another one so base and blind,
Another one so weak as I?

O Power, unchangeable, but just,
Impute this one good thing to me,
I sink my spirit to the dust
In utter dumb humility.

Archibald Lampman, 1861–1899

324. EVENSONG

The embers of the day are red
Beyond the murky hill.
The kitchen smokes; the bed
In the darkling house is spread:
The great sky darkens overhead,
And the great woods are shrill.
So far have I been led,
Lord, by Thy will:
So far I have followed, Lord, and wondered still.
The breeze from the embalméd land
Blows sudden towards the shore,
And claps my cottage door.
I hear the signal, Lord—I understand.
The night at Thy command
Comes. I will eat and sleep and will not question more.

Robert Louis Stevenson, 1850–1894

325. COMMUNION

Lord, I have knelt and tried to pray to-night,
But Thy love came upon me like a sleep,
And all desire died out; upon the deep
Of Thy mere love I lay, each thought in light
Dissolving like the sunset clouds, at rest
Each tremulous wish, and my strength weakness, sweet
As a sick boy with soon o'erwearied feet
Finds, yielding him unto his mother's breast
To weep for weakness there. I could not pray,
But with closed eyes I felt Thy bosom's love
Beating toward mine, and then I would not move
Till of itself the joy should pass away;
At last my heart found voice,—'Take me, O Lord,
And do with me according to Thy word.'

Edward Dowden, 1843–1913

326. OUR REFUGE

Psalm 46

God is our refuge and strength,
A very present help in trouble.
Therefore will we not fear, though the earth do change,
And though the mountains be moved in the heart of the seas:
Though the waters thereof roar and be troubled,
Though the mountains shake with the swelling thereof.
THE LORD OF HOSTS IS WITH US;
THE GOD OF JACOB IS OUR REFUGE.
There is a river, the streams whereof make glad the city of God,
The holy place of the tabernacles of the Most High.
God is in the midst of her; she shall not be moved:
God shall help her at the dawn of morning.
The nations raged, the kingdoms were moved;
He uttered his voice, the earth melted.
THE LORD OF HOSTS IS WITH US;
THE GOD OF JACOB IS OUR REFUGE.
Come, behold the works of the LORD,
What desolations he hath made in the earth.
He maketh wars to cease unto the end of the earth;
He breaketh the bow, and cutteth the spear in sunder;
He burneth the chariots in the fire.
Be still, and know that I am God:
I will be exalted among the nations,
I will be exalted in the earth.
THE LORD OF HOSTS IS WITH US;
THE GOD OF JACOB IS OUR REFUGE.

Moulton: The Modern Reader's Bible, 1895

327. A MIGHTY FORTRESS IS OUR GOD

A mighty Fortress is our God,
A Bulwark never failing;
Our Helper He amid the flood
Of mortal ills prevailing:
For still our ancient foe
Doth seek to work us woe;
His craft and power are great,
And, armed with cruel hate,
On earth is not his equal.

Did we in our own strength confide,
Our striving would be losing;
Were not the right Man on our side,
The Man of God's own choosing:
Dost ask who that may be?
Christ Jesus, it is He;
Lord Sabaoth His name,
From age to age the same,
And He must win the battle.

And though this world, with devils filled,
Should threaten to undo us;
We will not fear, for God hath willed
His truth to triumph through us:
The Prince of Darkness grim,
We tremble not for him;
His rage we can endure,
For lo! his doom is sure,
One little word shall fell him.

That word above all earthly powers,
No thanks to them, abideth;
The Spirit and the gifts are ours
Through Him who with us sideth:
Let goods and kindred go,
This mortal life also;
The body they may kill:
God's truth abideth still,
His Kingdom is forever.

Martin Luther, 1483–1546;
tr. by Frederick H. Hedge, 1805–1890

328. O GOD, OUR HELP

Psalm 90

O God, our help in ages past,
  Our hope for years to come,
Our shelter from the stormy blast,
  And our eternal home:

Beneath the shadow of Thy throne
  Thy saints have dwelt secure;
Sufficient is Thine arm alone,
  And our defence is sure.

Before the hills in order stood,
  Or earth received her frame,
From everlasting Thou art God,
  To endless years the same.

❖

A thousand ages in Thy sight
  Are like an evening gone;
Short as the watch that ends the night
  Before the rising sun.

❖

Time, like an ever-rolling stream,
  Bears all its sons away;
They fly forgotten, as a dream
  Dies at the opening day.

❖

Our God, our help in ages past;
  Our hope for years to come;
Be Thou our guard while troubles last,
  And our eternal home!

Isaac Watts, 1674–1748

329. GOD OUR REFUGE

If there had anywhere appeared in space
  Another place of refuge where to flee,
Our hearts had taken refuge in that place,
  And not with Thee.

For we against creation's bars had beat
  Like prisoned eagles, through great worlds had sought
Though but a foot of ground to plant our feet,
  Where Thou wert not.

And only when we found in earth and air,
  In heaven or hell, that such might nowhere be—
That we could not flee from Thee anywhere,
  We fled to Thee.

Richard Chenevix Trench, 1807–1886

330. THY SEA SO GREAT

Thy sea, O God, so great,
  My boat so small.
It cannot be that any happy fate
  Will me befall
Save as Thy goodness opens paths for me
Through the consuming vastness of the sea.

Thy winds, O God, so strong,
  So slight my sail.
How could I curb and bit them on the long
  And salty trail,
Unless Thy love were mightier than the wrath
Of all the tempests that beset my path?

Thy world, O God, so fierce,
  And I so frail.
Yet, though its arrows threaten oft to pierce
  My fragile mail,
Cities of refuge rise where dangers cease,
Sweet silences abound, and all is peace.

Winfred Ernest Garrison, 1874–

331. GOD IS MY STRONG SALVATION

God is my strong salvation;
  What foe have I to fear?
In darkness and temptation
  My light, my help is near.

Though hosts encamp around me,
  Firm to the fight I stand;
What terror can confound me,
  With God at my right hand?

Place on the Lord reliance;
  My soul, with courage wait;
His truth be thine affiance,
  When faint and desolate.

His might thine heart shall strengthen,
His love thy joy increase;
Mercy thy days shall lengthen;
The Lord will give thee peace.

James Montgomery, 1771–1854

332. THE PLACE OF PEACE

At the heart of the cyclone tearing the sky
And flinging the clouds and the towers by,
Is a place of central calm;
So here in the roar of mortal things,
I have a place where my spirit sings,
In the hollow of God's palm.

Edwin Markham, 1852–1940

333. NEARER, MY GOD, TO THEE

Nearer, my God, to Thee,
Nearer to Thee!
E'en though it be a cross
That raiseth me;
Still all my song shall be,
Nearer, my God, to Thee,
Nearer to Thee!

Though like the wanderer,
The sun gone down,
Darkness be over me,
My rest a stone;
Yet in my dreams I'd be
Nearer, my God, to Thee,
Nearer to Thee!

There let my way appear
Steps unto heaven;
All that Thou sendest me
In mercy given;
Angels to beckon me
Nearer, my God, to Thee,
Nearer to Thee!

Then, with my waking thoughts
Bright with Thy praise,
Out of my stony griefs,
Bethel I'll raise;
So by my woes to be
Nearer, my God, to Thee,
Nearer to Thee!

Or, if on joyful wing,
Cleaving the sky,
Sun, moon, and stars forgot,
Upward I fly,
Still all my song shall be
Nearer, my God, to Thee,
Nearer to Thee!

Sarah Flower Adams, 1805–1848

334. A HALLELUJAH CHORUS

Psalm 148

Hallelujah!
Praise the Lord from the heavens;
Praise him in the heights!
Praise him, all his angels;
Praise him, all his host!
Praise him, sun and moon;
Praise him, all you stars of light!
Praise him, highest heavens,
And waters that are above the heavens!
Let them praise the name of the Lord!
For he commanded and they were created.
And he fixed them fast forever and ever;
He gave a statute that they should not
transgress.
Praise the Lord from the earth;
Sea-monsters and all deeps!
Fire and hail, snow and fog,
Stormy wind, fulfilling his word!
Mountains and all hills,
Fruit-trees and all cedars!
Wild beasts and all cattle,
Reptiles and winged birds!
Kings of the earth and all peoples,
Princes and all rulers of the earth!
Young men and maidens, too,
Old men and boys!

Let them praise the name of the Lord;
For his name alone is exalted;
His majesty is over the earth and the heavens,
And he has raised up a horn for his people.
The praise is he of all his saints,
The sons of Israel, the people near him.
Hallelujah!

The Bible: An American Translation, 1935

335. HYMN BEFORE SUNRISE, IN THE VALE OF CHAMOUNI

Hast thou a charm to stay the morning-star
In his steep course? So long he seems to pause
On thy bald, awful head, O sovran Blanc!
The Arve and the Arveiron at thy base
Rave ceaselessly; but thou, most awful Form!
Risest from forth thy silent sea of pines,
How silently! Around thee and above,
Deep is the air and dark, substantial, black,
An ebon mass: methinks thou piercest it,
As with a wedge! But when I look again,
It is thine own calm home, thy crystal shrine,
Thy habitation from eternity!
O dread and silent Mount! I gazed upon thee,
Till thou, still present to the bodily sense,
Didst vanish from my thought: entranced in prayer
I worshipp'd the Invisible alone.

Yet, like some sweet beguiling melody,
So sweet, we know not we are listening to it,
Thou, the meanwhile, wast blending with my thought,
Yea, with my life and life's own secret joy:
Till the dilating Soul, enwrapt, transfused,
Into the mighty vision passing—there,
As in her natural form, swell'd vast to Heaven!

Awake, my soul! not only passive praise
Thou owest! not alone these swelling tears,
Mute thanks and secret ecstasy! Awake,
Voice of sweet song! Awake, my Heart, awake!
Green vales and icy cliffs, all join my Hymn.

Thou first and chief, sole sovran of the Vale!
O struggling with the darkness all the night,
And visited all night by troops of stars,
Or when they climb the sky or when they sink:
Companion of the morning-star at dawn,
Thyself Earth's rosy star, and of the dawn
Co-herald: wake, O wake, and utter praise!
Who sank thy sunless pillars deep in Earth?
Who fill'd thy countenance with rosy light?
Who made thee parent of perpetual streams?

And you, ye five wild torrents fiercely glad!
Who call'd you forth from night and utter death,
From dark and icy caverns call'd you forth,
Down those precipitous, black, jagged Rocks,
Forever shatter'd and the same forever?
Who gave you your invulnerable life,
Your strength, your speed, your fury, and your joy,
Unceasing thunder and eternal foam?
And who commanded, (and the silence came),
Here let the billows stiffen, and have rest?

Ye ice-falls! ye that from the mountain's brow
Adown enormous ravines slope amain—
Torrents, methinks, that heard a mighty voice,
And stopp'd at once amid their maddest plunge!
Motionless torrents! silent cataracts!
Who made you glorious as the gates of Heaven
Beneath the keen full moon? Who bade the sun
Clothe you with rainbows? Who, with living flowers
Of the loveliest blue, spread garlands at your feet?—
God! let the torrents, like a shout of nations,
Answer! and let the ice-plains echo, God!
God! sing ye meadow-streams, with gladsome voice!
Ye pine-groves, with soft and soul-like sounds!
And they too have a voice, yon piles of snow,
And in their perilous fall shall thunder, God!

Ye living flowers that skirt the eternal frost!
Ye wild goats sporting round the eagle's nest!
Ye eagles, playmates of the mountain-storm!
Ye lightnings, the dread arrows of the clouds!
Ye signs and wonders of the element!
Utter forth God, and fill the hills with praise!

Thou too, hoar Mount! with thy sky-pointing peaks,
Oft from whose feet the avalanche, unheard,
Shoots downward, glittering through the pure serene
Into the depths of clouds that veil thy breast—
Thou too again, stupendous Mountain! Thou
That, as I raise my head, awhile bow'd low
In adoration, upward from thy base
Slow travelling with dim eyes suffused with tears,
Solemnly seemest, like a vapory cloud,
To rise before me—Rise, O ever rise!
Rise like a cloud of incense, from the Earth!
Thou kingly Spirit throned among the hills,
Thou dread ambassador from Earth to Heaven,
Great hierarch! tell thou the silent sky,
And tell the stars and tell yon rising sun,
Earth, with her thousand voices, praises God.

Samuel Taylor Coleridge, 1772–1834

336. TE DEUM LAUDAMUS

We praise thee, O God; we acknowledge thee to be the Lord.
All the earth doth worship thee, the Father everlasting.
To thee all Angels cry aloud; the Heavens, and all the Powers therein.
To thee Cherubim and Seraphim continually do cry,
Holy, Holy, Holy, Lord God of Sabaoth;
Heaven and earth are full of the Majesty of thy Glory.
The glorious company of the Apostles praise thee.
The goodly fellowship of the Prophets praise thee.
The noble army of Martyrs praise thee.
The holy Church throughout all the world doth acknowledge thee;

The Father of an infinite Majesty;
Thine honorable, true, and only Son;
Also the Holy Ghost, the Comforter.
Thou art the King of Glory, O Christ.
Thou art the everlasting Son of the Father.
When thou tookest upon thee to deliver man, thou didst not abhor the Virgin's womb.
When thou hadst overcome the sharpness of death, thou didst open the Kingdom of Heaven to all believers.
Thou sittest at the right hand of God, in the Glory of the Father.
We believe that thou shalt come to be our Judge.
We therefore pray thee, help thy servants, whom thou hast redeemed with thy precious blood.
Make them to be numbered with thy Saints in glory everlasting.
O Lord, save thy people, and bless thine heritage.
Govern them, and lift them up forever.
Day by day we magnify thee;
And we worship thy Name ever, world without end.
Vouchsafe, O Lord, to keep us this day without sin.
O Lord, have mercy upon us, have mercy upon us.
O Lord, let thy mercy lighten upon us, as our trust is in thee.
O Lord, in thee have I trusted; let me never be confounded.

From the Latin, 4th century

337. HOLY, HOLY, HOLY

Holy, Holy, Holy! Lord God Almighty!
Early in the morning our song shall rise to Thee:
Holy, Holy, Holy! Merciful and Mighty!
God in THREE Persons, Blessed TRINITY!

Holy, Holy, Holy! all the Saints adore Thee,
Casting down their golden crowns around the glassy sea;
Cherubim and Seraphim falling down before Thee,
Which wert, and art, and evermore shalt be.

Holy, Holy, Holy! though the darkness hide Thee,
Though the eye of sinful man Thy glory may not see,
Only Thou art Holy, there is none beside Thee
Perfect in power, in love, and purity.

Holy, Holy, Holy! LORD GOD Almighty!
All Thy works shall praise Thy Name, in earth, and sky, and sea;
Holy, Holy, Holy! Merciful and Mighty!
God in THREE Persons, Blessed TRINITY!

Reginald Heber, 1783–1826

338. OLD HUNDREDTH

Psalm 100

All people that on earth do dwell,
Sing to the Lord with cheerful voice;
Him serve with mirth, His praise forth tell,
Come ye before Him, and rejoice.

Know that the Lord is God indeed;
Without our aid He did us make;
We are His folk, He doth us feed;
And for His sheep He doth us take.

O, enter then His gates with praise,
Approach with joy His courts unto;

Praise, laud, and bless His name always,
For it is seemly so to do.

For why? the Lord our God is good;
His mercy is forever sure;
His truth at all times firmly stood,
And shall from age to age endure.

William Kethe, 1510–1594

339. EVENING PRAYER

Glory to Thee, my God, this night
For all the blessings of the light;
Keep me, O keep me, King of kings,
Beneath Thine own almighty wings.

Forgive me, Lord, for Thy dear Son,
The ill that I this day have done,
That with the world, myself, and Thee,
I, ere I sleep at peace may be.

Teach me to live, that I may dread
The grave as little as my bed;
Teach me to die, that so I may
Rise glorious at the awful day.

O may my soul on Thee repose,
And may sweet sleep mine eyelids close,
Sleep that shall me more vigorous make
To serve my God when I awake.

When in the night I sleepless lie,
My soul with heavenly thoughts supply;
Let no ill dreams disturb my rest,
No powers of darkness me molest.

Praise God, from Whom all blessings flow,
Praise Him all creatures here below,
Praise Him above, ye heav'nly host,
Praise Father, Son, and Holy Ghost.

Thomas Ken, 1637–1711

340. THE HYMN OF CLEANTHES

Sometimes called "Hymn to Zeus"

O God most glorious, called by many a name,
Nature's great King, through endless years the same. . . .
We are thy children, we alone, of all
On earth's broad ways that wander to and fro,
Bearing thine image whereso'er we go.
Wherefore with songs of praise thy power I will forth shew.
Lo! yonder Heaven, that round the earth is wheeled,
Follows thy guidance, still to thee doth yield
Glad homage; thine unconquerable hand
Such flaming minister, the levin-brand,
Wieldeth, a sword two-edged, whose deathless might
Pulsates through all that Nature brings to light;
Vehicle of the universal Word, that flows
Through all, and in the light celestial glows
Of stars both great and small. O King of Kings
Through ceaseless ages, God, whose purpose brings
To birth, whate'er on land or in the sea
Is wrought, or in high heaven's immensity. . . .
Chaos to thee is order: in thine eyes
The unloved is lovely, who didst harmonize
Things evil with things good, that there should be
One Word through all things everlastingly. . . .
Zeus the all-bountiful, whom darkness shrouds,
Whose lightning lightens in the thunder-clouds;
Thy children save from error's deadly sway:
Turn thou the darkness from their souls away:

Vouchsafe that unto knowledge they attain;
For thou by knowledge art made strong to reign
O'er all, and all things rulest righteously.
So by thee honoured, we will honour thee,
Praising thy works continually with songs,
As mortals should; nor higher meed belongs
E'en to the gods, than justly to adore
The universal law for evermore.

Cleanthes of Assos,[1] *331?–232 B.C.;*
tr. from the Greek by James Adam

341. CANTICLE OF THE CREATURES

Sometimes called "Canticle of the Sun"

O most high, almighty, good Lord God, to Thee belong praise, glory, honour, and all blessing!

Praised be my Lord God with all His creatures; and specially our brother the sun, who brings us the day, and who brings us the light; fair is he, and shining with a very great splendour: O Lord, to us he signifies Thee!

Praised be my Lord for our sister the moon, and for the stars, the which He has set clear and lovely in heaven.

Praised be my Lord for our brother the wind, and for air and cloud, calms and all weather, by the which Thou upholdest in life all creatures.

Praised be my Lord for our sister water, who is very serviceable unto us, and humble, and precious, and clean.

Praised be my Lord for our brother fire, through whom Thou givest us light in the darkness; and he is bright, and pleasant, and very mighty, and strong.

Praised be my Lord for our mother the earth, the which doth sustain us and keep us, and bringeth forth divers fruits, and flowers of many colours, and grass.

Praised be my Lord for all those who pardon one another for His love's sake, and who endure weakness and tribulation; blessed are they who peaceably shall endure, for Thou, O most Highest, shalt give them a crown!

Praised be my Lord for our sister, the death of the body, from whom no man escapeth. Woe to him who dieth in mortal sin! Blessed are they who are found walking by Thy most holy will, for the second death shall have no power to do them harm.

Praise ye, and bless ye the Lord, and give thanks unto Him, and serve Him with great humility.

St. Francis of Assisi, 1182–1226;
tr. by Matthew Arnold, 1822–1888

[1] Cleanthes is one or two poets quoted by St. Paul in Acts 17: 28.

342. LIFT UP YOUR HEARTS!

"Lift up your hearts!" We lift them, Lord, to Thee;
Here at Thy feet none other may we see;
"Lift up your hearts!" E'en so, with one accord,
We lift them up, we lift them to the Lord.

Above the level of the former years,
The mire of sin, the slough of guilty fears,
The mist of doubt, the blight of love's decay,
O Lord of Light, lift up our hearts to-day.

Above the swamps of subterfuge and shame,
The deeds, the thoughts that honour may not name,
The halting tongue that dares not tell the whole,
O Lord of Truth, lift every Christian soul!

Above the storms that vex this lower state,
Pride, jealousy, and envy, rage, and hate,
And cold mistrust, that holds e'en friends apart,
O Lord of Love, lift every brother's heart.

Then, as the trumpet call, in after years,
"Lift up your hearts!" rings pealing in our ears,
Still shall those hearts respond, with full accord,
"We lift them up, we lift them to the Lord!"

Henry Montague Butler, 1833–1918

343. DIVINE LOVE

Lord, when the sense of Thy sweet grace
Sends up my soul to seek Thy face,
Thy blessed eyes breed such desire,
I die in love's delicious Fire.
O Love, I am thy Sacrifice.
Be still triumphant, blessed eyes.
Still shine on me, fair suns! that I
Still may behold, though still I die.

Though still I die, I live again;
Still longing so to be still slain,
So gainful is such loss of breath.
I die even in desire of death.
Still live in me this loving strife
Of living Death and dying Life.
For while Thou sweetly slayest me,
Dead to myself I live in Thee.

Richard Crashaw, 1613?–1649

344. ETERNAL LIGHT!

Eternal Light! Eternal Light!
How pure the soul must be,
When, placed within Thy searching sight
It shrinks not, but, with calm delight
Can live, and look on Thee!

The spirits that surround Thy throne,
May bear the burning bliss;
But that is surely theirs alone,
Since they have never, never known
A fallen world like this.

O! how shall I, whose native sphere
Is dark, whose mind is dim,
Before the Ineffable appear,
And on my naked spirit bear
That uncreated beam?

There is a way for man to rise
To that sublime abode:—
An offering and a sacrifice,
A Holy Spirit's energies,
An Advocate with God:—

These, these prepare us for the sight
Of Holiness above:

The sons of ignorance and night
May dwell in the Eternal Light,
Through the Eternal Love!

Thomas Binney, 1798–1874

345. THE WILL OF GOD

I worship thee, sweet will of God!
And all thy ways adore;
And every day I live, I long
To love thee more and more.

When obstacles and trials seem
Like prison-walls to be,
I do the little I can do,
And leave the rest to thee.

❖

He always wins who sides with God
To him no chance is lost:
God's will is sweetest to him when
It triumphs at his cost.

Ill that God blesses is our good,
And unblest good is ill;
And all is right that seems most wrong,
If it be His dear will!

Frederick William Faber, 1814–1863

346. SEND FORTH, O GOD, THY LIGHT AND TRUTH

Send forth, O God, Thy light and truth,
And let them lead me still,
Undaunted, in the paths of right,
Up to Thy holy hill:
Then to Thy altar will I spring,
And in my God rejoice;
And praise shall tune the trembling string,
And gratitude my voice.

O why, my soul, art thou cast down?
Within me why distressed?
Thy hopes the God of grace shall crown;
He yet shall make thee blessed:
To Him, my never-failing Friend,
I bow, and kiss the rod;
To Him shall thanks and praise ascend,
My Saviour and my God.

John Quincy Adams, 1767–1848

347. HYMN OF JOY

Joyful, joyful, we adore Thee,
God of glory, Lord of love;
Hearts unfold like flowers before Thee,
Praising Thee their sun above.
Melt the clouds of sin and sadness;
Drive the dark of doubt away;
Giver of immortal gladness,
Fill us with the light of day.

All Thy works with joy surround Thee,
Earth and heaven reflect Thy rays,
Stars and angels sing around Thee,
Center of unbroken praise:
Field and forest, vale and mountain,
Flowery meadow, flashing sea,
Chanting bird and flowing fountain,
Call us to rejoice in Thee.

Thou art giving and forgiving,
Ever blessing, ever blest,
Well-spring of the joy of living,
Ocean-depth of happy rest!
Thou our Father, Christ our Brother,—
All who live in love are Thine:
Teach us how to love each other,
Lift us to the Joy Divine.

Mortals, join the mighty chorus,
Which the morning stars began;
Father-love is reigning o'er us,
Brother-love binds man to man.
Ever singing march we onward,
Victors in the midst of strife;
Joyful music lifts us sunward
In the triumph song of life.

Henry van Dyke, 1852–1933

348. LET US WITH A GLADSOME MIND

Based on Psalm 136

Let us with a gladsome mind
Praise the Lord, for he is kind
For his mercies aye endure,
Ever faithful, ever sure.

Let us blaze his Name abroad,
For of gods he is the God; . . .
Who by all-commanding might,
Filled the new-made world with light.

He the golden tressèd sun
Caused all day his course to run;
Th' horned moon to shine by night,
'Mid her spangled sisters bright.

He his chosen race did bless,
In the wasteful wilderness;
He hath, with a piteous eye,
Looked upon our misery.

All things living he doth feed.
His full hand supplies their need;
For his mercies aye endure,
Ever faithful, ever sure.

John Milton, 1608–1674

349. O DAY OF REST AND GLADNESS

O day of rest and gladness,
  O day of joy and light,
O balm of care and sadness,
  Most beautiful, most bright!
On thee the high and lowly
  Before the eternal throne
Sing, 'Holy, holy, holy!'
  To the great Three in One.

On thee, at the creation,
  The light first had its birth;
On thee, for our salvation,
  Christ rose from depths of earth;
On thee our Lord victorious
  The Spirit sent from heaven:
And thus on thee most glorious
  A triple light was given.

Thou art a cooling fountain
  In life's dry dreary sand;
From thee, like Pisgah's mountain,
  We view our promised land.
A day of sweet refection,
  A day of holy love,
A day of resurrection
  From earth to things above.

To-day on weary nations
  The heavenly manna falls;
To holy convocations
  The silver trumpet calls,
Where gospel light is glowing
  With pure and radiant beams,
And living water flowing
  With soul-refreshing streams.

New graces ever gaining
  From this our day of rest,
We reach the rest remaining
  To spirits of the blest.
To Holy Ghost be praises,
  To Father and to Son;
The Church her voice upraises
  To Thee, blest Three in One.

Christopher Wordsworth, 1807–1885

350. WORSHIP THE LORD IN THE BEAUTY OF HOLINESS

Worship the Lord in the beauty of holiness,
Bow down before Him, His glory proclaim;
Gold of obedience, and incense of lowliness,
Kneel and adore Him,—the Lord is His name.

Low at His feet lay thy burden of carefulness,
High on His heart He will bear it for thee,
Comfort thy sorrows, and answer thy
  prayerfulness,
Guiding thy steps as may best for thee be.

Truth in its beauty, and love in its tenderness,
These are the offerings we lay on His shrine;
These, though we bring them in trembling
  and fearfulness,
He will accept in the Name all divine.

John S. B. Monsell, 1811–1875

351. FOR THE BEAUTY OF THE EARTH

For the beauty of the earth,
  For the beauty of the skies,
For the love which from our birth
  Over and around us lies,
Lord of all, to Thee we raise
This our sacrifice of praise.

For the beauty of each hour
  Of the day and of the night,
Hill and vale, and tree and flower,
  Sun and moon, and stars of light,
Lord of all, to Thee we raise
This our sacrifice of praise.

For the joy of ear and eye,
  For the heart and mind's delight,
For the mystic harmony
  Linking sense to sound and sight,

Lord of all, to Thee we raise
This our sacrifice of praise.

For the joy of human love,
  Brother, sister, parent, child,
Friends on earth, and friends above,
  For all gentle thoughts and mild,
Lord of all, to Thee we raise
This our sacrifice of praise.

For each perfect gift of Thine,
  To our race so freely given,
Graces human and divine,
  Flowers of earth, and buds of heaven,
Lord of all, to Thee we raise
This our sacrifice of praise.

Folliott Sandford Pierpoint, 1835–1917

352. GIVER OF ALL

O Lord of heaven, and earth, and sea!
To Thee all praise and glory be;
How shall we show our love to Thee,
  Who givest all?

The golden sunshine, vernal air,
Sweet flowers and fruit Thy love declare;
When harvests ripen, Thou art there,
  Who givest all.

For peaceful homes and healthful days,
For all the blessings earth displays,
We owe Thee thankfulness and praise,
  Who givest all.

For souls redeemed, for sins forgiven,
For means of grace and hopes of heaven,
What can to Thee, O Lord! be given,
  Who givest all?

We lose what on ourselves we spend,
We have, as treasures without end,
Whatever, Lord, to Thee we lend,
  Who givest all.

Whatever, Lord, we lend to Thee,
Repaid a thousandfold will be;
Then gladly will we give to Thee,
  Who givest all!

Christopher Wordsworth, 1807–1885

353. ETERNAL SPIRIT, EVERMORE CREATING

Eternal Spirit, evermore creating,
  Throughout Thy living universe far-flung
Thy purpose throbs in pulses unabating,
  Thy glory by the morning star is sung—
Yet this fair earth is in the shadow waiting
  Where human hearts by bitterness are wrung!

O Thou in whom a holy fullness dwelleth,
  Who hast the mystic fount of life within,
Whose quick'ning Spirit where it listeth telleth
  How man may triumph over death and sin—
Flood Thou our souls, Thou presence purifying,
  Help us our Battle for the right to win!

O Thou from whom all our discerning cometh,
  Thou Light of Lights, flood our dim souls this hour!
Out of the depths which Thy compassion plumbeth,
  Up from defeat to overcoming power
Lift us, we pray, unto a life triumphant,
  And go before us, though the war-clouds lower!

O Thou on whom our human good dependeth,
  Who from of old hast been Thy people's stay,
Whose bounty like the gentle rain descendeth,

And like the dew is fresh from day to day,
Quicken our spirits, as we wait expectant,
That we may go in strength upon our way!

Henry B. Robins, 1874–

354. VENI, CREATOR SPIRITUS

CREATOR Spirit, by whose aid
The World's foundations first were laid,
Come, visit every pious mind;
Come, pour Thy joys on human kind;
From sin and sorrow set us free,
And make Thy temples worthy Thee.

O Source of uncreated light,
The Father's promised Paraclete!
Thrice holy fount, thrice holy fire,
Our hearts with heavenly love inspire;
Come, and Thy sacred unction bring,
To sanctify us while we sing.

Plenteous of grace, descend from high,
Rich in Thy sevenfold energy!
Thou strength of His Almighty hand,
Whose power does heaven and earth
command;
Proceeding Spirit, our defence,
Who dost the gift of tongues dispense,
And crown'st Thy gift with eloquence!

Refine and purge our earthly parts;
But, oh, inflame and fire our hearts!
Our frailties help, our vice control,
Submit the senses to the soul;
And when rebellious they are grown,
Then lay Thy hand, and hold them down.

Chase from our minds th' infernal foe,
And peace, the fruit of love, bestow;
And, lest our feet should step astray,
Protect and guide us in the way.
Make us eternal truths receive,
And practise all that we believe:
Give us Thyself, that we may see
The Father, and the Son, by Thee.

Immortal honour, endless fame,
Attend th' Almighty Father's name!
The Saviour Son be glorified,
Who for lost man's redemption died!
And equal adoration be,
Eternal Paraclete, to Thee!

From the Latin, 4th century, by
John Dryden, 1631–1700

355. WORSHIP

From "Elegy On Thyrza"

Wilt thou accept not
The worship the heart lifts above
And the Heavens reject not:
The desire of the moth for the star,
Of the night for the morrow,
The devotion to something afar
From the sphere of our sorrow?

Percy Bysshe Shelley, 1792–1822

356. AD MAJOREM DEI GLORIAM

Thy glory alone, O God, be the end of all that I say;
Let it shine in every deed, let it kindle the prayers that I pray;
Let it burn in my innermost soul, till the shadow of self pass away,
And the light of Thy glory, O God, be unveiled in the dawning of day.

Frederick George Scott, 1861–1944

357. From THE MARSHES OF GLYNN

As the marsh-hen secretly builds on the watery sod,
Behold I will build me a nest on the greatness of God:
I will fly in the greatness of God as the marsh-hen flies
In the freedom that fills all the space 'twixt the marsh and the skies:
By so many roots as the marsh-grass sends in the sod

I will heartily lay me a-hold on the greatness of God:
Oh, like to the greatness of God is the greatness within
The range of the marshes, the liberal marshes of Glynn.

And the sea lends large, as the marsh: lo, out of his plenty the sea
Pours fast: full soon the time of the flood-tide must be:
Look how the grace of the sea doth go
About and about through the intricate channels that flow
  Here and there,
    Everywhere,
Till his waters have flooded the uttermost creeks and the low-lying lanes,
And the marsh is meshed with a million veins,
That like as with rosy and silvery essences flow
In the rose-and-silver evening glow.

    Farewell, my lord Sun!
The creeks overflow: a thousand rivulets run
'Twixt the roots of the sod; the blades of the marsh-grass stir;
Passeth a hurrying sound of wings that westward whirr;
Passeth, and all is still; and the currents cease to run;
And the sea and the marsh are one.
How still the plains of the waters be!
The tide in his ecstasy.
The tide is at his highest height:
    And it is night.

And now from the Vast of the Lord will the waters of sleep
Roll in on the souls of men,
But who will reveal to our waking ken
The forms that swim and the shapes that creep
    Under the waters of sleep?
And I would I could know what swimmeth below when the tide comes in
On the length and breadth of the marvelous marshes of Glynn.

Sidney Lanier, 1842–1881

358. A HEATHEN HYMN

O Lord, the Giver of my days,
My heart is ready, my heart is ready;
I dare not hold my peace, nor pause,
For I am fain to sing Thy praise.

I praise Thee not, with impious pride,
For that Thy partial hand has given
Bounties of wealth or form or brain,
Good gifts to other men denied.

Nor weary Thee with blind request,
For fancied goods Thy hand withholds;
I know not what to fear or hope,
Nor aught but that Thy will is best.

❖

I praise Thee, everlasting Lord,
In life and death, in heaven and hell:
What care I, since indeed Thou art,
And I the creature of Thy word.

Only if such a thing may be:
When all Thy infinite will is done,
Take back the soul Thy breath has given,
And let me lose myself in Thee.

Lewis Morris, 1833–1907

359. WORSHIP

God made my cathedral
  Under the stars;
He gave my cathedral
  Trees for its spires;
He hewed me an altar
  In the depth of a hill

He gave for a hymnal
  A rock-bedded rill;
He voiced me a sermon
  Of heavenly light
In the beauty around me—
  The calmness of night;
And I felt as I knelt
  On the velvet-like sod
I had supped of the Spirit
  In the Temple of God.

Ruth Furbee, contemporary American

360. THE CLOSING DOXOLOGY

Psalm 150

Hallelujah!
Praise God in his sanctuary!
Praise him in his mighty firmament!
Praise him for his mighty deeds!
Praise him for his abundant greatness!
Praise him with the blast of the horn!
Praise him with lyre and lute!
Praise him with drum and dance!
Praise him with strings and pipe!
Praise him with clanging cymbals!
Praise him with crashing cymbals!
Let everything that breathes praise the
  LORD!
Hallelujah!

The Bible: An American Translation, 1935

361. OUR PRAYER

Thou that hast given so much to me,
Give one thing more—a grateful heart;
Not thankful when it pleaseth me,
As if Thy blessings had spare days;
But such a heart, whose pulse may be
Thy praise.

George Herbert, 1593–1632

362. GRATITUDE

From "King Henry VI", Part II, Act II, sc. 1

Poor soul! God's goodness hath been great to
  thee:
Let never day nor night unhallow'd pass,
But still remember what the Lord hath done.

William Shakespeare, 1564–1616

363. THANKFULNESS

My God, I thank Thee who hast made
  The earth so bright;
So full of splendor and of joy,
  Beauty and light;
So many glorious things are here,
  Noble and right!

I thank Thee, too, that Thou hast made
  Joy to abound;
So many gentle thoughts and deeds
  Circling us round,
That in the darkest spot of earth
  Some love is found.

I thank Thee more that all our joy
  Is touched with pain;
That shadows fall on brightest hours;
  That thorns remain;
So that earth's bliss may be our guide,
  And not our chain.

I thank Thee, Lord, that Thou hast kept
  The best in store;
We have enough, yet not too much
  To long for more:
A yearning for a deeper peace,
  Not known before.

I thank Thee, Lord, that here our souls,
  Though amply blest,
Can never find, although they seek,
  A perfect rest,—
Nor ever shall, until they lean
  On Jesus' breast!

Adelaide Anne Procter, 1825–1864

364. O FATHER, THOU WHO GIVEST ALL

O Father, thou who givest all
  The bounty of thy perfect love,
We thank thee that upon us fall
  Such tender blessings from above.

We thank thee for the grace of home,
  For mother's love and father's care:
For friends and teachers—all who come
  Our joys and hopes and fears to share.

For eyes to see and ears to hear,
  For hands to serve and arms to lift,
For shoulders broad and strong to bear,
  For feet to run on errands swift.

For faith to conquer doubt and fear,
  For love to answer every call,
For strength to do, and will to dare,
  We thank thee, O thou Lord of all.

John Haynes Holmes, 1879–

365. A THANKSGIVING

For summer rain, and winter's sun,
For autumn breezes crisp and sweet;
For labors doing, to be done,
  And labors all complete;
For April, May, and lovely June,
For bud, and bird, and berried vine;
For joys of morning, night, and noon,
  My thanks, dear Lord, are Thine!

For loving friends on every side;
For children full of joyous glee;
For all the blessed Heavens wide,
  And for the sounding sea;
For mountains, valleys, forests deep;
For maple, oak, and lofty pine;
For rivers on their seaward sweep,
  My thanks, dear Lord, are Thine!

For light and air, for sun and shade,
For merry laughter and for cheer;
For music and the glad parade
  Of blessings through the year;
For all the fruitful earth's increase,
For home, and life, and love divine,
For hope, and faith, and perfect peace,
  My thanks, dear Lord, are Thine!

John Kendrick Bangs, 1862–1922

366. WE PLOW THE FIELDS

We plow the fields, and scatter
The good seed on the land,
But it is fed and watered
By God's almighty hand;
He sends the snow in winter,
The warmth to swell the grain,
The breezes and the sunshine,
And soft, refreshing rain.

He only is the Maker
Of all things near and far;
He paints the wayside flower,
He lights the evening star;
The winds and waves obey him,
By him the birds are fed;
Much more to us, his children,
He gives our daily bread.

We thank thee, then, O Father,
For all things bright and good,
The seed-time and the harvest,
Our life, our health, our food.
Accept the gifts we offer
For all thy love imparts,
And, what thou most desirest,
Our humble, thankful hearts.

Matthias Claudius, 1740–1815;
tr. by Jane M. Campbell

367. ONLY HEAVEN IS GIVEN AWAY

I bought a gay-roofed house upon a sunny hill,
Where heaven is very close to earth and all the world is still.
It took my savings, every cent, although the cost was small,
But, oh, the lovely things I bought, and paid for not at all!
The sleepy valleys that below in tawny sunshine lie,
The oaks that sprawl across their slopes and climb to meet the sky,
Stray winds that sing of other things than those our eyes may see,
Blue wisps of mist, and reveled clouds that, fleeing, beckon me.
White suns of mad, glad April, October's wine to quaff,
On crystal winter mornings my hearth fire's crackling laugh,
The silent stars that march at night so close above my head,
The sound of raindrops on the roof when I am snug in bed.
For joist and beam and shingles gay I spent my savings small,
But on the lovely things God gave He put no price at all!

Rose Darrough, contemporary American

368. THANKSGIVING

Be our daily bread withheld, be it given,
Thanks for the bread from heaven;
Though on sense disease and pain come stealing,
Thanks for the spirit's healing;
Thanks, when the springs of impulse are defiled,
For the renewing candor of the child;
Thanks, when the years sully the face of truth,
For the resurgent heart of youth.

Thanks, though we be cast off, unknown, alone,
Thanks that we are well known,
And though our outward man and lot decay,
The spirit kindles day by day;
Thanks that our sorrow by thine alchemy
Turns out to be the very fuel of glee,
That from our utter penury, we bless,
And having nothing, all things still possess.

Thanks for the faith that sees beyond these snows
The clemencies of God, the lily and the rose,
Beyond these graves, these ruins and this waste,
A garden of men, an empire undisgraced;
Thanks that each loss we own, each death we die,
Calls out of heaven amazing ministry,
Thanks, thanks that the costly travail wrought in dearth
Shatters old worlds and brings new worlds to birth.

Amos Niven Wilder, 1895–

369. THE THINGS OF THE SPIRIT

Thank God for life!
There! A meadowlark sings! Do you hear it?
For the sigh of the heart,
The contagion of laughter,
For the longing apart,
For the joy that comes after,
For the things that we feel
When we clasp, when we kneel—
Thank God for the sharing,
The caring, the giving,
For the things of Life's living.

Thank God for the riches
Of flowers in the ditches,
For the roof from the weather,
The fireside together,
For the step at the portal,
For the love we have treasured,
For something unmeasured,
For something immortal,
For our grief, for our mirth,
For heavens on earth,
For the things of the spirit!

There! A meadowlark sings! Do you hear it?

Douglas Malloch, 1877–1938

370. I THANK THEE, LORD, FOR STRENGTH OF ARM

I thank Thee, Lord, for strength of arm
To win my bread,
And that, beyond my need is meat
For friend unfed:
I thank Thee much for bread to live,
I thank Thee more for bread to give.

I thank Thee for my quiet home,
'Mid cold and storm,
And that, beyond my need, is room
For friend forlorn:

I thank Thee much for place to rest,
But more for shelter for my guest.

I thank Thee, Lord, for lavish love
On me bestowed,
Enough to share with loveless folk
To ease their load:
Thy love to me I ill could spare,
Yet dearer is Thy love I share.

Robert Davis, 1881–

371. PIED BEAUTY

Glory be to God for dappled things—
For skies of couple-colour as a brinded cow;
For rose-moles all in stipple upon trout that swim;
Fresh-firecoal chestnut-falls; finches' wings;
Landscape plotted and pieced—fold, fallow, and plow;
And all trades, their gear and tackle and trim.

All things counter, original, spare, strange;
Whatever is fickle, freckled (who knows how?)
With swift, slow; sweet, sour; adazzle, dim;
He fathers-forth whose beauty is past change:
Praise Him.

Gerard Manley Hopkins, 1844–1898

372. GRATITUDE

I thank You for these gifts, dear God,
Upon Thanksgiving Day—
For love and laughter and the faith
That makes me kneel to pray.

For life that lends me happiness,
And sleep that gives me rest,
These are the gifts that keep my heart
Serene within my breast.

Love, laughter, faith and life and sleep,
We own them, every one—
They carry us along the road
That leads from sun to sun.

Margaret E. Sangster, contemporary American

373. GIFTS WITHOUT SEASON

Lord, I would thank You for these things:
Not sunlight only, but sullen rain;
Not only laughter with lifted wings,
But the heavy muted hands of pain.

Lord, I would thank You for so much:
The toil no less than the well-earned ease;
The glory always beyond our touch
That bows the head and bends the knees.

Lord, there are gifts of brighter gold
Than the deepest mine or mint can yield:
Friendship and love and a dream to hold,
The look that heartened, the word that healed.

Lord, I would thank You for eyes to see
Miracles in our everyday earth:
The colors that crowd monotony,
The flame of the humblest flower's birth.

Lord, I would thank You for gifts without season:
The flash of a thought like a banner unfurled,
The splendor of faith and the sparkle of reason,
The tolerant mind in a turbulent world!

Joseph Auslander, 1897–

374. From A PRAYER

I kneel not now to pray that Thou
Make white one single sin,
I only kneel to thank thee, Lord,
For what I have not been—

For deeds which sprouted in my heart
But ne'er to bloom were brought,
For monstrous vices which I slew
In the shambles of my thought—

Dark seeds the world has never guessed,
By hell and passion bred,
Which never grew beyond the bud
That cankered in my head.

Some said I was a righteous man—
Poor fools! The gallows tree
(If thou hadst let one foot to slip)
Had grown a limb for me.

Harry Kemp, 1883–

375. THANKSGIVING

The roar of the world is in my ears.
  Thank God for the roar of the world!
Thank God for the mighty tide of fears
  Against me always hurled!

Thank God for the bitter and ceaseless strife,
  And the sting of His chastening rod!
Thank God for the stress and the pain of life,
  And Oh, thank God for God!

Joyce Kilmer, 1886–1918

376. BLIND

I cannot view the bloom upon the rose,
  But oh, the scent is very dear to me;
And I can feel the cooling breeze that blows
  Thro' pearl-tipped peaks of hills I cannot see.

I cannot see the wild birds on the wing,
  But I can hear the swallows in the eaves;
I hear the song that nature has to sing—
  The gentle music of the rustling leaves.

I cannot see the children going by,
  But I can hear their laughter as they pass;
I cannot see the sunset in the sky,
  But I can feel the swaying of the grass.

I cannot see the moonlight on the sea,
  But I can hear the waves beat on the shore;
I feast upon all nature's melody
  And thank my God and do not ask for more.

Norman V. Pearce

377. THE UNDISCOVERED COUNTRY

Lord, for the erring thought
Not unto evil wrought:
Lord, for the wicked will
Betrayed and baffled still:
For the heart from itself kept,
Our thanksgiving accept.
For ignorant hopes that were
Broken to our blind prayer:
For pain, death, sorrow sent
Unto our chastisement:
For all loss of seeming good,
Quicken our gratitude.

William Dean Howells, 1837–1920

378. FATHER, WE THANK THEE

Father, we thank Thee for the night,
And for the pleasant morning light;
For rest, and food, and loving care,
And all that makes the world so fair.

Help us to do the things we should,
To be to others kind and good;
In all we do, in work or play,
To love Thee better day by day.

Rebecca J. Weston, c. 1890

379. THANK GOD

    Thank God for life!
E'en though it bring much bitterness and strife,
  And all our fairest hopes be wrecked and lost,
E'en though there be more ill than good in life,
  We cling to life and reckon not the cost.
    Thank God for life!

    Thank God for love!
For though sometimes grief follows in its wake,
  Still we forget love's sorrow in love's joy,
And cherish tears with smiles for love's dear sake;
  Only in heaven is bliss without alloy.
    Thank God for love!

    Thank God for pain!
No tear hath ever yet been shed in vain,

And in the end each sorrowing heart shall find
No curse, but blessings in the hand of pain;
Even when he smiteth, then is God most kind.
Thank God for pain!

Thank God for death!
Who touches anguished lips and stills their breath
And giveth peace unto each troubled breast;
Grief flies before thy touch, O blessed death;
God's sweetest gift; thy name in heaven is Rest.
Thank God for death!

Author unknown

380. GOD, YOU HAVE BEEN TOO GOOD TO ME

God, You have been too good to me,
You don't know what You've done.
A clod's too small to drink in all
The treasure of the sun.

The pitcher fills the lifted cup
And still the blessings pour
They overbrim the shallow rim
With cool refreshing store.

You are too prodigal with joy,
Too careless of its worth,
To let the stream with crystal gleam
Fall wasted on the earth.

Let many thirsty lips draw near
And quaff the greater part!
There still will be too much for me
To hold in one glad heart.

Charles Wharton Stork, 1881–

381. THE QUEST ETERNAL

For man's unceasing quest for God,
For God's unceasing quest for man,
For records of his love and power
Surrounding life since life began,
We thank thee, Lord most high.

For ancient tales of long ago,
Man's guesses when the world was young,
For talks around the blazing fire,
For stories told and stories sung,
We thank thee, Lord most high.

For those great laws the Hebrews made,
Among the greatest ever known,
For early history wise men wrote,
Engraved on parchment, skin, or stone,
We thank thee, Lord most high.

For those old songs of tuneful verse,
The music of the shepherd king,
For songs the Boy of Nazareth sang,
And still succeeding ages sing,
We thank thee, Lord most high.

For those most precious books of all,
That show us Jesus Christ, our Lord,
Seen through the eyes of faithful friends
Who gave their lives to spread his word,
We thank thee, Lord most high.

Alice M. Pullen,
contemporary American

382. COMMUNION

From "The Excursion," Book I

Such was the Boy—but for the growing Youth
What soul was his, when, from the naked top
Of some bold headland, he beheld the sun
Rise up, and bathe the world in light! He
looked . . .
Beneath him:—Far and wide the clouds were
touched,
And in their silent faces could he read
Unutterable love. Sound needed none,
Nor any voice of joy; his spirit drank
The spectacle: sensation, soul, and form,
All melted into him; they swallowed up
His animal being; in them did he live,
And by them did he live; they were his life.
In such access of mind, in such high hour
Of visitation from the living God,

Thought was not; in enjoyment it expired.
No thanks he breathed, he proffered no
request;
Rapt into still communion that transcends
The imperfect offices of prayer and praise,
His mind was a thanksgiving to the power
That made him; it was blessedness and love!

William Wordsworth, 1770–1850

383. LINES WRITTEN AFTER THE DISCOVERY BY THE AUTHOR OF THE GERM OF YELLOW FEVER

This day relenting God
Hath placed within my hand
A wondrous thing; and God
Be praised. At His command,

Seeking His secret deeds
With tears and toiling breath,
I find thy cunning seeds,
O million-murdering Death.

I know this little thing
A myriad men will save.
O Death, where is thy sting?
Thy victory, O Grave?

Ronald Ross, 1857–1932

384. UNIVERSAL PRAYER

Father of all! In every age,
In every clime adored,
By saint, by savage, and by sage,
Jehovah, Jove, or Lord!

Thou Great First Cause, least understood,
Who all my sense confined
To know but this, that Thou art good,
And that myself am blind!

Yet gave me, in this dark estate,
To see the good from ill;
And, binding nature fast in fate,
Left free the human will.

What conscience dictates to be done,
Or warns me not to do,
This teach me more than hell to shun,
That, more than heaven pursue.

What blessings Thy free bounty gives,
Let me not cast away;
For God is paid when man receives;
To enjoy is to obey.

Yet not to earth's contracted span
Thy goodness let me bound,
Or think Thee Lord alone of man,
When thousand worlds are round.

Let not this weak, unknowing hand
Presume Thy bolts to throw,
And deal damnation round the land
On each I judge Thy foe.

If I am right, Thy grace impart
Still in the right to stay;
If I am wrong, oh, teach my heart
To find the better way!

Save me alike from foolish pride,
And impious discontent,
At aught Thy wisdom has denied,
Or aught Thy goodness lent.

Teach me to feel another's woe,
To hide the fault I see;
That mercy I to others show,
That mercy show to me.

Mean though I am, not wholly so,
Since quickened by Thy breath;
O, lead me wheresoe'er I go,
Through this day's life or death.

This day be bread and peace my lot:
All else beneath the sun
Thou know'st if best bestowed or not,
And let Thy will be done.

To Thee, whose temple is all space,—
Whose altar, earth, sea, skies,—
One chorus let all beings raise,
All Nature's incense rise!

Alexander Pope, 1688–1744

385. SPIRIT OF GOD, DESCEND UPON MY HEART

Spirit of God, descend upon my heart;
Wean it from earth; through all its pulses
move;
Stoop to my weakness, mighty as Thou art,
And make me love Thee as I ought to love.

I ask no dream, no prophet ecstasies,
No sudden rending of the veil of clay,
No angel visitant, no opening skies;
But take the dimness of my soul away.

Hast Thou not bid us love Thee, God and
King?
All, all Thine own, soul, heart, and strength,
and mind;
I see Thy cross—there teach my heart to
cling:
O let me seek Thee, and O let me find!

Teach me to feel that Thou art always nigh;
Teach me the struggles of the soul to bear,
To check the rising doubt, the rebel sigh;
Teach me the patience of unanswered prayer.

Teach me to love Thee as Thine angels love,
One holy passion filling all my frame;
The baptism of the heaven descended Dove,
My heart an altar, and Thy love the flame.

George Croly, 1780–1860

386. THE VOICE OF GOD IS CALLING

The voice of God is calling
Its summons unto men;
As once He spake in Zion,
So now He speaks again,
Whom shall I send to succor
My people in their need?
Whom shall I send to loosen
The bonds of shame and greed?

I hear my people crying
In cot and mine and slum;
No field or mart is silent,
No city street is dumb.
I see my people falling
In darkness and despair.
Whom shall I send to shatter
The fetters which they bear?

We heed, O Lord, Thy summons,
And answer: Here are we!
Send us upon Thine errand,
Let us Thy servants be.
Our strength is dust and ashes
Our years a passing hour:
But Thou canst use our weakness
To magnify Thy power.

From ease and plenty save us;
From pride of place absolve;
Purge us of low desire;
Lift us to high resolve;
Take us, and make us holy;
Teach us Thy will and way.
Speak, and behold! we answer;
Command, and we obey!

John Haynes Holmes, 1879–

387. BOY'S PRAYER

God of our boyhood, whom we yield
The tribute of our youthful praise,
Upon the well-contested field,
And 'mid the glory of these days,
God of our youth, be with us yet,
Lest we forget, lest we forget!

Sturdy of limb, with bounding health,
Eager to play the hero's part,
Grant to us each that greater wealth—
An undefiled and loyal heart,
God of our youth, be thou our might,
To do the right, to do the right!

When from the field of mimic strife,
Of strength with strength, and speed
with speed,
We face the sterner fights of life,
As still our strength in time of need,
God of our youth, be with us then,
And make us men, and make us men!

A. B. Ponsonby

388. A YOUTH'S PRAYER

"The Upward Road"

God, who touchest earth with beauty,
Make me lovely too;
With Thy Spirit re-create me,
Make my heart anew.

Like Thy springs and running waters,
Make me crystal pure;
Like Thy rocks of towering grandeur,
Make me strong and sure.

Like Thy dancing waves in sunlight,
Make me glad and free;
Like the straightness of the pine trees
Let me upright be.

Like the arching of the heavens,
  Lift my thoughts above;
Turn my dreams to noble action—
  Ministries of love.

God, who touchest earth with beauty,
  Make me lovely too;
Keep me ever, by Thy Spirit,
  Pure and strong and true.

Mary S. Edgar, contemporary Canadian

389. TAKE MY LIFE

Take my life, and let it be
Consecrated, Lord, to Thee.
Take my moments and my days;
Let them flow in ceaseless praise.
Take my hands, and let them move
At the impulse of Thy love.
Take my feet, and let them be
Swift and beautiful for Thee.

Take my voice, and let me sing,
Always, only, for my King.
Take my lips, and let them be
Filled with messages from Thee.
Take my silver and my gold;
Not a mite would I withhold.
Take my intellect, and use
Every power as Thou shalt choose.

Take my will, and make it Thine;
It shall be no longer mine.
Take my heart, it is Thine own;
It shall be Thy royal throne.
Take my love; my Lord, I pour
At Thy feet its treasure-store.
Take myself, and I will be
Ever, only, all for Thee.

Frances Ridley Havergal, 1836–1879

390. I WOULD BE TRUE

I would be true, for there are those who trust me;
I would be pure, for there are those who care;
I would be strong, for there is much to suffer;
I would be brave, for there is much to dare.

I would be friend of all—the foe, the friendless;
I would be giving, and forget the gift;
I would be humble, for I know my weakness;
I would look up, and laugh, and love, and lift.

I would be learning, day by day, the lessons
My heavenly Father gives me in his Word;
I would be quick to hear his lightest whisper,
And prompt and glad to do the things I've heard.

Howard Arnold Walter, 1883–1918

391. CONSECRATION

Just as I am, Thine own to be,
Friend of the young, who lovest me,
To consecrate myself to Thee,
O Jesus Christ, I come.

In the glad morning of my day,
My life to give, my vows to pay,
With no reserve and no delay,
With all my heart I come.

I would live ever in the light,
I would work ever for the right,
I would serve Thee with all my might;
Therefore, to Thee, I come.

Just as I am, young, strong and free,
To be the best that I can be
For truth, and righteousness, and Thee,
Lord of my life, I come.

Marianne Hearn, 1834–1909

392. LORD, SPEAK TO ME, THAT I MAY SPEAK

Lord, speak to me, that I may speak
  In living echoes of Thy tone;
As Thou hast sought, so let me seek
  Thy erring children lost and lone.

O teach me, Lord, that I may teach
  The precious things Thou dost impart;
And wing my words, that they may reach
  The hidden depths of many a heart.

O fill me with Thy fullness, Lord,
  Until my very heart o'erflow
In kindling thought and glowing word,
  Thy love to tell, Thy praise to show.

O use me, Lord, use even me,
  Just as Thou wilt, and when and where;
Until Thy blessed face I see,
  Thy rest, Thy joy, Thy glory share.

Frances Havergal, 1836–1879

393. A DEDICATION

My new-cut ashlar takes the light
  Where crimson-blank the windows flare;
By my own work, before the night,
  Great Overseer, I make my prayer.

If there be good in that I wrought,
  Thy hand compell'd it, Master, Thine;
Where I have fail'd to meet Thy thought
  I know, through Thee, the blame is mine.

One instant's toil to Thee denied
  Stands all Eternity's offence;
Of that I did with Thee to guide
  To Thee, through Thee, be excellence.

Who, lest all thought of Eden fade,
  Bring'st Eden to the craftsman's brain,
Godlike to muse o'er his own trade
  And manlike stand with God again.

The depth and dream of my desire,
  The bitter paths wherein I stray,
Thou knowest Who hast made the Fire,
  Thou knowest Who hast made the Clay.

One stone the more swings to her place
  In that dread Temple of Thy worth—
It is enough that through Thy grace
  I saw naught common on Thy earth.

Take not that vision from my ken;
  O, whatsoe'er may spoil or speed,
Help me to need no aid from men,
  That I may help such men as need!

Rudyard Kipling, 1865–1936

394. PRAYERS

God Who created me
  Nimble and light of limb,
In three elements free,
  To run, to ride, to swim:
Not when the sense is dim,
  But now from the heart of joy,
I would remember Him:
  Take the thanks of a boy.

Jesu, King and Lord,
  Whose are my foes to fight,
Gird me with Thy sword,
  Swift and sharp and bright.
Thee would I serve if I might;
  And conquer if I can,
From day-dawn till night,
  Take the strength of a man.

Spirit of Love and Truth,
  Breathing in grosser clay,
The light and flame of youth,
  Delight of men in the fray,
Wisdom in strength's decay;
  From pain, strife, wrong, to be free,
This best gift I pray,
  Take my spirit to Thee.

Henry Charles Beeching, 1859–1919

395. THE ELIXIR

Teach me, my God and King,
  In all things Thee to see,
And what I do in any thing
  To do it as for Thee.

Not rudely, as a beast,
  To run into an action;
But still to make Thee prepossest,
  And give it his perfection.

A man that looks on glass,
  On it may stay his eye;
Or, if he pleaseth, through it pass,
  And then the Heaven espy.

All may of Thee partake:
  Nothing can be so mean
Which with his tincture "for Thy sake,"
  Will not grow bright and clean.

A servant with this clause
  Makes drudgery divine;
Who sweeps a room, as for Thy laws,
  Makes that and the action fine.

This is the famous stone
  That turneth all to gold;
For that which God doth touch and own
  Cannot for less be told.

George Herbert, 1593–1632

396. AWARENESS

God—let me be aware.
Let me not stumble blindly down the ways,
Just getting somehow safely through the days,
Not even groping for another hand,
Not even wondering why it all was planned,
Eyes to the ground unseeking for the light,
Soul never aching for a wild-winged flight,
Please, keep me eager just to do my share.
God—let me be aware.

God—let me be aware.
Stab my soul fiercely with others' pain,
Let me walk seeing horror and stain.
Let my hands, groping, find other hands.
Give me the heart that divines, understands.
Give me the courage, wounded, to fight.
Flood me with knowledge, drench me in light.
Please—keep me eager just to do my share.
God—let me be aware.

Miriam Teichner, 1888–

397. HEROISM

Whether we climb, whether we plod,
  Space for one task the scant years lend—
To choose some path that leads to God,
  And keep it to the end.

Lizette Woodworth Reese, 1856–1935

398. MORNING HYMN

Awake, my soul, and with the sun
Thy daily stage of duty run;
Shake off dull sloth, and joyful rise
To pay thy morning sacrifice.

Wake, and lift up thyself, my heart,
And with the angels bear thy part,
Who all night long unwearied sing
High praise to the Eternal King.

All praise to Thee, Who safe hast kept
And hast refreshed me while I slept!
Grant, Lord, when I from death shall wake,
I may of endless life partake!

Lord, I my vows to Thee renew;
Disperse my sins as morning dew:
Guard my first springs of thought and will,
And with Thyself my spirit fill.

Direct, control, suggest this day
All I design, or do, or say;
That all my powers, with all their might,
In Thy sole glory may unite.

Praise God, from Whom all blessings flow!
Praise Him, all creatures here below!
Praise Him above, ye heavenly host!
Praise Father, Son, and Holy Ghost!

Thomas Ken, 1637–1711

399. HYMN FOR THE DAY

Through all this new-born day, O Lord,
Which, in Thy grace, Thou givest me,
Let all its moments throb with joy,
That better I may follow Thee.

Grant unto me the boon of health,
Faith, ardor, courage—gifts of youth—
Add unto these the gifts of age—
Reflection, wisdom, garnered truth.

Thrice happy I, at close of day,
If one foul hate hath vanquished been;
If light hath guided all my way,
If one more error I have slain.

If I have guarded well my tongue
That none need weep o'er heedless words,
Or scattered joy as I have sung
The tenderness my heart affords.

Along the highway of my days
Should pitfalls all about me throng
And treacherous rocks escape my gaze,
Make me a pilgrim brave and strong.

From every fall may I arise
Without a groan, without a tear;
Faith gilds the path before my eyes
And perfect love casts out all fear.

Let loving-kindness rule each hour,
Spare all my days for service free
As perfume round each blooming flower
Or fleecy clouds above the sea.

Forbid that I should ever let
The world's vain, glittering pageantry
Bewilder me, lest I forget
That dust I am and doomed to die.

O love all souls this day with me,
And search for light whate'er thy loss;
O love my joy, my agony,
Love thou the burden of my cross.

Gabriela Mistral (Chile), 1889–
tr. from the Spanish by James H. McLean
courtesy Gabriela Mistral

400. EXPECTANS EXPECTAVI

From morn to midnight, all day through,
I laugh and play as others do,
I sing and chatter, just the same
As others with a different name.

And all year long upon the stage,
I dance and tumble and do rage
So vehemently, I scarcely see
The inner and eternal me.

I have a temple I do not
Visit, a heart I have forgot,
A self that I have never met,
A secret shrine—and yet, and yet

This sanctuary of my soul
Unwitting I keep white and whole,
Unlatched and lit, if Thou should'st care
To enter or to tarry there.

With parted lips and outstretched hands
And listening ears Thy servant stands,
Call Thou early, call Thou late,
To Thy great service dedicate.

Charles Hamilton Sorley,[1] *1895–1915*

[1] Killed in France in World War I

401. DEDICATION

Lord, in the strength of grace,
With a glad heart and free,
Myself, my residue of days,
I consecrate to Thee.

Thy ransomed servant, I
Restore to Thee Thy own;
And, from this moment, live or die
To serve my God alone.

Charles Wesley, 1707–1788

402. AS WE PRAY

Only, O Lord, in Thy dear love
Fit us for perfect rest above;
And help us this and every day,
To live more nearly as we pray.

John Keble, 1792–1866

403. PETITION

I, for long days a stranger
To all high thoughts austere,
Lord, smite my soul with Danger
Touch Thou my heart with Fear!

Out of dull sloth upraise me;
Be my worth fully weighed;
Adjudge me and appraise me
With some keen tempered blade.

Lest in an hour of trial
I fail, I faint, I flee,
In blank shame faced denial
Of both mankind and Thee.

Clinton Scollard, 1860–1932

404. INNER LIGHT

Thus with the year
Seasons return, but not to me returns
Day or the sweet approach of even or morn,

Or sight of vernal bloom or summer's rose,
Or flocks or herds, or human face divine;
But cloud instead and ever during dark
Surrounds me, from the cheerful ways of men
Cut off, and for the book of knowledge fair
Presented with a universal blank
Of nature's works, to me expunged and rased,
And wisdom at one entrance quite shut out.
So much the rather Thou, celestial light,
Shine inward and the mind through all her
powers
Irradiate; there plant eyes, all must from
thence
Purge and disperse, that I may see and tell
Of things invisible to mortal sight.[1]

John Milton, 1608–1674

405. ST. FRANCIS' PRAYER

Lord, make me an instrument of Thy peace.
Where there is hate, may I bring love;
Where offense, may I bring pardon;
May I bring union in place of discord;
Truth, replacing error;
Faith, where once there was doubt;
Hope, for despair;
Light, where was darkness;
Joy to replace sadness.
Make me not to so crave to be loved as to
love.
Help me to learn that in giving I may receive;
In forgetting self, I may find life eternal.

St. Francis of Assisi, 1182–1226

406. THY WILL BE DONE IN ME

O Thou to whom, without reserve,
My all I would resign,
I ask for grace and faith to say,
"Thy will, O Lord, not mine!"
In joy or grief, in bliss or pain,
This prayer shall rise to Thee,
"Thy will, not mine, O blessed Lord,
Thy will be done in me!"

Though thorns may pierce my weary feet,
Yet would I ne'er repine,
But meekly say, as Thou hast said,
"Thy will, O Lord, not mine!"
And though I pass beneath Thy rod,
Amen, so let it be!
Whate'er Thou wilt, O blessed Lord,
I know is best for me.

So would I live that I may feel
Thy perfect peace divine,
And still Thy pure example show
In every act of mine;
And till I reach the silent vale,
And cross the narrow sea,
Be this my prayer, O blessed Lord,
"Thy will be done in me!"

Fanny Crosby, 1820–1918

407. THY WILL BE DONE

Thy will, O God, is best,
By Thee the victory's won,
In Thy strong will we find our rest,
Thy will, O God, be done.

Thy will, O God, is strong,
Resist Thy power can none,
Thy throne is raised above all wrong,
Thy will, O God, be done.

Thy will, O God, is law,
Thy word through worlds hath run,
Teach us to say with holy awe,
Thy will, O God, be done.

Thy will, O God, is love,
Thou art our shield and sun,
In earth below, in heaven above,
Thy will, O God, be done.

Thy will, O God, is life,
Thy life and ours is one,
Be Thou our master in the strife,
Until Thy will is done.

Hugh Thomson Kerr, 1871–

408. A PRAYER

Purge me, O God
With Thy refining fires!
Nor heavy rest Thy blame,
When flesh shrinks from the flame!

[1] "Sightless Milton dreamed visions no one else could see. Radiant with an inward light, he sent forth rays by which mankind beholds the realms of Paradise."—Helen Keller.

Sweep my soul clean
By cleansing winds!
Nor let me fret at storm and stress,
Whose purpose is to bless!

Give me a task too big,
Too hard for human hands.
Then I shall come at length
To lean on Thee;
And leaning, find my strength.

Wilbur Humphrey Fowler, contemporary American

409. SEND ME

Use me, God, in Thy great harvest field,
Which stretcheth far and wide like a wide sea;
The gatherers are so few; I fear the precious yield
Will suffer loss. Oh, find a place for me!
A place where best the strength I have will tell:
It may be one the older toilers shun;
Be it a wide or narrow place, 'tis well
So that the work it holds be only done.

Christina G. Rossetti, 1830–1894

410. MY LORD HIDES HIMSELF

My Lord hides Himself, and my Lord wonderfully reveals Himself:
My Lord has encompassed me with hardness, and my Lord has cast down my limitations.
My Lord brings to me words of sorrow and words of joy, and He Himself heals their strife.
I will offer my body and mind to my Lord: I will give up my life, but never can I forget my Lord!

Kabir (Indian), 1450–1518

Book II: JESUS

411. THE GLORY OF GOD REVEALED IN JESUS

God, who commanded the light to shine out of darkness,
hath shined in our hearts,
to give the light of the knowledge of the glory of God
in the face of Jesus Christ.

St. Paul, 1st century

412. THAT ONE FACE

From "Epilogue: Dramatis Personæ"

That one Face, far from vanish, rather grows,
Or decomposes but to recompose,
Become my universe that feels and knows.

Robert Browning, 1812–1889

413. CRUSADER'S HYMN

Fairest Lord Jesus,
Ruler of all nature,
O Thou of God and man the Son,
Thee will I cherish, Thee will I honor,
Thou, my soul's glory, joy, and crown.

Fair are the meadows,
Fairer still the woodlands,
Robed in the blooming garb of spring;
Jesus is fairer, Jesus is purer,
Who makes the woeful heart to sing.

Fair is the sunshine,
Fairer still the moonlight,
And all the twinkling, starry host;
Jesus shines brighter, Jesus shines purer,
Than all the angels heaven can boast.

From the German, 17th century;
tr. by R. Storrs Willis, c. 1850

414. CORONATION

All hail the Power of Jesus' name!
Let angels prostrate fall;
Bring forth the royal diadem,
And crown Him Lord of all!

Crown Him, ye martyrs of our God,
Who from His altar call;
Extol the stem of Jesse's rod,
And crown Him Lord of all.

Ye seed of Israel's chosen race,
Ye ransomed from the Fall,
Hail Him who saves you by His grace,
And crown Him Lord of all.

Sinners, whose love can ne'er forget
The wormwood and the gall,
Go, spread your trophies at His feet,
And crown Him Lord of all.

Let every kindred, every tribe,
On this terrestrial ball,
To Him all majesty ascribe,
And crown Him Lord of all.

Oh that with yonder sacred throng
We at His feet may fall,
Join in the everlasting song,
And crown Him Lord of all!

Edward Perronet, 1726–1792

415. WHEN MORNING GILDS THE SKIES

When morning gilds the skies,
My heart awaking cries,
May Jesus Christ be praised!
Alike at work and prayer
To Jesus I repair;
May Jesus Christ be praised!

❖

When sleep her balm denies,
My silent spirit sighs,
May Jesus Christ be praised!
When evil thoughts molest,
With this I shield my breast,
May Jesus Christ be praised!

The night becomes as day,
When from the heart we say,
May Jesus Christ be praised!
The pow'rs of darkness fear,
When this sweet chant they hear,
May Jesus Christ be praised!

In heav'n's eternal bliss
The loveliest strain is this,
May Jesus Christ be praised!
Let earth, and sea, and sky
From depth to height reply,
May Jesus Christ be praised!

Be this, while life is mine,
My canticle divine,
May Jesus Christ be praised!
Be this the eternal song
Through all the ages long,
May Jesus Christ be praised!

From the German, 1828;
tr. by E. Caswall, 1814–1878

416. CROWN HIM WITH MANY CROWNS

Crown Him with many crowns,
The Lamb upon His throne;
Hark! how the heavenly anthem drowns
All music but its own:
Awake, my soul, and sing
Of Him who died for thee,
And hail Him as thy matchless King
Through all eternity.

Crown Him the Lord of love:
Behold His hands and side,
Rich wounds, yet visible above,
In beauty glorified:
No angel in the sky
Can fully bear that sight,
But downward bends his burning eye
At mysteries so bright.

Crown Him the Lord of peace;
Whose power a scepter sways
From pole to pole, that wars may cease,
And all be prayer and praise:
His reign shall know no end;
And round His piercéd feet
Fair flowers of Paradise extend
Their fragrance ever sweet.

Crown Him the Lord of years,
The Potentate of time;
Creator of the rolling spheres,
Ineffably sublime:
All hail, Redeemer, hail!
For Thou hast died for me:
Thy praise shall never, never fail
Throughout eternity.

Matthew Bridges, 1800–1894

417. JESUS THE VERY THOUGHT OF THEE

Jesus, the very thought of Thee
With sweetness fills my breast;
But sweeter far Thy face to see,
And in Thy presence rest.

No voice can sing, no heart can frame,
Nor can the memory find,
A sweeter sound than Thy blest name,
O Saviour of mankind!

O Hope of every contrite heart!
O Joy of all the meek!
To those who ask how kind Thou art,
How good to those who seek!

But what to those who find? Ah, this
Nor tongue nor pen can show;
The love of Jesus, what it is,
None but His loved ones know.

Jesus, our only joy be Thou,
As Thou our prize wilt be;
In Thee be all our glory now,
And through eternity.

11th century Latin hymn, usually credited to Bernard of Clairvaux, 1091–1153; tr. Edward Caswall, 1814–1878

418. THE NAME OF JESUS

How sweet the Name of Jesus sounds
  In a believer's ear!
It soothes his sorrows, heals his wounds,
  And drives away his fear!

It makes the wounded spirit whole
  And calms the troubled breast;
'Tis manna to the hungry soul,
  And to the weary, rest.

Dear Name! the rock on which I build,
  My shield and hiding-place,
My never-failing treasury, fill'd
  With boundless stores of grace,—

By Thee my prayers acceptance gain,
  Although with sin defiled;
Satan accuses me in vain,
  And I am own'd a Child.

Weak is the effort of my heart,
  And cold my warmest thought;
But, when I see Thee as Thou art,
  I'll praise Thee as I ought.

Till then, I would Thy love proclaim
  With every fleeting breath;
And may the music of Thy Name
  Refresh my soul in death!

John Newton, 1725–1807

419. THE CRYSTAL CHRIST

From "The Crystal"

But Thee, but Thee, O sovereign Seer of Time,
But Thee, O poet's Poet, Wisdom's Tongue,
But Thee, O man's best Man, O love's best Love,
O perfect life in perfect labor writ,
O all men's Comrade, Servant, King, or Priest—
What *if* and *yet*, what mole, what flaw, what lapse,
What least defect or shadow of defect,
What rumor, tattled by an enemy,
Of inference loose, what lack of grace
Even in torture's grasp, or sleep's, or death's—
Oh, what amiss may I forgive in Thee,
Jesus, good Paragon, thou Crystal Christ?

Sidney Lanier, 1842–1881

420. EXCELLENCY OF CHRIST

From "Christ's Victorie and Triumph in Heaven and Earth"

He is a path, if any be misled;
  He is a robe, if any naked be;
If any chance to hunger, he is bread;
  If any be a bondman, he is free;
  If any be but weak, how strong is he!
To dead men life he is, to sick men, health;
To blind men, sight, and to the needy,
    wealth;
A pleasure without loss, a treasure without
    stealth.

Giles Fletcher, Jr., 1588?–1623

421. THE HOLY CHILD

He is the Ancient Wisdom of the World,
  The Word Creative, Beautiful and True,
The Nameless of Innumerable Names,
  Ageless forever, yet Forever New.

Charles Carroll Albertson, 1865–

422. THE WORD

John 1: 1–5

In the beginning was the Word,
  And the Word was with God,
  And the Word was God.
He was in the beginning with God.

All things came
  Through him;
  And apart from him
Came not a thing which has come.

In him was life;
  And the life was the light of men.
And the light shines in the darkness:
  And the darkness has not overcome it.

The Bible in Modern English, 1909

423. "AND THE WORD WAS MADE FLESH"

Light looked down and beheld Darkness.
  "Thither will I go," said Light.
Peace looked down and beheld War.
  "Thither will I go," said Peace.
Love looked down and beheld Hatred.
  "Thither will I go," said Love.
  So came Light and shone.
  So came Peace and gave rest.
  So came Love and brought Life.

Laurence Housman, 1865–

424. INCARNATION

Blow cold against the flame,
Throw sand upon the spark;
You cannot keep the Light
From shining in the dark.

Hunt out the heedless head,
And swing the acid knife;
You cannot abrogate
The ever-willful Life.

Immure the hallowed Word,
Bring faggot, rack and rope;
You cannot blur the Faith,
You cannot blunt the Hope.

No matter how untamed
Your ill intent may run,
You cannot stop the Pulse
That beats behind the sun.

Edith Lovejoy Pierce, 1904–

425. INCARNATE LOVE

Love came down at Christmas,
  Love all lovely, Love Divine;
Love was born at Christmas,
  Star and Angels gave the sign.

Worship we the Godhead,
  Love incarnate, Love Divine;
Worship we our Jesus:
  But wherewith for sacred sign?

Love shall be our token,
  Love be yours and Love be mine,
Love to God and all men,
  Love for plea and gift and sign.

Christina G. Rossetti, 1830–1894

426. A HYMN FOR CHRISTMAS DAY

Almighty Framer of the skies!
Oh, let our pure devotion rise
  Like incense in Thy sight!
Wrapt in impenetrable shade,
The texture of our souls were made,
  Till Thy command gave light.

The Sun of Glory gleam'd the ray,
Refined the darkness into day,
  And bid the vapours fly:
Impell'd by His eternal Love,
He left His palaces above
  To cheer our gloomy sky.

How shall we celebrate the day
When God appear'd in mortal clay,
  The mark of worldly scorn:
When the archangel's heavenly lays
Attempted the Redeemer's praise,
  And hail'd salvation's morn!

A humble form of Godhead wore,
The pains of poverty He bore,
  To gaudy pomp unknown:
Though in a human walk He trod,
Still was the Man Almighty God,
  In glory all His own.

Despis'd, oppress'd, the Godhead bears
The torments of this vale of tears,
  Nor bade His vengeance rise;
He saw the creatures He had made
Revile His power, His peace invade—
  He saw with Mercy's eyes.

How shall we celebrate His name,
Who groaned beneath a life of shame,

In all afflictions tried!
The soul is raptur'd to conceive
A truth which Being must believe—
The God eternal died.

My soul, exert thy powers—adore;
Upon Devotion's plumage soar
To celebrate the day;
The God from whom creation sprung
Shall animate my grateful tongue;
From Him I'll catch the lay!

Thomas Chatterton, 1752–1770

427. OUR CHRIST

In Christ I feel the heart of God
Throbbing from heaven through earth;
Life stirs again within the clod,
Renewed in beauteous birth;
The soul springs up, a flower of prayer,
Breathing His breath out on the air.

In Christ I touch the hand of God,
From His pure Height reached down,
By blessed ways before untrod,
To lift us to our crown;
Victory that only perfect is
Through loving sacrifice, like His.

Holding His hand, my steadied feet
May walk the air, the seas;
On life and death His smile falls sweet,
Lights up all mysteries;
Stranger nor exile can I be
In new worlds where He leadeth me.

Lucy Larcom, 1824–1893

428. THE COMING CHILD

Welcome! all Wonders in one sight!
Eternity shut in a span.
Summer in winter, day in night,
Heaven in earth, and God in man.
Great little one! whose all-embracing birth
Lifts earth to heaven, stoops heav'n to earth!

Richard Crashaw, 1613?–1649

429. TO JESUS

Thyself from love Thy heart didst not defend;
From heaven to earth it brought Thee from Thy throne.
Beloved, to what sheer depths didst Thou descend
To dwell with man, unhonored and unknown,
In life and death to enrich us without end.
Homeless and poor, with nothing of Thine own
Thou here didst come alone,
For Thou wert called
By Love unwalled,
That all Thy heart did move.
And as about the world Thy feet did go
'Twas Love that led Thee always, everywhere,
Thy only joy, for us Thy Love to show,
And for Thyself no whit at all to care.

From the Italian of Jacapone da Todi, 1250?–1306

430. THE DIVINE IMAGE

To Mercy, Pity, Peace, and Love
All pray in their distress;
And to these virtues of delight
Return their thankfulness.

For Mercy, Pity, Peace, and Love
Is God, our Father dear,
And Mercy, Pity, Peace, and Love
Is man, His child and care.

For Mercy has a human heart,
Pity a human face,
And Love, the human form divine,
And Peace, the human dress.

Then every man, of every clime,
That prays in his distress,
Prays to the human form divine,
Love, Mercy, Pity, Peace.

And all must love the human form,
In heathen, Turk, or Jew;
Where Mercy, Love, and Pity dwell
There God is dwelling too.

William Blake, 1757–1827

431. THE WORD INCARNATE

From "In Memoriam"

XXXVI

Tho' truths in manhood darkly join,
Deep-seated in our mystic frame,
We yield all blessing to the name
Of Him that made them current coin;

For Wisdom dealt with mortal powers,
Where truth in closest words shall fail,
When truth embodied in a tale
Shall enter in at lowly doors.

And so the Word had breath, and wrought
With human hands the creed of creeds
In loveliness of perfect deeds,
More strong than all poetic thought;

Which he may read that binds the sheaf,
Or builds the house, or digs the grave,
And those wild eyes that watch the wave
In roarings round the coral reef.

Alfred Tennyson, 1809–1892

432. QUATRAIN

Here is the Truth in a little creed,
Enough for all the roads we go:
In Love is all the law we need,
In Christ is all the God we know.

Edwin Markham, 1852–1940

433. BENEDICTUS

Luke 1: 68–79

Blessed be the Lord God of Israel; for he hath visited and redeemed his people,
And hath raised up an horn of salvation for us in the house of his servant David;
As he spake by the mouth of his holy prophets, which have been since the world began:
That we should be saved from our enemies, and from the hand of all that hate us;
To perform the mercy promised to our fathers, and to remember his holy covenant;
The oath which he sware to our father Abraham,
That he would grant unto us, that we being delivered out of the hand of our enemies might serve him without fear,
In holiness and righteousness before him, all the days of our life.
And thou, child, shalt be called the prophet of the Highest: for thou shalt go before the face of the Lord to prepare his ways;
To give knowledge of salvation unto his people by the remission of their sins,
Through the tender mercy of our God; whereby the dayspring from on high hath visited us,
To give light to them that sit in darkness and in the shadow of death, to guide our feet into the way of peace.

King James Version, 1611

434. IT CAME UPON THE MIDNIGHT CLEAR

It came upon the midnight clear,
That glorious song of old,
From angels bending near the earth,
To touch their harps of gold:
"Peace on the earth, good-will to men,
From heaven's all gracious King:"
The world in solemn stillness lay
To hear the angels sing.

Still through the cloven skies they come,
With peaceful wings unfurled;

And still their heavenly music floats
  O'er all the weary world:
Above its sad and lowly plains
  They bend on hovering wing,
And ever o'er its Babel sounds
  The blessed angels sing.

Yet with the woes of sin and strife
  The world hath suffered long;
Beneath the angel-strain have rolled
  Two thousand years of wrong;
And man, at war with man, hears not
  The love song which they bring:
O hush the noise, ye men of strife,
  And hear the angels sing.

And ye, beneath life's crushing load,
  Whose forms are bending low,
Who toil along the climbing way,
  With painful steps and slow,
Look now, for glad and golden hours
  Come swiftly on the wing;
O rest beside the weary road,
  And hear the angels sing.

For lo! the days are hastening on,
  By prophet bards foretold,
When with the ever-circling years
  Comes round the age of gold;
When peace shall over all the earth
  Its ancient splendors fling,
And the whole world give back the song
  Which now the angels sing.

Edmund H. Sears, 1810–1876

435. SILENT NIGHT! HOLY NIGHT!

Silent night! holy night!
All is calm, all is bright;
Round yon virgin mother and Child,
Holy Infant so tender and mild;
Sleep in heavenly peace,
Sleep in heavenly peace.

Silent night! holy night!
Darkness flies, all is light;
Shepherds hear the angels sing:
"Alleluia! hail the King!
Christ the Saviour is born,
Christ the Saviour is born."

Silent night! holy night!
Guiding Star, lend thy light!
See the eastern wise men bring
Gifts and homage to our King!
Christ the Saviour is born,
Christ the Saviour is born.

Silent night! holy night!
Wondrous Star, lend thy light!
With the angels let us sing
Alleluia to our King!
Christ the Saviour is born,
Christ the Saviour is born.

Joseph Mohr, 1792–1848

436. CHRISTMAS PASTORAL

The snow lies crisp beneath the stars,
  On roofs and on the ground;
Late footsteps crunch along the paths,
  There is no other sound.

So cold it is the roadside trees
  Snap in the rigid frost,
A dreadful night to think on them,—
  The homeless and the lost.

The dead sleep sheltered in the tomb,
  The rich drink in the hall;
The Virgin and the Holy Child
  Lie shivering in a stall.

Robert Hillyer, 1895–

437. BEFORE THE PALING OF THE STARS

Before the paling of the stars,
  Before the winter morn,
Before the earliest cockcrow,
  Jesus Christ was born:
Born in a stable,
  Cradled in a manger,
In the world His hands had made
  Born a stranger.

Priest and king lay fast asleep
  In Jerusalem,
Young and old lay fast asleep
  In crowded Bethlehem;
Saint and Angel, ox and ass,
  Kept a watch together
Before the Christmas daybreak
  In the winter weather.

Jesus on His mother's breast
  In the stable cold,
Spotless Lamb of God was He,
  Shepherd of the fold:
Let us kneel with Mary maid,
  With Joseph bent and hoary,
With Saint and Angel, ox and ass,
  To hail the King of Glory.

Christina G. Rossetti, 1830–1894

438. CHRISTMAS NIGHT

More lovely than the rose
  The fragrance that this night
Of nights is poured on earth;
  No noon-tide sun so bright

E'er shone as one clear star
  That led the Wise Men's way,
Before God's Wisdom hid
  In Babyhood to pray.

More lovely than the rose
  The Rose of Sharon lay
Bud of a virgin flower,
  Cradled in oxen's hay.

Marion Lochhead, contemporary Scottish

439. THERE'S A SONG IN THE AIR!

There's a song in the air!
There's a star in the sky!
There's a mother's deep prayer
And a baby's low cry!
And the star rains its fire while the beautiful
  sing,
For the manger of Bethlehem cradles a King!

There's a tumult of joy
O'er the wonderful birth,
For the Virgin's sweet boy
Is the Lord of the earth.
Ay! the star rains its fire while the beautiful
  sing,
For the manger of Bethlehem cradles a King!

In the light of that star
Lie the ages impearled;
And that song from afar
Has swept over the world.
Every hearth is aflame, and the beautiful
  sing
In the homes of the nations that Jesus is
  King!

We rejoice in the light,
And we echo the song
That comes down thro' the night
From the heavenly throng.
Ay! we shout to the lovely evangel they bring,
And we greet in His cradle our Saviour and
  King!

Josiah Gilbert Holland, 1819–1881

440. HARK! THE HERALD ANGELS SING

Hark! the herald angels sing,
"Glory to the new-born King;
Peace on earth, and mercy mild,
God and sinners reconciled!"
Joyful all ye nations rise,
Join the triumph of the skies;
With th' angelic host proclaim,
"Christ is born in Bethlehem."
Hark! the herald angels sing,
"Glory to the new-born King."

Christ, by highest heaven adored;
Christ, the ever-lasting Lord;
Come, Desire of Nations, come,
Fix in us Thy humble home.
Veiled in flesh the God-head see;
Hail th' Incarnate Deity,
Pleased as man with men to dwell;
Jesus, our Emmanuel.
Hark! the herald angels sing,
"Glory to the new-born King."

Hail, the heaven-born Prince of Peace!
Hail, the Sun of Righteousness!
Light and life to all He brings,
Risen with healing in His wings.
Mild He lays His glory by.
Born that man no more may die,
Born to raise the sons of earth,
Born to give them second birth.
Hark! the herald angels sing,
"Glory to the new-born King."

Charles Wesley, 1707–1788;
altered by George Whitefield, 1714–1770

441. ADESTE FIDELES

O come, all ye faithful,
  Joyful and triumphant;
O come ye, O come ye to Bethlehem;
  Come and behold Him

Born, the King of Angels;
O come, let us adore Him,
O come, let us adore Him,
O come, let us adore Him, Christ the Lord.

❖

Sing, choirs of angels;
Sing in exultation,
Sing, all ye citizens of Heav'n above:
"Glory to God
All glory in the highest";
O come, let us adore Him,
O come, let us adore Him,
O come, let us adore Him, Christ the Lord.

Yea, Lord, we greet Thee,
Born this happy morning;
Jesu, to Thee be glory given;
Word of the Father,
Now in flesh appearing;
O come, let us adore Him,
O come, let us adore Him,
O come, let us adore Him, Christ the Lord.

From the Latin, 18th century;
tr. by Frederick Oakeley, 1802–1880

442. MY MASTER

My Master was so very poor,
A manger was His cradling place;
So very rich my Master was
Kings came from far
To gain His grace.

My Master was so very poor
And with the poor He broke the bread;
So very rich my Master was
That multitudes
By Him were fed.

My Master was so very poor
They nailed Him naked to a cross;
So very rich my Master was
He gave His all
And knew no loss.

Harry Lee, 1874–1942

443. NATIVITY

Angels, from the realms of glory,
Wing your flight o'er all the earth,
Ye who sang creation's story,
Now proclaim Messiah's birth;
Come and worship,
Worship Christ the new-born King.

Shepherds, in the field abiding,
Watching o'er your flocks by night,
God with man is now residing,
Yonder shines the infant-light;
Come and worship,
Worship Christ the new-born King.

Sages, leave your contemplations,
Brighter visions beam afar;
Seek the great Desire of nations;
Ye have seen His natal star;
Come and worship,
Worship Christ the new-born King.

Saints before the altar bending,
Watching long in hope and fear,
Suddenly the Lord, descending,
In His temple shall appear;
Come and worship,
Worship Christ the new-born King.

James Montgomery, 1771–1854

444. WHAT CHILD IS THIS?

What Child is this who laid to rest
On Mary's lap is sleeping,
Whom angels greet with anthems sweet
While shepherds watch are keeping?
This, this is Christ the King
Whom shepherds guard and angels sing,
Haste, haste to bring Him laud,
The Babe, the Son of Mary.

Why lies He in such mean estate
Where ox and ass are feeding?
Good Christian fear, for sinners here
The silent word is pleading.
Nails, spear shall pierce Him through.
The cross He bore for me, for you.
Hail, hail, the Lord made flesh,
The Babe, the Son of Mary.

So bring Him incense, gold and myrrh,
Come peasant, king to own Him.
The King of kings salvation brings,
Let loving hearts enthrone Him.
Raise, raise the song on high,
The virgin sings her lullaby,
Joy, joy for Christ is born,
The Babe, the Son of Mary.

W. C. Dix, 1837–1898

445. AWAY IN A MANGER

"Cradle Song"

Away in a manger, no crib for a bed,
The little Lord Jesus laid down His sweet head.
The stars in the sky looked down where He lay,
The little Lord Jesus, asleep on the hay.

The cattle are lowing, the Baby awakes,
But little Lord Jesus, no crying He makes.
I love Thee, Lord Jesus, look down from the sky,
And stay by my cradle till morning is nigh.

Be near me, Lord Jesus, I ask Thee to stay
Close by me for ever, and love me, I pray.
Bless all the dear children in Thy tender care,
And fit us for heaven to live with Thee there.

Martin Luther, 1483–1546

446. BRIGHTEST AND BEST OF THE SONS OF THE MORNING

Brightest and best of the sons of the morning,
Dawn on our darkness, and lend us Thine aid!
Star of the East, the horizon adorning,
Guide where our infant Redeemer is laid!

Cold on His cradle the dewdrops are shining;
Low lies His head with the beasts of the stall;
Angels adore Him in slumber reclining,
Maker and Monarch and Saviour of all.

Say, shall we yield Him, in costly devotion,
Odors of Edom and offerings divine,
Gems of the mountain and pearls of the ocean,
Myrrh from the forest, and gold from the mine?

Vainly we offer each ample oblation,
Vainly with gifts would His favour secure;
Richer by far is the heart's adoration,
Dearer to God are the prayers of the poor.

Brightest and best of the sons of the morning,
Dawn on our darkness, and lend us Thine aid!
Star of the east, the horizon adorning,
Guide where our infant Redeemer is laid!

Reginald Heber, 1783–1826

447. THE LAMB

Little lamb, who made thee?
Dost thou know who made thee,
Gave thee life, and bid thee feed
By the streams and o'er the mead;
Gave thee clothing of delight,
Softest clothing, woolly, bright;
Gave thee such a tender voice,
Making all the vales rejoice?
Little lamb, who made thee?
Dost thou know who made thee?

Little lamb, I'll tell thee;
Little lamb, I'll tell thee.
He is callèd by thy name,
For He calls Himself a Lamb;
He is meek and He is mild,
He became a little child.
I a child, and thou a lamb,
We are callèd by His name.
Little lamb, God bless thee!
Little lamb, God bless thee!

William Blake, 1757–1827

448. A KNIGHT OF BETHLEHEM

There was a Knight of Bethlehem
Whose wealth was tears and sorrow;
His men-at-arms were little lambs,
His trumpeters were sparrows;
His castle was a wooden cross,
Whereon He hung so high;
His helmet was a crown of thorns
Whose crest did touch the sky.

H. N. Maugham, contemporary English

449. THAT HOLY THING

They all were looking for a king
To slay their foes and lift them high;
Thou cam'st, a little baby thing
That made a woman cry.

O Son of Man, to right my lot
Naught but Thy presence can avail;
Yet on the road Thy wheels are not,
Nor on the sea Thy sail!

My how or when Thou wilt not heed,
But come down Thine own secret stair,
That Thou mayst answer all my need—
Yea, every bygone prayer.

George Macdonald, 1824–1905

450. CHRIST CHILD

Warm as a little mouse he lay,
Hay kept him from the Winter's harm;
Bleating of puzzled lamb he heard,
And voices from the near-by farm.

His mother's eyes were bent on him
As to her frozen breast he clung;
His father stopped the draughty cracks
And sang a merry herding song.

Who would have thought upon that hour
Those little hands might stay a plague,
Those eyes would quell a multitude,
That voice would still a rising wave?

Only the omens of the night,
The lowing ox, the moaning tree,
Hinted the cruelty to come:
A raven croaked, "Gethsemane!"

Henry Treece, 1912–

451. THE OXEN

Christmas Eve, and twelve of the clock.
  "Now they are all on their knees,"
An elder said as we sat in a flock
  By the embers in hearthside ease.

We pictured the meek mild creatures where
  They dwelt in their strawy pen,
Nor did it occur to one of us there
  To doubt they were kneeling then.

So fair a fancy few would weave
  In these years! Yet, I feel,
If someone said on Christmas Eve,
  "Come; see the oxen kneel,

"In the lonely barton by yonder coomb
  Our childhood used to know,"
I should go with him in the gloom,
  Hoping it might be so.

Thomas Hardy, 1840–1928

452. A CHRISTMAS HYMN

Tell me what is this innumerable throng
Singing in the heavens a loud angelic song?
These are they who come with swift and shining feet
From round about the throne of God the Lord of Light to greet.

O, who are these that hasten beneath the starry sky,
As if with joyful tidings that through the world shall fly?
The faithful shepherds these, who greatly were afeared
When, as they watched their flocks by night, the heavenly host appeared.

Who are these that follow across the hills of night
A star that westward hurries along the fields of light?
Three wise men from the east who myrrh and treasure bring
To lay them at the feet of him, their Lord and Christ and King.

What babe new-born is this that in a manger cries?
Near on her bed of pain his happy mother lies.
O, see! the air is shaken with white and heavenly wings—
This is the Lord of all the earth, this is the King of Kings.

Tell me, how may I join in this holy feast
With all the kneeling world, and I of all the least?
Fear not, O faithful heart, but bring what most is meet;
Bring love alone, true love alone, and lay it at his feet.

Richard Watson Gilder, 1844–1909

453. HUSH, ALL YE SOUNDS OF WAR

Hush, all ye sounds of war,
Ye nations all be still,
A voice of heav'nly joy steals over vale and hill,
O hear the angels sing the captive world's release,
This day is born in Bethlehem the Prince of Peace.

No more divided be,
Ye families of men,
Old enmity forget, old friendship knit again,
In the new year of God let brothers' love increase,
This day is born in Bethlehem the Prince of Peace.

William H. Draper, 1855–1933

454. THE PEACE-GIVER

Thou whose birth on earth
  Angels sang to men,
While Thy stars made mirth,
Saviour, at Thy birth,
  This day born again;

As this night was bright
  With Thy cradle-ray,
Very Light of Light,
Turn the wild world's night
  To Thy perfect day.

Thou the Word and Lord
  In all time and space
Heard, beheld, adored,
With all ages poured
  Forth before Thy face,

Lord, what worth in earth
  Drew Thee down to die?
What therein was worth,
Lord, Thy death and birth?
  What beneath Thy sky?

Thou whose face gives grace
  As the sun's doth heat,
Let Thy sunbright face
Lighten time and space
  Here beneath Thy feet.

Bid our peace increase,
  Thou that madest morn;
Bid oppression cease;
Bid the night be peace;
  Bid the day be born.

Algernon Charles Swinburne, 1837–1909

455. SONGS OF JESUS

O sing a song of Bethlehem,
  Of shepherds watching there,
And of the news that came to them
  From angels in the air:
The light that shone on Bethlehem
  Fills all the world to-day;
Of Jesus' birth and peace on earth
  The angels sing alway.

O sing a song of Nazareth,
  Of sunny days of joy,
O sing of fragrant flowers' breath,
  And of the sinless Boy:
For now the flowers of Nazareth
  In every heart may grow;
Now spreads the fame of His dear Name
  On all the winds that blow.

O sing a song of Galilee,
  Of lake and woods and hill,
Of Him who walked upon the sea
  And bade its waves be still:
For though, like waves on Galilee,
  Dark seas of trouble roll,
When faith has heard the Master's word
  Falls peace upon the soul.

O sing a song of Calvary,
  Its glory and dismay;
Of Him who hung upon the Tree
  And took our sins away;
For He who died on Calvary
  Is risen from the grave,
And Christ, our Lord, by heaven adored,
  Is mighty now to save.

Louis F. Benson, 1855–1930

456. NEW PRINCE, NEW POMP

Behold a helpless,[1] tender Babe,
In freezing winter night,
In homely manger trembling lies;
Alas! a piteous sight.

The inns are full; no man will yield
This little Pilgrim bed;
But forced He is with silly beasts
In crib to shroud His head.

❖

Weigh not His crib, His wooden dish
Nor beasts that by Him feed;
Weigh not His mother's poor attire,
Nor Joseph's simple weed.

This stable is a Prince's court,
This crib His chair of state;
The beasts are parcel of His pomp,
The wooden dish His plate.

The persons in that poor attire
His royal liv'ries wear;
The Prince Himself is come from Heav'n;
This pomp is prizèd there.

With joy approach, O Christian wight!
Do homage to thy King;
And highly praise His humble pomp,
Which He from Heav'n doth bring.

Robert Southwell, 1561?–1595

457. THE PRINCE OF PEACE

Hark! the glad sound! the Saviour comes,
The Saviour promised long:
Let every heart prepare a throne,
And every voice a song.

He comes, the prisoners to release
In Satan's bondage held;
The gates of brass before Him burst,
The iron fetters yield.

He comes, from the thick films of vice
To clear the mental ray,
And on the eyeballs of the blind
To pour celestial day.

He comes, the broken heart to bind,
The bleeding soul to cure,
And with the treasures of His grace
To enrich the humble poor.

Our glad hosannas, Prince of Peace,
Thy welcome shall proclaim,
And Heaven's eternal arches ring
With Thy belovèd name.

Philip Doddridge, 1702–1751

458. CRADLE CAROL

The little birds praise you,
The wren and the sparrow,
The rabbits and squirrels
That run in the snow.
This house may be small
And this cradle be narrow.
You learned to be humble
A long time ago.

O little Lord Jesus,
Your moment is breaking.
The angels in heaven
Have polished your star.
Alone on their hill-sides
The shepherds are waking
The wise shall grow simple
And find where you are.

Eleanor Slater, 1903–

459. CHRISTMAS EVE MEDITATION

There is a hush that comes on Christmas Eve—
Life's hurry and its stress grow far away;
And something in the silence seems to weave
A mood akin to sadness, yet we say
A "Merry Christmas" to the friends we meet,
And all the while we feel that mystic spell,
As if the Christ Child came on noiseless feet,
With something old, yet ever new, to tell—
The eyes grow misty, yet they shed no tear,
And those that we have lost, somehow seem near.

Margaret E. Bruner,
contemporary American

[1] Early texts read "selly" or "silly" meaning "blessed," "innocent," "harmless," "helpless."

460. CHILDHOOD

To be Himself a star most bright
To bring the wise men to His sight,
To be Himself a voice most sweet
To call the shepherds to His feet,
To be a child—it was His will,
That folk like us might find Him still.

John Erskine, 1879-

461. IN THINE OWN HEART

Though Christ a thousand times
  In Bethlehem be born,
If He's not born in thee
  Thy soul is still forlorn.
The cross on Golgotha
  Will never save thy soul,
The cross in thine own heart
  Alone can make thee whole.

From the German of
Angelus Silesius, 1624-1677

462. A SONG FOR SIMEON

Lord, the Roman hyacinths are blooming in bowls and
The winter sun creeps by the snow hills;
The stubborn season has made stand.
My life is light, waiting for the death wind,
Like a feather on the back of my hand.
Dust in sunlight and memory in corners
Wait for the wind that chills towards the dead land.

Grant us thy peace.
I have walked many years in this city,
Kept faith and fast, provided for the poor,
Have given and taken honour and ease.
There went never any rejected from my door.
Who shall remember my house, where shall live my children's children
When the time of sorrow is come?
They will take to the goat's path, and the fox's home,
Fleeing from the foreign faces and the foreign swords.
Before the time of cords and scourges and lamentation
Grant us thy peace.
Before the stations of the mountain of desolation,
Before the certain hour of maternal sorrow,
Now at this birth season of decease,
Let the Infant, the still unspeaking and unspoken Word,
Grant Israel's consolation
To one who has eighty years and no to-morrow.

According to thy word.
They shall praise Thee and suffer in every generation
With glory and derision,
Light upon light, mounting the saints' stair.
Not for me the martyrdom, the ecstasy of thought and prayer,
Not for me the ultimate vision.
Grant me thy peace.
(And a sword shall pierce thy heart,
Thine also.)
I am tired with my own life and the lives of those after me,
I am dying in my own death and the deaths of those after me.
Let thy servant depart,
Having seen thy salvation.

T. S. Eliot, 1888-

463. THE MAGNIFICAT

Luke 1: 46–55

My soul doth magnify the LORD,
And my spirit hath rejoiced in God my Saviour.
For he hath regarded the low estate of his handmaiden:
for, behold, from henceforth all generations shall call me blessed.
For he that is mighty hath done to me great things; and holy is his name.
And his mercy is on them that fear him from generation to generation.
He hath shewed strength with his arm;
he hath scattered the proud in the imagination of their hearts.
He hath put down the mighty from their seats,
and exalted them of low degree.
He hath filled the hungry with good things;
and the rich he hath sent empty away.
He hath holpen his servant Israel, in remembrance of his mercy;
As he spake to our fathers, to Abraham, and to his seed for ever.

King James Version, 1611

464. A CHRISTMAS CAROL

The Christ-child lay on Mary's lap,
His hair was like a light.
(O weary, weary were the world,
But here is all aright.)

The Christ-child lay on Mary's breast,
His hair was like a star.
(O stern and cunning are the kings,
But here the true hearts are.)

The Christ-child lay on Mary's heart,
His hair was like a fire.
(O weary, weary is the world,
But here the world's desire.)

The Christ-child stood at Mary's knee,
His hair was like a crown,
And all the flowers looked up at Him,
And all the stars looked down.

Gilbert K. Chesterton, 1874–1936

465. MARY

Mary, when that little child
Lay upon your heart at rest,
Did the thorns, Maid-mother mild,
Pierce your breast?

Mary, when that little child
Softly kissed your cheek benign,
Did you know, O Mary mild,
Judas' sign?

Mary, when that little child
Cooed and prattled at your knee,
Did you see with heartbeat wild,
Calvary?

Rose Trumbull, contemporary American

466. CHRISTMAS MORNING

If Bethlehem were here today,
Or this were very long ago,
There wouldn't be a winter time
Nor any cold or snow.

I'd run out through the garden gate,
And down along the pasture walk;
And off beside the cattle barns
I'd hear a kind of gentle talk.

I'd move the heavy iron chain
And pull away the wooden pin;
I'd push the door a little bit
And tiptoe very softly in.

The pigeons and the yellow hens
And all the cows would stand away;
Their eyes would open wide to see
A lady in the manger hay,

If this were very long ago
And Bethlehem were here today.

And Mother held my hand and smiled—
I mean the lady would—and she
Would take the woolly blankets off
Her little boy so I could see.

His shut-up eyes would be asleep,
And he would look just like our John,
And he would be all crumpled too,
And have a pinkish color on.

I'd watch his breath go in and out.
His little clothes would all be white.
I'd slip my finger in his hand
To feel how he could hold it tight.

And she would smile and say, "Take care,"
The mother, Mary, would, "Take care";
And I would kiss his little hand
And touch his hair.

While Mary put the blankets back
The gentle talk would soon begin.
And when I'd tiptoe softly out
I'd meet the wise men going in.

Elizabeth Madox Roberts, 1885–1941

467. THE CHRISTMAS STORY

Luke 2: 8–14

And there were in the same country shepherds abiding in the field,
  keeping watch over their flock by night.
And, lo, the angel of the Lord came upon them,
  and the glory of the Lord shone round about them:
  and they were sore afraid.
And the angel said unto them,
Fear not: for, behold, I bring you good tidings of great joy,
  which shall be to all people.
For unto you is born this day in the city of David a Saviour,
  which is Christ the Lord.
And this shall be a sign unto you;
Ye shall find the babe wrapped in swaddling clothes, lying in a manger.
And suddenly there was with the angel a multitude of the heavenly
    host praising God, and saying,
Glory to God in the highest,
  and on earth peace,
  good will toward men.

King James Version, 1611

468. THE SHEPHERD SPEAKS

Out of the midnight sky a great dawn broke,
And a voice singing flooded us with song.
In David's city was He born, it sang,
A Saviour, Christ the Lord. Then while I sat
Shivering with the thrill of that great cry,
A mighty choir a thousandfold more sweet
Suddenly sang, Glory to God, and Peace—
Peace on the earth; my heart, almost
    unnerved
By that swift loveliness, would hardly beat.
Speechless we waited till the accustomed
    night
Gave us no promise more of sweet surprise;
Then scrambling to our feet, without a word
We started through the fields to find the
    Child.

John Erskine, 1879–

469. WHILE SHEPHERDS WATCHED THEIR FLOCKS BY NIGHT

While shepherds watched their flocks by night
  All seated on the ground,
The angel of the Lord came down,
  And glory shone around.

"Fear not," said he; (for mighty dread
Had seized their troubled mind);
"Glad tidings of great joy I bring
To you and all mankind.

"To you, in David's town, this day
Is born of David's line
A Saviour, who is Christ the Lord;
And this shall be the sign:

"The heavenly Babe you there shall find
To human view displayed,
All meanly wrapped in swathing bands,
And in a manger laid."

Thus spake the seraph; and forthwith
Appeared a shining throng
Of angels, praising God, who thus
Addressed their joyful song:

"All glory be to God on high,
And on the earth be peace;
Good-will henceforth from heaven to men
Begin and never cease."

Nahum Tate, 1652–1715

470. THE SHEPHERDS HAD AN ANGEL

The shepherds had an angel,
The wise men had a star,
But what have I, a little child,
To guide me home from far,
Where glad stars sing together,
And singing angels are?

Lord Jesus is my Guardian,
So I can nothing lack;
The lambs lie in His bosom
Along life's dangerous track:
The wilful lambs that go astray
He, bleeding, fetches back.

Those shepherds, through the lonely night
Sat watching by their sheep,
Until they saw the heavenly host
Who neither tire nor sleep,
All singing 'Glory, glory,'
In festival they keep.

Christ watches me, His little lamb,
Cares for me day and night,
That I may be His own in heaven:
So angels clad in white
Shall sing their 'Glory, glory,'
For my sake in the height.

Lord, bring me nearer day by day,
Till I my voice unite,
And sing my 'Glory, glory,'
With angels clad in white,
All 'Glory, glory,' given to Thee,
Through all the heavenly height.

Christina Georgina Rossetti, 1830–1894

471. THE KINGS OF THE EAST

The Kings of the East are riding
To-night to Bethlehem.
The sunset glows dividing,
The Kings of the East are riding;
A star their journey guiding,
Gleaming with gold and gem
The Kings of the East are riding
To-night to Bethlehem.

To a strange sweet harp of Zion
The starry host troops forth;
The golden glaived Orion
To a strange sweet harp of Zion;
The Archer and the Lion,
The watcher of the North;
To a strange sweet harp of Zion
The starry host troops forth.

There beams above a manger
The child-face of a star;
Amid the stars a stranger,
It beams above a manger;
What means this ether-ranger
To pause where poor folk are?
There beams above a manger
The child-face of a star.

Katharine Lee Bates, 1859–1929

472. WISE MEN SEEKING JESUS

Wise men seeking Jesus
Traveled from afar,
Guided on their journey
By a beauteous star.
But if we desire Him,
He is close at hand;
For our native country
Is our Holy Land.

Prayerful souls may find Him
  By our quiet lakes,
Meet Him on our hillsides
  Where the morning breaks.
In our fertile cornfields,
  While the sheaves are bound,
In our busy markets
  Jesus may be found.

Every peaceful village
  In our land might be,
Made by Jesus' presence
  Like sweet Bethany.
He is more than near us,
  If we love Him well;
For He seeketh ever
  In our hearts to dwell.

James East, 1860–1937

473. ALL MY HEART THIS NIGHT REJOICES

All my heart this night rejoices,
As I hear,
Far and near,
Sweetest angel voices:
"Christ is born" their choirs are singing,
Till the air,
Everywhere,
Now with joy is ringing.

Hark! a voice from yonder manger,
Soft and sweet,
Doth entreat,
"Flee from woe and danger;
Brethren, come; from all that grieves you
You are freed;
All you need
I will surely give you."

Come, then, let us hasten yonder;
Here let all,
Great and small,
Kneel in awe and wonder,
Love Him who with love is yearning;
Hail the Star
That from far
Bright with hope is burning.

Thee, dear Lord, with heed I'll cherish,
Live to Thee,
And with Thee
Dying, shall not perish,
But shall dwell with Thee forever
Far on high
In the joy
That can alter never.

Paul Gerhardt, 1607–1676;
tr. by Catherine Winkworth, 1829–1878

474. WHAT STAR IS THIS?

What star is this, with beams so bright,
Which shames the sun's less radiant light?
It shines to announce a new-born King,—
Glad tidings of our God to bring.

'Tis now fulfilled with God decreed,—
"From Jacob shall a star proceed."
And lo! the Eastern sages stand,
To read in heaven the Lord's command.

While outward signs the star displays,
And inward light the Lord conveys,
And urges them, with force benign,
To seek the giver of the sign.

True love can brook no dull delay,
Nor toil, nor dangers stop their way:
Home, kindred, fatherland, and all,
They leave at once, at God's high call.

O Jesu, while the Star of Grace
Invites us now to seek Thy face,
May we no more that grace repel,
Or quench that light that shines so well!

To God the Father, God the Son,
And Holy Spirit, Three in One,
May every tongue and nation raise
An endless song of thankful praise.

From the Latin;
tr. by J. Chandler, 1806–1876

475. THE CHRISTMAS STAR

High in the heavens a single star,
  Of pure, imperishable light;
Out on the desert strange and far
  Dim riders riding through the night:
Above a hilltop sudden song
  Like silver trumpets down the sky—
And all to welcome One so young
  He scarce could lift a cry!

Stars rise and set, that star shines on:
  Songs fail, but still that music beats
Through all the ages come and gone,
  In lane and field and city streets.
And we who catch the Christmas gleam,
  Watching with children on the hill,
We know, we know it is no dream—
  He stands among us still!

Nancy Byrd Turner, 1880–

476. CHRISTMAS

As shadows cast by cloud and sun
  Flit o'er the summer grass,
So, in Thy sight, Almighty One,
  Earth's generations pass.
And as the years, an endless host,
  Come swiftly pressing on,
The brightest names that earth can boast
  Just glisten and are gone.

Yet doth the star of Bethlehem shed
  A lustre pure and sweet:
And still it leads, as once it led,
  To the Messiah's feet.
O Father, may that holy star
  Grow every year more bright,
And send its glorious beams afar
  To fill the world with light.

William Cullen Bryant, 1794–1878

477. AS WITH GLADNESS MEN OF OLD

As with gladness men of old
Did the guiding star behold;
As with joy they hailed its light,
Leading onward, beaming bright;
So, most gracious Lord, may we
Evermore be led to Thee.

As with joyful steps they sped
To that lowly manger-bed,
There to bend the knee before
Him whom heaven and earth adore;
So may we with willing feet
Ever seek Thy mercy seat.

As they offered gifts most rare,
At that manger rude and bare,
So may we with holy joy,
Pure and free from sin's alloy,
All our costliest treasures bring,
Christ, to Thee, our heavenly King.

Holy Jesus, every day
Keep us in the narrow way;
And, when earthly things are past,
Bring our ransomed souls at last
Where they need no star to guide,
Where no clouds Thy glory hide.

William Chatterton Dix, 1837–1898

478. ROYAL PRESENTS

The off'rings of the Eastern kings of old
Unto our Lord were incense, myrrh and gold;
Incense because a God; gold as a king;
And myrrh as to a dying man they bring.
Instead of incense (Blessed Lord) if we
Can send a sigh or fervent prayer to thee,
Instead of myrrh if we can but provide
Tears that from penitential eyes do slide,
And though we have no gold; if for our part
We can present thee with a broken heart
Thou wilt accept: and say those Eastern kings
Did not present thee with more precious
    things.

Nathaniel Wanley, 1634–1680

479. ADVENT

I have no more gold;
I spent it all on foolish songs,
Gold I cannot give to you.

Incense, too, I burned
To the great idols of this world;
I must come with empty hands.

Myrrh I lost
In that darker sepulcher
Where another Christ
Died for man in vain.—

I can only give myself,
I have nothing left but this.
Naked I wait, naked I fall
Into Your Hands, Your Hands.

John Gould Fletcher, 1886–

480. WHO ARE THE WISE MEN?

Who were the Wise Men in the long ago?
Not Herod, fearful lest he lose his throne;
Not Pharisees too proud to claim their own;
Not priests and scribes whose province was to know;
Not money-changers running to and fro;
But three who traveled, weary and alone,
With dauntless faith, because before them shone
The Star that led them to a manger low.

Who are the Wise Men now, when all is told?
Not men of science; not the great and strong;
Not those who wear a kingly diadem;
Not those whose eager hands pile high the gold;
But those amid the tumult and the throng
Who follow still the Star of Bethlehem.

B. Y. Williams, contemporary American

481. MY GIFT

From "A Christmas Carol"

What can I give Him
Poor as I am?
If I were a shepherd,
I would give Him a lamb,
If I were a Wise Man,
I would do my part,—
But what I can I give Him,
Give my heart.

Christina G. Rossetti, 1830–1894

482. BETHLEHEM

O little town, O little town,
Upon the hills so far,
We see you like a thing sublime,
Across the great, gray wastes of time,
And men go up and men go down
But follow still the Star.

And this is humble Bethlehem
In the Judea wild:
And this is lowly Bethlehem
Wherein a mother smiled:
Yea, this is happy Bethlehem
That knew the little child.

Aye, this is glorious Bethlehem
Where He drew living breath
(Ah, precious, precious Bethlehem!
So every mortal saith)
Who brought to all that tread the earth
Life's triumph over death!

O little town, O little town,
Upon the hills afar,
You call to us, a thing sublime
Across the great, gray wastes of time
For men go up and men go down,
But follow still the Star.

Clinton Scollard, 1860–1932

483. O LITTLE TOWN OF BETHLEHEM!

O little town of Bethlehem,
How still we see thee lie!
Above thy deep and dreamless sleep
The silent stars go by:
Yet in thy dark streets shineth
The everlasting Light;
The hopes and fears of all the years
Are met in thee to-night.

For Christ is born of Mary;
And gathered all above,
While mortals sleep, the angels keep
Their watch of wondering love.
O morning stars together
Proclaim the holy birth;
And praises sing to God the King,
And peace to men on earth.

How silently, how silently,
  The wondrous Gift is given!
So God imparts to human hearts
  The blessings of His Heaven.
No ear may hear His coming,
  But in this world of sin,
Where meek souls will receive Him still,
  The dear Christ enters in.

O holy Child of Bethlehem,
  Descend to us, we pray;
Cast out our sins, and enter in,
  Be born in us to-day.
We hear the Christmas angels
  The great glad tidings tell;
O come to us, abide with us,
  Our Lord Emmanuel.

Phillips Brooks, 1835–1893

484. THE LIGHT OF BETHLEHEM

'Tis Christmas night! The snow,
  A flock unnumbered, lies:
The old Judean stars, aglow,
  Keep watch within the skies.

An icy stillness holds
  The pulses of the night:
A deeper mystery infolds
  The wondering hosts of light.

Till, lo, with reverence pale
  That dims each diadem,
The lordliest, earthward bending, hail
  The light of Bethlehem!

John Banister Tabb, 1845–1909

485. ONCE IN ROYAL DAVID'S CITY

Once in royal David's city
  Stood a lowly cattle-shed,
Where a mother laid her Baby
  In a manger for His bed.
Mary was that mother mild,
Jesus Christ her little Child.

He came down to earth from heaven
  Who is God and Lord of all,
And His shelter was a stable,
  And His cradle was a stall.
With the poor and mean and lowly
Lived on earth our Saviour holy.

And through all His wondrous childhood
  He would honour and obey,
Love, and watch the lowly maiden
  In whose gentle arms He lay.
Christian children all must be
Mild, obedient, good as He.

For He is our childhood's pattern:
  Day by day like us He grew:
He was little, weak, and helpless:
  Tears and smiles like us He knew;
And He feeleth for our sadness,
And He shareth in our gladness.

And our eyes at last shall see Him,
  Through His own redeeming love;
For that Child so dear and gentle
  Is our Lord in heaven above;
And He leads His children on
To the place where He is gone.

Not in that poor lowly stable,
  With the oxen standing by,
We shall see Him, but in heaven,
  Set at God's right hand on high,
When, like stars, His children crowned
All in white shall wait around.

Cecil F. Alexander, 1823–1895

486. HOW FAR IS IT TO BETHLEHEM?

How far is it to Bethlehem?
  Not very far.
Shall we find the stable-room
  Lit by a star?

Can we see the little Child,
  Is He within?
If we lift the wooden latch
  May we go in?

May we stroke the creatures there,
  Ox, ass, or sheep?
May we peep like them and see
  Jesus asleep?

If we touch His tiny hand
  Will He awake?
Will He know we've come so far
  Just for His sake?

Great Kings have precious gifts,
  And we have naught;
Little smiles and little tears
  Are all we brought.

For all weary children
  Mary must weep.
Here, on His bed of straw,
  Sleep, children, sleep.

God, in His Mother's arms
  Babes in the byre,
Sleep, as they sleep who find
  Their heart's desire.

Frances Chesterton, 1875–1938

487. HOW FAR TO BETHLEHEM?

"How far is it to Bethlehem Town?"
"Just over Jerusalem hills adown,
Past lovely Rachel's white-domed tomb—
Sweet shrine of motherhood's young doom.

"It isn't far to Bethlehem Town—
Just over the dusty roads adown,
Past Wise Men's well, still offering
Cool draughts from welcome wayside spring;
Past shepherds with their flutes of reed
That charm the woolly sheep they lead;
Past boys with kites on hilltops flying,
And soon you're there where Bethlehem's
  lying.
Sunned white and sweet on olived slopes,
Gold-lighted still with Judah's hopes.

"And so we find the Shepherd's field
And plain that gave rich Boaz yield,
And look where Herod's villa stood.
We thrill that earthly parenthood
Could foster Christ who was all-good;
And thrill that Bethlehem Town to-day
Looks down on Christmas homes that pray.

"It isn't far to Bethlehem Town!
It's anywhere that Christ comes down
And finds in people's friendly face
A welcome and abiding place.
The road to Bethlehem runs right through
The homes of folks like me and you."

Madeleine Sweeny Miller,
contemporary American

488. TODAY IN BETHLEHEM HEAR I

Today in Bethlehem hear I
  Sweet angel voices singing:
All glory be to God on high,
  Who peace on earth is bringing.

The Virgin Mary holdeth more
  Than highest heaven most holy:
Light shines on what was dark before,
  And lifteth up the lowly.

God wills that peace shall be on earth,
  And holy exultation:
Sweet Babe, I greet Thy spotless birth
  And wondrous Incarnation.
Today in Bethlehem hear I
  Even the lowly singing:
With angel-words they pierce the sky;
  All earth with joy is ringing.

From the Greek of
John of Damascus, d. 754 A.D.

489. THE EMPTY SOUL

At the end will be but rust,
Where earthly treasures are;
They whose eyes are in the dust
Will never see a star.
They who came to Bethlehem
And only dross have sought
Will take away alone with them
The emptiness they brought.

Walter R. Bowie, 1882–

490. JUDEAN HILLS ARE HOLY

Judean hills are holy,
  Judean fields are fair,
For one can find the footprints
  Of Jesus everywhere.

One finds them in the twilight
  Beneath the singing sky,
Where shepherds watch in wonder
  White planets wheeling by.

His trails are on the hillsides
  And down the dales and deeps;
He walks the high horizons
  Where vesper silence sleeps.

He haunts the lowly highways
  Where human hopes have trod
The Via Dolorosa
  Up to the heart of God.

He looms, a lonely figure,
 Along the fringe of night,
As lonely as a cedar
 Against the lonely light.

Judean hills are holy,
 Judean fields are fair,
For one can find the footprints
 Of Jesus everywhere.

William L. Stidger, 1885–

491. CHRISTMAS PRAYER

Let not our hearts be busy inns,
 That have no room for Thee,
But cradles for the living Christ
 And His nativity.

Still driven by a thousand cares
 The pilgrims come and go;
The hurried caravans press on;
 The inns are crowded so!

Here are the rich and busy ones,
 With things that must be sold,
No room for simple things within
 This hostelry of gold.

Yet hunger dwells within these walls,
 These shining walls and bright,
And blindness groping here and there
 Without a ray of light.

Oh, lest we starve, and lest we die,
 In our stupidity,
Come, Holy Child, within and share
 Our hospitality.

Let not our hearts be busy inns,
 That have no room for Thee,
But cradles for the living Christ
 And His nativity.

Ralph Spaulding Cushman, 1879–

492. THE ROAD TO BETHLEHEM

Above the road to Bethlehem
 When I was very young,
A twilight sky of tender blue
 With golden stars was hung;

And kneeling at the stable-door,
 I happily confessed
My humble worship of the Child
 Who slept at Mary's breast.

But now the road to Bethlehem
 Seems cold and steep and far;
It wanders through a wilderness
 Unlit by any star.

The earth I tread is frozen hard;
 The winter chills my breath;
On either hand rise evil shapes
 From valleys dark with death.

The air is tense with moans of pain
 And cries of bitter hate,
Where bloodstained hills and shattered
  stones
 Lie black and desolate.

How can the sacred heart of God
 Heal all this guilt and grief?
Lord, I believe. And yet, this night,
 Help Thou mine unbelief!

Purge Thou mine eyes, that they may see
 Thy Star across the gloom!
Touch Thou my heart, that I may lose
 These agonies of doom!

Now in the darkness guide my feet,
 Give holy strength to them
To walk with childlike faith once more
 The road to Bethlehem!

Watson Kirkconnell,
contemporary Canadian

493. AFTER CHRISTMAS

The angel song still trembles
 In Bethle'em's holy air;
The little hills lie sleeping,
 The bright stars still shine fair.

Gone is the rustle of the wings
 Heard in the watch serene;
The Golden Hour of God is past,
 His glory has been seen.

But, oh, the hearts that since have
  waked,
 The souls that have found rest
Because small Bethlehem one Day
 Took heaven to its breast!

Consuelo Valencia, 1918–

494. THE GUEST

Yet if his majesty, our sovereign lord,
  Should of his own accord
  Friendly himself invite,
And say, "I'll be your guest to-morrow night,"
How should we stir ourselves, call and
    command
All hands to work! "Let no man idle stand!

"Set me fine Spanish tables in the hall,
  See they be fitted all;
  Let there be room to eat,
And order taken that there want no meat.
See every sconce and candlestick made bright,
That without tapers they may give a light.

"Look to the presence: are the carpets spread,
  The dazie o'er the head,
  The cushions in the chairs,
And all the candles lighted on the stairs?
Perfume the chambers, and in any case
Let each man give attendance in his place."

Thus if the King were coming would we do,
  And 'twere good reason too;
  For 'tis a duteous thing
To show all honour to an earthly king,
And after all our travail and our cost,
So he be pleased, to think no labour lost.

But at the coming of the King of Heaven
  All's set at six and seven:
  We wallow in our sin,
Christ can not find a chamber in the inn.
We entertain Him always like a stranger,
And, as at first, still lodge Him in the
    manger.

Author unknown, 17th century
Christ Church manuscript

495. LET US KEEP CHRISTMAS

Whatever else be lost among the years,
Let us keep Christmas still a shining thing:
Whatever doubts assail us, or what fears,
Let us hold close one day, remembering
Its poignant meaning for the hearts of men.
Let us get back our childlike faith again.

Grace Noll Crowell, 1877–

496. HYMN FOR CHRISTMAS DAY

Christians awake, salute the happy Morn,
Whereon the Saviour of the World was born;
Rise, to adore the Mystery of Love,
Which Hosts of Angels chanted from above:
With them the joyful Tidings first begun
Of God incarnate, and the Virgin's Son:
Then to the watchful Shepherds it was told,
Who heard th' Angelic Herald's Voice—Behold!
I bring good Tidings of a Saviour's Birth
To you, and all the Nations upon Earth;
This Day hath God fulfill'd his promis'd Word;
This Day is born a Saviour, Christ, the Lord:
In David's City, Shepherds, ye shall find
The long foretold Redeemer of Mankind;
Wrapt up in swaddling Cloaths, the Babe divine
Lies in a Manger; this shall be your Sign.
He spake, and straightway the Celestial Choir,
In Hymns of Joy, unknown before, conspire:
The Praises of redeeming Love they sung,
And Heav'ns whole Orb with Hallelujahs rung:
God's highest Glory was their Anthem still;
Peace upon Earth, and mutual Good-will.
To Bethlehem straight th' enlightened Shepherds ran,

To see the Wonder God had wrought for Man;
And found, with Joseph and the blessed Maid,
Her Son, the Saviour, in a Manger laid.
Amaz'd, the wond'rous Story they proclaim;
The first Apostles of his Infant Fame:
While Mary keeps, and ponders in her Heart,
The heav'nly Vision, which the Swains impart;
They to their Flocks, still praising God, return,
And their glad Hearts within their Bosoms burn.
Let us, like these good Shepherds then, employ
Our grateful Voices to proclaim the Joy:
Like Mary, let us ponder in our Mind
God's wond'rous Love in saving lost Mankind;
Artless, and watchful, as these favour'd Swains,
While Virgin Meekness in the Heart remains:
Trace we the Babe, who has retriev'd our Loss,
From his poor Manger to his bitter Cross;
Treading his Steps, assisted by his Grace,
'Till Man's first heav'nly State again takes Place:
Then may we hope, th' Angelic Thrones among,
To sing, redeem'd, a glad triumphal Song:
He that was born, upon this joyful Day,
Around us all, his Glory shall display;
Sav'd by his Love, incessant we shall sing
Of Angels, and of Angel-Men, the King.

John Byrom, 1692–1763

497. CHRISTMAS EVERYWHERE

Everywhere, everywhere, Christmas to-night!
Christmas in lands of the fir-tree and pine,
Christmas in lands of the palm-tree and vine,
Christmas where snow-peaks stand solemn and white,
Christmas where cornfields lie sunny and bright,
Everywhere, everywhere, Christmas to-night!

Christmas where children are hopeful and gay,
Christmas where old men are patient and gray,
Christmas where peace, like a dove in its flight,
Broods o'er brave men in the thick of the fight.
Everywhere, everywhere, Christmas to-night!

For the Christ-child who comes is the Master of all,
No palace too great and no cottage too small;
The angels who welcome Him sing from the height,
"In the City of David, a King in His might."
Everywhere, everywhere, Christmas to-night!

Then let every heart keep its Christmas within,
Christ's pity for sorrow, Christ's hatred for sin,
Christ's care for the weakest, Christ's courage for right,
Christ's dread of the darkness, Christ's love of the light,
Everywhere, everywhere, Christmas to-night!

So the stars of the midnight which compass us round
Shall see a strange glory, and hear a sweet sound,
And cry, "Look! the earth is aflame with delight,
O sons of the morning, rejoice at the sight."
   Everywhere, everywhere, Christmas to-night!

Phillips Brooks, 1835–1893

498. GOD REST YOU MERRY, GENTLEMEN

God rest you merry, gentlemen!
   Let nothing you dismay,
For Jesus Christ, our Saviour,
   Was born upon this day.
To save us all from Satan's power
   When we were gone astray:
      O tidings of comfort and joy,
      For Jesus Christ our Saviour
      Was born on Christmas Day.

❖

From God our heavenly Father
   A blessèd Angel came,
And unto certain shepherds
   Brought tidings of the same,
How that in Bethlehem was born
   The Son of God by name:
      O tidings of comfort and joy,
      For Jesus Christ our Saviour
      Was born on Christmas Day.

"Fear not," then said the Angel!
   "Let nothing you affright,
This day is born a Saviour,
   Of virtue, power, and might;
So frequently to vanquish all
   The fiends of Satan quite:"
      O tidings of comfort and joy,
      For Jesus Christ our Saviour
      Was born on Christmas Day.

❖

Now to the Lord sing praises,
   All you within this place,
And with true love and brotherhood
   Each other now embrace;
This holy tide of Christmas
   All others doth deface:
      O tidings of comfort and joy,
      For Jesus Christ our Saviour
      Was born on Christmas Day.

Traditional English Carol, 18th century

499. CHRISTMAS CAROL

The earth has grown old with its burden of care,
   But at Christmas it always is young,
The heart of the jewel burns lustrous and fair,
And its soul full of music bursts forth on the air,
   When the song of the angels is sung.

It is coming, Old Earth, it is coming to-night!
   On the snowflakes that cover thy sod.
The feet of the Christ-child fall gentle and white,
And the voice of the Christ-child tell out with delight
   That mankind are the Children of God.

On the sad and the lonely, the wretched and poor,
   The voice of the Christ-child shall fall;
And to every blind wanderer open the door
Of hope that he dared not to dream of before,
   With a sunshine and welcome for all.

The feet of the humblest may walk in the field
  Where the feet of the Holiest trod,
This, then, is the marvel to mortals revealed
When the silvery trumpets of Christmas have pealed,
  That mankind are the children of God.

Phillips Brooks, 1835–1893

500. CHRISTMAS MORNING

The bells ring clear as bugle note;
Sweet song is filling every throat;
  'Tis welcome Christmas morning!
O, never yet was morn so fair;
Such silent music in the air;
  'Tis Merry Christmas morning!

Dear day of all days in the year;
Dear day of song, goodwill and cheer;
  'Tis golden Christmas morning!
The hope, the faith, the love that is,
The peace, the holy promises;
  'Tis glorious Christmas morning!

Joaquin Miller, 1839–1913

501. CHRISTMAS BELLS

I heard the bells on Christmas day
Their old familiar carols play,
  And wild and sweet
  The words repeat,
Of "Peace on earth, good will to men!"

And thought how, as the day had come,
The belfries of all Christendom
  Had rolled along
  The unbroken song,
Of "Peace on earth, good will to men!"

Till ringing, singing on its way,
The world revolved from night to day,—
  A voice, a chime,
  A chant sublime,
Of "Peace on earth, good will to men!"

And in despair I bowed my head;
"There is no peace on earth," I said,
  "For hate is strong
  And mocks the song
Of peace on earth, good will to men!"

Then pealed the bells more loud and deep:
"God is not dead; nor doth he sleep!
  The wrong shall fail,
  The right prevail,
With peace on earth, good will to men!"

Henry Wadsworth Longfellow, 1807–1882

502. CHRISTMAS BELLS

From "In Memoriam," XXVIII

The time draws near the birth of Christ:
  The moon is hid, the night is still;
  The Christmas bells from hill to hill
Answer each other in the mist.

Four voices of four hamlets round,
  From far and near, on mead and moor,
  Swell out and fail, as if a door
Were shut between me and the sound;

Each voice four changes on the wind,
  That now dilate, and now decrease,
  Peace and good will, good will and peace,
Peace and good will, to all mankind.

Alfred Tennyson, 1809–1892

503. THE HALLOWED SEASON

From "Hamlet," Act I, sc. 1

Some say that ever 'gainst that season comes
Wherein our Saviour's birth is celebrated,
The bird of dawning singeth all night long:
And then, they say, no spirit dare stir abroad,
The nights are wholesome, then no planets
    strike,
No fairy takes nor witch hath power to
    charm,
So hallow'd and so gracious is the time.

William Shakespeare, 1564–1616

504. THE HOUSE OF CHRISTMAS

There fared a mother driven forth
Out of an inn to roam;
In the place where she was homeless
All men are at home.
The crazy stable close at hand,
With shaking timber and shifting sand,
Grew a stronger thing to abide and stand
Than the square stones of Rome.

For men are homesick in their homes,
And strangers under the sun,
And they lay their heads in a foreign land
Whenever the day is done.
Here we have battle and blazing eyes,
And chance and honour and high surprise,
But our homes are under miraculous skies
Where the yule tale was begun.

A Child in a foul stable,
Where the beasts feed and foam,
Only where He was homeless
Are you and I at home;
We have hands that fashion and heads that
know,
But our hearts we lost—how long ago!—
In a place no chart nor ship can show
Under the sky's dome.

This world is wild as an old wives' tale,
And strange the plain things are.
The earth is enough and the air is enough
For our wonder and our war;
But our rest is as far as the fire-drake swings
And our peace is put in impossible things
Where clashed and thundered unthinkable
wings
Round an incredible star.

To an open house in the evening
Home shall men come,
To an older place than Eden
And a taller town than Rome.
To the end of the way of the wandering star,
To the things that cannot be and that are,
To the place where God was homeless
And all men are at home.

Gilbert K. Chesterton, 1874–1936

505. ODE ON THE MORNING OF CHRIST'S NATIVITY

I

This is the month, and this the happy morn,
Wherein the Son of Heaven's eternal King,
Of wedded maid and virgin mother born,
Our great redemption from above did bring;
For so the holy sages once did sing,
That he our deadly forfeit should release,
And with his Father work us a perpetual peace.

❖

III

Say, Heavenly Muse, shall not thy sacred vein
Afford a present to the Infant God?
Hast thou no verse, no hymn, or solemn strain,
To welcome him to this his new abode,
Now while the Heaven, by the sun's team untrod,
Hath took no print of the approaching light,
And all the spangled host keep watch in squadrons bright?

IV

See how from far, upon the eastern road,
The star-led wizards haste with odours sweet:
O run, prevent them with thy humble ode,
And lay it lowly at his blessed feet!

Have thou the honour first thy Lord to greet,
  And join thy voice unto the Angel Quire,
From out his secret altar touched with hallowed fire.

THE HYMN

I

It was the winter wild,
While the Heaven-born Child
  All meanly wrapt in the rude manger lies;
Nature, in awe to him,
Had doffed her gaudy trim,
  With her great Master so to sympathize. . . .

❖

V

But peaceful was the night
Wherein the Prince of Light
  His reign of peace upon the earth began;
The winds, with wonder whist,
Smoothly the waters kist,
  Whispering new joys to the mild ocean,
Who now hath quite forgot to rave,
While birds of calm sit brooding on the charmèd wave.

VI

The stars, with deep amaze,
Stand fixed in steadfast gaze,
  Bending one way their precious influence,
And will not take their flight,
For all the morning light,
  Or Lucifer that often warned them thence;
But in their glimmering orbs did glow,
Until their Lord himself bespake, and bid them go.

VII

And though the shady gloom
Had given day her room,
  The sun himself withheld his wonted speed,
And hid his head for shame,
As his inferior flame
  The new-enlightened world no more should need:
He saw a greater Sun appear
Than his bright throne or burning axletree could bear.

VIII

The shepherds on the lawn,
Or ere the point of dawn,
  Sat simply chatting in a rustic row;
Full little thought they than
That the mighty Pan
  Was kindly come to live with them below;
Perhaps their loves, or else their sheep,
Was all that did their silly thoughts so busy keep.

IX

When such music sweet
Their hearts and ears did greet,
  As never was by mortal finger strook,
Divinely-warbled voice
Answering the stringèd noise,
  As all their souls in blissful rapture took:
The air, such pleasure loath to lose,
With thousand echoes still prolongs each heavenly close.

❖

XIV

For if such holy song
Enwrap our fancy long,
  Time will run back and fetch the age of gold;
And speckled Vanity
Will sicken soon and die,
  And leprous Sin will melt from earthly mould;
And Hell itself will pass away,
And leave her dolorous mansions to the peering day.

XV

Yea, Truth and Justice then
Will down return to men,
  Orbed in a rainbow; and, like glories wearing,
Mercy will sit between,
Throned in celestial sheen,
  With radiant feet the tissued clouds down steering;
And Heaven, as at some festival,
Will open wide the gates of her high palace-hall.

❖

XXVII

But see! the Virgin blest
Hath laid her Babe to rest;
  Time is our tedious song should here have ending:
Heaven's youngest-teemèd star
Hath fixed her polished car,
  Her sleeping Lord with handmaid lamp attending;
And all about the courtly stable
Bright-harnessed angels sit in order serviceable.

John Milton, 1608–1674

506. CHRISTMAS IN THE HEART

It is Christmas in the mansion,
  Yule-log fires and silken frocks;
It is Christmas in the cottage,
  Mother's filling little socks.

It is Christmas on the highway,
  In the thronging, busy mart;
But the dearest truest Christmas
  Is the Christmas in the heart.

Author unknown

507. DECEMBER TWENTY-FOURTH

Tomorrow You are born again
 Who died so many times.
Do You like the candle-light,
 Do You like the chimes?

Do You stop to wonder
 Why men never see
How very closely Bethlehem
 Approaches Calvary?

Eleanor Slater, 1903—

508. A CHRISTMAS SONG

Oh, Christmas is a jolly time
 When forests hang with snow,
And other forests bend with toys,
 And lordly Yule logs glow.

And Christmas is a solemn time
 Because, beneath the star,
The first great Christmas Gift was given
 To all men, near and far.

But not alone at Christmas time
 Comes holiday and cheer,
For one who loves a little child
 Hath Christmas all the year.

Florence Evelyn Dratt,
contemporary American

509. ETERNAL CHRISTMAS

In the pure soul, although it sing or pray,
The Christ is born anew from day to day;
The life that knoweth Him shall bide apart
And keep eternal Christmas in the heart.

Elizabeth Stuart Phelps, 1844–1911

510. HORA CHRISTI

Sweet is the time for joyous folk
 Of gifts and minstrelsy;
Yet I, O lowly-hearted One,
 Crave but Thy company.
On lonesome road, beset with dread,
 My questing lies afar.
I have no light, save in the east
 The gleaming of Thy Star.

In cloistered aisles they keep today
 Thy feast, O living Lord!
With pomp of banner, pride of song,
 And stately sounding word.
Mute stand the kings of power and place,
 While priests of holy mind
Dispense Thy blessed heritage
 Of peace to all mankind.

I know a spot where budless twigs
 Are bare above the snow,
And where sweet winter-loving birds
 Flit softly to and fro;
There, with the sun for altar-fire,
 The earth for kneeling-place,
The gentle air for chorister,
 Will I adore Thy face.

Loud, underneath the great blue sky,
 My heart shall paean sing,
The gold and myrrh of meekest love
 Mine only offering.
Bliss of Thy birth shall quicken me;
 And for Thy pain and dole
Tears are but vain: so I will keep
 The silence of the soul.

Alice Brown, 1857–

511. PRAYER ON CHRISTMAS EVE

O Wondrous night of star and song,
 O blessed Christmas night!
Lord, make me feel my whole life long
 Its loveliness and light!
So all the years my heart shall thrill
Remembering angels on a hill,
And one lone star shall bless me still
 On every Christmas night!

Nancy Byrd Turner, 1880–

512. A CHRISTMAS PRAYER

We open here our treasures and our gifts;
And some of it is gold,
And some is frankincense,
And some is myrrh;
For some has come from plenty,
Some from joy,
And some from deepest sorrow of the soul.
But Thou, O God, dost know the gift is love,
Our pledge of peace, our promise of good-will.
Accept the gift and all the life we bring.

Herbert H. Hines,
contemporary American

513. ADVENT

From "St. Paul"

Lo! as some venturer, from his stars receiving
Promise and presage of sublime emprise,
Wears evermore the seal of his believing
Deep in the dark of solitary eyes,

So even I, and with a pang more thrilling,
So even I, and with a hope more sweet,
Yearn for the sign, O Christ, of Thy fulfilling,
Faint for the flaming of Thine advent feet.

F. W. H. Myers, 1843–1901

514. THE SILENT STARS GO BY

O Little Child of Bethlehem,
Why do your young eyes grieve?
What do your outstretched arms implore
Of us this Christmas Eve?

"Look! In the dark streets shineth
No Everlasting Light,
Hearts, crucified by daily fears,
Watch through the silent night.

"Their arms hold tight to little ones,
Tear-blinded eyes turn East,
Too tired to ask for more than crumbs,
Dropped from My Christmas Feast."

O Little Child of Bethlehem,
Descend to us, we pray,
And show our hearts how best to share
With these, on Christmas Day.

Harriet Hartridge Tompkins,
contemporary American

515. CHRISTIAN PARADOX

It is in loving—not in being loved,—
The heart is blest;
It is in giving—not in seeking gifts,—
We find our quest.

If thou art hungry, lacking heavenly food,—
Give hope and cheer.
If thou art sad and wouldst be comforted,—
Stay sorrow's tear.

Whatever be thy longing and thy need,—
That do thou give;
So shall thy soul be fed, and thou indeed,
Shalt truly live.

Author unknown

516. A CHRISTMAS SONNET

(For One in Doubt)

While you that in your sorrow disavow
Service and hope, see love and brotherhood
Far off as ever, it will do no good
For you to wear his thorns upon your brow
For doubt of him. And should you question how
To serve him best, he might say, if he could,
"Whether or not the cross was made of wood
Whereon you nailed me, is no matter now."

Though other saviors have in older lore
A Legend, and for older gods have died—
Though death may wear the crown it always wore
And ignorance be still the sword of pride—
Something is here that was not here before,
And strangely has not yet been crucified.

Edwin Arlington Robinson, 1869–1935

517. CHRISTMAS TODAY

How can they honor Him—the humble lad
Whose feet struck paths of beauty through the earth—
With all the drunken revelry, the mad
Barter of goods that marks His day of birth?
How can they honor Him with flame and din,
Whose soul was peaceful as a moon-swept sea,
Whose thoughts were somber with the world's great sin
Even while He trod the hill to Calvary?

I think if Jesus should return and see
This hollow blasphemy, this day of horror,
The heart that languished in Gethsemane
Would know again as great and deep a sorrow,
And He who charmed the troubled waves to sleep
With deathless words—would kneel again and weep.

Anderson M. Scruggs, 1897—

518. SONNET FOR CHRISTMAS

These are the things our Christmas Day should leave
Untarnished and untouched by dust and blight:
The warm, sweet kindliness of Christmas Eve,
Its heavenly glow of rapture and delight;
The breathless wonder that the stars awake;
The new-found faith that where a child is born
There is a little life for God's own sake,
Though lowly be its lot on Christmas morn;
The wide good-will we feel for all mankind
And that true peace that heals the aching mind.
And though the hurrying years be loud with strife,
A radiance lives that all men yet shall see,
A golden glory, rich with fullest life,
When each shall know his own divinity.

Vincent G. Burns, 1893-

519. CHRISTMAS AT BABBITT'S

On Christmas eve they filled the house, some fifty guests all told,
(O little Lord of Christmas, were you left out in the cold?)

And ate and sang, played cards and danced till early morning light.
(O little Lord of Christmas, did they think of you that night?)

Next morning came the presents on a glittering Christmas tree.
(O little Lord of Christmas, was there any gift for thee?)

The dinner was a Roman feast, and how those guests did eat!
(O little Lord of Christmas, were you hungry in the street?)

Then came some teas, a movie, and at night the last revue.
(O little Lord of Christmas, what had these to do with you?)

By midnight all were tired and cross and tumbled into bed.
(O little Lord of Christmas, did they think that you were dead?)

They all woke up with headaches and no joy in work or play.
(O little Lord of Christmas, did they mark your birth that day?)

The love, the joy were good, no doubt; the rest a pagan spree.
(O little Lord of Christmas, let us keep the day with Thee!)

Henry Hallam Tweedy, 1868–

520. TO JESUS ON HIS BIRTHDAY

For this your mother sweated in the cold,
For this you bled upon the bitter tree:
A yard of tinsel ribbon bought and sold;
A paper wreath; a day at home for me.
The merry bells ring out, the people kneel;
Up goes the man of God before the crowd;
With voice of honey and with eyes of steel
He drones your humble gospel to the proud.
Nobody listens. Less than the wind that blows
Are all your words to us you died to save.
O Prince of Peace! O Sharon's dewy Rose!
How mute you lie within your vaulted grave.
The stone the angel rolled away with tears
Is back upon your mouth these thousand years.

Edna St. Vincent Millay, 1892–

521. DAVID, AGED FOUR[1]

Christmas is a bitter day
For mothers who are poor,
The wistful eyes of children
Are daggers to endure.

Though shops are crammed with playthings
Enough for everyone,
If a mother's purse is empty
There might as well be none.

My purse is full of money
But I cannot buy a toy;
Only a wreath of holly
For the grave of my little boy.

Author unknown

522. THE LITTLE ONES

The little ones are put in bed,
And both are laughing, lying down;
Their father, and their mother too,
Are gone on Christmas eve to town.

"Old Santa Claus will bring a horse,
Gee up!" cried little Will, with glee;
"If I am good, I'll have a doll
From Santa Claus"—laughed Emily.

The little ones are gone to sleep,
Their father and their mother now
Are coming home, with many more—
They're drunk, and make a merry row.

The little ones on Christmas morn
Jump up, like skylarks from the grass;
And then they stand as still as stones,
And just as cold as stones, alas!

No horse, no doll beside their bed,
No sadder little ones could be;
"We did some wrong," said little Will—
"We must have sinned," sobbed Emily.

William H. Davies, 1871–1940

523. THE BURNING BABE

As I in hoary winter's night
Stood shivering in the snow,
Surprised I was with sudden heat
Which made my heart to glow;
And lifting up a fearful eye
To view what fire was near,

[1] Clipped from a column in the New York *Herald Tribune* by Alexander Woollcott, as a favorite, and quoted by Theodore Roosevelt II in his introduction to *The Desk Drawer Anthology*.

A pretty babe all burning bright
  Did in the air appear;
Who, scorchèd with excessive heat
  Such floods of tears did shed,
As though His floods should quench His
    flames,
  Which with His tears were bred:
"Alas!" quoth He, "but newly born
  In fiery heats I fry,
Yet none approach to warm their hearts
  Or feel My fire but I!

"My faultless breast the furnace is;
  The fuel, wounding thorns;
Love is the fire, and sighs the smoke;
  The ashes, shames and scorns;
The fuel Justice layeth on,
  And Mercy blows the coals,
The metal in this furnace wrought
  Are men's defilèd souls:
For which, as now on fire I am
  To work them to their good,
So will I melt into a bath,
  To wash them in My blood."
With this He vanished out of sight
  And swiftly shrunk away,
And straight I callèd unto mind
  That it was Christmas Day.

Robert Southwell, 1561?–1595

524. RECONCILIATION

Ye who have scorned each other,
Or injured friend or brother,
  In the fast fading year;
Ye who by word or deed,
Have made a kind heart bleed,
  Come gather here;
Let sinned against and sinning
Forget their strife's beginning,
  And join in friendship now—
Be links no longer broken;
Be sweet forgiveness spoken
  Under the Holly Bough.

Ye who have loved each other,
Sister and friend and brother,
  In this fast fading year;
Mother and sire and child,
Young man and maiden mild,
  Come gather here;
And let your hearts grow fonder,
As memory shall ponder
  Each past unbroken vow;
Old loves and younger wooing
Are sweet in the renewing,
  Under the Holly Bough.

Charles Mackay, 1814–1889

525. TWO INSCRIPTIONS FOR THE CHRISTMAS CANDLE

I

Come, Heavenly Child, and on this place
Shed the sweet halo of Thy grace.
O burning Love, O Heavenly Fire
Consume me with Thy deep desire.

II

As in the Holy Christ Child's name
This blessed wax shall feed the flame—
So let my heart its fires begin
And light the Heavenly Pilgrim in.

Anna Hempstead Branch, 1875?–1937

526. THE ROMANCE OF A CHRISTMAS CARD

The door is on the latch to-night,
  The hearth-fire is aglow,
I seem to hear soft passing feet—
  The Christ child in the snow.

My heart is open wide to-night
  For stranger, kith or kin.
I would not bar a single door
  Where Love might enter in.

Kate Douglas Wiggin, 1856–1923

527. LITTLE JESUS

Ex ore infantium Deus et lactentium perfecisti laudem.

Little Jesus, wast Thou shy
Once, and just as small as I?
And what did it feel like to be
Out of Heaven, and just like me?
Didst Thou sometimes think of *there*,
And ask where all the angels were?

I should think that I would cry
For my house all made of sky;
I would look about the air,
And wonder where my angels were;
And at waking 'twould distress me—
Not an angel there to dress me!

Hadst Thou ever any toys,
Like us little girls and boys?
And didst Thou play in Heaven with all
The angels that were not too tall,
With stars for marbles? Did the things
Play *Can you see me?* through their wings?

And did Thy mother let Thee spoil
Thy robes with playing on *our* soil?
How nice to have them always new
In Heaven, because 'twas quite clean blue!

Didst Thou kneel at night to pray,
And didst Thou join Thy hands, this way?
And did they tire sometimes, being young,
And make the prayer seem very long?
And dost Thou like it best that we
Should join our hands to pray to Thee?
I used to think, before I knew,
The prayer not said unless we do.
And did Thy mother at the night
Kiss Thee and fold the clothes in right?
And didst Thou feel quite good in bed,
Kiss'd, and sweet, and Thy prayers said?

Thou canst not have forgotten all
That it feels like to be small:
And Thou know'st I cannot pray
To Thee in my father's way—
When Thou wast so little, say,
Couldst Thou talk Thy Father's way?

So, a little Child, come down
And hear a child's tongue like Thy own;
Take me by the hand and walk,
And listen to my baby-talk.
To Thy Father show my prayer
(He will look, Thou art so fair),
And say: "O Father, I, Thy Son,
Bring the prayer of a little one."

And He will smile, that children's tongue
Has not changed since Thou wast young!

Francis Thompson, 1859–1907

528. THE LITTLE CHILD

A simple-hearted Child was He,
  And He was nothing more;
In summer days, like you and me,
  He played about the door,
Or gathered, when the father toiled,
  The shavings from the floor.

Sometimes He lay upon the grass,
  The same as you and I,
And saw the hawks above Him pass,
  Like specks against the sky;
Or, clinging to the gate, He watched
  The stranger passing by.

A simple Child, and yet, I think,
  The bird-folk must have known,
The sparrow and the bobolink,
  And claimed Him for their own,
And gathered round Him fearlessly
  When He was all alone.

The lark, the linnet, and the dove,
  The chaffinch and the wren,
They must have known His watchful love,
  And given their worship then;
They must have known and glorified
  The Child who died for men.

And when the sun at break of day
  Crept in upon His hair,
I think it must have left a ray
  Of unseen glory there—
A kiss of love on that little brow
  For the thorns that it must wear.

Albert Bigelow Paine, 1861–1937

529. A BOY WAS BORN AT BETHLEHEM

A Boy was born at Bethlehem
  that knew the haunts of Galilee.
He wandered on Mount Lebanon,
  and learned to love each forest tree.

But I was born at Marlborough,
  and love the homely faces there;
And for all other men besides
  'tis little love I have to spare.

I should not mind to die for them,
  my own dear *downs*, my comrades true;

But that great heart at Bethlehem,
He died for men He never knew.

And yet, I think, at Golgotha,
as Jesus' eyes were closed in death,
They saw with love most passionate
the village street at Nazareth.

Edward Hilton Young, 1879–

530. BY COOL SILOAM'S SHADY RILL

By cool Siloam's shady rill
How sweet the lily grows!
How sweet the breath beneath the hill
Of Sharon's dewy rose!

Lo, such the child whose early feet
The paths of peace have trod;
Whose secret heart, with influence sweet,
Is upward drawn to God.

By cool Siloam's shady rill
The lily must decay;
The rose that blooms beneath the hill
Must shortly fade away.

And soon, too soon, the wintry hour
Of man's maturer age
Will shake the soul with sorrow's power,
And stormy passion's rage.

O Thou, Whose infant feet were found
Within Thy Father's shrine!
Whose years, with changeless virtue crown'd,
Were all alike Divine;

Dependent on Thy bounteous breath,
We seek Thy grace alone,
In childhood, manhood, age, and death,
To keep us still Thine own!

Reginald Heber, 1783–1826

531. A LEGEND

Christ, when a Child, a garden made,
And many roses flourished there.
He watered them three times a day
To make a garland for His hair.
And when in time the roses bloomed,
He called the children in to share.
They tore the flowers from every stem,
And left the garden stript and bare.
"How wilt Thou weave Thyself a crown
Now that Thy roses are all dead?"
"Ye have forgotten that the thorns
Are left for Me," the Christ-child said.
They plaited then a crown of thorns
And laid it rudely on His head;
A garland for His forehead made;
For roses: drops of blood instead!

Tr. by Nathan Haskell Dole, 1852–1935

532. THE NATIVITY

From "To the Child Jesus"

Could every time-worn heart but see Thee once again,
A happy human child, among the homes of men,
The age of doubt would pass,—the vision of Thy face
Would silently restore the childhood of the race.

Henry van Dyke, 1852–1933

533. JOSES, THE BROTHER OF JESUS

Joses, the brother of Jesus, plodded from day to day
With never a vision within him to glorify his clay;
Joses, the brother of Jesus, was one with the heavy clod,
But Christ was the soul of rapture, and soared, like a lark, with God.
Joses, the brother of Jesus, was only a worker in wood,
And he never could see the glory that Jesus, his brother, could.
"Why stays he not in the workshop?" he often used to complain,

"Sawing the Lebanon cedar, imparting to woods their stain?
Why must he go thus roaming, forsaking my father's trade,
While hammers are busily sounding, and there is gain to be made?"

Thus ran the mind of Joses, apt with plummet and rule,
And deeming whoever surpassed him either a knave or a fool,—
For he never walked with the prophets in God's great garden of bliss—
And of all mistakes of the ages, the saddest, methinks, was this
To have such a brother as Jesus, to speak with him day by day,
But never to catch the vision which glorified his clay.

Harry Kemp, 1883–

534. O MASTER WORKMAN OF THE RACE

O Master workman of the race,
  Thou man of Galilee,
Who with the eyes of early youth
  Eternal things did see;
We thank Thee for Thy boyhood faith
  That shone Thy whole life through;
"Did ye not know it is My work
  My Father's work to do?"

O Carpenter of Nazareth,
  Builder of life divine,
Who shapest man to God's own law,
  Thyself the fair design,
Build us a tower of Christ-like height,
  That we the land may view,
And see like Thee our noblest work
  Our Father's work to do.

O Thou who dost the vision send
  And gives to each his task,
And with the task sufficient strength,
  Show us Thy will, we ask;
Give us a conscience bold and good,
  Give us a purpose true,
That it may be our highest joy,
  Our Father's work to do.

Jay T. Stocking, 1870–1936

535. MY YOKE IS EASY

The yokes He made were true.
Because the Man who dreamed
Was too
An artisan,
The burdens that the oxen drew
Were light.
At night
He lay upon his bed and knew
No beast of his stood chafing in a stall
Made restless by a needless gall.

The tenets of a man
May be full fine
But if he fails with plumb and line,
Scorns care,
Smooth planing,
And precision with the square,
Some neck will bear
The scar of blundering!

Gladys Latchaw

536. JESUS THE CARPENTER

If I could hold within my hand
  The hammer Jesus swung,
Not all the gold in all the land,
Nor jewels countless as the sand,
  All in the balance flung,
Could weigh the value of that thing
Round which his fingers once did cling.

If I could have the table Christ
  Once made in Nazareth,
Not all the pearls in all the sea,
Nor crowns of kings or kings to be
  As long as men have breath,
Could buy that thing of wood he made—
The Lord of Lords who learned a trade.

Yea, but his hammer still is shown
  By honest hands that toil,
And round his table men sit down;

And all are equals, with a crown
  Nor gold nor pearls can soil;
The shop of Nazareth was bare—
But brotherhood was builded there.

Charles M. Sheldon, 1857–1946

537. THE CARPENTER OF GALILEE

The Carpenter of Galilee
Comes down the street again,
In every land, in every age,
He still is building men.
On Christmas Eve we hear Him knock;
He goes from door to door:
"Are any workmen out of work?
The Carpenter needs more."

Hilda W. Smith, 1888–

538. WORK

Work! That makes the red blood glow,
Work! That makes the quick brain grow.
  Plough and hammer, hoe and flails,
  Axe and crowbar, saw and nails—
    A splitter of rails,
Lincoln was never a snob or a shirk,
Thank God for work!

Toil that binds mankind together,
Day by day in every weather.
  Pen and distaff, needle and thread,
  Visions of wonder over her head,
    A toiler for bread,
Joan of Arc was a peasant child
On whom God smiled.

Labor that God Himself has blest,
Honest endeavor that earns good rest.
  Bench and hammer, nails and cord,
  Hammer and chisel, plane and board—
    Christ our Lord
Had a carpenter's horny hands,
He understands.

Abbie Farwell Brown, 1872–1927

539. THE MASTER'S MAN

My Master was a worker,
  With daily work to do,
And he who would be like Him,
  Must be a worker too.
Then welcome honest labor,
  And honest labor's fare,
For where there is a worker
  The Master's man is there.

My Master was a comrade,
  A trusty friend and true,
And he who would be like Him,
  Must be a comrade too;
In happy hours of singing,
  In silent hours of care,
Where goes a loyal comrade,
  The Master's man is there.

My Master was a helper,
  The woes of life He knew,
And he who would be like Him
  Must be a helper too;
The burden will grow lighter,
  If each will take a share,
And where there is a helper
  The Master's man is there.

Then, brothers, brave and manly
  Together let us be,
For He, who is our Master,
  The Man of men was He;
The men who would be like Him
  Are wanted everywhere,
And where they love each other
  The Master's men are there.

William G. Tarrant, 1853–1928

540. JESUS, THOU DIVINE COMPANION

Jesus, Thou divine Companion,
  By Thy lowly human birth
Thou hast come to join the workers,
  Burden-bearers of the earth.
Thou, the Carpenter of Nazareth,
  Toiling for Thy daily food,
By Thy patience and Thy courage
  Thou hast taught us toil is good.

They who tread the path of labor,
  Follow where Thy feet have trod:
They who work without complaining
  Do the holy will of God.
Thou, the Peace that passeth knowledge,
  Dwellest in the daily strife;
Thou, the Bread of Heaven, art broken
  In the sacrament of life.

Every task, however simple,
  Sets the soul that does it free;

Every deed of love and kindness,
  Done to man is done to Thee.
Jesus, Thou divine Companion,
  Help us all to work our best;
Bless us in our daily labor,
  Lead us to our Sabbath rest.

Henry van Dyke, 1852–1933

541. GOOD TIDINGS

Luke 4: 18–19

The Spirit of the Lord is upon me,
  because he hath anointed me to preach the gospel to the poor;
he hath sent me to heal the brokenhearted,
  to preach deliverance to the captives,
and recovering of sight to the blind,
  to set at liberty them that are bruised,
To preach the acceptable year of the Lord.

King James Version, 1611

542. THE TEACHER

He sent men out to preach the living Word,
  Aflame with all the ardor of His fire;
They spoke the Truth, wherever truth was heard
  But back to Him they brought their hearts'-desire;
They turned to Him through all the lengthening days
  With each perplexity of life or creed.
His deep reward, not that they spoke His praise,
  But that they brought to Him their human need.

Hildegarde Hoyt Swift, contemporary American

543. PROGRESS

The Master stood upon the Mount, and taught.
He saw a fire in His disciple's eyes.
"The old Law," they said, "is wholly come to nought;
  Behold the new world rise!"

"Was it," the Lord then said, "with scorn ye saw
The old Law observed by Scribes and Pharisees?
I say unto you, see *ye* keep that Law
  More faithfully than these.

"Too hasty heads for ordering worlds, alas!
Think not that I to annul the Law have will'd.
No jot, no tittle, from the Law shall pass,
  Till all shall be fulfill'd."

So Christ said eighteen hundred years ago.
And what then shall be said to those to-day
Who cry aloud to lay the world low
  To clear the new world's way?

Matthew Arnold, 1822–1888

544. THE GREAT PHYSICIAN

From Thee all skill and science flow,
All pity, care, and love,
All calm and courage, faith and hope;
O pour them from above.

And part them, Lord, to each and all,
As each and all shall need,
To rise like incense, each to Thee,
In noble thought and deed.

And hasten, Lord, that perfect day
When pain and death shall cease,
And Thy just rule shall fill the earth
With health and light and peace.

Charles Kingsley, 1819–1875

545. AT EVEN, WHEN THE SUN WAS SET

At even, when the sun was set,
The sick, O Lord, around Thee lay;
O in what divers pains they met!
O with what joy they went away!

Once more 'tis eventide, and we,
Oppressed with various ills, draw near;
What if Thy form we cannot see,
We know and feel that Thou art here.

O Saviour Christ, our woes dispel;
For some are sick, and some are sad,
And some have never loved Thee well,
And some have lost the love they had;

And some are pressed with worldly care,
And some are tried with sinful doubt;
And some such grievous passions tear,
That only Thou canst cast them out;

And some have found the world is vain,
Yet from the world they break not free;
And some have friends who give them pain,
Yet have not sought a Friend in Thee;

And none, O Lord, have perfect rest,
For none are wholly free from sin;
And they who fain would serve Thee best
Are conscious most of wrong within.

O Saviour Christ, Thou too art Man;
Thou hast been troubled, tempted, tried;
Thy kind but searching glance can scan
The very wounds that shame would hide;

Thy touch has still its ancient power;
No word from Thee can fruitless fall;
Hear, in this solemn evening hour,
And in Thy mercy heal us all.

Henry Twells, 1823–1900

546. THE TEN LEPERS

Not white and shining like an ardent flame,
Not like thy mother and the saints in bliss,
But white from head to foot I bear my blame,
White as the leper is.

Unclean! unclean! But thou canst make me clean:
Yet if thou clean'st me, Lord, see that I be
Like that one grateful leper of the ten
Who ran back praising thee.

But if I must forget, take back thy word;
Be I unclean again but not ingrate.
Before I shall forget thee, keep me, Lord,
A sick man at thy gate.

Katharine Tynan Hinkson, 1861–1931

547. RELIGION AND DOCTRINE

He stood before the Sanhedrim;
The scowling rabbis gazed at him;
He recked not of their praise or blame;
There was no fear, there was no shame
For one upon whose dazzled eyes
The whole world poured its vast surprise.
The open heaven was far too near,
His first day's light too sweet and clear,
To let him waste his new-gained ken
On the hate-clouded face of men.

But still they questioned, Who art thou?
What hast thou been? What art thou now?
Thou art not he who yesterday
Sat here and begged beside the way,
For he was blind.

And I am he;
For I was blind, but now I see.

He told the story o'er and o'er;
It was his full heart's only lore;
A prophet on the Sabbath day
Had touched his sightless eyes with clay,
And made him see, who had been blind.

Their words passed by him on the wind
Which raves and howls, but cannot shock
The hundred-fathom-rooted rock.

Their threats and fury all went wide;
They could not touch his Hebrew pride;
Their sneers at Jesus and his band,
Nameless and homeless in the land,
Their boasts of Moses and his Lord,
All could not change him by one word.

I know not what this man may be,
Sinner or saint; but as for me,
One thing I know, that I am he
Who once was blind, and now I see.

They were all doctors of renown,
The great men of a famous town,
With deep brows, wrinkled, broad and wise,
Beneath their wide phylacteries;
The wisdom of the East was theirs,
And honor crowned their silver hairs;
The man they jeered and laughed to scorn
Was unlearned, poor, and humbly born;

But he knew better far than they
What came to him that Sabbath day;
And what the Christ had done for him,
He knew, and not the Sanhedrim.

John Hay, 1838–1905

548. THE HANDS OF CHRIST

A Baby's hands in Bethlehem
Were small and softly curled,
But held within their dimpled grasp
The hope of half the world.

A Carpenter's in Nazareth
Were skilled with tool and wood;
They laid the beams of simple homes
And found their labor good.

A Healer's hands in Galilee
Were stretched to all who came
For Him to cleanse their hidden wounds
Or cure the blind and lame.

Long, long ago the hands of Christ
Were nailed upon a tree,
But still their holy touch redeems
The hearts of you and me.

Leslie Savage Clark, contemporary American

549. THE BOAT

(Simon Peter's Testimony)

I owned a little boat a while ago,
And sailed the morning sea without a fear,
And whither any breeze might fairly blow
I steered my little craft afar or near.
Mine was the boat
And mine the air,
And mine the sea,
Nor mine a care.

My boat became my place of mighty toil,
I sailed at evening to the fishing ground,
At morn my boat was freighted with the spoil
Which my all-conquering work had found.
Mine was the boat
And mine the net,
And mine the skill
And power to get.

One day there came along that silent shore,
While I my net was casting in the sea,
A Man who spoke as never man before.
I followed Him; new life began in me.
Mine was the boat,
But His the voice,
And His the call,
Yet mine the choice.

Ah! 'twas a fearful night out on the lake,
And all my skill availed not, at the helm,
Till Him asleep I waked, crying, "Take
Thou the helm—lest water overwhelm!"
And His the boat,
And His the sea,
And His the peace
O'er all and me.

Once from the boat He taught the curious throng
Then bade me cast my net into the sea;
I murmured but obeyed, nor was it long
Before the catch amazed and humbled me.
His was the boat,
And His the skill.
And His the catch,
And His my will.

George Macdonald, 1824–1905

550. THE LOOK

The Saviour looked on Peter. Ay, no word,
No gesture of reproach; the Heavens serene
Though heavy with armed justice, did not lean
Their thunders that way: the forsaken Lord
Looked only, on the traitor. None record
What that look was, none guess; for those who have seen
Wronged lovers loving through a death-pang keen,
Or pale-cheeked martyrs smiling to a sword,
Have missed Jehovah at the judgment-call.
And Peter, from the height of blasphemy—
"I never knew this man"—did quail and fall
As knowing straight THAT GOD; and turnèd free
And went out speechless from the face of all,
And filled the silence, weeping bitterly.

Elizabeth Barrett Browning, 1806–1861

551. THE MEANING OF THE LOOK

I THINK that look of Christ might seem to say—
"Thou Peter! art thou then a common stone
Which I at last must break my heart upon,
For all God's charge to his high angels may
Guard my foot better? Did I yesterday
Wash *thy* feet, my beloved, that they should run
Quick to deny me 'neath the morning sun?
And do thy kisses, like the rest, betray?
The cock crows coldly.—Go, and manifest
A late contrition, but no bootless fear!
For when thy final need is dreariest,
Thou shalt not be denied, as I am here;
My voice to God and angels shall attest,
Because I KNOW *this man, let him be clear*."

Elizabeth Barrett Browning, 1806–1861

552. THE TWO SAYINGS

Two sayings of the Holy Scriptures beat
Like pulses in the Church's brow and breast;
And by them we find rest in our unrest
And, heart deep in salt-tears, do yet entreat
God's fellowship as if on heavenly seat.
The first is JESUS WEPT,—whereon is prest
Full many a sobbing face that drops its best
And sweetest waters on the record sweet:
And one is where the Christ, denied and scorned,
LOOKED UPON PETER. Oh, to render plain,
By help of having loved a little and mourned,
That look of sovran love and sovran pain
Which HE, who could not sin yet suffered, turned
On him who could reject but not sustain!

Elizabeth Barrett Browning, 1806–1861

553. PRAYER OF A MODERN THOMAS

If Thou, O God, the Christ didst leave,
In Him, not Thee, I do believe;
  To Jesus dying, all alone,
  To His dark Cross not Thy bright Throne,
My hopeless hands will cleave.

But if it was Thy love that died,
Thy voice that in the darkness cried,
  The print of nails I long to see,
  In Thy hands, God, who fashioned me,
Show me *Thy* piercèd side.

Edward Shillito, 1872–1948

554. JUDGE ME, O LORD

If I had been in Palestine
A poor disciple I had been.
I had not risked or purse or limb
All to forsake, and follow Him.

But with the vast and wondering throng
I too had stood and listened long;
I too had felt my spirit stirred
When the Beatitudes I heard.

With the glad crowd that sang the psalm,
I too had sung, and strewed the palm;
Then slunk away in dastard shame
When the High Priest denounced His name.

But when my late companions cried
"Away! Let him be crucified!"
I would have begged, with tremulous
Pale lips, "Release Him unto us!"

Beside the cross when Mary prayed
A great way off I too had stayed;
Not even in that hour had dared,
And for my dying Lord declared,

But beat upon my craven breast,
And loathed my coward heart, at least,
To think my life I dared not stake
And beard the Romans for His sake.

Sarah N. Cleghorn, 1876–1928

555. MAGDALEN

Magdalen at Michael's gate
Tirlèd at the pin;
On Joseph's thorn sang the blackbird,
"Let her in! Let her in!"

"Hast thou seen the wounds?" said Michael:
"Know'st thou thy sin?"
"It is evening, evening," sang the blackbird,
"Let her in! Let her in!"

"Yes, I have seen the wounds,
And I know my sin."
"She knows it well, well, well," sang the
  blackbird,
"Let her in! Let her in!"

"Thou bringest no offerings?" said Michael.
"Nought save sin."
And the blackbird sang, "She is sorry, sorry,
  sorry!
"Let her in! Let her in!"

When he had sung himself to sleep,
And night did begin,
One came and open'd Michael's gate,
And Magdalen went in.

Henry Kingsley, 1830–1876

556. DOST THOU REMEMBER ME?

Saviour, I've no one else to tell
And so I trouble Thee,
I am the one forgot Thee so.
Dost Thou remember me?

Not for myself I came so far,
That were the little load—
I brought Thee the imperial heart
I had not strength to hold.

The heart I carried in my own,
Till mine too heavy be,
Yet strangest—heavier
Since it went—
Is it too large for Thee?

Emily Dickinson, 1830–1886

557. SELF-RIGHTEOUSNESS

"He is a sinner," you are pleased to say.
Then love him for the sake of Christ, I pray.
If on His gracious words you place your
  trust,—
"I came to call the sinners, not the just,"—
Second His call; which if you will not do,
You'll be the greater sinner of the two.

John Byrom, 1692–1763

558. A HYMN TO GOD THE FATHER

Wilt Thou forgive that sin where I begun,
Which is my sin, though it were done before?
Wilt Thou forgive that sin, through which I run,
And do run still: though still I do deplore?
When Thou hast done, Thou hast not done,
For, I have more.

Wilt Thou forgive that sin by which I have won
Others to sin? and made my sin their door?
Wilt Thou forgive that sin which I did shun
A year, or two: But wallowed in, a score?
When Thou hast done, Thou hast not done,
For, I have more.

I have a sin of fear, that when I have spun
My last thread, I shall perish on the shore;
Swear by Thyself, that at my death Thy Son
Shall shine as He shines now, and heretofore;
And, having done that, Thou hast done,
I fear no more.

John Donne, 1573–1631

559. From THE BALLAD OF READING GAOL

I know not whether Laws be right,
Or whether Laws be wrong;
All that we know who lie in gaol
Is that the wall is strong;
And that each day is like a year,
A year whose days are long.

But this I know, that every Law
That men have made for Man,
Since first Man took his brother's life,
And the sad world began,
But straws the wheat and saves the chaff
With a most evil fan.

This too I know—and wise it were
If each could know the same—
That every prison that men build
Is built with bricks of shame,
And bound with bars lest Christ should see
How men their brothers maim.

With bars they blur the gracious moon,
And blind the goodly sun;
And they do well to hide their Hell,
For in it things are done
That Son of God nor Son of Man
Ever should look upon!

❖

The vilest deeds like poison weeds
Bloom well in prison-air:
It is only what is good in Man
That wastes and withers there:
Pale Anguish keeps the heavy gate,
And the Warder is Despair.

❖

And every human heart that breaks,
In prison-cell or yard,
Is as that broken box that gave
Its treasure to the Lord,
And filled the unclean leper's house
With the scent of costliest nard.

Ah! happy they whose hearts can break
And peace of pardon win:
How else may man make straight his plan
And cleanse his soul from Sin?
How else but through a broken heart
May Lord Christ enter in?

Oscar Wilde, 1856–1900

560. DE SHEEPFOL'

Po' lil' brack sheep dat strayed away,
Done los' in de win' an' de rain—
An' de Shepherd He say, "O hirelin',
Go fin' my sheep again."

An' de hirelin' say, "O Shepherd,
Dat sheep am brack an' bad,"
But de Shepherd He smile, like dat lil' brack sheep
Wuz de onliest lamb He had.

❖

An' de Shepherd go out in de darkness
Where de night wuz col' an' bleak,
An' dat lil' brack sheep, He fin' it,
An' lay it agains' His cheek.
An' de hirelin' frown; "O Shepherd,
Don' bring dat sheep to me!"
But de Shepherd He smile, an' He hol' it close.
An'—dat lil' brack sheep—was—me!

Sarah Pratt McLean Green, 1856–

561. THE HELP-GIVERS

(E. T. and F. B., ob. February 1923[1])

Pride held my will:
Too much was to disown,
Too many a need I still
Could not unsay:
High Help at hand,
I willed to stand alone;
Fearful for self, for self I would not pray.

Then came a day:
Judged and condemned, enduring without hope—
I learned how, near at hand, two prisoners lay
In separate cells, each waiting for the rope:
Fearful of that whose touch would put away
All griefs and fears.
And helpless I, to aid
Their hapless state—
Lighten, or lift from them that stroke of fate—
With heartfelt tears,
For those poor souls, I prayed,
That them from utter wreck
Some Help might save!

Then to my heart
There came a rending wave:
Across *my* neck
A sudden rope was flung;
Up went a light,
And I, of land, had sight,—
Where, dark against the sky, two murderers clung,
And in the baffling storm, hand over hand,
Hauled on the line
Which drew my feet to land!

Lord, in Thy Kingdom's day, remember them—
Whate'er they did—who helped me, in my need,
To touch Thy raiment's hem!

Laurence Housman, 1865–

562. LORD, COME AWAY!

Lord, come away;
Why dost Thou stay?
Thy road is ready and Thy paths made straight
With longing expectation wait
The consecration of Thy beauteous feet.
Ride on triumphantly: behold! we lay
Our lusts and proud wills in Thy way.
Hosannah! welcome to our hearts: Lord, here
Thou hast a temple too, and full as dear
As that of Sion; and as full of sin—
Nothing but thieves and robbers dwell therein;
Enter, and chase them forth, and cleanse the floor,
Crucify them, that they may never more
Profane that holy place
Where Thou hast chose to set Thy face.
And then if our still tongues shall be
Mute in the praises of Thy deity,
The stones out of the temple wall
Shall cry aloud and call
Hosannah! and Thy glorious footsteps greet.

Jeremy Taylor, 1613–1667

563. THE TRIUMPHANT ENTRY

Come, drop your branches, strow the way,
Plants of the day!
Whom sufferings make most green and gay

[1] The initials stand for the names of two lovers condemned for murder. The poem was written the night before they were hanged.

The king of grief, the man of sorrow
Weeping still, like the wet morrow,
Your shades and freshness comes to borrow.

Put on, put on your best array;
Let the joyed road make holy-day,
And flowers, that into fields do stray,
Or secret groves, keep the high-way.

Trees, flowers, and herbs; birds, beasts, and
stones,
That since man fell, expect with groans
To see the Lamb, come, all at once,
Lift up your heads and leave your moans!

For here comes he
Whose death will be
Man's life, and your full liberty.

Hark! how the children shrill and high
"Hosanna" cry;
Their joys provoke the distant sky,
Where thrones and seraphim reply;
And their own angels shine and sing
In a bright ring;
Such young, sweet mirth
Makes heaven and earth
Join in a joyful symphony.

Henry Vaughan, 1622–1695

564. PALM SUNDAY

Thy glory dawns, Jerusalem, awake, thy bells to ring!
Swift fashion thee a crown of gold,
And bring forth David's throne of old;
Jerusalem, make ready, make ready for the King!
From tower and roof thy banners fling,
For down the slopes of Olivet comes riding on, the King!

(*Jerusalem speaks:*)
A thorn-bush grows without the wall;
Of this his crown shall woven be.
For royal wine prepare we gall,
For throne a cross on Calvary.

Thy Saviour comes, Jerusalem, make haste, thine altar bring!
His body for an offering take,
The heart of all the world to break,
And on the cross uplifted our God shall own him King!
Ye lands afar, his triumph sing,
For with the love of all mankind our God shall crown him King!

John J. Moment, 1875–

565. GREEN BRANCHES

Today I saw a group of children running
Along the road with branches in their hands
That they were waving—green branches—and they were shouting
As children have shouted and run in many lands,
And many times; so it was strange that I kept thinking—
Watching these children, and listening to them—
Of those others who ran and shouted and waved green branches
One day, on the road into Jerusalem.

Joan Ramsay, 1902–

566. PALM SUNDAY AND MONDAY

They pluck their palm branches and hail Him as King,
Early on Sunday;
They spread out their garments; hosannas they sing,
Early on Sunday.

But where is the noise of their hurrying feet,
The crown they would offer, the sceptre, the seat?
Their King wanders hungry, forgot in the street,
Early on Monday

Edwin McNeill Poteat, 1892–

567. THE DONKEY

When fishes flew and forests walked
And figs grew upon thorn,
Some moment when the moon was blood
Then surely I was born.

With monstrous head and sickening cry
And ears like errant wings,
The devil's walking parody
On all four-footed things.

The tattered outlaw of the earth,
Of ancient crooked will;
Starve, scourge, deride me: I am dumb
I keep my secret still.

Fools! For I also had my hour;
One far fierce hour and sweet:
There was a shout about my ears,
And palms before my feet.

Gilbert K. Chesterton, 1874–1936

568. HOLY SATURDAY

O Earth, who daily kissed His feet
Like lowly Magdalen,—how sweet
(As oft His mother used) to keep
The silent watches of His sleep,
Till love demands the Prisoner,
And Death replies, "He is not here.
He passed my portal, where, afraid,
My footsteps faltered to invade
The region that beyond me lies:
Then, ere the dawn, I saw Him rise
In glory that dispelled my gloom
And made a Temple of the Tomb."

John Banister Tabb, 1845–1909

569. HOLY WEEK

I cannot wax ecstatic with the throng
Of parasites and servitors, who pray
And make such vast ado, this week and day,
Over the details of an ancient wrong,
Yet in their soddenness themselves prolong
Still, for the son of man, Golgotha's way;
Who yet the slaving multitudes betray,
That they may share in Herod's dance and song.
I count remembrance of the martyred dead
Remembrance only worthy of esteem
When it bears onward still the martyr's dream,
And dares like protest for the common good.
They who stand well today with Caesar's brood.
Call me in vain; so much they leave unsaid.

Robert Whitaker, 1863–1944

570. IN GETHSEMANE

Sweet Eden was the arbor of delight,
Yet in its honey flowers our poison blew:
Sad Gethsemane, the bower of baleful night,
Where Christ a health of poison for us drew,
Yet all our honey in that poison grew:
So we, from sweetest flower, could suck our bane,
And Christ, from bitter venom, could again
Extract life out of death, and pleasure out of pain.

Giles Fletcher, 1588?–1623

571. "COULD YE NOT WATCH ONE HOUR?"

Not for one hour; so much the daily task
Absorbs us, and the world fills all our mind,
Leaving no room for that which Thou dost ask:
Too busy or too indolent, to find
The path that leads to Olivet, or spare
One hour to watch with Thee in love and prayer.

No, not one hour: save when our heads are bowed
With our own sorrow; when the heart's sore need
Craves comfort from Thy presence, and the cloud
Hangs dark and heavy o'er us; then, indeed,
Oh, Saviour of the world, we turn to Thee,
To watch with us in our Gethsemane.

Godfrey Fox Bradby, 1863–

572. A BALLAD OF TREES AND THE MASTER

Into the woods my Master went,
Clean forspent, forspent.
Into the woods my Master came,
Forspent with love and shame.
But the olives they were not blind to Him;
The little gray leaves were kind to Him;
The thorn-tree had a mind to Him
When into the woods He came.

Out of the woods my Master went,
And He was well content.
Out of the woods my Master came,
Content with death and shame.
When Death and Shame would woo Him last,
From under the trees they drew Him last:
'Twas on a tree they slew Him—last
When out of the woods He came.

Sidney Lanier, 1842–1881

573. THY WILL BE DONE

Thy Will be done. No greater words than
these
Can pass from human lips, than these which
rent
Their way through agony and bloody sweat,
And broke the silence of Gethsemane
To save the world from sin.

G. A. Studdert-Kennedy, 1883–1929

574. GOD'S GARDEN

The Lord God planted a garden
In the first white days of the world,
And He set there an Angel warden
In a garment of light enfurled.

So near to the peace of Heaven
The hawk might nest with the wren,
For there in the cool of the even
God walked with the first of men.

And I dream that these garden closes
With their shade and their sun-flecked sod,
And their lilies and bowers of roses
Were laid by the hand of God.

The kiss of the sun for pardon,
The song of the birds for mirth,—
One is nearer God's heart in a garden
Than anywhere else on earth.[1]

For He broke it for us in a garden
Under the olive-trees
Where the angel of strength was the warden
And the soul of the world found ease.

Dorothy Frances Gurney, 1858–1932

575. GETHSEMANE'S GIFT

When is He nearest to all of us,
Our Brother and God's Son?
Why is He dearest, how is He most
Inalienably our own?

[1] The fourth stanza is inscribed at the Bok Singing Tower, Lake Wales, Florida.

Is it as little wondering Babe,
Innocent, impotent, wise,
Turning from angels and shepherds and kings
To laugh in His Mother's eyes?

Or during the hidden, mysterious years
When the Light of the World went veiled and dim,
When he walked with the village women and men
That their hearts might be open to Him?

Very close is the Christ Who wept
For his friend struck quiet by Death:
Who to ruler's daughter and widow's son
Gave back the incredible breath.

Who pitied our humblest hunger and thirst,
The tired flesh spent in the race—
And from water and wine and bread and love
Made Sacraments of His grace.

Our lips are pressed to His feet on the Cross,
And the heart of the world is pierced with his own,
And out of the Tomb, since He has led
We follow the Easter sun

To the Dream come true, to the Word fulfilled,
To the Life stretching endlessly, everywhere.

But I would not forget what the olive-trees heard—
His one unanswered prayer!

Katherine Brégy, contemporary American

576. GETHSEMANE

All those who journey, soon or late,
Must pass within the garden's gate;
Must kneel alone in darkness there,
And battle with some fierce despair.
God pity those who cannot say:
"Not mine but thine"; who only pray:
"Let this cup pass," and cannot see
The purpose in Gethsemane.

Ella Wheeler Wilcox, 1855–1919

577. EASTER EVE

"Ses meurtriers donc ses rencontraient de bon cœur."—
Alfonse Moreau

His murderers met. Their consciences were free:
The sun's eclipse was past, the tumult stilled
In Jewry, and their duty well fulfilled.

Quoth Caiaphas:—*It wrung my heart to see*
His mother's grief, God knows. Yet blasphemy
Was proven, the uprising imminent,
And all the church-supporting element
Demanded action, sir, of you and me.

Quoth Pilate:—*When this Nazarene denied*
Even Caesar's rule, reluctantly I knew
My duty to the state, sir. Still, I tried,
But found no way, to spare him yet stay true
In loyalty. . . . And still, the poor lad cried,
"Forgive them, for they know not what they do!"

James Branch Cabell, 1879–

578. BARABBAS SPEAKS

I heard a man explaining
(they said his name was Paul)
how Jesus, on that fateful day,
had died to save us all.

I found it hard to follow
His fine-spun theory,
but I am very, very sure
He died that day for me.

Edwin McNeill Poteat, 1892–

579. THE BACK OF GOD

I prayed to see the face of God,
Illumined by the central suns
Turning in their ancient track;
But what I saw was not His face at all—
I saw His bent figure on a windy hill,
Carrying a double load upon His back.

J. R. Perkins, contemporary American

580. SIMON THE CYRENIAN SPEAKS

He never spoke a word to me,
And yet He called my name;
He never gave a sign to me,
And yet I knew and came.

At first I said, "I will not bear
His cross upon my back;
He only seeks to place it there
Because my skin is black."

But He was dying for a dream,
And He was very meek,
And in His eyes there shone a gleam
Men journey far to seek.

It was Himself my pity bought;
I did for Christ alone
What all of Rome could not have wrought
With bruise of lash or stone.

Countee Cullen, 1903–1946

581. GOOD FRIDAY

This day upon the bitter tree
Died One who had He willed
Could have dried up the wide sea
And the wind stilled.

It was about the ninth hour
He surrendered the ghost,
And His face was a fading flower
Dropping and lost.

Who then was not afraid?
Targeted, heart and eye,
Struck, as with darts, by godhead
In human agony.

For Him, who with a cry
Could shatter if He willed
The sea and earth and sky
And them rebuild,

Who chose amid the tumult
Of the lowering sky
A chivalry more difficult—
As Man to die,

What answering meed of love
Can finite flesh return
That is not all unworthy of
The Friend I mourn?

A. J. M. Smith, 1902–

582. GOOD FRIDAY

There was no glory on the hills that day;
Only dark shame,
And three stark crosses rearing at the sky.
Only a whining wind,
And jeering,
And an anguished voice
Crying forgiveness.

Then darkness fell.

We sit today in cushioned pews
And for three hours we watch with Him,
Singing and praying,
Hearing quiet words.
There is a gentle rustle as we move in and out,
Too busy to stay long,
Or else too tired
To sit so long a time
In cushioned pews.

We see a golden cross
And pray to God
That some day,
In His own good time,
The world may do His will.
But we ourselves
Have little time to help—
Except to say a prayer
On cushioned pews.

The golden cross is all aglow
In candle flame.
It burns like flame.
Like flame it burns into my heart—
The golden cross has turned to fire
The candle glow—
Has set the cross on fire—
The burning cross up on the altar
Cries—
Cries out to me.
The flaming cross is burned into my heart!

The others have not seen.
There is the golden cross
And candle glow.

There was no glory on the hills that day;
But one stark cross
Against a vacant sky.

Martha Provine Leach Turner,
contemporary American

583. THERE IS A GREEN HILL FAR AWAY

There is a green hill far away,
Without a city wall,
Where the dear Lord was crucified,
Who died to save us all.

We may not know, we cannot tell,
What pains He had to bear;
But we believe it was for us
He hung and suffered there.

He died that we might be forgiven,
He died to make us good,
That we might go at last to heaven,
Saved by His precious blood.

There was no other good enough
To pay the price of sin;
He only could unlock the gate
Of heaven and let us in.

O dearly, dearly has He loved,
And we must love Him, too,
And trust in His redeeming blood,
And try His works to do.

Cecil F. Alexander, 1823–1895

584. MARY AT THE CROSS

And Mary stood beside the cross! Her soul
Pierced with the selfsame wound that rent His side
Who hung thereon. She watched Him as He died—
Her son! Saw Him paying the cruel toll
Exacted by the law, and unbelief,
Since He their evil will had dared defy.
There stood the mother helpless in her grief,
Beside the cross, and saw her firstborn die!

How many mothers in how many lands
Have bowed with Mary in her agony,
In silence borne the wrath of war's commands,
When every hill is made a Calvary!

O pity, Lord, these mothers of the slain,
And grant their dead shall not have died in vain.

Clyde McGee, 1875—

585. GOOD FRIDAY

Am I a stone, and not a sheep,
That I can stand, O Christ, beneath Thy cross,
To number drop by drop Thy Blood's slow loss,
And yet not weep?

Not so those women loved
Who with exceeding grief lamented Thee;
Not so fallen Peter weeping bitterly;
Not so the thief was moved;

Not so the Sun and Moon
Which hid their faces in a starless sky.
A horror of great darkness at broad noon—
I, only I.

Yet give not o'er
But seek Thy sheep, true Shepherd of the flock;
Greater than Moses, turn and look once more
And smite a rock.

Christina Rossetti, 1830–1894

586. NEAR THE CROSS

Near the Cross her vigil keeping,
Stood the mother, worn with weeping,
Where He hung, the dying Lord:
Through her soul, in anguish groaning,
Bowed in sorrow, sighing, moaning,
Passed the sharp and piercing sword.

O the weight of her affliction!
Hers, who won God's benediction,
Hers, who bore God's Holy One:
O that speechless, ceaseless yearning!
O those dim eyes never turning
From her wondrous, suffering Son!

Who upon that mother gazing,
In her trouble so amazing,
Born of woman, would not weep?
Who of Christ's dear mother thinking,
While her Son that cup is drinking,
Would not share her sorrow deep?

For His people's sin chastisèd
She beheld her Son despisèd,
Bound and bleeding 'neath the rod;

Saw the Lord's Anointed taken,
Dying desolate, forsaken,
Heard Him yield His soul to God.

Near Thy Cross, O Christ, abiding,
Grief and love my heart dividing,
I with her would take my place:
By Thy guardian Cross uphold me,
In Thy dying, Christ, enfold me
With the deathless arms of grace.

From the Latin, 13th century; tr. compiled by Louis F. Benson, 1855–1930

587. JESUS OF NAZARETH

Would you see the marks of the Roman scourge,
And the pits where the nails were driven?
They are all hidden under fresh wounds.

Much more than forty lashes have I borne since Calvary;
Blows aimed at striking labor have bruised my body sore;
I've known the torture of my kinsmen by the gentile mob;
My back is raw from lashings by heroes, masked, at night.
Wherever man was beaten, I was whipped.

You see this scar?
'Twas a bayonet in Flanders.
You see this bruise?
A slave's chain pinched me there.
My shoulders stoop?
Under the heavy load of labor.

You would see the marks of the Roman scourge,
And the pits where the nails were driven?
They are all hidden under fresh wounds.

Ernest Cadman Colwell, 1901–

588. GAMBLER

And sitting down, they watched Him there,
The soldiers did;
There, while they played with dice,
He made His sacrifice,
And died upon the Cross to rid
God's world of sin.

He was a gambler, too, my Christ,
He took His life and threw
It for a world redeemed.
And ere His agony was done,
Before the westering sun went down,
Crowning that day with crimson crown,
He knew that He had won.

G. A. Studdert-Kennedy, 1883–1929

589. THE CROWD

Always He feared you;
For you knew Him only as the man of loaves and fishes—
The man who did marvelous things.
He who raised Lazarus,
Healed the lame, and made the blind to see,
Fleeing from you, He sought the solace of the garden.

He must have known
That you would cry, "Release unto us Barabbas!"
And fling your cruel words at Him
As He climbed to Golgotha alone.
Perhaps He knew
That some day you would build creeds about Him,
And lose Him in massive structures of stone,
With costly windows, dignified ritual, and eloquent preachers;
While outside He waited . . .
Sad . . . and alone.

Irene McKeighan, contemporary American

590. SEQUEL TO FINALITY

They drove the hammered nails into His
hands,
His hands that shaped the hot sun overhead;
Then all prepared to return to their own
lands,
Glad in the knowledge God at last was dead.

"Now Babel can be built, and none deny!
In its cool gardens shall we take our ease;
Nor need we fear the everseeing eye,—
Our gods shall be whatever gods we please.

"Ishtar shall guard us, mother of all men,
And Bel rejoice us when the winds blow
spiced
From Indus. Wine and song shall glad us
then,—
We never loved this wistful, pallid Christ!"

So each rode homeward. And by each one's
side
Unseen One rode, Who had been crucified.

Patrick F. Kirby, 1891–

591. PILATE REMEMBERS

From "Pontius Pilate"

Some years after the crucifixion Pontius Pilate and his friend, Marcus, are spending an evening together talking over old times, as in the story by Anatole France, "The Procurator of Judea." Marcus asks Pilate if he remembers a certain Jew named Jesus whom he condemned to death. Pilate answers:

Do I remember such and such an one?
Nay, Marcus mine, how can I? Every day
The judgment hall was crowded. Every week
A motley throng of victims met their doom.
One Jesus? No. And yet,—and yet,—the name
Does sound familiar. Let me think again—
Jesus from Nazareth in Galilee?
Yes, I recall him now: a strange, still man
With eyes that searched one's very soul, a voice
Of marvelous sweetness, and a face so pure
It scarce seemed human. There again he stands!
All bruised and bleeding, he was dragged in chains
Before the judgment seat. The Jewish priests
Were thirsting for his blood. He claimed, it seems,
To be a king; and they had robed him out
In mocking purple, bound his brow with thorns!
Half mad with hate, they gnashed their teeth and cried,
"Away with him. Let him be crucified."
But evidence of legal fault or crime
They could not stablish. Innocent he was
As babe new born. I felt a certain awe
As there with folded hands he stood, and gazed
Right in my eyes, yet gave nor sign nor sound.
He seemed the judge, and I the criminal.
I would have freed him, by the Gods I would,
And strove to do so; but those cursed priests—
Nay, boy, enough, enough. Let memory rest.
Here pass the wine and let us drink to her,
The fair, young slave whom Publius brought from Spain,
Whose queenly grace, and rounded loveliness

Have turned all heads in Rome. Your questions, lad,
Have made me squeamish, turned to sourness
The milk of my content. Let be the past.
I thank the Gods, that two divinities
Have power to lay the peeping ghosts that slip
Through memory's doorway. Thank the Gods, I say,
For wine and women. Fill the cup again!

Thomas Durley Landels, contemporary American

592. THE CHOICE OF THE CROSS

From "The Devil to Pay"

Hard it is, very hard,
To travel up the slow and stony road
To Calvary, to redeem mankind; far better
To make but one resplendent miracle,
Lean through the cloud, lift the right hand of power
And with a sudden lightning smite the world perfect.
Yet this was not God's way, Who had the power,
But set it by, choosing the cross, the thorn,
The sorrowful wounds. Something there is, perhaps,
That power destroys in passing, something supreme,
To whose great value in the eyes of God
That cross, that thorn, and those five wounds bear witness.

Dorothy L. Sayers, 1893–

593. TOWARD JERUSALEM

Opening our windows toward Jerusalem,
And looking thitherward, we see
First Bethlehem,
Then Nazareth and Galilee,
And afterwards Gethsemane;
And then the little hill called Calvary.

Amy Carmichael, contemporary English

594. THE CROSS WAS HIS OWN

They borrowed a bed to lay His head
When Christ the Lord came down;
They borrowed the ass in the mountain pass
For Him to ride to town;
But the Crown that He wore and the Cross that He bore
Were His own—
The Cross was His own.

He borrowed the bread when the crowd He fed
On the grassy mountain side;
He borrowed the dish of broken fish
With which He satisfied;
But the Crown that He wore and the Cross that He bore
Were His own—
The Cross was His own.

He borrowed the ship in which to sit
To teach the multitude;
He borrowed a nest in which to rest,
He had never a home so crude;
But the Crown that He wore and the Cross that He bore
Were His own—
The Cross was His own.

He borrowed a room on His way to the tomb,
The Passover Lamb to eat;
They borrowed a cave for Him a grave;
They borrowed a winding sheet;
But the Crown that He wore and the Cross that He bore
Were His own—
The Cross was His own.

Author unknown

595. CRUCIFIXION

Dey crucified my Lord,
An' He never said a mumblin' word.
Dey crucified my Lord,
An' He never said a mumblin' word.
Not a word—not a word—not a word.

Dey nailed Him to de tree,
An' He never said a mumblin' word.
Dey nailed Him to de tree,
An' He never said a mumblin' word.
Not a word—not a word—not a word.

Dey pierced Him in de side,
An' He never said a mumblin' word.
Dey pierced Him in de side,
An' He never said a mumblin' word.
Not a word—not a word—not a word.

De blood came twinklin' down,
An' He never said a mumblin' word.
De blood came twinklin' down,
An' He never said a mumblin' word.
Not a word—not a word—not a word.

He bowed His head an' died,
An' He never said a mumblin' word.
He bowed His head an' died,
An' He never said a mumblin' word.
Not a word—not a word—not a word.

Negro Spiritual

596. HIS HANDS

The hands of Christ
Seem very frail
For they were broken
By a nail.

But only they
Reach heaven at last
Whom these frail, broken
Hands hold fast.

John Richard Moreland, 1880–1947

597. THREE CROSSES

Three crosses stood on Calvary
Stark against the sky.
Roman soldiers laughed to see
Three ways a man may die.

Crosses still stand on Calvary
Stark against the sky,
And some still laugh to see
Men die . . . hear little children cry.

Who builds the cross on Calvary
Stark against the sky?
Who laughs at pain and want?
Can it be you—or I?

Leila Avery Rotherburger,
contemporary American

598. THE SOVEREIGN EMBLEM

From "The Cathedral"

Whatsoe'er
The form of building or the creed professed,
The Cross, bold type of shame to homage turned,
Of an unfinished life that sways the world,
Shall tower as sovereign emblem over all.

James Russell Lowell, 1819–1891

599. ABOVE THE HILLS OF TIME

Above the hills of time the Cross is gleaming,
Fair as the sun when night has turned to day;
And from it love's pure light is richly streaming,
To cleanse the heart and banish sin away.
To this dear Cross the eyes of men are turning
To-day as in the ages lost to sight;
And for the love of Christ men's hearts are yearning
As shipwrecked seamen yearn for morning light.

The Cross, O Christ, Thy wondrous love revealing,
  Awakes our hearts as with the light of morn,
And pardon o'er our sinful spirits stealing
  Tells us that we, in Thee, have been re-born.
Like echoes to sweet temple bells replying,
  Our hearts, O Lord, make answer to Thy love;
And we will love Thee with a love undying,
  Till we are gathered to Thy home above.

Thomas Tiplady, 1882–

600. IN THE CROSS OF CHRIST I GLORY

In the cross of Christ I glory,
  Towering o'er the wrecks of time;
All the light of sacred story
  Gathers round its head sublime.

When the woes of life o'er take me,
  Hopes deceive, and fears annoy,
Never shall the cross forsake me:
  Lo! it glows with peace and joy.

When the sun of bliss is beaming
  Light and love upon my way,
From the cross the radiance streaming
  Adds more luster to the day.

Bane and blessing, pain and pleasure,
  By the cross are sanctified;
Peace is there that knows no measure,
  Joys that through all time abide.

In the cross of Christ I glory,
  Towering o'er the wrecks of time;
All the light of sacred story
  Gathers round its head sublime.

John Bowring, 1792–1872

601. "AND I, IF I BE LIFTED UP, SHALL DRAW ALL MEN"

"Three things there are," said one,
"That miracles are—
Dawn, and the setting sun
  And a falling star."

"Two things there be," he said,
"Beyond man's quest:
The white peace of the dead,
  And a heart at rest."

"One only thing," he cried,
"Draws all men still—
A stark cross standing wide
  On a windy hill."

E. P. Dickie, contemporary English

602. BENEATH THE CROSS

Beneath the Cross of Jesus,
  I fain would take my stand,
The shadow of a mighty rock
  Within a weary land;
A home within the wilderness,
  A rest upon the way,
From the burning of the noontide heat,
  And the burden of the day.

Upon the Cross of Jesus,
  Mine eye at times can see
The very dying form of One
  Who suffered there for me.
And from my smitten heart, with tears,
  Two wonders I confess,—
The wonder of His glorious love,
  And my own worthlessness.

I take, O Cross, thy shadow
  For my abiding-place;
I ask no other sunshine than
  The sunshine of His face:
Content to let the world go by,
  To know no gain nor loss,
My sinful self my only shame,
  My glory all, the Cross.

Elizabeth Cecilia Clephane, 1830–1869

603. WHEN I SURVEY THE WONDROUS CROSS

When I survey the wondrous cross
On which the Prince of glory died,
My richest gain I count but loss,
And pour contempt on all my pride.

Forbid it, Lord, that I should boast
Save in the cross of Christ my God;
All the vain things that charm me most,
I sacrifice them to His blood.

See from His head, His hands, His feet,
Sorrow and love flow mingled down;
Did e'er such love and sorrow meet,
Or thorns compose so rich a crown?

Were the whole realm of nature mine,
That were an present far too small;
Love so amazing, so divine,
Demands my soul, my life, my all.

Isaac Watts, 1674–1748

604. IN EVIL LONG I TOOK DELIGHT

In evil long I took delight,
Unawed by shame or fear,
Till a new object struck my sight,
And stopp'd my wild career:
I saw One hanging on a Tree
In agonies and blood,
Who fix'd His languid eyes on me,
As near His Cross I stood.

Sure never till my latest breath
Can I forget that look:
It seem'd to charge me with His death,
Though not a word He spoke:
My conscience felt and own'd the guilt,
And plunged me in despair:
I saw my sins His Blood had spilt,
And help'd to nail Him there.

Alas! I knew not what I did!
But now my tears are vain:
Where shall my trembling soul be hid?
For I the Lord have slain!
—A second look He gave, which said,
"I freely all forgive;
This blood is for thy ransom paid;
I die that thou may'st live."

Thus, while His death my sin displays
In all its blackest hue,
Such is the mystery of grace,
It seals my pardon too.
With pleasing grief, and mournful joy,
My spirit now is fill'd,
That I should such a life destroy,—
Yet live by Him I kill'd!

John Newton, 1725–1807

605. KNOWLEDGE THROUGH SUFFERING

I knew Thee not, Thou wounded Son of God,
Till I with Thee the path of suffering trod;
Till in the valley, through the gloom of night,
I walked with Thee, and turned to Thee for light.

I did not know the mystery of love,
The love that doth the fruitless branch remove;
The love that spares not e'en the fruitful tree,
But prunes, that it may yet more fruitful be.

I did not know the meaning of the Cross:
I counted it but bitterness and loss:
Till in Thy gracious discipline of pain
I found the loss I dreaded purest gain.

And shall I cry, e'en on the darkest day,
"Lord of all mercy, take my cross away"?
Nay, in the Cross I saw Thine open face,
And found therein the fulness of Thy grace.

George Wallace Briggs, 1875–

606. THE QUESTION

I saw the Son of God go by
  Crowned with the crown of Thorn.
"Was It not finished, Lord?" I said,
  "And all the anguish borne?"

He turned on me His awful eyes:
  "Hast thou not understood?
Lo! Every soul is Calvary,
  And every sin a Rood."

Rachel Annand Taylor, contemporary English

607. GESTURE

My arms were always quiet,
  Close, and never freed.
I was furled like a banner,
  Enfolded like a seed.

I thought, when Love shall strike me,
  Each arm will start and spring,
Unloosen like a petal,
  And open like a wing.

O Love—my arms are lifted,
  But not to sway and toss;
They strain out wide and wounded,
  Like arms upon a cross.

Winifred Welles, 1893–

608. BRIER

Because, dear Christ, your tender, wounded arm
  Bends back the brier that edges life's long way,
That no hurt comes to heart, to soul no harm,
  I do not feel the thorns so much to-day.

Because I never knew your care to tire,
  Your hand to weary guiding me aright,
Because you walk before and crush the brier,
  It does not pierce my feet so much to-night.

Because so often you have hearkened to
  My selfish prayers, I ask but one thing now,
That these harsh hands of mine add not unto
  The crown of thorns upon your bleeding brow.

E. Pauline Johnson, 1862–1913

609. THE CROSS

Talk not of Justice and her scales of woe,
We know no justice, weighing gain and loss,
Save the balancing arms of love held wide
That cannot sway or falter to and fro,
Mercy on this side and the other side,
The adamantine justice of the Cross.

Eva Gore-Booth, 1872–1926

610. A LITTLE PARABLE

I made the cross myself whose weight
  Was later laid on me.
This thought is torture as I toil
  Up life's steep Calvary.

To think mine own hands drove the nails!
  I sang a merry song,
And chose the heaviest wood I had
  To build it firm and strong.

If I had guessed—if I had dreamed
  Its weight was meant for me,
I should have made a lighter cross
  To bear up Calvary!

Anne Reeve Aldrich, 1866–1892

611. THE JEW TO JESUS

O man of my own people, I alone
Among these alien ones can know thy face,
I who have felt the kinship of our race
Burn in me as I sit where they intone
Thy praises—those who, striving to make known
A God for sacrifice, have missed the grace
Of thy sweet human meaning in its place,
Thou who art of our blood-bond and our own.

Are we not sharers of thy Passion? Yea,
In spirit-anguish closely by thy side
We have drained the bitter cup, and, tortured, felt
With thee the bruising of each heavy welt.
In every land is our Gethsemane.
A thousand times have we been crucified.

Florence Kiper Frank, contemporary American

612. STRENGTH

Ask of your soul this question, What is
strength?
Is it to slay ten thousand with the sword?
To steal at midnight Gaza's brazen gates?
To raze a temple on a heathen horde?
Or, in a garden drenched with evening dew
And bloody sweat, to pray beside a stone?
Defend a sinner from self-righteous priests?
Bear up to Calvary a cross, alone?

Jessie Wilmore Murton, 1886–

613. GOD'S WAY

I sought Him in the still, far place where flowers blow
In sun-bathed soil;
I found Him where the thousand life-streams flow
Through sin and toil.

I listened for His step within the still, deep-cloistered shrine
Of secret thought;
I heard it o'er the world's heart tumult, still divine,
The Voice I sought.

I thought, far off, alone, to feel His presence by my side,
His joy to gain;
I felt His touch upon life's weary pulse beside
A bed of pain.

So those who seek the Master following their own way—
Or gain, or loss—
Will find Him where their dreams of self are laid away,
And there—a cross.

Dorothy Clarke Wilson, contemporary American

614. IF HE SHOULD COME

If he should come tomorrow, the Meek and Lowly One,
To walk familiar pathways beneath an older sun,
What king would hail his coming, what seer proclaim his birth,
If he should come tomorrow, would he find faith on earth?

If he should come tomorrow, what marvels would he see,
White wings that soar the heavens, great ships that sail the sea,
A million spires arising to praise his holy name,
But human hearts unchastened, and human greed the same.

As in the days of Herod, the money-changers still
In God's own House contriving against the Father's will;
His messengers in exile, corruption on the throne,
And all the little company disbanded and alone.

Oh, let him come in glory with all the powers of God,
Begirt with shining legions to rule with iron rod,
Till greed be purged forever from out the souls of men;
Lest he who comes tomorrow be crucified again!

Lilith Lorraine, contemporary American

615. O LOVE THAT TRIUMPHS OVER LOSS

Lord Christ, when first thou cam'st to men,
  Upon a cross they bound thee,
And mock'd thy saving kingship then
  By thorns with which they crowned thee:
And still our wrongs may weave thee now
New thorns to pierce that steady brow,
  And robe of sorrow round thee.

O aweful Love, which found no room
  In life where sin denied thee,
And, doomed to death, must bring to doom
  The power which crucified thee,
Till not a stone was left on stone,
And all a nation's pride, o'erthrown,
  Went down to dust beside thee!

New advent of the love of Christ,
  Shall we again refuse thee,
Till in the night of hate and war
  We perish as we lose thee?
From old unfaith our souls release
To seek the kingdom of thy peace,
  By which alone we choose thee.

O wounded hands of Jesus, build
  In us thy new creation;
Our pride is dust, our vaunt is stilled,
  We wait thy revelation:
O love that triumphs over loss,
We bring our hearts before thy cross,
  To finish thy salvation.

Walter Russell Bowie, 1882–

616. AGAIN THE STORY IS TOLD

Pilate, Pilate, wash your hands,
  Cry "What is Truth?" again.
None asks or cares, these wiser days,
  Nor fears so small a stain.

Peter, Peter, save your skin,
  Then, futile, weep your shame.
No one will notice. After all
  We have done the same.

Judas, Judas, hang yourself.
  How many times is this?
The Lesson's yet to learn. We still
  Betray Him with a kiss.

Jesus, Jesus, nailed on high,
  Christ Whom the nations praise,
Which is the Cross that tore thee most—
  Golgotha's or today's?

Ada Jackson, contemporary American

617. INDIFFERENCE

When Jesus came to Golgotha they hanged Him on a tree,
They drave great nails through hands and feet, and made a Calvary;
They crowned Him with a crown of thorns, red were His wounds and deep,
For those were crude and cruel days, the human flesh was cheap.

When Jesus came to Birmingham, they simply passed Him by,
They never hurt a hair of Him, they only let Him die;
For men had grown more tender, and they would not give Him pain,
They only just passed down the street, and left Him in the rain.

Still Jesus cried, "Forgive them, for they know not what they do,"
And still it rained the winter rain that drenched Him through and through;
The crowds went home and left the streets without a soul to see,
And Jesus crouched against a wall and cried for Calvary.

G. A. Studdert-Kennedy, 1883–1929

618. CALVARY

Friendless and faint, with martyred steps and slow,
Faint for the flesh, but for the spirit free,
Stung by the mob that came to see the show,

The Master toiled along to Calvary;
We gibed him, as he went, with houndish glee,
Till his dimmed eyes for us did overflow;
We cursed his vengeless hand thrice wretchedly,—
And this was nineteen hundred years ago.

But after nineteen hundred years the shame
Still clings, and we have not made good the loss
That outraged faith had entered in his name.
Ah, when shall come love's courage to be strong!
Tell me, O Lord—tell me, O Lord, how long
Are we to keep Christ writhing on the cross!

Edwin Arlington Robinson, 1869–1935

619. CHRIST IS CRUCIFIED ANEW

Not only once, and long ago,
There on Golgotha's side,
Has Christ, the Lord, been crucified
Because He loved a lost world so.
But hourly souls, sin-satisfied,
Mock His great love, flout His commands.
And I drive nails deep in His hands,
You thrust the spear within His side.

John Richard Moreland, 1880–1947

620. AVE CRUX, SPES UNICA!

More than two crosses stand on either side
The Cross today on more than one dark hill;
More than three hours a myriad men have cried,
And they are crying still.

Before Him now no mocking faces pass;
Heavy on all who built the cross, it lies;
Pilate is hanging there, and Caiaphas,
Judas without his price.

Men scourge each other with their stinging whips;
To crosses high they nail, and they are nailed;
More than one dying man with parchèd lips,
"My God! My God!" has wailed.

Enlarged is Golgotha. But One alone
His healing shadow over all can fling;
One King Divine has made His Cross a Throne.
"Remember us, O King!"

Edward Shillito, 1872–1948

621. ANOTHER CROSS

In one of the most dramatic scenes in "The Everlasting Mercy," an autobiographical poem recounting the conversion of Saul Kane, Miss Bourne, the Quaker, on her nightly mission to the "pubs," came upon Saul half crazed with drink. Even the drunkards had always treated her with respect, but this night Saul was "beside himself." He greeted her with vile taunts, whereupon, grieved in spirit, she went to the bar and, emptying his half-filled tumbler upon the floor,—

"Saul Kane," she said, "when next you drink,
Do me the gentleness to think
That every drop of drink accursed
Makes Christ within you die of thirst,
That every dirty word you say
Is one more flint upon His way,
Another thorn about His head,
Another mock by where He tread,
Another nail, another cross.
All that you are is that Christ's loss."

John Masefield, 1875–

622. STILL THE CROSS

Calvary is a continent
Today. America
Is but a vast and terrible
New Golgotha.

The Legion (not of Rome today)
Jests. The Beatitudes
Are called by our new Pharisees
Sweet platitudes.

We tear the seamless robe of love
With great guns' lightning-jets;
We set upon Christ's head a crown
Of bayonets.

"Give us Barabbas!" So they cried
Once in Jerusalem:
In Alcatraz and Leavenworth
We copy them.

With pageant and with soldiers still
We march to Golgotha
And crucify Him still upon
A cross of war.

O blasphemous and blind! shall we
Rejoice at Eastertide
When Christ is risen but to be
Recrucified?

E. Merrill Root, 1895–

623. CRUCIFIXION

In the crowd's multitudinous mind
  Terror and passion embrace,
Whilst the darkness heavily blind
  Hides face from horror-struck face;
And all men, huddled and dumb,
  Shrink from the death-strangled cry,
And the hidden terror to come,
  And the dead men hurrying by.
White gleams from the limbs of the dead
  Raised high o'er the blood-stained sod,
And the soldier shuddered and said,
  'Lo, this was the Son of God.'
Nay, but all Life is one,
  A wind that wails through the vast,
And this deed is never done,
  This passion is never past.
When any son of man by man's blind doom
  On any justest scaffold strangled dies,
Once more across the shadow-stricken gloom
  Against the sun the dark-winged Horror flies,
A lost voice cries from the far olive trees
  Weary and harsh with pain, a desolate cry,
What ye have done unto the least of these
  Is done to God in Heaven, for earth and sky,
And bird and beast, green leaves and golden sun,
  Men's dreams, the starry dust, the bread, the wine,
Rivers and seas, my soul and his, are one;
  Through all things flows one life austere, divine,—
Strangling the murderer you are slaying me,
  Scattering the stars and leaves like broken bread,
Casting dark shadows on the sun-lit sea,
  Striking the swallows and the sea-gulls dead,
Making the red rose wither to its fall,
  Darkening the sunshine, blasting the green sod,—
Wounding one soul, you wound the soul of all,
  The unity of Life, the soul of God.

Eva Gore-Booth, 1872–1926

624. THE SECOND CRUCIFIXION

Loud mockers in the roaring street
  Say Christ is crucified again:
Twice pierced His gospel-bearing feet,
  Twice broken His great heart in vain.

I hear, and to myself I smile,
For Christ talks with me all the while.

No angel now to roll the stone
  From off His unawaking sleep,
In vain shall Mary watch alone,
  In vain the soldiers vigil keep.

Yet while they deem my Lord is dead
My eyes are on His shining head.

Ah! never more shall Mary hear
  That voice exceeding sweet and low
Within the garden calling clear:
  Her Lord is gone, and she must go.

Yet all the while my Lord I meet
In every London lane and street.

Poor Lazarus shall wait in vain,
  And Bartimæus still go blind;
The healing hem shall ne'er again
  Be touch'd by suffering humankind.

Yet all the while I see them rest,
The poor and outcast, on His breast.

No more unto the stubborn heart
  With gentle knocking shall He plead,
No more the mystic pity start,
  For Christ twice dead is dead indeed.

So in the street I hear men say:
Yet Christ is with me all the day.

Richard Le Gallienne, 1866–1947

625. THE CROSS AT THE CROSSWAYS

See There! God's signpost, standing at the ways
Which every man of his free will must go—
Up the steep hill, or down the winding ways,
One or the other, every man must go.

He forces no man, each must choose his way,
And as he chooses so the end will be;
One went in front to point the Perfect Way,
Who follows fears not where the end will be.

John Oxenham, 1852–1941

626. THERE IS A MAN ON THE CROSS

Whenever there is silence around me
By day or by night—
I am startled by a cry.
It came down from the cross—
The first time I heard it.
I went out and searched—
And found a man in the throes of crucifixion,
And I said, "I will take you down,"
And I tried to take the nails out of his feet.
But he said, "Let them be
For I cannot be taken down
Until every man, every woman, and every child
Come together to take me down."
And I said, "But I cannot hear you cry.
What can I do?"
And he said, "Go about the world—
Tell everyone that you meet—
There is a man on the cross."

Elizabeth Cheney[1]

627. EVIDENCE

"Where is God!" inquired the mind:
"To His presence I am blind.
I can tell each blade of grass,
Read the tempests as they pass;
I have learned what metals lie
In the earth's deep mystery;
Every voice of field and wood
I have heard and understood;
Ancient secrets of the sea
Are no longer dark to me:
But the wonders of the earth
Bring no thought of God to birth."
Then the heart spake quietly,
"Hast thou thought of Calvary?"

"Where is God?" inquired the mind;
"To His presence I am blind.
I have scanned each star and sun,
Traced the certain course they run;
I have weighed them in my scale,
And can tell when each will fail;
From the caverns of the night
I have brought new worlds to light;
I have measured earth and sky,
Read each zone with steady eye;
But no sign of God appears
In the glory of the spheres."
But the heart spake wistfully,
"Hast thou looked on Calvary?"

Thomas Curtis Clark, 1877–

628. O SACRED HEAD, NOW WOUNDED

O sacred Head, now wounded,
With grief and shame weighed down,
Now scornfully surrounded
With thorns, Thy only crown,
How art Thou pale with anguish,
With sore abuse and scorn!
How does that visage languish
Which once was bright as morn!

What Thou, my Lord, hast suffered
Was all for sinners' gain:
Mine, mine was the transgression,
But Thine the deadly pain.
Lo, here I fall, my Saviour!
'Tis I deserve Thy place;
Look on me with Thy favor,
Vouchsafe to me Thy grace.

What language shall I borrow
To thank Thee, dearest Friend,
For this Thy dying sorrow,
Thy pity without end?
O make me Thine forever;
And, should I fainting be,
Lord, let me never, never,
Outlive my love to Thee!

Ascribed to Arnulf von Loewen, 1200–1250; tr. into German by Paul Gerhardt, 1607–1676; tr. from the German by James W. Alexander, 1804–1859

[1] Not to be confused with Elizabeth Cheney (born 1859) who wrote poem No. 264.

629. A PRAYER FOR THE HEALING OF THE WOUNDS OF CHRIST

Is not the work done? Nay, for still the Scars
Are open; still Earth's Pain stands deified,
With Arms spread wide:
And still, like falling stars,
Its Blood-drops strike the doorposts, where abide
The watchers with the Bride,
To wait the final coming of their kin,
And hear the sound of kingdoms gathering in.

While Earth wears wounds, still must Christ's Wounds remain,
Whom Love made Life, and of Whom Life made Pain,
And of Whom Pain made Death.
No breath,
Without Him, sorrow draws; no feet
Wax weary, and no hands hard labour bear,
But He doth wear
The travail and the heat:
Also, for all things perishing, He saith,
'*My* grief, *My* pain, *My* death.'

O kindred Constellation of bright stars,
Ye shall not last for aye!
Far off there dawns a comfortable day
Of healing for those Scars:
When, faint in glory, shall be wiped away
Each planetary fire,
Now, all the aching way, the balm of Earth's desire!

For from the healèd nations there shall come
The healing touch: the blind, the lame, the dumb,
With sight, and speed, and speech,
And ardent reach
Of yearning hands shall cover up from sight
Those Imprints of a night
Forever past. And all the Morians' lands
Shall stretch out hands of healing to His Hands:
And to His Feet
The timid, sweet
Four-footed ones of earth shall come and lay,
Forever by, the sadness of their day:
And, they being healèd, healing spring from them.
So round the Stem
And Rod of Jesse, roots and trees and flowers,
Touched with compassionate powers,
Shall cause the thorny Crown
To blossom down
Laurel and bay.

So lastly to His Side,—
Stricken when, from the Body that had died,
Going down He saw sad souls being purified,—
Shall rise, out of the deeps no man

Can sound or scan,
The morning star of Heaven that once fell
And fashioned Hell:—
Now, star to star
Mingling to melt where shadeless glories are.

O Earth, seek deep, and gather up thy soul,
And come from high and low, and near and far,
And make Christ whole!

Laurence Housman, 1865–

630. CRUCIFIXION

Lord, must I bear the whole of it, or none?
"Even as I was crucified, My son."

Will it suffice if I the thorn-crown wear?
"To take the scourge, My shoulders were made bare."

My hands, O Lord, must I be pierced in both?
"Twain gave I to the hammer, nothing loth."

But surely, Lord, my feet need not be nailed?
"Had Mine not been, then love had not prevailed."

What need I more, O Lord, to fill my part?
"Only the spear-point in thy broken heart."

Frederick George Scott, 1861–1944

631. TO HIM THAT WAS CRUCIFIED

My spirit to yours, dear brother;
Do not mind because many, sounding your name, do not understand you;
I do not sound your name, but I understand you, (there are others also;)
I specify you with joy, O my comrade, to salute you, and to salute those who are with you before and since—and those to come also,
That we all labor together, transmitting the same charge and succession;
We few, equals, indifferent of lands, indifferent of times;
We, enclosers of all continents, all castes—allowers of all theologies,
Compassionaters, perceivers, rapport of men,
We walk silent among disputes and assertions, but reject not the disputers, nor any thing that is asserted;
We hear the bawling and din—we are reach'd at by divisions, jealousies, recriminations on every side,
They close peremptorily upon us, to surround us, my comrade,
Yet we walk unheld, free, the whole earth over, journeying up and down, till we make our ineffaceable mark upon time and the diverse eras,
Till we saturate time and eras, that the men and women of races, ages to come, may prove brethren and lovers, as we are.

Walt Whitman, 1819–1892

632. SUBSTITUTION

When some belovèd voice that was to you
Both sound and sweetness, faileth suddenly,
And silence, against which you dare not cry,
Aches round you like a strong disease and new—
What hope? what help? what music will undo
That silence to your sense? Not friendship's sight,
Not reason's subtle count; not melody
Of viols, nor of pipes that Faunus blew;
Not songs of poets, nor of nightingales
Whose hearts leap upward through the cypress-trees
To the clear moon; nor yet the spheric laws
Self-chanted, nor the angels' sweet "All-hails,"
Met in the smile of God: nay, none of these.
Speak THOU, availing Christ!—and fill this pause.

Elizabeth Barrett Browning, 1806–1861

633. I SEE HIS BLOOD UPON THE ROSE

I see His blood upon the rose
And in the stars the glory of His eyes,
His body gleams amid eternal snows,
His tears fall from the skies.

I see His face in every flower;
The thunder and the singing of the birds
Are but His voice—and carven by His power
Rocks are His written words.

All pathways by His feet are worn,
His strong heart stirs the ever-beating sea,
His crown of thorns is twined with every
thorn,
His cross is every tree.

Joseph Mary Plunkett, 1887–1916

634. ONE CROWN NOT ANY SEEK

One crown not any seek,
And yet the highest head
Its isolation coveted,
Its stigma deified.

While Pontius Pilate lives,
In whatsoever hell,
That coronation pierces him.
He recollects it well.

Emily Dickinson, 1830–1886

635. AFTER THE MARTYRDOM

They threw a stone, you threw a stone,
I threw a stone that day.
Although their sharpness bruised His flesh
He had no word to say.

But for the moan He did not make
To-day I make my moan;
And for the stone I threw at Him
My heart must bear a stone.

Scharmel Iris, contemporary American

636. DEATH'S CONQUEROR

I Corinthians 15:20, 21, 53, 55

Now is Christ risen from the dead,
and become the firstfruits of them that
slept.
For since by man came death,
by man came also the resurrection of the
dead.
For this corruptible must put on incorruption,
and this mortal must put on immortality.
O death, where is thy sting?
O grave, where is thy victory?

Saint Paul, 1st century A.D.,
King James Version, 1611

637. VICTORY

The strife is o'er, the battle done;
The victory of life is won;
The song of triumph has begun.
Alleluia!

The powers of death have done their worst,
But Christ their legions hath dispersed;
Let shouts of holy joy outburst.
Alleluia!

The three sad days are quickly sped;
He rises glorious from the dead;
All glory to our risen Head!
Alleluia!

He closed the yawning gates of hell;
The bars from heaven's high portals fell
Let hymns of praise His triumph tell!
Alleluia!

Lord! by the stripes which wounded Thee,
From death's dread sting Thy servants free,
That we may live and sing to Thee!
Alleluia!

From the Latin, 17th century;
tr. by Francis Pott, 1832–1909

638. EASTER MORNING

Tomb, thou shalt not hold Him longer:
Death is strong, but life is stronger;
Stronger than the dark, the light;
Stronger than the wrong, the right;
Faith and hope triumphant say,
"Christ will rise on Easter Day!"

While the patient earth lies waking
Till the morning shall be breaking,
Shuddering 'neath the burden dread
Of her Master, cold and dead,
Hark! she hears the angels say,
"Christ will rise on Easter Day!"

And when sunrise smites the mountains,
Pouring light from heavenly fountains,
Then the earth blooms out to greet
Once again the blessed feet;
And her countless voices say:
"Christ has risen on Easter Day!"

Phillips Brooks, 1835–1893

639. EASTER HYMN

Christ the Lord is risen to-day,
Sons of men and angels say:
Raise your joys and triumphs high,
Sing, ye heavens, and earth reply.

Love's redeeming work is done,
Fought the fight, the battle won;
Lo! our Sun's eclipse is o'er;
Lo! He sets in blood no more.

Vain the stone, the watch, the seal;
Christ hath burst the gates of hell!
Death in vain forbids His rise;
Christ hath opened Paradise!

Lives again our glorious King:
Where, O Death, is now thy sting?
Once He died, our souls to save:
Where thy victory, O Grave?

Charles Wesley, 1707–1788

640. THE DAY OF RESURRECTION

The day of resurrection!
Earth, tell it out abroad;
The passover of gladness,
The passover of God.
From death to life eternal,
From this world to the sky,
Our Christ hath brought us over
With hymns of victory.

Our hearts be pure from evil,
That we may see aright
The Lord in rays eternal
Of resurrection light,
And, list'ning to His accents,
May hear, so calm and plain,
His own "All hail!" and, hearing,
May raise the victor strain.

Now let the heav'ns be joyful,
Let earth her song begin,
Let the round world keep triumph
And all that is therein;
Invisible and visible,
Their notes let all things blend;
For Christ the Lord hath risen—
Our Joy that hath no end.

John of Damascus, 8th century;
tr. by John M. Neale, 1818–1866

641. EASTER CHORUS FROM FAUST

Christ is arisen.
  Joy to thee, mortal!
Out of His prison,
  Forth from its portal!
Christ is not sleeping,
  Seek Him no longer;
Strong was His keeping,
  Jesus was stronger.

Christ is arisen.
  Seek Him not here;
Lonely His prison,
  Empty His bier;
Vain His entombing,
  Spices and lawn,
Vain the perfuming,
  Jesus is gone.

Christ is arisen.
  Joy to thee, mortal!
Empty His prison,
  Broken its portal!
Rising, He giveth
  His shroud to the sod;
Risen, He liveth,
  And liveth to God.

Johann Wolfgang von Goethe, 1749–1832;
tr. by Arthur Cleveland Coxe, 1818–1896

642. AN EASTER REVEILLE

FIRST TRUMPET:
Souls in the east, awake.
Make ready to meet the dawn.
The sun of God is rising,
The bridegroom from his chamber,
Rejoicing as a strong man
To run his race.
  He is risen.

SECOND TRUMPET:
Souls in the north, awake.
Souls of the dead, remember,
He goeth before you into Galilee.
Is he here? Is he there?
He is everywhere;
  He is risen.

THIRD TRUMPET:
Souls in the south, awake.
Winter is dead, Spring lives.
Purple and gold the crocus comes.
The beauty of the world returns;
  He is risen.

FOURTH TRUMPET:
Souls in the west, awake.
Souls of the years to come,
Christ guide you on your way
Into this world, and out again.
He knows the way to come and go—
Comes with a star, goes with a cross,
And comes again with a triumph;
  He is risen.

ALL FOUR TRUMPETS:
Awake, all souls that sleep.
Across the year but once or twice
Can men hear angels calling.
Heed that *first* trumpet, nor await the last.
The resurrection moment soon is past.
Life calls again, to all that would be living,
  He is risen.

John R. Slater, 1872–

643. THE RESURRECTION

Awake and praise, O dwellers in the dust!
The dew of this new everlasting spring
Is singing on the garden hill, the trust
Of death is broken; now will seas disclose
Their dead, earth's slain will rise again.
                                        For He
Who has not known corruption is not here—He goes
Before to Galilee.

                    Awake, and see
The sepulcher unsealed, the stone rolled back,
The winding sheets still reeled, the angels limned in light.

O Mary, Mary and Salome, seek
Him not among the dead, the heavy night
Of Adam's guilt is fled, the Temple is rebuilt,
The stone rejected of the builders now is made
The corner stone.
Rejoice, rejoice, this is the day!

O Magdalen, who knew not where they laid
Your Lord, discard your spices, gather bay,
The Victim has become the Victor! He,
The Way, the Truth, the Life, is risen! O behold!
The Shepherd glorified has shown His sheep to fold!

John Gilland Brunini, 1899-

644. EASTER MORNING

Most glorious Lord of life, that on this day
Didst make thy triumph over death and sin,
And, having harrowed hell, didst bring away
Captivity thence captive, us to win;
This joyous day, dear Lord, with joy begin,
And grant that we, for whom thou didst die,
Being with thy dear blood clean washed from sin,
May live forever in felicity:
And that thy love we weighing worthily,
May likewise love thee for the same again:
And for thy sake, that all like dear didst buy,
With love may one another entertain.
So let us love, dear love, like as we ought;
Love is the lesson which the Lord us taught.

Edmund Spenser, 1552?–1599

645. EASTER HYMN

If in that Syrian garden, ages slain,
You sleep, and know not you are dead in vain,
Nor even in dreams behold how dark and bright
Ascends in smoke and fire by day and night
The hate you died to quench and could but fan,
Sleep well and see no morning, son of man.

But if, the grave rent and the stone rolled by,
At the right hand of majesty on high
You sit, and sitting so remember yet
Your tears, your agony and bloody sweat,
Your cross and passion and the life you gave,
Bow hither out of heaven and see and save.

A. E. Housman, 1859–1936

646. RESURGAM

We doubted our God in secret,
We scoffed in the market-place,
We held our hearts from His keeping,
We held our eyes from His face;
We looked to the ways of our fathers,
Denying where they denied,
And we said as He passed, "He is stilled at last,
And a man is crucified."

But now I give you certain news
To bid a world rejoice:
Ye may crush Truth to silence,
Ye may cry above His voice,
Ye may close your ears before Him,
Lest ye tremble at the word,
But late or soon, by night or noon;
The living Truth is heard.

We buried our God in darkness,
In secret and all affright;
We crept on a path of silence,
Fearful things in the night;
We buried our God in terror,
After the fashion of men;
As we said each one, "The deed is done,
And the grave is closed again."

But now I give you certain news
To spread by land and sea;
Ye may scourge Truth naked,
Ye may nail Him to the tree,
Ye may roll the stone above Him,
And seal it priestly-wise,
But against the morn, unmaimed, new-born,
The living Truth shall rise!

Theodosia Garrison, 1874–1944

647. CHORUS FOR EASTER

Awareness is on us, now, of the several
heavens
Unto which we ascended,
Unfailingly, after the long Golgothas
And the vinegar-drinking ended.

None made it known, none made it
understood,
Clearly, what dying is,
Nor how the hurting, heaped-up hill of bone
Was climbing unto this.

We have forgotten, now, or nearly forgotten
Each Gethsemane,
As Christ forgot . . . as this new springing
bough,
It well may be,
Forgets the leafless winter, to avow
The green leaf that we see.

David Morton, 1886–

648. HE IS NOT RISEN

Too well, O Christ, we know Thee; on our
eyes
There sits a film, through which we dimly
see,
Of frozen faith and stagnant memory.
Thou art among us in the homely guise
Of One whose nearness, like a shadow, lies
Between our minds and His own mystery;
And our familiar knowledge is to Thee
A second tomb, from which Thou dost not
rise.

Thou hast a sepulchre not made with hands,
Built of our staled beliefs, and we lay there
Our formal wreaths of customary prayer.
But in that hollow place no angel stands;
It is not visions that our faith demands,
But plain instruction from the gardener!

W. S. Handley Jones,
contemporary English

649. IF EASTER BE NOT TRUE

If Easter be not true,
Then all the lilies low must lie;
The Flanders poppies fade and die;
The spring must lose her fairest bloom
For Christ were still within the tomb—
If Easter be not true.

If Easter be not true.
Then faith must mount on broken wing;
Then hope no more immortal spring;
Then love must lose her mighty urge;
Life prove a phantom, death a dirge—
If Easter be not true.

If Easter be not true.
'Twere foolishness the cross to bear;
He died in vain who suffered there;
What matter though we laugh or cry,
Be good or evil, live or die,
If Easter be not true?

If Easter be not true—
But it is true, and Christ is risen!
And mortal spirit from its prison
Of sin and death with him may rise!
Worthwhile the struggle, sure the prize,
Since Easter, aye, is true!

Henry H. Barstow, 1866–1944

650. RESURRECTION

If it be all for naught, for nothingness
At last, why does God make the world so fair?
Why spill this golden splendor out across
The western hills, and light the silver lamp
Of eve? Why give me eyes to see, and soul
To love so strong and deep? Then, with a pang
This brightness stabs me through, and wakes
within
Rebellious voice to cry against all death?
Why set this hunger for eternity
To gnaw my heartstrings through, if death
ends all?
If death ends all, then evil must be good,
Wrong must be right, and beauty ugliness.
God is a Judas who betrays his Son,
And with a kiss, damns all the world to hell,—
If Christ rose not again.

Unknown soldier, killed in World War I

651. AN EASTER CAROL

Spring bursts today,
For Christ is risen and all the earth's at play.

Flash forth, thou sun,
The rain is over and gone, its work is done.

Winter is past,
Sweet spring is come at last, is come at last.

Bud, fig and vine,
Bud, olive, fat with fruit and oil, and wine.

Break forth this morn
In roses, thou but yesterday a thorn.

Uplift thy head,
O pure white lily through the winter dead.

Beside your dams
Leap and rejoice, you merry-making lambs.

All herds and flocks
Rejoice, all beasts of thickets and of rocks.

Sing, creatures, sing,
Angels and men and birds, and everything....

Christina G. Rossetti, 1830–1894

652. From AN EASTER CANTICLE

In every trembling bud and bloom
  That cleaves the earth, a flowery sword,
I see Thee come from out the tomb,
  Thou risen Lord.

❖

Thou art not dead! Thou art the whole
  Of life that quickens in the sod;
Green April is Thy very soul,
  Thou great Lord God.

Charles Hanson Towne, 1877–

653. RESURRECTION

From "Rue," Part III

Spring comes with silent rush of leaf
  Across the earth, and cries,
"Lo, Love is risen!" But doubting Grief
  Returns, "If with mine eyes

"I may not see the marks, nor reach
  My hand into His side,
I will not hear your lips that preach
  Love raised and glorified.

"Except by all the wounds that brake
  His heart, and marred His brow
Most grievously for sorrow's sake,
  How shall I know Him now?"

Love came, and said, "Reach hither, Grief,
  Thy hand into My side.
Oh, slow of heart to win belief,
  Seeing that for grief I died!

"Lo, all the griefs of which I died
  Rise with Me from the dead!"
Then Grief drew near, and touched the side
  And touched the wounds that bled,

And cried, "My God, O blessèd sign,
  O Body raised, made whole,
Now do I know that Thou art mine,
  Upholder of my soul!"

Laurence Housman, 1865–

654. A SONG AT EASTER

If this bright lily
  Can live once more,
And its white promise
  Be as before,
Why can not the great stone
  Be moved from His door?

If the green grass
  Ascend and shake
Year after year,
  And blossoms break
Again and again
  For April's sake,

Why can not He,
  From the dark and mould,
Show us again
  His manifold
And gleaming glory,
  A stream of gold?

Faint heart, be sure
  These things must be.
See the new bud
  On the old tree! . . .
If flowers can wake,
  Oh, why not He?

Charles Hanson Towne, 1877–

655. THOUGHT FOR EASTER

O happy world to-day if we could know
The message of that morning long ago!
There is no dark despair that cannot be
Evicted from the heart's Gethsemane;
For faith is always more than unbelief,
And vibrant courage triumphs over grief.

Mary E. McCullough, 1915–1942

656. ON A GLOOMY EASTER

I hear the robins singing in the rain.
The longed-for Spring is hushed so drearily
That hungry lips cry often wearily,
"Oh, if the blessed sun would shine again!"

I hear the robins singing in the rain.
The misty world lies waiting for the dawn;
The wind sobs at my window and is gone,
And in the silence come old throbs of pain.

But still the robins sing on in the rain,
Not waiting for the morning sun to break,
Nor listening for the violets to wake,
Nor fearing lest the snow may fall again.

My heart sings with the robins in the rain,
For I remember it is Easter morn,
And life and love and peace are all new born,
And joy has triumphed over loss and pain.

Sing on, brave robins, sing on in the rain!
You know behind the clouds the sun must shine,
You know that death means only life divine
And all our losses turn to heavenly gain.

I lie and listen to you in the rain.
Better than Easter bells that do not cease,
Your message from the heart of God's great peace,
And to his arms I turn and sleep again.

Alice Freeman Palmer, 1855–1902

657. EASTER MUST BE RECLAIMED

Easter must be redeemed
From revelry that marks the end of Lent,
And worshippers who yearly are content
To journey to God's house, and then forget
That Christ still lives when Easter's sun has set.
The vision fades, the power soon is lost
If Easter does not lead to Pentecost.

Easter must be reclaimed.
Too long the world has missed the Easter glow,
Claimed by the glitter of a fashion show;
A dress parade; a gala holiday,
With church-bound manikins upon display.
The faith of Easter never will be caught
By making Christ a fleeting afterthought.

George W. Wiseman, contemporary American

658. THE CROSS AND THE CROWN

The Head that once was crowned with thorns
Is crowned with glory now;
A royal diadem adorns
The mighty Victor's brow.

The highest place that heaven affords
Is His, is His by right,
The King of kings, and Lord of lords,
And heaven's eternal Light,

The joy of all who dwell above,
The joy of all below
To whom He manifests His love,
And grants His Name to know.

To them the Cross, with all its shame,
With all its grace, is given,
Their name an everlasting name,
Their joy the joy of heaven.

They suffer with their Lord below,
  They reign with Him above,
Their profit and their joy to know
  The mystery of His love.

The Cross He bore is life and health,
  Though shame and death to Him,
His people's hope, His people's wealth,
  Their everlasting theme.

Thomas Kelly, 1769–1854

659. CHRIST'S VICTORY

Christ when He died
Deceived the cross,
And on death's side
Threw all the loss:
The captive world awak'd and found
The prisoners loose, the jailor bound.

O dear and sweet dispute
'Twixt death's and love's far different fruit,
Different as far
As antidote and poisons are:
By the first fatal Tree
Both life and liberty
Were sold and slain,
By this they both look up, and live again.

O strange and mysterious strife,
Of open death and hidden life:
When on the cross my King did bleed,
Life seemed to die, Death died indeed.

Richard Crashaw, 1613?–1649

660. THE COMING OF HIS FEET

In the crimson of the morning, in the whiteness of the noon,
  In the amber glory of the day's retreat,
In the midnight, robed in darkness, or the gleaming of the moon,
  I listen to the coming of His feet.

I heard His weary footsteps on the sands of Galilee,
  On the Temple's marble pavement, on the street,
Worn with weight of sorrow, faltering up the slopes of Calvary,
  The sorrow of the coming of His feet.

Down the minster aisles of splendor, from betwixt the cherubim,
  Through the wondering throng, with motion strong and fleet,
Sounds His victor tread approaching, with a music far and dim—
  The music of the coming of His feet.

Sandaled not with sheen of silver, girded not with woven gold,
  Weighted not with shimmering gems and odors sweet,
But white-winged and shod with glory in the Tabor light of old—
  The glory of the coming of His feet.

He is coming, O my spirit, with His everlasting peace,
  With His blessedness immortal and complete;
He is coming, O my spirit, and His coming brings release—
  I listen for the coming of His feet.

Lyman W. Allen, 1854–1930

661. JESUS SHALL REIGN WHERE'ER THE SUN

Jesus shall reign where'er the sun
Doth his successive journeys run;
His kingdom stretch from shore to shore,
Till moon shall wax and wane no more.

To Him shall endless prayer be made,
And praises throng to crown His head;
His name, like sweet perfume, shall rise
With every morning sacrifice;

People and realms of every tongue
Dwell on His love with sweetest song,

And infant voices shall proclaim
Their early blessings on His name.

Blessings abound where'er He reigns;
The prisoner leaps to lose his chains;
The weary find eternal rest,
And all the sons of want are blest.

Let every creature rise and bring
Peculiar honors to our King;
Angels descend with songs again,
And earth repeat the loud amen.

Isaac Watts, 1674–1748

662. THE NAIL-TORN GOD

Here in life's chaos make no foolish boast
That there is any God omnipotent,
Seated serenely in the firmament,
And looking down on men as on a host
Of grasshoppers blown on a windy coast,
Damned by disasters, maimed by mortal ill,
Yet who could end it with one blast of Will.
This God is all a man-created ghost.

But there is a God who struggles with the All,
And sounds across the world his danger-call:
He is the builder of roads, the breaker of bars,
The One forever hurling back the Curse—
The nail-torn Christus pressing toward the stars,
The Hero of the battling universe.

Edwin Markham, 1852–1940

663. THE KING ETERNAL

Hail to the Lord's Anointed,
Great David's greater Son!
Hail, in the time appointed,
His reign on earth begun!
He comes to break oppression,
To set the captive free,
To take away transgression,
And rule in equity.

He comes with succour speedy
To those who suffer wrong,
To help the poor and needy,
And bid the weak be strong,
To give them songs for sighing,
Their darkness turn to light
Whose souls, condemned and dying,
Were precious in His sight.

He shall come down like showers
Upon the fruitful earth;
And love, joy, hope, like flowers
Spring in His path to birth.
Before Him, on the mountains,
Shall peace, the herald, go;
And righteousness, in fountains,
From hill to valley flow.

Kings shall fall down before Him,
And gold and incense bring;
All nations shall adore Him,
His praise all people sing:
For He shall have dominion
O'er river, sea, and shore,
Far as the eagle's pinion
Or dove's light wing can soar.

For Him shall prayer unceasing
And daily vows ascend;
His Kingdom still increasing,
A Kingdom without end:
The mountain dews shall nourish
A seed in weakness sown,
Whose fruit shall spread and flourish,
And shake like Lebanon.

O'er every foe victorious,
He on His throne shall rest,
From age to age more glorious,
All blessing and all-blest.
The tide of time shall never
His covenant remove;
His Name shall stand for ever;
That Name to us is Love.

James Montgomery, 1771–1854

664. THE CONQUERORS

I saw the Conquerors riding by
With trampling feet of horse and men:
Empire on empire like the tide
Flooded the world and ebbed again.

A thousand banners caught the sun,
And cities smoked along the plain,
And laden down with silk and gold
And heaped-up pillage groaned the wain.

I saw the Conquerors riding by,
  Splashing through loathsome floods of
    war—
The Crescent leaning o'er its hosts,
  And the barbaric scimitar—

And continents of moving spears,
  And storms of arrows in the sky,
And all the instruments sought out
  By cunning men that men may die!

I saw the Conquerors riding by
  With cruel lips and faces wan:
Musing on kingdoms sacked and burned
  There rode the Mongol Genghis Khan;

And Alexander, like a god,
  Who sought to weld the world in one;
And Caesar with his laurel wreath;
  And like a thing from Hell, the Hun;

And leading, like a star the van,
  Heedless of upstretched arm and groan,
Inscrutable Napoleon went
  Dreaming of empire, and alone . . .

Then all they perished from the earth
  As fleeting shadows from a glass,
And, conquering down the centuries,
  Came Christ, the Swordless, on an ass!

Harry Kemp, 1883–

665. THE CAPTAINS OF THE YEARS

I watched the Captains
  A-riding, riding
  Down the years;
The men of mystic grip
  Of soul, a-riding
Between a hedge of spears.

I saw their banners
  A-floating, floating
  Over all,
Till each of them had passed,
  And Christ came riding
A donkey lean and small.

I watched the Captains
  A-turning, staring,
  Proud and set,
At Christ a-riding there—
  So calmly riding
The Road men can't forget.

I watched the Captains
  Dismounting, waiting—
  None now led—
The Captains bowing low!
  The Caesars waiting!
While Christ rode on ahead.

Arthur R. Macdougall, Jr., 1880–

666. WORLD CONQUEROR

The crown of empire—must thou yield it now?
(Mine was of thorns they pressed upon my
    brow.)

Did friends, as foes, desert thee in thy power?
(Mine could not watch with me one single
    hour.)

Is all thy life stripped stark through shame
    and loss?
(Between two thieves I hung upon a Cross.)

Laura Simmons, 1877–

667. THE COINS OF LOVE

From "What of the Night?"

Arrogant kings
  With hate and lust,
Stamp on intrinsic
  Things of dust

Their impress.
  Tiny coins of brass
Show forth their face
  As in a glass.

While superscriptions
  Boast their name,
The years they ruled;
  Their weight of fame.

Only One King
  Has shed his blood
That men might walk
  In brotherhood;

Whose coin is love,
  And graved thereon:
A scourge, a cross,
  A crown of thorn;

Whose reign
Is without period. . . .
The King of Heaven;
The Son of God!

John Richard Moreland, 1880–1947

668. KINGS

"They perish all, but He remains." Omar Khâyyâm.

Who has not marvelled at the might of kings
When voyaging down the river of dead years?
What deeds of death to still an hour of fears,
What waste of wealth to gild a moth's frail wings?
A Caesar to the breeze his banner flings,
An Alexander with his bloody spears,
A Herod heedless of his people's tears!
And Rome in ruin while Nero laughs and sings:
Ye actors of a drama, cruel and cold,
Your names are by-words in Love's temple now,
Your pomp and glory but a winding sheet;
Then Christ came scorning regal power and gold
To wear warm blood-drops on a willing brow,
And we, in love, forever kiss His feet.

John Richard Moreland, 1880–1947

669. THE VETERAN OF HEAVEN

O captain of the wars, whence won Ye so great scars?
In what fight did Ye smite, and what manner was the foe?
Was it on a day of rout they compassed Thee about,
Or gat Ye these adornings when Ye wrought their overthrow?

"'Twas on a day of rout they girded Me about,
They wounded all My brow, and they smote Me through the side:
My hand held no sword when I met their armèd horde,
And the conqueror fell down, and the Conquered bruised his pride."

What is this, unheard before, that the Unarmed makes war,
And the Slain hath the gain, and the Victor hath the rout?
What wars, then, are these, and what the enemies,
Strange Chief, with the scars of Thy conquest trenched about?

"The Prince I drave forth held the Mount of the North,
Girt with the guards of flame that roll round the pole.
I drave him with My wars from all his fortress-stars,
And the sea of death divided that My march might strike its goal.

"In the heart of Northern Guard, many a great dæmonian sword
Burns as it turns round the Mount occult, apart:
There is given him power and place still for some certain days,
And his name would turn the Sun's blood back upon its heart."

What is *Thy* Name? Oh, show!—"My Name ye may not know;
'Tis a going forth with banners, and a baring of much swords:
But My titles that are high, are they not upon My thigh?
'King of Kings!' are the words, 'Lord of Lords!';
It is written 'King of Kings, Lord of Lords.' "

Francis Thompson, 1859–1907

670. THE COMING DAY

Beyond the war-clouds and the reddened
ways,
I see the Promise of the Coming Days!
I see His Sun arise, new charged with grace
Earth's tears to dry and all her woes efface!
Christ lives! Christ loves! Christ rules!
No more shall Might,
Though leagued with all the Forces of the
Night,
Ride over Right. No more shall Wrong
The world's gross agonies prolong.
Who waits His Time shall surely see
The triumph of His Constancy;—
When without let, or bar, or stay,
The coming of His Perfect Day
Shall sweep the Powers of Night away;—
And Faith, replumed for nobler flight,
And Hope, aglow with radiance bright,
And Love, in loveliness bedight,
Shall greet the morning light!

John Oxenham, 1852–1941

671. ASCENSION HYMN

A hymn of glory let us sing;
New hymns throughout the world shall ring;
By a new way none ever trod
Christ mounteth to the throne of God.

❖

May our affections thither tend,
And thither constantly ascend,
Where, seated on the Father's throne,
Thee, reigning in the heavens, we own!

Be Thou our present joy, Oh Lord,
Who wilt be ever our reward;
And, as the countless ages flee,
May all our glory be in Thee!

The Venerable Bede, 673–735;
tr. by Elizabeth Charles

672. THE GREATEST

When Jesus walked upon the earth
He didn't talk with kings,
He talked with simple people
Of doing friendly things.

He didn't praise the conquerors
And all their hero host,
He said the very greatest
Were those who loved the most.

He didn't speak of mighty deeds
And victories. He spoke
Of feeding hungry people
And cheering lonely folk.

I'm glad his words were simple words
Just meant for me and you,
The things he asked were simple things
That even I can do!

Marion Brown Shelton d. 1940

673. JESUS PRAYING

He sought the mountain and the loneliest height,
For He would meet his Father all alone,
And there, with many a tear and many a groan,
He strove in prayer throughout the long long night.
Why need He pray, who held by filial right,
O'er all the world alike of thought and sense,
The fulness of his Sire's omnipotence?
Why crave in prayer what was his own by might?
Vain is the question,—Christ was man in need,
And being man his duty was to pray.
The son of God confess'd the human need,
And doubtless ask'd a blessing every day.
Nor ceases yet for sinful man to plead,
Nor will, till heaven and earth shall pass away.

Hartley Coleridge, 1796–1849

674. ALONE INTO THE MOUNTAIN

All day from that deep well of life within
Himself has He drawn healing for the press
Of folk, restoring strength, forgiving sin,
Quieting frenzy, comforting distress.
Shadows of evening fall, yet wildly still
They throng Him, touch Him, clutch His garment's hem,
Fall down and clasp His feet, cry on Him, till
The Master, spent, slips from the midst of them
And climbs the mountain for a cup of peace,
Taking a sheer and rugged track untrod
Save by a poor lost sheep with thorn-torn fleece
That follows on and hears Him talk with God.

Katharine Lee Bates, 1859–1929

675. THE SONG OF A HEATHEN

(Sojourning in Galilee, A.D. 32)

If Jesus Christ is a man—
And only a man,—I say
That of all mankind I cleave to him,
And to him will I cleave alway.

If Jesus Christ is a God—
And the only God,—I swear
I will follow him through heaven and hell,
The earth, the sea, the air!

Richard Watson Gilder, 1844–1909

676. FAITH

And must I say that God is Christ
Or Jesus God in human guise,
When I can say He has sufficed
To bring the light to shadowed eyes?

I do not care to speculate
On things mysterious to the mind;
But O the rapture, early, late,
Of light to eyes that once were blind.

Edwin McNeill Poteat, 1892–

677. CHRIST THE MAN

Lord, I say nothing; I profess
No faith in Thee nor Christ Thy Son:
Yet no man ever heard me mock
A true believing one.

If knowledge is not great enough
To give a man believing power,
Lord, he must wait in Thy great hand
Till revelation's hour.

Meanwhile he'll follow Christ the man,
In that humanity He taught,
Which to the poor and the oppressed,
Gives its best time and thought.

William H. Davies, 1871–1940

678. AN UNBELIEVER

All these on whom the sacred seal was set,
They could forsake thee while thine eyes were wet.
Brother, not once have I believed in thee,
Yet having seen I cannot once forget.

I have looked long into those friendly eyes,
And found thee dreaming, fragile, and unwise.
Brother, not once have I believed in thee,
Yet have I loved thee for thy gracious lies.

One broke thee with a kiss at eventide,
And he that loved thee well has thrice denied.
Brother, I have no faith in thee at all,
Yet must I seek thy hands, thy feet, thy side.

Behold that John that leaned upon thy breast—
His eyes grew heavy and he needs must rest.
I watched unseen through dark Gethsemane
And might not slumber, for I loved thee best.

Peace thou wilt give to them of troubled
mind,
Bread to the hungry, spittle to the blind.
My heart is broken for my unbelief,
But that thou canst not heal, though thou
art kind.

They asked one day to sit beside thy throne.
I made one prayer, in silence and alone.
Brother, thou knowest my unbelief in thee.
Bear not my sins, for thou must bear thine
own.

Even he that grieves thee most "Lord, Lord,"
he saith.
So will I call on thee with my last breath!
Brother, not once have I believed in thee,
Yet I am wounded for thee unto death.

Anna Hempstead Branch, 1875?–1937

679. THE BETTER PART

Long fed on boundless hopes, O race of man,
How angrily thou spurn'st all simpler fare!
"Christ," someone says, "was human as we
are;
No judge eyes us from heaven, our sin to scan;
We live no more, when we have done our
span."
"Well, then, for Christ," thou answerest,
"who can care?
From sin which Heaven records not, why
forbear?
Live we like brutes our life without a plan!"

So answerest thou; but why not rather say—
"Hath man no second life? *Pitch this one high!*
Sits there no judge in heaven, our sin to see?
More strictly, then, the inward judge obey!
Was Christ a man like us? *Ah! let us try*
If we then, too, can be such men as He!"

Matthew Arnold, 1822–1888

680. OUR CHRIST

A Harvard Prize Hymn

I know not how that Bethlehem's Babe
Could in the God-head be;
I only know the Manger Child
Has brought God's life to me.

I know not how that Calvary's cross
A world from sin could free:
I only know its matchless love
Has brought God's love to me.

I know not how that Joseph's tomb
Could solve death's mystery:
I only know a living Christ,
Our immortality.

Harry Webb Farrington, 1880–1931

681. THE MAN CHRIST

He built no temple, yet the farthest sea
Can yield no shore that's barren of His place
For bended knee.

He wrote no book, and yet His words and
prayer
Are intimate on many myriad tongues,
Are counsel everywhere.

The life He lived has never been assailed,
Nor any precept, as He lived it, yet
Has ever failed.

He built no kingdom, yet a King from youth
He reigned, is reigning yet; they call His
realm
The kingdom of the Truth.

Therese Lindsey, 1870–

682. A VIRILE CHRIST

Give us a virile Christ for these rough days!
You painters, sculptors, show the warrior
bold;
And you who turn mere words to gleaming
gold,
Too long your lips have sounded in the praise
Of patience and humility. Our ways
Have parted from the quietude of old;
We need a man of strength with us to hold
The very breach of Death without amaze.
Did he not scourge from temple courts the
thieves?
And make the arch-fiend's self again to fall?
And blast the fig-tree that was only leaves?
And still the raging tumult of the seas?
Did he not bear the greatest pain of all,
Silent, upon the cross on Calvary?

Rex Boundy, contemporary American

683. THE BARGAIN

"Tell me your name," I challenged Christ.
"Were you prophet, saint supreme?
Did you wear true flesh and blood?
Are you that which we call God?
Or but a hope, a sigh,
A thing compacted of man's dream?"

"I will declare myself," said Christ
"When you confess your name and station."
Easy terms. I thought and thought
But still the sum of me was nought.
"A dying sinner, I"
And straight he told his name, "Salvation."

Anna Bunston de Bary,
contemporary English

684. From JESUS THE COMFORTER

Jesu, to Thee I cry and greed;
Prince of Peace, to Thee I pray;
Thou wouldest bleed for mannis need,
And suffer many a fearful fray;
Thou me freed in all my dread,
With patience now and aye,
My life to lead in word and deed,
As is most pleasant to Thy pay,
And to die well when it is my day.
Jesu, that died on tree for us,
Let me not be the Fiendis prey,
But be my comfort, Christ Jesus . . .

Early 15th century

685. ROCK OF AGES

Rock of Ages, cleft for me,
Let me hide myself in Thee!
Let the water and the blood
From Thy riven side which flow'd,
Be of sin the double cure,
Cleanse me from its guilt and power.

Not the labours of my hands
Can fulfil Thy law's demands;
Could my zeal no respite know,
Could my tears for ever flow,
All for sin could not atone;
Thou must save, and Thou alone.

Nothing in my hand I bring;
Simply to Thy Cross I cling;
Naked, come to Thee for dress;
Helpless, look to Thee for grace;
Foul, I to the Fountain fly;
Wash me, Saviour, or I die!

While I draw this fleeting breath,
When my eyelids close in death,
When I soar through tracts unknown,
See Thee on Thy Judgement-throne;
Rock of Ages, cleft for me,
Let me hide myself in Thee!

Augustus Montague Toplady, 1740–1778

686. JESUS, REFUGE OF THE WEARY

Jesus, refuge of the weary,
Treasure of the spirit's love,
Fountain in life's desert dreary,
Saviour from the world above;
O how oft Thine eyes, offended,
Gaze upon the sinner's fall!
Yet upon the cross extended,
Thou didst bear the pain of all.

Do we pass that cross unheeding,
Breathing no repentant vow,
Though we see Thee, wounded, bleeding,
See Thy thorn-encircled brow!
Yet Thy sinless death has brought us
Life eternal, peace and rest;
Only what Thy grace has taught us
Calms the sinner's stormy breast.

Jesus, may our hearts be burning
With more fervent love for Thee!
May our eyes be ever turning
To Thy cross of agony;
Till in glory, parted never
From the blessed Saviour's side,
Graven in our hearts for ever,
Dwell the cross, the Crucified.

Girolamo Savonarola, 1452–1498

687. I KNOW A NAME

I know a soul that is steeped in sin,
  That no man's art can cure;
But I know a Name, a Name, a Name
  That can make that soul all pure.

I know a life that is lost to God,
  Bound down by the things of earth;
But I know a Name, a Name, a Name
  That can bring that soul new birth.

I know of lands that are sunk in shame,
Of hearts that faint and tire;
But I know a Name, a Name, a Name
That can set those lands on fire.

Its sound is a brand, its letters flame
Like glowing tongues of fire.
I know a Name, a Name, a Name
That will set those lands on fire.

Author unknown

688. I WAS A STRICKEN DEER

From "The Task," Book III

I was a stricken deer, that left the herd
Long since; with many an arrow deep infixt
My panting side was charg'd, when I withdrew
To seek a tranquil death in distant shades.
There was I found by one who had himself
Been hurt by th' archers. In his side he bore,
And in his hands and feet, the cruel scars.
With gentle force soliciting the darts,
He drew them forth, and heal'd, and bade me live.
Since then, with few associates, in remote
And silent woods I wander, far from those
My former partners of the peopled scene;
With few associates, and not wishing more.
Here much I ruminate, as much I may,
With other views of men and manners now
Than once, and others of a life to come.

William Cowper, 1731–1800

689. FIERCE WAS THE WILD BILLOW

Fierce was the wild billow,
Dark was the night,
Oars labored heavily,
Foam glimmered white;
Trembled the mariners,
Peril was nigh;
Then said the God of God,
"Peace! It is I."

Ridge of the mountain-wave,
Lower thy crest!
Wail of Euroclydon,
Be thou at rest!
Sorrow can never be,
Darkness must fly,
Where saith the Light of Light,
"Peace! It is I."

Jesus, Deliverer,
Come Thou to me;
Soothe Thou my voyaging
Over life's sea;
Thou, when the storm of death
Roars, sweeping by,
Whisper, O Truth of Truth,
"Peace! It is I."

Anatolius, 8th century;
tr. by John M. Neale, 1818–1866

690. LOVE DIVINE

Love Divine, all loves excelling,
Joy of heaven, to earth come down,
Fix in us Thy humble dwelling,
All Thy faithful mercies crown.
Jesus, Thou art all compassion;
Pure, unbounded love Thou art;
Visit us with Thy salvation,
Enter every trembling heart.

Come, Almighty to deliver;
Let us all Thy grace receive;
Suddenly return, and never,
Never more Thy temples leave.
Thee we would be always blessing,
Serve Thee as Thy hosts above,
Pray, and praise Thee, without ceasing,
Glory in Thy perfect love.

Finish, then, Thy new creation;
Pure and spotless let us be;
Let us see Thy great salvation,
Perfectly restored in Thee,
Changed from glory into glory,
Till in heaven we take our place,
Till we cast our crowns before Thee,
Lost in wonder, love, and praise.

Charles Wesley, 1707–1788

691. E TENEBRIS

Come down, O Christ, and help me! reach my hand,
For I am drowning in a stormier sea
Than Simon on thy lake of Galilee:

The wine of life is spilt upon the sand,
My heart is as some famine-murdered land
  Whence all good things have perished utterly,
  And well I know my soul in Hell must lie
If I this night before God's throne should stand.
"He sleeps perchance, or rideth to the chase,
  Like Baal, when his prophets howled that name
  From morn to noon on Carmel's smitten height."
Nay, peace, I shall behold, before the night,
  The feet of brass, the robe more white than flame,
  The wounded hands, the weary human face.

Oscar Wilde, 1856–1900

692. SALUTATION TO JESUS CHRIST

I greet thee, my Redeemer sure,
  I trust in none but thee,
Thou who hast borne such toil and shame
  And suffering for me:
Our hearts from cares and cravings vain
  And foolish fears set free.

Thou art the King compassionate,
  Thou reignest everywhere,
Almighty Lord, reign thou in us,
  Rule all we have and are:
Enlighten us and raise to heaven,
  Amid thy glories there.

Thou art the life by which we live;
  Our stay and strength's in thee;
Uphold us so in face of death,
  What time soe'er it be,
That we may meet it with strong heart,
  And may die peacefully.

❖

Our hope is in none else but thee;
  Faith holds thy promise fast;
Be pleased, Lord, to strengthen us,
  Whom Thou redeemed hast,
To bear all troubles patiently,
  And overcome at last. . . .

John Calvin, 1509–1564

693. SAUL

I

Said Abner, "At last thou art come! Ere I tell, ere thou speak,
Kiss my cheek, wish me well!" Then I wished it, and did kiss his cheek.
And he: "Since the King, O my friend, for thy countenance sent,
Neither drunken nor eaten have we; nor until from his tent
Thou return with the joyful assurance the King liveth yet,
Shall our lip with the honey be bright, with the water be wet.
For out of the black mid-tent's silence, a space of three days,
Not a sound hath escaped to thy servants, of prayer nor of praise,
To betoken that Saul and the Spirit have ended their strife,
And that, faint in his triumph, the monarch sinks back upon life.

II

"Yet now my heart leaps, O beloved! God's child with his dew
On thy gracious gold hair, and those lilies still living and blue
Just broken to twine around thy harp-strings, as if no wild heat
Were now raging to torture the desert!"

III

Then I, as was meet,
Knelt down to the God of my fathers, and rose on my feet,
And ran o'er the sand burnt to powder. The tent was unlooped;
I pulled up the spear that obstructed, and under I stooped;
Hands and knees on the slippery grass-patch, all withered and gone,
That extends to the second enclosure, I groped my way on
Till I felt where the foldskirts fly open. Then once more I prayed,
And opened the foldskirts and entered, and was not afraid
But spoke, "Here is David, thy servant!"
And no voice replied.
At the first I saw naught but the blackness: but soon I descried
A something more black than the blackness—the vast, the upright
Main prop which sustains the pavilion: and slow into sight
Grew a figure against it, gigantic and blackest of all.
Then a sunbeam, that burst through the tent-roof, showed Saul.

IV

He stood as erect as that tent-prop, both arms stretched out wide
On the great cross-support in the centre, that goes to each side;
He relaxed not a muscle, but hung there as, caught in his pangs
And waiting his change, the king-serpent all heavily hangs,
Far away from his kind, in the pine, till deliverance come
With the spring-time,—so agonized Saul, drear and stark, blind and dumb.

V

Then I tuned my harp,—took off the lilies we twine round its chords
Lest they snap 'neath the stress of the noontide—those sunbeams like swords!
And I first played the tune all our sheep know, as, one after one,
So docile they come to the pen-door till folding be done.
They are white and untorn by the bushes, for lo, they have fed
Where the long grasses stifle the water within the stream's bed;
And now one after one seeks its lodging, as star follows star
Into eve and the blue far above us,—so blue and so far!

VI

—Then the tune for which quails on the cornland will each leave his mate
To fly after the player; then, what makes the crickets elate
Till for boldness they fight one another; and then, what has weight
To set the quick jerboa a-musing outside his sand house—
There are none such as he for a wonder, half bird and half mouse—!
God made all the creatures and gave them our love and our fear,
To give sign, we and they are his children, one family here.

VII

Then I played the help-tune of our reapers, their wine-song, when hand
Grasps at hand, eye lights eye in good friendship, and great hearts expand
And grow one in the sense of this world's life.
—And then, the last song
When the dead man is praised on his journey—
"Bear, bear him along,
With his few faults shut up like dead flowerets!
Are balm seeds not here

To console us? The land has none left such as he on the bier.
Oh, would we might keep thee, my brother!"
 —And then, the glad chaunt
Of the marriage,—first go the young maidens next, she whom we vaunt
As the beauty, the pride of our dwelling.—And then, the great march
Wherein man runs to man to assist him and buttress an arch
Naught can break; who shall harm them, our friends? Then, the chorus intoned
As the Levites go up to the altar in glory enthroned.
But I stopped here: for here in the darkness Saul groaned.

VIII

And I paused, held my breath in such silence, and listened apart;
And the tent shook, for mighty Saul shuddered: and sparkles 'gan dart
From the jewels that woke in his turban, at once with a start,
All its lordly male-sapphires, and rubies courageous at heart.
So the head: but the body still moved not, still hung there erect.
And I bent once again to my playing, pursued it unchecked,
As I sang:—

IX

"Oh, our manhood's prime vigor! No spirit feels waste,
Not a muscle is stopped in its playing nor sinew unbraced.
Oh, the wild joys of living! the leaping from rock up to rock,
The strong rending of boughs from the fir-tree, the cool silver shock
Of the plunge in a pool's living water, the hunt of the bear,
And the sultriness showing the lion is couched in his lair.
And the meal, the rich dates yellowed over with gold dust divine,
And the locust-flesh steeped in the pitcher, the full draught of wine,
And the sleep in the dried river-channel where bulrushes tell
That the water was wont to go warbling so softly and well.
How good is man's life, the mere living! how fit to employ
All the heart and the soul and the senses forever in joy!
Hast thou loved the white locks of thy father, whose sword thou didst guard
When he trusted thee forth with the armies, for glorious reward?
Didst thou see the thin hands of thy mother held up as men sung
The low song of the nearly-departed, and hear her faint tongue
Joining in while it could to the witness, 'Let one more attest,
I have lived, seen God's hand through a lifetime, and all was for best'?
Then they sung through their tears in strong triumph, not much, but the rest.
And thy brothers, the help and the contest, the working whence grew
Such result as, from seething grape-bundles, the spirit strained true:
And the friends of thy boyhood—that boyhood of wonder and hope,
Present promise and wealth of the future beyond the eye's scope,—
Till lo, thou art grown to a monarch; a people is thine;
And all gifts, which the world offers singly, on one head combine!
On one head, all the beauty and strength, love and rage (like the throe
That, a-work in the rock, helps its labor and lets the gold go)
High ambition and deeds which surpass it, fame crowning them,—all
Brought to blaze on the head of one creature—King Saul!"

X

And lo, with that leap of my spirit,—heart, hand, harp and voice,
Each lifting Saul's name out of sorrow, each bidding rejoice
Saul's fame in the light it was made for—as when, dare I say,

The Lord's army, in rapture of service, strains through its array,
And upsoareth the cherubim-chariot—"Saul!" cried I, and stopped,
And waited the thing that should follow. Then Saul, who hung propped
By the tent's cross-support in the centre, was struck by his name.
Have ye seen when Spring's arrowy summons goes right to the aim,
And some mountain, the last to withstand her, that held (he alone,
While the vale laughed in freedom and flowers) on a broad bust of stone
A year's snow bound about for a breastplate,—leaves grasp of the sheet?
Fold on fold all at once it crowds thunderously down to his feet,
And there fronts you, stark, black, but alive yet, your mountain of old,
With his rents, the successive bequeathings of ages untold—
Yea, each harm got in fighting your battles, each furrow and scar
Of his head thrust 'twixt you and the tempest—all hail, there they are!
—Now again to be softened with verdure, again hold the nest
Of the dove, tempt the goat and its young to the green on his crest
For their food in the ardors of summer. One long shudder thrilled
All the tent till the very air tingled, then sank and was stilled
At the King's self left standing before me, released and aware.
What was gone, what remained? All to traverse 'twixt hope and despair,
Death was past, life not come: so he waited.
  Awhile his right hand
Held the brow, helped the eyes left too vacant forthwith to remand
To their place what new objects should enter: 'twas Saul as before.
I looked up and dared gaze at those eyes, nor was hurt any more
Than by slow pallid sunsets in autumn, ye watch from the shore,
At their sad level gaze o'er the ocean—a sun's slow decline
Over hills which, resolved in stern silence, o'erlap and entwine
Base with base to knit a strength more intensely so, arm folded arm
O'er the chest whose slow heavings subsided.

XI

    What spell or what charm,
(For awhile there was trouble within me,) what next should I urge
To sustain him where song had restored him?—Song filled to the verge
His cup with the wine of this life, pressing all that it yields
Of mere fruitage, the strength and the beauty: beyond, on what fields,
Glean a vintage more potent and perfect to brighten the eye
And bring blood to the lip, and commend them the cup they put by?
He saith, "It is good;" still he drinks not: he lets me praise life,
Gives assent, yet would die for his own part.

XII

    Then fancies grew rife
Which had come long ago on the pasture, when round me the sheep
Fed in silence—above, the one eagle wheeled slow as in sleep;
And I lay in my hollow and mused on the world that might lie
'Neath his ken, though I saw but the strip 'twixt the hill and the sky:
And I laughed—"Since my days are ordained to be passed with my flocks,
Let me people at least, with my fancies, the plains and the rocks,
Dream the life I am never to mix with, and image the show
Of mankind as they live in those fashions I hardly shall know!
Schemes of life, its best rules and right uses, the courage that gains,
And the prudence that keeps what men strive for." And now these old trains
Of vague thought came again; I grew surer; so, once more the string
Of my harp made response to my spirit, as thus—

XIII

"Yea, my King,"
I began—"thou dost well in rejecting mere comforts that spring
From the mere mortal life held in common by man and by brute:
In our flesh grows the branch of this life, in our soul it bears fruit.
Thou hast marked the slow rise of the tree,—how its stem trembled first
Till it passed the kid's lip, the stag's antler; then safely outburst
The fan-branches all round; and thou mindest when these too, in turn,
Broke a-bloom and the palm-tree seemed perfect: yet more was to learn,
E'en the good that comes in with the palm-fruit. Our dates shall we slight,
When their juice brings a cure for all sorrow? or care for the plight
Of the palm's self whose slow growth produced them? Not so! stem and branch
Shall decay, nor be known in their place, while the palm-wine shall stanch
Every wound of man's spirit in winter. I pour thee such wine.
Leave the flesh to the fate it was fit for! the spirit be thine!
By the spirit, when age shall o'ercome thee, thou still shalt enjoy
More indeed, than at first when inconscious, the life of a boy.
Crush that life, and behold its wine running! Each deed thou hast done
Dies, revives, goes to work in the world; until e'en as the sun
Looking down on the earth, though clouds spoil him, though tempests efface,
Can find nothing his own deed produced not, must everywhere trace
The results of his past summer-prime,—so, each ray of thy will,
Every flash of thy passion and prowess, long over, shall thrill
Thy whole people, the countless, with ardor, till they too give forth
A like cheer to their sons, who in turn, fill the South and the North
With the radiance thy deed was the germ of. Carouse in the past!
But the license of age has its limit; thou diest at last:
As the lion when age dims his eyeball, the rose at her height,
So with man—so his power and his beauty forever take flight.
No! Again a long draught of my soul-wine! Look forth o'er the years!
Thou hast done now with eyes for the actual; begin with the seer's!
Is Saul dead? In the depth of the vale make his tomb—bid arise
A gray mountain of marble heaped four-square, till, built to the skies,
Let it mark where the great First King slumbers: whose fame would ye know?
Up above see the rock's naked face, where the record shall go
In great characters cut by the scribe,—Such was Saul, so he did;
With the sages directing the work, by the populace chid,—
For not half, they'll affirm, is comprised there! Which fault to amend,
In the grove with his kind grows the cedar, whereon they shall spend
(See, in tablets 'tis level before them) their praise, and record
With the gold of the graver, Saul's story,—the statesman's great word
Side by side with the poet's sweet comment. The river's a-wave
With smooth paper-reeds grazing each other when prophet-winds rave:
So the pen gives unborn generations their due and their part
In thy being! Then, first of the mighty, thank God that thou art!"

XIV

And behold while I sang . . . but O Thou who didst grant me that day,
And before it not seldom hast granted thy help to essay,
Carry on and complete an adventure,—my shield and my sword
In that act where my soul was thy servant, thy word was my word,—
Still be with me, who then at the summit of human endeavor
And scaling the highest, man's thought could, gazed hopeless as ever
On the new stretch of heaven above me—till, mighty to save,

Just one lift of thy hand cleared that distance—God's throne from man's grave!
Let me tell out my tale to its ending—my voice to my heart
Which can scarce dare believe in what marvels last night I took part,
As this morning I gather the fragments, alone with my sheep,
And still fear lest the terrible glory evanish like sleep!
For I wake in the gray dewy covert, while Hebron upheaves
The dawn struggling with night on his shoulder, and Kidron retrieves
Slow the damage of yesterday's sunshine.

XV

I say then,—my song
While I sang thus, assuring the monarch, and ever more strong
Made a proffer of good to console him—he slowly resumed
His old motions and habitudes kingly. The right hand replumed
His black locks to their wonted composure, adjusted the swathes
Of his turban, and see—the huge sweat that his countenance bathes,
He wipes off with the robe; and he girds now his loins as of yore,
And feels slow for the armlets of price, with the clasp set before.
He is Saul, ye remember in glory,—ere error had bent
The broad brow from the daily communion; and still, though much spent
Be the life and the bearing that front you, the same, God did choose,
To receive what a man may waste, desecrate, never quite lose.
So sank he along by the tent-prop till, stayed by the pile
Of his armor and war-cloak and garments, he leaned there awhile,
And sat out my singing,—one arm round the tent-prop, to raise
His bent head, and the other hung slack—till I touched on the praise
I foresaw from all men in all time, to the man patient there;
And thus ended, the harp falling forward. Then first I was 'ware
That he sat, as I say, with my head just above his vast knees
Which were thrust out on each side around me, like oak roots which please
To encircle a lamb when it slumbers. I looked up to know
If the best I could do had brought solace: he spoke not, but slow
Lifted up the hand slack at his side, till he laid it with care
Soft and grave, but in mild settled will, on my brow: through my hair
The large fingers were pushed, and he bent back my head, with kind power—
All my face back, intent to peruse it, as men do a flower.
Thus held he me there with his great eyes that scrutinized mine—
And oh, all my heart how it loved him! but where was the sign?
I yearned—"Could I help thee, my father, inventing a bliss,
I would add, to that life of the past, both the future and this;
I would give thee new life altogether, as good, ages hence,
As this moment,—had love but the warrant, love's heart to dispense!"

XVI

Then the truth came upon me. No harp more—no song more! outbroke—

XVII

"I have gone the whole round of creation: I saw and I spoke:
I, a work of God's hand for that purpose, received in my brain
And pronounced on the rest of his handwork—returned him again
His creation's approval or censure: I spoke as I saw:
I report, as a man may of God's work—all's love, yet all's law.
Now I lay down the judgeship he lent me. Each faculty tasked
To perceive him, has gained an abyss, where a dewdrop was asked.

Have I knowledge? confounded it shrivels at Wisdom laid bare.
Have I forethought? how purblind, how blank, to the Infinite Care!
Do I task any faculty highest, to image success?
I but open my eyes,—and perfection, no more and no less,
In the kind I imagined, full-fronts me, and God is seen God
In the star, in the stone, in the flesh, in the soul and the clod.
And thus looking within and around me, I ever renew
(With that stoop of the soul which in bending upraises it too)
The submission of man's nothing-perfect to God's all-complete,
As by each new obeisance in spirit, I climb to his feet.
Yet with all this abounding experience, this deity known,
I shall dare to discover some province, some gift of my own.
There's a faculty pleasant to exercise, hard to hoodwink,
I am fain to keep still in abeyance, (I laugh as I think)
Lest, insisting to claim and parade in it, wot ye, I worst
E'en the Giver in one gift.—Behold, I could love if I durst!
But I sink the pretension as fearing a man may o'ertake
God's own speed in the one way of love: I abstain for love's sake.
—What, my soul? see thus far and no farther? when doors great and small,
Nine-and-ninety flew ope at our touch, should the hundredth appall?
In the least things have faith, yet distrust in the greatest of all?
Do I find love so full in my nature, God's ultimate gift,
That I doubt his own love can compete with it? Here, the parts shift?
Here, the creature surpass the Creator,—the end, what Began?
Would I fain in my impotent yearning do all for this man,
And dare doubt he alone shall not help him, who yet alone can?
Would it ever have entered my mind, the bare will, much less power,
To bestow on this Saul what I sang of, the marvellous dower
Of the life he was gifted and filled with? to make such a soul,
Such a body, and then such an earth for insphering the whole?
And doth it not enter my mind (as my warm tears attest)
These good things being given, to go on, and give one more, the best?
Ay, to save and redeem and restore him, maintain at the height
This perfection,—succeed with life's dayspring, death's minute of night?
Interpose at the difficult minute, snatch Saul the mistake,
Saul the failure, the ruin he seems now,—and bid him awake
From the dream, the probation, the prelude, to find himself set
Clear and safe in new light and new life,—a new harmony yet
To be run, and continued, and ended—who knows?—or endure!
The man taught enough by life's dream, of the rest to make sure;
By the pain-throb, triumphantly winning intensified bliss,
And the next world's reward and repose, by the struggles in this.

XVIII

"I believe it! 'Tis thou, God, that givest, 'tis I who receive:
In the first is the last, in thy will is my power to believe.
All's one gift: thou canst grant it moreover, as prompt to my prayer
As I breathe out this breath, as I open these arms to the air.
From thy will stream the worlds, life and nature, thy dread Sabaoth:
I will?—the mere atoms despise me! Why am I not loth
To look that, even that in the face too? Why is it I dare
Think but lightly of such impuissance? What stops my despair?
This;—'tis not what man Does which exalts him, but what man Would do!
See the King—I would help him but cannot, the wishes fall through.

Could I wrestle to raise him from sorrow, grow poor to enrich,
To fill up his life, starve my own out, I would—knowing which,
I know that my service is perfect. Oh, speak through me now!
Would I suffer for him that I love? So wouldst thou—so wilt thou!
So shall crown thee the topmost, ineffablest, uttermost crown—
And thy love fill infinitude wholly, nor leave up nor down
One spot for the creature to stand in! It is by no breath,
Turn of eye, wave of hand, that salvation joins issue with death!
As thy Love is discovered almighty, almighty be proved
Thy power, that exists with and for it, of being Beloved!
He who did most, shall bear most; the strongest shall stand the most weak.
'Tis the weakness in strength, that I cry for! my flesh, that I seek
In the Godhead! I seek and I find it. O Saul, it shall be
A Face like my face that receives thee; a Man like to me,
Thou shalt love and be loved by, forever: a Hand like this hand
Shall throw open the gates of new life to thee! See the Christ stand!"

XIX

I know not too well how I found my way home in the night.
There were witnesses, cohorts about me, to left and to right,
Angels, powers, the unuttered, unseen, the alive, the aware:
I repressed, I got through them as hardly, as strugglingly there,
As a runner beset by the populace famished for news—
Life or death. The whole earth was awakened, hell loosed with her crews;
And the stars of night beat with emotion, and tingled and shot
Out in fire the strong pain of pent knowledge: but I fainted not,
For the Hand still impelled me at once and supported, suppressed
All the tumult, and quenched it with quiet, and holy behest,
Till the rapture was shut in itself, and the earth sank to rest.
Anon at the dawn, all that trouble had withered from earth—
Not so much, but I saw it die out in the day's tender birth;
In the gathered intensity brought to the gray of the hills;
In the shuddering forests' held breath; in the sudden wind-thrills;
In the startled wild beasts that bore off, each with eye sidling still
Though averted with wonder and dread; in the birds stiff and chill
That rose heavily, as I approached them, made stupid with awe:
E'en the serpent that slid away silent,—he felt the new law.
The same stared in the white humid faces upturned by the flowers;
The same worked in the heart of the cedar and moved the vine-bowers:
And the little brooks witnessing murmured, persistent and low,
With their obstinate, all but hushed voices—
"E'en so, it is so!"

Robert Browning, 1812–1889

694. I LIFT MY GAZE

I lift my gaze beyond the night, and see,
Above the banners of Man's hate unfurled,
The holy figure that on Calvary
Stretched arms out wide enough for all the world.

John Hall Wheelock, 1886–

695. OUT OF BOUNDS

A little Boy of heavenly birth,
But far from home to-day,
Comes down to find His ball, the earth,
That sin has cast away.
O comrades, let us one and all
Join in to get Him back His ball!

John Banister Tabb, 1845–1909

696. "A MAN MUST LIVE"

"A man must live!" We justify
Low shift and trick, to treason high;
A little vote for a little gold,
Or a whole Senate bought and sold,
With this self-evident reply—
"A man must live!"

But is it so? Pray tell me why
Life at such cost you have to buy.
In what religion were you told
A man must live?
There are times when a man must die!
There are times when a man will die!
Imagine for a battle-cry
From soldiers with a sword to hold,
From soldiers with a flag unfurled,
This coward's whine, this liar's lie,
"A man must live!"

The Saviour did not "live!"
He died!
But in his death was life—
Life for himself and all mankind!
He found his life by losing it!
And we, being crucified
Afresh with him, may find
Life in the cup of death,
And, drinking it,
Win life forever more.

Charlotte Stetson Gilman, 1860–1935

697. From CHARITAS NIMIA

or The Dear Bargain

Lord, what is man? why should he cost thee
So dear? what had his ruin lost thee?
Lord, what is man? that thou hast overbought
So much a thing of naught?

❖

What if my faithless soul and I
Would needs fall in
With guilt and sin,
What did the lamb, that he should die?
What did the lamb, that he should need,
When the wolf sins, himself to bleed?

If my base lust,
Bargain'd with death and well-beseeming dust
Why would the white
Lamb's bosom write
The purple name
Of my sin's shame?

Why should his unstain'd breast make good
My blushes with his own heart-blood?
O my Saviour, make me see
How dearly thou hast paid for me

That lost again my life may prove
As then in death, so now in love.

Richard Crashaw, 1613?–1649

698. SEND ME

O Thou best gift from heaven,
Thou who Thyself hast given,
For Thou hast died—

This hast Thou done for me,—
What have I done for Thee,
Thou crucified?

I long to serve Thee more,
Reveal an open door
Saviour, to me.

Then counting all but loss,
I'll glory in Thy cross,
And follow Thee.

Author unknown

699. From SAINT PATRICK'S BREASTPLATE

I bind unto myself to-day
The power of God to hold and lead,
His eye to watch, His might to stay,
His ear to hearken to my need,
The wisdom of my God to teach,
His hand to guide, His shield to ward;
The word of God to give me speech,
His heavenly host to be my guard.

I bind unto myself the name,
The strong name of the Trinity;
By invocation of the same
The Three in One and One in Three,
Of whom all nature hath creation;
Eternal Father, Spirit, Word;
Praise to the Lord of my salvation,
Salvation is of CHRIST the LORD.

Ascribed to St. Patrick, 389?–461?

700. THE TRUE GIFT

I gave a beggar from my scanty store
Of hard-earned gold. He spent the shining ore
And came again, and yet again, still cold
And hungry, as before.

I gave the Christ, and through that Christ of
mine
He found himself, a man, supreme, divine,
Fed, clothed, and crowned with blessings
manifold,
And now he begs no more.

Author unknown

701. THE CAPTAIN

Written after reading Henley's "Invictus"

Out of the light that dazzles me,
Bright as the sun from pole to pole
I thank the God I know to be
For Christ—the Conqueror of my soul.

Since His the sway of circumstance
I would not wince, nor cry aloud.
Under that rule which men call chance,
My head, with joy, is humbly bowed.

Beyond this place of sin and tears,
That life with Him—and His the aid
That, spite the menace of the years,
Keeps, and will keep me, unafraid.

I have no fear though strait the gate:
He cleared from punishment the scroll.
Christ is the Master of my fate!
Christ is the Captain of my soul.

Dorothea Day, c. 1900

702. THE WORLD SITS AT THE FEET OF CHRIST

From "The Overheart"

The world sits at the feet of Christ,
Unknowing, blind and unconsoled;
It yet shall touch His garment's fold,
And feel the heavenly Alchemist
Transform its very dust to gold.

John Greenleaf Whittier, 1807–1892

703. "I AM THE WAY"

Thou art the Way
Hadst Thou been nothing but the goal,
I cannot say
If Thou hadst ever met my soul.

I cannot see—
I, child of process—if there lies
An end for me,
Full of repose, full of replies.

I'll not reproach
The road that winds, my feet that err.
Access, Approach
Art Thou, Time, Way, and Wayfarer.

Alice Meynell, 1847–1922

704. VIA, ET VERITAS, ET VITA

"You never attained to Him?" "If to attain
Be to abide, then that may be."
"Endless the way, followed with how much
pain!"
"The way was He."

Alice Meynell, 1847–1922

705. THE WAY O CHRIST THOU ART

With thee, O Christ, I fain would walk,
Thy pathway constant tread;
Thy spirit in my spirit live,
My life to thee be led.

The thought sublime that filled thy soul,
May this my soul inspire;
The purpose high that thee consumed
Burn in my heart as fire.

Thy blood for me thou gladly shedst,
My life, to thee I'd give,
In toil's hard road or on the cross;
Be mine to die or live.

Then for me earth's toils and joys
Howe'er it be, shall end;
Like thee, O Christ, my soul to God
In peace I will commend.

May those who after me shall come
Find blazed on rock and tree
Signs of the path that thou didst tread
And finding follow thee.

And while the years roll on, may men
Of cloister, field and mart
The way of life more clear e'er find—
The Way, O Christ, thou art!

Ernest De Witt Burton, 1856–1925

706. DIES IRAE

There were no footprints left upon the waters
When Jesus walked on Lake Gennesareth.
The unrecorded words His finger penciled
In dust upon the road are gone like breath.

Yet when the charts and books are all discarded,
And, dreadful in the dawn, the horn is heard
Above the ended roads, the cancelled phrases,
Behold! the endless Way, the deathless Word!

James L. Duff, 1891–

707. ASPIRATION

But O my God! though grovelling I appear
Upon the ground, and have a rooting here
Which pulls me downward, yet in my desire
To that which is above me I aspire:
And all my best affections I profess
To Him that is the Sun of Righteousness.
Oh! keep the morning of His incarnation,
The burning noontide of His bitter passion,
The night of His descending, and the height
Of His ascension—ever in my sight!
That, imitating Him in what I may,
I never follow an inferior way.

George Wither, 1588–1667

708. MY LIGHT! MY WAY!

O Thou, to whose all-searching sight
The darkness shineth as the light,
Search, prove my heart; it pants for Thee;
O burst these bonds, and set it free!

Wash out its stains, refine its dross,
Nail my affections to the Cross;
Hallow each thought; let all within
Be clean, as Thou, my Lord, art clean!

If in this darksome wild I stray,
Be Thou my Light, be Thou my Way;
No foes, no violence I fear,
No fraud, while Thou, my God, art near.

When rising floods my soul o'erflow,
When sinks my heart in waves of woe,
Jesus, Thy timely aid impart,
And raise my head, and cheer my heart.

Saviour, where'er Thy steps I see,
Dauntless, untired, I follow Thee;
O let Thy hand support me still,
And lead me to Thy holy hill!

If rough and thorny be the way,
My strength proportion to my day;
Till toil, and grief, and pain shall cease,
Where all is calm, and joy, and peace.

Nicolaus Ludwig von Zinzendorf, 1700–1760;
tr. by John Wesley, 1703–1791

709. THE WAY, THE TRUTH, THE LIFE

Thou art the Way: to Thee alone
From sin and death we flee;
And he who would the Father seek
Must seek Him, Lord, by Thee.

Thou art the Truth: Thy Word alone
True wisdom can impart;
Thou only canst inform the mind,
And purify the heart.

Thou art the Life: the rending tomb
Proclaims Thy conquering arm;
And those who put their trust in Thee
Nor death nor hell shall harm.

Thou art the Way, the Truth, the Life:
Grant us that way to know,
That truth to keep, that life to win,
Whose joys eternal flow.

George Washington Doane, 1799–1859

710. O CHRIST, THE WAY

O Christ, the Way, the Truth, the Life,
Show me the living way,
That in the tumult and the strife
I may not go astray.

Teach me Thy Truth, O Christ, my Light,
The Truth that makes me free,
That in the darkness and the night
My trust shall be in Thee.

The Life that Thou alone canst give,
Impart in love to me,
That I may in Thy presence live,
And ever be like Thee.

George L. Squier, c. 1900

711. THE WAY, THE TRUTH, AND THE LIFE

O Thou great Friend to all the sons of men,
Who once appeared in humblest guise below,
Sin to rebuke, to break the captive's chain,
And call thy brethren forth from want and woe,—

We look to thee! thy truth is still the Light
Which guides the nations, groping on their way,
Stumbling and falling in disastrous night,
Yet hoping ever for the perfect day.

Yes; thou art still the Life, thou art the Way
The holiest know; Light, Life, the Way of heaven!
And they who dearest hope and deepest pray,
Toil by the Light, Life, Way, which thou hast given.

Theodore Parker, 1810–1860

712. HE IS THE WAY

Chorus from "For the Time Being, A Christmas Oratorio"

He is the Way.
Follow Him through the Land of Unlikeness;
You will see rare beasts, and have unique adventures.

He is the Truth.
Seek Him in the Kingdom of Anxiety;
You will come to a great city that has expected your return for years.

He is the Life.
Love Him in the World of the Flesh;
And at your marriage all its occasions shall dance for joy.

W. H. Auden, 1907–

713. IMPLICIT FAITH

Of all great Nature's tones that sweep
Earth's resonant bosom, far or near,
Low-breathed or loudest, shrill or deep,
How few are grasped by mortal ear.

Ten octaves close our scale of sound:
Its myriad grades, distinct or twined,
Transcend our hearing's petty bound,
To us as colours to the blind.

In Sound's unmeasured empire thus
The heights, the depths alike we miss;
Ah, but in measured sound to us
A compensating spell there is!

In holy music's golden speech
Remotest notes to notes respond:
Each octave is a world; yet each
Vibrates to worlds its own beyond.

Our narrow pale the vast resumes;
Our seashell whispers of the sea:
Echoes are ours of angel-plumes
That winnow far infinity!

—Clasp thou of Truth the central core!
Hold fast that centre's central sense!
An atom there shall fill thee more
Than realms on Truth's circumference.

That cradled Saviour, mute and small,
Was God—is God while worlds endure!
Who holds Truth truly holds it all
In essence, or in miniature.

Know what thou know'st! He knoweth much
Who knows not many things: and he
Knows most whose knowledge hath a touch
Of God's divine simplicity.

Aubrey Thomas de Vere, 1814–1902

714. LIGHT OF THE WORLD, HOW LONG THE QUEST

Light of the world, how long the quest
down weary years to learn Thy name!
From sacred fire on mountain crest;
or temple altar's lambent flame.

Cringing before the riven oak,
man fain the lightning would appease;
In fear the flaming dawn invoke,
or greet the morning on his knees.

Yet all the while, though hearts were dark,
soft glints of light were entering;
Each gleam of truth a glowing spark
of Thy divine illumining.

In Thee, O Christ, we hail the dawn,
with uncreated light aflame;
Before Thee terror is withdrawn;
Light of all times and hearts the same.

Edwin McNeill Poteat, 1892–

715. THOU LIGHT OF AGES

(For Candle-lighting Service)

Thou Light of Ages, Source of living truth,
Shine into every groping, seeking mind;
Let plodding age and pioneering youth
Each day some clearer, brighter pathway find.

Thou Light of Ages, shining forth in Christ,
Whose brightness darkest ages could not dim,
Grant us the spirit which for Him sufficed,—
Rekindle here the torch of love for Him.

Rolland W. Schloerb, 1893–

716. AT EVENTIDE

Now cheer our hearts this eventide,
Lord Jesus Christ, and with us bide:
Thou that canst never set in night,
Our heav'nly Sun, our glorious Light.

May we and all who bear thy name
By gentle love thy cross proclaim,
Thy gift of peace on earth secure,
And for thy Truth the world endure.

From the German, 1560;
tr. by Robert Bridges, 1844–1930

717. From THE PASSING CHRIST

Behold Him now as He comes!
Not the Christ of our subtle creeds,
But the Light of our hearts and our homes,
Our hopes, our fears, our needs,
The brother of want and blame,
The lover of women and men,
With a love that puts to shame
All passions of mortal ken . . . .

Ah, no, thou life of the heart,
Never shalt thou depart!
Not till the heaven of God
Shall lighten each human clod;
Not till the world shall climb
To the height serene, sublime,
Shall the Christ who enters our door
Pass to return no more.

Richard Watson Gilder, 1844–1909

718. THE LIGHT OF GOD IS FALLING

The light of God is falling
Upon life's common way;
The Master's voice still calling,
"Come, walk with Me to-day";
No duty can seem lowly
To him who lives with Thee,
And all of life grows holy,
O Christ of Galilee!

Who shares his life's pure pleasures,
And walks the honest road,
Who trades with heaping measures,
And lifts his brother's load,
Who turns the wrong down bluntly,
And lends the right a hand,
He dwells in God's own country,
He tills the Holy Land.

Where human lives are thronging
In toil and pain and sin,
While cloistered hearts are longing
To bring the Kingdom in,
O Christ, the Elder Brother
Of proud and beaten men,
When they have found each other,
Thy Kingdom will come then!

Thy ransomed host in glory,
All souls that sin and pray,
Turn toward the cross that bore Thee;
"Behold the Man!" they say:
And while Thy Church is pleading
For all who would do good,
We hear Thy true voice leading
Our song of brotherhood.

Louis F. Benson, 1855–1930

719. NEVER NIGHT AGAIN

The soft light from a stable door
Lies on the midnight lands.
The Wise Men's star burns evermore
Over all desert sands.

Unto all peoples of the earth
  A little Child brought light,
And never in the darkest place
  Can it be utter night.

No flickering torch, no wavering fire,
  But Light—the Life of men.
Whatever clouds may veil the sky,
  Never is night again!

Lilian Cox, contemporary English

720. O LOVE, THAT WILT NOT LET ME GO

O Love, that wilt not let me go,
  I rest my weary soul in Thee;
I give Thee back the life I owe,
That in Thine ocean depth its flow
    May richer, fuller be.

O Light, that followest all my way,
  I yield my flickering torch to Thee;
My heart restores its borrowed ray,
That in Thy sunshine's blaze its day
    May brighter, fairer be.

O Joy, that seekest me through pain,
  I cannot close my heart to Thee;
I trace the rainbow through the rain,
And feel the promise is not vain,
    That morn shall tearless be.

O Cross, that liftest up my head,
  I dare not ask to fly from Thee;
I lay in dust life's glory dead,
And from the ground there blossoms red
    Life that shall endless be.

George Matheson, 1842–1906

721. COME UNTO ME

Matthew 11: 28–30

Come unto me, all ye that labour and are heavy laden,
  and I will give you rest.
Take my yoke upon you, and learn of me;
  for I am meek and lowly in heart:
  and ye shall find rest unto your souls.
For my yoke is easy, and my burden is light.

King James Version, 1611

722. I HEARD THE VOICE OF JESUS

I heard the voice of Jesus say,
"Come unto Me and rest;
Lay down, thou weary one, lay down
Thy head upon my breast:"
I came to Jesus as I was,
Weary, and worn, and sad;
I found in Him a resting-place,
And He has made me glad.

I heard the voice of Jesus say,
"Behold, I freely give
The living water, thirsty one,
Stoop down, and drink, and live:"
I came to Jesus, and I drank
Of that life-giving stream;
My thirst was quench'd, my soul revived,
And now I live in Him.

I heard the voice of Jesus say,
"I am this dark world's light;
Look unto Me, thy morn shall rise,
And all thy day be bright:"
I look'd to Jesus, and I found
In Him my star, my sun;
And in that light of life I'll walk
Till travelling days are done.

Horatius Bonar, 1808–1889

723. JESUS CALLS US O'ER THE TUMULT

Jesus calls us o'er the tumult
Of our life's wild, restless sea,
Day by day His sweet voice soundeth,
Saying, "Christian, follow Me."

As, of old, St. Andrew heard it
By the Galilean lake,
Turned from home and toil and kindred,
Leaving all for His dear sake.

Jesus calls us from the worship
Of the vain world's golden store,
From each idol that would keep us,
Saying, "Christian, love Me more."

In our joys and in our sorrows,
Days of toil and hours of ease,
Still He calls, in cares and pleasures,
"Christian, love Me more than these."

Jesus calls us; by Thy mercies,
Saviour, may we hear Thy call,
Give our hearts to Thy obedience,
Serve and love Thee best of all.

Cecil F. Alexander, 1823–1895

724. THE TRIMMED LAMP

I dare not slight the stranger at my gate—
Threadbare of garb, and sorrowful of lot
Lest it be Christ that stands, and goes His way
Because I, all unworthy, knew Him not.

I dare not miss one flash of loving cheer
From alien souls, in challenge fine and high:
Ah—what if God be moving very near—
And I, so blind, so deaf—had passed Him by?

Laura Simmons, 1877–

725. O YOUNG AND FEARLESS PROPHET

O young and fearless Prophet
Of ancient Galilee:
Thy life is still a summons
To serve humanity,
To make our thoughts and actions
Less prone to please the crowd,
To stand with humble courage
For Truth with hearts uncowed.

We marvel at the purpose
That held Thee to Thy course,
While ever on the hilltop
Before Thee loomed the cross;
Thy steadfast face set forward
Where love and duty shone,
While we betray so quickly
And leave Thee there alone.

Stir up in us a protest
Against the greed of wealth,
While men go starved and hungry
Who plead for work and health:
Whose wives and little children
Cry out for lack of bread,
Who spend their years o'er-weighted
Beneath a gloomy dread.

O help us stand unswerving
Against war's bloody way,
Where hate and lust and falsehood
Hold back Christ's holy sway;
Forbid that love of country
Should blind us to His call
Who lifts above the nation
The brotherhood of all.

Create in us the splendor
That dawns when hearts are kind,
That knows not race nor station
As boundaries of the mind;
That learns to value beauty,
In heart, or brain, or soul,
And longs to bind God's children
Into one perfect whole.

O young and fearless Prophet,
We need Thy presence here,
Amid our pride and glory
To see Thy face appear;
Once more to hear Thy challenge
Above our noisy day,
Triumphantly to lead us
Along God's holy way.

S. Ralph Harlow, 1885–

726. FOLLOW THE GLEAM

From "Merlin and The Gleam," IX

Not of the sunlight,
Not of the moonlight,
Not of the starlight!
O young Mariner,
Down to the haven,
Call your companions,
Launch your vessel
And crowd your canvas,

And, ere it vanishes
Over the margin,
After it, follow it,
Follow the Gleam.

Alfred Tennyson, 1809–1892

727. DESPISED AND REJECTED

My sun has set, I dwell
In darkness as a dead man out of sight;
And none remains, not one, that I should tell
To him mine evil plight
This bitter night.
I will make fast my door
That hollow friends may trouble me no more.

"Friend, open to Me."—Who is this that calls?
Nay, I am deaf as are my walls:
Cease crying, for I will not hear
Thy cry of hope or fear.
Others were dear,
Others forsook me: what art thou indeed
That I should heed
Thy lamentable need?
Hungry should feed,
Or stranger lodge thee here?

"Friend, My Feet bleed.
Open thy door to Me and comfort Me."
I will not open, trouble me no more.
Go on thy way footsore,
I will not rise and open unto thee.

"Then is it nothing to thee? Open, see
Who stands to plead with thee.
Open, lest I should pass thee by, and thou
One day entreat My Face
And howl for grace,
And I be deaf as thou art now.
Open to Me."

Then I cried out upon him: Cease,
Leave me in peace:
Fear not that I should crave
Aught thou mayst have.
Leave me in peace, yea trouble me no more,
Lest I arise and chase thee from my door.
What, shall I not be let
Alone, that thou dost vex me yet?

But all night long that voice spake urgently:
"Open to Me."
Still harping in mine ears:
"Rise, let Me in."
Pleading with tears:
"Open to Me that I may come to thee."
While the dew dropped, while the dark hours were cold:
"My Feet bleed, see My Face,
See My Hands bleed that bring thee grace,
My Heart doth bleed for thee,
Open to Me."

So till the break of day:
Then died away
That voice, in silence as of sorrow;
Then footsteps echoing like a sigh
Passed me by,
Lingering footsteps slow to pass.
On the morrow
I saw upon the grass
Each footprint marked in blood, and on my door
The mark of blood forevermore.

Christina G. Rossetti, 1830–1894

728. THE MASTER'S TOUCH

In the still air the music lies unheard;
In the rough marble beauty hides unseen:
To make the music and the beauty, needs
The master's touch, the sculptor's chisel keen.

Great Master, touch us with Thy skilful hand;
Let not the music that is in us die!
Great Sculptor, hew and polish us; nor let,
Hidden and lost, Thy form within us lie!

Spare not the stroke! do with us as Thou wilt!
Let there be naught unfinished, broken, marred;
Complete Thy purpose, that we may become
Thy perfect image, Thou our God and Lord!

Horatius Bonar, 1808–1889

729. OH, HAUNTING SPIRIT OF THE EVER TRUE

Oh, Haunting Spirit of the Ever True,
Keep thou the pressure of thy way upon us.
We see a world too big to grasp;

We glimpse a city too far off to reach;
We trudge a way too long to walk;
We feel a truth too pure to understand,
We have a purpose that we cannot prove;
A life to live beyond the power of living;
A vision, time nor energy cannot contain;
But faith that all our effort will not be in vain.
Oh, Haunting Spirit of the Ever True,
Keep thou the pressure of thy way upon us.

Allan Knight Chalmers, 1897–

730. WE WOULD SEE JESUS

We would see Jesus! We would look upon
The light in that divinely human face,
Where lofty majesty and tender grace
In blended beauty shone.

We would see Jesus, and would hear again
The voice that charmed the thousands by the sea,
Spoke peace to sinners, set the captives free,
And eased the sufferers' pain.

We would see Jesus, yet not Him alone—
But see ourselves as in our Maker's plan;
And in the beauty of the Son of Man
See man upon his throne.

We would see Jesus, and let Him impart
The truth He came among us to reveal,
Till in the gracious message we should feel
The beating of God's heart.

W. J. Suckow, contemporary American

731. WE WOULD SEE JESUS

We would see Jesus; lo! His star is shining
Above the stable while the angels sing;
There in a manger on the hay reclining;
Haste, let us lay our gifts before the King.

We would see Jesus, Mary's Son most holy,
Light of the village life from day to day;
Shining revealed through every task most lowly,
The Christ of God, the Life, the Truth, the Way.

We would see Jesus, on the mountain teaching,
With all the listening people gathered round;
While birds and flowers and sky above are preaching,
The blessedness which simple trust has found.

We would see Jesus, in His work of healing,
At the eventide before the sun was set;
Divine and human, in His deep revealing,
Of God and man in loving service met.

We would see Jesus; in the early morning
Still as of old He calleth, "Follow me";
Let us arise, all meaner service scorning:
Lord, we are Thine, we give ourselves to Thee.

John Edgar Park, 1879–

732. NOT YOURS BUT YOU

He died for me: what can I offer Him?
Towards Him swells incense of perpetual prayer;
His court wear crowns and aureoles round their hair:
His ministers are subtle Cherubim;
Ring within ring, white intense Seraphim
Leap like immortal lightnings through the air.
What shall I offer Him? Defiled and bare
My spirit broken and my brightness dim?
"Give Me thy youth." "I yield it to Thy rod,
As Thou didst yield Thy prime of youth for me."
"Give Me thy life." "I give it breath by breath;
As Thou didst give Thy life so give I Thee."
"Give Me thy love." "So be it, my God, my God
As Thou hast loved me, even to bitter death."

Christina G. Rossetti, 1830–1894

733. LET US SEE JESUS

We would see Jesus—for the shadows lengthen
Across the little landscape of our life;
We would see Jesus—our weak faith to strengthen,
For the last weariness, the final strife.

❖

We would see Jesus—other lights are paling,
Which for long years we have rejoiced to see;
The blessings of our pilgrimage are failing,
We would not mourn them, for we come to thee.

❖

We would see Jesus—the great Rock-foundation
Whereon our feet are set by sovereign grace;
Nor life, nor death, with all their agitation,
Can thence remove us, if we see his face.

❖

We would see Jesus—that is all we're needing,
Strength, joy, and willingness come with the sight;
We would see Jesus—dying, risen, pleading—
Then welcome day, and farewell mortal night!

Anna B. Warner, 1820–1915

734. THE SEARCH

I sought Him where my logic led.
"This friend is always sure and right,
His lantern is sufficient light. . . .
I need no star," I said.

I sought Him in the city square.
Logic and I went up and down
The market-place of many a town,
And He was never there.

I tracked Him to the Mind's far rim.
The valiant intellect went forth
To east and west and south and north,
And found no trace of Him!

We walked the world from sun to sun,
Logic and I, with little faith;
But never came to Nazareth,
Or found the Holy One.

I sought in vain. And finally
Back to the Heart's small house I crept,
And fell upon my knees and wept,
And lo, He came to me!

Sara Henderson Hay,
contemporary American

735. BONDS

As a stream that runs to sea
Ever by its banks is led,
And by windings shepherded;
So, in bonds though bound I be,
I through limits reach to Thee.

These dear bonds wherein I chafe,
Wishing, "Would that I were free!"
These it is which hold me safe,
Bringing me at last to Thee,
As the stream is brought to sea.

Shepherding its little streams,
Penning it from side to side,
Every bank a barrier seems:
Yet the stream would soon be dried
If the channel were too wide.

Here, fast bound by bank and fence,
Where I have not space to spread,
Still my body, chafed by sense,
Feels a spirit cross its bed,
As a stream goes current-led.

Human minds so move about,
Only if denied their grasp;

Only if fenced round with doubt,
  Gain the everlasting clasp.
Only streams which fettered be
Fret their way at last to sea.

So, with limits for my guide,
Safe, I shall not wander wide;
  But, where we are meant to meet,
Find in Thee the Life denied:
  Falling low shall kiss Thy Feet,
Reaching far shall touch Thy Side.

Laurence Housman, 1865–

736. PER CONTRA

They say Thou art a Myth—
  That every prayer is vain:
Yet still I seek Thee with
  My pleas, again, again.

"There is no Christ—nay, none!"
  The lips of men have said:
But see, Thou fabled One,
  I kiss the Hands that bled!

Mahlon Leonard Fisher, 1874–

737. JESUS OF THE SCARS

If we have never sought, we seek Thee now;
  Thine eyes burn through the dark, our only stars;
We must have sight of thorn-pricks on Thy brow,
  We must have Thee, O Jesus of the Scars.

The heavens frighten us; they are too calm;
  In all the universe we have no place.
Our wounds are hurting us; where is the balm?
  Lord Jesus, by Thy Scars we claim Thy grace.

If when the doors are shut, Thou drawest near,
  Only reveal those hands, that side of Thine;
We know to-day what wounds are, have no fear,
  Show us Thy Scars, we know the countersign.

The other gods were strong; but Thou wast weak;
  They rode, but Thou didst stumble to a throne;
But to our wounds only God's wounds can speak,
  And not a god has wounds, but Thou alone.

Edward Shillito, 1872–1948

738. WHEN GATHERING CLOUDS

When gathering clouds around I view
And days are dark and friends are few,
On Him I lean, Who not in vain
Experienced every human pain;
He sees my wants, allays my fears,
And counts and treasures up my tears.

If aught should tempt my soul to stray
From heavenly wisdom's narrow way;
To fly the good I would pursue,
Or do the sin I would not do;
Still He, Who felt temptation's power,
Shall guard me in that dangerous hour.

If wounded love my bosom swell,
Deceived by those I prized too well;
He shall His pitying aid bestow,
Who felt on earth severer woe;
At once betrayed, denied, or fled
By those who shared His daily bread.

If vexing thoughts within me rise,
And, sore dismayed, my spirit dies;
Still He, Who once vouchsafed to bear
The sickening anguish of despair,
Shall sweetly soothe, shall gently dry,
The throbbing heart, the streaming eye.

When sorrowing o'er some stone I bend,
Which covers what was once a friend,
And from his voice, his hand, his smile,
Divides me for a little while;
Thou, Saviour, mark'st the tears I shed,
For Thou didst weep o'er Lazarus dead!

And O! when I have safely past
Through every conflict but the last;
Still, still unchanging, watch beside
My painful bed, for Thou hast died!
Then point to realms of cloudless day,
And wipe the latest tear away!

Robert Grant, 1779–1838

739. CHRIST THE ANSWER

Thou Christ, my soul is hurt and bruised;
With words the scholars wear me out.
Brain of me weary and confused,
Thee and myself and all I doubt.

And must I back to darkness go
Because I cannot say their creed?
I know not what I think, I know
Only that Thou art all I need.

Oh, let me live in Thy realities,
Nor substitute my notions for Thy facts
Notion with notion making leagues and pacts,
They are to Truth as dream-deeds are to acts,
And questioned, make me doubt of everything.
"O Lord, my God," my soul gets up and cries,
"Come Thy own self and with Thee my faith bring."

George Macdonald, 1824–1905

740. DOUBT

O distant Christ, the crowded, darkening years
Drift slow between Thy gracious face and me;
My hungry heart leans back to look for Thee,
But finds the way set thick with doubts and fears.

My groping hands would touch Thy garment's hem,
Would find some token Thou art walking near;
Instead, they clasp but empty darkness drear,
And no diviner hands reach out to them.

Sometimes my listening soul, with bated breath,
Stands still to catch a footfall by my side,
Lest, haply, my earth-blinded eyes but hide
Thy stately figure, leading Life and Death;

My straining eyes, O Christ, but long to mark
A shadow of Thy presence, dim and sweet,
Or far-off light to guide my wandering feet,
Or hope for hands prayer-beating 'gainst the dark.

O Thou! unseen by me, that like a child
Tries in the night to find its mother's heart,
And weeping wanders only more apart,
Not knowing in the darkness that she smiled—

Thou, all unseen, dost hear my tired cry.
As I, in darkness of a half-belief,
Grope for Thy heart, in love and doubt and grief:
O Lord! speak soon to me—"Lo, here am I!"

Margaret Deland, 1857–1945

741. SPIRITUAL VISION

Shall the mole, in his dark underground, call the beasts from the day-glare to flee?
Shall the owl charge the birds: "I am wise. Come dwell in the shadows with me"?
Shall a man bind his eyes and proclaim: "It is vain that men weary to see"?

Let him walk in the gloom, whoso will; peace be with him. But whence is his right
To declare that the world is in darkness, because he has turned from the light,
Or to seek to o'ershadow my day with the pall of his self-chosen night?

❖

"Yea, I know!" cried the true man of old; and whoso'er wills it, may know,
"My Redeemer—He liveth!" I seek for a sign of His presence, and lo,
As He spake to the light, and it was, so He speaks to my soul—and I know!

Solomon Solis-Cohen, 1857–

742. OUR MASTER

Immortal Love, forever full,
Forever flowing free,
Forever shared, forever whole,
A never-ebbing sea!

Our outward lips confess the name
All other names above;
Love only knoweth whence it came,
And comprehendeth love.

❖

We may not climb the heavenly steeps
To bring the Lord Christ down:
In vain we search the lowest deeps,
For Him no depths can drown.

❖

But warm, sweet, tender, even yet
A present help is He;
And faith has still its Olivet,
And love its Galilee.

The healing of His seamless dress
Is by our beds of pain;
We touch Him in life's throng and press,
And we are whole again.

Through Him the first fond prayers are said
Our lips of childhood frame,
The last low whispers of our dead
Are burdened with His name.

O Lord and Master of us all!
Whate'er our name or sign,
We own Thy sway, we hear Thy call,
We test our lives by Thine.

John Greenleaf Whittier, 1807–1892

743. TELL ME THE STORIES OF JESUS

Tell me the stories of Jesus
I love to hear;
Things I would ask Him to tell me
If He were here;
Scenes by the wayside,
Tales of the sea,
Stories of Jesus,
Tell them to me.

First let me hear how the children
Stood round His knee,
And I shall fancy His blessing
Resting on me:
Words full of kindness,
Deeds full of grace,
All in the lovelight
Of Jesus' face.

Into the city I'd follow
The children's band,
Waving a branch of the palm-tree
High in my hand;
One of His heralds,
Yes, I would sing
Loudest hosannas,
Jesus is King!

Tell me, in accents of wonder,
How rolled the sea
Tossing the boat in a tempest
On Galilee!
And how the Master,
Ready and kind,
Chided the billows
And hushed the wind.

Tell how the sparrow that twitters
On yonder tree,
And the sweet meadow-side lily
May speak to me:
Give me their message,
For I would hear
How Jesus taught us
Our Father's care.

Show me that scene in the garden
Of bitter pain;
And of the Cross where my Saviour
For me was slain.
Sad ones or bright ones,
So that they be
Stories of Jesus,
Tell them to me.

William Henry Parker, 1845–1929

744. I THINK WHEN I READ THAT SWEET STORY OF OLD

I think, when I read that sweet story of old,
When Jesus was here among men,
How He called little children as lambs to His fold,
I should like to have been with them then;
I wish that His hands had been placed on my head,
That His arms had been thrown around me,
And that I might have seen His kind look when He said,
"Let the little ones come unto Me."

Yet still to His footstool in prayer I may go,
And ask for a share in His love;
And, if I now earnestly seek Him below,
I shall see Him and hear Him above,
In that beautiful place He is gone to prepare
For all who are washed and forgiven;
And many dear children are gathering there,
For of such is the Kingdom of heaven.

But thousands and thousands, who wander and fall,
Never heard of that heavenly home;
I should like them to know there is room for them all,
And that Jesus has bid them to come.
I long for the joy of that glorious time,
The sweetest and brightest and best,
When the dear little children of every clime
Shall crowd to His arms and be blest.

Jemima Luke, 1813–1906

745. MY GOD, I LOVE THEE

My God, I love Thee; not because
I hope for heaven thereby,
Nor yet because who love Thee not
Are lost eternally.

Thou, O my Jesus, Thou didst me
Upon the cross embrace;
For me didst bear the nails, and spear,
And manifold disgrace,

And griefs and torments numberless,
And sweat of agony;
Yea, death itself; and all for me
Who was thine enemy.

Then why, O blessèd Jesu Christ,
Should I not love Thee well?
Not for the sake of winning heaven,
Nor of escaping hell;

Not from the hope of gaining aught,
Not seeking a reward;
But as Thyself hast lovèd me,
O ever-loving Lord.

So would I love Thee, dearest Lord,
And in Thy praise will sing;
Solely because Thou art my God,
And my most loving King.

Spanish sonnet ascribed to
Francis Xavier, 1506–1552;
tr. by Edward Caswall, 1814–1878

746. DEAR LORD AND FATHER OF MANKIND

From "The Brewing of Soma"

Dear Lord and Father of mankind!
Forgive our foolish ways!
Reclothe us in our rightful mind,
In purer lives Thy service find,
In deeper reverence, praise.

In simple trust like theirs who heard,
  Beside the Syrian sea,
The gracious calling of the Lord,
Let us, like them, without a word,
  Rise up and follow Thee.

O Sabbath rest by Galilee!
  O calm of hills above,
Where Jesus knelt to share with Thee
The silence of eternity
  Interpreted by love!

With that deep hush subduing all
  Our words and works that drown
The tender whisper of Thy call,
As noiseless let Thy blessing fall
  As fell Thy manna down.

Drop Thy still dews of quietness,
  Till all our strivings cease;
Take from our souls the strain and stress,
And let our ordered lives confess
  The beauty of Thy peace.

Breathe through the heats of our desire
  Thy coolness and Thy balm;
Let sense be dumb, let flesh retire;
Speak through the earthquake, wind and fire,
  O still small voice of calm!

John Greenleaf Whittier, 1807–1892

747. O CHRIST, THOU ART WITHIN ME LIKE A SEA

O Christ, thou art within me like a sea,
Filling me as a slowly rising tide.
No rock or stone or sandbar may abide
Safe from thy coming and undrowned in thee.

Thou dost not break me by the might of
    storm,
But with a calm upsurging from the deep
Thou shuttest me in thy eternal keep
Where is no ebb, for fullness is thy norm.

And never is thy flood of life withdrawn;
Thou holdest me till I am all thy own.
This gradual overcoming is foreknown.
Thou art within me like a sea at dawn.

Edith Lovejoy Pierce, 1904–

748. CHRIST ALL-SUFFICIENT

From "Saint Paul"

Christ, I am Christ's and let the name suffice you;
  Aye, for me, too, it greatly hath sufficed.
Lo, with no winning words would I entice you,
  Paul hath no honour and no friend but Christ.

Yea, through life, death, through sorrow and through sinning,
  Christ shall suffice me, for He hath sufficed;
Christ is the end, for Christ was the beginning,
  Christ the beginning, for the end is Christ.

Frederick W. H. Myers, 1843–1901

749. KINSMAN

And didst Thou love the race that loved not Thee?
  And didst Thou take to heaven a human brow?
Dost plead with man's voice by the marvellous sea?
  Art Thou his Kinsman now?

O God, O Kinsman loved, but not enough,
  O Man, with eyes majestic after death,
Whose feet have toiled along our pathways rough,
  Whose lips drawn human breath!—

By that one likeness which is ours and Thine,
  By that one nature which doth hold us kin,
By that high heaven where, sinless, Thou dost shine
  To draw us sinners in;

By Thy last silence in the judgment hall,
  By long foreknowledge of the deadly Tree,
By darkness, by the wormwood and the gall,
  I pray Thee visit me.

Come, lest this heart should, cold and cast away,
  Die ere the Guest adored she entertain—
Lest eyes which never saw Thine earthly day
  Should miss Thy heavenly reign.

Jean Ingelow, 1820–1897

750. JESUS

From "The Testament of Beauty"

So it was when Jesus came in his gentleness
with his divine compassion and great Gospel of Peace,
men hail'd him WORD OF GOD, and in the title of Christ
crown'd him with love beyond all earth-names of renown.
For He, wandering unarm'd save by the Spirit's flame,
in few years with few friends founded a world-empire
wider than Alexander's and more enduring;
since from his death it took its everlasting life.
HIS kingdom is God's kingdom, and his holy temple
not in Athens or Rome but in the heart of man.
They who understand not cannot forget, and they
who keep not his commandment call him Master and Lord.

Robert Bridges, 1844–1930

751. OBEDIENCE

I said, "Let me walk in the fields."
  He said, "No, walk in the town."
I said, "There are no flowers there."
  He said, "No flowers, but a crown."

I said, "But the skies are black;
  There is nothing but noise and din."
And He wept as he sent me back;
  "There is more," He said; "there is sin."

I said, "But the air is thick,
  And fogs are veiling the sun."
He answered, "Yet souls are sick,
  And souls in the dark undone."

I said, "I shall miss the light,
  And friends will miss me, they say."
He answered, "Choose to-night
  If *I* am to miss you, or they."

I pleaded for time to be given.
  He said, "Is it hard to decide?
It will not seem hard in heaven
  To have followed the steps of your Guide."

I cast one look at the fields,
  Then set my face to the town;
He said, "My child, do you yield?
  Will you leave the flowers for the crown?"

Then into His hand went mine,
  And into my heart came He;
And I walk in a light divine
  The path I had feared to see.

George Macdonald, 1824–1905

752. I NEED THEE

My Lord, I have no clothes to come to thee;
My shoes are pierced and broken with the
road;
I am torn and weathered, wounded with the
goad,
And soiled with tugging at my weary load:
The more I need thee! A very prodigal
I stagger into thy presence, Lord of me:
One look, my Christ, and at thy feet I fall!

George Macdonald, 1824–1905

753. HOW FIRM A FOUNDATION

How firm a foundation, ye saints of the Lord,
Is laid for your faith in His excellent word!
What more can He say than to you He hath
said,
To you who for refuge to Jesus have fled?

"Fear not, I am with thee, O be not dismayed,
For I am thy God, I will still give thee aid:
I'll strengthen thee, help thee, and cause thee
to stand,
Upheld by My righteous, omnipotent hand.

"When through the deep waters I call thee to
go,
The rivers of sorrow shall not overflow;
For I will be with thee, thy troubles to bless,
And sanctify to thee thy deepest distress.

"When through fiery trials thy pathway shall
lie,
My grace, all-sufficient, shall be thy supply;
The flame shall not hurt thee; I only design
Thy dross to consume, and thy gold to refine.

"E'en down to old age all My people shall
prove
My sovereign, eternal, unchangeable love;
And when hoary hairs shall their temples
adorn,
Like lambs they shall still in My bosom be
borne.

"The soul that on Jesus hath leaned for
repose,
I will not, I will not desert to his foes;
That soul, though all hell should endeavor to
shake,
I'll never, no, never, no, never forsake."

"K." in Rippon's Selections, 1787

754. NOW THE DAY IS OVER

Now the day is over,
Night is drawing nigh,
Shadows of the evening
Steal across the sky.

Now the darkness gathers,
Stars begin to peep.
Birds, and beasts, and flowers
Soon will be asleep.

Jesus, give the weary
Calm and sweet repose;
With thy tend'rest blessing
May mine eyelids close.

Grant to little children
Visions bright of Thee;
Guard the sailors tossing
On the deep blue sea.

Comfort every sufferer
Watching late in pain;
Those who plan some evil,
From their sin restrain.

Through the long night watches
May Thine angels spread
Their white wings above me,
Watching round my bed.

When the morning wakens,
Then may I arise,
Pure and fresh and sinless
In Thy holy eyes.

Sabine Baring-Gould, 1834–1924

755. DREAMS AND DEEDS

Dear Master, in Whose life I see
All that I long and fail to be;
Let Thy clear light for ever shine
To shame and guide this life of mine.

Though what I dream and what I do
In my poor days are always two,
Help me, oppressed by things undone,
O Thou, Whose dreams and deeds were one.

John Hunter, 1728–1793

756. SAVIOUR, BREATHE AN EVENING BLESSING

Saviour, breathe an evening blessing,
Ere repose our spirits seal;
Sin and want we come confessing,
Thou canst save, and Thou canst heal.

Though the night be dark and dreary,
Darkness cannot hide from Thee;
Thou art He who, never weary,
Watchest where Thy people be.

Though destruction walk around us,
Though the arrow past us fly,
Angel-guards from Thee surround us,
We are safe if Thou art nigh.

Blessed Spirit, brooding o'er us,
Chase the darkness of our night,
Till the perfect day before us
Breaks in ever-lasting light.

James Edmeston, 1791–1867

757. CHRIST'S BONDSERVANT

Make me a captive, Lord,
  And then I shall be free;
Force me to render up my sword,
  And I shall conqueror be.
I sink in life's alarms
  When by myself I stand;
Imprison me within Thine arms,
  And strong shall be my hand.

My heart is weak and poor
  Until it master find;
It has no spring of action sure—
  It varies with the wind:
It cannot freely move
  Till Thou hast wrought its chain;
Enslave it with Thy matchless love,
  And deathless it shall reign.

My power is faint and low
  Till I have learned to serve:
It wants the needed fire to glow,
  It wants the breeze to nerve;
It cannot drive the world
  Until itself be driven;
Its flag can only be unfurled
  When Thou shalt breathe from heaven.

My will is not my own
  Till Thou hast made it Thine;
If it would reach a monarch's throne
  It must its crown resign:
It only stands unbent
  Amid the clashing strife,
When on Thy bosom it has leant
  And found in Thee its life.

George Matheson, 1842–1906

758. CONVERSION

From "Nicodemus"

Nicodemus. Tell me one thing; why do you follow Jesus?
John. It was because of John the Baptist first.
Nicodemus. But why because of him?
John. One day when we were standing by the Jordan,
John and my cousin Andrew and myself,
We saw a man pass by, tall as a spirit;
He did not see us though he passed quite near;
Indeed we thought it strange;
His eyes were open but he looked on nothing;
And as he passed, John, pointing with his finger,
Cried—I can hear him cry it now—
"Behold, the Lamb of God!"
Nicodemus. And He, what did He say? What did He do?
John. Nothing; we watched Him slowly climb the hill;
His shadow fell before Him; it was evening.
Sometimes He stopped

To raise His head to the home-flying rooks
Or greet a countryman with plough on shoulder.
Nicodemus. John said, "Behold, the Lamb of God"?
John. He said so.
Nicodemus. And from that day you followed Him?
John. No, that was afterwards in Galilee.
Nicodemus. But tell me why; why did you follow Him?
John. I think it was our feet that followed Him;
It was our feet; our hearts were too afraid.
Perhaps indeed it was not in our choice;
He tells us that we have not chosen Him,
But He has chosen us. I only know
That as we followed Him that day He called us
We were not walking on the earth at all;
It was another world,
Where everything was new and strange and shining;
We pitied men and women at their business,
For they knew nothing of what we knew—
Nicodemus. Perhaps it was some miracle He did.
John. It was indeed; more miracles than one;
I was not blind and yet He gave me sight;
I was not deaf and yet He gave me hearing;
Nor was I dead, yet me He raised to life.

Andrew Young, 1885–

759. MY MASTER'S FACE

No pictured likeness of my Lord have I;
He carved no record of His ministry
On wood or stone.
He left no sculptured tomb nor parchment dim,
But trusted for all memory of Him
Men's hearts alone.

Who sees the face but sees in part; who reads
The spirit which it hides, sees all; he needs
No more. Thy grace—
Thy life in my life, Lord, give Thou to me;
And then, in truth, I may forever see
My Master's face!

William Hurd Hillyer, 1880–

760. TO JESUS

Rise, O my soul, with thy desires to heaven,
And with divinest contemplation use
Thy time where time's eternity is given,
And let vain thoughts no more thy thoughts abuse;
But down in midnight darkness let them lie;
So live thy better, let thy worse thoughts die!

And thou, my soul, inspired with holy flame,
View and review with most regardful eye
That holy Cross, whence thy salvation came,
On which thy Saviour and thy sin did die!
For in that sacred object is much pleasure,
And in that Saviour is my life, my treasure.

To Thee, O Jesu! I direct my eye,
To Thee my hands, to Thee my humble knees;
To Thee my heart shall offer sacrifice;
To Thee my thoughts, Who my thoughts only sees:
To Thee myself, myself and all I give;
To Thee I die; to Thee I only live!

Sir Walter Raleigh, 1552–1618

761. O MASTER, LET ME WALK WITH THEE

O Master, let me walk with thee
In lowly paths of service free;
Tell me thy secret; help me bear
The strain of toil, the fret of care.

Help me the slow of heart to move
By some clear, winning word of love;
Teach me the wayward feet to stay
And guide them in the homeward way.

Teach me thy patience; still with thee
In closer, dearer company,
In work that keeps faith sweet and strong,
In trust that triumphs over wrong;

In hope that sends a shining ray
Far down the future's broadening way;
In peace that only thou canst give,—
With thee, O Master, let me live!

Washington Gladden, 1836–1918

762. LOYALTY HYMN

While nations rage, while empires rock and fall,
While hatred burns, and greed and war increase,
With heart and voice we dedicate our all
Once more to Thee, O mighty Prince of Peace.

Fast grow abysmal rifts in every land,
O'er creed and class, o'er wealth and soil and blood.
Through all the earth, made one in Thee, we stand—
Thy Church in its transcendent brotherhood.

Into the soon forgotten past they die,
False gods that rise and flourish for a day.
Not so Thy Cross, firm rooted in the sky;
Thy words, O Christ, shall never pass away.

While nations rage, while empires rock and fall,
While hatred burns, and greed and war increase,
With heart and voice we dedicate our all
Once more to Thee, O mighty Prince of Peace.

Edith Lovejoy Pierce, 1904–

763. A LIGHT UPON THE MOUNTAINS

There's a light upon the mountains,
And the day is at the spring,
When our eyes shall see the beauty
And the glory of the King:
Weary was our heart with waiting,
And the night-watch seemed so long,
But His triumph-day is breaking,
And we hail it with a song.

In the fading of the star-light
We may see the coming morn;
And the lights of men are paling
In the splendors of the dawn;
For the eastern skies are glowing
As with light of hidden fire,
And the hearts of men are stirring
With the throbs of deep desire.

There's a hush of expectation
And a quiet in the air,
And the breath of God is moving
In the fervent breath of prayer;
For the suffering, dying Jesus
Is the Christ upon the throne,
And the travail of our spirit
Is the travail of His own.

He is breaking down the barriers,
He is casting up the way;
He is calling for His angels
To build up the gates of day:
But His angels here are human,
Not the shining hosts above;
For the drum-beats of His army
Are the heart-beats of our love.

Hark! we hear a distant music,
And it comes with fuller swell;
'Tis the triumph-song of Jesus,
Of our King, Immanuel!
Go ye forth with joy to meet Him!
And, my soul, be swift to bring
All thy sweetest and thy dearest
For the triumph of our King!

Henry Burton, 1840–1930

764. EVENING HYMN

Sun of my soul! Thou Saviour dear!
It is not night if Thou be near!
Oh, may no earth-born cloud arise
To hide Thee from Thy servant's eyes!

❖

When the soft dews of kindly sleep
My wearied eyelids gently steep,
Be my last thought, how sweet to rest
For ever on my Saviour's breast.

Abide with me from morn till eve,
For without Thee I cannot live!
Abide with me when night is nigh,
For without Thee I dare not die!

Thou Framer of the light and dark,
Steer through the tempest Thine own ark:
Amid the howling wintry sea,
We are in port if we have Thee!

❖

If some poor wandering child of Thine
Has spurned to-day the voice divine,
Now, Lord, the gracious work begin;
Let him no more lie down in sin!

Watch by the sick: enrich the poor
With blessings from Thy boundless store;
Be every mourner's sleep to-night
Like infant's slumbers, pure and light!

Come near and bless us when we wake,
Ere through the world our way we take,
Till in the ocean of Thy love
We lose ourselves in heaven above.

John Keble, 1792–1866

765. SAVIOUR, TEACH ME

Saviour, teach me, day by day,
Love's sweet lesson,—to obey;
Sweeter lesson cannot be,
Loving Him who first loved me.

With a child's glad heart of love
At Thy bidding may I move,
Prompt to serve and follow Thee,
Loving Him who first loved me.

Teach me thus Thy steps to trace,
Strong to follow in Thy grace,
Learning how to love from Thee,
Loving Him who first loved me.

Love in loving finds employ,
In obedience all her joy;
Ever new that joy will be,
Loving Him who first loved me.

Thus may I rejoice to show
That I feel the love I owe;
Singing, till Thy face I see,
Of His love who first loved me.

Jane Eliza Leeson, 1807–1882

766. PRAYER

White Captain of my soul, lead on;
I follow Thee, come dark or dawn.
Only vouchsafe three things I crave:
Where terror stalks, help me be brave!
Where righteous ones can scarce endure
The siren call, help me be pure!
Where vows grow dim, and men dare do
What once they scorned, help me be true!

Robert Freeman, 1878–1940

767. ART THOU WEARY, ART THOU TROUBLED

Art thou weary, art thou troubled,
Art thou sore distressed?
"Come to me," saith One, "and, coming,
Be at rest."

Hath He marks to lead me to Him,
If He be my Guide?
"In His feet and hands are wound-prints,
And His side."

Hath He diadem, as monarch,
That His brow adorns?
"Yea, a crown, in very surety,
But of thorns."

If I find Him, if I follow,
What His guerdon here?
"Many a sorrow, many a labor,
Many a tear."

If I still hold closely to Him,
What hath He at last?
"Sorrow vanquished, labor ended,
Jordan passed."

If I ask Him to receive me,
Will He say me nay?
"Not till earth and not till heaven
Pass away."

St. Stephen the Sabaite, 725–794;
tr. from the Greek by
John M. Neale, 1818–1866

768. MY GUIDE

There is no path in this desert waste;
For the winds have swept the shifting sands,
The trail is blind where the storms have raced,
And a stranger, I, in these fearsome lands.
But I journey on with a lightsome tread;
I do not falter nor turn aside,
For I see His figure just ahead—
He knows the way—my Guide.

There is no path in this trackless sea;
No map is lined on the restless waves;
The ocean snares are strange to me
Where the unseen wind in its fury raves.
But it matters naught; my sails are set,
And my swift prow tosses the seas aside,
For the changeless stars are steadfast yet,
And I sail by His star-blazed trail—my Guide.

There is no way in this starless night;
There is naught but cloud in the inky skies;
The black night smothers me, left and right,
I stare with a blind man's straining eyes.
But my steps are firm, for I cannot stray;
The path to my feet seems light and wide;
For I hear His voice—"I am the Way!"
And I sing as I follow Him on—my Guide.

Robert J. Burdette, 1844–1914

769. O THOU WHOSE FEET HAVE CLIMBED LIFE'S HILL

O Thou whose feet have climbed life's hill,
And trod the path of youth,
Our Saviour and our Brother still,
Now lead us into truth.

The call is Thine: be Thou the way,
And give us men to guide;
Let wisdom broaden with the day,
Let human faith abide.

Who learn of Thee the truth shall find,
Who follow, gain the goal;
With reverence crown the earnest mind,
And speak within the soul.

Awake the purpose high which strives,
And, falling, stands again;
Confirm the will of eager lives
To quit themselves like men:

Thy life the bond of fellowship,
Thy love the law that rules,
Thy Name, proclaimed by every lip,
The Master of our schools.

Louis F. Benson, 1855–1930

770. SHEPHERD OF EAGER YOUTH[1]

(Excerpts)

Shepherd of eager youth,
Guiding in love and truth
Through devious ways;
Christ, our triumphant King,
We come Thy name to sing,
And here our children bring,
To sound Thy praise.

Thou art our Holy Lord,
The all-subduing Word,
Healer of strife;
Thou didst Thyself abase,
That from sin's deep disgrace
Thou mightest save our race,
And give us life.

Ever be Thou our Guide,
Our Shepherd and our Pride,
Our Staff and Song;
Jesus, Thou Christ of God,
By Thy enduring word,
Lead us where Thou hast trod,
Make our faith strong.

Clement of Alexandria, 200 A.D.;
tr. by Henry M. Dexter, 1821–1890

771. LORD OF US ALL

Lord of the strong, when earth you trod,
You calmly faced the angry sea,
The fierce unmasked hypocrisy,
The traitor's kiss, the rabble's hiss,
The awful death upon the tree:
All glory be to God.

[1] Said to be the earliest known Christian hymn.

Lord of the weak, when earth you trod,
Oppressors writhed beneath your scorn;
The weak, despised, depraved, forlorn,
You taught to hope and know the scope
Of love divine for all who mourn:
All glory be to God.

Lord of the rich, when earth you trod,
To Mammon's power you never bowed,
But taught how men with wealth endowed
In meekness' school might learn to rule
The demon that enslaves the proud:
All glory be to God.

Lord of the poor, when earth you trod,
The lot you chose was hard and poor;
You taught us hardness to endure,
And so to gain through hurt and pain
The wealth that lasts for evermore:
All glory be to God.

Lord of us all, when earth you trod,
The life you led was perfect, free,
Defiant of all tyranny:
Now give us grace that we may face
Our foes with like temerity,
And glory give to God.

Donald Hankey, 1884–1916

772. THE PRAYER OF THE QUEST

Take us on the Quest of Beauty,
Poet Seer of Galilee,
Making all our dreams creative,
Through their fellowship with Thee

Take us on the Quest of Knowledge,
Clearest Thinker man has known!
Make our minds sincere and patient,
Satisfied by Truth alone.

Take us on the Quest of Service,
Kingly Servant of man's needs,
Let us work with Thee for others,
Anywhere Thy purpose leads.

All along our Quest's far pathway,
Christ our Leader and our guide,
Make us conscious of Thy presence,
Walking always at our side.

Eleanor B. Stock, 1900–

773. HE LEADS

The fairest things are those that silent come;
You may not hear the first approach of morn,
And though you listen as the golden sum
Of hours fade into dusk, no sound is born.
When the stars dance on high no bugles blow;
The footsteps of the flowers fall silently,
As softly come the blossoms of the snow;
And clouds float by in pale tranquility.
No voices herald moonlight on a lake;
The silvery dew is still; these gifts are given
As quietly as Christ, who for our sake
Was sent to us, the greatest gift of heaven.
Tenderly now, as in the yesterday,
He leads earth-weary children in His way.

Elizabeth Scollard

774. CHRIST OF EVERYWHERE

"Christ of the Andes," Christ of Everywhere,
Great lover of the hills, the open air,
And patient lover of impatient men
Who blindly strive and sin and strive again,—
Thou Living Word, larger than any creed,
Thou Love Divine, uttered in human deed,—
Oh, teach the world, warring and wandering still,
Thy way of Peace, the footpath of Good Will!

Henry van Dyke, 1852–1933

775. THE HOLY SPIRIT

Our blest Redeemer, ere He breathed
His tender last farewell,
A Guide, a Comforter bequeathed,
With us to dwell.

He came in tongues of living flame,
To teach, convince, subdue;
All-powerful as the wind He came,
As viewless too.

He came sweet influence to impart,
A gracious, willing Guest,
While He can find one humble heart
Wherein to rest.

And His that gentle voice we hear,
Soft as the breath of even,
That checks each fault, that calms each fear,
And speaks of heaven.

And every virtue we possess,
  And every victory won,
And every thought of holiness
  Are His alone.

Spirit of purity and grace,
  Our weakness pitying see;
O make our hearts Thy dwelling-place,
  And worthier Thee.

Harriet Auber, 1773–1862

776. JESUS, THOU JOY OF LOVING HEARTS

Jesus, Thou Joy of loving hearts,
Thou Fount of life, Thou Light of men,
From the best bliss that earth imparts
We turn unfilled to Thee again.

Thy truth unchanged hath ever stood;
Thou savest those that on Thee call;
To them that seek Thee Thou art good,
To them that find Thee all in all.

We taste Thee, O Thou living Bread,
And long to feast upon Thee still;
We drink of Thee, the Fountain-head,
And thirst our souls from Thee to fill.

Our restless spirits yearn for Thee,
Where'er our changeful lot is cast,
Glad when Thy gracious smile we see,
Blest when our faith can hold Thee fast.

O Jesus, ever with us stay,
Make all our moments calm and bright;
Chase the dark night of sin away,
Shed o'er the world Thy holy light.

From the Latin, 11th century;
tr. by Ray Palmer, 1808–1887

777. JESU, LOVER OF MY SOUL

Jesu, Lover of my soul,
  Let me to Thy bosom fly,
While the nearer waters roll,
  While the tempest still is high:
Hide me, O my Saviour, hide
  Till the storm of life is past,
Safe into the haven guide,
  O receive my soul at last!

Other refuge have I none;
  Hangs my helpless soul on Thee;
Leave, ah! leave me not alone,
  Still support and comfort me!
All my trust on Thee is stay'd,
  All my help from Thee I bring:
Cover my defenceless head
  With the shadow of Thy wing!

Wilt Thou not regard my call?
  Wilt Thou not accept my prayer?
Lo! I sink, I faint, I fall—
  Lo! on Thee I cast my care!
Reach me out Thy gracious hand:
  While I of Thy strength receive,
Hoping against hope I stand,
  Dying, and behold I live!

Plenteous grace with Thee is found,
  Grace to cover all my sin;
Let the healing streams abound;
  Make and keep me pure within:—
Thou of Life the Fountain art,
  Freely let me take of Thee;
Spring Thou up within my heart,—
  Rise to all eternity!

Charles Wesley, 1707–1788

778. THE COTTAGER'S HYMN

My food is but spare,
  And humble my cot,
Yet Jesus dwells there
  And blesses my lot:
Though thinly I'm clad,
  And tempests oft roll,
He's raiment, and bread,
  And drink to my soul.

His presence is wealth,
  His grace is a treasure,
His promise is health
  And joy out of measure.
His word is my rest,
  His spirit my guide:
In Him I am blest,
  Whatever betide.

Since Jesus is mine,
  Adieu to all sorrow;
I ne'er shall repine,
  Nor think of to-morrow:
The lily so fair,

And raven so black,
He nurses with care,
Then how shall I lack?

Each promise is sure
That shines in His word,
And tells me, though poor,
I'm rich in my Lord.
Hence! Sorrow and Fear!
Since Jesus is nigh
I'll dry up each tear
And stifle each sigh.

❖

The trials which frown,
Applied by His blood,
But plait me a crown
And work for my good.
In praise I shall tell,
When throned in my rest,
The things which befell
Were always the best.

Patrick Brontë, 1777-1861

779. JESUS, THESE EYES HAVE NEVER SEEN

Jesus, these eyes have never seen
That radiant form of Thine;
The veil of sense hangs dark between
Thy blessèd face and mine.

I see Thee not, I hear Thee not,
Yet art Thou oft with me;
And earth hath ne'er so dear a spot
As where I meet with Thee.

Like some bright dream that comes unsought
When slumbers o'er me roll,
Thine image ever fills my thought,
And charms my ravished soul.

Yet, though I have not seen, and still
Must rest in faith alone,
I love Thee, dearest Lord, and will,
Unseen but not unknown.

When death these mortal eyes shall seal,
And still this throbbing heart,
The rending veil shall Thee reveal
All glorious as Thou art.

Ray Palmer, 1808–1887

780. A CHILD'S EVENING PRAYER

Jesus, tender Shepherd, hear me;
Bless Thy little lamb to-night;
Through the darkness be Thou near me,
Watch my sleep till morning light.

All this day Thy hand has led me,
And I thank Thee for Thy care;
Thou hast cloth'd and warm'd and fed me;
Listen to my evening prayer.

Let my sins be all forgiven!
Bless the friends I love so well!
Take me, when I die, to Heaven;
Happy, there with Thee to dwell.

Mary Lundie Duncan, 1814–1840

781. O SON OF MAN

O Son of Man, our Hero strong and tender,
Whose servants are the brave in all the earth,
Our living sacrifice to Thee we render,
Who sharest all our sorrows, all our mirth.

O feet so strong to climb the path of duty,
O lips divine that taught the words of truth,
Kind eyes that marked the lilies in their beauty,
And heart that kindled at the zeal of youth;

Lover of children, boyhood's inspiration,
Of all mankind the Servant and the King;

O Lord of joy and hope and consolation,
To Thee our fears and joys and hopes we bring.

Not in our failures only and our sadness
We seek Thy presence, Comforter and Friend;
O rich man's Guest, be with us in our gladness,
O poor man's Mate, our lowliest tasks attend.

Frank Fletcher, 1870–1936

782. CHRIST SPEAKS

Think not on me, as countless men have thought
To their mind's torture and their spirit's loss,
As a pathetic figure, frail, distraught,
Nailed to the sky upon a naked cross.

That transient travail is too sharply limned
Upon the canvas of man's consciousness;
Think rather on my laughing eyes, undimmed,
My hands, unpierced, devising tenderness!

Wade Oliver, 1890–

783. THE KING OF LOVE

The King of love my Shepherd is,
Whose goodness faileth never;
I nothing lack if I am His,
And He is mine forever.

Where streams of living water flow
My ransomed soul He leadeth,
And where the verdant pastures grow
With food celestial feedeth.

Perverse and foolish oft I strayed,
But yet in love He sought me,
And on His shoulder gently laid,
And home rejoicing brought me.

In death's dark vale I fear no ill,
With Thee, dear Lord, beside me;
Thy rod and staff my comfort still,
Thy cross before to guide me.

Thou spread'st a table in my sight;
Thy unction grace bestoweth;
And O what transport of delight
From Thy pure chalice floweth.

And so, through all the length of day,
Thy goodness faileth never;
Good Shepherd, may I sing Thy praise
Within Thy house forever.

Henry W. Baker, 1821–1877

784. A BALLAD OF WONDER

My Lord came to me once a King.
A crown was on His hair.
I never knew that anything
Could be so regal fair.
My Lord came to me once a King.
I stopped my dream to stare.

My Lord came to me once a Child.
His eyes were dark and wide.
He was so sweet and small and mild
I dreamed I could have cried,
But when He looked at me, He smiled,
And all my tears were dried.

My Lord came once—(Shall it be said
I did but dream He came?)—
A crown of thorns was on His head,
But in His heart a flame,
He came alone, unheralded,
And signed me with His name.
I am no more the same.

Eleanor Slater, 1903–

785. THE SON OF GOD GOES FORTH TO WAR

The Son of God goes forth to war,
A kingly crown to gain;
His blood-red banner streams afar;
Who follows in His train?

Who best can drink his cup of woe
Triumphant over pain,
Who patient bears his cross below,—
He follows in His train.

The martyr first, whose eagle eye
Could pierce beyond the grave,
Who saw his Master in the sky,
And called on Him to save;
Like Him, with pardon on his tongue,
In midst of mortal pain,
He prayed for them that did the wrong;
Who follows in his train?

A glorious band, the chosen few
On whom the Spirit came,
Twelve valiant saints, their hope they knew,
And mocked the cross and flame;
They met the tyrant's brandished steel,
The lion's gory mane;
They bowed their necks the stroke to feel;
Who follows in their train?

A noble army, men and boys,
The matron and the maid,
Around the Saviour's throne rejoice,
In robes of light arrayed:
They climbed the steep ascent of heaven
Through peril, toil, and pain.
O God, to us may grace be given
To follow in their train.

Reginald Heber, 1783–1826

786. WHO IS ON THE LORD'S SIDE

Who is on the Lord's side?
Who will serve the King
Who will be His helpers
Other lives to bring?
Who will leave the world's side?
Who will face the foe?
Who is on the Lord's side?
Who for Him will go?
By Thy call of mercy,
By Thy grace Divine,
We are on the Lord's side,
Saviour, we are Thine.

Not for weight of glory,
Not for crown and palm,
Enter we the army,
Raise the warrior psalm;
But for love that claimeth
Lives for whom He died;
He whom Jesus nameth
Must be on His side.
By Thy love constraining,
By Thy grace divine,
We are on the Lord's side,
Saviour, we are Thine.

Jesus, Thou hast bought us,
Not with gold or gem,
But with Thine own life-blood,
For Thy diadem.
With Thy blessing filling
Each who comes to Thee,
Thou hast made us willing,
Thou hast made us free.
By Thy grand redemption,
By Thy grace divine,
We are on the Lord's side,
Saviour, we are Thine.

Fierce may be the conflict,
Strong may be the foe,
But the King's own army,
None can overthrow.
Round His standard ranging
Victory is secure;
For His truth unchanging
Makes the triumph sure.
Joyfully enlisting
By Thy grace divine,
We are on the Lord's side,
Saviour, we are Thine.

Frances R. Havergal, 1836–1879

787. THE MAN OF SORROWS

Christ claims our help in many a strange disguise;
Now, fever-ridden, on a bed He lies;
Homeless He wanders now beneath the stars;
Now counts the number of His prison bars;
Now bends beside us, crowned with hoary hairs.
No need have we to climb the heavenly stairs,
And press our kisses on His feet and hands;
In every man that suffers, He, the Man of Sorrows, stands!

Author unknown

788. THE SUFFERING GOD

If He could speak, that victim torn and bleeding,
  Caught in His pain and nailed upon the Cross,
Has He to give the comfort souls are needing?
  Could He destroy the bitterness of loss?

Once and for all men say He came and bore it,
  Once and for all set up His throne on high,
Conquered the world and set His standard o'er it,
  Dying that once, that men might never die.

Yet men are dying, dying soul and body,
  Cursing the God who gave to them their birth,
Sick of the world with all its sham and shoddy,
  Sick of the lies that darken all the earth.

Peace we were pledged, yet blood is ever flowing,
  Where on the earth has Peace been ever found?
Men do but reap the harvest of their sowing,
  Sadly the songs of human reapers sound.

Sad as the winds that sweep across the ocean,
  Telling to earth the sorrow of the sea.
Vain is my strife, just empty idle motion,
  All that has been is all there is to be.

So on the earth the time waves beat in thunder,
  Bearing wrecked hopes upon their heaving breasts,
Bits of dead dreams, and true hearts torn asunder,
  Flecked with red foam upon their crimson crests.

How can it be that God can reign in glory,
  Calmly content with what His Love has done,
Reading unmoved the piteous shameful story,
  All the vile deeds men do beneath the sun?

Are there no tears in the heart of the Eternal?
  Is there no pain to pierce the soul of God?
Then must He be a fiend of Hell infernal,
  Beating the earth to pieces with His rod.

Or is it just that there is nought behind it,
  Nothing but forces purposeless and blind?
Is the last thing, if mortal man could find it,
  Only a power wandering as the wind?

Father, if He, the Christ, were Thy Revealer,
  Truly the First Begotten of the Lord,
Then must Thou be a Suff'rer and a Healer,
  Pierced to the heart by the sorrow of the sword.

Then must it mean, not only that Thy sorrow
  Smote Thee that once upon the lonely tree,
But that to-day, to-night, and on the morrow,
  Still it will come, O Gallant God, to Thee.

Swift to its birth in spite of human scorning
  Hastens the day the storm-clouds roll apart;
Rings o'er the earth the message of the morning,
  Still on the Cross the Saviour bares His heart.

Passionately fierce the voice of God is pleading,
  Pleading with men to arm them for the fight;
See how those hands, majestically bleeding,
  Call us to rout the armies of the night.

Not to the work of sordid selfish saving
  Of our own souls to dwell with Him on high,
But to the soldier's splendid selfless braving,
  Eager to fight for Righteousness and die.

Peace does not mean the end of all our striving,
  Joy does not mean the drying of our tears;
Peace is the power that comes to souls arriving
  Up to the light where God Himself appears.

Joy is the wine that God is ever pouring
  Into the hearts of those who strive with Him,
Light'ning their eyes to vision and adoring,
  Strength'ning their arms to warfare glad and grim.

So would I live and not in idle resting,
  Stupid as swine that wallow in the mire;
Fain would I fight, and be for ever breasting
  Danger and death for ever under fire.

Bread of Thy Body give me for my fighting,
  Give me to drink Thy Sacred Blood for wine,
While there are wrongs that need me for the righting,
  While there is warfare splendid and divine.

Give me, for light, the sunshine of Thy sorrow,
  Give me, for shelter, shadow of Thy Cross;
Give me to share the glory of Thy morrow,
  Gone from my heart the bitterness of Loss.

G. A. Studdert-Kennedy, 1883-1929

789. OFT HAVE I STOOD BY THEE

From "Pauline"

  Oft have I stood by thee—
Have I been keeping lonely watch with thee
In the damp night by weeping Olivet,
Or leaning on thy bosom, proudly less,
Or dying with thee on the lonely cross,
Or witnessing thine outburst from the tomb.

Robert Browning, 1812–1889

790. OUR BROTHER CHRIST

We bear the strain of earthly care,
But bear it not alone;
Beside us walks our brother Christ
And makes our task His own.

Through din of market, whirl of wheels,
And thrust of driving trade,
We follow where the Master leads,
Serene and unafraid.

The common hopes that make us men
Were His in Galilee;
The tasks He gives are those He gave
Beside the restless sea.

Our brotherhood still rests in Him,
The Brother of us all,
And o'er the centuries still we hear
The Master's winsome call.

Ozora Stearns Davis, 1866–1931

791. NO DISTANT LORD

No distant Lord have I,
Loving afar to be.
Made flesh for me He cannot rest
Until He rests in me.

I need not journey far
This dearest friend to see.
Companionship is always mine;
He makes His home with me.

I envy not the twelve.
Nearer to me is He.
The life He once lived here on earth.
He lives again in me.

Ascended now to God
My witness there to be,
His witness here am I because
His Spirit dwells in me.

O glorious Son of God,
Incarnate Deity,
I shall forever be with Thee
Because Thou art with me.

Maltbie D. Babcock, 1858–1901

792. DEAR LORD, WHO SOUGHT AT DAWN

Dear Lord, who sought at dawn of day
The solitary woods to pray,
In quietness we come to ask
Thy presence for the daily task.

O Master, who with kindly face
At noon trod in the market-place,
We crave a brother's smile and song
When mingling in the lonely throng.

Thou wearied Christ at eventide
Renewed upon the mountain side,
Restore us with thy mystic might
Before the falling of the night.

Strong Pilot, who at midnight hour
Could calm the sea with gentle power,
Grant us the skill to aid the bark
Of those who drift in storm and dark.

Harry Webb Farrington, 1880–1931

793. A PRAYER FOR THE PRESENCE OF CHRIST

Reveal Thy Presence now, O Lord,
As in the Upper Room of old;
Break Thou our bread, grace Thou our board,
And keep our hearts from growing cold.

Thomas Tiplady, 1882–

794. THE WHITE PRESENCE

Will not our hearts within us burn
On the darkening road,
If a White Presence we can discern—
Despite an ancient load?

Whither goest Thou, Pilgrim Friend?
Lone Figure far ahead,
Wilt Thou not tarry until the end—
And break our bread?

Follow we must amid sun or shade,
Our faith to complete,
Journeying where no path is made—
Save by His feet!

Joseph Fort Newton, 1880–

795. THE VOICE OF CHRISTMAS

I cannot put the Presence by, of Him, the Crucified,
Who moves men's spirits with His Love as doth the moon the tide;
Again I see the Life He lived, the godlike Death He died.

Again I see upon the cross that great Soul-battle fought,
Into the texture of the world the tale of which is wrought
Until it hath become the woof of human deed and thought,—

And, joining with the cadenced bells that all the morning fill,
His cry of agony doth yet my inmost being thrill,
Like some fresh grief from yesterday that tears the heart-strings still.

I cannot put His Presence by, I meet Him everywhere;
I meet Him in the country town, the busy market-square;
The Mansion and the Tenement attest His Presence there.

Upon the funneled ships at sea He sets His shining feet;
The Distant Ends of Empire not in vain His Name repeat,—
And, like the presence of a rose, He makes the whole world sweet.

He comes to break the barriers down raised up by barren creeds;
About the globe from zone to zone like sunlight He proceeds;
He comes to give the World's starved heart the perfect love it needs,

The Christ, whose friends have played Him false, whom Dogmas have belied,
Still speaking to the hearts of men—though shamed and crucified,
The Master of the Centuries who will not be denied!

Harry Kemp, 1883-

796. CHRISTIAN, DOST THOU SEE THEM?

Christian, dost thou see them
On the holy ground,
How the powers of darkness
Compass thee around?
Christian, up and smite them,
Counting gain but loss,
In the strength that cometh
By the holy cross.

Christian, dost thou feel them,
How they work within,
Striving, tempting, luring,
Goading into sin?
Christian, never tremble,
Never be downcast;
Gird thee for the battle,
Watch and pray and fast.

Christian, dost thou hear them,
How they speak thee fair,
"Always fast and vigil,
Always watch and prayer?"
Christian, answer boldly,
"While I breathe I pray!"
Peace shall follow battle,
Night shall end in day.

"Well I know thy trouble,
O my servant true;
Thou art very weary,
I was weary, too;
But that toil shall make thee
Some day all mine own,
And the end of sorrow
Shall be near my throne."

Andrew of Crete, 660–732;
tr. by John M. Neale, 1818–1866

797. TO AN ENEMY

Some passionate hour before my own deep
stripe
Has taken on its healing, I shall trace
Him out, and with clean linen I shall wipe
The stain from that raw cut upon his face;
And with the hand that smote him I shall turn
The audit strong against him, offering
Once more a wound for wound and burn for
burn
Out of the heart's own codeless bargaining.

And he, with wound adjuring wound, shall
draw
His equal measure to the sacrament

From an old well to which some mortals went
When, with their thirsts ablaze, they looked
and saw
An Orient form uplifted in the skies,
And quenched their hate in his forgiving eyes.

E. J. Pratt, contemporary Canadian

798. NO EAST OR WEST

In Christ there is no East or West,
In Him no South or North,
But one great Fellowship of Love
Throughout the whole wide earth.

In Him shall true hearts everywhere
Their high communion find.
His service is the golden cord
Close-binding all mankind.

Join hands then, Brothers of the Faith,
Whate'er your race may be!—
Who serves my Father as a son
Is surely kin to me.

In Christ now meet both East and West,
In Him meet South and North,
All Christly souls are one in Him,
Throughout the whole wide earth.

John Oxenham, 1852–1941

799. AFRICA

I slept. I dreamed. I seemed to climb a hard, ascending track
And just behind me labored one whose face was black.
I pitied him, but hour by hour he gained upon my path.
He stood beside me, stood upright, and then I turned in wrath.
"Go back," I cried, "what right have you to stand beside me here?"
I paused, struck dumb with fear, for lo! the black man was not there—
But Christ stood in his place!
And oh! the pain, the pain, the pain that looked from that dear face.

Author unknown

800. IN HIM WE LIVE

But souls that of His own good life partake,
He loves as His own self; dear as His eye
They are to Him: He'll never them forsake:
When they shall die, then God himself shall
die;
They live, they live in blest eternity.

Henry More, 1614–1687

801. I HAVE A LIFE WITH CHRIST TO LIVE

I have a life with Christ to live,
But, ere I live it, must I wait
Till learning can clear answer give
Of this and that book's date?

I have a life in Christ to live,
I have a death in Christ to die;—
And must I wait, till science give
All doubts a full reply?

Nay rather, while the sea of doubt
Is raging wildly round about,
Questioning of life and death and sin,
Let me but creep within
Thy fold, O Christ, and at Thy feet
Take but the lowest seat,
And hear Thine awful voice repeat
In gentlest accents, heavenly sweet,
Come unto Me, and rest:
Believe Me, and be blest.

John Campbell Shairp, 1819–1885

802. THE COLLAR

I struck the board, and cry'd, "No more,
I will abroad."
What, shall I ever sigh and pine?
My lines and life are free; free as the road,
Loose as the wind, as large as store.
Shall I be still in suit?
Have I no harvest but a thorn

To let me blood, and not restore
What I have lost with cordial fruit?
Sure there was wine
Before my sighs did dry it; there was corn
Before my tears did drown it;
Is the year only lost to me?
Have I no bays to crown it?
No flowers, no garlands gay? all blasted,
All wasted?
Not so, my heart; but there is fruit,
And thou hast hands.
Recover all thy sigh-blown age
On double pleasures; leave thy cold dispute
Of what is fit and not; forsake thy cage,
Thy rope of sands
Which petty thoughts have made: and made to thee
Good cable, to enforce and draw,
And be thy law,
While thou didst wink and wouldst not see.
Awake: take heed:
I will abroad.
Call in thy death's-head there, tie up thy fears.
He that forbears
To suit and serve his need
Deserves his load.
But as I rav'd and grew more fierce and wild
At every word,
Methought I heard one calling, "Child":
And I replied, "My Lord."

George Herbert, 1593–1692

803. FOLLOW THE CHRIST

From: "Idylls of the King: Gareth and Lynette"

Man am I grown, a man's work must I do,
Follow the deer? follow the Christ, the King,
Live pure, speak true, right wrong, follow the King—
Else, wherefore born?

Alfred Tennyson, 1809–1892

804. TAKE UP THY CROSS

Thou say'st, "Take up thy cross,
O man, and follow Me";
The night is black, the feet are slack,
Yet we would follow Thee.

But, O dear Lord, we cry,
That we Thy face could see!
Thy blessèd face one moment's space
Then might we follow Thee!

Dim tracts of time divide
Those golden days from me;
Thy voice comes strange o'er years of change;
How can we follow Thee?

Comes faint and far Thy voice
From vales of Galilee;
Thy vision fades in ancient shades;
How should we follow Thee?

Ah! sense-bound heart and blind!
Is naught but what we see?
Can time undo what once was true;
Can we not follow Thee?

If not as once Thou cam'st
In true humanity,
Come yet as Guest within the breast
That burns to follow Thee.

Within our heart of hearts
In nearest nearness be:
Set up Thy throne within Thine own:
Go, Lord, we follow Thee.

Francis Turner Palgrave, 1824–1897

805. FOLLOW ME!

Lord, I would follow, but—
First, I would see what means that wondrous call
That peals so sweetly through Life's rainbow hall,
That thrills my heart with quivering golden chords,
And fills my soul with joys seraphical.

Lord, I would follow, but—
First, I would leave things straight before I go,—
Collect my dues, and pay the debts I owe;
Lest when I'm gone, and none is here to tend,
Time's ruthless hand my garnering o'erthrow.

Lord, I would follow, but—
First, I would see the end of this high road
That stretches straight before me, fair and broad;
So clear the way I cannot go astray,
It surely leads me equally to God.

Lord, I would follow,—yea,
Follow I *will*,—but first so much there is
That claims me in life's vast emergencies,—
Wrongs to be righted, great things to be done;
Shall I neglect these vital urgencies?

Who answers Christ's insistent call
Must give himself, his life, his all,
Without one backward look.
Who sets his hand unto the plow,
And glances back with anxious brow,
His calling hath mistook.
Christ claims him wholly for His own;
He must be Christ's, and Christ's alone.

John Oxenham, 1852–1941

806. APPROACHES

When thou turn'st away from ill,
Christ is this side of thy hill.

When thou turnest toward good,
Christ is walking in thy wood.

When thy heart says, "Father, pardon!"
Then the Lord is in thy garden.

When stern Duty wakes to watch,
Then His hand is on the latch.

But when Hope thy song doth rouse,
Then the Lord is in the house.

When to love is all thy wit,
Christ doth at thy table sit.

When God's will is thy heart's pole,
Then is Christ thy very soul.

George Macdonald, 1824–1905

807. A HYMN FOR THE NEW AGE

O Master of the modern day,
Our hearts are kindled as we know
Thou walkest still along life's way
As in the ages long ago!
And by the magic of Thy will
New worlds Thou art creating still.

We thank Thee that the truth moves on
With wireless wave and healing ray;
That yester's noon was but the dawn
Of brighter glories in our day.
And now by faith, in holy dream
We glimpse tomorrow's grander gleam.

We thank Thee that Thou rulest still
This goodly orb on which we dwell—
That Thou dost still reveal Thy will
To those who would the dark dispel—
That upward o'er the peaks of time
Thy plan unfolds in form sublime.

Help us to keep Thee as our guest
While speeding o'er the highways grand,
Or cleave the air at Thy behest
To give some soul a helping hand!
Thy tireless Spirit leads the way
To heal the woes that throng our day!

Enlarge our minds to grasp Thy thought,
Enlarge our hearts to work Thy plan,
Assured Thy purpose faileth not
To put Thy spirit into man!
God of the present age and hour,
Thrill us anew with holy power!

William Steward Gordon

808. From THE TESTAMENT OF BEAUTY, IV

Our happiest earthly comradeships hold a foretaste
of the feast of salvation and by thatt virtue in them
provoke desire beyond them to out-reach and surmount
their humanity in some superhumanity
and ultimat perfection: which, hoe'er 'tis found
or strangely imagin'd, answereth to the need of each
and pulleth him instinctively as to a final cause.
Thus unto all who hav found their high ideal in Christ,
Christ is to them the essence discern'd or undiscern'd
of all their human friendships; and each lover of him
and of his beauty must be as a bud on the Vine
and hav participation in him; for Goddes love
is unescapable as nature's environment,

Which if a man ignore or think to thrust it off
he is the ill-natured fool that runneth blindly on death.
  This Individualism is man's true Socialism.
This is the rife Idea whose spiritual beauty
multiplieth in communion to transcendant might.
This is thatt excelent way whereon if we wil walk
all things shall be added unto us—thatt Love which inspired
the wayward Visionary in his doctrinal ode
to the three christian Graces, the Church's first hymn
and only deathless athanasian creed,—the which
"except a man believe he cannot be savèd".
This is the endearing bond whereby Christ's company
yet holdeth together on the truth of his promise
that he spake of his great pity and trust in man's love,
Lo, I am with you always ev'n to the end of the world.

Robert Bridges, 1844–1930

809. LO, I AM WITH YOU ALWAYS

Wide fields of corn along the valleys spread;
  The rain and dews mature the swelling vine;
I see the Lord is multiplying bread;
  I see Him turning water into wine;
  I see Him working all the works divine
He wrought when Salamward His steps were led;
  The selfsame miracles around Him shine;
He feeds the famished; He revives the dead;
  He pours the flood of light on darkened eyes;
He chases tears, diseases, fiends away;
  His throne is raised upon these orient skies;
His footstool is the pave whereon we pray.
  Ah, tell me not of Christ in Paradise,
For He is all around us here to-day.

John Charles Earle, 1824-1903

810. THE CONTINUING CHRIST

Far, far away is Bethlehem,
  And years are long and dim,
Since Mary held the Holy Child
  And angels sang for Him.
But still to hearts where love and faith
  Make room for Christ in them,
He comes again, the Child from God,
  To find His Bethlehem.

Beyond the sea is Galilee
  And ways which Jesus trod,
And hidden there are those high hills
  Where He communed with God;
Yet on the plains of common life,
  Through all the world of men,
The voice that once said, "Follow me,"
  Speaks to our hearts again.

Gethsemane and Calvary
  And death and bitter loss,
Are these but echoes drifting down
  From a forgotten cross?
Nay, Lord, for all our living sins
  Thy cross is lifted up,
And as of old we hear Thee say,
  "Can ye, too, drink My cup?"

O Life that seems so long ago,
  And yet is ever new,
The fellowship of love with Thee,
  Through all the years is true.
O Master over death and time,
  Reveal Thyself, we pray,
And as before amongst Thine own,
  Dwell Thou in us today!

W. Russell Bowie, 1882-

811. THE CHRIST OF THE WORLD'S HIGHWAY

He treads no more the paths of Galilee;
But where the sullen Ganges bares its breast
To burning skies, His sandaled feet are pressed
Into the dust, and seeking souls to-day
Have met a turbaned Comrade on the way.

He sits no more beside Samaria's wells;
Yet where a thousand far-off fountains spring
From jungle silence, wondering mothers bring
The children of a dark, bewildered race
Unto a Friend with kindly, dusky face.

He walks no more along the Syrian road;
Yet where a dim pagoda's haunting spire
Hides crumbling gods and dying altar fire,
A people old in burdens, race, and pride
Have found a Brother walking by their side.

Dorothy Clarke Wilson, 1904–

812. TO AND FRO ABOUT THE CITY

Shakespeare is dust, and will not come
To question from his Avon tomb,
And Socrates and Shelley keep
An Attic and Italian sleep.

They will not see us, nor again
Shall indignation light the brain
Where Lincoln on his woodland height
Tells out the spring and winter night.

They see not. But, O Christians, who
Throng Holborn and Fifth Avenue,
May you not meet, in spite of death,
A traveler from Nazareth?

John Drinkwater, 1882–1937

813. VIA LUCIS

And have the bright immensities
Received our risen Lord
Where light-years frame the Pleiades
And point Orion's sword?

Do flaming suns His footsteps trace
Through corridors sublime,
The Lord of interstellar space
And Conqueror of time?

The heaven that hides Him from our sight
Knows neither near nor far:
An altar candle sheds its light
As surely as a star;

And where His loving people meet
To share the gift divine,
There stands He with unhurrying feet,
There heavenly splendors shine.

Howard Chandler Robbins, 1876–

814. ALIVE FOR EVERMORE

Whom God hath raised up, having loosed the pangs of death: because it was not possible that he should be holden of it. Acts 2: 24

His spirit lives; he died and is alive,
That pure will haunts this guilty world forever.
How could men's idle fury drive
That mighty shepherd from his sheep? Or sever
His heart from Mary's, Peter's? Or deprive
Iscariot and the thief of his blest rod,
Far in the ultimate night apart from God?
Never, never
Could death's thin shadows dim that ardent Sun!
He walks amid the Golden Candlesticks
Today, and lights all souls while time shall run
Who on the tree by his own troth affixed
Has knit the life of God and man forever.

Amos Niven Wilder, 1895–

815. COME THOU MY LIGHT

Come, Thou my Light, that I may see
Thy truth divine, Thy love so free.
Dispel the clouds of doubt and sin
And let the face of God shine in.

Come Thou my Life, that I may be
Made one in living faith with Thee.
Renew my will and make it Thine,
Thou living Source of life divine.

Come Thou my Guide, that I may know
The way my seeking soul should go:
And never from Thee let me stray,
Thyself the Life, the Truth, the Way.

Come Thou my King, and I will make
My heart a shrine, for Thy dear sake:
Until this Earthly life of mine
Shall be forever wholly Thine.

Hugh Thomson Kerr, 1871–

816. WHEN THE DAYLIGHT WANES

O Risen Saviour, when the daylight wanes,
Go Thou before,
To meet us in our streets and quiet lanes

Or by the shore;
Among Thine own at eventide to be;
As in the ancient days in Galilee.

❖

No more in Galilee we look for Thee,
O Risen Lord;
In every land and on each moonlit sea
Thy voice is heard;
And when Thy saints are gathered in Thy
Name,
Closer Thou art to each than fire to flame.

Thomas Tiplady, 1882–

817. MY GALILEES

Although my eyes may never see
That hallowed Lake of Galilee,

Still I have found each little lake
More fraught with meaning for His sake.

Upon a floor of amethyst
He walks in early morning mist,

While on a grassy slope is spread
Once more the Feast of Living Bread.

Belle Chapman Morrill,
contemporary American

818. THE LILIES OF THE FIELD

When I went up to Nazareth—
A pilgrim of the spring—
When I went up to Nazareth
The earth was blossoming!
I saw the blue flower of the flax
Beside a shepherd's fold;
Along the hillsides' stony tracks
I found the marigold;
The iris raised a shimmering spire
Of beauty at my feet;
The poppy was a cup of fire
Among the cooling wheat!

When I went up to Nazareth
I marked how time came down
With blighting dust and withering breath
Upon the hallowed town!
The years that buried Babylon
Were drifting to efface
The steps of Mary's Heavenly Son,
But still his truth held place,
And still I read his permanence
By signs that never dim:
With all their ancient eloquence;
The lilies spoke of him.

Daniel Henderson, 1880–

819. CHRIST OUR CONTEMPORARY

Christ's Spirit taketh breath again
Within the lives of holy men.

Each changing age beholds afresh
Its word of God in human flesh,

Amid the meek of earth, whose ear
Pure wisdom maketh quick to hear,

Who know the founts of good and ill,
And live in the eternal will,

Sharing themselves and all their good
In universal brotherhood;

In whose sweet lives we still may see
The One who walked in Galilee,

❖

And preaching through the human page
Christ's living gospel to our age.

W. C. Braithwaite, 1862–1922

820. THE ILLIMITABLE GOD

From "A Death in the Desert," conclusion

If Christ, as thou affirmest, be of men
Mere man, the first and best but nothing more—
Account Him, for reward of what He was,
Now and for ever, wretchedest of all.
For see; Himself conceived of life as love,

Conceived of love as what must enter in,
Fill up, make one with His each soul He loved:
Thus much for man's joy, all men's joy for Him.
Well, He is gone, thou sayest, to fit reward.
But by this time are many souls set free,
And very many still retained alive:
Nay, should His coming be delayed awhile,
Say, ten years longer (twelve years some compute),
See if, for every finger of thy hands,
There be not found, that day the world shall end,
Hundreds of souls, each holding by Christ's word
That He will grow incorporate with all,
With me as Pamphylax, with him as John,
Groom for each bride! Can a mere man do this?
Yet Christ saith this He lived and died to do.
Call Christ, then, the illimitable God,
Or lost!

Robert Browning, 1812–1889

Book III: MAN

821. WHAT IS MAN?

Psalm 8

O Lord our Lord,
how excellent is thy name in all the earth!
who hast set thy glory above the heavens.
Out of the mouth of babes and sucklings hast thou ordained strength
because of thine enemies,
that thou mightest still the enemy and the avenger.
When I consider thy heavens, the work of thy fingers,
the moon and the stars, which thou hast ordained;
What is man, that thou art mindful of him?
and the son of man, that thou visitest him?
For thou hast made him a little lower than the angels,
and hast crowned him with glory and honour.
Thou madest him to have dominion over the works of thy hands;
thou hast put all things under his feet:
All sheep and oxen,
Yea, and the beasts of the field;
The fowl of the air, and the fish of the sea,
and whatsoever passeth through the paths of the seas.
O Lord our Lord,
how excellent is thy name in all the earth!

King James Version, 1611

822. From THE LOOM OF YEARS

O, woven in one wide Loom thro' the throbbing weft of the whole,
One in spirit and flesh, one in body and soul,
The leaf on the winds of autumn, the bird in its hour to die,
The heart in its muffled anguish, the sea in its mournful cry,
One with the dream that triumphs beyond the light of the spheres,
We come from the Loom of the Weaver that weaves the Web of the Years.

Alfred Noyes, 1880–

823. THE MAKING OF MAN

Flame of the spirit, and dust of the earth,—
This is the making of man,
This is his problem of birth;
Born to all holiness, born to all crime,
Heir of both worlds, on the long slope of time
Climbing the path of God's plan;
Dust of the earth in his error and fear,
Weakness and malice and lust;
Yet, quivering up from the dust,
Flame of the spirit, unleaping and clear,
Yearning to God, since from God is its birth—
This is man's portion, to shape as he can,
Flame of the spirit, and dust of the earth—
This is the making of man.

Priscilla Leonard, 1852–

824. THE CREATION

A Negro Sermon

And God stepped out on space,
And He looked around and said:
I'm lonely—
I'll make me a world.

And far as the eye of God could see
Darkness covered everything,

Blacker than a hundred midnights
Down in a cypress swamp.

Then God smiled,
And the light broke,
And the darkness rolled up on one side,
And the light stood shining on the other,
And God said: *That's good!*

Then God reached out and took the light in
His hands,
And God rolled the light around in His hands
Until He made the sun;
And He set that sun a-blazing in the heavens.
And the light that was left from making the
sun
God gathered it up in a shining ball
And flung it against the darkness,
Spangling the night with the moon and stars.
Then down between
The darkness and the light
He hurled the world;
And God said: *That's good!*

Then God himself stepped down—
And the sun was on His right hand,
And the moon was on His left;
The stars were clustered about His head,
And the earth was under His feet.
And God walked, and where He trod
His footsteps hollowed the valleys out
And bulged the mountains up.

Then He stopped and looked and saw
That the earth was hot and barren.
So God stepped over to the edge of the world
And He spat out the seven seas—
He batted His eyes, and the lightnings
flashed—
He clapped His hands, and the thunders
rolled—
And the waters above the earth came down,
The cooling waters came down.

Then the green grass sprouted,
And the little red flowers blossomed,
The pine tree pointed his finger to the sky,
And the oak spread out his arms,
The lakes cuddled down in the hollows of the
ground,
The rivers ran down to the sea;
And God smiled again,
And the rainbow appeared,
And curled itself around His shoulder.

Then God raised His arm and He waved His
hand
Over the sea and over the land,
And He said: *Bring forth! Bring forth!*
And quicker than God could drop His hand,
Fishes and fowls
And beasts and birds
Swam the rivers and the seas,
Roamed the forests and the woods,
And split the air with their wings.
And God said: *That's good!*

Then God walked around,
And God looked around
On all that He had made.
He looked at His sun,
And He looked at His moon,
And He looked at His little stars;
He looked on His world
With all its living things,
And God said: *I'm lonely still.*

Then God sat down—
On the side of a hill where He could think;
By a deep, wide river He sat down;
With His head in His hands,
God thought and thought,
Till He thought: *I'll make me a man!*

Up from the bed of the river
God scooped the clay;
And by the bank of the river
He kneeled Him down;
And there the great God Almighty
Who lit the sun and fixed it in the sky,
Who flung the stars to the most far corner of
the night,
Who rounded the earth in the middle of His
hand;
This Great God,
Like a mammy bending over her baby,
Kneeled down in the dust
Toiling over a lump of clay
Till He shaped it in His own image;

Then into it He blew the breath of life,
And man became a living soul
Amen. Amen.

James Weldon Johnson, 1871–1938

825. THE PULLEY

When God at first made man,
Having a glass of blessings standing by;
Let us (said He) pour on him all we can:
Let the world's riches, which dispersèd lie,
Contract into a span.

So strength first made a way;
Then beauty flowed, then wisdom, honour, pleasure:
When almost all was out, God made a stay,
Perceiving that alone of all His treasure
Rest in the bottom lay.

For if I should (said He)
Bestow this jewel also on My creature,
He would adore My gifts instead of Me,
And rest in Nature, not the God of Nature.
So both should losers be.

Yet let him keep the rest,
But keep them with repining restlessness:
Let him be rich and weary, that at least,
If goodness lead him not, yet weariness
May toss him to My breast.

George Herbert, 1593–1632

826. From BY AN EVOLUTIONIST

If my body come from brutes, tho' somewhat finer than their own,
I am heir, and this my kingdom. Shall the royal voice be mute?
No, but if the rebel subject seek to drag me from the throne,
Hold the sceptre, Human Soul, and rule thy province of the brute.

I have climb'd to the snows of Age, and I gaze at a field in the Past,
Where I sank with the body at times in the sloughs of a low desire,
But I hear no yelp of the beast, and the Man is quiet at last,
As he stands on the heights of his life with a glimpse of a height that is higher.

Alfred Tennyson, 1809–1892

827. ODE ON INTIMATIONS OF IMMORTALITY FROM RECOLLECTIONS OF EARLY CHILDHOOD

There was a time when meadow, grove, and stream,
The earth, and every common sight,
To me did seem
Apparelled in celestial light,
The glory and the freshness of a dream.
It is not now as it hath been of yore;—
Turn whereso'er I may,
By night or day,
The things which I have seen I now can see no more.
The Rainbow comes and goes,
And lovely is the Rose,
The Moon doth with delight
Look round her when the heavens are bare;
Waters on a starry night
Are beautiful and fair;
The sunshine is a glorious birth;
But yet I know, where'er I go,
That there hath past away a glory from the earth.

❖

Our birth is but a sleep and a forgetting:
The Soul that rises with us, our life's Star,
Hath had elsewhere its setting,
And cometh from afar:
Not in entire forgetfulness,
And not in utter nakedness,
But trailing clouds of glory do we come
From God, who is our home:

Heaven lies about us in our infancy!
Shades of the prison-house begin to close
    Upon the growing Boy,
But he beholds the light, and whence it flows,
    He sees it in his joy;
The Youth, who daily farther from the east
    Must travel, still is Nature's Priest,
    And by the vision splendid
    Is on his way attended;
At length the Man perceives it die away,
And fade into the light of common day.

❖

    O joy! that in our embers
    Is something that doth live,
    That nature yet remembers
    What was so fugitive!
The thought of our past years in me doth breed
Perpetual benediction: not indeed
For that which is most worthy to be blest—
Delight and liberty, the simple creed
Of Childhood, whether busy or at rest,
With new-fledged hope still fluttering in his breast:—
    Not for these I raise
    The song of thanks and praise;
  But for those obstinate questionings
  Of sense and outward things,
  Fallings from us, vanishings;
  Blank misgivings of a Creature
Moving about in worlds not realized,
High instincts before which our mortal Nature
Did tremble like a guilty Thing surprised:
  But for those first affections,
    Those shadowy recollections,
  Which, be they what they may,
Are yet the fountain light of all our day,
Are yet a master light of all our seeing;
  Uphold us, cherish, and have power to make
Our noisy years seem moments in the being
Of the eternal Silence: truths that wake,
    To perish never;
Which neither listlessness, nor mad endeavor,
    Nor Man nor Boy,
Nor all that is at enmity with joy,
Can utterly abolish or destroy!
    Hence in a season of calm weather
    Though inland far we be,
Our Souls have sight of that immortal sea
    Which brought us hither,
    Can in a moment travel thither,
And see the Children sport upon the shore,
And hear the mighty waters rolling evermore.

Then sing, ye Birds, sing, sing a joyous song!
And let the young Lambs bound
As to the tabor's sound!
We in thought will join your throng,
Ye that pipe and ye that play,
Ye that through your hearts to-day
Feel the gladness of the May!
What though the radiance which was once so bright
Be now forever taken from my sight,
Though nothing can bring back the hour
Of splendor in the grass, of glory in the flower;
We will grieve not, rather find
Strength in what remains behind;
In the primal sympathy
Which having been must ever be;
In the soothing thoughts that spring
Out of human suffering;
In the faith that looks through death,
In years that bring the philosophic mind.
And O, ye Fountains, Meadows, Hills, and Groves,
Forebode not any severing of our loves!
Yet in my heart of hearts I feel your might;
I only have relinquished one delight
To live beneath your more habitual sway.
I love the Brooks which down their channels fret,
Even more than when I tripped lightly as they;
The innocent brightness of a new-born Day
Is lovely yet;
The Clouds that gather round the setting sun
Do take a sober coloring from an eye
That hath kept watch o'er man's mortality;
Another race hath been, and other palms are won.
Thanks to the human heart by which we live,
Thanks to its tenderness, its joys, and fears,
To me the meanest flower that blows can give
Thoughts that do often lie too deep for tears.

William Wordsworth, 1770–1850

828. THE PILGRIM

Man comes a pilgrim of the universe,
Out of the mysteries that were before
The world, out of the wonder of old stars.
Far roads have felt his feet, forgotten wells
Have glassed his beauty bending down to drink.
At altar-fires anterior to Earth
His soul was lighted, and it will burn on
After the suns have wasted in the void.
His feet have felt the pressure of old worlds,
And are to tread on others yet unnamed—
Worlds sleeping yet in some new dream of God.

Edwin Markham, 1852–1940

829. FORM

The buried statue through the marble gleams,
Praying for freedom, an unwilling guest,
Yet flooding with the light of her strange dreams
The hard stone folded round her uncarved breast.

Founded in granite, wrapped in serpentine,
Light of all life and heart of every storm,
Doth the uncarven image, the Divine,
Deep in the heart of each man, wait for form.

Eva Gore-Booth, 1872–1926

830. From SONG OF MYSELF

44

It is time to explain myself—Let us stand up.

What is known I strip away;
I launch all men and women forward with me into THE UNKNOWN.

The clock indicates the moment—but what does eternity indicate?

We have thus far exhausted trillions of winters and summers;
There are trillions ahead, and trillions ahead of them.

❖

I am an acme of things accomplish'd, and I an encloser of things to be.

❖

Rise after rise bow the phantoms behind me;
Afar down I see the huge first Nothing—I know I was even there;
I waited unseen and always, and slept through the lethargic mist,
And took my time, and took no hurt from the fetid carbon.

Long I was hugg'd close—long and long.
Immense have been the preparations for me,
Faithful and friendly the arms that have help'd me.

Cycles ferried my cradle, rowing and rowing like cheerful boatmen;
For room to me stars kept aside in their own rings;
They sent influences to look after what was to hold me.

Before I was born out of my mother, generations guided me;
My embryo has never been torpid—nothing could overlay it.

For it the nebula cohered to an orb,
The long slow strata piled to rest it on,
Vast vegetables gave it sustenance,
Monstrous sauroids transported it in their mouths, and deposited it with care.

All forces have been steadily employ'd to complete and delight me;
Now on this spot I stand with my robust Soul.

Walt Whitman, 1819–1892

831. KINSHIP

I am part of the sea and stars
  And the winds of the South and North,
Of mountain and moon and Mars,
  And the ages sent me forth!

Blind Homer, the splendor of Greece,
  Sang the songs I sang ere he fell;
She whom men call Beatrice,
  Saw me in the depths of hell.

I was hanged at dawn for a crime—
  Flesh dies, but the soul knows no death;
I piped to great Shakespeare's chime
  The witches' song in Macbeth.

All, all who have suffered and won,
  Who have struggled and failed and died,
Am I, with work still undone,
  And a spear-mark in my side.

I am part of the sea and stars
  And the winds of the South and North,
Of mountains and moon and Mars,
  And the ages sent me forth!

Edward H. S. Terry, 20th century

832. THE CHALLENGE OF LIFE

From "Ulysses"

I am a part of all that I have met;
Yet all experience is an arch wherethro'
Gleams that untravell'd world whose margin
  fades
For ever and for ever when I move.
How dull it is to pause, to make an end,
To rust unburnish'd, not to shine in use!
As tho' to breathe were life! Life piled on life
Were all too little, and of one to me
Little remains; but every hour is saved
From that eternal silence, something more,
A bringer of new things; and vile it were
For some three suns to store and hoard
  myself,
And this gray spirit yearning in desire
To follow knowledge like a sinking star,
Beyond the utmost bound of human thought.

Alfred Tennyson, 1809–1892

833. A SONG OF DERIVATIONS

I come from nothing, but from where
Come the undying thoughts I bear?
  Down, through long links of death and
    birth,
  From the past poets of earth,
My immortality is there.

I am like the blossom of an hour
But long, long vanished sun and shower
  Awoke my breath i' the young world's air.
  I track the past back everywhere
Through seed and flower and seed and flower.

Or, I am like a stream that flows
Full of the cold springs that arose
  In morning lands, in distant hills;
  And down the plain my channel fills
With melting of forgotten snows.

Voices I have not heard, possessed
My own fresh songs; my thoughts are blessed
  With relics of the far unknown.
  And mixed with memories not my own
The sweet streams throng into my breast.

Before this life began to be,
The happy songs that wake in me
  Woke long ago and far apart.
  Heavily on this little heart
Presses this immortality.

Alice Meynell, 1847–1922

834. THE LOST KEY

The key of yesterday
I threw away;
And now, too late,
Before tomorrow's fast-closed gate
Helpless I stand—in vain to pray!
  In vain to sorrow!
Only the key of yesterday
  Unlocks tomorrow.

Priscilla Leonard, 1852–

835. PIONEERS

For the first man to climb the hill
And seek a prospect wider still;
For the first man to brave the sea
Unscared by its immensity;

For he who, conquering craven fear,
First found in fire a friend to cheer;
For he who first from stubborn stone
Wrought tool and weapon of his own;
For those the first with patient toil
To break the clod and till the soil;
For all such men, since men began,
We thank the God who made the man.

Author unknown

836. NO GREAT, NO SMALL

From "History"

There is no great and no small
To the Soul that maketh all:
And where it cometh, all things are;
And it cometh everywhere.

I am owner of the sphere,
Of the seven stars and the solar year,
Of Caesar's hand, and Plato's brain,
Of Lord Christ's heart, and Shakespeare's strain.

Ralph Waldo Emerson, 1803–1882

837. SONNET

Upon our fullness smiles the dawning day,
Our superdreadnaughts dominate the main,
The whirring of the infant aeroplane
Threatens with chains the breezes at their play;
Our towers rise; we prosper while we may,
Grown drunken with the wine of loss and gain,
Nor fearful lest we haply rear in vain
A brazen idol upon feet of clay.

The ages are not mocked; the years that fleet
Are harsh or gentle as it seemeth well,
The victors in Thermopylae's defeat
Are weaker than the Spartan few who fell;
And still above the turmoil of the street
Smiles the Madonna of a Raphael.

Francis Lyman Windolph, 1889–

838. GOSHEN!

"How can you live in Goshen?"
Said a friend from afar,
"This wretched country town
Where folks talk little things all year,
And plant their cabbage by the moon!"
Said I:
"I do not live in Goshen,—
I eat here, sleep here, work here;
I live in Greece,
Where Plato taught,
And Phidias carved,
And Epictetus wrote.
I dwell in Italy,
Where Michael Angelo wrought
In color, form and mass;
Where Cicero penned immortal lines,
And Dante sang undying songs.
Think not my life is small
Because you see a puny place;
I have my books; I have my dreams;
A thousand souls have left for me
Enchantment that transcends
Both time and place.
And so I live in Paradise,
Not here."

Edgar Frank, contemporary American

839. IN THIS STERN HOUR

In this stern hour when the spirit falters
Before the weight of fear, the nameless dread;
When lights burn low upon accustomed altars
And meaningless are half the prayers we've said—
Faith seeks a rock, immovable, unchanging,
On which to build the fortress of its strength,
Some pole-star, fixed, beyond the planets' ranging,
Steadfast and true throughout the journey's length.

Older than any creed of man's evolving,
Wiser than any prophet in his day:
The human heart, the brown sweet earth revolving!
Take these, O faith! Although they both be clay
Yet through them both there runs a fire supernal—
Part of the very stars' bright diagram
They spell that Word, primordial and eternal,
Which said "Before Jehovah was, I AM!"

Josephine Johnson, contemporary American

840. WHAT KNOW WE GREATER THAN THE SOUL?

From "Ode On The Death Of The Duke Of Wellington"

Tho' world on world in myriad myriads roll
Round us, each with different powers,
And other forms of life than ours,
What know we greater than the soul?
On God and Godlike men we build our trust.

Alfred Tennyson, 1809–1892

841. From THE VANITY OF HUMAN LEARNING

I know my soul hath power to know all things,
Yet is she blind and ignorant in all:
I know I'm one of Nature's little kings,
Yet to the least and vilest things am thrall.

I know my life's a pain, and but a span;
I know my sense is mock'd in ev'ry thing:
And to conclude, I know myself a man,
Which is a proud, and yet a wretched thing.

John Davies, 1569–1626

842. MAN

From "Night Thoughts"

How poor, how rich, how abject, how august,
How complicate, how wonderful is man!
How passing wonder He, who made him such,
Who centred in our make such strange extremes!
From different natures marvellously mixt,
Connection exquisite of distant worlds!
Distinguished link in being's endless chain!
Midway from nothing to the Deity!
A beam, ethereal, sullied, and absorpt!
Though sullied and dishonoured, still divine!
Dim miniature of greatness absolute!
And heir of glory! a frail child of dust!
Helpless immortal! insect infinite!
A worm!—a god!—I tremble at myself,
And in myself am lost! at home a stranger,
Thought wanders up and down, surprised, aghast,
And wond'ring at her own: how reason reels!
O what a miracle to man is man,
Triumphantly distressed! what joy, what dread!
Alternately transported, and alarmed!
What can preserve my life? or what destroy?
An angel's arm can't snatch me from the grave:
Legions of angels can't confine me there.

Edward Young, 1683–1765

843. THE PERFECT TRIBUTE

From "Julius Caesar," Act V, sc. 5

His life was gentle; and the elements
So mix'd in him, that Nature might stand up,
And say to all the world, "This was a man!"

William Shakespeare, 1564–1616

844. KNOW THEN THYSELF

From "Essay on Man"

Know then thyself, presume not God to scan,
The proper study of mankind is man.
Placed on this isthmus of a middle state,
A being darkly wise, and rudely great:
With too much knowledge for the skeptic side,
With too much weakness for the stoic's pride,
He hangs between, in doubt to act or rest:

In doubt to deem himself a god or beast;
In doubt his mind or body to prefer;
Born but to die, and reasoning but to err;
Alike in ignorance, his reason such,
Whether he thinks too little or too much:
Chaos of thought and passion, all confused;
Still by himself abused or disabused;
Created half to rise, and half to fall;
Great lord of all things, yet a prey to all;
Sole judge of truth, in endless error hurled;
The glory, jest and riddle of the world!

Alexander Pope, 1688–1744

845. DESTINY

From "Upon an 'Honest Man's Fortune'"

An honest and a perfect man
Commands all light, all influence, all fate.
Nothing to him falls early, or too late.
Our acts our angels are, or good or ill,
Our fatal shadows that walk by us still.
Our deeds pursue us from afar,
And what we have been makes us what we are.

John Fletcher, 1579–1625

846. MY NAME IS LEGION

Within my earthly temple there's a crowd;
There's one of us that's humble, one that's proud,
There's one that's broken-hearted for his sins,
There's one that unrepentant sits and grins;
There's one that loves his neighbor as himself,
And one that cares for naught but fame and pelf.
From much corroding care I should be free
If I could once determine which is me.

Edward Sanford Martin, 1856–1939

847. THE KINGDOM WITHIN

Count not thyself a starveling soul,
Baulked of the wealth and glow of life,
Destined to grasp, of this rich whole,
Some meagre measure through thy strife.

Ask not of flower or sky or sea
Some gift that in their giving lies;
Their light and wonder are of thee,
Made of thy spirit through thine eyes.

All meaningless the primrose wood,
All messageless the chanting shore,
Hadst thou not in thee gleams of good
And whispers of God's evermore.

The hours bring nothing in their hands;
A silent suppliant at thy gate,
Each one for its brief lifetime stands—
Thou art its master and its fate.

One looketh on the evening skies
And saith, "to-morrow will be fair";
Another's westering gaze descries
God's angels on the golden stair.

The only heaven thou shalt behold
Is builded of thy thoughts and deeds;
Hopes are its pearls and faith its gold,
And love is all the light it needs.

That Voice that broke the world's blind dream
Of gain the stronger hand may win,
For things that are 'gainst things that seem,
Pleaded, The Kingdom is within.

There is no depth, there is no height,
But dwells within thy soul, He saith;
And there dwell time and day and night,
And life is there, and there is death.

Percy Clough Ainsworth, 1873–1909

848. MY KINGDOM

I do not ask for any crown
But that which all may win;
Nor try to conquer any world
Except the one within.
Be Thou my guide until I find
Led by a tender hand,
The happy kingdom in myself
And dare to take command.

Louisa May Alcott,[1] *1832–1888*

849. WARNING

"In the image of God created He him . . ." Genesis 1: 27

These hands are shaped like God's, and so
Let them be careful what they do.

[1] Written at the age of thirteen years.

Let them be quick to lift the weak,
Let them be kind as they are strong.
Let them defend the silent meek
Against the many-languaged wrong.

These hands are shaped like God's. Be sure
They bear the mark of no man's pain
Who asked their help to make secure
His little roof . . . and asked in vain.

These hands are shaped like God's. Take care
They catch the sparrow hurled from air.

Lest God look down from heaven and see
What things are wrought beneath the sun
By us, His images, and be
Ashamed of what His hands have done.

Sara Henderson Hay,
contemporary American

850. INCONSTANCY

From "Holy Sonnets," XIX

Oh, to vex me, contraries meet in one;
Inconstancy unnaturally hath begot
A constant habit; that when I would not
I change in vows, and in devotion.
As humorous is my contrition
As my profane Love, and as soon forgot:
As riddlingly distemper'd, cold and hot,
As praying, as mute; as infinite, as none.
I durst not view heaven yesterday; and to-day
In prayers, and flattering speeches I court
God:
To-morrow I quake with true fear of His rod.
So my devout fits come and go away
Like a fantastic Ague: save that here
Those are my best days, when I shake with
fear.

John Donne, 1573–1631

851. CONSCIENCE AND REMORSE

"Good-bye," I said to my conscience—
"Good-bye for aye and aye,"
And I put her hands off harshly,
And turned my face away;
And conscience smitten sorely
Returned not from that day.

But a time came when my spirit
Grew weary of its pace;
And I cried: "Come back, my conscience;
I long to see thy face."
But conscience cried: "I cannot;
Remorse sits in my place."

Paul Laurence Dunbar, 1872–1906

852. TOO LATE

From "Guinevere"

Late, late, so late! and dark the night and
chill!
Late, late, so late! but we can enter still.
Too late, too late! ye cannot enter now.

No light had we; for that we do repent,
And learning this, the bridegroom will relent.
Too late, too late! ye cannot enter now.

No light! so late! and dark and chill the night!
O, let us in, that we may find the light!
Too late, too late! ye cannot enter now.

Have we not heard the bridegroom is so
sweet?
O, let us in, tho' late, to kiss his feet!
No, no, too late! ye cannot enter now.

Alfred Tennyson, 1809–1892

853. REMORSE

From "On This Day I Complete My Thirty-sixth Year"
(January 22, 1824)

My days are in the yellow leaf;
The flowers and fruits of love are gone;
The worm, the canker, and the grief,
Are mine alone!

The fire that in my bosom preys
Is like to some volcanic isle;
No torch is kindled at its blaze,—
A funeral pile.

The hope, the fear, the jealous care,
The exalted portion of the pain
And power of love, I cannot share,
But wear the chain.

George Gordon, Lord Byron, 1788–1824

854. REMORSE

From "Macbeth," Act V, sc. 3

Macbeth: Canst thou not minister to a mind diseased,
Pluck from the memory a rooted sorrow,
Raze out the written troubles of the brain,
And with some sweet oblivious antidote
Cleanse the stuffed bosom of that perilous stuff,
Which weighs upon the heart?
Doctor: Therein the patient
Must minister to himself.

William Shakespeare, 1564–1616

855. REMORSE

From "Guinevere"

Shall I kill myself?
What help in that? I cannot kill my sin,
If soul be soul, nor can I kill my shame;
No, nor by living can I live it down.
The days will grow to weeks, the weeks to months,
The months will add themselves, and make the years,
The years will roll into the centuries,
And mine shall ever be a name of scorn.

Alfred Tennyson, 1809–1892

856. MYSELF AM HELL

From "Paradise Lost," Book I; Book IV

[SATAN:] "The mind is its own place, and in itself
Can make a heaven of hell, a hell of heaven."

❖

"Me Miserable! which way shall I fly
Infinite wrath, and infinite despair?
Which way I fly is hell; myself am hell;
And in the lowest deep a lower deep
Still threat'ning to devour me, opens wide,
To which the hell I suffer seems a heaven.
O, then, at last relent! Is there no place
Left for repentance, none for pardon left?"

John Milton, 1608–1674

857. HEAVEN AND HELL

From "The Rubáiyát"

LXVI

I sent my Soul through the Invisible,
Some letter of that After-life to spell:
And by and by my Soul return'd to me.
And answer'd "I Myself am Heav'n and Hell."

Omar Khayyam, 1070–1123;
tr. by Edward Fitzgerald, 1809–1883

858. AS A MAN SOWETH

We must not hope to be mowers,
And to gather the ripe gold ears,
Unless we have first been sowers
And watered the furrows with tears.

It is not just as we take it,
This mystical world of ours,
Life's field will yield as we make it
A harvest of thorns or of flowers.

Johann W. von Goethe, 1749–1832

859. THE DEBT

This is the debt I pay
Just for one riotous day,—
Years of regret and grief,
Sorrow without relief.

Pay it I will to the end—
Until the grave, my friend,
Gives me a true release,
Gives me the clasp of peace.

Slight was the thing I bought,
Small was the debt, I thought,
Poor was the loan at best—
God! but the interest!

Paul Laurence Dunbar, 1872–1906

860. STAINS

The three ghosts on the lonesome road,
Spake each to one another,
"Whence came that stain about your mouth
No lifted hand may cover?"
"From eating of forbidden fruit,
Brother, my brother."

The three ghosts on the sunless road
Spake each to one another,
"Whence came that red burn on your foot
No dust or ash may cover?"
"I stamped a neighbor's hearth-flame out,
Brother, my brother."

The three ghosts on the windless road
Spake each to one another,
"Whence came that blood upon your hand
No other hand may cover?"
"From breaking of a woman's heart,
Brother, my brother."

"Yet on the earth clean men we walked,
Glutton and Thief and Lover;
White flesh and fair it hid our stains
That no man might discover."
"Naked the soul goes up to God,
Brother, my brother."

Theodosia Garrison, 1874–1944

861. DESTINY

From "Raphael"

We shape ourselves the joy or fear
Of which the coming life is made,
And fill our future's atmosphere
With sunshine or with shade.

The tissue of the life to be
We weave with colors all our own,
And in the field of destiny
We reap as we have sown.

John Greenleaf Whittier, 1807–1892

862. A LITTLE

A little work, a little play
To keep us going—and
So, good-day!

A little warmth, a little light
Of love's bestowing—and
So, good-night!

A little fun, to match the sorrow
Of each day's growing—and
So, good-morrow!

A little trust that when we die
We reap our sowing—and
So, good-bye!

George du Maurier, 1834–1896

863. KNELL

Dust is the end of all pursuit,
Ash and worm the doom of faces,
Quakes and holes the fate of places—
Yes, hounded like a wounded brute,
At last with all his worldly loot
Man is caught by what he chases.

George Chapman, 1559?–1634

864. THREE THINGS COME NOT BACK

Remember three things come not back:
The arrow sent upon its track—
It will not swerve, it will not stay
Its speed; it flies to wound, or slay
The spoken word so soon forgot
By thee; but it has perished not;
In other hearts 'tis living still
And doing work for good or ill.
And the lost opportunity
That cometh back no more to thee,
In vain thou weepest, in vain dost yearn,
Those three will nevermore return.

From the Arabian

865. MY TASK

To be honest, to be kind;
To earn a little and to spend a little less;
To make upon the whole a family happier for his presence;
To renounce when that shall be necessary and not to be embittered;
To keep a few friends, but those without capitulation,—
Above all, on the same grim conditions, to keep friends with himself—
Here is a task for all that a man has of fortitude and delicacy.

Robert Louis Stevenson, 1850–1894

866. DREAMERS OF DREAMS

We are all of us dreamers of dreams,
On visions our childhood is fed;
And the heart of the child is unhaunted, it
seems,
By the ghosts of dreams that are dead.

From childhood to youth's but a span
And the years of our life are soon sped;
But the youth is no longer a youth, but a man,
When the first of his dreams is dead.

There's no sadder sight this side the grave
Than the shroud o'er a fond dream spread,
And the heart should be stern and the eyes
be brave
To gaze on a dream that is dead.

'Tis a cup of wormwood and gall
When the doom of a great dream is said,
And the best of a man is under the pall
When the best of his dreams is dead.

He may live on by compact and plan
When the fine bloom of living is shed,
But God pity the little that's left of a man
When the last of his dreams is dead.

Let him show a brave face if he can,
Let him woo fame or fortune instead,
Yet there's not much to do but to bury a man
When the last of his dreams is dead.

William Herbert Carruth, 1859–1924

867. THE CHILD IN THE GARDEN

When to the garden of untroubled thought
I came of late, and saw the open door,
And wished again to enter, and explore
The sweet, wild ways with stainless bloom
inwrought,
And bowers of innocence with beauty fraught,
It seemed some purer voice must speak before
I dared to tread that garden loved of yore,
That Eden lost unknown and found unsought.
Then just within the gate I saw a child,—
A stranger-child, yet to my heart most
dear,—
Who held his hands to me and softly smiled
With eyes that knew no shade of sin or fear;
"Come in," he said, "and play awhile with
me;
I am the little child you used to be."

Henry van Dyke, 1852–1933

868. SOMETIMES

Across the fields of yesterday
He sometimes comes to me,
A little lad just back from play—
The lad I used to be.

And yet he smiles so wistfully
Once he has crept within,
I wonder if he hopes to see
The man I might have been.

Thomas S. Jones, Jr., 1882–1932

869. REMEMBER NOW THY CREATOR

Ecclesiastes 12: 1–7

Remember now thy Creator in the days of thy youth,
while the evil days come not,
nor the years draw nigh,
when thou shalt say, I have no pleasure in them;

While the sun,
or the light,
or the moon,
or the stars,
be not darkened,
nor the clouds return after the rain:

In the day when the keepers of the house shall tremble,
and the strong men shall bow themselves,

and the grinders cease because they are few,
and those that look out of the windows be darkened,

And the doors shall be shut in the streets,
when the sound of the grinding is low,
and he shall rise up at the voice of a bird,
and all the daughters of musick shall be brought low;

Also when they shall be afraid of that which is high,
and fears shall be in the way,
and the almond tree shall flourish,
and the grasshopper shall be a burden,
and desire shall fail:
because man goeth to his long home,
and the mourners go about the streets:

Or ever the silver cord be loosed,
or the golden bowl be broken,
or the pitcher be broken at the fountain,
or the wheel broken at the cistern.

Then shall the dust return to the earth
as it was:
and the spirit shall return unto God
who gave it.

King James Version, 1611

870. IF

If you can keep your head when all about you
Are losing theirs and blaming it on you;
If you can trust yourself when all men doubt you,
But make allowance for their doubting too;
If you can wait and not be tired by waiting,
Or being lied about, don't deal in lies,
Or being hated don't give way to hating,
And yet don't look too good, nor talk too wise;

If you can dream—and not make dreams your master;
If you can think—and not make thoughts your aim;
If you can meet with Triumph and Disaster
And treat those two impostors just the same;
If you can bear to hear the truth you've spoken
Twisted by knaves to make a trap for fools,
Or watch the things you gave your life to, broken,
And stoop and build 'em up with worn-out tools;

If you can make one heap of all your winnings
And risk it on one turn of pitch-and-toss,
And lose, and start again at your beginnings
And never breathe a word about your loss;
If you can force your heart and nerve and sinew

To serve your turn long after they are gone,
And so hold on when there is nothing in you
Except the Will which says to them: "Hold on!"

If you can talk with crowds and keep your virtue,
Or walk with Kings—nor lose the common touch;
If neither foes nor loving friends can hurt you;
If all men count with you, but none too much;
If you can fill the unforgiving minute
With sixty seconds' worth of distance run—
Yours is the Earth and everything that's in it,
And—which is more—you'll be a Man, my son!

Rudyard Kipling, 1865–1936

871. ON HIS BEING ARRIVED TO THE AGE OF TWENTY-THREE

How soon hath Time, the subtle thief of youth,
Stolen on his wing my three and twentieth year!
My hasting days fly on with full career,
But my late spring no bud or blossom shew'th.
Perhaps my semblance might deceive the truth,
That I to manhood am arrived so near;
And inward ripeness doth much less appear,
That some more timely-happy spirits endu'th.
Yet it be less or more, or soon or slow,
It shall be still in strictest measure even
To that same lot, however mean or high,
Toward which Time leads me, and the will of heaven:
All is, if I have grace to use it so,
As ever in my great Taskmaster's eye.

John Milton, 1608–1674

872. THE LEADEN-EYED

Let not young souls be smothered out before
They do quaint deeds and fully flaunt their pride.
It is the world's one crime its babes grow dull,
Its poor are ox-like, limp and leaden-eyed.

Not that they starve, but starve so dreamlessly,
Not that they sow, but that they seldom reap,
Not that they serve, but have no gods to serve,
Not that they die, but that they die like sheep.

Vachel Lindsay, 1879–1931

873. LIFE-SCULPTURE

Chisel in hand stood a sculptor boy
With his marble block before him,
And his eyes lit up with a smile of joy,
As an angel dream passed o'er him.

He carved the dream on that shapeless stone,
With many a sharp incision;
With heaven's own light the sculpture shone,—
He'd caught that angel-vision.

Children of life are we, as we stand
  With our lives uncarved before us,
Waiting the hour when, at God's command,
  Our life-dream shall pass o'er us.

If we carve it then on the yielding stone,
  With many a sharp incision,
It's heavenly beauty shall be our own,—
  Our lives, that angel-vision.

George W. Doane, 1799–1859

874. LET ME LIVE OUT MY YEARS

Let me live out my years in heat of blood!
Let me die drunken with the dreamer's wine!
Let me not see this soul-house built of mud
Go toppling to the dust—a vacant shrine!

Let me go quickly like a candle light
Snuffed out just at the heyday of its glow!
Give me high noon—and let it then be night!
Thus would I go.

And grant me, when I face the grisly Thing,
One haughty cry to pierce the gray Perhaps!
O let me be a tune-swept fiddlestring
That feels the Master Melody—*and snaps!*

John G. Neihardt, 1881–

875. THE FLIGHT OF YOUTH

There are gains for all our losses.
  There are balms for all our pain:
But when youth, the dream, departs
It takes something from our hearts,
  And it never comes again.

We are stronger, and are better,
  Under manhood's sterner reign:
Still we feel that something sweet
Followed youth, with flying feet,
  And will never come again.

Something beautiful is vanished,
  And we sigh for it in vain;
We behold it everywhere,
On the earth, and in the air,
  But it never comes again!

Richard Henry Stoddard, 1825–1903

876. SAD IS OUR YOUTH

Sad is our youth, for it is ever going,
Crumbling away beneath our very feet;
Sad is our life, for onward it is flowing
In current unperceived, because so fleet;
Sad are our hopes for they were sweet in sowing,
But tares, self-sown, have overtopp'd the wheat;
Sad are our joys, for they were sweet in blowing;
And still, O still, their dying breath is sweet:
And sweet is youth, although it hath bereft us
Of that which made our childhood sweeter still;
And sweet our life's decline, for it hath left us
A nearer Good to cure an older Ill:
And sweet are all things, when we hope to prize them
Not for their sake, but His who grants them or denies them.

Aubrey Thomas de Vere, 1814–1902

877. I REMEMBER, I REMEMBER

I remember, I remember
The house where I was born,
The little window where the sun
Came peeping in at morn;
He never came a wink too soon
Nor brought too long a day;
But now, I often wish the night
Had borne my breath away.

I remember, I remember
The roses, red and white,
The violets, and the lily-cups—

Those flowers made of light!
The lilacs where the robin built,
And where my brother set
The laburnum on his birthday,—
The tree is living yet!

I remember, I remember
Where I was used to swing,
And thought the air must rush as fresh
To swallows on the wing;
My spirit flew in feathers then
That is so heavy now,
And summer pools could hardly cool
The fever on my brow.

I remember, I remember
The fir-trees dark and high;
I used to think their slender tops
Were close against the sky:
It was a childish ignorance,
But now 'tis little joy
To know I'm farther off from Heaven
Than when I was a boy.

Thomas Hood, 1799–1845

878. THE RETURN

He sought the old scenes with eager feet,—
The scenes he had known as a boy;
"Oh! for a draught of those fountains sweet,
And a taste of that vanished joy."
He roamed the fields, he mused by the
streams,
He threaded the paths and lanes;
On the hills he sought his youthful dreams,
In the woods to forget his pains.
Oh, sad, sad hills; oh, cold, cold hearth!
In sorrow he learned the truth,—
One may go back to the place of his birth,—
He cannot go back to his youth.

John Burroughs, 1837–1921

879. AS I GROW OLD

God keep my heart attuned to laughter
When youth is done;
When all the days are gray days, coming after
The warmth, the sun.
God keep me then from bitterness, from
grieving,
When life seems cold;
God keep me always loving and believing
As I grow old.

Author unknown

880. UNSUBDUED

I have hoped, I have planned, I have striven,
To the will I have added the deed;
The best that was in me I've given,
I have prayed, but the gods would not
heed.

I have dared and reached only disaster,
I have battled and broken my lance;
I am bruised by a pitiless master
That the weak and the timid call chance.

I am old, I am bent, I am cheated
Of all that Youth urged me to win;
But name me not with the defeated,
Tomorrow again, I begin.

S. E. Kiser, 1862–

881. MEN TOLD ME, LORD!

Men told me, Lord, it was a vale of tears
Where thou hadst placed me; wickedness and woe
My twain companions whereso I might go;
That I through ten and three-score weary years
Should stumble on, beset by pains and fears,
Fierce conflict round me, passions hot within,
Enjoyment brief and fatal, but in sin.
When all was ended then I should demand
Full compensation from thine austere hand:
For 'tis thy pleasure, all temptation past,
To be not just but generous at last.

Lord, here am I, my three score years and ten
Are counted to the full; I've fought thy fight,
Crossed thy dark valleys, scaled thy rocks' harsh height,
Borne all the burdens thou dost lay on men
With hand unsparing, three score years and ten.
Before thee now I make my claim, Oh, Lord!
What shall I pay thee as a meet reward?

David Starr Jordan, 1851–1931

882. From ULYSSES[1]

There lies the port; the vessel puffs her sail;
There gloom the dark, broad seas. My mariners,
Souls that have toil'd, and wrought, and thought with me,—
That ever with a frolic welcome took
The thunder and the sunshine, and opposed
Free hearts, free foreheads,—you and I are old;
Old age hath yet his honor and his toil:
Death closes all; but something ere the end,
Some work of noble note, may yet be done,
Not unbecoming men that strove with Gods.
The lights begin to twinkle from the rocks;
The long day wanes; the slow moon climbs; the deep
Moans round with many voices. Come, my friends.
'Tis not too late to seek a newer world.
Push off, and sitting well in order smite
The sounding furrows; for my purpose holds
To sail beyond the sunset, and the baths
Of all the western stars, until I die.
It may be that the gulfs will wash us down;
It may be we shall touch the Happy Isles,
And see the great Achilles, whom we knew.
Tho' much is taken, much abides; and tho'
We are not now that strength which in old days
Moved earth and heaven, that which we are, we are,—
One equal temper of heroic hearts,
Made weak by time and fate, but strong in will
To strive, to seek, to find, and not to yield.

Alfred Tennyson, 1809–1892

883. OLD AGE

From "Of The Last Verses In The Book"

The seas are quiet when the winds give o'er;
So calm are we when passions are no more.
For then we know how vain it was to boast
Of fleeting things, so certain to be lost.
Clouds of affection from our younger eyes
Conceal that emptiness which age descries.
The soul's dark cottage, battered, and
decayed,
Lets in new light through chinks that Time
hath made:
Stronger by weakness, wiser men become
As they draw near to their eternal home.
Leaving the old, both worlds at once they
view
That stand upon the threshold of the new.

Edmund Waller, 1606–1687

[1] On a cross erected in the South Polar regions to commemorate the sacrifice of Captain Robert F. Scott and his party who perished in 1912 on their way back from the Pole, are the following words:
"To strive, to seek, to find, and not to yield."
They are taken from the above poem.

884. THE DAY IS DONE

The day is done, and the darkness
  Falls from the wings of Night,
As a feather is wafted downward
  From an eagle in his flight.

I see the lights of the village
  Gleam through the rain and the mist,
And a feeling of sadness comes o'er me
  That my soul cannot resist.

A feeling of sadness and longing,
  That is not akin to pain,
And resembles sorrow only
  As the mist resembles the rain.

Come, read to me some poem,
  Some simple and heartfelt lay,
That shall soothe this restless feeling,
  And banish the thoughts of day.

❖

Such songs have power to quiet
  The restless pulse of care,
And come like the benediction
  That follows after prayer.

Then read from the treasured volume
  The poem of thy choice,
And lend to the rhyme of the poet
  The beauty of thy voice.

And the night shall be filled with music,
  And the cares, that infest the day,
Shall fold their tents, like the Arabs,
  And as silently steal away.

Henry Wadsworth Longfellow, 1807–1882

885. WAITING

Serene I fold my arms and wait,
  Nor care for wind, or tide, or sea:
I rave no more 'gainst time or fate,
  For lo! my own shall come to me.

I stay my haste, I make delays,
  For what avails this eager pace?
I stand amid the eternal ways,
  And what is mine shall know my face.

Asleep, awake, by night or day,
  The friends I seek are seeking me;
No wind can drive my bark astray,
  Nor change the tide of destiny.

What matter if I stand alone?
  I wait with joy the coming years;
My heart shall reap where it has sown,
  And garner up its fruit of tears.

The waters know their own, and draw
  The brook that springs in yonder height;
So flows the good with equal law
  Unto the soul of pure delight.

The floweret nodding in the wind
  Is ready plighted to the bee;
And, maiden, why that look unkind?
  For lo! thy lover seeketh thee.

The stars come nightly to the sky;
  The tidal wave unto the sea;
Nor time, nor space, nor deep, nor high
  Can keep my own away from me.

John Burroughs, 1837–1921

886. From AT EIGHTY-THREE

Thank God for life, with all its endless store
Of great experiences, of hill and dale,
Of cloud and sunshine, tempest, snow and
  hail.
Thank God for straining sinews, panting
  breast,
No less for weary slumber, peaceful rest;
Thank God for home and parents, children,
  friends,
For sweet companionship that never ends:
Thank God for all the splendor of the earth,
For nature teeming with prolific birth:
Thank God for sea and sky, for changing
  hours,
For trees and singing birds and fragrant
  flowers.
And so in looking back at eighty-three
My final word to you, my friends, shall be:
Thank God for life; and when the gift's
  withdrawn,
Thank God for twilight bell, and coming
  dawn.

Thomas Durley Landels, 1862–

887. THE LIGHT OF OTHER DAYS

Oft in the stilly night,
  Ere slumber's chain has bound me,
Fond Memory brings the light
  Of other days around me:

The smiles, the tears
Of boyhood's years,
The words of love then spoken;
The eyes that shone
Now dimm'd and gone,
The cheerful hearts now broken!
Thus in the stilly night
Ere slumber's chain has bound me,
Sad Memory brings the light
Of other days around me.

When I remember all
The friends so link'd together
I've seen around me fall
Like leaves in wintry weather,
I feel like one
Who treads alone
Some banquet hall deserted,
Whose lights are fled,
Whose garlands dead,
And all but he departed!
Thus in the stilly night
Ere slumber's chain has bound me,
Sad Memory brings the light
Of other days around me.

Thomas Moore, 1779–1852

888. BREAK, BREAK, BREAK

Break, break, break,
On thy cold gray stones, O Sea!
And I would that my tongue could utter
The thoughts that arise in me.

O, well for the fisherman's boy,
That he shouts with his sister at play!
O, well for the sailor lad,
That he sings in his boat on the bay!

And the stately ships go on
To their haven under the hill;
But O for the touch of a vanish'd hand,
And the sound of a voice that is still!

Break, break, break,
At the foot of thy crags, O Sea!
But the tender grace of a day that is dead
Will never come back to me.

Alfred Tennyson, 1809–1892

889. THE RAINY DAY

The day is cold and dark and dreary;
It rains, and the wind is never weary;
The vine still clings to the moldering wall,
But at every gust the dead leaves fall,
And the day is dark and dreary.

My life is cold and dark and dreary;
It rains, and the wind is never weary;
My thoughts still cling to the moldering past,
But the hopes of youth fall thick in the blast,
And the days are dark and dreary.

Be still, sad heart! and cease repining;
Behind the clouds is the sun still shining:
Thy fate is the common fate of all:
Into each life some rain must fall,
Some days must be dark and dreary.

Henry W. Longfellow, 1807–1882

890. WHY

From the French, apparently itself a translation from the Japanese.

Why have
I thought the dew
Ephemeral when I
Shall rest so short a time, myself,
On earth?

Adelaide Crapsey, 1878–1914

891. From RENASCENCE

Conclusion

The world stands out on either side
No wider than the heart is wide;
Above the world is stretched the sky,—
No higher than the soul is high.
The heart can push the sea and land
Farther away on either hand;
The soul can split the sky in two,
And let the face of God shine through.
But East and West will pinch the heart
That can not keep them pushed apart;
And he whose soul is flat—the sky
Will cave in on him by and by.

Edna St. Vincent Millay, 1892–

892. WORTH MAKES THE MAN

From "Essay on Man"

Honor and shame from no condition rise;
Act well your part, there all the honor lies.
Fortune in men has some small difference made,
One flaunts in rags, one flutters in brocade;
The cobbler aproned, and the parson gowned;
The friar hooded, and the monarch crowned.
"What differ more," you cry, "than crown and cowl!"
I'll tell you, friend! a wise man and a fool.
You'll find, if once the monarch acts the monk,
Or, cobbler-like, the parson will be drunk,
Worth makes the man, and want of it the fellow;
The rest is all but leather or prunella.

Alexander Pope, 1688–1744

893. A MAN'S A MAN FOR A' THAT

Is there, for honest poverty,
That hangs his head, and a' that?
The coward-slave, we pass him by,
We dare be poor for a' that!
For a' that, and a' that,
Our toils obscure, and a' that;
The rank is but the guinea's stamp;
The man's the gowd[1] for a' that.

What tho' on hamely[2] fare we dine,
Wear hodden[3]-gray, and a' that;
Gie fools their silks, and knaves their wine,
A man's a man for a' that.
For a' that, and a' that,
Their tinsel show, and a' that;
The honest man, tho' e'er sae poor,
Is King of men for a' that.

Ye see yon birkie,[4] ca'd a lord,
Wha struts, an' stares, and a' that;
Tho' hundreds worship at his word,
He's but a coof[5] for a' that:
For a' that, and a' that,
His riband, star, and a' that,
The man of independent mind,
He looks and laughs at a' that.

A prince can mak a belted knight,
A marquis, duke, and a' that;
But an honest man's aboon[6] his might,
Guid faith he mauna fa'[7] that!
For a' that, and a' that,
Their dignities, and a' that,
The pith o' sense, and pride o' worth,
Are higher rank than a' that.

Then let us pray that come it may,
As come it will for a' that,
That sense and worth, o'er a' the earth,
May bear the gree,[8] and a' that.
For a' that, and a' that,
It's coming yet, for a' that,
That man to man, the warld o'er,
Shall brothers be for a' that.

Robert Burns, 1759–1796

894. MYSELF

I have to live with myself, and so
I want to be fit for myself to know,
I want to be able, as days go by,
Always to look myself straight in the eye;
I don't want to stand, with the setting sun,
And hate myself for the things I've done.

I don't want to keep on a closet shelf,
A lot of secrets about myself,
And fool myself, as I come and go,
Into thinking that nobody else will know
The kind of a man that I really am;
I don't want to dress up myself in sham.

I want to go out with my head erect,
I want to deserve all men's respect;
But here in the struggle for fame and pelf,

[1] gold; [2] homely; [3] homespun; [4] fellow; [5] fool; [6] above; [7] must not claim; [8] prize.

I want to be able to like myself.
I don't want to look at myself and know
That I'm bluster and bluff and empty show.

I never can hide myself from me;
I see what others may never see;
I know what others may never know;
I never can fool myself, and so,
Whatever happens, I want to be
Self-respecting and conscience free.

Edgar A. Guest, 1881–

895. THE FOE WITHIN

None but one can harm you,
None but yourself who are your greatest foe;
He that respects himself is safe from others:
He wears a coat of mail that none can pierce.

Henry Wadsworth Longfellow, 1807–1882

896. TRUE GREATNESS

Were I so tall to reach the pole,
Or grasp the ocean with my span,
I must be measured by my soul:
The mind's the standard of the man.

Isaac Watts, 1674–1748

897. TRUE GREATNESS

That man is great, and he alone,
Who serves a greatness not his own,
For neither praise nor pelf:
Content to know and be unknown:
Whole in himself.

Owen Meredith (Lord Bulwer Lytton), 1831–1891

898. THRICE ARMED

From "King Henry VI," Part II, Act III, sc. 2

What stronger breastplate than a heart untainted!
Thrice is he arm'd that hath his quarrel just,
And he is naked, though locked up in steel,
Whose conscience with injustice is corrupted.

William Shakespeare, 1564–1616

899. POLONIUS' ADVICE TO HIS SON

From "Hamlet," Act I, sc. 3

There,—my blessing with you!
And these few precepts in thy memory
See thou character.—Give thy thoughts no tongue,
Nor any unproportion'd thought his act.
Be thou familiar, but by no means vulgar.
The friends thou hast, and their adoption tried,
Grapple them to thy soul with hoops of steel;
But do not dull thy palm with entertainment
Of each new-hatched, unfledged comrade. Beware
Of entrance to a quarrel; but being in,
Bear't that the opposed may beware of thee.
Give every man thine ear, but few thy voice:
Take each man's censure, but reserve thy judgment.
Costly thy habit as thy purse can buy,
But not expressed in fancy; rich, not gaudy:
For the apparel oft proclaims the man. . . .
Neither a borrower nor a lender be,
For loan oft loses both itself and friend,
And borrowing dulls the edge of husbandry.
This above all: to thine own self be true,
And it must follow, as the night the day,
Thou canst not then be false to any man.

William Shakespeare, 1564–1616

900. "THEY WENT FORTH TO BATTLE BUT THEY ALWAYS FELL"

They went forth to battle but they always fell.
Their eyes were fixed above the sullen shields.
Nobly they fought and bravely, but not well,
And sank heart-wounded by a subtle spell.
They knew not fear that to the foeman yields,
They were not weak, as one who vainly wields
A faltering weapon: yet the sad scrolls tell
How on the hard-fought field they always fell.

It was a secret music that they heard,
The murmurous voice of pity and of peace,
And that which pierced the heart was but a word,
Though the white breast was red-lipped where the sword
Pressed a fierce cruel kiss and did not cease
Till its hot thirst was surfeited. Ah these
By an unwarlike troubling doubt were stirred,
And died for hearing what no foeman heard.

They went forth to battle but they always fell.
Their might was not the might of lifted spears.
Over the battle-clamor came a spell
Of troubling music, and they fought not well.
Their wreaths are willows and their tribute, tears.
Their names are old sad stories in men's ears.
Yet they will scatter the red hordes of Hell,
Who went to battle forth and always fell.

Shaemas O'Sheel, 1886–

901. IO VICTIS

I sing the hymn of the conquered, who fell in the Battle of Life,—
The hymn of the wounded, the beaten, who died overwhelmed in the strife;
Not the jubilant song of the victors, for whom the resounding acclaim
Of nations was lifted in chorus, whose brows wear the chaplet of fame,
But the hymn of the low and the humble, the weary, the broken in heart,
Who strove and who failed, acting bravely a silent and desperate part;
Whose youth bore no flower in its branches, whose hopes burned in ashes away,
From whose hands slipped the prize they had grasped at, who stood at the dying of day
With the wreck of their life all around them, unpitied, unheeded, alone,
With Death swooping down o'er their failure, and all but their faith overthrown,
While the voice of the world shouts its chorus,—its pæan for those who have won;
While the trumpet is sounding triumphant, and high to the breeze and the sun
Glad banners are waving, hands clapping, and hurrying feet
Thronging after the laurel crowned victors, I stand on the field of defeat,
In the shadow, with those who are fallen, and wounded, and dying, and there
Chant a requiem low, place my hand on their pain-knotted brows, breathe a prayer,
Hold the hand that is helpless, and whisper, "They only the victory win,
Who have fought the good fight, and have vanquished the demon that tempts us within;
Who have held to their faith unseduced by the prize that the world holds on high;
Who have dared for a high cause to suffer, resist, fight—if need be, to die."

Speak, History! Who are Life's victors? Unroll thy long annals and say;
Are they those whom the world called the victors, who won the success of a day?
The martyrs, or Nero? The Spartans, who fell at Thermopylæ's tryst,
Or the Persians and Xerxes? His judges or Socrates, Pilate or Christ?

William Wetmore Story, 1819–1895

902. FOR THOSE WHO FAIL

"All honor to him who shall win the prize,"
The world has cried for a thousand years;
But to him who tries and who fails and dies,
I give great honor and glory and tears.

❖

O great is the hero who wins a name,
But greater many and many a time,
Some pale-faced fellow who dies in shame,
And lets God finish the thought sublime.

And great is the man with the sword undrawn,
And good is the man who refrains from wine;
But the man who fails and yet fights on,
Lo! he is the twin-born brother of mine!

Joaquin Miller, 1841–1913

903. THE LAST WORD

Creep into thy narrow bed,
Creep, and let no more be said!
Vain thy onset! all stands fast.
Thou thyself must break at last.

Let the long contention cease!
Geese are swans, and swans are geese
Let them have it how they will!
Thou art tired; best be still.

They out-talked thee, hissed thee, tore thee?
Better man fared thus before thee;
Fired their ringing shot and passed,
Hotly charged—and sank at last.

Charge once more, then, and be dumb!
Let the victors, when they come,
When the forts of folly fall,
Find thy body by the wall!

Matthew Arnold, 1822–1888

904. HE HAD HIS DREAM

He had his dream, and all through life,
Worked up to it through toil and strife.
Afloat fore'er before his eyes,
It colored for him all his skies:
The storm-cloud dark
Above his bark,
The calm and listless vault of blue
Took on its hopeful hue,
It tinctured every passing beam—
He had his dream.

He labored hard and failed at last,
His sails too weak to bear the blast,
The raging tempests tore away
And sent his beating bark astray.
But what cared he
For wind or sea!
He said, "The tempest will be short,
My bark will come to port."
He saw through every cloud a gleam—
He had his dream.

Paul Laurence Dunbar, 1872–1906

905. TO A BAFFLED IDEALIST

Because the upper and the nether stones
Of things that are, ground close and slew
That dreamer who was you;
Because the flowers your heart set in your
mind,

So aptly ordered and so beautiful,
Were withered in the wind
That life sends hot and blighting over those
Who must dispose
A grand and god-like spirit in their kind;
You have turned inward-seeking and have
cried
Out of your simple pride,
"See, Lord, how men are bitter and unsouled:
There is none just save me."
While we,
Expecting little, happen on the gold,
Seamy and tough of assay that runs through
The coarse ore of the mine-run that is Man,
Often enough to make our hearts grow glad
Out of humility,
Remembering that in Man are many men
Who live and die and hope for heaven, too.

J. G. E. Hopkins, 1909–

906. SONS OF FAILURE

There is a close companionship of pain,
There is a clinging brotherhood of woe,
That children of success may never know,
That darlings of the world may never gain.

There lies in misery a subtle tie
Only the brokenhearted understand;
Look feeds on look, hand waits for trembling hand,
Unnoticed of the careless passer-by.

And they, the sons of Failure, sit around,
And in Life's antechamber sleep and wait,
As day melts into night. It grows too late:
No bed or board on earth for them is found.

Sometimes the doorstep is at midnight crossed.
Follows a muffled movement on the stair:
Jesus, the Son of Heaven, enters there
And takes the lowliest seat among the lost.

Edith Lovejoy Pierce, 1904–

907. WE MET THEM ON THE COMMON WAY

We met them on the common way,
They passed and gave no sign,—
The heroes that had lost the day,
The failures half divine.

Ranged in a quiet place we see
Their mighty ranks contain
Figures too great for victory,
Hearts too unspoiled for gain.

Here are earth's splendid failures, come
From glorious foughten fields;
Some bear the wounds of combat, some
Are prone upon their shields.

To us that still do battle here,
If we in aught prevail,
Grant, God, a triumph not too dear,
Or strength, like theirs, to fail!

Elizabeth C. Cardozo, 1867–1918

908. IN MEN WHOM MEN CONDEMN

"Byron"

In men whom men condemn as ill
I find so much of goodness still,
In men whom men pronounce divine
I find so much of sin and blot,
I do not dare to draw a line
Between the two, where God has not.

Joaquin Miller, 1841–1913

909. TO THOMAS HARDY

Thanks: not for thoughts that give the mind more mirth—
Or help us to be glad, and wish our day
Were but a little longer; or to say
"Life is worth living," while on doubtful earth
Back to the homely dust man wins his way:
Not because we are happier, having read
Your book of life, when—all its pages turned—
Deeply our thoughts go back to find its dead
Are dearer than its living:
But to have learned
This help in grief—that life, though full of ill,
Storm-dogged, star-darkened, cannot break man's will,
Nor wrest him from that firm heroic mould
Wherein rich earth endued his mind of old!
There, furrowed deep, the tilth by Fortune spurned:
Patience, endurance, kindness, courage still,
And pity—when life's fire to ash has burned.

Laurence Housman, 1865–

910. "I THINK CONTINUALLY OF THOSE——"

I think continually of those who were truly great.
Who, from the womb, remembered the soul's history
Through corridors of light where the hours are suns
Endless and singing. Whose lovely ambition
Was that their lips, still touched with fire,
Should tell of the Spirit clothed from head to foot in song.
And who hoarded from the Spring branches
The desires falling across their bodies like blossoms.

What is precious is never to forget
The essential delight of the blood drawn from ageless springs
Breaking through rocks in worlds before our earth.
Never to deny its pleasure in the morning simple light
Nor its grave evening demand for love.
Never to allow gradually the traffic to smother
With noise and fog the flowering of the spirit.

Near the snow, near the sun, in the highest fields
See how these names are fêted by the waving grass
And by the streamers of white cloud
And whispers of wind in the listening sky.
The names of those who in their lives fought for life
Who wore at their hearts the fire's centre.
Born of the sun they travelled a short while toward the sun,
And left the vivid air signed with their honour.

Stephen Spender, 1909–

911. From ALUMNUS FOOTBALL

For when the One Great Scorer comes
To write against your name,
He writes—not that you won or lost—
But how you played the game.

Grantland Rice, 1880–

912. THE INEVITABLE

I like the man who faces what he must,
With step triumphant and a heart of cheer;
Who fights the daily battle without fear;
Sees his hopes fail, yet keeps unfaltering trust
That God is God,—that somehow, true and just
His plans work out for mortals; not a tear
Is shed when fortune, which the world holds dear,
Falls from his grasp—better, with love, a crust
Than living in dishonor: envies not,
Nor loses faith in man; but does his best,
Nor ever murmurs at his humbler lot;
But, with a smile and words of hope, gives zest
To every toiler: he alone is great
Who by a life heroic conquers fate.

Sarah Knowles Bolton, 1841–1916

913. BEGIN AGAIN

Every day is a fresh beginning,
Every morn is the world made new.
You who are weary of sorrow and sinning,
Here is a beautiful hope for you,—
A hope for me and a hope for you.

❖

Every day is a fresh beginning;
Listen, my soul, to the glad refrain,
And, spite of old sorrow and older sinning,
And puzzles forecasted and possible pain,
Take heart with the day, and begin again.

Susan Coolidge, 1845–1905

914. VITAÏ LAMPADA

There's a breathless hush in the close to-night—
Ten to make and the match to win—
A bumping pitch and a blinding light,
An hour to play and the last man in.
And it's not for the sake of a ribboned coat,
Or the selfish hope of a season's fame,
But his captain's hand on his shoulder smote
"Play up! play up! and play the game!"

The sand of the desert is sodden red—
Red with the wreck of a square that broke—
The gatling's jammed and the colonel dead,
And the regiment blind with dust and smoke:
The river of death has brimmed its banks,
And England's far, and honour a name,
But the voice of a schoolboy rallies the ranks,
"Play up! play up! and play the game!"

This is the word that year by year
While in her place the school is set
Every one of her sons must hear,
And none that hears it dare forget.
This they all with a joyful mind
Bear through life like a torch in flame,
And, falling, fling to the host behind,
"Play up! play up! and play the game!"

Henry Newbolt, 1862–1938

915. VICTORY IN DEFEAT

Defeat may serve as well as victory
To shake the soul and let the glory out.
When the great oak is straining in the wind,
The boughs drink in new beauty, and the trunk
Sends down a deeper root on the windward side.
Only the soul that knows the mighty grief
Can know the mighty rapture. Sorrows come
To stretch our spaces in the heart for joy.

Edwin Markham, 1852–1940

916. THE ONE

I knew his face the moment that he passed
Triumphant in the thoughtless, cruel throng,—
Triumphant, though the quiet, tired eyes

Showed that his soul had suffered overlong.
And though across his brow faint lines of care
Were etched, somewhat of Youth still lingered there.
I gently touched his arm—he smiled at me—
He was the Man that Once I Meant to Be!

Where I had failed, he'd won from life, Success;
Where I had stumbled, with sure feet he stood;
Alike—yet unalike—we faced the world,
And through the stress he found that life was good.
And I? The bitter wormwood in the glass,
The shadowed way along which failures pass!
Yet as I saw him thus, joy came to me—
He was the Man that Once I Meant to Be!

I knew him! And I knew he knew me for
The man HE might have been. Then did his soul
Thank silently the gods that gave him strength
To win, while I so sorely missed the goal?
He turned, and quickly in his own firm hand
He took my own—the gulf of Failure spanned, . . .
And that was all—strong, self-reliant, free,
He was the Man that Once I Meant to Be!

We did not speak. But in his sapient eyes
I saw the spirit that had urged him on,
The courage that had held him through the fight
Had once been mine, I thought, "Can it be gone?"
He felt that unasked question—felt it so
His pale lips formed the one-word answer, "No!"

❖

Too late to win? No! Not too late for me—
He is the Man that Still I Mean to Be!

Everard Jack Appleton, 20th century American

917. NO STAR IS EVER LOST

Have we not all, amid life's petty strife,
Some pure ideal of a noble life
That once seemed possible? Did we not hear
The flutter of its wings and feel it near,
And just within our reach? It was. And yet
We lost it in this daily jar and fret.
But still our place is kept and it will wait,
Ready for us to fill it, soon or late.
No star is ever lost we once have seen:
We always may be what we might have been.

Adelaide A. Procter, 1825–1864

918. LIFE'S PURPOSE

From "A Minor Prophet"

The earth yields nothing more Divine
Than high prophetic vision—than the Seer
Who fasting from man's meaner joy beholds
The paths of beauteous order, and constructs
A fairer type, to shame our low content. . .

The faith that life on earth is being shaped
To glorious ends, that order, justice, love,
Mean man's completeness, mean effect as sure
As roundness in the dew-drop—that great faith
Is but the rushing and expanding stream
Of thought, of feeling, fed by all the past.
Our finest hope is finest memory. . . .

❖

Even our failures are a prophecy,
Even our yearnings and our bitter tears
After that fair and true we cannot grasp;
As patriots who seem to die in vain
Make liberty more sacred by their pangs.

George Eliot, 1819–1880

919. HE WHOM A DREAM HATH POSSESSED

He whom a dream hath possessed knoweth no more of doubting,
For mist and the blowing of winds and the mouthing of words he scorns;
Not the sinuous speech of schools he hears, but a knightly shouting,
And never comes darkness down, but he greeteth a million morns.

He whom a dream hath possessed knoweth no more of roaming;
All roads and the flowing of waves and the speediest flight he knows,
But wherever his feet are set, his soul is forever homing,
And going, he comes, and coming he heareth a call and goes.

He whom a dream hath possessed knoweth no more of sorrow,
At death and the dropping of leaves and the fading of suns he smiles,
For a dream remembers no past, and scorns the desire of a morrow,
And a dream in a sea of doom sets surely the ultimate isles.

He whom a dream hath possessed treads the impalpable marches,
From the dust of the day's long road he leaps to a laughing star,
And the ruin of worlds that fall he views from eternal arches,
And rides God's battlefield in a flashing and golden car.

Shaemas O'Sheel, 1886–

920. WHO HAS KNOWN HEIGHTS

Who has known heights and depths, shall not again
  Know peace—not as the calm heart knows
  Low, ivied walls; a garden close;
  The old enchantment of a rose.
And though he tread the humble ways of men,
He shall not speak the common tongue again.

Who has known heights, shall bear forevermore
  An incommunicable thing
  That hurts his heart, as if a wing

Beat at the portal, challenging;
And yet—lured by the gleam his vision wore,—
Who once has trodden stars seeks peace no more.

Mary Brent Whiteside, contemporary American

921. LIFE

From "The Three Best Things"

Let me but live my life from year to year,
With forward face and unreluctant soul;
Not hurrying to, nor turning from, the goal;
Not mourning for the things that disappear
In the dim past, nor holding back in fear
From what the future veils; but with a whole
And happy heart, that pays its toll
To Youth and Age, and travels on with cheer.

So let the way wind up the hill or down,
O'er rough or smooth, the journey will be joy:
Still seeking what I sought when but a boy,
New friendship, high adventure, and a crown,
My heart will keep the courage of the quest,
And hope the road's last turn will be the best.

Henry van Dyke, 1852–1933

922. LIFE NOT DEATH

From "The Two Voices"

Whatever crazy sorrow saith,
No life that breathes with human breath
Has ever truly long'd for death.

'Tis life, whereof our nerves are scant,
O, life, not death, for which we pant;
More life, and fuller, that I want.

Alfred Tennyson, 1809–1892

923. I HAVE A RENDEZVOUS WITH LIFE

I have a rendezvous with Life,
In days I hope will come,
Ere youth has sped, and strength of mind,
Ere voices sweet grow dumb.
I have a rendezvous with Life,
When Spring's first heralds hum.
Sure some would cry it's better far
To crown their days with sleep
Than face the road, the wind and rain,
To heed the calling deep.
Though wet nor blow nor space I fear,
Yet fear I deeply, too,
Lest Death should meet and claim me ere
I keep Life's rendezvous.

Countee Cullen, 1903–1946

924. LIFE

Life is too brief
Between the budding and the falling leaf.
Between the seed time and the golden sheaf,
For hate and spite.
We have no time for malice and for greed;
Therefore, with love make beautiful the deed;
Fast speeds the night.

Life is too swift
Between the blossom and the white snow's drift,
Between the silence and the lark's uplift,
For bitter words.

In kindness and in gentleness our speech
Must carry messages of hope, and reach
The sweetest chords.

Life is too great
Between the infant's and the man's estate,
Between the clashing of earth's strife and fate,
For petty things.
Lo! we shall yet who creep with cumbered feet
Walk glorious over heaven's golden street,
Or soar on wings!

W. M. Vories, 1880–

925. TO-DAY

Why fear to-morrow, timid heart?
Why tread the future's way?
We only need to do our part
To-day, dear child, to-day.

The past is written! Close the book
On pages sad and gay;
Within the future do not look,
But live to-day—to-day.

'Tis this one hour that God has given;
His Now we must obey;
And it will make our earth his heaven
To live to-day—to-day.

Lydia Avery Coonley Ward, 1845–1924

926. LIFE AND DEATH

So he died for his faith. That is fine—
More than most of us do.
But say, can you add to that line
That he lived for it, too?
In his death he bore witness at last
As a martyr to truth.
Did his life do the same in the past
From the days of his youth?
It is easy to die. Men have died
For a wish or a whim—
From bravado or passion or pride.
Was it harder for him?
But to live—every day to live out
All the truth that he dreamt,
While his friends met his conduct with doubt
And the world with contempt—
Was it thus that he plodded ahead,
Never turning aside?
Then we'll talk of the life that he led.
Never mind how he died.

Ernest H. Crosby, 1856–1907

927. THE GREATER GLORY

It's easy to die 'mid the world's applause
For a noble deed, with trumpets blaring!
It's the harder part to fight for a cause
And inwardly bleed with no one caring!
It's easy, perhaps, to die for a dream
With banners unfurled—and be forgiving!
It's the harder part to follow the gleam
When scorned by the world—and go on living!

Myra Brooks Welch,
contemporary American

928. THE BUILDERS

All are architects of Fate,
Working in these walls of Time;
Some with massive deeds and great,
Some with ornaments of rhyme.

Nothing useless is, or low;
Each thing in its place is best;
And what seems but idle show
Strengthens and supports the rest.

For the structure that we raise,
Time is with materials filled;
Our to-days and yesterdays
Are the blocks with which we build.

Truly shape and fashion these;
Leave no yawning gaps between;
Think not, because no man sees,
Such things will remain unseen.

In the elder days of art,
Builders wrought with greatest care
Each minute and unseen part;
For the Gods see everywhere.

Let us do our work as well,
Both the unseen and the seen;
Make the house, where Gods may dwell,
Beautiful, entire, and clean.

Else our lives are incomplete,
  Standing in these walls of Time,
Broken stairways, where the feet
  Stumble as they seek to climb.

Build to-day, then, strong and sure,
  With a firm and ample base;
And ascending and secure
  Shall to-morrow find its place.

Thus alone can we attain
  To those turrets, where the eye
Sees the world as one vast plain,
  And one boundless reach of sky.

Henry Wadsworth Longfellow, 1807–1882

929. I SHALL NOT PASS THIS WAY AGAIN

A Symphony

I shall not pass this way again—
  Although it bordered be with flowers,
  Although I rest in fragrant bowers,
    And hear the singing
    Of song-birds winging
To highest heaven their gladsome flight;
Though moons are full and stars are bright,
And winds and waves are softly sighing,
While leafy trees make low replying;
Though voices clear in joyous strain
Repeat a jubilant refrain;
Though rising suns their radiance throw
On summer's green and winter's snow,
In such rare splendor that my heart
Would ache from scenes like these to part
    Though beauties heighten,
    And life-lights brighten,
And joys proceed from every pain,—
I shall not pass this way again.

Then let me pluck the flowers that blow,
And let me listen as I go
    To music rare
    That fills the air;
    And let hereafter
    Songs and laughter
Fill every pause along the way;
And to my spirit let me say:
"O soul, be happy; soon 'tis trod,
The path made thus for thee by God.
Be happy, thou, and bless His name
By whom such marvellous beauty came."
And let no chance by me be lost
To kindness show at any cost.
I shall not pass this way again;
Then let me now relieve some pain,
Remove some barrier from the road,
Or brighten some one's heavy load;
A helping hand to this one lend,
Then turn some other to befriend.

    O God, forgive
    That now I live
As if I might, sometime, return
To bless the weary ones that yearn
For help and comfort every day,—
For there be such along the way.
O God, forgive that I have seen
The beauty only, have not been
Awake to sorrow such as this;
That I have drunk the cup of bliss
Remembering not that those there be
Who drink the dregs of misery.

I love the beauty of the scene,
Would roam again o'er fields so green;
But since I may not, let me spend
My strength for others to the end,—
For those who tread on rock and stone,
And bear their burdens all alone,
Who loiter not in leafy bowers,
Nor hear the birds nor pluck the flowers.
A larger kindness give to me,
A deeper love and sympathy;
    Then, O, one day
    May someone say—
Remembering a lessened pain—
"Would she could pass this way again."

Eva Rose York, 1858–

930. VICTORY

I sheath my sword. In mercy go.
  Turn back from me your hopeless eyes,
  For in them all my anger dies:
I cannot face a beaten foe.

My cause was just, the fight was sweet.
  Go from me, O mine enemy,
  Before, in shame of victory,
You find me kneeling at your feet.

Aline Kilmer, 1888–1941

931. UNREST

A fierce unrest seethes at the core
  Of all existing things:
It was the eager wish to soar
  That gave the gods their wings.

From what flat wastes of cosmic slime,
  And stung by what quick fire,
Sunward the restless races climb!—
  Men risen out of mire!

There throbs through all the worlds that are
  This heart-beat hot and strong
And shaken systems, star by star,
  Awake and glow in song.

But for the urge of this unrest
  These joyous spheres are mute;
But for the rebel in his breast
  Had man remained a brute.

When baffled lips demanded speech,
  Speech trembled into birth—
(One day the lyric word shall reach
  From earth to laughing earth.)—

When man's dim eyes demanded light,
  The light he sought was born—
His wish, a Titan, scaled the height
  And flung him back the morn!

From deed to dream, from dream to deed,
  From daring hope to hope,
The restless wish, the instant need,
  Still lashed him up the slope!

❖

I sing no governed firmament,
  Cold, ordered, regular—
I sing the stinging discontent
  That leaps from star to star!

Don Marquis, 1878–1937

932. 'TIS BETTER TO HAVE LOVED AND LOST

From "In Memoriam"

XXVII

I envy not in any moods
  The captive void of noble rage,
  The linnet born within the cage,
That never knew the summer woods;

I envy not the beast that takes
  His license in the field of time,
  Unfetter'd by the sense of crime,
To whom a conscience never wakes;

Nor, what may count itself as blest,
  The heart that never plighted troth
  But stagnates in the weeds of sloth;
Nor any want-begotten rest.

I hold it true, whate'er befall;
  I feel it, when I sorrow most;
  'Tis better to have loved and lost
Than never to have loved at all.

Alfred Tennyson, 1809–1892

933. A RHYME OF LIFE

If life be as a flame that death doth kill,
  Burn little candles, lit for me,
  With a pure flame, that I may rightly see
  To word my song, and utterly
    God's plan fulfil.

If life be a flower that blooms and dies,
  Forbid the cunning frost that slays
  With Judas kiss, and trusting love betrays;
    Untainted rise.

If life be a voyage, foul or fair,
  Oh, bid me not my banners furl
  For adverse gale, or wave in angry whirl,
  Till I have found the gates of pearl,
    And anchored there.

Charles Warren Stoddard, 1843–1909

934. LORD OF THE FAR HORIZONS

Lord of the far horizons,
  Give us the eyes to see
Over the verge of sundown
  The beauty that is to be.
Give us the skill to fashion
  The task of Thy command,
Eager to follow the pattern
  We may not understand.

Master of ancient wisdom
  And the lore lost long ago,
Inspire our foolish reason
  With faith to seek and know.

When the skein of truth is tangled,
And the lead of sense is blind,
Foster the fire to lighten
Our unillumined mind.

Bliss Carman, 1861–1929

935. From RUGBY CHAPEL

What is the course of the life
Of mortal men on the earth?—
Most men eddy about
Here and there—eat and drink,
Chatter and love and hate,
Gather and squander, are raised
Aloft, are hurled in the dust,
Striving blindly, achieving
Nothing; and then they die—
Perish;—and no one asks
Who or what they have been,
More than he asks what waves,
In the moonlit solitudes mild
Of the midmost ocean, have swelled,
Foam'd for a moment, and gone.

And there are some, whom a thirst
Ardent, unquenchable, fires,
Not with the crowd to be spent,
Not without aim to go round
In an eddy of purposeless dust,
Effort unmeaning and vain.
Ah, yes! some of us strive
Not without action to die
Fruitless, but something to snatch
From dull oblivion, nor all
Glut the devouring grave!
We, we have chosen our path—
Path to a clear-purposed goal,
Path of advance!—but it leads
A long steep journey, through sunk
Gorges, o'er mountains of snow,
Cheerful, with friends, we set forth—
Then, on the height, comes the storm.
Thunder crashes from rock
To rock, the cataracts reply,
Lightnings dazzle our eyes.
Roaring torrents have breached
The track, the stream-bed descends
In the place where the wayfarer once
Planted his footstep—the spray
Boils o'er its borders! aloft
The unseen snow-beds dislodge
Their hanging ruin; alas,
Havoc is made in our train!
Friends who set forth at our side,
Falter, are lost in the storm.

We, we only are left!
With frowning foreheads, with lips
Sternly compressed, we strain on,
On—and at nightfall at last
Come to the end of our way,
To the lonely inn 'mid the rocks;
Where the gaunt and taciturn host
Stands on the threshold, the wind
Shaking his thin white hairs—
Holds his lantern to scan
Our storm-beat figures, and asks;
Whom in our party we bring?
Whom have we left in the snow?

Sadly we answer: we bring
Only ourselves! we lost
Sight of the rest in the storm.
Hardly ourselves we fought through,
Stripped, without friends, as we are.
Friends, companions, and train,
The avalanche swept from our side.

But thou wouldst not *alone*
Be saved, my father! *alone*
Conquer and come to thy goal,
Leaving the rest in the wild.
We were weary, and we
Fearful, and we in our march
Fain to drop down and to die.
Still thou turnedst, and still
Beckonedst the trembler, and still
Gavest the weary thy hand.
If, in the paths of the world,
Stones might have wounded thy feet,
Toil or dejection have tried
Thy spirit, of that we saw
Nothing: to us thou wast still
Cheerful, and helpful, and firm!
Therefore to thee it was given
Many to save with thyself,
And, at the end of the day,
O faithful shepherd, to come
Bringing thy sheep in thy hand.
And through thee I believe
In the noble and great who are gone;
Pure souls honoured and blest
By former ages, who else—
Such, so soulless, so poor,
Is the race of men whom I see—
Seem'd but a dream of the heart,

Seem'd but a cry of desire.
Yes! I believe that there lived
Others like thee in the past,
Not like the men of the crowd
Who all round me today
Bluster or cringe, and make life
Hideous, and arid, and vile;
But souls tempered with fire,
Fervent, heroic, and good,
Helpers and friends of mankind.

Matthew Arnold, 1822–1888

936. THE WAYS

To every man there openeth
A Way, and Ways, and a Way.
And the High Soul climbs the High Way,
And the Low Soul gropes the Low,
And in between, on the misty flats,
The rest drift to and fro.
But to every man there openeth
A High Way, and a Low.
And every man decideth
The way his soul shall go.

John Oxenham, 1852–1941

937. THE TREE-TOP ROAD

Beyond the little window
  Of my dull House of Care
One road is always beckoning
  When days are gray and bare:
And then I leave the dusty street
  The struggle and the load—
I pin my wings upon my feet
  And take the Tree-top Road!

Life's sweetest joys are hidden
  In unsubstantial things;
An April rain, a fragrance,
  A vision of blue wings:
And what are memory and hope
  But dreams? And yet the bread
On which these little lives of ours
  Are fed and comforted!

Without imagination
  The soul becomes a clod,
Missing the trail of beauty
  Losing the way to God.
And I have built a templed-stair
  Out of a lilac bloom
And climbed to heaven with purple pomp
  And censers of perfume!

Philosophers and sages
  Seeking to find out God
With puzzling chart and compass
  And strange divining rod,
I think He must come down to see
  His orchards bloom in May,—
O souls of ours, put on your wings
  And try the Tree-top Way!

I have no feud with Labor,
  But at the Gates of June
I fling away my dusty pack
  And join in Youth's glad tune.
And just forgetting for awhile
  That I am worn and gray
Go sailing off with Peter Pan
  Along the Tree-top Way!

May Riley Smith, 1842–1927

938. ROAD MAKERS

We shall not travel by the road we make.
Ere day by day the sound of many feet
Is heard upon the stones that now we break,
We shall but come to where the cross-roads meet.

For us the heat by day, the cold by night,
The inch-slow progress and the heavy load,
And death at last to close the long, grim fight
With man and beast and stone: for them—the road.

For them the shade of trees that now we plant,
The safe, smooth journey and the ultimate goal—
Yea, birthright in the land of covenant:
For us day-labour, travail of the soul.

And yet the road is ours, as never theirs;
Is not one thing on us alone bestowed?
For us the master-joy, oh, pioneers—
We shall not travel, but we make the road!

V. H. Friedlaender, contemporary English

939. WHAT MAN MAY CHOOSE

No man can choose what coming hours may bring
To him of need, of joy, of suffering;
But what his soul shall bring unto each hour
To meet its challenge—this is in his power.

Priscilla Leonard, 1852–

940. THE SALUTATION OF THE DAWN

Listen to the Exhortation of the Dawn!
Look to this Day!
For it is Life, the very Life of Life.
In its brief course lie all the
Verities and Realities of your Existence:
The Bliss of Growth,
The Glory of Action,
The Splendor of Beauty,
For Yesterday is but a Dream,
And To-morrow is only a Vision:
But To-day well-lived makes
Every Yesterday a Dream of Happiness,
And every To-morrow a Vision of Hope.
Look well therefore to this Day!
Such is the Salutation of the Dawn!

Based on the Sanskrit, c. 1200 B.C.

941. DAWN

The immortal spirit hath no bars
To circumscribe its dwelling-place;
My soul hath pastured with the stars
Upon the meadow-lands of space.

My mind and ear at times have caught,
From realms beyond our mortal reach,
The utterance of eternal thought
Of which all nature is the speech.

And high above the seas and lands,
On peaks just tipped with morning light,
My dauntless spirit mutely stands
With eagle wings outspread for flight.

Frederick G. Scott, 1861–1944

942. OPPORTUNITY

Master of human destinies am I.
Fame, love, and fortune on my footsteps wait,
Cities and fields I walk; I penetrate
Deserts and seas remote, and, passing by
Hovel, and mart, and palace, soon or late
I knock unbidden once at every gate!
If sleeping, wake—if feasting, rise before
I turn away. It is the hour of fate,
And they who follow me reach every state
Mortals desire, and conquer every foe
Save death; but those who doubt or hesitate,
Condemned to failure, penury and woe,
Seek me in vain and uselessly implore—
I answer not, and I return no more.

John James Ingalls, 1833–1900

943. OPPORTUNITY

They do me wrong who say I come no more
When once I knock and fail to find you in,
For every day I stand outside your door
And bid you wake, and rise to fight and win.

Wail not for precious chances passed away,
Weep not for golden ages on the wane!
Each night I burn the records of the day;
At sunrise every soul is born again.

Laugh like a boy at splendors that have sped,
To vanished joys be blind and deaf and dumb;
My judgments seal the dead past with its dead,
But never bind a moment yet to come.

Tho' deep in mire, wring not your hands and weep;
I lend my arm to all who say, "I can!"
No shamefaced outcast ever sank so deep
But yet might rise and be again a man.

Dost thou behold thy lost youth all aghast?
Dost reel from righteous retribution's blow?
Then turn from blotted archives of the past
And find the future's pages white as snow.

Art thou a mourner? Rouse thee from thy spell;
Art thou a sinner? Sins may be forgiven;
Each morning gives thee wings to flee from hell,
Each night a star to guide thy feet to Heaven.

Walter Malone, 1866–1915

944. LIVE TODAY

Forget the past and live the present hour;
Now is the time to work, the time to fill
The soul with noblest thoughts, the time to
will
Heroic deeds, to use whatever dower
Heaven has bestowed, to test our utmost
power.

Now is the time to love, and better still,
To serve our loved ones, over passing ill
To rise triumphant; thus the perfect flower
Of life shall come to fruitage; wealth amass
For grandest giving ere the time be gone.

Be glad today, tomorrow may bring tears;
Be brave today, the darkest night will pass,
And golden rays will usher in the dawn;
Who conquers now shall rule the coming
years.

Sarah Knowles Bolton, 1841–1916

945. A SPORTSMAN'S PRAYER

Let me live, O Mighty Master,
Such a life as men should know,
Tasting triumph and disaster,
Joy—and not too much of woe;
Let me run the gamut over,
Let me fight and love and laugh
And when I'm beneath the clover
Let this be my epitaph.

Here lies one who took his chances
In life's busy world of men;
Battled fate and circumstances,
Fought and fell and fought again.
Won sometimes, but did no crowing,
Lost sometimes, but didn't wail,
Took his beating, but kept going
Never let his courage fail.

He was fallible and human
Therefore loved and understood
Both his fellow man and woman
Whether good or not so good.
Kept his spirit undiminished,
Never failed to help a friend,
Played the game till it was finished,
Lived a Sportsman to the end.

Author unknown

946. USE WELL THE MOMENT

Use well the moment; what the hour
Brings for thy use is in thy power;
And what thou best canst understand
Is just the thing lies nearest to thy hand.

Johann W. von Goethe, 1749–1832

947. THERE IS A TIDE

From "Julius Caesar," Act IV, sc. 3

There is a tide in the affairs of men,
Which, taken at the flood, leads on to fortune;
Omitted, all the voyage of their life
Is bound in shallows and in miseries:
And we must take the current when it serves,
Or lose our ventures.

William Shakespeare, 1564–1616

948. LAST JUDGMENT

No grim last judge recording on a slate
His evil deeds, he met beyond the Gate,
But an appraiser still more stern and just:
His own accusing conscience roused too late.

Stanton A. Coblentz, 1896–

949. BETRAYAL

Still as of old
Men by themselves are priced—
For thirty pieces Judas sold
Himself, not Christ.

Hester H. Cholmondeley, 19th century

950. A PRAYER

Great God, I ask thee for no meaner pelf
Than that I may not disappoint myself,
That in my action I may soar as high
As I can now discern with this clear eye.

❖

That my weak hand may equal my firm faith,
And my life practice more than my tongue
saith;
That my low conduct may not show,
Nor my relenting lines,
That I thy purpose did not know,
Or overrated thy designs.

Henry David Thoreau, 1817–1862

951. GROWING

Lord of all growing things,
By such sweet, secret influences as those
That draw the scilla through the melting
snows,
And bid the fledgling bird trust untried wings,
When quick my spirit grows,
Help me to trust my wings.

Author unknown

952. SELF-MASTERY

Who, harnessed in his mail of Self, demands
To be men's master and their sovran guide?—
Proclaims his place, and by sole right of pride
A candidate for love and reverence stands,
As if the power within his empty hands
Had fallen from the sky, with all beside,
So oft to longing and to toil denied,
That makes the leaders and the lords of lands?
He who would lead must first himself be led;
Who would be loved be capable to love
Beyond the utmost he receives, who claims
The rod of power must first have bowed
And being honored, honor what's above:
This know the men who leave the world their
names.

Bayard Taylor, 1825–1878

953. THE LAMP OF LIFE

Always we are following a light,
Always the light recedes; with groping hands
We stretch toward this glory, while the lands
We journey through are hidden from our sight
Dim and mysterious, folded deep in night,
We care not, all our utmost need demands
Is but the light, the light! So still it stands
Surely our own if we exert our might.
Fool! Never can'st thou grasp this fleeting
gleam,
Its glowing flame would die if it were caught,
Its value is that it doth always seem
But just a little farther on. Distraught,
But lighted ever onward, we are brought
Upon our way unknowing, in a dream.

Amy Lowell, 1874–1925

954. A NOISELESS, PATIENT SPIDER

A noiseless, patient spider,
I mark'd, where, on a little promontory, it stood, isolated;
Mark'd how, to explore the vacant, vast surrounding,
It launch'd forth filament, filament, filament, out of itself;
Ever unreeling them—ever tirelessly speeding them.

And you, O my Soul, where you stand,
Surrounded, surrounded, in measureless oceans of space,
Ceaselessly musing, venturing, throwing—seeking the spheres, to connect them;
Till the bridge you will need, be form'd—till the ductile anchor hold;
Till the gossamer thread you fling, catch somewhere, O my Soul.

Walt Whitman, 1819–1892

955. From FOR AN AUTOGRAPH

Life is a leaf of paper white
Whereon each one of us may write
His word or two, and then comes night.

❖

Greatly begin! though thou have time
But for a line, be that sublime,—
Not failure, but low aim, is crime.

James Russell Lowell, 1819–1891

956. IN TUNE WITH THE INFINITE

From "The Merchant of Venice," Act V, sc. I

How sweet the moonlight sleeps upon this
bank!
Here will we sit, and let the sounds of music
Creep in our ears: soft stillness and the night
Become the touches of sweet harmony.
Sit, Jessica. Look how the floor of heaven
Is thick inlaid with patines of bright gold:

There's not the smallest orb which thou
beholds't
But in his motion like an angel sings,
Still quiring to the young-eyed cherubims;
Such harmony is in immortal souls;
But whilst this muddy vesture of decay
Doth grossly close it in, we cannot hear it.

William Shakespeare, 1564–1616

957. WINGS

Be like the bird
That, pausing in her flight
Awhile on boughs too slight,
Feels them give way
Beneath her and yet sings,
Knowing that she hath wings.

Victor Hugo, 1802–1885

958. From ANXIETY

Some of your hurts you have cured,
And the sharpest you still have survived,
But what torments of grief you endured
From evils that never arrived!

Ralph Waldo Emerson, 1803–1882

959. WE NEEDS MUST LOVE THE HIGHEST

From "Guinevere"

Ah, my God,
What might I not have made of thy fair world,
Had I but loved thy highest creature here?
It was my duty to have loved the highest:
It surely was my profit had I known;
It would have been my pleasure had I seen.
We needs must love the highest when we see
it.

Alfred Tennyson, 1809–1892

960. THE PSALM OF LIFE

Tell me not, in mournful numbers,
Life is but an empty dream!—
For the soul is dead that slumbers,
And things are not what they seem.

Life is real! Life is earnest!
And the grave is not its goal;
Dust thou art, to dust returnest,
Was not spoken of the soul.

Not enjoyment, and not sorrow,
Is our destined end or way;
But to act, that each tomorrow
Find us farther than today.

Art is long, and Time is fleeting,
And our hearts, though stout and brave,
Still, like muffled drums, are beating
Funeral marches to the grave.

In the world's broad field of battle,
In the bivouac of life,
Be not like dumb, driven cattle!
Be a hero in the strife!

Trust no Future, howe'er pleasant!
Let the dead Past bury its dead!
Act, act in the living Present!
Heart within, and God o'erhead!

Lives of great men all remind us
We can make our lives sublime,
And, departing, leave behind us
Footprints on the sands of time.

Footprints, that perhaps another,
Sailing o'er life's solemn main,
A forlorn and shipwrecked brother,
Seeing, shall take heart again.

Let us then be up and doing,
With a heart for any fate;
Still achieving, still pursuing,
Learn to labor and to wait.

Henry Wadsworth Longfellow, 1807–1882

961. THE MAN OF LIFE UPRIGHT

The man of life upright,
Whose guiltless heart is free
From all dishonest deeds,
Or thought of vanity;

The man whose silent days
In harmless joys are spent,
Whom hopes cannot delude
Nor sorrow discontent:

That man needs neither towers
Nor armour for defence,
Nor secret vaults to fly
From thunder's violence.

He only can behold
With unaffrighted eyes
The horrors of the deep
And terrors of the skies.

Thus scorning all the cares
That fate or fortune brings,
He makes the heaven his book,
His wisdom heavenly things;

Good thoughts his only friends,
His wealth a well-spent age,
The earth his sober inn
And quiet pilgrimage.

Thomas Campion, 1567–1620

962. YOUR HOUSE OF HAPPINESS

Take what God gives, O heart of mine,
And build your house of happiness.
Perchance some have been given more;
But many have been given less.
The treasure lying at your feet,
Whose value you but faintly guess,
Another builder, looking on,
Would barter heaven to possess.

Have you found work that you can do?
Is there a heart that loves you best?
Is there a spot somewhere called home
Where, spent and worn, your soul may rest?
A friendly tree? A book? A song?
A dog that loves your hand's caress?
A store of health to meet life's needs?
Oh, build your house of happiness!

Trust not tomorrow's dawn to bring
The dreamed-of joy for which you wait;
You have enough of pleasant things
To house your soul in goodly state;
Tomorrow Time's relentless stream
May bear what now you have away;
Take what God gives, O heart, and build
Your house of happiness today!

B. Y. Williams, contemporary American

963. ACHIEVEMENT

I have builded my house; deep, deep have I digged in the earth
That the stones I have laid may endure both the tempest and flood;
I have toiled; I have strained; I have silently suffered men's mirth;
And the mortar I molded was mixed with my tears and my blood.

I have builded my house; and the labor was weary and long;
Stone by stone, beam by beam, foot by foot, oh, how slowly it grew;
I have welded the stones, braced the walls; they are solid and strong,
And how weary and proud am I now that the building is through.

I have builded my house; I have planted my trees in a row
That the twitter of birds may awake me to glorious dawns;
I have veiled it with vines where the shy early roses may blow,
I have compassed its walls with the emerald velvet of lawns

I have builded my house; 'twas a glorious vision of mine,
And I dreamed and I planned and I dared, and I caused it to be;
Now it stands in the deep-rooted strength of the quarry and pine,
And its peace is the peace of the stars in their soft summer sea.

I have builded my house; I have set it aloft on a hill
Where its lights may shine out in the dark, the lone rider to guide;
I have stretched out my hands; I have opened my doors with a will
That the weary and worn may come in and in peace may abide.

I have builded my house; O thou great Master Builder of all,
  Look thou down on my building, and bless it, and strengthen its bands
Through the aeons to come, though the tempest may threaten its wall,
  For this mansion of mine is a dwelling not builded with hands.

Berta Hart Nance

964. A BAG OF TOOLS

Isn't it strange
That princes and kings,
And clowns that caper
In sawdust rings,
And common people
Like you and me
Are builders for eternity?

Each is given a bag of tools,
A shapeless mass,
A book of rules;
And each must make,
Ere life is flown,
A stumbling-block
Or a stepping-stone.

R. L. Sharpe

965. OUR SWEETEST SONGS

From "To a Skylark"

We look before and after,
  And pine for what is not;
Our sincerest laughter
  With some pain is fraught;
Our sweetest songs are those that tell of
    saddest thought.

Yet if we could scorn
  Hate and pride and fear;
If we were things born
  Not to shed a tear,
I know not how thy joy we ever should come
    near.

Percy Bysshe Shelley, 1792–1822

966. CREATION'S LORD, WE GIVE THEE THANKS

Creation's Lord, we give Thee thanks
That this Thy world is incomplete;
That battle calls our marshaled ranks,
That work awaits our hands and feet;

That Thou hast not yet finished man,
That we are in the making still,
As friends who share the Maker's plan,
As sons who know the Father's will.

Beyond the present sin and shame,
Wrong's bitter, cruel, scorching blight,
We see the beckoning vision flame,
The blessed kingdom of the right.

What though the Kingdom long delay,
And still with haughty foes must cope?
It gives us that for which to pray,
A field for toil and faith and hope.

Since what we choose is what we are,
And what we love we yet shall be,
The goal may ever shine afar;
The will to win it makes us free.

William De Witt Hyde, 1858–1917

967. SOME FAITH AT ANY COST

No vision and you perish;
  No ideal, and you're lost;
Your heart must ever cherish
  Some faith at any cost.

Some hope, some dream to cling to,
  Some rainbow in the sky,
Some melody to sing to,
  Some service that is high.

Harriet du Autermont

968. THE LOST CHORD

Seated one day at the Organ,
  I was weary and ill at ease,
And my fingers wandered idly
  Over the noisy keys.

I know not what I was playing,
  Or what I was dreaming then;
But I struck one chord of music,
  Like the sound of a great Amen.

It flooded the crimson twilight,
Like the close of an angel's Psalm,
And it lay on my fevered spirit
With a touch of infinite calm.

It quieted pain and sorrow,
Like love overcoming strife;
It seemed the harmonious echo
From our discordant life.

It linked all perplexed meanings
Into one perfect peace,
And trembled away into silence,
As if it were loath to cease.

I have sought, but I seek it vainly,
That one lost chord divine,
That came from the soul of the Organ
And entered into mine.

It may be that Death's bright angel
Will speak in that chord again,—
It may be that only in Heaven
I shall hear that grand Amen.

Adelaide A. Procter, 1825–1864

969. STAND FORTH!

Stand forth, my soul, and grip thy woe,[1]
Buckle thy sword and face thy foe.
What right hast thou to be afraid
When all the universe will aid?
Ten thousand rally to thy name,
Horses and chariots of flame.
Do others fear? Do others fail?
My soul must grapple and prevail.
My soul must scale the mountain side
And with the conquering army ride—
Stand forth, my soul!

Stand forth, my soul, and take command.
'Tis I, thy master, bid thee stand.
Claim thou thy ground and thrust thy foe,
Plead not thine enemy should go.
Let others cringe! My soul is free,
No hostile host can conquer me.
There lives no circumstance so great
Can make me yield, or doubt my fate.
My soul must know what kings have known,
Must reach and claim its rightful throne—
Stand forth, my soul!

I ask no truce, I have no qualms,
I seek no quarter and no alms.
Let those who will, obey the sod;
My soul sprang from the living God.
'Tis I, the king, who bid thee stand;
Grasp with thy hand my royal hand—
Stand forth!

Angela Morgan, contemporary American

970. CARRY ON!

It's easy to fight when everything's right,
And you're mad with the thrill and the glory;
It's easy to cheer when victory's near,
And wallow in fields that are gory.
It's a different song when everything's wrong,
When you're feeling infernally mortal;
When it's ten against one, and hope there is none,
Buck up, little soldier, and chortle:

Carry on! Carry on!
There isn't much punch in your blow.
You're glaring and staring and hitting out blind;
You're muddy and bloody, but never you mind.
Carry on! Carry on!
You haven't the ghost of a show.
It's looking like death, but while you've a breath,
Carry on, my son! Carry on!

And so in the strife of the battle of life
It's easy to fight when you're winning;
It's easy to slave, and starve and be brave,
When the dawn of success is beginning.
But the man who can meet despair and defeat
With a cheer, there's the man of God's choosing;
The man who can fight to Heaven's own height
Is the man who can fight when he's losing.

Carry on! Carry on!
Things never were looming so black.
But show that you haven't a cowardly streak,
And though you're unlucky you never are weak.
Carry on! Carry on!
Brace up for another attack.

[1] Written in tribute to Franklin D. Roosevelt on his courage after being stricken with infantile paralysis.

It's looking like hell, but—you never can
tell:
Carry on, old man! Carry on!

There are some who drift out in the deserts
of doubt,
And some who in brutishness wallow;
There are others, I know, who in piety go
Because of a Heaven to follow.
But to labor with zest, and to give of your
best,
For the sweetness and joy of the giving;
To help folks along with a hand and a song;
Why, there's the real sunshine of living.

Carry on! Carry on!
Fight the good fight and true;
Believe in your mission, greet life with a
cheer;
There's big work to do, and that's why you
are here.
Carry on! Carry on!
Let the world be the better for you;
And at last when you die, let this be your cry:
Carry on, my soul! Carry on!

Robert Service, 1874–

971. MY ORDERS

My orders are to fight;
Then if I bleed, or fail,
Or strongly win, what matters it?
God only doth prevail.

The servant craveth naught
Except to serve with might.
I was not told to win or lose,—
My orders are to fight.

Ethelwyn Wetherald, 1857–1940

972. BE STRONG!

Be strong!
We are not here to play, to dream, to drift,
We have hard work to do, and loads to lift.
Shun not the struggle, face it, 'tis God's gift.

Be strong!
Say not the days are evil—who's to blame!
And fold the hands and acquiesce—O shame!
Stand up, speak out, and bravely, in God's
name.

Be strong!
It matters not how deep entrenched the
wrong,
How hard the battle goes, the day, how long;
Faint not, fight on! To-morrow comes the
song.

Maltbie D. Babcock, 1858–1901

973. From CHARACTER OF THE HAPPY WARRIOR

Who is the happy warrior? Who is he
That every man in arms should wish to be?
It is the generous spirit, who, when brought
Among the tasks of real life, hath wrought
Upon the plan that pleased his boyish
thought:
Whose high endeavours are an inward light
That makes the path before him always
bright:
Who, with a natural instinct to discern
What knowledge can perform, is diligent to
learn;
Abides by this resolve, and stops not there,
But makes his moral being his prime care;
Who, doomed to go in company with pain,
And fear, and bloodshed, miserable train!
Turns his necessity to glorious gain:

❖

Who, if he be called upon to face
Some awful moment to which heaven has
joined
Great issues, good or bad for human-kind,
Is happy as a lover; and attired
With sudden brightness, like a man inspired.

❖

This is the happy warrior; this is he
That every man in arms should wish to be.

William Wordsworth, 1770–1850

974. I THOUGHT THAT NATURE WAS ENOUGH

I THOUGHT that nature was enough
Till human nature came,
But that the other did absorb
As firmament a flame.

Of human nature just aware
There added the divine
Brief struggle for capacity.
The power to contain

Is always as the contents,
But give a giant room
And you will lodge a giant
And not a lesser man.

Emily Dickinson, 1830–1886

975. From BISHOP BLOUGRAM'S APOLOGY

When the fight begins within himself,
A man's worth something. God stoops o'er
his head,
Satan looks up between his feet—both tug—
He's left, himself, i' the middle: the soul wakes
And grows. Prolong that battle through his
life!
Never leave growing till the life to come!

Robert Browning, 1812–1889

976. NO ENEMIES

You have no enemies, you say?
Alas! my friend, the boast is poor—
He who has mingled in the fray
Of duty, that the brave endure,
Must have made foes! If you have none,
Small is the work that you have done;
You've hit no traitor on the hip;
You've dashed no cup from perjured lip;
You've never turned the wrong to right—
You've been a coward in the fight!

Charles Mackay, 1814–1889

977. SAY NOT THE STRUGGLE NAUGHT AVAILETH

Say not the struggle naught availeth,
The labor and the wounds are vain,
The enemy faints not, nor faileth,
And as things have been they remain.

If hopes were dupes, fears may be liars;
It may be, in von smoke conceal'd,
Your comrades chase e'en now the fliers,
And, but for you, possess the field.

For while the tired waves, vainly breaking,
Seem here no painful inch to gain,
Far back, through creeks and inlets making,
Comes silent, flooding in, the main.

And not by eastern windows only,
When daylight comes, comes in the light;
In front, the sun climbs slow, how slowly!
But westward, look, the land is bright!

Arthur Hugh Clough, 1819–1861

978. YONDER SEE THE MORNING BLINK

Yonder see the morning blink:
The sun is up, and up must I,
To wash and dress and eat and drink
And look at things and talk and think
And work, and God knows why.

Oh, often have I washed and dressed
And what's to show for all my pain?
Let me lie abed and rest:
Ten thousand times I've done my best
And all's to do again.

A. E. Housman, 1859–1936

979. THE EMPTY LIFE

From "Macbeth," Act V, sc. 5

To-morrow, and to-morrow, and to-morrow
Creeps on this petty pace from day to day
To the last syllable of recorded time;
And all our yesterdays have lighted fools
The way to dusty death. Out, out, brief
candle!
Life's but a walking shadow, a poor player
That struts and frets his hour upon the stage
And then is heard no more: it is a tale
Told by an idiot, full of sound and fury,
Signifying nothing.

William Shakespeare, 1564–1616

980. CARDINAL WOLSEY'S FAREWELL

From "King Henry VIII," Act III, sc. 2

Farewell! a long farewell, to all my greatness!
This is the state of man: to-day he puts forth
The tender leaves of hopes; to-morrow blossoms
And bears his blushing honours thick upon him;
The third day comes a frost, a killing frost;
And, when he thinks, good easy man, full surely
His greatness is a-ripening, nips his root,
And then he falls, as I do. I have ventured,
Like little wanton boys that swim on bladders,
This many summers in a sea of glory,
But far beyond my depth: my high-blown pride
At length broke under me, and now has left me,
Weary and old with service, to the mercy
Of a rude stream, that must for ever hide me.
Vain pomp and glory of this world, I hate ye:
I feel my heart new open'd. O! how wretched
Is that poor man that hangs on prince's favours!
There is, betwixt that smile we would aspire to,
That sweet aspect of princes, and their ruin,
More pangs and fears than wars or women have—
And when he falls, he falls like Lucifer,
Never to hope again.

William Shakespeare, 1564–1616

981. GONE IN THE WIND

Solomon! where is thy throne? It is gone in the wind.
Babylon! where is thy might? It is gone in the wind.
Like the swift shadows of Noon, like the dreams of the Blind,
Vanish the glories and pomps of the earth in the wind.

Man! canst thou build upon aught in the pride of thy mind?
Wisdom will teach thee that nothing can tarry behind;
Though there be thousand bright actions embalmed and enshrined,
Myriads and millions of brighter are snow in the wind.

Solomon! where is thy throne? It is gone in the wind.
Babylon! where is thy might? It is gone in the wind.
All that the genius of Man hath achieved and designed
Waits for its hour to be dealt with as dust by the wind.

Pity thou, reader! the madness of poor Humankind,
Raving of Knowledge,—and Satan so busy to blind!
Raving of Glory,—like me,—for the garlands I bind
(Garlands of song) are but gathered, and—strewn in the wind!

James Clarence Mangan, 1803–1849

982. OZYMANDIAS

I met a traveler from an antique land
Who said: "Two vast and trunkless legs of stone
Stand in the desert. Near them, on the sand,
Half sunk, a shattered visage lies, whose frown,
And wrinkled lip, and sneer of cold command,
Tell that the sculptor well those passions read
Which yet survive, stamped on these lifeless things,
The hand that mocked them, and the heart that fed.
And on the pedestal these words appear—
'My name is Ozymandias, king of kings:
Look on my works, ye Mighty, and despair!'
Nothing beside remains. Round the decay
Of that colossal wreck, boundless and bare
The lone and level sands stretch far away."

Percy Bysshe Shelley, 1792–1822

983. THE WORLDLY HOPE

From "The Rubáiyát"

XVI

The Worldly Hope men set their Hearts upon
Turns Ashes—or it prospers; and anon,
  Like Snow upon the desert's dusty Face,
Lighting a little hour or two—is gone.

XVII

Think, in this batter'd Caravanserai
Whose Portals are alternate Night and Day,
  How Sultán with his Pomp
Abode his destined Hour, and went his way.

Omar Khayyám, 1070–1123;
tr. by Edward Fitzgerald, 1809–1883

984. WHEN PLANES OUTSOAR THE SPIRIT

When planes outsoar the spirit, flying blind,
When ships outsail the dreams that gave
    them birth,
When towers dwarf the upward-reaching
    mind,
When wealth is mightier than simple worth—

We almost hear the turning of a page,
We almost know what every seraph knows,
That somewhere on a universal stage
A tiresome play is drawing to its close.

Lilith Lorraine, contemporary American

985. EPITAPH, FOUND SOMEWHERE IN SPACE

In desolation, here a lost world lies.
All wisdom was its aim: with noble plan,
It sounded ocean deeps; measured the skies;
And fathomed every mystery but Man.

Hugh Wilgus Ramsaur,
contemporary American

986. FATALISM

From "The Rubáiyát"

LXVIII

We are no other than a moving row
Of Magic Shadow-shapes that come and go
  Round with this Sun-illumined Lantern
    held
In Midnight by the Master of the Show;

LXIX

But helpless Pieces of the Game He plays
Upon this Checker-board of Nights and Days;
  Hither and thither moves, and checks, and
    slays,
And one by one back in the Closet lays.

LXX

The Ball no question makes of Ayes and Noes,
But Here or There as strikes the Player goes;
  And He that tossed you down into the
    Field,
He knows about it all—HE knows—HE
    knows!

LXXI

The Moving Finger writes; and, having writ,
Moves on: nor all your Piety nor Wit
Shall lure it back to cancel half a Line,
Nor all your Tears wash out a Word of it.

LXXII

And that inverted Bowl they call the Sky,
Whereunder crawling coop'd we live and die,
Lift not your hands to *It* for help—for It
As impotently rolls as you or I.

Omar Khayyám, 1070–1123;
tr. by Edward Fitzgerald, 1809–1883

987. From ODE

Written during the Battle of Dunkirk, May 1940

V

Happy are those who can relieve
suffering with prayer
Happy those who can rely on God
to see them through.

They can wait patiently for the end.

But we who have put our faith
in the goodness of man
and now see man's image debased
lower than the wolf or the hog—

Where can we turn for consolation?

Herbert Read, contemporary English

988. PERSUASION

From "Ecclesiastical Sonnets," XVI

Man's life is like a Sparrow, mighty King!
That—while at banquet with your Chiefs you sit
Housed near a blazing fire—is seen to flit
Safe from the wintry tempest. Fluttering,
Here did it enter: there, on hasty wing,
Flies out, and passes on from cold to cold;
But whence it came we know not, nor behold
Whither it goes. Even such, that transient Thing,
The human Soul; not utterly unknown
While in the Body lodged, her warm abode;
But from what world she came, what woe or weal
On her departure waits, no tongue hath shown;
This mystery if the Stranger can reveal,
His be a welcome cordially bestowed!

William Wordsworth, 1770–1850

989. THE DOOMED MAN

There is a time, we know not when,
A point we know not where,
That marks the destiny of men,
For glory or despair.

There is a line, by us unseen,
That crosses every path;
The hidden boundary between
God's patience and His wrath.

Joseph Addison Alexander, 1800–1860

990. LIFE'S PURPOSE

From "The Cathedral"

This life were brutish did we not sometimes
Have intimations clear of wider scope,
Hints of occasion infinite, to keep
The soul alert with noble discontent
And onward yearnings of unstilled desire;
Fruitless, except we now and then divined
A mystery of Purpose, gleaming through
The secular confusions of the world,
Whose will we darkly accomplish, doing ours.

James Russell Lowell, 1819–1891

991. BAD TIMES

Why slander we the times?
What crimes
Have days and years, that we
Thus charge them with iniquity?
If we would rightly scan,
It's not the times are bad, but man.
If thy desire it be
To see
The times prove good, be thou
But such thyself, and surely know
That all thy days to thee
Shall spite of mischief happy be.

Joseph Beaumont, 1616–1699

992. QUICKSAND YEARS

Quicksand years that whirl me I know not whither,
Your schemes, politics, fail—lines give way—substances mock and elude me;
Only the theme I sing, the great and strong-possess'd Soul, eludes not;
One's-self must never give way—that is the final substance—that out of all is sure;
Out of politics, triumphs, battles, life—what at last finally remains?
What shows break up, what but One's-Self is sure?

Walt Whitman, 1819–1892

993. PSALM AGAINST THE DARKNESS

1

What shall we fear, son, now that the stars go down and silence is chilling the breath to a pattern of frost?
Stalactites glisten from caverns of night for the grief of the world is hardened again into swords.
Cankers of malice are boring their icy augers deep in the bosoms of men, and the hooves of the four horsemen are heard on the roofs of the brain.
What is this prescience of doom, this stalk of evil that sucks the sap of the spirit, and spreads the pollen of anger?
Some witch is abroad in the world, paroled for an hour of mischief to scatter her cockle in furrows of greed.
We have taken the earth in our stride, but the boot is crusted in clay, and the cleat has bruised the dream bogged low in the darkness.
Heads downward, we count the treadmill steps to the sky in a litany mixed with a laugh and wordy bluster of braggarts.

2

Standing on the rim of the world we beat hollow drums in our breasts, we shout into caverns a challenge of God.
Nimble are we in the centuries to alter our skin, our tongue and our shrine, but never the bloody oblation as Abraham also remembered.
Peace, peace, we cry, till our voice is shrilled to a paean, but the map men wrangle by mountain and river.
Knowledge we gather as a conquering host, and pile the loot of the years in bins of oak and of marble, but wisdom we cannot bequeath.
The heat of blood is the same as the night it spilled on the lichened rocks in a world too small for the fingers of Cain.

3

Which is more difficult, son, to save the world, or end it swift in a vacuum, sans mark or memory of men?
What is the goal of the centaur whose fingers have changed the wine of Cana to gall, who sold his art to Magus and fouled the steps of the temple?
What shall we fear too much? Hate's guarantee of our doom? Love's indestructible dawn? The half-god who stumbles on pride cannot end his world by the wishing.
A finger rising from conscience and shadowing the sun shall mark the hour with less than His praise, yet curve a rainbow high over Golgotha.
The finger has written again on the curved deception of blue, and the words are the old, old cry of "Eli, Eli, lama sabachthani?"

4

There are two majorities, son, though you ask me no question. The nameless dead, the unborn legions of time, but we are the thin minority, the living, who hold God's sceptre of light.

A. M. Sullivan, 1896–

994. THE DAY SHALL YET BE FAIR

The darkness passes; storms shall not abide,
A little patience and the fog is past;
After the sorrow of the ebbing tide
The singing floods return in joy at last.

The night is long, and pain weighs heavily,
But God will hold his world above despair.
Look to the east, where up the lurid sky
The morning climbs! The day shall yet be fair.

Celia Thaxter, 1835–1894

995. THE WINDS OF FATE

This poem was written by Mrs. Wilcox on the steamer *Richard Peck* between New Haven and New York, following her husband's observation that one ship went west and another east in the same wind.

One ship drives east and another drives west
With the selfsame winds that blow.
'Tis the set of the sails
And not the gales
Which tells us the way to go.

Like the winds of the sea are the ways of fate,
As we voyage along through life:
'Tis the set of a soul
That decides its goal,
And not the calm or the strife.

Ella Wheeler Wilcox, 1855–1919

996. LONDON, 1940

[*Si monumentum requiris, circumspice*]

Old London's time-encrusted walls
Are but the work of human hands.
What man has fashioned for us falls;
What God has breathed into us stands.

What if the splendour of the past
Is shattered into dust, we raise
A monument that shall outlast
Even the Abbey's span of days.

On broken homes we set our feet[1]
And raise proud heads that all may see,
Immortal in each little street,
The soul in its integrity.

A. A. Milne, 1882–

997. PROGRESSION

Look upward at the hill that must be climbed
Today, forgetting thorns and grief that marked
The steeps of yesterday, as drifted snow
Is unremembered when the feet of Spring
Have passed. . . . We are the pioneers of this
New age and we have wider trails to blaze,
Which lead to happiness . . . new cities that
Must stand upon the hill of faith . . .
New bridges to be built to span the seas
Of hatred surging in the hearts of men,
And there are songs that we must weave . . . new songs
That are as runners bearing messages
Of hope and love and peace . . .

Inez Clark Thorson, contemporary American

[1] On returning to his house in London after an air raid Mr. Milne found only the steps left. Sitting on them he wrote the above lines.

998. FOR A MATERIALIST

I

I know your barren belief—that a rose will grow
From what was once the miracle of a man;
That only in this way shall we thwart the grave;
Believe, my friend, and be satisfied, if you can.

But I have a mystical hunger, so great and intense
That only Almighty God with a purpose would fill
My fragile shell with its poignant immensity—
A hunger to find, emerging from death, that I still
Am the sum of myself! myself, to aspire and climb
Some farther and undreamed slope of the range of Time.

I have faith that I shall. Is a rose worth the patience of Him
Who evolved through the aeons a man and endowed him with soul?
Would He who created the splendor of spirit and mind
Envisage a sweet-scented waft as its trivial goal?

2

You say that the soul is forever commingled with matter,
That it lives since the body lives and dies when that dies,
That it feels and thinks with the flesh and perceives creations
With the body's eyes.

The two are knit, I know, for the length of a lifetime;
But tell me—have you not seen a spirit unfold
Its beauty and grow more vital although the body
Was faded and old?
Whence this splendor apart, this effervescence,
This gaining in strength through the years that the end can show,
If it depend so wholly on forces receding,
On sap running low?
The body may be assailed by the frosts of winter
And the spirit be steeped in the sunniness of May;
Why shall it not maintain, when matter has crumbled,
Its separate way?

3

A dusty dissolution! So Death means
No more than this dry thing to you—no more.
Oh, I am one who confidently gleans
A rich surmise from shadows cast before;
From this insatiate seeking, this sublime
Persistence of man's soul, intent to find
The shining Core from which the rays of Time
And Life proceed; from this assault of mind,
The strong, well tempered weapon which man brings
To all adventure, his Excalibur
With which in his eternal questionings
He storms for answers earth and sea and star!
Would any God who breathes in us such need

And power to learn of Him, who let us look
Upon some pages freely, bid us read
The preface only—and then shut the book?

Adelaide Love, contemporary American

999. ELEGY WRITTEN IN A COUNTRY CHURCHYARD

The curfew tolls the knell of parting day,
The lowing herd wind slowly o'er the lea,
The plowman homeward plods his weary way,
And leaves the world to darkness and to me.

Now fades the glimmering landscape on the sight,
And all the air a solemn stillness holds,
Save where the beetle wheels his droning flight,
And drowsy tinklings lull the distant folds;

Save that from yonder ivy-mantled tower
The moping owl does to the moon complain
Of such as, wandering near her secret bower,
Molest her ancient solitary reign.

Beneath those rugged elms, that yew-tree's shade
Where heaves the turf in many a mouldering heap,
Each in his narrow cell for ever laid,
The rude forefathers of the hamlet sleep.

The breezy call of incense-breathing morn,
The swallow twittering from the straw-built shed,
The cock's shrill clarion, or the echoing horn,
No more shall rouse them from their lowly bed.

For them no more the blazing hearth shall burn,
Or busy housewife ply her evening care:
No children run to lisp their sire's return,
Or climb his knees the envied kiss to share.

Oft did the harvest to their sickle yield,
Their furrow oft the stubborn glebe has broke;
How jocund did they drive their team afield!
How bowed the woods beneath their sturdy stroke!

Let not ambition mock their useful toil,
Their homely joys, and destiny obscure;
Nor grandeur hear with a disdainful smile,
The short and simple annals of the poor.

The boast of heraldry, the pomp of power,
And all that beauty, all that wealth e'er gave,
Await alike th' inevitable hour:—
The paths of glory lead but to the grave.

Nor you, ye proud, impute to these the fault,
  If memory o'er their tomb no trophies raise,
Where through the long-drawn aisle and fretted vault
  The pealing anthem swells the note of praise.

Can storied urn or animated bust
  Back to its mansion call the fleeting breath?
Can honour's voice provoke the silent dust,
  Or flattery soothe the dull cold ear of death?

Perhaps in this neglected spot is laid
  Some heart once pregnant with celestial fire;
Hands, that the rod of empire might have swayed,
  Or wak'd to ecstasy the living lyre.

But knowledge to their eyes her ample page
  Rich with the spoils of time, did ne'er unroll;
Chill penury repressed their noble rage,
  And froze the genial current of the soul.

Full many a gem of purest ray serene
  The dark unfathomed caves of ocean bear:
Full many a flower is born to blush unseen,
  And waste its sweetness on the desert air.

Some village-Hampden, that with dauntless breast
  The little tyrant of his fields withstood;
Some mute inglorious Milton here may rest,
  Some Cromwell guiltless of his country's blood.

Th' applause of listening senates to command,
  The threats of pain and ruin to despise,
To scatter plenty o'er a smiling land,
  And read their history in a nation's eyes,

Their lot forbade: nor circumscribed alone
  Their growing virtues, but their crimes confined;
Forbade to wade through slaughter to a throne,
  And shut the gates of mercy on mankind;

The struggling pangs of conscious truth to hide,
  To quench the blushes of ingenuous shame,
Or heap the shrine of luxury and pride
  With incense kindled at the Muse's flame.

Far from the madding crowd's ignoble strife,
  Their sober wishes never learn'd to stray;
Along the cool sequestered vale of life
  They kept the noiseless tenor of their way.

Yet ev'n these bones from insult to protect
  Some frail memorial still erected nigh,
With uncouth rhymes and shapeless sculpture decked,
  Implores the passing tribute of a sigh.

Their name, their years, spelt by th' unlettered Muse,
  The place of fame and elegy supply:
And many a holy text around she strews,
  That teach the rustic moralist to die.

For who, to dumb forgetfulness a prey,
  This pleasing anxious being e'er resigned,
Left the warm precincts of the cheerful day,
  Nor cast one longing, ling'ring look behind?

On some fond breast the parting soul relies,
  Some pious drops the closing eye requires;
Ev'n from the tomb the voice of Nature cries,
  Ev'n in our ashes live their wonted fires.

For thee, who, mindful of th' unhonoured dead,
  Dost in these lines their artless tale relate;
If chance, by lonely contemplation led,
  Some kindred spirit shall inquire thy fate,

Haply some hoary-headed swain may say,
  "Oft have we seen him at the peep of dawn
Brushing with hasty steps the dews away,
  To meet the sun upon the upland lawn;

"There at the foot of yonder nodding beech
  That wreathes its old fantastic roots so high,
His listless length at noontide would he stretch,
  And pore upon the brook that babbles by.

"Hard by yon wood, now smiling as in scorn,
  Muttering his wayward fancies he would rove;
Now drooping, woeful, wan, like one forlorn,
  Or crazed with care, or crossed in hopeless love.

"One morn I missed him on the customed hill,
  Along the heath, and near his favorite tree;
Another came; nor yet beside the rill,
  Nor up the lawn, nor at the wood was he;

"The next, with dirges due in sad array
  Slow through the church-way path we saw him borne.
Approach and read (for thou canst read) the lay
  Graved on the stone beneath yon aged thorn."

The Epitaph

Here rests his head upon the lap of earth
  A youth, to fortune and to fame unknown;
Fair science frowned not on his humble birth,
  And melancholy marked him for her own.

Large was his bounty, and his soul sincere;
  Heaven did a recompense as largely send:

He gave to misery all he had, a tear;
He gained from heaven ('twas all he wished) a friend.

No farther seek his merits to disclose,
Or draw his frailties from their dread abode,
(There they alike in trembling hope repose),
The bosom of his Father and his God.

Thomas Gray, 1716–1771

1000. From ODE TO THE WEST WIND

Make me thy lyre, even as the forest is:
What if my leaves are falling like its own!
The tumult of thy mighty harmonies

Will take from both a deep, autumnal tone,
Sweet though in sadness. Be thou, Spirit fierce,
My spirit! Be thou me, impetuous one!

Drive my dead thoughts over the universe
Like withered leaves to quicken a new birth!
And, by the incantation of this verse,

Scatter, as from an unextinguished hearth
Ashes and sparks, my words among mankind!
Be through my lips to unawakened earth

The trumpet of a prophecy! O wind,
If Winter comes, can Spring be far behind?

Percy Bysshe Shelley, 1792–1822

1001. WORLDLY WISDOM

From "The Rubáiyát"

XXVII

Myself when young did eagerly frequent
Doctor and Saint, and heard great argument
About it and about; but evermore
Came out by the same door as in I went.

XXVIII

With them the seed of Wisdom did I sow,
And with mine own hand wrought to make it grow;
And this was all the Harvest that I reap'd—
"I came like Water, and like Wind I go."

XXIX

Into this Universe, and *Why* not knowing
Nor *Whence*, like Water willy-nilly flowing;
And out of it, as Wind along the Waste,
I know not *Whither*, willy-nilly blowing.

XXXI

Up from Earth's Centre through the Seventh Gate
I rose, and on the Throne of Saturn sate,
And many a Knot unravel'd by the Road;
But not the Master-knot of Human Fate.

XXXII

There was the Door to which I found no Key;
There was the Veil through which I might not see;
Some little talk awhile of Me and Thee
There was—and then no more of Thee and Me.

Omar Khayyám, 1070–1123;
tr. by Edward Fitzgerald, 1809–1883

1002. THE STRONG

We were spawned in lava mountains, from the surf line of the sea,
We were cast on desert islands when the world began to be.
Rocks were hard to make us harder. Storms were strong to make us strong.
And our will was set and tempered where the frosts were sore and long.

Glaciers drove us. We retreated till we overtopped the snow.
Past the passes, pierced the mountains; found the valleys warm below.

We went marching past perdition with a purpose ill conceived
Till we made us gods of granite, and a Law that we believed.

Then we made us camps and cities, for our cattle, for our wives.
And we found us gold and silver, and we purchased power with lives.
And we made us ships and seamen. Master craftsmen we became.
And we wrought us arts and letters; blew a bubble that was fame

And our strength became our weakness. We were wasted in the night.
And we lost the stars in lewdness that blasphemed all law and light.
And we bred us filth and fevers till our children were as slaves
In the streets of dying cities, and our gods we laid in graves.

Still we lusted for the open, for the sea, and for the sun.
There we marveled at the mountains and the deeds that men have done.
There we sought a Voice, a Vision; till our doctors of disease
Out of travail pangs of ages brought to birth a Soul that sees:

Made a mind that masters slowly want and weakness, storm and time:
Wrests her secrets from the midnight; fills all space with rhythm and rhyme:
Tears the rotting veils of vision from its Truth it dares to face·
Sees in man his own salvation, finds in fear its last disgrace.

Binds new burdens on the strong, and sets them sterner handicaps;
Spends their strength in ceaseless striving till they meet the great Perhaps;
Lends itself to lift the fallen in its last crusade of light.
For the mind of man is marching past perdition through the night.

John Curtis Underwood, 1874–

1003. MAN'S DESTINY

From "Paracelsus," Pt. V

Progress is
The law of life, man is not Man as yet.
Nor shall I deem his object served, his end
Attained, his genuine strength put fairly fortn,
While only here and there a star dispels
The darkness, here and there a towering mind
O'erlooks its prostrate fellows: when the host
Is out at once to the despair of night,
When all mankind alike is perfected,
Equal in full-blown powers—then, not till then,
I say, begins man's general infancy.
For wherefore make account of feverish starts
Of restless members of a dormant whole,
Impatient nerves which quiver while the body
Slumbers as in a grave? Oh, long ago
The brow was twitched, the tremulous lids astir,
The peaceful mouth disturbed; half uttered speech
Ruffled the lip, and then the teeth were set,
The breath drawn sharp, the strong right-hand clenched stronger,

As it would pluck a lion by the jaw;
The glorious creature laughed out, even in sleep!
But when full roused, each giant-limb awake,
Each sinew strung, the great heart pulsing fast,
He shall start up and stand on his own earth,
Then shall his long triumphant march begin,
Thence shall his being date,—thus wholly roused,
What he achieves shall be set down to him.
When all the race is perfected alike
As man, that is; all tended to mankind,
And, man produced, all has its end thus far:
But in completed man begins anew
A tendency to God. Prognostics told
Man's near approach; so in man's self arise
August anticipations, symbols, types
Of a dim splendor ever on before
In that eternal circle life pursues.
For men begin to pass their nature's bound,
And find new hopes and cares which fast supplant
Their proper joys and griefs; they grow too great
For narrow creeds of right and wrong, which fade
Before the unmeasured thirst for good: while peace
Rises within them ever more and more.
Such men are even now upon the earth,
Serene amid the half-formed creatures round
Who should be saved by them and joined with them.

Robert Browning, 1812–1889

1004. ONWARD AND UPWARD

I pass the vale. I breast the steep.
  I bear the cross: the cross bears me.
Light leads me on to light. I weep
  For joy at what I hope to see

When, scaled at last the arduous height,
  For every painful step I trod,
I traverse worlds on worlds of light,
  And pierce some deeper depth of God.

John Charles Earle, 1824–1903

1005. THERE IS A BEAUTY

From "The Largest Life"

There is a beauty at the goal of life,
  A beauty growing since the world began,
Through every age and race, through lapse and strife,
  Till the great human soul complete her span.
Beneath the waves of storm that lash and burn,
  The currents of blind passion that appall,
To listen and keep watch till we discern
  The tide of sovereign truth that guides it all;
So to address our spirits to the height,
  And so attune them to the valiant whole,
That the great light be clearer for our light,

And the great soul the stronger for our soul:
To have done this is to have lived, though fame
Remember us with no familiar name.

Archibald Lampman, 1861–1899

1006. ETERNAL HOPE

Eternal Hope! When yonder spheres, sublime,
Pealed their first notes to sound the march of Time,
Thy joyous youth began,—but not to fade.
When all the sister planets have decayed;
When, wrapped in fire, the realms of ether glow,
And Heaven's last thunder shakes the world below,
Thou, undismayed, shalt o'er the ruins smile,
And light thy torch at Nature's funeral pile.

Author unknown

1007. From CONTEMPLATIONS

When I behold the heavens as in their prime,
And then the earth, though old, still clad in green,
The stones and trees insensible of time,
Nor age nor wrinkle on their front are seen;
If winter come, and greenness then do fade,
A spring returns, and they more youthful made;
But man grows old, lies down, remains where once he's laid.

By birth more noble than those creatures all,
Yet seems by nature and by custom cursed—
No sooner born but grief and care makes fall
That state obliterate he had at first;
Nor youth, nor strength, nor wisdom spring again,
Nor habitations long their names retain,
But in oblivion to the final day remain.

Shall I then praise the heavens, the trees, the earth,
Because their beauty and their strength last longer?
Shall I wish therefor never to had birth,
Because they're bigger and their bodies stronger?
Nay, they shall darken, perish, fade, and die,
And when unmade so ever shall they lie;
But man was made for endless immortality.

Anne Bradstreet, 1612–1672

1008. I KNOW I AM DEATHLESS

From "Song of Myself," 20

I know I am deathless;
I know this orbit of mine cannot be swept by a carpenter's compass;
I know I shall not pass like a child's curlacue cut with a burnt stick at night.

I know I am august;
I do not trouble my spirit to vindicate itself or be understood;
I see that the elementary laws never apologize. . . .

I exist as I am—that is enough;
If no other in the world be aware, I sit content;
And if each and all be aware I sit content.

One world is aware, and by far the largest to me, and that is myself;
And whether I come to my own to-day, or in ten thousand or ten million years,
I can cheerfully take it now, or with equal cheerfulness I can wait.

My foothold is tenon'd and mortis'd in granite;
I laugh at what you call dissolution;
And I know the amplitude of time.

Walt Whitman, 1819–1892

1009. PATIENT IS TIME

From "The Pageant of Man"

Patient is time: it knows that truth will stand
Against all tempests, like the iron core
Of the firm earth; that beauty's luminous ore
Shall still remain, though many a raiding hand
Crumble to dust; that love will surge and soar
Across the universe like pulsing light,
Though hatred snarl, wolves prowl, and scorpions bite.

Patient is time!—and what if cyclones slay
With smoke-grim funnels? What if breakers smash
At pillars of the land, and torrents splash
Over the fields, with lips of muddy spray?
That which is real is real, though planets crash
And eons die, and shall endure unchanged
When continents and their oceans are estranged!

❖

So be not sad if time seem long and slow.
Too often man, forgetting light and hope,
Is like a searcher at a microscope,
Whose world is an atomic phantom-show.
The master Workman does not halt nor grope,
But builds, and builds, and subtly builds again
In ways unrecognized, unknown to men.

Stanton A. Coblentz, 1896–

1010. "WHERE GOEST THOU?"

You say, "Where goest thou?" I cannot tell,
And still go on. If but the way be straight
I cannot go amiss: before me lies
Dawn and the day: the night behind me: that
Suffices me: I break the bounds: I see,
And nothing more; believe and nothing less.
My future is not one of my concerns.

Victor Hugo, 1802–1885

1011. THE UNKNOWN SCULPTOR

What sculptor carved the arches of a tree
And gave the rocks their mossy cameos?
Turned the soft-curling eyelids of the rose,
And raised the beetling ridges of the sea?—
Thus the old wonder flashes over me,
When under yellowing domes where autumn blows
Or in the summer woodlands' lulled repose
I bow before the timeless mystery.

No answer comes—except this word alone:
That power which scatters stars across the dark,
Notches the hills, and guides the firefly's spark—
Surely, we may not deem it all unknown,
Nor hold the arm that tends the worm and stone
Leads mankind finally to a dead-sea mark.

Stanton A. Coblentz, 1896–

1012. IN HARMONY WITH NATURE

TO A PREACHER

"In harmony with Nature?" Restless fool,
Who with such heat dost preach what were to thee,
When true, the last impossibility—
To be like Nature strong, like Nature cool!

Know, man hath all which Nature hath, but more,
And in that *more* lie all his hopes of good.
Nature is cruel, man is sick of blood;
Nature is stubborn, man would fain adore;

Nature is fickle, man hath need of rest;
Nature forgives no debt, and fears no grave;
Man would be mild, and with safe conscience blest.

Man must begin, know this, where Nature ends;
Nature and man can never be fast friends.
Fool, if thou canst not pass her, rest her slave!

Matthew Arnold, 1822–1888

1013. A PSALM OF CONFIDENCE

The spirit of man shall triumph and reign o'er all the earth.
The earth was made for Man, he is heir to all that therein is.
He is the end of creation, the purpose of the ages since the dawn of time.
He is the fulfillment of all prophecy and in himself the goal of every great hope born in high desire.

Who art Thou, O Spirit of Man?
Thou art the Child of the Infinite, in thy nostrils is the breath of God.
Thou didst come at Love's behest, yea! to fulfill the Love of the Eternal didst Thou come.
Yet Man's beginnings were in lowliness, in nature akin to that of the brute.
His body and appetite bore the marks of the beast, yet in his soul was the unquenchable Spark of Divine Fire.
His ascending hath been with pain, with struggle and conflict hath he marched toward the Ideal.
At times he hath turned his face away from the promise of Destiny.
He hath given reins to the lust of the brute; he hath appeared at times as the child of Hate.
He hath forgotten his Divine Origin, he hath forsaken the dream of Eternal Love.
Then hath he lifted his hands against his fellows and war and bloodshed have dwelt upon the earth.
In moments of blind passion he hath destroyed the work of his own hands, the fruit of the centuries hath he cast to the winds.
He hath marred the Divine Image, deaf to the call of the promise of God.
Upon the altars of Self hath he sacrificed Brotherhood, and ruled by avarice and greed he hath slain Justice and Right.
Thus have wickedness and sin dwelt in his midst, and his soul hath been chained in the bondage of low desires.
Yet all this could not destroy the unquenchable Spark of Divine Fire.
For it belongs to the Eternal and that which is Eternal cannot die.
Therefore, great though Thy shortcomings, manifold though Thy failures, wicked though Thy crimes,
I will not despair, O Spirit of Man!
Thou canst not forever deny the God that is within Thee, nor turn Thy back upon the Ideal.
Though Thou destroyest fairest hopes, yet shall they live again.
Though Thou returnest to the level of the beast, Thou shalt arise to the heights of Thy Divine Humanity.
For the Spirit of Man breathes the untiring purpose of the Living God and to the fulfillment of that purpose the whole creation moves.

Horace Westwood, 1884–

1014. ON A STEAMSHIP

All night, without the gates of slumber lying,
I listen to the joy of falling water,
And to the throbbing of an iron heart.
In ages past, men went upon the sea,
Waiting the pleasure of the chainless winds;
But now the course is laid, the billows part;
Mankind has spoken: "Let the ship go there!"

I am grown haggard and forlorn, from dreams
That haunt me, of the time that is to be,
When man shall cease from wantonness and strife,
And lay his law upon the course of things.
Then shall he live no more on sufferance,
An accident, the prey of powers blind;
The untamed giants of nature shall bow down—
The tides, the tempest and the lightning cease
From mockery and destruction, and be turned
Unto the making of the soul of man.

Upton Sinclair, 1878–

1015. EARTH IS ENOUGH

We men of Earth have here the stuff
Of Paradise—we have enough!
We need no other stones to build
The Temple of the Unfulfilled—
No other ivory for the doors—
No other marble for the floors—
No other cedar for the beam
And dome of man's immortal dream.

Here on the paths of every-day—
Here on the common human way
Is all the stuff the gods would take
To build a Heaven, to mold and make
New Edens. Ours the stuff sublime
To build Eternity in time!

Edwin Markham, 1852–1940

1016. MAN

We are born and pass on so quickly!
Those of us who sail upon rough seas;
Who slyly amass great wealth;
Who preach breathlessly of God;
Who shout songs unto all the world.
We are born, pass on, and are forgotten.

And yet, in the combination of our littleness
There looms a vast greatness:
We alter the face of the earth;
We subdue the rivers and oceans;
We transcend and encompass the skies!
We are born, pass on and our works are not
forgotten!

Marvin Stevens, contemporary American

1017. GREATNESS PASSING BY

When the high heart we magnify,
And the clear vision celebrate,
And worship greatness passing by,
Ourselves are great.

John Drinkwater, 1882–1937

1018. THE WAY TO POWER

From "Œnone"

Self-reverence, self-knowledge, self-control,
These three alone lead life to sovereign power.
Yet not for power (power of herself
Would come uncall'd for) but to live by law,
Acting the law we live by without fear;
And, because right is right, to follow right
Were wisdom in the scorn of consequence.

Alfred Tennyson, 1809–1892

1019. THE SUPERMAN

He will come;
I know not when, or how;
But he will walk breast-high with God, stepping among the stars.
Clothed in light and crowned with glory he will stride down the Milky Way,
Creating with a thought, building with a word.

A hundred million ages it may be until he comes; what does it matter?
Consider the deliberate stars—how eternity waits their fulfilments.
A hundred million ages, and yet, sometimes,
Here and now, in these small, primeval days—in this dull gloaming of creation's dawn—
Here and now, sometimes, there crackles out a tiny shimmering spark,
Some hint in our blind, protoplasmic lives,
Of that far, infinite torch
Whose ray shall one day touch the utmost reaches of space
Where life is born.

One that has made brotherhood with the eagle and the hawk;
One that has made voices speak across the emptiness;
One that has laid cheer and comfort to the tired heart—
These and a thousand others are the prophecy:
These tell of the day
When the poor expedient of birth and the sorry trouble of dying have been dismissed,
And all the sad adventures of the body are long forgot.
Walking as angels walk, but greater than the angels,
He that will come will know not space nor time, nor any limitation,
But will step across the sky, infinite, supreme—one with God.

Albert Bigelow Paine, 1861–1937

1020. RESPICE FINEM

My soul, sit thou a patient looker-on;
Judge not the Play before the Play is done;
Her Plot has many changes; every day
Speaks a new scene; the last act crowns the
Play.

Francis Quarles, 1592–1644

1021. From MORALITY

We cannot kindle when we will
The fire which in the heart resides,
The spirit bloweth and is still;
In mystery our soul abides:
But tasks in hours of insight willed
Can be through hours of gloom fulfilled.

With aching hands and bleeding feet
We dig and heap, lay stone on stone;
We bear the burden and the heat
Of the long day, and wish 'twere done.
Not till the hours of light return,
All we have built do we discern.

Matthew Arnold, 1822–1888

1022. BEAR UP AWHILE

Ye good distress'd!
Ye noble few! who here unbending stand
Beneath Life's pressure, yet bear up awhile,
And what your bounded view, which only saw
A little part, deem'd evil, is no more;
The storms of wintry Time will quickly pass,
And one unbounded Spring encircle all.

James Thomson, 1834–1882

1023. DESTINY

Somewhere there waiteth in this world of ours
For one lone soul, another lonely soul—

Each chasing each through all the weary hours,
  And meeting strangely at one sudden goal;
Then blend they—like green leaves with golden flowers,
  Into one beautiful and perfect whole—
And life's long night is ended, and the way
Lies open onward to eternal day.

Edwin Arnold, 1832–1904

1024. LOVE

From "The Song of Solomon," 8: 6–7

Set me as a seal upon thine heart, as a seal upon thine arm:
  for love is strong as death;
  jealousy is cruel as the grave:
  the coals thereof are coals of fire, which hath a most vehement flame.
Many waters cannot quench love, neither can the floods drown it:
  if a man would give all the substance of his house for love, it would utterly be contemned.

King James Version, 1611

1025. LOVE SERVICEABLE

From "The Angel In The House"

What measure Fate to him did mete
  Is not the lover's noble care;
He's heart-sick with a longing sweet
  To make her happy as she's fair.
Oh, misery, should she him refuse,
  And so her dearest good mistake!
His own success he thus pursues
  With frantic zeal for her sole sake.
To lose her were his life to blight,
  Being lost to hers; to make her his,
Except as helping her delight,
  He calls but accidental bliss;
And, holding life as so much pelf
  To buy her posies, learns this lore:
He does not rightly love himself
  Who does not love another more.

Coventry Patmore, 1823–1896

1026. TRUE LOVE

True love is but a humble, low-born thing,
And hath its food served up in earthenware;
It is a thing to walk with, hand in hand,
Through the everydayness of this work-day world,
Baring its tender feet to every roughness,
Yet letting not one heart-beat go astray
From beauty's law of plainness and content—
A simple, fireside thing, whose quiet smile
Can warm earth's poorest hovel to a home.

James Russell Lowell, 1819–1891

1027. IF THOU MUST LOVE ME[1]

From "Sonnets from the Portuguese"

XIV

If thou must love me, let it be for naught
Except for love's sake only. Do not say,
"I love her for her smile—her look—her way
Of speaking gently,—for a trick of thought
That falls in well with mine, and certes brought
A sense of pleasant ease on such a day"—
For these things in themselves, Belovèd, may
Be changed, or change for thee,—and love, so wrought,
May be unwrought so. Neither love me for
Thine own dear pity's wiping my cheeks dry,—
A creature might forget to weep, who bore
Thy comfort long, and lose thy love thereby!
But love me for love's sake, that evermore
Thou mayst love on, through love's eternity.

Elizabeth Barrett Browning, 1806–1861

[1] These sonnets are not, as sometimes supposed, translations from the Portuguese. On account of her olive complexion Elizabeth Barrett was frequently referred to by Robert Browning as "my Portuguese," which prompted her later when she became his wife to show him the now famous sonnets, entitling them "Sonnets from the Portuguese."

1028. HOW DO I LOVE THEE?

From "Sonnets from the Portuguese"

XLIII

How do I love thee? Let me count the ways.
I love thee to the depth and breadth and height
My soul can reach, when feeling out of sight
For the ends of Being and ideal Grace.
I love thee to the level of everyday's
Most quiet need, by sun and candlelight.
I love thee freely, as men strive for Right;
I love thee purely, as they turn from Praise.
I love thee with the passion put to use
In my old griefs, and with my childhood's faith.
I love thee with a love I seemed to lose
With my lost saints,—I love thee with the breath,
Smiles, tears, of all my life!—and, if God choose,
I shall but love thee better after death.

Elizabeth Barrett Browning, 1806–1861

1029. FOR THY SWEET LOVE

Sonnet 29

When in disgrace with fortune and men's eyes
I all alone beweep my outcast state,
And trouble deaf heaven with my bootless cries,
And look upon myself and curse my fate,
Wishing me like to one more rich in hope,
Featured like him, like him with friends possessed,
Desiring this man's art, and that man's scope,
With what I most enjoy contented least;
Yet in these thoughts myself almost despising,
Haply I think on thee—and then my state,
Like to the lark at break of day arising
From sullen earth, sings hymns at heaven's gate;
For thy sweet love remembered, such wealth brings
That then I scorn to change my state with kings.

William Shakespeare, 1564–1616

1030. THE TRUTHS THAT NEVER CAN BE PROVED

From "In Memoriam"

CXXIX

Dear friend, far off, my lost desire,
So far, so near in woe and weal,
O loved the most, when most I feel
There is a lower and a higher;

Known and unknown, human, divine;
Sweet human hand and lips and eye;
Dear heavenly friend that canst not die,
Mine, mine, for ever, ever mine;

Strange friend, past, present and to be;
Loved deeplier, darklier understood;
Behold, I dream a dream of good,
And mingle all the world with thee.

CXXX

Thy voice is on the rolling air;
  I hear thee where the waters run;
  Thou standest in the rising sun,
And in the setting thou art fair.

What art thou then? I cannot guess;
  But tho' I seem in star and flower
  To feel thee some diffusive power,
I do not therefore love thee less.

My love involves the love before;
  My love is vaster passion now;
  Tho' mix'd with God and Nature thou,
I seem to love thee more and more.

Far off thou art, but ever nigh;
  I have thee still, and I rejoice;
  I prosper, circled with thy voice;
I shall not lose thee tho' I die.

CXXXI

O living will that shalt endure
  When all that seems shall suffer shock,
  Rise in the spiritual rock,
Flow thro' our deeds and make them pure,

That we may lift from out of dust
  A voice as unto him that hears,
  A cry above the conquer'd years
To one that with us works, and trust,

With faith that comes of self-control,
  The truths that never can be proved
  Until we close with all we loved,
And all we flow from, soul in soul.

❖

That God, which ever lives and loves,
  One God, one law, one element,
  And one far-off divine event,
To which the whole creation moves.

Alfred Tennyson, 1809–1892

1031. JOHN ANDERSON MY JO

John Anderson my jo,[1] John,
  When we were first acquent,
Your locks were like the raven,
  Your bonnie brow was brent;
But now your brow is beld, John,
  Your locks are like the snaw;
But blessings on your frosty pow,
  John Anderson my jo.

John Anderson my jo, John,
  We clamb the hill thegither,
And monie a cantie day, John,
  We've had wi' ane anither;
Now we maun totter down, John,
  And hand in hand we'll go,
And sleep thegither at the foot,
  John Anderson my jo!

Robert Burns, 1759–1796

[1] "Jo" means "dear," "beloved," "darling."

1032. LOVE

Come, let us make love deathless, thou and I,
Seeing that our footing on earth is brief. . . .

Herbert Trench, 1865–1923

1033. RUTH TO NAOMI

Ruth 1: 16–17

Intreat me not to leave thee,
  And to return from following after thee:
For whither thou goest, I will go;
  And where thou lodgest, I will lodge;
Thy people shall be my people,
  And thy God my God;
Where thou diest, will I die,
  And there will I be buried:
The LORD do so to me,
And more also,
  If aught but death part thee and me.

Moulton: The Modern Reader's Bible, 1895

1034. LOVE

I love you,
Not only for what you are,
But for what I am
When I am with you.

I love you,
Not only for what
You have made of yourself,
But for what
You are making of me.

I love you
For the part of me
That you bring out;
I love you
For putting your hand
Into my heaped-up heart
And passing over
All the foolish, weak things
That you can't help
Dimly seeing there,
And for drawing out
Into the light
All the beautiful belongings
That no one else had looked
Quite far enough to find.

I love you because you
Are helping me to make
Of the lumber of my life
Not a tavern
But a temple;
Out of the works
Of my every day
Not a reproach
But a song. . . .

Author unknown

1035. BELOVÈD

From "Sonnets from the Portuguese"

XX

Belovèd, my Belovèd, when I think
That thou wast in the world a year ago,
What time I sat alone here in the snow
And saw no footprint, heard the silence sink
No moment at thy voice, but, link by link,
Went counting all my chains as if that so
They never could fall off at any blow
Struck by thy possible hand,—why, thus I drink
Of life's great cup of wonder! Wonderful,
Never to feel thee thrill the day or night
With personal act or speech,—nor ever cull
Some prescience of thee with the blossoms white
Thou sawest growing! Atheists are as dull,
Who cannot guess God's presence out of sight.

Elizabeth Barrett Browning, 1806–1861

1036. SONG

Let my voice ring out and over the earth,
  Through all the grief and strife,
With a golden joy in a silver mirth:
  Thank God for life!

Let my voice swell out through the great abyss
  To the azure dome above,
With a chord of faith in the harp of bliss:
  Thank God for Love!

Let my voice thrill out beneath and above,
  The whole world through
O my Love and Life, O my Life and Love,
  Thank God for you!

James Thomson, 1834–1882

1037. From THE WHITE CLIFFS

Young and in love—how magical the phrase!
How magical the fact! Who has not yearned
Over young lovers when to their amaze
They fall in love, and find their love returned,
And the lights brighten, and their eyes are clear
To see God's image in their common clay.
Is it the music of the spheres they hear?
Is it the prelude to that noble play
The drama of Joined Lives?

Alice Duer Miller, 1874–1942

1038. HOLY MATRIMONY

The voice that breathed o'er Eden,
  That earliest wedding-day,
The primal marriage blessing,
  It hath not passed away.

Still in the pure espousal
  Of Christian man and maid,
The holy Three are with us,
  The threefold grace is said.

For dower of blessèd children,
  For love and faith's sweet sake,
For high mysterious union,
  Which naught on earth may break.

Be present, awful Father,
  To give away this bride,
As Eve thou gav'st to Adam
  Out of his own pierced side:

Be present, Son of Mary,
  To join their loving hands,
As thou didst bind two natures
  In thine eternal bands:

Be present, Holiest Spirit,
  To bless them as they kneel,
As thou for Christ, the Bridegroom,
  The heavenly Spouse dost seal.

Oh, spread thy pure wing o'er them,
  Let no ill power find place,
When onward to thine altar
  The hallowed path they trace,

To cast their crowns before thee
  In perfect sacrifice,
Till to the home of gladness
  With Christ's own Bride they rise.

John Keble, 1792–1866

1039. O GOD OF LOVE, TO THEE WE BOW

O God of Love, to Thee we bow,
And pray for these before Thee now,
That closely knit in holy vow,
They may in Thee be one.

When days are filled with pure delight,
When paths are plain and skies are bright,
Walking by faith and not by sight,
May they in Thee be one.

When stormy winds fulfil Thy will,
And all their good seems turned to ill,
Then, trusting Thee completely still,
May they in Thee be one.

What e'er in life shall be their share
Of quickening joy or burdening care,
In power to do and grace to bear,
May they in Thee be one.

Eternal Love, with them abide;
In Thee forever may they hide,
For even death cannot divide
Those whom Thou makest one.

William Vaughan Jenkins, 1868–1920

1040. A WEDDING HYMN

Jesus, stand beside them
  On this day of days,
That in happy wedlock
  They may live always.

Join their hands together,
  And their hearts make one;
Guard the troth now plighted
  And the life begun.

On their pleasant homestead
  Let Thy radiance rest;
Making joy and sorrow
  By Thy presence blest.

Gild their common duties
  With a light divine,
As, in Cana, water
  Thou didst change to wine.

Leave them nor forsake them;
  Ever be their Friend;
Guarding, guiding, blessing
  To their journey's end.

Thomas Tiplady, 1882–

1041. NOT OURS THE VOWS

Not ours the vows of such as plight
  Their troth in sunny weather,
While leaves are green, and skies are bright,
  To walk on flowers together.

But we have loved as those who tread
  The thorny path of sorrow,
With clouds above, and cause to dread
  Yet deeper gloom to-morrow.

That thorny path, those stormy skies,
  Have drawn our spirits nearer;
And rendered us, by sorrow's ties,
  Each to the other dearer.

Love, born in hours of joy and mirth,
  With mirth and joy may perish;
That to which darker hours gave birth,
  Still more and more we cherish.

It looks beyond the clouds of time,
  And through death's shadowy portal;
Made by adversity sublime,
  By faith and hope immortal.

Bernard Barton, 1784–1849

1042. O PERFECT LOVE

O perfect Love, all human thought transcending,
Lowly we kneel in prayer before Thy throne,
That theirs may be the love which knows no ending,
Whom Thou forever more dost join in one.

O perfect Life, be Thou their full assurance
Of tender charity and steadfast faith,
Of patient hope, and quiet, brave endurance,
With child-like trust that fears nor pain nor death.

Grant them the joy which brightens earthly sorrow;
Grant them the peace which calms all earthly strife,
And to life's day the glorious unknown morrow
That dawns upon eternal love and life.

Dorothy F. Gurney, 1858–1932

1043. From A WEDDING HYMN

O Thou, Who love in mercy hast created
To be the joy and comfort of our way,
Be present now to bind in happy wedlock
These whom we bring in love and prayer to-day.

Be as a ring of sacred flame around them
To guard their hearts and 'stablish peace within;
May every joy and sorrow serve to strengthen
Their love for Thee and purify from sin.

Be with them in the tasks that lie before them;
May faith and hope and love attend their way;
Till, labour ended, evening shadows gather
And call them to the land of endless day.

Thomas Tiplady, 1882–

1044. TRUE LOVE

Sonnet 116

Let me not to the marriage of true minds
Admit impediments. Love is not love
Which alters when it alteration finds,
Or bends with the remover to remove.
O, no! it is an ever-fixèd mark,
That looks on tempests and is never shaken;
It is the star to every wandering bark,
Whose worth's unknown, although his height be taken.
Love's not Time's fool, though rosy lips and cheeks
Within his bending sickle's compass come;
Love alters not with his brief hours and weeks,
But bears it out even to the edge of doom.
If this be error and upon me proved,
I never writ, nor no man ever loved.

William Shakespeare, 1564–1616

1045. THEIR CONSCIENCE AS THEIR KING

From "Guinevere"

I made them lay their hands in mine and swear
To reverence the King, as if he were
Their conscience, and their conscience as their King,
To break the heathen and uphold the Christ,
To ride abroad redressing human wrongs,
To speak no slander, no, nor listen to it,
To honor his own word as if his God's,
To lead sweet lives of purest chastity,
To love one maiden only, cleave to her,
And worship her by years of noble deeds,
Until they won her; for indeed I knew
Of no more subtle master under heaven
Than is the maiden passion for a maid,
Not only to keep down the base in man,
But teach high thought, and amiable words
And courtliness, and the desire of fame,
And love of truth, and all that makes a man.

Alfred Tennyson, 1809–1892

1046. THE NEWLY-WEDDED

Now the rite is duly done,
  Now the word is spoken,
And the spell has made us one
  Which may ne'er be broken;
Rest we, dearest, in our home,
  Roam we o'er the heather:
We shall rest, and we shall roam
  Shall we not? together.

From this hour the summer rose
  Sweeter breathes to charm us;
From this hour the winter snows
  Lighter fall to harm us:
Fair or foul—on land or sea—
  Come the wind or weather,
Best and worst, whate'er they be,
  We shall share together.

Death, who friend from friend can part,
  Brother rend from brother,
Shall but link us, heart and heart,
  Closer to each other:
We will call his anger play,
  Deem his dart a feather,
When we meet him on our way
  Hand in hand together.

Winthrop Mackworth Praed, 1802–1839

1047. GOOD NIGHT

Good-Night. Good-night. Ah, good the night
That wraps thee in its silver light.
Good-night. No night is good for me
That does not hold a thought of thee.
      Good-night.
Good-night. Be every night as sweet
As that which made our love complete,
Till that last night when death shall be
One brief "Good-night," for thee and me.
      Good-night.

S. Weir Mitchell, 1829–1914

1048. GOD KEEP YOU

God keep you, dearest, all this lonely night:
  The winds are still,
  The moon drops down behind the western hill;
God keep you safely, dearest, till the light.

God keep you then when slumber melts away,
  And care and strife
  Take up new arms to fret our waking life,
God keep you through the battle of the day.

God keep you. Nay, beloved soul, how vain,
  How poor is prayer!
I can but say again, and yet again,
  God keep you every time and everywhere.

Madeline Bridges, 1844–1920

1049. MARRIAGE

Going my way of old,
  Contented more or less,
I dreamt not life could hold
  Such happiness.

I dreamt not that love's way
  Could keep the golden height
Day after happy day,
  Night after night.

Wilfred Wilson Gibson, 1878?–

1050. GOLDEN WEDDING

This is no fallow field through which we travel,
  No barren land made waste by nature's rust;
This is no grassless plain where sand and gravel
  Are trod upon and ground to atom dust.

This is, instead, the fertile field of living
  Where you and I have scattered precious seed;
Where we have raised affection, and are giving,
  One to the other, what our spirits need.

Our grain is cut—the loam of life is mellow,
  A kindly sun is beaming from above.
We've reaped abundant years of ripened yellow,
  For crops are rich when two have planted love.

William W. Pratt, contemporary American

1051. THE VIRTUOUS WIFE

Proverbs 31: 10–31

Who can find a virtuous woman?
  for her price is far above rubies.
The heart of her husband doth safely trust in her,
  so that he shall have no need of spoil.
She will do him good and not evil
  all the days of her life.
She seeketh wool, and flax,
  and worketh willingly with her hands.
She is like the merchants' ships;
  she bringeth her food from afar.
She riseth also while it is yet night,
  and giveth meat to her household, and a portion to her maidens.
She considereth a field, and buyeth it:
  with the fruit of her hands she planteth a vineyard.
She girdeth her loins with strength,
  and strengtheneth her arms.
She perceiveth that her merchandise is good:
  her candle goeth not out by night.
She layeth her hands to the spindle,
  and her hands hold the distaff.
She stretcheth out her hand to the poor;
  yea, she reacheth forth her hands to the needy.
She is not afraid of the snow for her household:
  for all her household are clothed with scarlet.
She maketh herself coverings of tapestry;
  her clothing is silk and purple.
Her husband is known in the gates,
  when he sitteth among the elders of the land.
She maketh fine linen, and selleth it;
  and delivereth girdles unto the merchant.
Strength and honour are her clothing;
  and she shall rejoice in time to come.
She openeth her mouth with wisdom;
  and in her tongue is the law of kindness.
She looketh well to the ways of her household,
  and eateth not the bread of idleness.
Her children arise up, and call her blessed;
  her husband also, and he praiseth her.
Many daughters have done virtuously,
  but thou excellest them all.
Favour is deceitful, and beauty is vain:

but a woman that feareth the Lord, she shall be
praised.
Give her of the fruit of her hands;
and let her own works praise her in the gates.
King James Version, 1611

1052. A PRAYER

I pray for you, and yet I do not frame
In words the thousand wishes of my heart.
It is a prayer only to speak your name,
To think of you when we are far apart.
God has not need of words. He hears our love,
And tho' my lips are mute, I bow my head,
And know he leans to listen from above,
And understand the things that are not said,
For love is prayer—and so prayers for you
Mount upward unto Him eternally—
They are not many, and they are not few,
All are as one that ever seems to be.
Thus do I pray for you, and cannot say
When I begin, or when I cease, to pray.
Mary Dixon Thayer, 1897–

1053. LOVE SONG

Distance nor death shall part us, dear,
Nor yet the traitor word;
And love shall live within our home
As blithe as any bird.

The sight of you is in my eyes,
Your touch is in my hand;
They cannot part us now, my love,
With miles of weary land.

Man with his sword and Death his scythe,
Are but the tricks of time,
To tease me with the empty years
Before we shared one name.
Henry Treece, 1912–

1054. TO MY WIFE

Trusty, dusky, vivid, true,
With eyes of gold and bramble-dew,
Steel true and blade straight
The Great Artificer made my mate

Honor, anger, valor, fire,
A love that life could never tire,
Death quench 'or evil stir,
The Mighty Master gave to her.

Teacher, tender comrade, wife,
A fellow-farer true through life,
Heart-whole and soul-free,
The August Father gave to me.
Robert Louis Stevenson, 1850–1894

1055. THE WORD

My friend, my bonny friend, when we are old,
And hand and hand go tottering down the hill,
May we be rich in love's refined gold,
May love's gold coin be current with us still.
May love be sweeter for the vanished days,
And your most perfect beauty still as dear
As when your troubled singer stood at gaze
In the dear March of a most sacred year.
May what we are be all we might have been,
And that potential, perfect, O my friend,
And may there still be many sheafs to glean
In our love's acre, comrade, till the end.
And may we find, when ended is the page,
Death but a tavern on our pilgrimage.
John Masefield, 1875–

1056. PRAYER OF ANY HUSBAND

Lord, may there be no moment in her life
When she regrets that she became my wife,
And keep her dear eyes just a trifle blind
To my defects, and to my failings kind!

Help me to do the utmost that I can
To prove myself her measure of a man,
But, if I often fail as mortals may,
Grant that she never sees my feet of clay!

And let her make allowance—now and then—
That we are only grown-up boys, we men,
So, loving all our children, she will see,
Sometimes, a remnant of the child in me!

Since years must bring to all their load of care,
Let us together every burden bear,
And when Death beckons one its path along,
May not the two of us be parted long!
Mazie V. Caruthers

1057. NEVERMORE ALONE

Go from me. Yet I feel that I shall stand
Henceforward in thy shadow. Nevermore
Alone upon the threshold of my door
Of individual life I shall command
The uses of my soul, nor lift my hand
Serenely in the sunshine as before,
Without the sense of that which I forebore—
Thy touch upon the palm. The widest land
Doom takes to part us, leaves thy heart in mine
With pulses that beat double. What I do
And what I dream include thee, as the wine
Must taste of its own grapes. And when I sue
God for myself, He hears that name of thine,
And sees within my eyes the tears of two.

Elizabeth Barrett Browning, 1806–1861

1058. DOVER BEACH

The sea is calm to-night.
The tide is full, the moon lies fair
Upon the straits;—on the French coast the light
Gleams and is gone; the cliffs of England stand,
Glimmering and vast, out in the tranquil bay.
Come to the window, sweet is the night-air!

Only, from the long line of spray
Where the sea meets the moon-blanch'd land,
Listen! you hear the grating roar
Of pebbles which the waves draw back, and fling,
At their return, up the high strand,
Begin, and cease, and then again begin,
With tremulous cadence slow, and bring
The eternal note of sadness in.

Sophocles long ago
Heard it on the Ægean, and it brought
Into his mind the turbid ebb and flow
Of human misery; we
Find also in the sound a thought,
Hearing it by this distant northern sea.

The Sea of Faith
Was once, too, at the full, and round earth's shore
Lay like the folds of a bright girdle furled.
But now I only hear
Its melancholy, long, withdrawing roar,
Retreating, to the breath
Of the night-wind, down the vast edges drear
And naked shingles of the world.

Ah, love, let us be true
To one another! for the world, which seems
To lie before us like a land of dreams,
So various, so beautiful, so new,
Hath really neither joy, nor love, nor light,
Nor certitude, nor peace, nor help for pain;
And we are here as on a darkling plain
Swept with confused alarms of struggle and flight,
Where ignorant armies clash by night.

Matthew Arnold, 1822–1888

1059. DITTY

The time was long and long ago,
And we were young, my dear;
The place stands fair in memory's glow,
But it is far from here.

The springtimes fade, the summers come,
Autumn is here once more;
The voice of ecstasy is dumb,
The world goes forth to war;

And what is Time, when Speed is king,
And what is Space to Power?
Who harks now when the thrushes sing,
Or sees the lilacs flower?

But though the flowers and birds were dead,
And all the hours we knew,
And though a hundred years had fled,
I'd still come back to you!

Ted Robinson, contemporary American

1060. WHEN YOU ARE OLD

When you are old and gray and full of sleep
And nodding by the fire, take down this book,
And slowly read, and dream of the soft look
Your eyes had once, and of their shadows deep;

How many loved your moments of glad grace,
And loved your beauty with love false or true;
But one man loved the pilgrim soul in you,
And loved the sorrows of your changing face.

And bending down beside the glowing bars,
  Murmur, a little sadly, how love fled
  And paced upon the mountains overhead,
And hid his face amid a crowd of stars.

William Butler Yeats, 1865–1939

1061. HOME THEY BROUGHT HER WARRIOR DEAD

Song from "The Princess"

Home they brought her warrior dead;
  She nor swooned nor utter'd cry.
All her maidens, watching, said,
  "She must weep or she will die."

Then they praised him, soft and low,
  Call'd him worthy to be loved,
Truest friend and noblest foe;
  Yet she neither spoke nor moved.

Stole a maiden from her place,
  Lightly to the warrior stept,
Took the face-cloth from the face;
  Yet she neither moved nor wept.

Rose a nurse of ninety years,
  Set his child upon her knee;—
Like summer tempest came her tears:—
  "Sweet my child, I live for thee."

Alfred Tennyson, 1809–1892

1062. SMALL SONG

If it were but a wall between us,
The heart might hurtle it,
Or if it were a gateway,
Swing it wide;
A door, our barrier, dim-lit,
I could step inside
And say: "Forgive me, love. . ."
In tenderness
Your answer might be yes,
With pity stirred.
But O, how strange that evermore
Through all our days
Our hearts must go their separate ways
Divided by no mountain's height,
No continent of dark or light,
But by the soundless ocean
Of a word.

Daniel Whitehead Hicky, 1902–

1063. FORBEARANCE

The kindest and the happiest pair
Will find occasion to forbear;
And something, every day they live,
To pity, and perhaps forgive.

William Cowper, 1731–1800

1064. A DREAM

My dear love came to me, and said:
  "God gives me one hour's rest
To spend with thee on earth again:
  How shall we spend it best?"

"Why, as of old," I said; and so
  We quarreled, as of old:
But when I turned to make my peace,
  That one short hour was told.

Stephen Phillips, 1868–1915

1065. FAITH OF OUR MOTHERS

Faith of our mothers, living yet
  In cradle song and bedtime prayer,
In nursery love and fireside lore,
  Thy presence still pervades the air.
Faith of our mothers, living faith,
We will be true to thee till death.

Faith of our mothers, lavish faith,
  The fount of childhood's trust and grace,
O may thy consecration prove
  The wellspring of a nobler race.
Faith of our mothers, lavish faith,
We will be true to thee till death.

Faith of our mothers, guiding faith,
  For youthful longings—youthful doubts,
How blurred our vision, blind our way,
  Thy providential care without.
Faith of our mothers, guiding faith,
We will be true to thee till death.

Faith of our mothers, Christian faith,
  In truth beyond our man-made creeds,
Still serve the home and save the church,
  And breathe thy spirit through our deeds.
Faith of our mothers, Christian faith,
We will be true to thee till death.

Arthur B. Patten, 1920–

1066. THE GREATEST BATTLE THAT EVER WAS FOUGHT

The greatest battle that ever was fought—
Shall I tell you where and when?
On the maps of the world you will find it not:
It was fought by the Mothers of Men.

Not with cannon or battle shot,
With sword or nobler pen;
Not with eloquent word or thought
From the wonderful minds of men;

But deep in a walled-up woman's heart;
A woman that would not yield;
But bravely and patiently bore her part;
Lo! there is the battlefield.

No marshalling troops, no bivouac song,
No banner to gleam and wave;
But, Oh, these battles they last so long—
From babyhood to the grave!

But faithful still as a bridge of stars
She fights in her walled-up town;
Fights on, and on, in the endless wars;
Then silent, unseen goes down!

Ho! ye with banners and battle shot,
With soldiers to shout and praise,
I tell you the kingliest victories fought
Are fought in these silent ways.

Joaquin Miller, 1841–1913

1067. MY ALTAR

I have worshipped in churches and chapels;
I've prayed in the busy street;
I have sought my God and have found him
Where the waves of his ocean beat;
I have knelt in the silent forest
In the shade of some ancient tree;
But the dearest of all my altars
Was raised at my mother's knee.

I have listened to God in his temple;
I've caught his voice in the crowd;
I have heard him speak when the breakers
Were booming long and loud;
Where the winds play soft in the treetops
My father has talked to me;
But I never have heard him clearer
Than I did at my mother's knee.

The things in my life that are worthy
Were born in my mother's breast,
And breathed into mine by the magic
Of the love her life expressed.
The years that have brought me to manhood
Have taken her far from me;
But memory keeps me from straying
Too far from my mother's knee.

God, make me the man of her vision
And purge me of selfishness!
God, keep me true to her standards
And help me to live to bless!
God, hallow the holy impress
Of the days that used to be,
And keep me a pilgrim forever
To the shrine at my mother's knee!

John H. Styles, Jr.

1068. TO MY MOTHER

Because I feel that, in the Heavens above,
The angels, whispering to one another,
Can find, among their burning terms of love,
None so devotional as that of "Mother,"
Therefore by that dear name I long have called you—
You who are more than mother unto me,
And fill my heart of hearts, where Death installed you,
In setting my Virginia's spirit free.

My mother—my own mother, who died early,
Was but the mother of myself; but you
Are mother to the one I loved so dearly,
And thus are dearer than the mother I knew
By that infinity with which my wife
Was dearer to my soul than its soul-life.

Edgar Allan Poe, 1809–1849

1069. TO MOTHER

You painted no Madonnas
On chapel walls in Rome,
But with a touch diviner
You lived one in your home.

You wrote no lofty poems
That critics counted art,
But with a nobler vision
You lived them in your heart.

You carved no shapeless marble
 To some high souled design,
But with a finer sculpture
 You shaped this soul of mine.

You built no great cathedrals
 That centuries applaud
But with a grace exquisite
 Your life cathedraled God.

Had I the gift of Raphael,
 Or Michelangelo,
Oh, what a rare Madonna
 My mother's life would show!

T. W. Fessenden, 1876–

1070. THE BLIND CHILD

I know what mother's face is like,
 Although I cannot see;
It's like the music of a bell;
It's like the roses I can smell—
 Yes, these it's like to me.

I know what father's face is like;
 I'm sure I know it all;
It's like his whistle on the air;
It's like his arms which take such care
 And never let me fall.

And I can tell what God is like—
 The God whom no one sees.
He's everything my parents seem;
He's fairer than my fondest dream,
 And greater than all these.

Author unknown

1071. MOTHER O' MINE

From "The Light That Failed"

If I were hanged on the highest hill,
 Mother o' mine, O mother o' mine!
I know whose love would follow me still,
 Mother o' mine, O mother o' mine!
If I were drowned in the deepest sea,
 Mother o' mine, O mother o' mine!
I know whose tears would come down to me,
 Mother o' mine, O mother o' mine!
If I were damned o'body and soul,
I know whose prayers would make me whole,
 Mother o' mine, O mother o' mine!

Rudyard Kipling, 1865–1936

1072. MOTHER

One wept whose only child was dead,
New-born, ten years ago.
"Weep not; he is in bliss," they said.
She answered, "Even so,

"Ten years ago was born in pain
A child, not now forlorn.
But oh, ten years ago, in vain,
A mother, a mother was born."

Alice Meynell, 1847–1922

1073. THE WATCHER

She always leaned to watch for us,
 Anxious if we were late,
In winter by the window,
 In summer by the gate;

And though we mocked her tenderly,
 Who had such foolish care,
The long way home would seem more safe
 Because she waited there.

Her thoughts were all so full of us,
 She never could forget!
And so I think that where she is
 She must be watching yet,

Waiting till we come home to her,
 Anxious if we are late—
Watching from Heaven's window,
 Leaning from Heaven's gate.

Margaret Widdemer,
contemporary American

1074. MY MOTHER

Who fed me from her gentle breast
And hushed me in her arms to rest,
And on my cheek sweet kisses prest?
  My mother.

❖

Who taught my infant lips to pray,
To love God's holy word and day,
And walk in wisdom's pleasant way?
  My mother.

And can I ever cease to be
Affectionate and kind to thee
Who wast so very kind to me,—
  My mother.

Oh no, the thought I cannot bear;
And if God please my life to spare
I hope I shall reward thy care,
My mother.

When thou art feeble, old and gray,
My healthy arm shall be thy stay,
And I will soothe thy pains away,
My mother.

And when I see thee hang thy head,
'Twill be my turn to watch thy bed,
And tears of sweet affection shed,—
My mother.

Jane Taylor, 1783–1824

1075. A MOTHER'S BIRTHDAY

Lord Jesus, Thou hast known
A mother's love and tender care:
And Thou wilt hear,
While for my own
Mother most dear
I make this birthday prayer.

Protect her life, I pray,
Who gave the gift of life to me;
And may she know,
From day to day,
The deepening glow
Of joy that comes from Thee.

As once upon her breast
Fearless and well content I lay,
So let her heart,
On Thee at rest,
Feel fear depart
And trouble fade away.

Ah, hold her by the hand,
As once her hand held mine;
And though she may
Not understand
Life's winding way,
Lead her in peace divine.

I cannot pay my debt
For all the love that she has given;
But Thou, love's Lord,
Wilt not forget
Her due reward,—
Bless her in earth and heaven.

Henry van Dyke, 1852–1933

1076. A MOTHER'S PRAYER

Father in Heaven, make me wise,
So that my gaze may never meet
A question in my children's eyes.
God keep me always kind and sweet,

And patient, too, before their need;
Let each vexation know its place,
Let gentleness be all my creed,
Let laughter live upon my face!

A mother's day is very long,
There are so many things to do!
But never let me lose my song
Before the hardest day is through.

Margaret E. Sangster,
contemporary American

1077. A MOTHER'S REWARD

I do not ask that you repay
The hours of toil and pain.
The sacrifice of youth and strength
Shall not have been in vain.
I do not ask for gratitude
But only this, my child,
That you shall live your life so well
My gifts be not defiled.

The nights I watched beside your crib,
The years of love and care
Will amply be repaid if once
I see you standing there—
An upright and an honest soul
On whom success has smiled,
That I may say with humble pride
—"THAT is my child!"

Ona Freeman Lathrop,
contemporary American

1078. THE MOTHER'S HYMN

Lord who ordainst for mankind
Benignant toils and tender cares,
We thank thee for the ties that bind
The mother to the child she bears.

We thank thee for the hopes that rise
Within her heart, as, day by day,
The dawning soul, from those young eyes,
Looks with a clearer, steadier ray.

And grateful for the blessing given
  With that dear infant on her knee,
She trains the eye to look to heaven,
  The voice to lisp a prayer to Thee.

Such thanks the blessed Mary gave
  When from her lap the Holy Child,
Sent from on high to seek and save
  The lost of earth, looked up and smiled.

All-Gracious! grant to those who bear
  A mother's charge, the strength and light
To guide the feet that own their care
  In ways of Love and Truth and Right.

William Cullen Bryant, 1794–1878

1079. THE BIBLE

We search the world for truth. We cull
The good, the true, the beautiful,
From graven stone and written scroll,
And all old flower-fields of the soul;
And, weary seekers of the best,
We come back laden from our quest,
To find that all the sages said
Is in the Book our mothers read.

John Greenleaf Whittier, 1807–1892

1080. FAITH OF OUR FATHERS

Faith of our fathers, living still
  In spite of dungeon, fire and sword,
O how our hearts beat high with joy
  Whene'er we hear that glorious word!
Faith of our fathers, holy faith,
  We will be true to thee till death.

Our fathers, chained in prisons dark,
  Were still in heart and conscience free,
And blest would be their children's fate,
  If they, like them, should die for thee:
Faith of our fathers, holy faith,
  We will be true to thee till death.

Faith of our fathers, we will strive
  To win all nations unto thee;
And through the truth that comes from God
  Mankind shall then indeed be free:
Faith of our fathers, holy faith,
  We will be true to thee till death.

Faith of our fathers, we will love
  Both friend and foe in all our strife,
And preach thee, too, as love knows how,
  By kindly words and virtuous life:
Faith of our fathers, holy faith,
  We will be true to thee till death.

Frederick W. Faber, 1814–1863

1081. MY SON

I that had yearned for youth, my own, again,
  And mourned the wasted hours of younger days,
I that had sighed for Spring, for Summer, when
  The snows of Winter covered all my ways—
I that had prayed for years, for only one,
  Have found that prayer answered in my son.

He is myself again, with hopes of old,
  With old temptations and with old desires;
He is myself again—the clay to mold
  Into the man, and all the man aspires.
Who says that youth returns to us no more?
  He is as I was in the days of yore.

In my own days, in my own days of youth,
  Ah, how I wished a comrade and a friend!—
To help me keep the quiet path of truth
  And through temptation my own feet attend.
So shall I journey onward by his side,
  His father—yea, his comrade and his guide.

I that have failed shall shape success in him,
  I that have wandered point the proper path,
I signal when the signal lights are dim,
  A roof to fend him from the storms of wrath—
So we shall journey upward, I and he,
  And he shall be the man I meant to be.

Douglas Malloch, 1877–1938

1082. THE TOYS

My little Son, who look'd from thoughtful eyes
And moved and spoke in quiet grown-up wise,
Having my law the seventh time disobey'd,
I struck him, and dismiss'd
With hard words and unkiss'd,
—His Mother, who was patient, being dead.
Then, fearing lest his grief should hinder sleep,
I visited his bed,
But found him slumbering deep,
With darken'd eyelids, and their lashes yet
From his late sobbing wet.
And I, with moan,
Kissing away his tears, left others of my own;
For, on a table drawn beside his head,
He had put, within his reach,
A box of counters and a red-vein'd stone,
A piece of glass abraded by the beach
And six or seven shells,
A bottle with bluebells,
And two French copper coins, ranged there with careful art,
To comfort his sad heart.
So when that night I pray'd
To God, I wept, and said:
Ah, when at last we lie with trancèd breath,
Not vexing Thee in death,
And Thou rememberest of what toys
We made our joys,
How weakly understood
Thy great commanded good,
Then, fatherly not less
Than I whom Thou hast moulded from the clay,
Thou'lt leave Thy wrath, and say,
"I will be sorry for their childishness."

Coventry Patmore, 1823–1896

1083. THE BRIDGE BUILDER

An old man, going a lone highway,
Came at the evening, cold and gray,
To a chasm, vast and deep and wide,
Through which was flowing a sullen tide.
The old man crossed in the twilight dim;
The sullen stream had no fears for him;
But he turned when safe on the other side
And built a bridge to span the tide.

"Old man," said a fellow pilgrim near,
"You are wasting strength with building here;
Your journey will end with the ending day;
You never again must pass this way;
You have crossed the chasm, deep and wide—
Why build you the bridge at the eventide?"

The builder lifted his old gray head:
"Good friend, in the path I have come," he said,
"There followeth after me today
A youth whose feet must pass this way.
This chasm that has been naught to me
To that fair-haired youth may a pitfall be.
He, too, must cross in the twilight dim;
Good friend, I am building the bridge for him."

Will Allen Dromgoole, ?–d. 1934

1084. THE KINGDOM

"Where is the Kingdom?" asked the solemn priest,
Weighted with lore and spent with fast and feast.
The happy Christ at his pretensions smiled
And simply said, "In the heart of a child."

Thomas Curtis Clark, 1877–

1085. THE CHILD'S APPEAL

I am the Child.
All the world waits for my coming.
All the earth watches with interest to see what I shall become.
Civilization hangs in the balance,
For what I am, the world of tomorrow will be.

I am the Child.
I have come into your world, about which I know nothing.
Why I came I know not;
How I came I know not.
I am curious; I am interested.

I am the Child.
You hold in your hand my destiny.
You determine, largely, whether I shall succeed or fail.
Give me, I pray you, those things that make for happiness.
Train me, I beg you, that I may be a blessing to the world.

Mamie Gene Cole

1086. LITTLE HANDS

Soft little hands that stray and clutch,
Like fern fronds curl and uncurl bold,
While baby faces lie in such
Close sleep as flowers at night that fold,
What is it you would clasp and hold,
Wandering outstretched with wilful touch?
O fingers small of shell-tipped rose,
How should you know you hold so much?
Two full hearts beating you inclose,
Hopes, fears, prayers, longings, joys and woes,—
All yours to hold, O little hands!
More, more than wisdom understands
And love, love only knows.

Laurence Binyon, 1869–1943

1087. I FOUND GOD

Sophisticated, worldly-wise,
I searched for God and found Him not,
Until one day, the world forgot,
I found Him in my baby's eyes.

Mary Afton Thacker, contemporary American

1088. VIGIL

I think that life has spared those mortals much—
And cheated them of more—who have not kept
A breathless vigil by the little bed
Of some belovèd child; they go, it seems,
Scot-free, who have not known fear-haunted days
And nights of terror, when the dim lamp burns
And shadows menace from the waiting walls,
While Life and Death, majestic, in the room
Gigantic rise above the fret and rub,
The petty prickings of small goads, and all
One has, and yearns to have, is, ruthless, flung
Into a fragile balance.

Hours pass
While on the thread of weary, childish breaths
The issue hangs. Then, one comes close to God,
Waiting and watching; and the hoping heart
Seems branded with the clutch of helpless hands
That leave long scars.

And when the turning tide
Bears life upon its slow, triumphant surge,—
When tortured eyes grow calm, and when a voice
Speaks feebly—but speaks again—I think
The watchers' eyes see, radiant, a dawn
Break on a newer world, a world more fair
Than ever world has seemed to them before.

God's mercy is as sunlight in the room;
And hearts that through the endless night were crushed
Between the millstones of despair and hope
Are free to sing.

Oh, life has spared so much—
And less revealed—to those who have not known
A breathless vigil by some little bed.

Faith Baldwin, contemporary American

1089. AS THROUGH THE LAND AT EVE WE WENT

From "The Princess"

As thro' the land at eve we went,
And pluck'd the ripen'd ears,
We fell out, my wife and I,
O, we fell out, I know not why,
And kiss'd again with tears.
And blessings on the falling out
That all the more endears,
When we fall out with those we love
And kiss again with tears!
For when we came where lies the child
We lost in other years,
There above the little grave,
O, there above the little grave,
We kiss'd again with tears.

Alfred Tennyson, 1809–1892

1090. THE OPEN DOOR

You, my son,
Have shown me God.
Your kiss upon my cheek
Has made me feel the gentle touch
Of Him who leads us on.
The memory of your smile, when young,
Reveals His face,
As mellowing years come on apace.
And when you went before,
You left the gates of heaven ajar
That I might glimpse,
Approaching from afar,
The glories of His grace.
Hold, son, my hand,
Guide me along the path,
That, coming,
I may stumble not,
Nor roam,
Nor fail to show the way
Which leads us home.

Grace Coolidge, contemporary American

1091. A PRAYER FOR FAMILY LOVE

Father,
Grant unto us true family love,
That we may belong more entirely to those whom Thou hast given us,
Understanding each other, day by day, more instinctively,
Forbearing each other, day by day, more patiently,
Growing, day by day, more closely into oneness with each other.

Father,
Thou too art love:
Thou knowest the depth of pain and the height of glory
Which abide continually in love:
Make us perfect in love for these our dear ones,
As knowing that without them we can never be made perfect in Thee.

Father,
Bring to full fruit in us Thine own nature—
That nature of humble redemptive devotion,

Which, out of two responsive souls,
Can create a new heaven and a new earth,
One eternal glory of divine self-sharing.

John S. Hoyland, 1887–

1092. THE CUP OF HAPPINESS

Lord God, how full our cup of happiness!
We drink and drink—and yet it grows not less;
But every morn the newly risen sun
Finds it replenished, sparkling, over-run!
Hast Thou not given us raiment, warmth, and meat,
And in due season all earth's fruits to eat?—
Work for our hands and rainbows for our eyes,
And for our souls the wings of butterflies?—
A father's smile, a mother's fond embrace,
The tender light upon a lover's face?—
The talk of friends, the twinkling eye of mirth,
The whispering silence of the good green earth?—
Hope for our youth, and memories for age,
And psalms upon the heavens' moving page?

And dost Thou not of pain a mingling pour,
To make the cup but overflow the more?

Gilbert Thomas, 1891–

1093. SEARCH

I sought Him in a great cathedral, dim
With age, where oft-repeated prayers arise,
But caught no glimpse of Him.

I sought Him then atop a lonely hill,
Like Moses once, but though I scanned the skies,
My search was fruitless still.

There was a little home where grief and care
Had bred but courage, love, and valiant will,
I sought—and found Him there.

Anne Marriott, contemporary Canadian

1094. HOME

From "The Death Of The Hired Man"

Home is the place where, when you have to go there,
They have to take you in.

Robert Frost, 1875–

1095. HOUSE BLESSING

Bless the four corners of this house,
And be the lintel blest;
And bless the hearth, and bless the board,
And bless each place of rest;

And bless the door that opens wide
To stranger, as to kin;
And bless each crystal windowpane
That lets the starlight in;

And bless the rooftree overhead,
And every sturdy wall.
The peace of man, the peace of God,
The peace of love on all.

Arthur Guiterman, 1871–1943

1096. DEDICATION

O thou whose gracious presence blest
The home at Bethany,
This shelter from the world's unrest,
This home made ready for its Guest,
We dedicate to thee.

We build an altar here, and pray
  That thou wilt show thy face.
Dear Lord, if thou wilt come to stay,
This home we consecrate today
  Will be a holy place.

Louis F. Benson, 1855–1930

1097. THE HOUSE

The hollow shell of a house
Is not the body and blood;
The brain, the fire and the flesh
Live not in bones of wood.

The soul is never seen,
Intangible as air;
It is the love of the man
Whose children live there.

Henry Treece, 1912–

1098. HOUSE AND HOME

A house is built of logs and stone,
  Of tiles and posts and piers;
A home is built of loving deeds
  That stand a thousand years.

Victor Hugo, 1802–1885

1099. PRAYER FOR THIS HOUSE

May nothing evil cross this door,
And may ill fortune never pry
About these windows; may the roar
    And rain go by.

Strengthened by faith, these rafters will
Withstand the batt'ring of the storm;
This hearth, though all the world grow chill,
    Will keep us warm.

Peace shall walk softly through these rooms,
Touching our lips with holy wine,
Till ev'ry casual corner blooms
    Into a shrine.

Laughter shall drown the raucous shout;
And, though these shelt'ring walls are thin,
May they be strong to keep hate out
    And hold love in.

Louis Untermeyer, 1885–

1100. GOD BLESS OUR HOME

Eternal Father, who hast given
To homes on earth foretaste of heaven,
Whose gentle Spirit from above
Doth breathe Thy peace in hearts that love;
  While here we bide, or far we roam,
  Hear this our prayer: God Bless Our Home!

O Saviour, who didst smile to see
The bridal feast in Galilee,
Whose grace we crave on all who bow,
For life and death to take their vow;
  While here we bide, or far we roam,
  Hear this our prayer: God Bless Our Home!

O Tender Shepherd, who dost hold
Each little lamb within Thy fold,
With rod and staff who followest still
The wandering sheep o'er vale and hill;
  While here we bide, or far we roam,
  Hear this our prayer: God Bless Our Home!

Eternal Father, ever near,
With arm outstretched and listening ear,
Whose mercy keeps, whose power defends
Our sons, our daughters, and our friends,
  While here we bide, or far we roam,
  Hear this our prayer: God Bless Our Home!

Robert Freeman, 1878–1940

1101. From A THANKSGIVING TO GOD FOR HIS HOUSE

Lord, Thou hast given me a cell
  Wherein to dwell,
A little house whose humble roof
  Is weather-proof. . . .
Low is my porch, as is my fate,
  Both void of state;
And yet the threshold of my door
  Is worn by th' poor,
Who hither come and freely get
  Good words, or meat. . . .
'Tis Thou that crown'st my glittering hearth
  With guileless mirth. . . .
All these, and better Thou dost send
  Me, to this end,
That I should render, for my part,
  A thankful heart.

Robert Herrick, 1591–1674

1102. PRAYER FOR A LITTLE HOME

God send us a little home,
To come back to, when we roam—

Low walls and fluted tiles;
Wide windows, a view for miles;

Red firelight and deep chairs;
Small white beds upstairs;

Great talk in little nooks;
Dim colors, rows of books;

One picture on each wall;
Not many things at all.

God send us a little ground,
Tall trees standing round.

Homely flowers in brown sod,
Overhead, Thy stars, O God.

God bless thee, when winds blow,
Our home, and all we know!

Florence Bone, contemporary English

1103. HYMN FOR A HOUSEHOLD

Lord Christ, beneath Thy starry dome
We light this flickering lamp of home,
And where bewildering shadows throng
Uplift our prayer and evensong.
Dost Thou, with heaven in Thy ken
Seek still a dwelling-place with men,
Wandering the world in ceaseless quest?
O Man of Nazareth, be our guest!

Lord Christ, the bird his nest has found,
The fox is sheltered in his ground,
But dost Thou still this dark earth tread
And have no place to lay Thy head?
Shepherd of mortals, here behold
A little flock, a wayside fold
That wait Thy presence to be blest—
O Man of Nazareth, be our guest!

Daniel Henderson, 1880—

1104. THE "OLD, OLD SONG"

When all the world is young, lad,
  And all the trees are green;
And every goose a swan, lad,
  And every lass a queen;
Then hey for boot and horse, lad,
  And round the world away;
Young blood must have its course, lad,
  And every dog its day.

When all the world is old, lad,
  And all the trees are brown;
And all the sport is stale, lad,
  And all the wheels run down:
Creep home, and take your place there,
  The spent and maim'd among:
God grant you find one face there
  You loved when all was young.

Charles Kingsley, 1819–1875

1105. O HAPPY HOME

O happy home, where Thou art loved the dearest,
  Thou loving Friend, and Saviour of our race,
And where among the guests there never cometh
  One who can hold such high and honored place!

O happy home, where two in heart united
  In holy faith and blessed hope are one,
Whom death a little while alone divideth,
  And cannot end the union here begun!

O happy home, where Thou art not forgotten
  When joy is overflowing, full, and free;
O happy home, where every wounded spirit
  Is brought, Physician, Comforter, to Thee—

Until at last, when earth's day's work is ended
All meet Thee in the blessed home above,
From whence Thou camest, where Thou hast ascended,
Thy everlasting home of peace and love!

Karl J. P. Spitta, 1801–1859

1106. HOME, SWEET HOME!

Mid pleasures and palaces though we may roam,
Be it ever so humble, there's no place like home;
A charm from the sky seems to hallow us there,
Which, seek through the world, is ne'er met with elsewhere.
Home, Home, sweet, sweet Home!
There's no place like Home! there's no place like Home!

An exile from home, splendour dazzles in vain;
O, give me my lowly thatched cottage again!
The birds singing gayly, that came at my call,—
Give me them,—and the peace of mind, dearer than all!
Home, Home, sweet, sweet Home!
There's no place like Home! there's no place like Home!

How sweet 't is to sit 'neath a fond father's smile,
And the cares of a mother to soothe and beguile!
Let others delight mid new pleasures to roam,
But give me, oh, give me, the pleasures of home!
Home! Home! sweet, sweet Home!
There's nc place like Home! there's no place like Home!

To thee I'll return, overburdened with care;
The heart's dearest solace will smile on me there;
No more from that cottage again will I roam;
Be it ever so humble, there's no place like home.
Home! Home! sweet, sweet Home!
There's no place like Home! there's no place like Home!

John Howard Payne, 1792–1852

1107. HOME IS WHERE THERE'S ONE TO LOVE US

Home's not merely four square walls,
Though with pictures hung and gilded;
Home is where Affection calls,
Filled with shrines the Heart hath builded!
Home!—go watch the faithful dove,
Sailing 'neath the heaven above us;
Home is where there's one to love!
Home is where there's one to love us!

Home's not merely roof and room—
It needs something to endear it;
Home is where the heart can bloom,
Where there's some kind lip to cheer it!
What is home with none to meet,
None to welcome, none to greet us?
Home is sweet—and only sweet—
Where there's one we love to meet us!

Charles Swain, 1801–1874

1108. BETTER THAN GOLD

Better than grandeur, better than gold,
Than rank and titles a thousandfold,
Is a healthy body and a mind at ease,
And simple pleasures that always please.

A heart that can feel for another's woe,
And share his joys with a genial glow;
With sympathies large enough to enfold
All men as brothers, is better than gold.

Better than gold is a conscience clear,
Though toiling for bread in an humble sphere,
Doubly blessed with content and health,
Untried by the lusts and cares of wealth,
Lowly living and lofty thought
Adorn and ennoble a poor man's cot;
For mind and morals in nature's plan
Are the genuine tests of an earnest man.

Better than gold is a peaceful home
Where all the fireside characters come,
The shrine of love, the heaven of life,
Hallowed by mother, or sister, or wife.
However humble the home may be,
Or tried with sorrow by heaven's decree,
The blessings that never were bought or sold,
And center there, are better than gold.

Abram J. Ryan, 1838–1886

1109. From PRAYER FOR THE HOME

Lord, this humble house we'd keep
Sweet with play and calm with sleep.
Help us so that we may give
Beauty to the lives we live.
Let Thy love and let Thy grace
Shine upon our dwelling place.

Edgar A. Guest, 1881–

1110. SO LONG AS THERE ARE HOMES

So long as there are homes to which men turn
At close of day;
So long as there are homes where children are,
Where women stay—
If love and loyalty and faith be found
Across those sills—
A stricken nation can recover from
Its gravest ills.

So long as there are homes where fires burn
And there is bread;
So long as there are homes where lamps are lit
And prayers are said;
Although people falter through the dark—
And nations grope—
With God himself back of these little homes—
We have sure hope.

Grace Noll Crowell, 1877–

1111. PRAYER FOR OUR HOME

Father, this day
For our home we pray Thee—
Our home, which, small and unknown
though it be,
May yet most plainly show forth
Thine eternal glory.

May Thy love everlasting
Be reborn in our home this day;
May we take of the sacrament, all day long,
Of Thine own great love in the life of our
home.

May we meet with Thee here,
May we know Thee here,
Be drawn very close to Thy side;
See revealed, in mysterious splendour,
Incarnate once more upon earth,
Thy life, Thy love, in our home this day.

Father, we pray Thee,
Give us grace for this highest holiest task,
To build up a perfect home life,
That shall give to Thyself, the Omnipotent
God,
Power to create, through weak human lives,
Thine own perfection of love.

J. S. Hoyland, 1887–

Book IV: THE CHRISTIAN LIFE

1112. THE DAY'S DEMAND

God give us men! A time like this demands
Strong minds, great hearts, true faith and ready hands;
Men whom the lust of office does not kill;
Men whom the spoils of office cannot buy;
Men who possess opinions and a will;
Men who have honor—men who will not lie;
Men who can stand before a demagogue
And damn his treacherous flatteries without winking;
Tall men, sun-crowned, who live above the fog
In public duty and in private thinking;
For while the rabble, with their thumb-worn creeds,
Their large professions and their little deeds,
Mingle in selfish strife, lo! Freedom weeps,
Wrong rules the land, and waiting Justice sleeps.

Josiah Gilbert Holland, 1819–1881

1113. DIES IRAE—DIES PACIS

"Only through Me!". . . . The clear, high call comes pealing,
Above the thunders of the battle-plain;—
"Only through Me can Life's red wounds find healing;
Only through Me shall Earth have peace again.

"Only through Me! . . . . Love's Might, all might transcending,
Alone can draw the poison-fangs of Hate.
Yours the beginning!—Mine a nobler ending,—
Peace upon Earth, and Man regenerate!

"Only through Me can come the great awaking;
Wrong cannot right the wrongs that Wrong hath done;
Only through Me, all other gods forsaking,
Can ye attain the heights that must be won.

"Only through Me shall Victory be sounded;
Only through Me can Right wield righteous sword;
Only through Me shall Peace be surely founded;
Only through Me. . . . *Then bid Me to the Board!*"

Can we not rise to such great height of glory?
Shall this vast sorrow spend itself in vain?
Shall future ages tell the woeful story,—
"*Christ by His own was crucified again*"*?*

John Oxenham, 1852–1941

1114. HOLD HIGH THE TORCH

Hold high the torch!
You did not light its glow—
'Twas given you by other hands, you know.

'Tis yours to keep it burning bright,
Yours to pass on when you no more need light;
For there are other feet that we must guide,
And other forms go marching by our side;
Their eyes are watching every smile and tear
And efforts which we think are not worthwhile,
Are sometimes just the very helps they need,
Actions to which their souls would give most heed;
So that in turn they'll hold it high
And say, "I watched someone else carry it this way."
If brighter paths should beckon you to choose,
Would your small gain compare with all you'd lose?
Hold high the torch!
You did not light its glow—
'Twas given you by other hands, you know.
I think it started down its pathway bright,
The day the Maker said: "Let there be light."
And He once said, who hung on Calvary's tree—
"Ye are the light of the world." . . . Go! . . . Shine—for me.

Author unknown

1115. RISE UP, O MEN OF GOD

Rise up, O men of God!
Have done with lesser things,
Give heart and soul and mind and strength
To serve the King of kings.

Rise up, O men of God!
His kingdom tarries long.
Bring in the day of brotherhood
And end the night of wrong.

Rise up, O men of God!
The church for you doth wait,
Her strength unequal to her task;
Rise up, and make her great!

Lift high the cross of Christ!
Tread where His feet have trod;
As brothers of the Son of Man
Rise up, O men of God!

William Pierson Merrill, 1867–

1116. THINGS THAT NEVER DIE

The pure, the bright, the beautiful
That stirred our hearts in youth,
The impulses to wordless prayer,
The streams of love and truth,
The longing after something lost,
The spirit's yearning cry,
The striving after better hopes—
These things can never die.

The timid hand stretched forth to aid
A brother in his need;
A kindly word in grief's dark hour
That proves a friend indeed;
The plea for mercy softly breathed,
When justice threatens high,
The sorrow of a contrite heart—
These things shall never die.

Let nothing pass, for every hand
Must find some work to do,
Lose not a chance to waken love—
Be firm and just and true.
So shall a light that cannot fade
Beam on thee from on high,
And angel voices say to thee—
"These things shall never die."

Charles Dickens, 1812–1870

1117. FIGHT THE GOOD FIGHT

Fight the good fight with all thy might,
Christ is thy strength, and Christ thy right;
Lay hold on life, and it shall be
Thy joy and crown eternally.

Run the straight race through God's good grace,
Lift up thine eyes and seek His face;
Life with its way before us lies,
Christ is the path, and Christ the prize.

Cast care aside, lean on thy Guide,
His boundless mercy will provide;
Trust, and thy trusting soul shall prove
Christ is its life, and Christ its love.

Faint not nor fear, His arms are near,
He changeth not and thou art dear;
Only believe, and thou shalt see
That Christ is all in all to thee.

John S. B. Monsell, 1811–1875

1118. EPISTLE

Christian, be up before the end of day,
Before the last, the fading hour dies;
Sleep not until the light has fled away,
And night's black trumpet cries.

Christian, arise while yet the sunset chime
With mellow music all the distance fills,
And while God walks, as in an older time,
In beauty on the hills.

Lie not so long with dim, unmindful eye;
Sleep not so late while others wake and hark;
There is a grief of voices in the sky,
An evil in the dark.

Christian, awake and watch upon the height;
The day is dying in the darkening air.
There is but little time before the night;
There is but time for prayer.

Robert Nathan, 1894–

1119. THE CHRISTIAN SOLDIER

Passionately fierce the voice of God is pleading,
  Pleading with men to arm them for the fight,
See how those hands, majestically bleeding,
  Call us to rout the armies of the night.

Not to the work of sordid selfish saving
  Of our own souls to dwell with Him on high,
But to the soldier's splendid selfless braving,
  Eager to fight for righteousness and die.

Peace does not mean the end of all our striving,
  Joy does not mean the drying of our tears,
Peace is the power that comes to souls arriving,
  Up to the light where God Himself appears.

G. A. Studdert-Kennedy, 1883–1929

1120. TO-DAY

To be alive in such an age!
With every year a lightning page
Turned in the world's great wonder book
Whereon the leaning nations look.
When men speak strong for brotherhood,
For peace and universal good,
When miracles are everywhere,
And every inch of common air
Throbs a tremendous prophecy
Of greater marvels yet to be.
    O thrilling age,
    O willing age!
When steel and stone and rail and rod
Become the avenue of God—
A trump to shout His thunder through
To crown the work that man may do.

To be alive in such an age!
When man, impatient of his cage,
Thrills to the soul's immortal rage
For conquest—reaches goal on goal,
Travels the earth from pole to pole,
Garners the tempests and the tides
And on a Dream Triumphant rides.
When, hid within the lump of clay,
A light more terrible than day
Proclaims the presence of that Force

Which hurls the planets on their course.
O age with wings
O age that flings
A challenge to the very sky,
Where endless realms of conquest lie!
When, earth on tiptoe, strives to hear
The message of a sister sphere,
Yearning to reach the cosmic wires
That flash Infinity's desires.

To be alive in such an age!
That blunders forth its discontent
With futile creed and sacrament,
Yet craves to utter God's intent,
Seeing beneath the world's unrest
Creation's huge, untiring quest,
And through Tradition's broken crust
The flame of Truth's triumphant thrust;
Below the seething thought of man
The push of a stupendous Plan.
O age of strife!
O age of life!
When Progress rides her chariots high,
And on the borders of the sky
The signals of the century
Proclaim the things that are to be—
The rise of woman to her place,
The coming of a nobler race.

To be alive in such an age—
To live in it,
To give to it!
Rise, soul, from thy despairing knees.
What if thy lips have drunk the lees?
Fling forth thy sorrows to the wind
And link thy hope with humankind—
The passion of a larger claim
Will put thy puny grief to shame.
Breathe the world thought, do the world deed,
Think hugely of thy brother's need.
And what thy woe, and what thy weal?
Look to the work the times reveal!
Give thanks with all thy flaming heart—
Crave but to have in it a part.
Give thanks and clasp thy heritage—
To be alive in such an age!

Angela Morgan, contemporary American

1121. THE PRESENT AGE

We are living, we are dwelling,
In a grand and awful time,
In an age on ages telling;
To be living is sublime.
Hark! the waking up of nations,
Gog and Magog to the fray.
Hark! what soundeth is creation
Groaning for its latter day.

Will ye play, then, will ye dally
With your music and your wine?
Up! it is Jehovah's rally!
God's own arm hath need of thine.
Hark! the onset! will ye fold your
Faith-clad arms in lazy lock?
Up, oh up, thou drowsy soldier!
Worlds are charging to the shock.

Worlds are charging—heaven beholding;
Thou hast but an hour to fight;
Now the blazoned cross unfolding,
On—right onward for the right!
On! let all the soul within you
For the truth's sake go abroad!
Strike! let every nerve and sinew
Tell on ages—tell for God.

Arthur Cleveland Coxe, 1818–1896

1122. STANZAS ON FREEDOM

Men! whose boast it is that ye
Come of fathers brave and free,
If there breathe on earth a slave,
Are ye truly free and brave?
If ye do not feel the chain
When it works a brother's pain,
Are ye not base slaves indeed,
Slaves unworthy to be freed!

Is true Freedom but to break
Fetters for our own dear sake,
And, with leathern hearts, forget
That we owe mankind a debt?
No! True Freedom is to share
All the chains our brothers wear,
And, with heart and hand, to be
Earnest to make others free!

They are slaves who fear to speak
For the fallen and the weak;
They are slaves who will not choose
Hatred, scoffing and abuse,
Rather than in silence shrink
From the truth they needs must think:
They are slaves who dare not be
In the right with two or three.

James Russell Lowell, 1819–1891

1123. IT IS TIME TO BUILD

I am tired of echoes in the old house:
Echoes of ancient hatreds and historic feuds;
Echoes of outworn slogans;
Echoes of pompous fools long dead;
Echoes of statesmen whose folly is more
enduring than bronze.

Man's mind reaches past the stars,
Probes into the atom,
Measures waves of ether in the infinite
spaces;
His soul trembles at a brother's pain,
Sees light through jungle darkness,
Sings with faith and tenderness the vastness
of divinity,
But he still lives in an old house,
An old house full of echoes.

Tear down the rotted boards;
Scrap the bat-haunted chambers;
Stop the babbling of simian tongues
Pretending to blabber wisdom.

It is time to build new towers for a new age.
I am tired of echoes . . . echoes . . . echoes . . .
In the old house.

Elias Lieberman, 1883–

1124. WE SHALL BUILD ON!

We shall build on!
On through the cynic's scorning.
On through the coward's warning.
On through the cheat's suborning.

We shall build on!
Firm on the Rock of Ages,
City of saints and sages.
Laugh while the tempest rages,
We shall build on!

Christ, though my hands be bleeding,
Fierce though my flesh be pleading,
Still let me see Thee leading,
Let me build on!

Till through death's cruel dealing,
Brain wrecked and reason reeling,
I hear Love's trumpets pealing,
And I pass on.

G. A. Studdert-Kennedy, 1883–1929

1125. From IS LIFE WORTH LIVING

Is life worth living? Yes, so long
As there is wrong to right,
Wail of the weak against the strong,
Or tyranny to fight;
Long as there lingers gloom to chase,
Or streaming tear to dry,
One kindred woe, one sorrowing face
That smiles as we draw nigh;
Long as a tale of anguish swells
The heart, and lids grow wet,
And at the sound of Christmas bells
We pardon and forget;
So long as Faith with Freedom reigns,
And loyal Hope survives,
And gracious Charity remains
To leaven lowly lives;
While there is one untrodden tract
For Intellect or Will,
And men are free to think and act
Life is worth living still.

Alfred Austin, 1835–1913

1126. THE RIDERLESS HORSE

Close ranks and ride on!
Though his saddle be bare,
The bullet is sped,
Now the dead
Cannot care.
Close ranks and ride on!
Let the pitiless stride
Of the host that he led,
Though his saddle be red,
Sweep on like the tide.
Close ranks and ride on!
The banner he bore
For God and the right
Never faltered before.
Quick, up with it, then!
For the right! For the light!
Lest legions of men
Be lost in the night!

Harold Trowbridge Pulsifer, 1886–1948

1127. A POET'S PROVERB

God's Road is all uphill,
But do not tire,
Rejoice that we may still
Keep climbing higher.

Arthur Guiterman, 1871–1943

1128. THE LAST DEFILE

"He died climbing"—A Swiss Guide's Epitaph.

Make us Thy mountaineers;
We would not linger on the lower slope,
Fill us afresh with hope, O God of Hope,
That undefeated we may climb the hill
As seeing Him who is invisible.

Let us die climbing. When this little while
Lies far behind us, and the last defile
Is all alight, and in that light we see
Our Leader and our Lord, what will it be?

Amy Carmichael, contemporary English

1129. HEARTS COURAGEOUS

Foes in plenty we shall meet,
Hearts courageous scorn defeat,
So we press with eager feet
Up, and On.

Ever onward to the fight,
Ever upward to the Light,
Ever true to God and Right,—
Up!—and On!

John Oxenham, 1852–1941

1130. JACOB'S LADDER

We are climbing Jacob's ladder,
Soldier of the cross.

Every round goes higher, higher,
Soldier of the cross.

Sinner, do you love my Jesus?
Soldier of the cross.

If you love Him, why not serve Him?
Soldier of the cross.

We are climbing higher, higher,
Soldier of the cross.

Negro Spiritual

1131. INTROVERSION

What do you seek within, O Soul, my
Brother?
What do you seek within?
I seek a life that shall never die,
Some haven to win
From mortality.

What do you find within, O Soul, my
Brother?
What do you find within?
I find great quiet where no noises come.
Without, the world's din:
Silence in my home.

Whom do you find within, O Soul, my
Brother?
Whom do you find within?
I find a friend that in secret came:
His scarred hands within
He shields a faint flame.

What would you do within, O Soul, my
Brother?
What would you do within?
Bar door and window that none may see:
That alone we may be
(Alone! face to face,
In that flame-lit place!)
When first we begin
To speak one with another.

Evelyn Underhill, 1875–1941

1132. WE LIVE IN DEEDS

From "Festus"

We live in deeds, not years; in thoughts, not breaths;
In feelings, not in figures on a dial.
We should count time by heart-throbs. He most lives
Who thinks most, feels the noblest, acts the best.
And he whose heart beats quickest lives the longest:
Lives in one hour more than in years do some
Whose fat blood sleeps as it slips along their veins.

Life's but a means unto an end; that end,
Beginning, mean, and end to all things—God.
The dead have all the glory of the world.

Philip James Bailey, 1816–1902

1133. THREE DAYS

Three days, I ween, make up our life,
  When shadow and sunshine play;
The day that is past, and the day to come,
  And the one that is called "Today."

Three days, I ween, make up our life,
  But two are not ours at all;
For yesterday, laden with good or ill,
  Has passed beyond recall.

And tomorrow sits shrouded near God's
    throne,
  And her veil none can tear away;
But today is the golden day for men—
  For God's work may be *done today.*

W. Boyd Carpenter, 1841–1918

1134. TO-DAY

So here hath been dawning
  Another blue day:
Think, wilt thou let it
  Slip useless away?

Out of Eternity
  This new day is born;
Into Eternity,
  At night, will return.

Behold it aforetime
  No eye ever did;
So soon it forever
  From all eyes is hid.

Here hath been dawning
  Another blue day:
Think, wilt thou let it
  Slip useless away?

Thomas Carlyle, 1795–1881

1135. LIFE

Forenoon and afternoon and night,—
    Forenoon,
And afternoon, and night,—Forenoon, and—
    what!
The empty song repeats itself. No more?
Yea, that is Life: make this forenoon sublime,
This afternoon a psalm, this night a prayer,
And Time is conquered, and thy crown is won.

Edward Rowland Sill, 1841–1887

1136. MY PURPOSE

To awaken each morning with a smile brightening my face;
To greet the day with reverence for the opportunities it contains;
To approach my work with a clean mind;
To hold ever before me, even in the doing of little things, the Ultimate Purpose toward which
    I am working;
To meet men and women with laughter on my lips and love in my heart;
To be gentle, kind, and courteous through all the hours;
To approach the night with weariness that ever woos sleep, and the joy that comes from
    work well done—
This is how I desire to waste wisely my days.

Thomas Dekker, 1572?–1632?

1137. THE CELESTIAL SURGEON

If I have faltered more or less
In my great task of happiness;
If I have moved among my race
And shown no glorious morning face;
If beams from happy human eyes
Have moved me not; if morning skies,
Books, and my food, and summer rain

Knocked on my sullen heart in vain:—
Lord, thy most pointed pleasure take
And stab my spirit broad awake;
Or, Lord, if still too obdurate I,
Choose thou, before that spirit die,
A piercing pain, a killing sin,
And to my dead heart run them in!

Robert Louis Stevenson, 1850–1894

1138. YOUR PLACE

Is your place a small place?
  Tend it with care;—
    He set you there.

Is your place a large place?
  Guard it with care!—
    He set you there.

Whate'er your place, it is
  Not yours alone, but His
    Who set you there.

John Oxenham, 1852–1941

1139. THE SLUGGARD—A SONNET

Proverbs 6: 6–11

Go to the ant, thou Sluggard;
Consider her ways, and be wise:
  Which having no chief,
  Overseer,
  Or ruler,
Provideth her meat in the summer,
And gathereth her food in the harvest.

How long wilt thou sleep, O Sluggard?
When wilt thou arise out of thy sleep?
  "Yet a little sleep,
  A little slumber,
  A little folding of the hands to sleep"—
So shall thy poverty come as a robber,
And thy want as an armed man!

Moulton: The Modern Reader's Bible, 1895

1140. THE NEW CHALLENGE

Our fathers to their graves have gone;
Their strife is past, their triumph won;
But sterner trials await the race
Which rises in their honored place—
A moral warfare with the crime
And folly of an evil time.
So let it be. In God's own might
We gird us for the coming fight,
And strong in Him Whose cause is ours,
In conflict with unholy powers,
We grasp the weapons He has given—
The light and truth and love of Heaven.

John Greenleaf Whittier, 1807–1892

1141. TRUE REST

Rest is not quitting
The busy career;
Rest is the fitting
Of self to one's sphere.

'Tis the brook's motion
Clear without strife,
Fleeting to ocean,
After this life.

'Tis loving and serving,
The highest and best;
'Tis onward, unswerving,
And this is true rest.

Johann Wolfgang von Goethe, 1749–1832

1142. CHRIST—AND WE

Christ has no hands but our hands
  To do His work today;
He has no feet but our feet
  To lead men in His way;
He has no tongue but our tongues
  To tell men how He died;
He has no help but our help
  To bring them to His side.

We are the only Bible
  The careless world will read;
We are the sinner's gospel,
  We are the scoffer's creed;
We are the Lord's last message
  Given in deed and word—
What if the line is crooked?
  What if the type is blurred?

What if our hands are busy
  With other work than His?
What if our feet are walking
  Where sin's allurement is?

What if our tongues are speaking
  Of things His lips would spurn?
How can we hope to help Him
  Unless from Him we learn?

Annie Johnson Flint, 1862–1932

1143. MAKING LIFE WORTH WHILE

Every soul that touches yours—
Be it the slightest contact—
Gets therefrom some good;
Some little grace; one kindly thought;
One aspiration yet unfelt;
One bit of courage
For the darkening sky;
One gleam of faith
To brave the thickening ills of life;
One glimpse of brighter skies—
To make this life worth while
And heaven a surer heritage.

George Eliot, 1819–1880

1144. SERMONS WE SEE

I'd rather see a sermon than hear one any day;
I'd rather one should walk with me than merely tell the way.
The eye's a better pupil and more willing than the ear,
Fine counsel is confusing, but example's always clear;
And the best of all the preachers are the men who live their creeds,
For to see good put in action is what everybody needs.

I soon can learn to do it if you'll let me see it done;
I can watch your hands in action, but your tongue too fast may run.
And the lecture you deliver may be very wise and true,
But I'd rather get my lessons by observing what you do;
For I might misunderstand you and the high advice you give,
But there's no misunderstanding how you act and how you live.

When I see a deed of kindness, I am eager to be kind.
When a weaker brother stumbles and a strong man stays behind
Just to see if he can help him, then the wish grows strong in me
To become as big and thoughtful as I know that friend to be.
And all travelers can witness that the best of guides to-day
Is not the one who tells them, but the one who shows the way.

One good man teaches many, men believe what they behold;
One deed of kindness noticed is worth forty that are told.
Who stands with men of honor learns to hold his honor dear,
For right living speaks a language which to every one is clear.
Though an able speaker charms me with his eloquence, I say,
I'd rather see a sermon than to hear one, any day.

Edgar A. Guest, 1881–

1145. THE EFFECT OF EXAMPLE

We scatter seeds with careless hand,
  And dream we ne'er shall see them more;
    But for a thousand years
    Their fruit appears,
In weeds that mar the land,
  Or healthful shore.

The deeds we do, the words we say,—
  Into still air they seem to fleet,
    We count them ever past;
    But they shall last,—
In the dread judgment they
  And we shall meet.

I charge thee by the years gone by,
  For the love's sake of brethren dear,
    Keep thou the one true way,
    In work and play,
Lest in that world their cry
  Of woe thou hear.

John Keble, 1792–1866

1146. YOUR OWN VERSION

You are writing a Gospel,
  A chapter each day,
By deeds that you do,
  By words that you say.

Men read what you write,
  Whether faithless or true;
Say, what is the Gospel
  According to You?

Paul Gilbert

1147. GET SOMEBODY ELSE

The Lord had a job for me,
  But I had so much to do,
I said, "You get somebody else,
  Or wait till I get through."
I don't know how the Lord came out,
  But He seemed to get along,
But I felt kind o' sneakin' like—
  Knowed I'd done God wrong.

One day I needed the Lord—
  Needed Him right away;
But He never answered me at all,
  And I could hear Him say,
Down in my accusin' heart:
  "Nigger, I'se got too much to do;
You get somebody else,
  Or wait till I get through."

Now, when the Lord He have a job for me,
  I never tries to shirk;
I drops what I have on hand,
  And does the good Lord's work.
And my affairs can run along,
  Or wait till I get through;
Nobody else can do the work
  That God marked out for you.

Attributed to Paul Laurence Dunbar

1148. THE GOAL

I care not that the storm sways all the trees,
  And floods the plain and blinds my trusting sight;
I only care that o'er the land and seas
  Comes somewhere Love's perpetual peace and light.

I care not that sharp thorns grow thick below,
  And wound my hands and scar my anxious feet;
I only care to know God's roses grow,
  And I may somewhere find their odor sweet.

I care not if they be not white, but red,
  Red as the blood-drops from a wounded heart;
I only care to ease my aching head
  With faith that somewhere God hath done His part.

I care not if, in years of such despair,
  I reach in vain and seize no purpose vast;
I only care that I sometime, somewhere,
  May find a meaning, shining at the last.

Frank W. Gunsaulus, 1856–1921

1149. THE NECESSITY OF RELIGION

From "Starting From Paumanok"

I say the whole earth, and all the stars in the sky, are for Religion's sake.

I say no man has ever yet been half devout enough;
None has ever yet adored or worship'd half enough;
None has begun to think how divine he himself is, and how certain the future is.

I say that the real and permanent grandeur of These States must be their Religion;
Otherwise there is no real and permanent grandeur:
(Nor character, nor life worthy the name, without Religion;
Nor land, nor man or woman, without Religion.)

Walt Whitman, 1819–1892

1150. RELIGION

From "Mr. Sludge, 'The Medium'"

Religion's all or nothing; it's no mere smile
O' contentment, sigh of aspiration, sir—
No quality o' the finelier-tempered clay
Like its whiteness or its lightness; rather, stuff
O' the very stuff, life of life, and self of self.

Robert Browning, 1812–1889

1151. HOW DOES THE SOUL GROW?

How does the soul grow? Not all in a minute;
Now it may lose ground, and now it may win it;
Now it resolves, and again the will faileth;
Now it rejoiceth, and now it bewaileth;
Now its hopes fructify, then they are blighted;
Now it walks sullenly, now gropes benighted;
Fed by discouragements, taught by disaster;
So it goes forward, now slower, now faster,
Till all the pain is past, and failure made whole,
It is full grown, and the Lord rules the soul.

Susan Coolidge, 1845–1905

1152. MY TASK

To love some one more dearly ev'ry day,
To help a wandering child to find his way,
To ponder o'er a noble thought, and pray,
And smile when evening falls.
This is my task.

To follow truth as blind men long for light,
To do my best from dawn of day till night,
To keep my heart fit for His holy sight,
And answer when He calls.
This is my task.

Maude Louise Ray

1153. SCHOOL DAYS

Lord, let me make this rule:
To think of life as school,
And try my best
To stand each test,
And do my work
And nothing shirk.

❖

If weary with my book
I cast a wistful look
Where posies grow,
Oh, let me know
That flowers within
Are best to win.

❖

These lessons thou dost give
To teach me how to live,
To do, to bear,
To get and share,
To work and play
And trust alway.

❖

Some day the bell will sound,
Some day my heart will bound,
As with a shout,
That school is out,
And, lessons done,
I homeward run.

Maltbie D. Babcock, 1858–1901

1154. DAY BY DAY

I heard a voice at evening softly say:
Bear not thy yesterday into to-morrow,
Nor load this week with last week's load of sorrow;
Lift all thy burdens as they come, nor try

To weight the present with the by and by.
One step, and then another, take thy way—
Live day by day.

Live day by day.
Though the autumn leaves are withering round thy way,
Walk in the sunshine. It is all for thee.
Push straight ahead as long as thou canst see.
Dread not the winter where thou mayst go;
But when it comes, be thankful for the snow.
Onward and upward. Look and smile and pray—
Live day by day.

Live day by day.
The path before thee doth not lead astray.
Do the next duty. It must surely be
The Christ is in the one that's close to thee.
Onward, still onward, with a sunny smile,
Till step by step shall end in mile by mile.
"I'll do my best," unto my conscience say—
Live day by day.

Live day by day.
Why art thou bending toward the backward way?
One summit and another thou shalt mount.
Why stop at every round the space to count
The past mistakes if thou must still remember?
Watch not the ashes of the dying ember.
Kindle thy hope. Put all thy fears away—
Live day by day.

Julia Harris May, 1833–1912

1155. THE NOBLE NATURE

From "A Pindaric Ode"

It is not growing like a tree
In bulk, doth make man better be;
Or standing long an oak, three hundred year,
To fall a log at last, dry, bald, and sear;
A lily of a day
Is fairer far, in May,
Although it fall and die that night,
It was a plant and flower of Light.
In small proportions we just beauties see;
And in short measures life may perfect be.

Ben Jonson, 1573?–1637

1156. HYMN TO LABOR

They are living the poems we write,
They are doing the glories we sing—
Diggers of ditches and builders of roads,
Toilers who carry humanity's loads,
Mothers who give with no thought of return,
Daughters who help them and fathers who earn,
Sons who endure in the dust of the fight,
Are *living* the poems we write.

They are living the sermons you preach,
Minister, prophet and sage;
You who would summon your gods to the earth,
Blind to the sum of humanity's worth;
You who are praying for angels again
To rescue a planet now peopled with men . . .
See how the humblest of all you may teach
Are *living* the sermons you preach!

They are doing the deeds you inspire,
They are brave as the angels are brave;
Drivers of engines and hewers of wood,
Farmers who labor to furnish us food,

Miners who suffer that we shall be warm,
Builders of houses that shield us from
storm . . .
Prophet, behold how in letters of fire
They are living the deeds you inspire.

They are living the sagas and psalms,
They embody the terms we employ:
Sympathy, brotherhood, courage, control,
Strength of the spirit and joy of the soul.
Saintly, superior, humble and brave,
They are Christs and Messiahs whose souls
we would save.
And the hour is at hand when the mighty in
turn
Shall listen to labor and learn!

Angela Morgan, contemporary American

1157. INFLUENCE

Drop a pebble in the water,
And its ripples reach out far;
And the sunbeams dancing on them
May reflect them to a star.

Give a smile to someone passing,
Thereby making his morning glad;
It may greet you in the evening
When your own heart may be sad.

Do a deed of simple kindness;
Though its end you may not see,
It may reach, like widening ripples,
Down a long eternity.

Joseph Norris, 1909–

1158. THE NOBLE LIFE

True worth is in being, not seeming;
In doing each day that goes by
Some little good—not in the dreaming
Of great things to do by-and-by.
For whatever men say in blindness,
And spite of the fancies of youth,
There's nothing so kingly as kindness,
And nothing so royal as truth.

We get back our mete as we measure;
We cannot do wrong and feel right;
Nor can we give pain and gain pleasure,
For justice avenges each slight.

The air for the wing of the sparrow,
The bush for the robin and wren,
But always the path that is narrow
And strait for the children of men.

Alice Cary, 1820–1871

1159. HOW—WHEN—WHERE

It is not so much WHERE you live,
As HOW, and WHY, and WHEN you live,
That answers in the affirmative,
Or maybe in the negative,
The question—Are you fit to live?

It is not so much WHERE you live,
As HOW you live, and whether good
Flows from you through your neighborhood.

And WHY you live, and whether you
Aim high and noblest ends pursue,
And keep Life brimming full and true.

And WHEN you live, and whether Time
Is at its nadir or its prime,
And whether you descend or climb.

It is not so much WHERE you live,
As whether while you live you *live*
And to the world your highest give,
And so make answer positive
That you are truly fit to live.

John Oxenham, 1852–1941

1160. LIFE'S MIRROR

There are loyal hearts, there are spirits brave,
There are souls that are pure and true;
Then give to the world the best you have,
And the best will come back to you.

Give love, and love to your life will flow,
A strength in your utmost need;
Have faith, and a score of hearts will show
Their faith in your word and deed.

Give truth, and your gift will be paid in kind,
And honor will honor meet;
And a smile that is sweet will surely find
A smile that is just as sweet.

Give sorrow and pity to those who mourn;
You will gather in flowers again
The scattered seeds of your thought outborne,
Though the sowing seemed but vain.

For life is the mirror of king and slave—
'Tis just what we are and do;
Then give to the world the best you have,
And the best will come back to you.
Madeline Bridges, 1844–1920

1161. THREE LESSONS

There are three lessons I would write—
Three words as with a burning pen,
In tracings of eternal light,
Upon the hearts of men.

Have Hope. Though clouds environ now,
And gladness hides her face in scorn,
Put thou the shadow from thy brow—
No night but hath its morn.

Have Faith. Where'er thy bark is driven—
The calm's disport, the tempest's mirth—
Know this: God rules the host of heaven,
The inhabitants of earth.

Have Love. Not love alone for one,
But man as man thy brother call;
And scatter like the circling sun
Thy charities on all.

Thus grave these lessons on thy soul—
Faith, Hope, and Love—and thou shalt find
Strength when life's surges rudest roll,
Light when thou else wert blind.
Johann Christopher Friedrich von Schiller, 1759–1805

1162. FOUR THINGS

Four things a man must learn to do
If he would make his record true:
To think without confusion clearly;
To love his fellowmen sincerely;
To act from honest motives purely;
To trust in God and Heaven securely.
Henry van Dyke, 1852–1933

1163. BE STRONG

Be strong to *hope*, O Heart!
Though day is bright,
The stars can only shine
In the dark night.
Be strong, O Heart of mine,
Look toward the light!

Be strong to *bear*, O Heart!
Nothing is vain:
Strive not, for life is care,
And God sends pain;
Heaven is above, and there
Rest will remain!

Be strong to *love*, O Heart!
Love knows not wrong;
Didst thou love—creatures even,
Life were not long;
Didst thou love God in heaven,
Thou wouldst be strong!
Adelaide Anne Procter, 1825–1864

1164. AFTER THE ORDER OF MELCHISEDEC

I have no temple and no creed,
I celebrate no mystic rite;
The human heart is all I need
Wherein I worship day and night:

The human heart is all I need,
For I have found God ever there—
Love is the one sufficient creed,
And comradeship the purest prayer!

I bow not down to any book,
No written page holds me in awe;
For where on one friend's face I look
I read the Prophets and the Law!

Love is the Word God gave and said:
"With it thou shalt mankind assoil!"
Then forthwith poured upon my head
Anointing of His holy oil!
Robert Norwood, 1874–1932

1165. ORTHODOX

They questioned my theology,
And talked of modern thought:
Bade me recite a dozen creeds—
I could not as I ought.
"I've but one creed," I answer made,
"And do not want another:
I know I've passed from death to life
Because I love my brother."
Mark Guy Pearse, 1842–1930

1166. "THERE IS ONE CREED, AND ONLY ONE"

There is one creed, and only one,
That glorifies God's excellence;
So cherish, that His will be done,
The common creed of common sense.

It is the crimson, not the gray,
That charms the twilight of all time;
It is the promise of the day
That makes the starry sky sublime.

It is the faith within the fear
That holds us to the life we curse;—
So let us in ourselves revere
The Self which is the Universe!

Let us, the Children of the Night,
Put off the cloak that hides the scar!
Let us be Children of the Light,
And tell the ages what we are!

Edwin Arlington Robinson, 1869–1935

1167. LABORARE EST ORARE

Christian, rise, and act thy creed,
Let thy prayer be in thy deed;
Seek the right, perform the true,
Raise thy work and life anew.

Hearts around thee sink with care;
Thou canst help their load to bear,
Thou canst bring inspiring light,
Arm their faltering wills to fight.

Let thine alms be hope and joy,
And thy worship God's employ;
Give him thanks in humble zeal,
Learning all his will to feel.

Come then, Law divine, and reign,
Freest faith assailed in vain,
Perfect love bereft of fear,
Born in heaven and radiant here.

Francis Albert Rollo Russell, 1849–1914

1168. WHAT I LIVE FOR

I live for those who love me,
Whose hearts are kind and true;
For the Heaven that smiles above me,
And awaits my spirit too;
For all human ties that bind me,
For the task by God assigned me,
For the bright hopes yet to find me,
And the good that I can do.

I live to learn their story
Who suffered for my sake;
To emulate their glory
And follow in their wake:
Bards, patriots, martyrs, sages,
The heroic of all ages,
Whose deeds crowd History's pages
And Time's great volume make.

I live to hold communion
With all that is divine,
To feel there is a union
'Twixt Nature's heart and mine;
To profit by affliction,
Reap truth from fields of fiction,
Grow wiser from conviction,
And fulfill God's grand design.

I live to hail the season,
By gifted ones foretold,
When man shall live by reason,
And not alone by gold;
When man to man united,
And every wrong thing righted,
The whole world shall be lighted,
As Eden was of old.

I live for those who love me,
For those who know me true;
For the heaven that smiles above me,
And awaits my spirit too;
For the cause that lacks assistance,
For the wrong that needs resistance,
For the future in the distance,
And the good that I can do.

G. Linnaeus Banks, 1821–1881

1169. MY CREED

To live as gently as I can;
To be, no matter where, a man;
To take what comes of good or ill
And cling to faith and honor still;
To do my best, and let that stand
The record of my brain and hand;
And then, should failure come to me,
Still work and hope for victory.

To have no secret place wherein
I stoop unseen to shame or sin;
To be the same when I'm alone
As when my every deed is known;
To live undaunted, unafraid
Of any step that I have made;
To be without pretense or sham
Exactly what men think I am.

To leave some simple mark behind
To keep my having lived in mind;
If enmity to aught I show,
To be an honest, generous foe,
To play my little part, nor whine
That greater honors are not mine.
This, I believe, is all I need
For my philosophy and creed.

Edgar A. Guest, 1881–

1170. MY DAILY CREED

Let me be a little kinder,
Let me be a little blinder
To the faults of those about me;
Let me praise a little more;
Let me be, when I am weary,
Just a little bit more cheery;
Let me serve a little better
Those that I am striving for.

Let me be a little braver
When temptation bids me waver;
Let me strive a little harder
To be all that I should be;
Let me be a little meeker
With the brother that is weaker;
Let me think more of my neighbor
And a little less of me.

Author unknown

1171. CREDO

Not what, but *Whom*, I do believe,
That, in my darkest hour of need,
Hath comfort that no mortal creed
To mortal man may give;—
Not what, but *Whom*!
For Christ is more than all the creeds,
And His full life of gentle deeds
Shall all the creeds outlive.

Not what I do believe, but *Whom*!
Who walks beside me in the gloom?
Who shares the burden wearisome?
Who all the dim way doth illume,
And bids me look beyond the tomb
The larger life to live?—
Not what I do believe,
But *Whom*!
Not what
But *Whom*!

John Oxenham, 1852–1941

1172. MY SYMPHONY

To live content with small means;
To seek elegance rather than luxury, and refinement rather than fashion;
To be worthy, not respectable, and wealthy, not rich;
To study hard, think quietly, talk gently, act frankly;
To listen to stars and birds, to babes and sages, with open heart;
To bear all cheerfully, do all bravely, await occasions, hurry never.
In a word, to let the spiritual, unbidden and unconscious, grow up through the common.
This is to be my symphony.

William Ellery Channing, 1818–1901

1173. A CONFESSION OF FAITH

From "My Religion"

I believe in God, who is for me spirit, love, the principle of all things.
I believe that God is in me, as I am in Him.
I believe that the true welfare of man consists in fulfilling the will of God.

I believe that from the fulfillment of the will of God there can follow nothing but that which is good for me and for all men.

I believe that the will of God is that every man should love his fellow men, and should act toward others as he desires that they should act toward him.

I believe that the reason of life is for each of us simply to grow in love.

I believe that this growth in love will contribute more than any other force to establish the Kingdom of God on earth—

To replace a social life in which division, falsehood and violence are all-powerful, with a new order in which humanity, truth and brotherhood will reign.

Leo Tolstoy, 1828–1910

1174. PRAYER

God, though this life is but a wraith,
  Although we know not what we use,
Although we grope with little faith,
  Give me the heart to fight—and lose.

Ever insurgent let me be,
  Make me more daring than devout;
From sleek contentment keep me free,
  And fill me with a buoyant doubt.

Open my eyes to visions girt
  With beauty, and with wonder lit—
But let me always see the dirt,
  And all that spawn and die in it.

Open my ears to music; let
  Me thrill with Spring's first flutes and drums—
But never let me dare forget
  The bitter ballads of the slums.

From compromise and things half-done,
  Keep me, with stern and stubborn pride.
And when, at last the fight is won.
  God, keep me still unsatisfied.

Louis Untermeyer, 1885–

1175. MATINS

Flowers rejoice when night is done,
Lift their heads to greet the sun;
Sweetest looks and odours raise,
In a silent hymn of praise.

So my heart would turn away
From the darkness to the day;
Lying open in God's sight
Like a flower in the light.

Henry van Dyke, 1852–1933

1176. A CHILD'S OFFERING

The wise may bring their learning,
  The rich may bring their wealth,
And some may bring their greatness,
  And some bring strength and health;
We, too, would bring our treasures
  To offer to the King;
We have no wealth or learning:
  What shall we children bring?

We'll bring Him hearts that love Him;
  We'll bring Him thankful praise,
And young souls meekly striving
  To walk in holy ways:
And these shall be the treasures
  We offer to the King,
And these are gifts that even
  The poorest child may bring.

We'll bring the little duties
  We have to do each day;
We'll try our best to please Him,
  At home, at school, at play:
And better are these treasures
  To offer to our King,
Than richest gifts without them;
  Yet these a child may bring.

The Book of Praise for Children, 1881

1177. THE CHAMBERED NAUTILUS

This is the ship of pearl, which, poets feign,
  Sails the unshadowed main,—
  The venturous bark that flings
On the sweet summer wind its purpled wings
In gulfs enchanted, where the Siren sings,
  And coral reefs lie bare,
Where the cold sea-maids rise to sun their streaming hair.

Its webs of living gauze no more unfurl;
Wrecked is the ship of pearl!
And every chambered cell,
Where its dim, dreaming life was wont to dwell,
As the frail tenant shaped his growing shell,
Before thee lies revealed,—
Its irised ceiling rent, its sunless crypt unsealed!

Year after year beheld the silent toil
That spread his lustrous coil;
Still, as the spiral grew,
He left the past year's dwelling for the new,
Stole with soft step its shining archway through,
Built up its idle door,
Stretched in his last-found home, and knew the old no more.

Thanks for the heavenly message brought by thee,
Child of the wandering sea,
Cast from her lap, forlorn!
From thy dead lips a clearer note is born
Than ever Triton blew from wreathèd horn!
While on mine ear it rings,
Through the deep caves of thought I hear a voice that sings:—

Build thee more stately mansions, O my soul,
As the swift seasons roll!
Leave thy low-vaulted past!
Let each new temple, nobler than the last,
Shut thee from heaven with a dome more vast,
Till thou at length art free,
Leaving thine outgrown shell by life's unresting sea!

Oliver Wendell Holmes, 1809–1894

1178. GENTLE JESUS

Gentle Jesus, meek and mild,
Look upon a little child;
Pity my simplicity,
Suffer me to come to Thee.

Lamb of God, I look to Thee:
Thou shalt my example be;
Thou art gentle, meek and mild;
Thou wast once a little child.

Fain I would be as Thou art;
Give me Thy obedient heart.
Thou art pitiful and kind,
Let me have Thy loving mind.

Loving Jesus, gentle Lamb,
In Thy gracious hands I am:
Make me, Saviour, what Thou art;
Live Thyself within my heart.

Charles Wesley, 1707–1788

1179. A LITTLE PRAYER

That I may not in blindness grope,
But that I may with vision clear
Know when to speak a word of hope
Or add a little wholesome cheer.

That tempered winds may softly blow
Where little children, thinly clad,
Sit dreaming, when the flame is low,
Of comforts they have never had.

That through the year which lies ahead
No heart shall ache, no cheek be wet,
For any word that I have said
Or profit I have tried to get.

S. E. Kiser, 1862–

1180. ALMIGHTY LORD, WITH ONE ACCORD

Almighty Lord, with one accord
We offer Thee our youth,
And pray that Thou wouldst give us now
The warfare of the truth.

Thy cause doth claim our souls by name,
Because that we are strong;
In all the land, one steadfast band,
May we to Christ belong.

Let fall on ev'ry college hall
The luster of Thy cross,
That love may dare Thy work to share
And count all else as loss.

Our hearts be ruled, our spirits schooled
Alone Thy will to seek;
And when we find Thy blessed mind,
Instruct our lips to speak.

M. Woolsey Stryker, 1851–1929

1181. GOD'S WAY

Thy way, not mine, O Lord!
However dark it be;
Lead me by Thine own hand,
Choose out the path for me.

Smooth let it be, or rough,
It will be still the best;
Winding or straight it matters not,
It leads me to Thy rest.

I dare not choose my lot,
I would not, if I might;
Choose Thou for me, O God!
So shall I walk aright.

The kingdom that I seek
Is Thine; so let the way
That leads to it be Thine;
Else I must surely stray.

Take Thou my cup, and it
With joy or sorrow fill;
As best to Thee may seem;
Choose Thou my good or ill.

❖

Not mine, not mine the choice
In things or great or small;
Be Thou my guide, my strength,
My wisdom and my all.

Horatius Bonar, 1808–1889

1182. THE MYSTIC'S PRAYER

Lay me to sleep in sheltering flame,
O Master of the Hidden Fire!
Wash pure my heart, and cleanse for me
My soul's desire.

In flame of sunrise bathe my mind,
O Master of the Hidden Fire,
That, when I wake, clear-eyed may be
My soul's desire.

Fiona Macleod, 1855–1905

1183. From PIPPA PASSES, PT. IV

All service ranks the same with God:
If now, as formerly he trod
Paradise, his presence fills
Our earth, each only as God wills
Can work—God's puppets, best and worst,
Are we; there is no last nor first.

Say not "a small event!" Why "small"?
Costs it more pain that this, ye call
A "great event," should come to pass,
Than that? Untwine me from the mass
Of deeds which make up life, one deed
Power shall fall short in or exceed!

Robert Browning, 1812–1889

1184. THE PASSIONATE SWORD

Temper my spirit, O Lord,
Burn out its alloy,
And make it a pliant steel for Thy wielding,
Not a clumsy toy;
A blunt, iron thing in my hands
That blunder and destroy.

Temper my spirit, O Lord,
Keep it long in the fire;
Make it one with the flame. Let it share
That up-reaching desire.
Grasp it, Thyself, O my God;
Swing it straighter and higher!

Jean Starr Untermeyer, 1886–

1185. THE BATTLE WITHIN

God strengthen me to bear myself;
That heaviest weight of all to bear,
Inalienable weight of care.

All others are outside myself;
I lock my door and bar them out,
The turmoil, tedium, gad-about.

I lock my door upon myself,
And bar them out; but who shall wall
Self from myself, most loathed of all?

If I could once lay down myself,
And start self-purged upon the race
That all must run! Death runs apace.

If I could set aside myself,
And start with lightened heart upon
The road by all men overgone!

God harden me against myself,
This coward with pathetic voice
Who craves for ease, and rest, and joys:

Myself, arch-traitor to myself;
My hollowest friend, my deadliest foe,
My clog whatever road I go.

Yet One there is can curb myself,
Can roll the strangling load from me,
Break off the yoke and set me free.

Christina G. Rossetti, 1830–1894

1186. I AM NOT BOUND TO WIN

I am not bound to win,
But I am bound to be true.
I am not bound to succeed,
But I am bound to live up to what light I
have.
I must stand with anybody that stands right;
Stand with him while he is right,
And part with him when he goes wrong.

Abraham Lincoln, 1809–1865

1187. PRAYER FOR STRENGTH

This is my prayer to Thee, my Lord—
Strike, strike at the root of penury in my heart.
Give me the strength lightly to bear my joys and sorrows.
Give me the strength to make my love fruitful in service.
Give me the strength never to disown the poor or bend my knees before insolent might.
Give me the strength to raise my mind above daily trifles.
And give me the strength to surrender my strength to Thy will with love.

Rabindranath Tagore,[1] *(India), 1861–1941*

1188. MY WORK

Lord, let me not die until I've done for Thee
My earthly work, whatever it may be.
Call me not hence with mission unfulfilled;
Let me not leave my space of ground untilled;
Impress this truth upon me that not one
Can do my portion that I leave undone.

Author unknown

1189. "I DIE DAILY"

Since who'd begin must make an end,
Who'd reign must first resign his crown,
Who'd gain, his all must give:
Each dawn of day I would commend
My soul to Christ and lay me down
To die that I might live.

Low in the grave while morning flowers
I'd lie, and all this self remit
To nothingness at noon:
Its memory wane through waning hours
Till not a ghost remain to flit
Before the rising moon.

But I-in-Christ would quickened rise
And live by His creative will
A very day of days:
His love my morning's enterprise,
His peace my vespers rapt and still,
My night His starry praise.

Phil. J. Fisher, 1883–

[1] Nobel Prize Laureate, 1913.

1190. STRONG SON OF GOD

From "In Memoriam" Proem

Strong Son of God, immortal Love,
Whom we, that have not seen thy face,
By faith, and faith alone, embrace,
Believing where we cannot prove;

Thine are these orbs of light and shade;
Thou madest Life in man and brute;
Thou madest Death; and, lo, thy foot
Is on the skull which thou hast made.

Thou wilt not leave us in the dust:
Thou madest man, he knows not why,
He thinks he was not made to die;
And thou hast made him: thou art just.

Thou seemest human and divine,
The highest, holiest manhood, thou.
Our wills are ours, we know not how;
Our wills are ours, to make them thine.

Our little systems have their day;
They have their day and cease to be;
They are but broken lights of thee,
And thou, O Lord, art more than they.

We have but faith: we cannot know,
For knowledge is of things we see;
And yet we trust it comes from thee,
A beam in darkness: let it grow.

Let knowledge grow from more to more,
But more of reverence in us dwell;
That mind and soul, according well,
May make one music as before,

But vaster. We are fools and slight;
We mock thee when we do not fear:
But help thy foolish ones to bear;
Help thy vain worlds to bear thy light.

Forgive what seem'd my sin in me,
What seem'd my worth since I began;
For merit lives from man to man,
And not from man, O Lord, to thee.

Forgive my grief for one removed,
Thy creature, whom I found so fair.
I trust he lives in thee, and there
I find him worthier to be loved.

Forgive these wild and wandering cries,
Confusions of a wasted youth;
Forgive them where they fail in truth,
And in thy wisdom make me wise.

Alfred Tennyson, 1809–1892

1191. I BIND MY HEART

I bind my heart this tide
To the Galilean's side,
To the wounds of Calvary—
To the Christ who died for me.

I bind my soul this day
To the brother far away,
To the brother near at hand,
In this town, and in this land.

I bind my heart in thrall
To the God, the Lord of all,
To the God, the poor man's Friend,
And the Christ whom He didst send.

I bind myself to peace,
To make strife and envy cease,
God! knit Thou sure the cord
Of my thralldom to my Lord.

Lauchlan MacLean Watt, 1867–

1192. A PRAYER FOR TODAY

Lord, in an age of steel and stone,
When girders tell the dreamer's plan:
Give me the grace to stand alone,
Give me the strength to be a man.

As mighty trains on shining rails
Haste onward through the night and day:
Send me on work that never fails
Because of indolent delay.

As planes that plunge into the sky
To find themselves upborne on air:
Teach me the life of trust to try,
And find the soul upheld through prayer.

From distant places voices speak—
They fill the mind with mystery:
Then may I now Thy message seek,
O, let me keep in tune with Thee.

Amid the motion of machine,
The whirl of wheel, the rush of wings:
Help me to live the life serene,
Because victorious over things.

May something of the vast designs
That motivate and move our days,
Be but inevitable signs
Which call life into lordlier ways.

Charles Nelson Pace, 1877–

1193. From THE VISION OF SIR LAUNFAL

And the voice that was softer than silence
said,
"Lo it is I, be not afraid!
In many climes, without avail,
Thou hast spent thy life for the Holy Grail;

Behold, it is here,—this cup which thou
Didst fill at the streamlet for Me but now;
This crust is My body broken for thee,
This water His blood that died on the tree;
The Holy Supper is kept, indeed,
In whatso we share with another's need;
Not what we give, but what we share,
For the gift without the giver is bare;
Who gives himself with his alms feeds three,
Himself, his hungering neighbor, and Me."

James Russell Lowell, 1819–1891

1194. THE SEARCH

I sought his love in sun and stars,
And where the wild seas roll,
I found it not, as mute I stood,
Fear overwhelmed my soul;
But when I gave to one in need,
I found the Lord of Love indeed.

I sought his love in lore of books,
In charts of science's skill;
They left me orphaned as before—
His love eluded still;
Then in despair I breathed a prayer;
The Lord of Love was standing there!

Thomas Curtis Clark, 1877–

1195. ECCE HOMO

I bent to lift a comrade from the water
Still hotly crimson with the recent slaughter;
Hands joined to mine, with no nail-marks
deviced;
Yet when I stared I knew him for the Christ.

Again, when one from clouds of living steam
Brought out his watch-mate and in pain
extreme
Sank down, I stripped him; though his
blistered side
No spear-wound shows, I hail the Crucified.

I find Him now where deeds are done for man,
At once the Master and the Artisan;
Look for no stigma, nor for royal graces,
Dressed like the next, His face like all men's
faces.

John Ackerson, 1898–

1196. THANKS BE TO GOD

I do not thank Thee, Lord,
That I have bread to eat while others starve;
Nor yet for work to do
While empty hands solicit Heaven;
Nor for a body strong
While other bodies flatten beds of pain.
No, not for these do I give thanks!

But I am grateful, Lord,
Because my meagre loaf I may divide;
For that my busy hands
May move to meet another's need;
Because my doubled strength
I may expend to steady one who faints.
Yes, for all these do I give thanks!

For heart to share, desire to bear
And will to lift,
Flamed into one by deathless Love—
Thanks be to God for this!
Unspeakable! His Gift!

Janie Alford

1197. ON GIVING

From "The Prophet"

You give but little when you give of your possessions.
It is when you give of yourself that you truly give.
For what are your possessions but things you keep and guard for fear you may need them tomorrow?
And tomorrow, what shall tomorrow bring to the overprudent dog burying bones in the trackless sand as he follows the pilgrims to the holy city?
And what is fear of need but need itself?
Is not dread of thirst when your well is full, the thirst that is unquenchable?

There are those who give little of the much which they have—and they give it for recognition and their hidden desire makes their gifts unwholesome.
And there are those who have little and give it all.
These are the believers in life and the bounty of life, and their coffer is never empty.
There are those who give with joy, and that joy is their reward.
And there are those who give with pain, and that pain is their baptism.
And there are those who give and know not pain in giving, nor do they seek joy, nor give with mindfulness of virtue;
They give as in yonder valley the myrtle breathes its fragrance into space.
Through the hands of such as these God speaks, and from behind their eyes He smiles upon the earth.

It is well to give when asked, but it is better to give unasked, through understanding;
And to the open-handed the search for one who shall receive is joy greater than giving.
And is there aught you would withhold?
All you have shall some day be given;
Therefore give now, that the season of giving may be yours and not your inheritors'.

Kahlil Gibran, 1883–1931

1198. GIVING

To give a little from a shining store,
Is that to give? To give and feel no loss,
Is that to give as Christ gave on the Cross?
To share the crumbs of happiness we gain
With those who weep apart, to give our best
Of healing sympathy to hearts in pain,
To give our labor when we fain would rest,
This is the charity men knew when He
First breathed that word by starlit Galilee!

William F. Kirk, 1877–

1199. PENNILESS

Penniless . . .
A while
Without food
I can live;
But it breaks my heart
To know
I cannot give.

Penniless . . .
I can share my rags,
But I—
I cannot bear to hear
Starved children cry.

Penniless . . .
And rain falls,
But trust is true.
Helpless I wait to see
What God will do.

Toyohiko Kagawa, 1888–

1200. MERCY

From "The Merchant of Venice," Act IV, sc. 1

The quality of mercy is not strain'd,
It droppeth as the gentle rain from heaven
Upon the place beneath. It is twice bless'd:
It blesseth him that gives and him that takes.
'Tis mightiest in the mightiest: it becomes
The thronéd monarch better than his crown:
His sceptre shows the force of temporal power,
The attribute to awe and majesty,
Wherein doth sit the dread and fear of kings;
But mercy is above this sceptred sway,
It is enthronéd in the hearts of kings,
It is an attribute to God himself;
And earthly power doth then show likest
God's,
When mercy seasons justice.

William Shakespeare, 1564–1616

1201. COURAGE

Courage is the price that Life exacts for
granting peace.
The soul that knows it not
Knows no release from little things:
Knows not the livid loneliness of fear,
Nor mountain heights where bitter joy can
hear
The sound of wings.

How can Life grant us boon of living,
compensate

For dull gray ugliness and pregnant hate
Unless we dare
The soul's dominion? Each time we make a choice, we pay
With courage to behold resistless day,
And count it fair.

Amelia Earhart,[1] *1898–1937*

1202. COURAGE

Courage is armor
A blind man wears;
The calloused scar
Of outlived despairs:
Courage is Fear
That has said its prayers.

Karle Wilson Baker, 1878–

1203. THE PURE HEART

From "Sir Galahad"

My good blade carves the casques of men,
My tough lance thrusteth sure,
My strength is as the strength of ten,
Because my heart is pure.

Alfred Tennyson, 1809–1892

1204. A BATTLE CRY

Give me a battle to fight,
Worthy of courage high,
There let me prove my right
Or let me striving die.
What of the weak who fall?
What of the danger rife?
I am in love with it all—
I am in love with life!

Heroes are common clay,
Conquerors are but men:
Courage has blazed their way,
Courage will win again!
Will makes the man a god—
Then shall I shirk the strife?
Better beneath the sod—
I am in love with life!

Weaklings the combat are fleeing,
Cowardice leans on time;
Strength is the glory of being,
Love makes our strength sublime!
On with the battle of might,
Brave hearts for drum and fife!
Glorious is the fight—
I am in love with life!

Lee Shippey, 1884–

1205. PRAYER FOR COURAGE

Let me not pray to be sheltered from dangers but to be fearless in facing them.
Let me not beg for the stilling of my pain but for the heart to conquer it.
Let me not look for allies in life's battle-field, but to my own strength.
Let me not crave in anxious fear to be saved, but hope for the patience to win my freedom.
Grant me that I may not be a coward, feeling your mercy in my success alone; but let me find the grasp of your hand in my failure.

Rabindranath Tagore, 1861–1941

1206. OPPORTUNITY

This I beheld, or dreamed it in a dream:—
There spread a cloud of dust along a plain;
And underneath the cloud, or in it, raged
A furious battle, and men yelled, and swords
Shocked upon swords and shields. A prince's banner
Wavered, then staggered backward, hemmed by foes.
A craven hung along the battle's edge,
And thought, "Had I a sword of keener steel—
That blue blade that the king's son bears,—but this
Blunt thing!" he snapped and flung it from his hand,
And lowering crept away and left the field.

[1] First woman to cross Atlantic in airplane. Lost on Pacific flight July 1937.

Then came the king's son, wounded, sore
 bestead,
And weaponless, and saw the broken sword,
Hilt-buried in the dry and trodden sand,
And ran and snatched it, and with battle-
 shout
Lifted afresh he hewed his enemy down,
And saved a great cause that heroic day.

Edward Rowland Sill, 1841–1887

1207. HOW DID YOU DIE?

Did you tackle that trouble that came your
 way
 With a resolute heart and cheerful?
Or hide your face from the light of day
 With a craven soul and fearful?
Oh, a trouble's a ton, or a trouble's an ounce,
 Or a trouble is what you make it.
And it isn't the fact that you're hurt that
 counts,
 But only how did you take it?

You are beaten to earth? Well, well, what's
 that?
 Come up with a smiling face.
It's nothing against you to fall down flat,
 But to lie there—that's disgrace.
The harder you're thrown, why the higher
 you bounce;
 Be proud of your blackened eye!
It isn't the fact that you're licked that counts;
 It's how did you fight—and why?

And though you be done to the death, what
 then?
 If you battled the best you could;
If you played your part in the world of men,
 Why, the Critic will call it good.
Death comes with a crawl, or comes with a
 pounce,
 And whether he's slow or spry,
It isn't the fact that you're dead that counts,
 But only, how did you die?

Edmund Vance Cooke, 1866–1932

1208. COWARDS

From "Julius Caesar," Act II, sc. 2

Cowards die many times before their deaths;
The valiant never taste of death but once.

William Shakespeare, 1564–1616

1209. THE PILGRIM

Who would true valour see,
 Let him come hither;
One here will constant be,
 Come wind, come weather;
There's no discouragement
Shall make him once relent
His first avowed intent
 To be a Pilgrim.

Whoso beset him round
 With dismal stories
Do but themselves confound;
 His strength the more is.
No lion can him fright,
He'll with a giant fight,
But he will have a right
 To be a Pilgrim.

Hobgoblin nor foul fiend
 Can daunt his spirit;
He knows he at the end
 Shall life inherit.
Then fancies fly away,
He'll fear not what men say;
He'll labour night and day
 To be a Pilgrim.

John Bunyan, 1628–1688

1210. THE BRIDGE YOU'LL NEVER CROSS

If life seems drab and difficult,
 Just face it with a will;
You do not have to work alone
 Since God is with you still.
Press on with courage toward the goal,
 With Truth your shield emboss;
Be strong, look up and just ignore
 The bridge you'll never cross.

Grenville Kleiser, 1868–

1211. THE BLITHE MASK

He went so blithely on the way
 That people call the Road of Life,
That good folks, who had stopped to pray,
Shaking their heads would look and say
It wasn't right to be so gay
 Upon this weary road of strife.

He whistled as he went, and still
He bore the young where streams were deep,
He helped the feeble up the hill;
He seemed to go with heart athrill,
Careless of deed and wild of will.
He whistled that he might not weep.

Dollett Fuguet

1212. THE SWEETEST LIVES

The sweetest lives are those to duty wed,
Whose deeds, both great and small,
Are close-knit strands of unbroken thread
Where love ennobles all.
The world may sound no trumpets, ring no bells;
The book of life the shining record tells.

The love shall chant its own beatitudes
After its own life working. A child's kiss
Set on thy sighing lips shall make thee glad;
A sick man helped by thee shall make thee strong;
Thou shalt be served thyself by every sense
Of service which thou renderest.

Attributed to Elizabeth Barrett Browning

1213. From VOLUNTARIES

In an age of fops and toys,
Wanting wisdom, void of right,
Who shall nerve heroic boys
To hazard all in Freedom's fight—
Break sharply off their jolly games,
Forsake their comrades gay
And quit proud homes and youthful dames
For famine, toil, and fray?
Yet on the nimble air benign
Speed nimbler messages,
That waft the breath of grace divine
To hearts in sloth and ease.
So nigh is grandeur to our dust,
So near is God to man,
When Duty whispers low, *Thou must,*
The youth replies, *I can.*

Ralph Waldo Emerson, 1803–1882

1214. ODE TO DUTY

Stern Daughter of the Voice of God!
O Duty! if that name thou love
Who art a light to guide, a rod
To check the erring and reprove;
Thou who art victory and law
When empty terrors overawe;
From vain temptations dost set free;
And calm'st the weary strife of frail humanity!

There are who ask not if thine eye
Be on them; who, in love and truth,
Where no misgiving is, rely
Upon the genial sense of youth;
Glad hearts, without reproach or blot,
Who do thy work and know it not:
Oh! if through confidence misplaced
They fail, thy saving arms, dread Power, around them cast.

Serene will be our days, and bright
And happy will our nature be,
When love is an unerring light,
And joy its own security;
And they a blissful course may hold
Even now, who, not unwisely bold,
Live in the spirit of this creed;
Yet seek thy firm support according to their need.

I, loving freedom, and untried,
No sport of every random gust,
Yet being to myself a guide,
Too blindly have reposed my trust;
And oft, when in my heart was heard
Thy timely mandate, I deferred
The task, in smoother walks to stray;
But thee I now would serve more strictly, if I may.

Through no disturbance of my soul,
Or strong compunction in me wrought,
I supplicate for thy control,
But in the quietness of thought.
Me this unchartered freedom tires;
I feel the weight of chance-desires:
My hopes no more must change their name,
I long for a repose that ever is the same.

Stern Lawgiver! yet thou dost wear
The Godhead's most benignant grace;
Nor know we anything so fair
As is the smile upon thy face:

Flowers laugh before thee on their beds
And fragrance in thy footing treads;
Thou dost preserve the stars from wrong;
And the most ancient heavens, through
thee, are fresh and strong.

To humbler functions, awful Power!
I call thee; I myself commend
Unto thy guidance from this hour;
Oh, let my weakness have an end!
Give unto me, made lowly wise,
The spirit of self-sacrifice;
The confidence of reason give;
And in the light of truth thy bondman let me
live.

William Wordsworth, 1770–1850

1215. HOPE EVERMORE AND BELIEVE!

Go from the east to the west, as the sun and the stars direct thee,
Go with the girdle of man, go and encompass the earth.
Not for the gain of the gold; for the getting, the hoarding, the having,
But for the joy of the deed; but for the Duty to do.
Go with the spiritual life, the higher volition and action,
With the great girdle of God, go and encompass the earth.

❖

Go with the sun and the stars, and yet evermore in thy spirit
Say to thyself: It is good: yet is there better than it.
This that I see is not all, and this that I do is but little;
Nevertheless it is good, though there is better than it.

Arthur Hugh Clough, 1819–1861

1216. HE GIVES NOTHING

From "The Vision of Sir Launfal"

He gives nothing but worthless gold
Who gives from a sense of duty;
But he who gives a slender mite,
And gives to that which is out of sight,
That thread of the all-sustaining Beauty
Which runs through all and doth all unite,—
The hand cannot clasp the whole of his alms,
The heart outstretches its eager palms,
For a god goes with it and makes it store
To the soul that was starving in darkness
before.

James Russell Lowell, 1819–1891

1217. FAITH

Lord, give me faith!—to live from day to day,
With tranquil heart to do my simple part,
And, with my hand in thine, just go Thy way.

Lord, give me faith!—to trust, if not to know;
With quiet mind in all things Thee to find,
And, child-like, go where Thou wouldst have
me go.

Lord, give me faith!—to leave it all to Thee,
The future is Thy gift, I would not lift
The veil Thy love has hung 'twixt it and me.

John Oxenham, 1852–1941

1218. UNBELIEF

There is no unbelief;
Whoever plants a seed beneath the sod
And waits to see it push away the clod,
He trusts in God.

Whoever says when clouds are in the sky,
"Be patient, heart; light breaketh by and by,"
Trusts the Most High.

Whoever sees 'neath winter's field of snow,
The silent harvest of the future grow,
God's power must know.

Whoever lies down on his couch to sleep,
Content to lock each sense in slumber deep,
Knows God will keep.

Whoever says "To-morrow," "The
unknown,"

"The future," trusts that Power alone
He dares disown.

The heart that looks on when the eye-lids close,
And dares to live when life has only woes,
God's comfort knows.

There is no unbelief;
For thus by day and night unconsciously
The heart lives by the faith the lips deny.
God knoweth why!

Elizabeth York Case, 1840–1911

1219. I NEVER SAW A MOOR

I never saw a moor,
I never saw the sea;
Yet know I how the heather looks,
And what a wave must be.

I never spoke with God,
Nor visited in heaven;
Yet certain am I of the spot
As if the chart were given.

Emily Dickinson, 1830–1886

1220. FAITH

From "The Ancient Sage"

Thou canst not prove the Nameless, O my son,
Nor canst thou prove the world thou movest in,
Thou canst not prove that thou art body alone,
Nor canst thou prove that thou art spirit alone,
Nor canst thou prove that thou art both in one.
Thou canst not prove thou art immortal, no,
Nor yet that thou art mortal—nay, my son,
Thou canst not prove that I, who speak with thee,
Am not thyself in converse with thyself,
For nothing worthy proving can be proven,
Nor yet disproven. Wherefore thou be wise,
Cleave ever to the sunnier side of doubt,
And cling to Faith beyond the forms of Faith!
She reels not in the storm of warring words,
She brightens at the clash of "Yes" and "No,"
She sees the best that glimmers thro' the worst
She feels the sun is hid but for a night,
She spies the summer thro' the winter bud,
She tastes the fruit before the blossom falls,
She hears the lark within the songless egg,
She finds the fountain where they wail'd "Mirage!"

Alfred Tennyson, 1809–1892

1221. EXPERIENCE

From "Saint Paul"

Oh could I tell ye surely would believe it!
Oh could I only say what I have seen!
How should I tell or how can ye receive it,
How, till he bringeth you where I have been?

Frederick W. H. Myers, 1843–1901

1222. CHALLENGE TO YOUTH

From "The Castle Builder"

Build on, and make thy castles high and fair,
Rising and reaching upward to the skies;
Listen to voices in the upper air,
Nor lose thy simple faith in mysteries.

Henry Wadsworth Longfellow, 1807–1882

1223. FAITH SHALL BUILD A FAIRER THRONE

The waves unbuild the wasting shore;
Where mountains towered, the billows sweep,
Yet still their borrowed spoils restore,
And build new empires from the deep.
So while the floods of thought lay waste
The proud domain of priestly creeds,
Its heaven-appointed tides will haste
To plant new homes for human needs.
Be ours to mark with hearts unchilled
The change an outworn church deplores;
The legend sinks, but Faith shall build
A fairer throne on new found shores.

Oliver Wendell Holmes, 1809–1894

1224. THE TIDE OF FAITH

So faith is strong
Only when we are strong, shrinks when we shrink.
It comes when music stirs us, and the chords,
Moving on some grand climax, shake our souls
With influx new that makes new energies.
It comes in swellings of the heart and tears
That rise at noble and at gentle deeds.
It comes in moments of heroic love,
Unjealous joy in joy not made for us;
In conscious triumph of the good within,
Making us worship goodness that rebukes.
Even our failures are a prophecy,
Even our yearnings and our bitter tears
After that fair and true we cannot grasp.
Presentiment of better things on earth
Sweeps in with every force that stirs our souls
To admiration, self-renouncing love.

George Eliot, 1819–1880

1225. IF THIS WERE FAITH

God, if this were enough,
That I see things bare to the buff
And up to the buttocks in mire;
That I ask nor hope nor hire,
Nut in the husk,
Nor dawn beyond the dusk,
Nor life beyond death:
God, if this were faith?

Having felt thy wind in my face
Spit sorrow and disgrace,
Having seen thine evil doom
In Golgotha and Khartoum,
And the brutes, the work of thine hands,
Fill with injustice lands
And stain with blood the sea:
If still in my veins the glee
Of the black night and the sun
And the lost battle, run:
If, an adept,
The iniquitous lists I still accept
With joy, and joy to endure and be withstood,
And still to battle and perish for a dream of good:
God, if that were enough?

If to feel, in the ink of the slough,
And the sink of the mire,
Veins of glory and fire
Run through and transpierce and transpire,
And a secret purpose of glory in every part,
And the answering glory of battle fill my heart;
To thrill with the joy of girded men
To go on forever and fail and go on again,
And be mauled to the earth and arise,
And contend for the shade of a word and a thing not seen with the eyes:
With the half of a broken hope for a pillow at night
That somehow the right is the right
And the smooth shall bloom from the rough:
Lord, if that were enough?

Robert Louis Stevenson, 1850–1894

1226. FAITH

How do I know that God is good? I don't.
I gamble like a man. I bet my life
Upon one side in life's great war. I must,
I can't stand out. I must take sides. The man
Who is a neutral in this fight is not
A man.

❖

I know not why the Evil,
I know not why the Good, both mysteries
Remain unsolved, and both insoluble.
I know that both are there, the battle set,
And I must fight on this side or on that.
I can't stand shiv'ring on the bank, I plunge
Head first. I bet my life on Beauty, Truth,
And Love, not abstract but incarnate Truth,
Not Beauty's passing shadow but its Self.

Its very self made flesh, Love realized.
I bet my life on Christ—Christ Crucified.
Behold your God! My soul cries out. He hangs,
Serenely patient in his agony,
And turns the soul of darkness into light.
I look upon that body, writhing, pierced
And torn with nails, and see the battlefields
Of time, the mangled dead, the gaping wounds,
The sweating, dazed survivors straggling back,
The widows worn and haggard, still dry-eyed,
Because their weight of sorrow will not lift
And let them weep; I see the ravished maid,
The honest mother in her shame; I see
All history pass by, and through it all
Still shines that face, the Christ Face, like a star
Which pierces drifting clouds, and tells the Truth.
They pass, but it remains and shines untouched,
A pledge of that great hour which surely comes
When storm winds sob to silence, fury spent
To silver silence, and the moon sails calm
And stately through the soundless seas of Peace.
So through the clouds of Calvary—there shines
His face, and I believe that Evil dies,
And Good lives on, loves on, and conquers all—
All War must end in Peace. These clouds are lies.
They cannot last. The blue sky is the Truth.
For God is Love. Such is my Faith, and such
My reasons for it, and I find them strong
Enough. And you? You want to argue? Well,
I can't. It is a choice. I choose the Christ.

G. A. Studdert-Kennedy, 1883–1929

1227. THE VENTURE OF FAITH

From the Phi Beta Kappa poem, Harvard, 1924

Is not one's life itself an act of daring,
A voyage of hazards, without chart or lee;
A risk of tempest, vanquishing or sparing
Our precious argosy?

Not in the harbors of secure seclusion,
Not for the timorous in their sheltered bays,
But after weathering the storm's confusion
Arrive the halcyon days.

And thou, my soul, a heavy-laden vessel,
Beating to windward under shortened sail,
Shall we not run to port, and cease to wrestle
With the unsparing gale?

Ah, better the fierce tempests of contrition,
The treacherous currents of adversity,
Than the entanglements of inanition
Of a Sargasso Sea.

Not to desert the ship in its disaster,
But to win through to port, invites the brave;
Is it not written of the soul's great Master,
"Himself he could not save?"

And when the voyage is ended, by what token
Shall one receive the Master's praise, "Well done?"
"To him that overcometh," God has spoken,
"Lo, he shall be my son."

The crown of piercing thorns which is his burden
Blooms into roses as by magic breath;
And, at the last, rewards with ample guerdon
The faithful unto death.

To hold life only for the sake of giving,
To find in loss a gain, in gain a loss,
That is the paradox of Christian living,
The venture of the Cross.

Francis Greenwood Peabody, 1847–1936

1228. ULTIMA VERITAS

When the anchors that faith has cast
Are dragging in the gale,
I am quietly holding fast
To the things that cannot fail:

I know that right is right;
That it is not good to lie;
That love is better than spite,
And a neighbor than a spy;

I know that passion needs
The leash of a sober mind;

I know that generous deeds
  Some sure reward will find;

❖

In the darkest night of the year,
  When the stars have all gone out,
That courage is better than fear,
  That faith is truer than doubt;

And fierce though the fiends may fight,
  And long though the angels hide,
I know that Truth and Right
  Have the universe on their side;

And that somewhere, beyond the stars,
  Is a Love that is better than fate;
When the night unlocks her bars
  I shall see Him, and I will wait.

Washington Gladden, 1836–1918

1229. TWO PRAYERS

Last night my little boy confessed to me
Some childish wrong;
And kneeling at my knee,
He prayed with tears—
"Dear God, make me a man
Like Daddy—wise and strong;
I know you can."

Then while he slept
I knelt beside his bed,
Confessed my sins,
And prayed with low-bowed head.
"O God, make me a child
Like my child here—
Pure, guileless,
Trusting Thee with faith sincere."

Andrew Gillies, 1870–1942

1230. FAITH

From "The Excursion," Part Fourth

I have seen
A curious child, who dwelt upon a tract
Of inland ground, applying to his ear
The convolutions of a smooth-lipped shell;
To which, in silence hushed, his very soul
Listened intensely; and his countenance soon
Brightened with joy; for from within were heard
Murmurings, whereby the monitor expressed
Mysterious union with its native sea.
Even such a shell the universe itself
Is to the ear of Faith; and there are times,
I doubt not, when to you it doth impart
Authentic tidings of invisible things;
Of ebb and flow, and ever-during power;
And central peace, subsisting at the heart
Of endless agitation.

William Wordsworth, 1770–1850

1231. STRENGTH IN WEAKNESS

Not in the morning vigor, Lord, am I
Most sure of Thee, but when the day goes by
To evening and, all spent with work, my head
Is bowed, my limbs are laid upon my bed.
Lo! in my weariness is faith at length,
Even as children's weakness is their strength.

Richard Burton, 1861–1940

1232. FAITH

What if I say—
  "The Bible is God's Holy Word,
Complete, inspired, without a flaw"—
  But let its pages stay
Unread from day to day,
And fail to learn therefrom God's law;
What if I go not there to seek
  The truth of which I glibly speak,
  For guidance on this earthly way,—
  Does it matter what I say?

What if I say
  That Jesus Christ is Lord divine;
  Yet fellow-pilgrims can behold
  Naught of the Master's love in me,
  No grace of kindly sympathy?
  If I am of the Shepherd's fold,
  Then shall I know the Shepherd's voice
  And gladly make his way my choice.
We are saved by faith, yet faith is one
With life, like daylight and the sun.
Unless they flower in our deeds,
  Dead, empty husks are all the creeds.
  To call Christ, Lord, but strive not to obey,
  Belies the homage that with words I pay.

Maud Frazer Jackson,
contemporary American

1233. THE BOOK OF BOOKS

Within this ample volume lies
The mystery of mysteries.
Happiest they of human race
To whom their God has given grace
To read, to fear, to hope, to pray,
To lift the latch, to force the way;
But better had they ne'er been born
That read to doubt or read to scorn.

Sir Walter Scott, 1771–1832

1234. O WORLD

O world, thou choosest not the better part!
It is not wisdom to be only wise,
And on the inward vision close the eyes;
But it is wisdom to believe the heart.
Columbus found a world, and had no chart
Save one that faith deciphered in the skies;
To trust the soul's invincible surmise
Was all his science and his only art.
Our knowledge is a torch of smoky pine
That lights the pathway but one step ahead
Across a void of mystery and dread.
Bid, then, the tender light of faith to shine
By which alone the mortal heart is led
Unto the thinking of the thought divine.

George Santayana, 1863–

1235. DESERTS

A desert does not have to be
A sandy waste where springs are dry;
A life can shrink to barrenness
If love goes by.

A desert does not have to be
A place where buzzards wheel at dawn;
A heart can hold as dreadful things
When faith is gone.

Anne Hamilton, 1843–1876

1236. FAITH

The road winds up the hill to meet the height,
Beyond the locust hedge it curves from sight—
And yet no man would foolishly contend
That where he sees it not, it makes an end.

Emma Carleton

1237. FAITH AND SIGHT

So I go on, not knowing,
—I would not, if I might—
I would rather walk in the dark with God
Than go alone in the light;
I would rather walk with Him by faith
Than walk alone by sight.

Mary Gardner Brainard, 1837–1905

1238. BETTER A DAY OF FAITH

Better a day of faith
Than a thousand years of doubt!
Better one mortal hour with Thee
Than an endless life without!

Thou art a mighty Wall,
Skirting life's darkened stair;
Groping my way alone,
Lo, I have found Thee there!

Henry Burke Robins, 1874–

1239. TRUST

Better trust all and be deceived,
And weep that trust and that deceiving,
Than doubt one heart, that if believed
Had blessed one's life with true believing.

Oh, in this mocking world too fast
The doubting fiend o'ertakes our youth;
Better be cheated to the last
Than lose the blessed hope of truth.

Frances Anne Kemble, 1809–1893

1240. THE DOUBTER'S PRAYER

Eternal Power, of earth and air!
Unseen, yet seen in all around;
Remote, but dwelling everywhere;
Though silent heard in every sound;

If e'er Thine ear in Mercy lent,
When wretched mortals cried to Thee,
And if indeed, Thy Son was sent,
To save lost sinners such as me:

Then hear me now, while kneeling here,
I lift to Thee my heart and eye,
And all my soul ascends in prayer,
Oh, give me—Give me Faith! I cry.

While Faith is with me, I am blest;
It turns my darkest night to day;
But while I clasp it to my breast,
I often feel it slide away.

Then, cold and dark, my spirit sinks,
To see my light of life depart;
And every fiend of Hell, methinks,
Enjoys the anguish of my heart.

What shall I do if all my love,
My hopes, my toil, are cast away,
And if there be no God above,
To hear and bless me while I pray?

If this be vain delusion all,
If death be an eternal sleep
And none can hear my secret call,
Or see the silent tears I weep!

O help me God! for Thou alone
Canst my distracted soul relieve;
Forsake it not, it is Thine own,
Though weak, yet longing to believe.

Anne Brontë, 1820–1849

1241. BLIND

Give no pity because my feet
Stumble along the dark, hard street,
And stub against the hostile stones,
Coldly deaf to the world's numb moans.

The days move by on sullen wing
Like migrant birds that cannot sing,
Merging at last with a starless night,
Forever denied the gift of light.

Silent—I climb the anguished dark,
Still I can hear a heaven-bound lark.
Sightless—I see! And, seeing, find
Soul-vision though my eyes are blind!

Fanny Crosby, 1820–1918

1242. CREDO

I cannot find my way: there is no star
In all the shrouded heavens anywhere;
And there is not a whisper in the air
Of any living voice but one so far
That I can hear it only as a bar
Of lost, imperial music, played when fair
And angel fingers wove, and unaware,
Dead leaves to garlands where no roses are.

No, there is not a glimmer, nor a call,
For one that welcomes, welcomes when he fears,
The black and awful chaos of the night;
For through it all,—above, beyond it all,—
I know the far-sent message of the years,
I feel the coming glory of the Light!

Edwin Arlington Robinson, 1869–1935

1243. GOD AND MAN

Whenever I am prone to doubt and wonder,
I check myself, and say, the mighty One
Who made the solar system cannot blunder,
And for the best all things are being done.
He who set the stars on their eternal courses,
Has fashioned this strange earth by some sure plan.
Bow low—bow low to those majestic forces,
Nor dare to doubt their wisdom, puny man.

You cannot put one little star in motion,
You cannot shape one single forest leaf,
Nor fling a mountain up, nor sink an ocean,
Presumptuous pygmy, large with unbelief!
You cannot bring one dawn of regal splendor,
Nor bid the day to shadowy twilight fall,
Nor send the pale moon forth with radiance tender;
And dare you doubt the One who has done all?

S. A. Nagel, contemporary American

1244. FAITH

I will not doubt, though all my ships at sea
Come drifting home with broken masts and sails;
I shall believe the Hand which never fails,
From seeming evil worketh good to me;
And, though I weep because those sails are battered,
Still will I cry, while my best hopes lie shattered,
"I trust in Thee."

I will not doubt, though all my prayers return
Unanswered from the still, white realm above;
I shall believe it is an all-wise Love
Which has refused those things for which I yearn;
And though, at times, I cannot keep from grieving,
Yet the pure ardor of my fixed believing
Undimmed shall burn.

I will not doubt, though sorrows fall like rain,
And troubles swarm like bees about a hive;
I shall believe the heights for which I strive,
Are only reached by anguish and by pain;
And, though I groan and tremble with my crosses,
I yet shall see, through my severest losses,
The greater gain.

I will not doubt; well anchored in the faith,
Like some stanch ship, my soul braves every gale,
So strong its courage that it will not fail
To breast the mighty, unknown sea of death.
Oh, may I cry when body parts with spirit,
"I do not doubt," so listening worlds may hear it
With my last breath.

Ella Wheeler Wilcox, 1855–1919

1245. IN DOUBT OF DOUBT

From "Bishop Blougram's Apology"

And now what are we? unbelievers both,
Calm and complete, determinately fixed
To-day, to-morrow, and forever, pray?
You'll guarantee me that? Not so, I think!
In no wise! all we've gained is, that belief,
As unbelief before, shakes us by fits,
Confounds us like its predecessor. Where's
The gain? how can we guard our unbelief,
Make it bear fruit to us?—the problem here.
Just when we are safest, there's a sunset-touch,
A fancy from a flower-bell, some one's death,
A chorus-ending from Euripides,—
And that's enough for fifty hopes and fears
As old and new at once as Nature's self,
To rap and knock and enter in our soul,
Take hands and dance there, a fantastic ring,
Round the ancient idol, on his base again,—
The grand Perhaps! We look on helplessly.
There the old misgivings, crooked questions are—
This good God,—what he could do, if he would,
Would, if he could—then must have done long since:
If so, when, where, and how? some way must be,—
Once feel about, and soon or late you hit
Some sense, in which it might be, after all.
Why not, "The Way, the Truth, the Life?"

Robert Browning, 1812–1889

1246. FAITH

If I lay waste and wither up with doubt
The blessed fields of heaven where once my faith
Possessed itself serenely safe from death;
If I deny the things past finding out;
Or if I orphan my own soul of One
That seemed a Father, and make void the place
Within me where He dwelt in power and grace,
What do I gain by that I have undone?

William Dean Howells, 1837–1920

1247. From INSPIRATION

I will not doubt for evermore,
Nor falter from a steadfast faith,
For though the system be turned o'er,
God takes not back the word which once He saith.

I will not doubt the love untold
Which not my worth nor want has bought,
Which wooed me young, and wooes me old,
And to this evening hath me brought.

Henry David Thoreau, 1817–1862

1248. A STRONGER FAITH

From "In Memoriam," XCVI

Perplext in faith, but pure in deeds,
At last he beat his music out.
There lives more faith in honest doubt,
Believe me, than in half the creeds.

He fought his doubts and gather'd strength,
He would not make his judgment blind,
He faced the specters of the mind
And laid them; thus he came at length

To find a stronger faith his own,
And Power was with him in the night,
Which makes the darkness and the light,
And dwells not in the light alone.

Alfred Tennyson, 1809–1892

1249. DOUBTS

From "Measure For Measure," Act I, sc. 4

Our doubts are traitors,
And make us lose the good we oft might win,
By fearing to attempt.

William Shakespeare, 1564–1616

1250. THE GREATEST LOSS

Upon the white sea sand there sat a pilgrim band,
Telling the losses that their lives had known;
While evening waned away from breezy cliff and bay
And the strong tides went out with weary moan.

One spoke with quivering lip of a fair-freighted ship,
With all his household to the deep gone down;
But one had wider woe for a fair face, long ago
Lost in the darker depths of a great town.

There were who mourned their youth with a most tender ruth,
For its brave hopes and memories ever green;
And one upon the West turned an eye that would not rest
For far off hills whereon its joys had been.

Some talked of vanished gold, some of proud honors told.
Some spake of friends who were their trust no more;
And one, of a green grave beside a foreign wave,
That made me sit so lonely on the shore.

But when their tales were done, there spake among them one,
A stranger seeming from all sorrow free;
"Sad losses ye have met, but mine is heavier yet,
For a believing heart hath gone from me."

"Alas!" these pilgrims said, "for the living and the dead,
For fortune's cruelty, for love's sure cross,
For the wrecks of land and sea! but, however it came to thee,
Thine, stranger, is life's last and heaviest loss!
For the believing heart has gone from thee."

Frances Brown, 1816–1864

1251. DON'T TROUBLE TROUBLE

Don't you trouble trouble till trouble troubles you.
Don't you look for trouble; let trouble look for you.
Who feareth hath forsaken the heavenly Father's side;
What He hath undertaken He surely will provide.

The very birds reprove thee with their happy song;
The very flowers teach thee that fretting is a wrong.
"Cheer up," the sparrow chirpeth; "Thy Father feedeth me;
Think how much He careth, oh, lonely child, for thee."

"Fear not," the flowers whisper; "since thus He hath arrayed
The buttercup and daisy, how canst thou be afraid?"
Then don't you trouble trouble till trouble troubles you;
You'll only double trouble, and trouble others too.

Mark Guy Pearse, 1842–1930

1252. CLOSING THE DOORS

I have closed the door on Doubt.
I will go by what light I can find,
And hold up my hands and reach them out
To the glimmer of God in the dark, and call,
"I am Thine, though I grope and stumble and fall.
I serve, and Thy service is kind."

I have closed the door on Fear.
He has lived with me far too long.
If he were to break forth and reappear,
I would lift my eyes and look at the sky,
And sing aloud and run lightly by;
He will never follow a song.

I have closed the door on Gloom.
His house has too narrow a view.
I must seek for my soul a wider room,
With windows to open and let in the sun,
And radiant lamps when the day is done,
And the breeze of the world blowing through.

Irene Pettit McKeehan, 1882–

1253. MAKE FRIENDS

He who has a thousand friends has not a friend to spare,
And he who has one enemy shall meet him everywhere.

Ali Ben Abu Taleb, A.D. 660;
tr. by Ralph W. Emerson, 1803–1882

1254. THE BEST TREASURE

There are veins in the hills where jewels hide,
And gold lies buried deep;
There are harbor-towns where the great ships ride,

And fame and fortune sleep;
But land and sea though we tireless rove,
And follow each trail to the end,
Whatever the wealth of our treasure-trove,
The best we shall find is a friend.

John J. Moment, 1875–

1255. THREE GATES

If you are tempted to reveal
A tale to you someone has told
About another, make it pass,
Before you speak, three gates of gold.
These narrow gates: First, "Is it true?"
Then, "Is it needful?" In your mind
Give truthful answer. And the next
Is last and narrowest, "Is it kind?"
And if to reach your lips at last
It passes through these gateways three,
Then you may tell the tale, nor fear
What the result of speech may be.

From the Arabian

1256. LET SOMETHING GOOD BE SAID

When over the fair fame of friend or foe
The shadow of disgrace shall fall; instead
Of words of blame, or proof of so and so,
Let something good be said.

Forget not that no fellow-being yet
May fall so low but love may lift his head;
Even the cheek of shame with tears is wet,
If something good be said.

No generous heart may vainly turn aside
In ways of sympathy; no soul so dead
But may awaken strong and glorified,
If something good be said.

And so I charge ye, by the thorny crown,
And by the cross on which the Saviour bled,
And by your own soul's hope for fair renown,
Let something good be said.

James Whitcomb Riley, 1849–1916

1257. FRIENDSHIP

From "The Testament of Beauty"

Friendship is in loving rather than in being lov'd,
which is its mutual benediction and recompense;
and tho' this be, and tho' love is from lovers learn'd,
it springeth none the less from the old essence of self.
No friendless man ('twas well said) can be truly himself;
what a man looketh for in his friend and findeth,
and loving self best, loveth better than himself,
is his own better self, his live lovable idea,
flowering by expansion in the loves of his life.

Robert Bridges, 1844–1930

1258. PASS IT ON

Have you had a kindness shown?
Pass it on.
'Twas not given for thee alone,
Pass it on.
Let it travel down the years,
Let it wipe another's tears,
'Till in heav'n the deed appears—
Pass it on.

Did you hear the loving word?
Pass it on—
Like the singing of a bird?
Pass it on.
Let its music live and grow,
Let it cheer another's woe;
You have reaped what others sow—
Pass it on.

'Twas the sunshine of a smile—
Pass it on.
Staying but a little while!
Pass it on.
April beam a little thing,
Still it wakes the flowers of spring,
Makes the silent birds to sing—
Pass it on.

Have you found the heavenly light?
  Pass it on.
Souls are groping in the night,
  Daylight gone—
Hold thy lighted lamp on high,
Be a star in someone's sky,
He may live who else would die—
  Pass it on.

Be not selfish in thy greed,
  Pass it on.
Look upon thy brother's need,
  Pass it on.
Live for self, you live in vain;
Live for Christ, you live again;
Live for Him, with Him you reign—
  Pass it on.

Henry Burton, 1840–1930

1259. TOUCHING SHOULDERS

There's a comforting thought at the close of the day,
When I'm weary and lonely and sad,
That sort of grips hold of my crusty old heart
And bids it be merry and glad.
It gets in my soul and it drives out the blues,
And finally thrills through and through.
It is just a sweet memory that chants the refrain:
"I'm glad I touch shoulders with you!"

Did you know you were brave, did you know you were strong?
Did you know there was one leaning hard?
Did you know that I waited and listened and prayed,
And was cheered by your simplest word?
Did you know that I longed for that smile on your face,
For the sound of your voice ringing true?
Did you know I grew stronger and better because
I had merely touched shoulders with you?

I am glad that I live, that I battle and strive
For the place that I know I must fill;
I am thankful for sorrows; I'll meet with a grin
What fortune may send, good or ill.
I may not have wealth, I may not be great,
But I know I shall always be true,
For I have in my life that courage you gave
When once I rubbed shoulders with you.

Author unknown

1260. THE HUMAN TOUCH

'Tis the human touch in this world that counts,
  The touch of your hand and mine,
Which means far more to the fainting heart
  Than shelter and bread and wine;
For shelter is gone when the night is o'er,
  And bread lasts only a day,
But the touch of the hand and the sound of the voice
  Sing on in the soul alway.

Spencer Michael Free, 1856–

1261. THE BANQUET

One dwelt in darkness and sang within his dwelling,
  An old one, a blind one, in a hut beside the way.
The king rode wearily; sad and full of care was he
  When he heard the cheerful roundelay.

"Oh," sang the blind man, "I have had a good life!
  Mine has been a merry life, with pleasant things beguiled.
Once a lass kissed me, once I heard a lark sing,
  Once I found a flower, and once I comforted a child."

Then the king paused suddenly and held his hand for his men to see,
  Left his horse, and went to the blind man's door.
"Friend," he called, "good-day to thee. May I come and sup with thee?"
  "Aye, friend and welcome. Why came ye not before?"

Then sat the great king, the wise king, the sad king.
Stroking slow his long beard while the blind man bent his head.
Salt and wet his eyes were on the bread and wine before him.
"Thank Thee," said the blind man, "Who has sent me friend and bread."

Then the king rode hurriedly, then the king rode comforted.
"Oh," sang the blind man, "life goes merrily."
He dwelt in darkness and he sang within his dwelling.
"I have bread a-plenty, and a friend has supped with me."

Louise Driscoll, 1875–

1262. THE UNDERSTANDING HEART

Give me, O God, the understanding heart—
The quick discernment of the soul to see
Another's inner wish, the hidden part
Of him who, wordless, speaks for sympathy.
I would be kind, but kindness is not all:
In arid places may I find the wells,
The deeps within my neighbor's soul that call
To me, and lead me where his spirit dwells.
When Jesus lifted Mary Magdalene
And Mary came with alabaster flask,
A deed was wrought—but more; that there was seen
The bond of holy love for which I ask.
Give me, O God, the understanding heart,
Lit with the quickening flame Thou dost impart.

Georgia Harkness, 1891–

1263. I SOUGHT MY SOUL

I sought my soul,
But my soul I could not see.
I sought my God,
But my God eluded me.
I sought my brother,
And I found all three.

Author unknown

1264. A ROSE TO THE LIVING

A rose to the living is more than
Sumptuous wreaths to the dead;
In filling love's infinite store
A rose to the living is more—
If graciously given before the
Hungering spirit is fled,
A rose to the living is more than
Sumptuous wreaths to the dead.

Nixon Waterman, 1859–1944

1265. WALL

My friend and I have built a wall
Between us thick and wide:
The stones of it are laid in scorn
And plastered high with pride.

We talk across the stubborn stones
So arrogantly tall—
Only we cannot touch our hands
Since we have built the wall.

Elizabeth Morrow,
contemporary American

1266. THE ARROW AND THE SONG

I shot an arrow into the air,
It fell to earth, I knew not where;
For, so swiftly it flew, the sight
Could not follow it in its flight.

I breathed a song into the air,
It fell to earth, I knew not where;
For who has sight so keen and strong,
That it can follow the flight of song?

Long, long afterward, in an oak
I found the arrow, still unbroke;
And the song, from beginning to end,
I found again in the heart of a friend.

Henry Wadsworth Longfellow, 1807–1882

1267. From MENDING WALL

Something there is that doesn't love a wall,
That sends the frozen-ground-swell under it,
And spills the upper boulders in the sun;
And makes gaps even two can pass abreast.

❖

Before I built a wall I'd ask to know
What I was walling in or walling out,

And to whom I was like to give offence.
Something there is that doesn't love a wall,
That wants it down!

Robert Frost, 1875–

1268. ATONEMENT

How often we neglect a friend
When living—but should death appear,
The penitent heart is quick to send
A wreath to lay upon his bier.

Margaret E. Bruner,
contemporary American

1269. TELL HIM SO

If you have a word of cheer
That may light the pathway drear,
Of a brother pilgrim here,
Let him know.
Show him you appreciate
What he does, and do not wait
Till the heavy hand of fate
Lays him low.
If your heart contains a thought
That will brighter make his lot,
Then, in mercy, hide it not;
Tell him so.

❖

Wait not till your friend is dead
Ere your compliments are said;
For the spirit that has fled,
If it know,
Does not need to speed it on
Our poor praise; where it has gone
Love's eternal, golden dawn
Is aglow.
But unto our brother here
That poor praise is very dear;
If you've any word of cheer
Tell him so.

J. A. Egerton, 1869–

1270. TODAY AND TOMORROW

Withhold all eulogies when I am dead,
All noisy sorrow;
Give me the tender word today instead
Of tears tomorrow.

Come not with flowers to strew above my breast,
And sigh for me there.
The hawk or crow may haunt the piney crest;
I shall not be there.

Speak not my name, when I have passed from earth,
In tones of sadness;
At thought of me repress no note of mirth,
No burst of gladness.

Delay not, thou whom I have wounded sore,
Till thou outlive me
To grant the pardon that I here implore;
But now forgive me.

Edward N. Pomeroy

1271. AN OLD STORY

Strange that I did not know him then,
That friend of mine.
I did not even show him then
One friendly sign;

But cursed him for the ways he had
To make me see
My envy of the praise he had
For praising me.

I would have rid the earth of him
Once, in my pride.
I never knew the worth of him
Until he died.

Edwin Arlington Robinson, 1869–1935

1272. A PRAYER

Oh, not for more or longer days, dear Lord,
My prayer shall be—
But rather teach me how to use the days
Now given me.

I ask not more of pleasure or of joy
For this brief while—
But rather let me for the joys I have
Be glad and smile.

I ask not ownership of vast estates
Nor piles of gold—
But make me generous with the little store
My hands now hold.

Nor shall I ask that life should give to me
Another friend—
Just keep me true to those I have, dear Lord,
Until the end.

B. Y. Williams,
contemporary American

1273. HOPE

From "Essay on Man"

Hope springs eternal in the human breast:
Man never is, but always to be blest.

Alexander Pope, 1688–1744

1274. HOPE

Hope, like a gleaming taper's light,
Adorns and cheers our way;
And still, as darker grows the night,
Emits a brighter ray.

Oliver Goldsmith, 1728–1774

1275. HOPE

Soft as the voice, as the voice of a
Zephyr, breathing unheard,
Hope gently whispers, through the shadows,
Her comforting word:
Wait till the darkness is over,
Wait till the tempest is done,
Hope for the sunshine, hope for the morrow,
After the storm has gone.

Author unknown

1276. THE SONGS WE NEED

Myriad singers pour their treasures
Into wearied ears—
Sweet, uncertain, minor measures,
Trembling doubts and fears.

Why repeat these strains of sadness,
Which but feed our fears?
Are there no clear notes of gladness
Straying down the years?

Sing of Sorrow? All men know it.
Share with them their tears;
Then—ah! then, forget not, poet—
Sing the Hope that cheers.

Bernard Freeman Trotter, 1890–1917

1277. SONG OF HOPE

Children of yesterday,
Heirs of tomorrow,
What are you weaving?
Labor and sorrow?
Look to your looms again.
Faster and faster
Fly the great shuttles
Prepared by the Master;
Life's in the loom,
Room for it—
Room!

Children of yesterday,
Heirs of tomorrow,
Lighten the labor
And sweeten the sorrow.
Now, while the shuttles fly
Faster and faster,
Up and be at it,
At work with the Master;
He stands at your loom,
Room for Him—
Room!

Children of yesterday,
Heirs of tomorrow,
Look at your fabric
Of labor and sorrow.
Seamy and dark
With despair and disaster,
Turn it, and—lo,
The design of the Master!
The Lord's at the loom;
Room for Him—
Room!

Mary Artemisia Lathbury, 1841–1913

1278. HOPE

I shall wear laughter on my lips
Though in my heart is pain—
God's sun is always brightest after rain.

I shall go singing down my little way
Though in my breast the dull ache grows—
The song birds come again after the snows.

I shall walk eager still for what Life holds
Although it seems the hard road will not
end—
One never knows the beauty round the bend!

Anna Blake Mezquida,
contemporary American

1279. THE LARGER HOPE

From "In Memoriam," LIV; LV

O, yet we trust that somehow good
Will be the final goal of ill,
To pangs of nature, sins of will,
Defects of doubt, and taints of blood;

That nothing walks with aimless feet;
That not one life shall be destroy'd,
Or cast as rubbish to the void
When God hath made the pile complete;

That not a worm is cloven in vain;
That not a moth with vain desire
Is shrivel'd in a fruitless fire,
Or but subserves another's gain.

Behold, we know not anything;
I can but trust that good shall fall
At last—far off—at last, to all,
And every winter change to spring.

So runs my dream; but what am I?
An infant crying in the night;
An infant crying for the light,
And with no language but a cry.

❖

I falter where I firmly trod,
And falling with my weight of cares
Upon the great world's altar-stairs
That slope thro' darkness up to God,

I stretch lame hands of faith, and grope,
And gather dust and chaff, and call
To what I feel is Lord of all,
And faintly trust the larger hope.

Alfred Tennyson, 1809–1892

1280. HOPE

From "The Ballad of Reading Gaol"

We did not dare to breathe a prayer
Or give our anguish scope!
Something was dead in each of us,
And what was dead was Hope.

Oscar Wilde, 1856–1900

1281. O GOD OF EARTH AND ALTAR

O God of earth and altar,
Bow down and hear our cry,
Our earthly rulers falter,
Our people drift and die;
The walls of gold entomb us,
The swords of scorn divide,
Take not Thy thunder from us,
But take away our pride.

From all that terror teaches,
From lies of tongue and pen,
From all the easy speeches
That comfort cruel men,
From sale and profanation
Of honor and the sword,
From sleep and from damnation,
Deliver us, good Lord!

Tie in a living tether
The priest and prince and thrall,
Bind all our lives together,
Smite us and save us all;
In ire and exultation
Aflame with faith, and free,
Lift up a living nation,
A single sword to Thee.

Gilbert K. Chesterton, 1874–1936

1282. THE LOWEST PLACE

Give me the lowest place, not that I dare
Ask for that lowest place, but Thou hast died
That I might live and share
Thy glory by Thy side.

Give me the lowest place; or if for me
That lowest place too high, make one more low
Where I may sit and see
My God and love Thee so.[1]

Christina G. Rossetti, 1830–1894

1283. THE SWEEPER OF THE FLOOR

Methought that in a solemn church I stood.
Its marble acres, worn with knees and feet,
Lay spread from door to door, from street to street.

[1] The last four lines are inscribed over the poet's grave at Highgate, England.

Midway the form hung high upon the rood
Of Him who gave His life to be our good;
Beyond, priests flitted, bowed, murmured meet
Among the candles shining still and sweet.
Men came and went, and worshipped as they could;
And still their dust a woman with her broom,
Bowed to her work, kept sweeping to the door.
Then saw I slow through all the pillared gloom
Across the church a silent figure come.
"Daughter," it said, "Thou sweepest well my floor!"
"It is the Lord!" I cried, and saw no more.

George Macdonald, 1824–1905

1284. From THE MONK IN THE KITCHEN

There is no small work unto God.
He required of us greatness;
Of His least creature
A high angelic nature,
Stature superb and bright completeness,
He sets to us no humble duty.
Each act that He would have us do
Is haloed round with strangest beauty;
Terrific deeds and cosmic tasks
Of His plainest child He asks.
When I polish the brazen pan
I hear a creature laugh afar
In the gardens of a star,
And from his burning presence run
Flaming wheels of many a sun.
Whoever makes a thing more bright,
He is an angel of all light.
When I cleanse this earthen floor
My spirit leaps to see
Bright garments trailing over it,
A cleanness made by me.
Purger of all men's thoughts and ways,
With labor do I sound Thy praise,
My work is done for Thee.
Whoever makes a thing more bright,
He is an angel of all light.
Therefore let me spread abroad
The beautiful cleanness of my God.

Anna Hempstead Branch, 1875?–1937

1285. THE POWER-HOUSE

Out for my evening stroll
I discovered on 84th Street
A power-house, quietly humming to itself,
And though I lived near-by
I had never known it was there.

Some people are like that.

Christopher Morley, 1890–

1286. ABOU BEN ADHEM

Abou Ben Adhem (may his tribe increase!)
Awoke one night from a deep dream of peace,
And saw within the moonlight in his room,
Making it rich and like a lily in bloom,
An angel writing in a book of gold;
Exceeding peace had made Ben Adhem bold,
And to the Presence in the room he said,
"What writest thou?" The vision raised its head,
And with a look made of all sweet accord,
Answered, "The names of those who love the Lord."
"And is mine one?" said Abou. "Nay, not so,"
Replied the angel. Abou spoke more low,
But cheerily still, and said, "I pray thee, then,
Write me as one that loves his fellow-men."
The angel wrote, and vanished. The next night
It came again with a great wakening light,
And showed the names whom love of God had blessed;
And, lo! Ben Adhem's name led all the rest!

Leigh Hunt, 1784–1859

1287. THE BLADES OF GRASS

In Heaven,
Some little blades of grass
Stood before God.
"What did you do?"
Then all save one of the little blades
Began eagerly to relate
The merits of their lives.
This one stayed a small way behind,
Ashamed.
Presently, God said,
"And what did you do?"
The little blade answered, "Oh, my Lord,
Memory is bitter to me,
For, if I did good deeds,
I know not of them."
Then God, in all His splendor,
Arose from His throne.
"Oh, best little blade of grass!" He said.

Stephen Crane, 1871–1900

1288. THE FOOL'S PRAYER

The royal feast was done; the King
Sought some new sport to banish care,
And to his jester cried: "Sir Fool,
Kneel now, and make for us a prayer!"

The jester doffed his cap and bells,
And stood the mocking court before;
They could not see the bitter smile
Behind the painted grin he wore.

He bowed his head, and bent his knee
Upon the monarch's silken stool;
His pleading voice arose: "O Lord,
Be merciful to me, a fool!

❖

"'Tis not by guilt the onward sweep
Of truth and right, O Lord, we stay;
'Tis by our follies that so long
We hold the earth from heaven away.

"These clumsy feet, still in the mire,
Go crushing blossoms without end;
These hard, well-meaning hands we thrust
Among the heart-strings of a friend.

"The ill-timed truth we might have kept—
Who knows how sharp it pierced and stung?
The word we had not sense to say—
Who knows how grandly it had rung?

"Our faults no tenderness should ask,
The chastening stripes must cleanse them all;
But for our blunders—oh, in shame
Before the eyes of heaven we fall.

"Earth bears no balsam for mistakes;
Men crown the knave, and scourge the tool
That did his will; but Thou, O Lord,
Be merciful to me, a fool!"

The room was hushed; in silence rose
The King, and sought his gardens cool,
And walked apart, and murmured low,
"Be merciful to me, a fool!"

Edward Rowland Sill, 1841–1887

1289. THE SHEPHERD BOY'S SONG

From "The Pilgrim's Progress"

He that is down needs fear no fall,
He that is low, no pride;
He that is humble ever shall
Have God to be his guide.

I am content with what I have,
Little be it or much:
And, Lord, contentment still I crave,
Because Thou savest such.

Fullness to such a burden is
That go on pilgrimage:
Here little, and hereafter bliss,
Is best from age to age.

John Bunyan, 1628–1688

1290. THE HAPPIEST HEART

Who drives the horses of the sun
Shall lord it but a day.
Better the lowly deed were done
And kept the humble way.

The rust will find the sword of fame;
The dust will hide the crowd,
Aye, none shall nail so high his name
Time will not tear it down.

The happiest heart that ever beat
Was in some quiet breast
That found the common daylight sweet
And left to heaven the rest.

John Vance Cheney, 1848–1922

1291. THE NEWER VAINGLORY

Two men went up to pray; and one gave thanks,
Not with himself—aloud,
With proclamation, calling on the ranks
Of an attentive crowd.

"Thank God, I clap not my own humble breast,
But other ruffians' backs,
Imputing crime—such is my tolerant haste—
To any man that lacks.

"For I am tolerant, generous, keep no rules,
And the age honours me.
Thank God, I am not as these rigid fools,
Even as this Pharisee."

Alice Meynell, 1847–1922

1292. THESE TIMES

Our motors pierce the clouds. They penetrate
The depth of oceans. Microscopes reveal
New worlds to conquer, while we dedicate
Our intellects to strength of stone and steel.
We are as proud as those who built a tower
To reach to heaven. Recklessly we rear
Our lofty Babels, arrogant with power.
How dare we boast of cities while we hear
The nations groping through the dark along
The road of life? What right have we for pride
Till Truth is steel, and Faith is iron-strong,
Till God and man are working side by side?
Then let our prayers and labors never cease;
We act the prologue of a masterpiece.

Gertrude Ryder Bennett,
contemporary American

1293. WISDOM

From "The Task," Book 6

Knowledge and wisdom, far from being one,
Have oft times no connection. Knowledge dwells
In heads replete with thoughts of other men:
Wisdom in minds attentive to their own.
Knowledge is proud that he has learn'd so much;
Wisdom is humble that he knows no more.

William Cowper, 1731–1800

1294. MORTALITY[1]

Oh why should the spirit of mortal be proud?
Like a swift-flitting meteor, a fast-flying cloud,
A flash of the lightning, a break of the wave,
Man passeth from life to his rest in the grave.

The leaves of the oak and the willow shall fade,
Be scattered around, and together be laid;
And the young and the old, and the low and the high,
Shall molder to dust and together shall lie.

The infant a mother attended and loved,
The mother that infant's affection who proved,
The husband that mother and infant have blessed—
Each, all, are away to their dwellings of rest.

The maid on whose cheek, on whose brow, in whose eye,
Shone beauty and pleasure—her triumphs are by;
And alike from the minds of the living erased
Are the memories of mortals who loved her and praised.

[1] A favorite poem of Abraham Lincoln.

The hand of the king, that the scepter hath borne;
The brow of the priest, that the miter hath worn;
The eye of the sage, and the heart of the brave,—
Are hidden and lost in the depths of the grave.

The peasant whose lot was to sow and to reap;
The herdsman, who climbed with his goats up the steep;
The beggar, who wandered in search of his bread,—
Have faded away like the grass that we tread.

The saint who enjoyed the communion of heaven,
The sinner who dared to remain unforgiven;
The wise and the foolish, the guilty and just,
Have quietly mingled their bones in the dust.

So the multitude goes, like the flower or the weed
That withers away to let others succeed;
So the multitude comes, even those we behold,
To repeat every tale that has often been told.

For we are the same things our fathers have been;
We see the same sights our fathers have seen;
We drink the same stream, and feel the same sun,
And run the same course our fathers have run.

The thoughts we are thinking our fathers did think;
From the death we are shrinking our fathers did shrink;
To the life we are clinging our fathers did cling;
But it speeds from us all like a bird on the wing.

They loved,—but the story we cannot unfold;
They scorned,—but the heart of the haughty is cold;
They grieved,—but no wail from their slumbers will come;
They joyed,—but the tongue of their gladness is dumb.

They died, aye! they died; and we, things that are now,
That walk on the turf that lies over their brow,
That make in their dwellings a transient abode,
Meet the changes they met on their pilgrimage road.

Yea! hope and despondency, pleasure and pain,
Are mingled together in sunshine and rain;
And the smile and the tear, the song and the dirge,
Still follow each other like surge upon surge.

'Tis the wink of an eye, 'tis the draught of a breath,
From the blossom of health to the paleness of death,
From the gilded saloon to the bier and the shroud—
Oh, why should the spirit of mortal be proud?

William Knox, 1789–1825

1295. THE HIGHER LOYALTY

From "Henry VIII," Act III, sc. 2

Cromwell, I charge thee, fling away ambition:
By that sin fell the angels; how can man, then,
The image of his Maker, hope to win by 't?
Love thyself last; cherish those hearts that hate thee:
Corruption wins not more than honesty.
Still in thy right hand carry gentle peace,
To silence envious tongues. Be just, and fear not:
Let all the ends thou aim'st at be thy country's,
Thy God's, and truth's; then if thou fall'st, O Cromwell!
Thou fall'st a blessed martyr.
Serve the king; and—pr'ythee, lead me in:
There take an inventory of all I have,
To the last penny; 'tis the king's: my robe,
And my integrity to heaven, is all
I dare now call mine own. O Cromwell, Cromwell!
Had I but served my God with half the zeal
I served my king, he would not in mine age
Have left me naked to mine enemies!

William Shakespeare, 1564–1616

1296. MY WORLD

God gave my world to me,
And I rebelliously cried out
"How small, and is this all?"
His voice was sad, yet mild:
"All that you love, my child."
Myself that moment died,
And born anew, I cried,
"Love take control and lead my soul
To serve my small estate."
And lo, my world is great!

Chauncey R. Piety

1297. SATAN'S PRIDE

From "Paradise Lost," Book IV

Is there no place
Left for repentance, none for pardon left?
None left but by submission; and that word
Disdain forbids me, and my dread of shame
Among the Spirits beneath, whom I seduced
With other promises and other vaunts
Than to submit, boasting I could subdue
The Omnipotent. Ay me! they little know
How dearly I abide that boast so vain,
Under what torments inwardly I groan.
While they adore me on the throne of Hell,
With diadem and sceptre high advanced,
The lower still I fall, only supreme
In misery: such joy ambition finds!
But say I could repent, and could obtain,
By act of grace, my former state; how soon
Would highth recal high thoughts, how soon unsay
What feigned submission swore! Ease would recant
Vows made in pain, as violent and void
(For never can true reconcilement grow
Where wounds of deadly hate have pierced so deep);
Which would but lead me to a worse relapse
And heavier fall: so should I purchase dear
Short intermission, bought with double smart.
This knows my Punisher; therefore as far
From granting he, as I from begging, peace.
All hope excluded thus, behold, instead
Of us, outcast, exiled, his new delight,
Mankind, created, and for him this World!
So farewell hope, and, with hope, farewell fear,
Farewell remorse! All good to me is lost;
Evil, be thou my Good.

John Milton, 1608–1674

1298. AS OTHERS SEE US

From "To A Louse"
On Seeing One On A Lady's Bonnet At Church

O wad some Power the giftie gie us
To see oursels as ithers see us!
It wad frae monie a blunder free us,
An' foolish notion.
What airs in dress an' gait wad lea'e us,
An' ev'n devotion!

Robert Burns, 1759–1796

1299. HUMILITY

From "God's Two Dwellings"

Though Heaven be high, the gate is low,
And he that comes in there must bow:
The lofty looks shall ne'er
Have entrance there.

O God! since Thou delight'st to rest
In the humble contrite breast,
First make me so to be,
Then dwell with me.

Thomas Washbourne, 1606–1687

1300. THE GREATNESS OF LOVE

I Corinthians 13

I may speak with the tongues of men and of angels, but if I have no love,
I am a noisy gong or a clanging cymbal;
I may prophesy, fathom all mysteries and secret lore,
I may have such absolute faith that I can move hills from their place,
but if I have no love,
I count for nothing;
I may distribute all I possess in charity,
I may give up my body to be burnt,
but if I have no love,
I make nothing of it.
Love is very patient, very kind
Love knows no jealousy;
Love makes no parade, gives itself no airs, is never rude, never selfish, never irritated, never resentful;
Love is never glad when others go wrong,
Love is gladdened by goodness, always slow to expose, always eager to believe the best, always hopeful, always patient.
Love never disappears.
As for prophesying, it will be superseded;
As for 'tongues,' they will cease;
As for knowledge, it will be superseded.
For we only know bit by bit, and we only prophesy bit by bit;
But when the perfect comes, the imperfect will be superseded.
When I was a child,
I talked like a child,
I thought like a child,
I argued like a child;
Now that I am a man, I am done with childish ways.
At present we only see the baffling reflections in a mirror, but then it will be face to face;
At present I am learning bit by bit,
But then I shall understand, as all along I have myself been understood.
Thus 'faith and hope and love last on, these three,' but the greatest of all is love.

Saint Paul, 1st century A.D.,
The New Testament, A New Translation by James Moffatt, 1922

1301. THE WAY

Who seeks for heaven alone to save his soul,
May keep the path, but will not reach the goal;
While he who walks in love may wander far,
But God will bring him where the Blessed are.

Henry van Dyke, 1852–1933

1302. From THE ROAMER

Love is the bread that feeds the multitudes;
Love is the healing of the hospitals;
Love is the light that breaks through prison doors;
Love knows not rich nor poor, nor good nor bad,
But only the beloved, in every heart
One and the same, the incorruptible
Spirit divine, whose tabernacle is life.
Love, more than hunger, feeds the soul's desire;
Love more the spirit than the body heals;
Love is a star unto the darkened mind;
And they who truly are Love's servants leal,
And follow him, undoubting, to the end,
Beyond the bounds of human righteousness,
Past Justice and past Mercy, find at last,
Past Charity, past Pardon, Love enthroned,
Lord of all hearts, incarnate in man's soul.

George Edward Woodberry, 1855–1930

1303. LOVE'S MIRACLE

Upon the marsh mud, dank and foul,
  A golden sunbeam softly fell,
And from the noisome depths arose
  A lily miracle.

Upon a dark bemired life
  A gleam of human love was flung,
And lo, from that ungenial soil
  A noble life upsprung.

L. M. Montgomery, 1874–1942

1304. THE FINAL LESSON

I have sought beauty through the dust of strife,
  I have sought meaning for the ancient ache,
And music in the grinding wheels of life;
  Long have I sought, and little found as yet
Beyond this truth: that Love alone can make
  Earth beautiful, and life without regret!

Arthur Stringer, 1874–

1305. WHEN THE HEART IS FULL OF LOVE

There is beauty in the forest
When the trees are green and fair,
There is beauty in the meadow
When wild flowers scent the air.
There is beauty in the sunlight
And the soft blue beams above.
Oh, the world is full of beauty
When the heart is full of love.

Author unknown

1306. LOVE FOUND ME

Love found me in the wilderness, at cost
Of painful quests, when I myself had lost.

Love on its shoulders joyfully did lay
Me, weary with the greatness of my way.

Love lit the lamp, and swept the house all round,
Till the lost money in the end was found.

'Twas Love, whose quick and ever-watchful eye
The wanderer's first step homeward did espy.

From its own wardrobe Love gave word to bring
What things I needed—shoes, and robe, and ring.

Richard C. Trench, 1807–1886

1307. OUTWITTED

He drew a circle that shut me out—
Heretic, rebel, a thing to flout.
But Love and I had the wit to win:
We drew a circle that took him in!

Edwin Markham, 1852–1940

1308. LOVE THYSELF LAST

Love thyself last; look near, behold thy duty
To those who walk beside thee down life's road,
Make glad their days by little acts of beauty,
And help them bear the burden of earth's load.

Love thyself last; look far and find the stranger
Who staggers 'neath his sin and his despair;
Go, lend a hand and lead him out of danger
To heights where he may see the world is fair

Love thyself last; the vastnesses above thee
Are filled with spirit forces, strong and pure;
And fervently these faithful friends shall love thee,
Keep thy watch over others and endure.

Love thyself last; and thou shalt grow in spirit
To see, to hear, to know and understand;
The message of the stars, lo, thou shalt hear it,
And all God's joys shall be at thy command.

Ella Wheeler Wilcox, 1855–1919

1309. LOVE'S ARGUMENT

I took Love to task;
"Behold," I said,
"How many a weary one
Hath only straw to lie upon."
"There will I lay my head,"
Said Love, "'tis straw I ask."

I took Love to task;
"Behold," I said,
"How many thorns there be
To rend and pierce with treachery
Our lives." Love bent Him down
And took the thorns and made of them
A crown!

I took Love to task;
"Behold," I said,
"Yon gibbet with its burden dread.
Hate reigns!" Love answered me,
"I found a throne like that
On Calvary."

I said to Love,
"Thy law is much too hard,
I cannot follow Thee."
Love stretched forth mighty arms
And said, "Come, child,
I'll carry thee!"

Father Andrew, S.D.C.,
20th century English

1310. SONG

Love that is hoarded, moulds at last
Until we know some day
The only thing we ever have
Is what we give away.

And kindness that is never used
But hidden all alone
Will slowly harden till it is
As hard as any stone.

It is the things we always hold
That we will lose some day;
The only things we ever keep
Are what we give away.

Harold Cornelius Sandall, 1902

1311. THE MASTER-PLAYER

An old, worn harp that had been played
Till all its strings were loose and frayed,
Joy, Hate, and Fear, each one essayed,
To play. But each in turn had found
No sweet responsiveness of sound.

Then Love the Master-Player came
With heaving breast and eyes aflame;
The Harp he took all undismayed,
Smote on its strings, still strange to song,
And brought forth music sweet and strong.

Paul Laurence Dunbar, 1872–1906

1312. LOVE AND HATE

From "Christus"

The sole thing I hate is Hate;
For Hate is death; and Love is life,
A peace, a splendor from above;
And Hate, a never ending strife,
A smoke, a blackness from the abyss
Where unclean serpents coil and hiss!
Love is the Holy Ghost within;
Hate the unpardonable sin!
Who preaches otherwise than this
Betrays his Master with a kiss!

Henry Wadsworth Longfellow, 1807–1882

1313. LIGHT AND LOVE

The night has a thousand eyes,
And the day but one;
Yet the light of the bright world dies
With the dying sun.

The mind has a thousand eyes,
And the heart but one;
Yet the light of a whole life dies
When love is done.

Francis W. Bourdillon, 1852–1921

1314. I NEVER KNEW A NIGHT SO BLACK

I never knew a night so black
Light failed to follow on its track.
I never knew a storm so gray
It failed to have its clearing day.
I never knew such bleak despair
That there was not a rift, somewhere.
I never knew an hour so drear
Love could not fill it full of cheer!

John Kendrick Bangs, 1862–1922

1315. APPREHENSION

I do not fear
To walk the lonely road
Which leads far out into
The sullen night. Nor do
I fear the rebel, wind-tossed
Sea that stretches onward, far,
Beyond the might of human hands
Or human loves. It is the
Brooding, sharp-thorned discontent
I fear, the nagging days without
A sound of song; the sunlit
Noon of ease; the burden of
Delight and—flattery. It is
The hate-touched soul I dread,
The joyless heart; the unhappy
Faces in the streets; the
Smouldering fires of unforgiven
Slights. These do I fear. Not
Night, nor surging seas, nor
Rebel winds. But hearts unlovely,
And unloved.

James A. Fraser, 1907–

1316. BY NIGHT

The tapers in the great God's hall
Burn ageless, beautiful and white,
But only with the fall of dusk
Disclose to earth their faithful light.

Earth keeps her lamps of beauty, too,
  Fairer than stars in fields above;
Dark hours of grief and pain reveal
  The undreamed constancy of love.

Philip Jerome Cleveland, 1903–

1317. THE HOUSE OF PRIDE

I lived with Pride; the house was hung
  With tapestries of rich design.
Of many houses, this among
  Them all was richest, and 'twas mine.
But in the chambers burned no fire,
  Tho' all the furniture was gold:
I sickened of fulfilled desire,
  The House of Pride was very cold.

I lived with Knowledge; very high
  Her house rose on a mountain's side.
I watched the stars roll through the sky,
  I read the scroll of Time flung wide.
But in that house, austere and bare,
  No children played, no laughter clear
Was heard, no voice of mirth was there,
  The House was high but very drear.

I lived with Love; all she possest
  Was but a tent beside a stream.
She warmed my cold hands in her breast,
  She wove around my sleep a dream.
And One there was with face divine
  Who softly came, when day was spent,
And turned our water into wine,
  And made our life a sacrament.

William J. Dawson, 1854–1928

1318. FOLKS NEED A LOT OF LOVING

Folks need a lot of loving in the morning;
  The day is all ahead, with cares beset—
The cares we know, and those that give no warning;
  For love is God's own antidote for fret.

Folks need a heap of loving at the noontime—
  The battle lull, the moment snatched from strife—
Halfway between the waking and the croontime,
  When bickering and worriment are rife.

Folks hunger so for loving at the nighttime,
  When wearily they take them home to rest—
At slumber song and turning-out-the-light time.
  Of all the times for loving, that's the best.

Folks want a lot of loving every minute—
  The sympathy of others and their smile!
Till life's end, from the moment they begin it,
  Folks need a lot of loving all the while.

Strickland Gillilan, 1869–

1319. MADNESS

She called from her cell,
"Let me give you a rose,"
To the cold tract-man
In his Sabbath clothes.

And the tract-man said
To the one gone mad,
"How can you give
What you never had?"

"As you give Christ,"
The madwoman said,
"While love in your heart
Lies cold and dead."

Harry Lee, 1874–1942

1320. DIRGE

O sad, sad world, O world that knows not Love,
But fashions shell and armor, spear and nail,
With unrelenting hearts which these entail,
O world of hate, O world that knows not Love.
Light shines; the darkness comprehends it not:
Too swiftly was thy provenance forgot,
O tragic world, O world that knows not Love.
Proud, hard, the city set upon a hill
Denies the humble Rider, weeping still:
O foolish world, O world that knows not Love.
Drives him to death beyond the outer gate,
Unmindful of his high and hidden state,—
O fearful world, O world that knows not Love.
And so the armored years march thousands strong,
While the sick heart cries, "How long? How long?"
O sad, sad world, O world that knows not Love.

Edith Lovejoy Pierce, 1904–

1321. CLOISTERED

Seal thou the window! Yea, shut out the light
And bar my door to all the airs of spring.
Yet in my cell, concealed from curious sight,
Here will I sit and sing.

Deaf, blind, and wilt Thou have me dumb, also,
Telling in silence these sad beads of days?
So let it be: though no sweet numbers flow,
My breath shall be Thy praise.

Yea, though Thou slay the life wherein men see
The upward-mounting flame, the failing spark,
My heart of love, that heart Thou gavest me,
Shall beat on in the dark.

Alice Brown, 1857–

1322. GOD'S PLANS

If we could push ajar the gates of life,
And stand within, and all God's workings see,
We could interpret all this doubt and strife,
And for each mystery could find a key.
But not today. Then be content, poor heart!
God's plans, like lilies pure and white, unfold:
We must not tear the close-shut leaves apart—
Time will reveal the calyxes of gold.

Mary Riley Smith, 1842–1927

1323. HASTE NOT, REST NOT

Without haste! Without rest!
Bind the motto to thy breast;
Bear it with thee as a spell;
Storm or sunshine, guard it well!
Heed not the flowers that round thee bloom,
Bear it onward to the tomb.

Haste not! Let no thoughtless deed
Mar for aye the spirit's speed!
Ponder well and know the right,
Onward, then, with all thy might!
Haste not! Years can ne'er atone
For one reckless action done.

Rest not! Life is sweeping by,
Go and dare before you die
Something mighty and sublime
Leave behind to conquer time!
Glorious 'tis to live for aye,
When these forms have passed away.

Haste not! Rest not! Calmly wait;
Meekly bear the stones of fate!
Duty be thy polar guide—
Do the right whate'er betide!
Haste not! Rest not! Conflicts past,
God shall crown thy work at last.

Johann W. von Goethe, 1749–1832

1324. A PRAYER FOR PEACE

Keep me quiet, Master,
Patient day by day,
When I would go faster,
Teach me Thy delay.

Restless, oft I borrow
From the future care.
Teach me that to-morrow
Shall its burden bear.

From Thy full provision
Daily richly fed,
By Thy clearer vision
Ever safely led,

Let me to my brothers
Turn a face serene,
Sharing thus with others
Peace from the Unseen.

William Adams Brown, 1865–1943

1325. ON HIS BLINDNESS[1]

When I consider how my light is spent,
E're half my days, in this dark world and wide,
And that one Talent which is death to hide,
Lodg'd with me useless, though my Soul more bent
To serve therewith my Maker, and present
My true account, lest he returning chide,
Doth God exact day-labour, light deny'd,

I fondly ask; but patience, to prevent
That murmur, soon replies, God doth not need
Either man's work or his own gifts, who best
Bear his mild yoke, they serve him best, his State
Is Kingly. Thousands at his bidding speed,
And post o'er Land and Ocean without rest:
They also serve who only stand and wait.

John Milton, 1608–1674

[1] Milton was 44 when his blindness became total.

1326. MEDITATION

When I am sore beset I seek some quiet place,
Some lonely room or barren, windswept hill,
And there in silence wait alone until
I see again the smile upon God's face.

I feel his presence fill me like the dawn
And hear once more his whispered, "Peace, be still,"
And know again the strength to do his will.
I turn to take my load and find it gone.

Antoinette Goetschius, contemporary American

1327. WHAT IS PRAYER?

Prayer is the soul's sincere desire,
Uttered or unexpressed;
The motion of a hidden fire,
That trembles in the breast.

Prayer is the burden of a sigh,
The falling of a tear;
The upward glancing of an eye,
When none but God is near.

Prayer is the simplest form of speech
That infant lips can try;
Prayer, the sublimest strains that reach
The Majesty on high.

Prayer is the contrite sinner's voice,
Returning from his ways;
While angels in their songs rejoice,
And cry, "Behold! He prays!"

Prayer is the Christian's vital breath,
The Christian's native air;
His watchword at the gate of death—
He enters heaven with prayer.

The saints in prayer appear as one
In word and deed and mind;
Where with the Father and the Son
Sweet fellowship they find.

Nor prayer is made by man alone:
The Holy Spirit pleads;
And Jesus, on the eternal Throne,
For sinners intercedes.

O Thou by whom we come to God—
The Life, the Truth, the Way!
The path of prayer Thyself hast trod;
Lord, teach us how to pray!

James Montgomery, 1771–1854

1328. THE UNSEEN BRIDGE

There is a bridge, whereof the span
Is rooted in the heart of man,
And reaches, without pile or rod,
Unto the Great White Throne of God.
Its traffic is in human sighs
Fervently wafted to the skies;
'Tis the one pathway from despair;
And it is called the Bridge of Prayer.

Gilbert Thomas, 1891–

1329. From ANCHORED TO THE INFINITE

The builder who first bridged Niagara's gorge,
Before he swung his cable, shore to shore,
Sent out across the gulf his venturing kite
Bearing a slender cord for unseen hands
To grasp upon the further cliff and draw
A greater cord and then a greater yet;
Till at last across the chasm swung
The cable—then the mighty bridge in air!

So we may send our little timid thought
Across the void, out to God's reaching
hands—
Send out our love and faith to thread the
deep—
Thought after thought until the little cord
Has greatened to a chain no chance can break,
And we are anchored to the Infinite!

Edwin Markham, 1852–1940

1330. PROOF

If radio's slim fingers can pluck a melody
From night—and toss it over a continent or
sea;
If the petalled white notes of a violin
Are blown across the mountains or the city's
din;
If songs, like crimson roses, are culled from
thin blue air—
Why should mortals wonder if God hears
prayer?

Ethel Romig Fuller, 1883–

1331. THIS WERE TO PRAY

If we with earnest effort could succeed
To make our life one long-connected prayer,
As lives of some perhaps have been and are;
If, never leaving Thee, we had no heed
Our wandering spirits back again to lead
Into Thy presence, but continue there,
Like angels standing on the highest stair
Of the sapphire throne—this were to pray
indeed.

But if distractions manifold prevail,
And if in this we must confess we fail,
Grant us to keep at least a prompt desire,
Continual readiness for prayer and praise,
An altar heaped and waiting to take fire
With the least spark, and leap into a blaze.

Richard Chenivix Trench, 1807–1886

1332. From THE FORCE OF PRAYER

Oh! there is never sorrow of heart
That shall lack a timely end,
If but to God we turn, and ask
Of Him to be our friend!

William Wordsworth, 1770–1850

1333. THOU KNOWEST, LORD

Thou knowest, Lord! the weariness and sorrow
Of all sad hearts that come to Thee for rest;
Cares of today, and burdens of tomorrow. . . .
O Saviour, Thou hast wept and Thou hast loved;
And love and sorrow still to Thee may come,
And find a hiding-place, a rest, a home.

Therefore we come, Thy gentle call obeying,
And lay our sins and sorrows at Thy feet,

On everlasting strength our weakness staying,
Clothed in Thy robe of righteousness complete;
Then rising and refreshed we leave Thy throne,
And follow on to know as we are known.

Author unknown

1334. SANCTUARY

Let us put by some hour of every day
For holy things—whether it be when dawn
Peers through the window pane, or when noon
Flames, like a burnished topaz, in the vault,
Or when the thrush pours in the ear of eve
Its plaintive melody; some little hour
Wherein to hold rapt converse with the soul,
From sordidness and self a sanctuary,
Swept by the winnowings of unseen things,
And touched by the White Light ineffable!

Clinton Scollard, 1860–1932

1335. THE SENTINEL

The morning is the gate of day,
But ere you enter there
See that you set to guard it well,
The sentinel of prayer.

So shall God's grace your steps attend,
But nothing else pass through
Save what can give the countersign;
The Father's will for you.

When you have reached the end of day
Where night and sleep await,
Set there the sentinel again
To bar the evening's gate.

So shall no fear disturb your rest,
No danger and no care.
For only peace and pardon pass
The watchful guard of prayer.

Author unknown

1336. REST AND WORK

The camel, at the close of day,
Kneels down upon the sandy plain
To have his burden lifted off,
And rest to gain.

My soul, thou too, shouldst to thy knees
When daylight draweth to a close,
And let thy Master lift thy load
And grant repose.

Else how canst thou tomorrow meet,
With all tomorrow's work to do,
If thou thy burden all the night
Dost carry through?

The camel kneels at break of day
To have his guide replace his load
Then rises up anew to take
The desert road.

So thou shouldst kneel at morning dawn,
That God may give thee daily care,
Assured that He no load too great
Will make thee bear.

Anne Whitney

1337. BEGIN THE DAY WITH GOD

Every morning lean thine arms awhile
Upon the window-sill of heaven
And gaze upon thy Lord,
Then, with the vision in thy heart,
Turn strong to meet thy day.

Author unknown

1338. THE SECRET

I met God in the morning
When my day was at its best,
And His presence came like sunrise,
Like a glory in my breast.

All day long the Presence lingered,
All day long He stayed with me,
And we sailed in perfect calmness
O'er a very troubled sea.

Other ships were blown and battered,
Other ships were sore distressed,
But the winds that seemed to drive them
Brought to us a peace and rest.

Then I thought of other mornings,
With a keen remorse of mind,
When I too had loosed the moorings,
With the Presence left behind.

So I think I know the secret,
Learned from many a troubled way:
You must seek Him in the morning
If you want Him through the day!

Ralph Spaulding Cushman, 1879–

1339. From THE VISION SPLENDID[1]

'Mid all the traffic of the ways,
Turmoils without, within,
Make in my heart a quiet place,
And come and dwell therein:

A little shrine of quietness,
All sacred to Thyself,
Where Thou shalt all my soul possess,
And I may find myself:

A little shelter from life's stress,
Where I may lay me prone,
And bare my soul in loneliness,
And know as I am known:

A little place of mystic grace,
Of self and sin swept bare,
Where I may look upon Thy face,
And talk with Thee in prayer.

John Oxenham, 1852–1941

1340. PRAYER

O God, I love Thee in the stars at night
Under the still eternity of sky;
Teach me to love Thee in the passer-by,
For Thou hast said that this is loving right.
I hear Thee in the stars whose silence sings,
And in the shout of dawn Thy voice I know;
Teach me to hear Thee in the joy and woe
Of men who speak of trivial earthly things.
I see Thee when the world is full of sleep
Walking upon the moon-path of the sea;
Teach me by all the tears of Calvary
To know Thee in the eyes of all that weep.

There are so many things that I would say,
God-soul of beauty, teach me how to pray!

Nadejda de Bragança, d. 1946

1341. PRAYER

Lord, what a change within us one short hour
Spent in Thy presence will prevail to make!
What heavy burdens from our bosoms take,
What parched grounds refresh as with a shower!
We kneel, and all around us seems to lower;
We rise, and all, the distant and the near,
Stands forth in sunny outline brave and clear;
We kneel, how weak! we rise, how full of power!
Why, therefore, should we do ourselves this wrong,
Or others, that we are not always strong,
That we are ever overborne with care,
That we should ever weak or heartless be,
Anxious or troubled, when with us is prayer,
And joy and strength and courage are with Thee!

Richard Chenevix Trench, 1807–1886

1342. PRAYER

Be not afraid to pray—to pray is right.
Pray, if thou canst, with hope; but ever pray,
Though hope be weak, or sick with long delay;
Pray in the darkness, if there be no light.
Far is the time, remote from human sight,
When war and discord on the earth shall cease;
Yet every prayer for universal peace
Avails the blessed time to expedite.
Whate'er is good to wish, ask that of Heaven,
Though it be what thou canst not hope to see;
Pray to be perfect, though material leaven
Forbid the spirit so on earth to be:
But if for any wish thou darest not pray,
Then pray to God to cast that wish away.

Hartley Coleridge, 1796–1849

1343. PRAYER

From "Morte D'Arthur"

The old order changeth, yielding place to new,
And God fulfils himself in many ways,
Lest one good custom should corrupt the world.
Comfort thyself: what comfort is in me?

[1] Written in 1917 in a London chapel where the poet had gone to think and pray on receiving word that his son had been killed in action.

I have lived my life, and that which I have
done
May He within himself make pure! but thou,
If thou shouldst never see my face again,
Pray for my soul. More things are wrought
by prayer
Than this world dreams of. Wherefore, let
thy voice
Rise like a fountain for me night and day.
For what are men better than sheep or goats
That nourish a blind life within the brain,
If, knowing God, they lift not hands of prayer
Both for themselves and those who call them
friend?
For so the whole round earth is every way
Bound by gold chains about the feet of
God. . . .

Alfred Tennyson, 1809–1892

1344. PRAYER

I often say my prayers,
But do I ever pray;
And do the wishes of my heart
Go with the words I say?

I may as well kneel down
And worship gods of stone,
As offer to the living God
A prayer of words alone.

For words without the heart
The Lord will never hear:
Nor will he to those lips attend
Whose prayers are not sincere.

John Burton, 1894-

1345. UNANSWERED PRAYERS

I thank Thee, Lord, for mine unanswered prayers,
Unanswered, save Thy quiet, kindly "Nay,"
Yet it seemed hard among my heavy cares
That bitter day.

I wanted joy: but Thou didst know for me
That sorrow was the lift I needed most,
And in its mystic depths I learned to see
The Holy Ghost.

I wanted health; but Thou didst bid me sound
The secret treasuries of pain,
And in the moans and groans my heart oft found
Thy Christ again.

I wanted wealth; 'twas not the better part;
There is a wealth with poverty oft given,
And Thou didst teach me of the gold of heart,
Best gift of Heaven.

I thank Thee, Lord, for these unanswered prayers,
And for Thy word, the quiet, kindly "Nay."
'Twas Thy withholding lightened all my cares
That blessed day.

Author unknown

1346. JOHN THE PILGRIM

Beneath the sand-storm John the Pilgrim prays
But when he rises, lo! an Eden smiles,
Green leafy slopes, meadows of chamomiles,

Claspt in a silvery river's winding maze:
"Water, water! Blessed be God!" he says,
  And totters gasping toward those happy isles.
  Then all is fled! Over the sandy piles
The bald-eyed vultures come and stand at gaze.

"God heard me not," says he, "blessed be God!"
  And dies. But as he nears the pearly strand,
  Heav'n's outer coast where waiting angels stand,
He looks below: "Farewell, thou hooded clod,
  Brown corpse the vultures tear on bloody sand:
God heard my prayer for life—blessed be God!"

Theodore Watts-Dunton, 1832–1914

1347. THE LARGER PRAYER

At first I prayed for Light:
  Could I but see the way,
How gladly, swiftly would I walk
  To everlasting day!

And next I prayed for Strength:
  That I might tread the road
With firm, unfaltering feet, and win
  The heaven's serene abode.

And then I asked for Faith:
  Could I but trust my God,
I'd live enfolded in His peace,
  Though foes were all abroad.

But now I pray for Love:
  Deep love to God and man,
A living love that will not fail,
  However dark His plan.

And Light and Strength and Faith
  Are opening everywhere;
God only waited for me, till
  I prayed the larger prayer.

Edna D. Cheney, 1824–1904

1348. "TWO WENT UP TO THE TEMPLE TO PRAY"

Two went to pray? Oh, rather say
One went to brag, the other to pray;
One stands up close and treads on high
Where the other dares not send his eye;
One nearer to God's altar trod,
The other to the altar's God.

Richard Crashaw, 1613?–1649

1349. PEACE THROUGH PRAYER

From the Introduction to the Translation of Dante's "Divine Comedy"

Oft have I seen at some cathedral door
A laborer, pausing in the dust and heat,
Lay down his burden, and with reverent feet
Enter, and cross himself, and on the floor
Kneel to repeat his paternoster o'er;
Far off the noises of the world retreat;
The loud vociferations of the street
Become an undistinguishable roar.
So, as I enter here from day to day,
And leave my burden at this minster gate,
Kneeling in prayer, and not ashamed to pray,
The tumult of the time disconsolate
To inarticulate murmurs dies away,
While the eternal ages watch and wait.

Henry Wadsworth Longfellow, 1807–1882

1350. REFLECTIONS

Stars lie broken on a lake
Whenever passing breezes make
  The wavelets leap;
But when the lake is still, the sky
Gives moon and stars that they may lie
  On that calm deep.

If, like the lake that has the boon
Of cradling the little moon
  Above the hill,
I want the Infinite to be
Reflected undisturbed in me,
  I must be still.

Edna Becker, 1898–

1351. A PRAYER

Let me do my work each day;
And if the darkened hours of despair overcome me,
May I not forget the strength that comforted me
In the desolation of other times.
May I still remember the bright hours that found me
Walking over the silent hills of my childhood,
Or dreaming on the margin of the quiet river,
When a light glowed within me,
And I promised my early God to have courage
Amid the tempests of the changing years.
Spare me from bitterness
And from the sharp passions of unguarded moments.
May I not forget that poverty and riches are of the spirit.
Though the world know me not,
May my thoughts and actions be such
As shall keep me friendly with myself.
Lift my eyes from the earth,
And let me not forget the uses of the stars.
Forbid that I should judge others,
Lest I condemn myself.
Let me not follow the clamor of the world,
But walk calmly in my path.
Give me a few friends who will love me for what I am;
And keep ever burning before my vagrant steps
The kindly light of hope.
And though age and infirmity overtake me,
And I come not within sight of the castle of my dreams,
Teach me still to be thankful for life,
And for time's olden memories that are good and sweet;
And may the evening's twilight find me gentle still.

Max Ehrmann, 1872–1945

1352. THE LORD'S PRAYER

Matthew 6: 9–13

Our Father which art in heaven,
Hallowed be thy name.
Thy kingdom come.
Thy will be done
in earth, as it is in heaven.

Give us this day
our daily bread.
And forgive us our debts,
as we forgive our debtors.
And lead us not into temptation,
but deliver us from evil:

For thine is the kingdom,
and the power,
and the glory,
forever. Amen.

King James Version, 1611

1353. MYSTIC'S PRAYER

If my feeble prayer can reach Thee,
O, my Saviour, I beseech Thee,
Even as Thou hast died for me
More sincerely
Let me follow where Thou leadest,
Let me bleeding as Thou bleedest,
Die, if dying I may give
Life to one who asks to live;
And more nearly
Dying thus, resemble Thee.

Fourteenth Century

1354. THE PRAYER PERFECT

Dear Lord! Kind Lord!
  Gracious Lord! I pray
Thou wilt look on all I love,
  Tenderly today!
Weed their hearts of weariness;
  Scatter every care
Down a wake of angel-wings
  Winnowing the air.

Bring unto the sorrowing
  All release from pain;
Let the lips of laughter
  Overflow again;
And with all the needy
  O divide, I pray,
This vast measure of content
  That is mine today!

James Whitcomb Riley, 1849–1916

1355. WHAT DOTH THE LORD REQUIRE?

Micah 6: 6–8

Wherewith shall I come before the Lord,
And bow myself before the high God?
Shall I come before him with burnt offerings,
With calves of a year old?
Will the Lord be pleased with thousands of rams,
With ten thousands of rivers of oil?
Shall I give my firstborn for my transgression,
The fruit of my body for the sin of my soul?
He hath shewed thee, O man, what is good;
And what doth the Lord require of thee,
But to do justly, and to love mercy, and to walk humbly with thy God?

From the Hebrew, 8th century B.C.

1356. LENT

To search our souls,
To meditate,
Will not suffice
For Lent.

To share the cross,
To sacrifice,
These are the things
God meant.

Jane McKay Lanning

1357. THE CHRISTIAN PARADOX

All through life I see a cross—
  Where sons of God yield up their breath;
There is no gain except by loss;
  There is no life except by death;
  There is no vision but by faith.

Walter Chalmers Smith, 1824–1908

1358. THE MARTYR'S HYMN

All human progress up to God
Has stained the stairs of time with blood;
For every gain for Christendom
Is bought by someone's martyrdom.

For us he poured the crimson cup,
And bade us take and drink it up.
Himself he poured to set us free.
Help us, O Christ, to drink with Thee.

Ten thousand saints come thronging home,
From lion's den and catacomb.
The fire and sword and beasts defied;
For Christ, their King, they gladly died.

With eye of faith we see today
That cross-led column wind its way
Up life's repeated Calvary.
We rise, O Christ, to follow Thee!

Adapted from a poem by Dr. Francis H. Rose, one of the eleven missionaries put to death on the Island of Panay, Philippine Islands, December 1943.

1359. TO KEEP A TRUE LENT

Is this a Fast, to keep
  The larder lean,
    And clean
From fat of veals and sheep?

Is it to quit the dish
  Of flesh, yet still
    To fill
The platter high with fish?

Is it to fast an hour,
  Or ragg'd to go,
    Or show
A downcast look and sour?

No: 'tis a Fast to dole
  Thy sheaf of wheat
    And meat,
Unto the hungry soul.

It is to fast from strife,
From old debate
And hate;
To circumcise thy life.

To show a heart grief-rent;
To starve thy sin,
Not bin:
And that's to keep thy Lent.

Robert Herrick, 1591–1674

1360. THE SEARCH

I went to seek for Christ,
And Nature seemed so fair
That first the woods and fields my youth enticed,
And I was sure to find him there:
The temple I forsook,
And to the solitude
Allegiance paid; but Winter came and shook
The crown and purple from my wood;
His snows, like desert sands, with scornful drift,
Besieged the columned aisle and palace-gate;
My Thebes, cut deep with many a solemn rift,
But epitaphed her own sepulchred state:
Then I remembered whom I went to seek,
And blessed blunt Winter for his counsel bleak.

Back to the world I turned,
For Christ, I said, is King;
So the cramped alley and the hut I spurned,
As far beneath his sojourning:
'Mid power and wealth I sought,
But found no trace of him,
And all the costly offerings I had brought
With sudden rust and mould grew dim:
I found his tomb, indeed, where, by their laws,
All must on stated days themselves imprison,
Mocking with bread a dead creed's grinning jaws,
Witless how long the life had thence arisen;
Due sacrifice to this they set apart,
Prizing it more than Christ's own living heart.

So from my feet the dust
Of the proud World I shook;
Then came dear Love and shared with me his crust,
And half my sorrow's burden took.
After the World's soft bed,
Its rich and dainty fare,
Like down seemed Love's coarse pillow to my head
His cheap food seemed as manna rare;
Fresh-trodden prints of bare and bleeding feet,
Turned to the heedless city whence I came,
Hard by I saw, and springs of worship sweet
Gushed from my cleft heart smitten by the same;
Love looked me in the face and spake no words,
But straight I knew those footprints were the Lord's.

I followed where they led
And in a hovel rude,
With naught to fence the weather from his head,
The King I sought for meekly stood;
A naked, hungry child
Clung round his gracious knee,
And a poor hunted slave looked up and smiled
To bless the smile that set him free;
New miracles I saw his presence do,—
No more I knew the hovel bare and poor,
The gathered chips into a woodpile grew,
The broken morsel swelled to goodly store;
I knelt and wept: my Christ no more I seek,
His throne is with the outcast and the weak.

James Russell Lowell, 1819–1891

1361. A PRAYER

Teach me, Father, how to go
Softly as the grasses grow;
Hush my soul to meet the shock
Of the wild world as a rock;
But my spirit, propt with power,
Make as simple as a flower.
Let the dry heart fill its cup,
Like a poppy looking up;
Let life lightly wear her crown,
Like a poppy looking down,
When its heart is filled with dew,
And its life begins anew.

Teach me, Father, how to be
Kind and patient as a tree.
Joyfully the crickets croon
Under shady oak at noon;
Beetle, on his mission bent,
Tarries in that cooling tent.
Let me, also, cheer a spot,
Hidden field or garden grot—
Place where passing souls can rest
On the way and be their best.

Edwin Markham, 1852–1940

1362. COUNT THAT DAY LOST

If you sit down at set of sun
And count the acts that you have done,
And counting find
One self-denying deed, one word
That eased the heart of him who heard;
One glance most kind,
That fell like sunshine where it went—
Then you may count that day well spent.

But if, through all the livelong day,
You've cheered no heart, by yea or nay—
If, through it all
You've nothing done that you can trace
That brought the sunshine to one face—
No act most small
That helped some soul and nothing cost—
Then count that day as worse than lost.

George Eliot, 1819–1880

1363. A MORNING PRAYER

Let me today do something that will take
A little sadness from the world's vast store
And may I be so favored as to make
Of joy's too scanty sum a little more.

Let me not hurt, by any selfish deed
Or thoughtless word, the heart of foe or friend;
Nor would I pass, unseeing, worthy need,
Or sin by silence when I should defend.

However meager be my worldly wealth,
Let me give something that shall aid my kind—
A word of courage, or a thought of health
Dropped as I pass for troubled hearts to find.

Let me tonight look back across the span
'Twixt dawn and dark, and to my conscience say—
Because of some good act to beast or man—
"The world is better that I lived today."

Ella Wheeler Wilcox, 1855–1919

1364. LEND A HAND

I am only one,
But still I am one.
I cannot do everything,
But still I can do something;
And because I cannot do everything
I will not refuse to do the something
that I can do.

Edward Everett Hale, 1822–1909

1365. OTHERS

Lord, help me live from day to day
In such a self-forgetful way
That even when I kneel to pray
My prayers will be for OTHERS.

Help me in all the work I do
To ever be sincere and true
And know that all I do for YOU
Must needs be done for OTHERS.

Let Self be crucified and slain
And buried deep, and all in vain
May efforts be to rise again
Unless to live for OTHERS.

And when my work on earth is done
And my new work in heaven begun
May I forget the crown I've won
While thinking still of OTHERS.

Others, Lord, yes, others
Let this my motto be;
Help me to live for Others
That I may live like Thee.

Charles D. Meigs, 1846–1920

1366. "WHOSO LOSETH HIS LIFE"

From "Super Flumina Babylonis"

Unto each man his handiwork, unto each his crown,
The just Fate gives;
Whoso takes the world's life on him and his own lays down,
He, dying so, lives.

Whoso hears the whole heaviness of the wronged world's weight
And puts it by,
It is well with him suffering, though he face man's fate;
How should he die?

Seeing death has no part in him any more, no power
Upon his head;
He has bought his eternity with a little hour,
And is not dead.

For an hour, if ye look for him, he is no more found,
For one hour's space;
Then ye lift up your eyes to him and behold him crowned,
A deathless face.

Algernon Charles Swinburne, 1837–1909

1367. AS I GO ON MY WAY

My life shall touch a dozen lives before this day is done—
Leave countless marks for good or ill ere sets this evening sun.
Shall fair or foul its imprint prove, on those my life shall hail?
Shall benison my impress be, or shall a blight prevail?

When to the last great reckoning the lives I meet must go,
Shall this wee, fleeting touch of mine have added joy or woe?
Shall He who looks their records o'er—of name and time and place—
Say "Here a blessed influence came" or "Here is evil's trace"?

From out each point of contact of my life with other lives
Flows ever that which helps the one who for the summit strives.
The troubled souls encountered—does it sweeten with its touch,
Or does it more embitter those embittered overmuch?

Does love in every handclasp flow in sympathy's caress?
Do those that I have greeted know a newborn hopefulness?
Are tolerance and charity the keynote of my song
As I go plodding onward with earth's eager, anxious throng?

My life shall touch a million lives in some way ere I go
From this dear world of struggle to the land I do not know.
So this the wish I always wish, the prayer I ever pray:
Let my life help the other lives it touches by the way.

Strickland Gillilan, 1869–

1368. From THE PARTING OF THE WAYS

Be thou guardian of the weak,
Of the unbefriended, thou the friend;
No guerdon for thy valor seek,
No end beyond the avowèd end.
Wouldst thou thy Godlike power preserve,
Be Godlike in the will to serve.

Jeannette Gilder, 1849–1916

1369. "I SHALL NOT PASS AGAIN THIS WAY"

The bread that bringeth strength I want to give,
The water pure that bids the thirsty live;
I want to help the fainting day by day;
I'm sure I shall not pass again this way.

I want to give the oil of joy for tears,
The faith to conquer crowding doubts and fears,
Beauty for ashes may I give always;
I'm sure I shall not pass again this way.

I want to give good measure running o'er
And into angry hearts I want to pour
The answer soft that turneth wrath away;
I'm sure I shall not pass again this way.

I want to give to others hope and faith;
I want to do all that the Master saith;
I want to live aright from day to day;
I'm sure I shall not pass again this way.

Ellen H. Underwood, 1845–1930

1370. A PRAYER

Lord, not for light in darkness do we pray,
Not that the veil be lifted from our eyes,
Nor that the slow ascension of our day
Be otherwise.

Not for a clearer vision of the things
Whereof the fashioning shall make us great,
Not for remission of the peril and stings
Of time and fate.

Not for a fuller knowledge of the end
Whereto we travel, bruised yet unafraid,
Nor that the little healing that we lend
Shall be repaid.

Not these, O Lord. We would not break the bars
Thy wisdom sets about us; we shall climb
Unfettered to the secrets of the stars
In Thy good time.

We do not crave the high perception swift
When to refrain were well, and when fulfill,
Nor yet the understanding strong to sift
The good from ill.

Not these, O Lord. For these Thou hast revealed.
We know the golden season when to reap
The heavy-fruited treasure of the field,
The hour to sleep.

Not these. We know the hemlock from the rose,
The pure from stained, the noble from the base,
The tranquil holy light of truth that glows
On Pity's face.

We know the paths wherein our feet should press,
Across our hearts are written Thy decrees.
Yet now, O Lord, be merciful to bless
With more than these.

Grant us the will to fashion as we feel,
Grant us the strength to labour as we know,
Grant us the purpose, ribbed and edged with steel,
To strike the blow.

Knowledge we ask not—knowledge Thou hast lent;
But Lord, the will—there lies our bitter need.
Give us to build above the deep intent
The deed, the deed.

John Drinkwater, 1882–1937

1371. A HUNDRED NOBLE WISHES

A hundred noble wishes fill my heart:
I long to help each soul in need of aid:
In all good works my zeal would have a part,
Before no weight of toil it stands afraid.

But noble wishes are not noble deeds,
And he does least who seeks to do the whole:
Who works the best, his simplest duties heeds;
Who moves the world, first moves a single soul.

Charles Francis Richardson, 1851–1913

1372. IF I CAN STOP ONE HEART FROM BREAKING

If I can stop one heart from breaking,
I shall not live in vain;
If I can ease one life the aching,
Or cool one pain,
Or help one fainting robin
Unto his nest again,
I shall not live in vain.

Emily Dickinson, 1830–1886

1373. THE BROKEN PINION

I walked through the woodland meadows,
Where sweet the thrushes sing;
And I found on a bed of mosses
A bird with a broken wing.
I healed its wound, and each morning
It sang its old sweet strain,
But the bird with the broken pinion
Never soared as high again.

I found a young life broken
By sin's seductive art;
And, touched with a Christ-like pity,
I took him to my heart.
He lived with a noble purpose
And struggled not in vain;
But the life that sin had stricken
Never soared as high again.

But the bird with the broken pinion
Kept another from the snare;
And the life that sin had stricken
Raised another from despair.
Each loss has its compensation,
There is healing for every pain;
But the bird with a broken pinion
Never soars as high again.

Hezekiah Butterworth, 1839–1905

1374. THE SISTERS

The waves forever move;
The hills forever rest:
Yet each the heavens approve,
And Love alike hath blessed
A Martha's household care,
A Mary's cloistered prayer.

John Banister Tabb, 1845–1909

1375. DO THE WORK THAT'S NEAREST

Do the work that's nearest,
Though it's dull at whiles,
Helping, when you meet them,
Lame dogs over stiles;
See in every hedgerow
Marks of angels' feet,
Epics in each pebble
Underneath our feet.

Charles Kingsley, 1819–1875

1376. From "ANDREW RYKMAN'S PRAYER"

If there be some weaker one,
Give me strength to help him on;
If a blinder soul there be,
Let me guide him nearer Thee.
Make my mortal dreams come true
With the work I fain would do;
Clothe with life the weak intent,
Let me be the thing I meant;
Let me find in Thy employ
Peace that dearer is than joy;
Out of self to love be led
And to heaven acclimated,
Until all things sweet and good
Seem my natural habitude.

John Greenleaf Whittier, 1807–1892

1377. MAN-MAKING

We are all blind, until we see
That in the human plan
Nothing is worth the making if
It does not make the man.

Why build these cities glorious
If man unbuilded goes?
In vain we build the work, unless
The builder also grows.

Edwin Markham, 1852–1940

1378. THE GREATEST WORK

He built a house; time laid it in the dust;
He wrote a book, its title now forgot;
He ruled a city, but his name is not
On any table graven, or where rust
Can gather from disuse, or marble bust.
He took a child from out a wretched cot,
Who on the state dishonor might have brought,
And reared him to the Christian's hope and trust.
The boy, to manhood grown, became a light
To many souls, and preached for human need
The wondrous love of the Omnipotent.
The work has multiplied like stars at night
When darkness deepens; every noble deed
Lasts longer than a granite monument.

Ray M. Johnson, contemporary American

1379. A PRAYER OF BUSY HANDS

Dear God, Thou know'st how many tasks
Await my hands today;
If all are done at set of sun
No time is left to pray.
Thou know'st how many duties press,
How urgent is each need;
I may not dare a moment spare
To fashion me a creed.

Thou know'st the hungry must be fed,
The naked clothed must be;
My scant store wanes; no gift remains
Of sacrifice for Thee;
So if, when life is done, I come
With no gift in my hand,
No prayer nor creed—Just this I'll plead:
Thou, God, dost understand.

B. Y. Williams, contemporary American

1380. FATHER, WHOSE WILL IS LIFE AND GOOD

Father, whose will is life and good
For all of mortal breath,
Bind strong the bond of brotherhood
Of those who fight with death.

Empower the hands and hearts and wills,
Of friends both near and far,
Who battle with the body's ills,
And wage Thy holy war.

Where'er they heal the maimed and blind,
Let love of Christ attend:
Proclaim the good Physician's mind.
And prove the Saviour friend.

O Father, look from heaven and bless,
Where'er Thy servants be,
Their works of pure unselfishness,
Made consecrate to Thee.

Hardwicke Drummond Rawnsley, 1851–1920

1381. THE HEALER

To a young physician, with Doré's picture of Christ healing the sick.

So stood of old the holy Christ
Amidst the suffering throng;
With whom His lightest touch sufficed
To make the weakest strong.

That healing gift He lends to them
Who use it in His name;
The power that filled His garment's hem
Is evermore the same.

For lo! in human hearts unseen
The Healer dwelleth still,
And they who make His temples clean
The best subserve His will.

The holiest task by Heaven decreed,
And errand all divine,
The burden of our common need
To render less is thine.

The paths of pain are thine. Go forth
With patience, trust, and hope;
The sufferings of a sin-sick earth
Shall give thee ample scope.

Beside the unveiled mysteries
Of life and death go stand,
With guarded lips and reverent eyes
And pure of heart and hand.

So shalt thou be with power endued
From Him who went about
The Syrian hillsides doing good,
And casting demons out.

That Good Physician liveth yet
Thy friend and guide to be;
The Healer by Gennesaret
Shall walk the rounds with thee.

John Greenleaf Whittier, 1807–1892

1382. THE PATIENT SCIENTISTS

How they have learned the secrets of the ether!
Ships in the clouds, afloat as on a sea;
Voices through miles of distance singing, captured,
Brought to our homes to gladden you and me.

How selflessly they seek profounder meanings
Hid in the clump of moss—the iron ore!
How they have found in energy the secrets
God smiled to know a billion years before.

Counting their lives not dear, so they discover
Some bit of truth through eons all unguessed,
Something to make the lives to come the richer,
Ere they themselves shall shut their eyes and rest.

Ah, still the Lord God walks with noiseless footfall,
Visits the workshops of these patient men—
Smiles on the test tubes, the revealing lenses,
And "It is good," he murmurs once again.

Bertha Gerneaux Woods, 1873–

1383. THE NAMELESS SAINTS

What was his name? I do not know his name.
I only know he heard God's voice and came,
Brought all he had across the sea
To live and work for God and me;
Felled the ungracious oak;
Dragged from the soil
With horrid toil
The thrice-gnarled roots and stubborn rock;
With plenty piled the haggard mountain-side;
And at the end, without memorial, died.
No blaring trumpets sounded out his fame,
He lived,—he died,—I do not know his name.

No form of bronze and no memorial stones
Show me the place where lie his mouldering bones.
Only a cheerful city stands
Builded by his hardened hands.
Only ten thousand homes
Where every day
The cheerful play
Of love and hope and courage comes.
These are his monuments, and these alone,
There is no form of bronze and no memorial stone.

And I?
Is there some desert or some pathless sea
Where Thou, good God of angels, wilt send me?
Some oak for me to rend; some sod,
Some rock for me to break;
Some handful of His corn to take
And scatter far afield,
Till it, in turn, shall yield
Its hundredfold
Of grains of gold
To feed the waiting children of my God?
Show me the desert, Father, or the sea.
Is it Thine enterprise? Great God, send me.
And though this body lie where ocean rolls,
Count me among all Faithful Souls.

Edward Everett Hale, 1822–1909

1384. THE SIN OF OMISSION

It isn't the thing you do;
It's the thing you leave undone,
Which gives you a bit of heartache
At the setting of the sun.

The tender word forgotten,
The letter you did not write,
The flower you might have sent,
Are your haunting ghosts at night.

The stone you might have lifted
Out of a brother's way,
The bit of heartsome counsel
You were hurried too much to say;

The loving touch of the hand,
The gentle and winsome tone,
That you had no time or thought for
With troubles enough of your own.

The little acts of kindness,
So easily out of mind;
Those chances to be helpful
Which everyone may find—

No, it's not the thing you do,
It's the thing you leave undone,
Which gives you the bit of heartache
At the setting of the sun.

Margaret E. Sangster, 1838–1912

1385. GUILTY

I never cut my neighbor's throat;
My neighbor's gold I never stole;
I never spoiled his house and land;
But God have mercy on my soul!

For I am haunted night and day
By all the deeds I have not done;
O unattempted loveliness!
O costly valor never won!

Marguerite Wilkinson, 1883–1928

1386. LEANERS OR LIFTERS

There are two kinds of people on earth today;
Just two kinds of people, no more, I say.

Not the sinner and saint, for it's well understood,
The good are half bad, and the bad are half good.

Not the rich and the poor, for to rate a man's wealth,
You must first know the state of his conscience and health.

Not the humble and proud, for in life's little span,
Who puts on vain airs, is not counted a man.

Not the happy and sad, for the swift flying years
Bring each man his laughter and each man his tears.

No; the two kinds of people on earth I mean,
Are the people who lift, and the people who lean.

Wherever you go, you will find the earth's masses
Are always divided in just these two classes.

And, oddly enough, you will find too, I ween,
There's only one lifter to twenty who lean.

In which class are you? Are you easing the load
Of overtaxed lifters, who toil down the road?

Or are you a leaner, who lets others share
Your portion of labor, and worry and care?

Ella Wheeler Wilcox, 1855–1919

1387. THE HOUSE BY THE SIDE OF THE ROAD

"He was a friend to man, and lived in a house by the side of the road."—Homer

There are hermit souls that live withdrawn
  In the peace of their self-content;
There are souls, like stars, that dwell apart,
  In a fellowless firmament;
There are pioneer souls that blaze their paths
  Where highways never ran;—
But let me live by the side of the road
  And be a friend to man.

Let me live in a house by the side of the road,
  Where the race of men go by—
The men who are good and the men who are bad,
  As good and as bad as I.
I would not sit in the scorner's seat,
  Or hurl the cynic's ban;—
Let me live in a house by the side of the road
  And be a friend to man.

I see from my house by the side of the road,
  By the side of the highway of life,
The men who press with the ardor of hope,
  The men who are faint with the strife.

But I turn not away from their smiles nor their tears—
  Both parts of an infinite plan;—
Let me live in my house by the side of the road
  And be a friend to man.

I know there are brook-gladdened meadows ahead
  And mountains of wearisome height;
That the road passes on through the long afternoon
  And stretches away to the night.
But still I rejoice when the travellers rejoice,
  And weep with the strangers that moan,
Nor live in my house by the side of the road
  Like a man who dwells alone.

Let me live in my house by the side of the road
  Where the race of men go by—
They are good, they are bad, they are weak, they are strong,
  Wise, foolish—so am I.
Then why should I sit in the scorner's seat
  Or hurl the cynic's ban?—
Let me live in my house by the side of the road
  And be a friend to man.

Sam Walter Foss, 1858–1911

1388. LEAD ON, O KING ETERNAL

Lead on, O King Eternal,
The day of march has come;
Hence-forth in fields of conquest
Thy tents shall be our home;
Through days of preparation
Thy grace has made us strong,
And now, O King Eternal,
We lift our battle song.

Lead on, O King Eternal,
Till sin's fierce war shall cease,
And holiness shall whisper
The sweet Amen of peace;
For not with swords loud clashing,
Nor roll of stirring drums,
With deeds of love and mercy,
The heav'nly kingdom comes.

Lead on, O King Eternal,
We follow, not with fears,
For gladness breaks like morning
Where'er Thy face appears;
Thy cross is lifted o'er us;
We journey in its light;
The crown awaits the conquest;
Lead on, O God of might.

Ernest W. Shurtleff, 1862–1917

1389. THE HARDER TASK

Teach me to live! 'Tis easier far to die—
  Gently and silently to pass away—
On earth's long night to close the heavy eye,
  And waken in the glorious realms of day.

Teach me that harder lesson—how to live
  To serve Thee in the darkest paths of life.
Arm me for conflict, now fresh vigor give,
  And make me more than conqu'ror in the strife.

Author unknown

1390. WHEN LIFE IS DONE

I'd like to think when life is done
  That I had filled a needed post,
That here and there I'd paid my fare
  With more than idle talk and boast;
That I had taken gifts divine,
The breath of life and manhood fine,
And tried to use them now and then
In service for my fellow men.

Edgar A. Guest, 1881–

1391. NOT THINE OWN

From "Measure for Measure," Act I, sc. I

Thyself and thy belongings
Are not thine own so proper as to waste
Thyself upon thy virtues, they on thee.
Heaven doth with us as we with torches do
Not light them for themselves; for if our virtues
Did not go forth of us, 'twere all alike
As if we had them not. Spirits are not finely touched
But to fine issues, nor Nature never lends
The smallest scruple of her excellence
But, like a thrifty goddess, she determines
Herself the glory of a creditor,
Both thanks and use.

William Shakespeare, 1564–1616

1392. A PRISONER'S SONG

Written in the Bastille, France

A little bird I am,
Shut from the fields of air;
And in my cage I sit and sing
To Him Who placed me there;
Well pleased a prisoner to be,
Because, my God, it pleases Thee.

Naught have I else to do:
I sing the whole day long;
And He Whom I most love to please
Doth listen to my song:
He caught and bound my wandering wing;
But still He bends to hear me sing.

Thou hast an ear to hear,
A heart to love and bless;
And though my notes were e'er so rude,
Thou wouldst not hear the less;
Because Thou knowest as they fall,
That love, sweet love, inspires them all.

My cage confines me round;
Abroad I cannot fly;
But though my wing is closely bound,
My heart's at liberty;
My prison walls cannot control
The flight, the freedom of the soul.

Oh, it is good to soar
These bolts and bars above,
To Him Whose purpose I adore,
Whose providence I love;
And in Thy mighty will to find
The joy, the freedom of the mind.

Madame Jeanne Marie Guyon, 1648–1717

1393. From TO ALTHEA FROM PRISON

Stone walls do not a prison make,
Nor iron bars a cage;
Minds innocent and quiet take
That for an hermitage:
If I have freedom in my love,
And in my soul am free,
Angels alone, that soar above,
Enjoy such liberty.

Richard Lovelace, 1618–1658

1394. HE THAT HAS LIGHT WITHIN

From "Comus"

He that has light within his own clear breast
May sit i' the centre, and enjoy bright day:
But he that hides a dark soul and foul thoughts
Benighted walks under the mid-day sun;
Himself is his own dungeon.

John Milton, 1608–1674

1395. FREEDOM'S HERO

From "The Prisoner of Chillon"

Eternal Spirit of the chainless mind!
Brightest in dungeons, Liberty! thou art,
For there thy habitation is the heart—
The heart which love of thee alone can bind;

And when thy sons to fetters are consigned—
To fetters, and the damp vault's dayless gloom,
Their country conquers with their martyrdom,
And Freedom's fame finds wings on every wind.

Chillon! thy prison is a holy place,
  And thy sad floor an altar—for 'twas trod,
Until his very steps have left a trace
  Worn, as if thy cold pavement were a sod,
By Bonnivard!—May none those marks efface!
  For they appeal from tyranny to God.

George Gordon, Lord Byron, 1788–1824

1396. THE KEEPER

Wide is the world and wide its open seas,
  Yet I who fare from pole to pole remain
A prisoned Hope that paces ill at ease,
  A captive Fear that fumbles with its chain.

I once for Freedom madly did aspire,
  And stormed His bars in many a burst of rage:
But see, my Keeper with his brands of fire
  Has cowed me quiet . . . and bade me love my cage!

Arthur Stringer, 1874–

1397. THE SLAVE

They set the slave free, striking off his chains . . .
Then he was as much of a slave as ever.

He was still chained to servility,
He was still manacled to indolence and sloth,
He was still bound by fear and superstition,
By ignorance, suspicion, and savagery . . .
His slavery was not in the chains,
But in himself. . . .

They can only set free men free . . .
And there is no need of that:
Free men set themselves free.

James Oppenheim, 1882–1932

1398. WE GIVE THEE BUT THINE OWN

We give Thee but Thine own,
Whate'er the gift may be:
All that we have is Thine alone,
A trust, O Lord, from Thee.

May we Thy bounties thus
As stewards true receive,
And gladly, as Thou blessest us,
To Thee our first-fruits give.

To comfort and to bless,
To find a balm for woe,
To tend the lone and fatherless,
Is angels' work below.

The captive to release,
To God the lost to bring,
To teach the way of life and peace,
It is a Christ-like thing.

And we believe Thy word,
Though dim our faith may be,
Whate'er for Thine we do, O Lord,
We do it unto Thee.

William Walsham How, 1823–1897

1399. REQUIEM FOR A MODERN CROESUS

  To him the moon was a silver dollar, spun
Into the sky by some mysterious hand; the sun
  Was a gleaming golden coin—
    His to purloin;
The freshly minted stars were dimes of delight
  Flung out upon the counter of the night.

    In yonder room he lies,
    With pennies on his eyes.

Lew Sarett, 1888–

1400. MAMMON

From "Paradise Lost," Book I

Mammon, the least erected spirit that fell
From heaven; for ev'n in heaven his looks and thoughts
Were always downward bent, admiring more
The riches of heaven's pavement, trodden gold,
Than aught divine or holy else enjoy'd
In vision beatific.

John Milton, 1608–1674

1401. TO ONE WHO WORSHIPPED GODS OF GOLD

A miser till his last quick breath,
Then for a tomb his wealth was given;
Bankrupt he hurried on with death
To beg upon the streets of Heaven.

John Richard Moreland, 1880–1947

1402. GOLD

Gold! gold! gold! gold!
Bright and yellow, hard and cold,
Molten, graven, hammered and rolled,
Heavy to get, and light to hold;
Hoarded, bartered, bought and sold,
Stolen, borrowed, squandered, doled:
Spurned by the young, but hugged by the old
To the very verge of the churchyard mold;
Price of many a crime untold.

Thomas Hood, 1799–1845

1403. WINE AND WOE

Proverbs 23: 29–35

Who hath woe?
Who hath sorrow?
Who hath contentions?
Who hath complaining?
Who hath wounds without cause?
Who hath redness of eyes?

They that tarry long at the wine;
They that go to seek out mixed wine.

Look not thou upon the wine
When it is red,
When it giveth its colour in the cup,
When it goeth down smoothly:

At the last it biteth like a serpent,
And stingeth like an adder,
Thine eyes shall behold strange things,
And thine heart shall utter froward things.
Yea, thou shalt be as he that lieth down in the midst of the sea,
Or as he that lieth upon the top of a mast.
"They have stricken me,
And I was not hurt;
They have beaten me,
And I felt it not;
When shall I awake?
I will seek it yet again."

Moulton: The Modern Reader's Bible, 1895

1404. INTEMPERANCE

Isaiah 5: 11–12

Woe unto them
That rise up early in the morning,
That they may follow strong drink;
That tarry late into the night,
Till wine inflame them.
And the harp and the lute, the tabret and the pipe,
And wine, are in their feasts:
But they regard not the work of the LORD,
Neither have they considered the operation of his hands!

Moulton: The Modern Reader's Bible, 1895

1405. GOD SPEAKS IN ALL RELIGIONS

I love the chalice and the pyx,
The altar and the crucifix.
A spirit haunts the aged bowers,
Born from the ashes of the flowers.
What once was holy still retains
Some virtue of the primal days,
Though malice blights and greed profanes,
Though age consumes, though hate betrays—
Symbols that grew long ere the birth
Of Him who was the Light of Earth;
Old as Religion, they endure,
And still to pureness all are pure.

Have we a faith?—One bud is ours,
Plucked from Religion's world of flowers.
Have we a creed?—Therein some ray
Born from the universal day.
Have we a rite?—That owned sincere,
Brings the Eternal Presence near.
The shining clue is in the hand
That leads the soul to Morning Land.

By beads or crucifix I pray
With the hushed crowd, yet not as they.
Conformed to Islam's lowly rite,
Its crescent shows me loftier light.

In the rude fetish I divine
What Christians find in bread and wine.
As Joseph worshipped, I adore
By sphinx and obelisk of yore.
Still, where dread Isis veils her face,
I hail the Mother of the race.

I love the Parsee's quenchless flame:
The sunrise lifts God's hidden name.
I taste the mystic raptures known
Where Buddha's sons the prayer intone.
With mild Samaritans I dwell,
Kneeling as they by Jacob's well.
Where sound the trumpets and the shawms,
From David's faith I gather alms,
And so the loud hosannas swell—
Still God is great in Israel.

All faiths are one when from disguise
And narrowness their spirit flies.
All faiths are one by their ascent,
Piercing the stellar firmament.
All faiths are one in last decline,
Tainting the hearts they should refine.
Each faith is of the all possest,
Since one pure truth holds all the rest.

Are Scriptures all a mortal clod?—
Ay, but each atom holds the God.
Are Scriptures all in vision spun?—
Ay, but the morn-mist holds the sun.
Do Scriptures move before the sight,
Shifting their meanings with the light?
Do they, in mystery and awe,
Disclose but fragments of the Law
Of that pure harmony we trace
In Heaven and nature, time and space?—
Ay, but no man can hold the light
Save as by symbols borne to sight. . . .

Your care, O Mother, mighty yet mild,
Curtains the cradle of the child,
Whose searching hands through darkness
  prest,
Touch Heaven, and—lo, it is your Breast!

Thomas Lake Harris, 1823–1906

1406. INTOLERANCE

And when religious sects ran mad,
  He held, in spite of all his learning,
That if a man's belief is bad,
  It will not be improved by burning.

W. M. Praed, 1802–1839

1407. WHO IS THE ANGEL THAT COMETH?

I

Who is the Angel that cometh?
    Life!
Let us not question what he brings,
    Peace or Strife,
Under the shadow of his mighty wings,
    One by one,
  Are his secrets told;
    One by one,
Lit by the rays of each morning sun,
  Shall a new flower its petals unfold,
  With the mystery hid in its heart of gold.
We will arise and go forth to greet him,
  Singly, gladly, with one accord;—
"Blessed is he that cometh
  In the name of the Lord."

II

Who is the Angel that cometh?
    Joy!
Look at his glittering rainbow wings—
    No alloy
Lies in the radiant gifts he brings;
    Tender and sweet,
  He is come to-day,
    Tender and sweet:
While chains of love on his silver feet
  Will hold him in lingering fond delay.
  But greet him quickly, he will not stay,
Soon he will leave us; but though for others
  All his brightest treasures are stored;—
"Blessed is he that cometh
  In the name of the Lord!"

III

Who is the Angel that cometh?
    Pain!
Let us arise and go forth to greet him;
    Not in vain
Is the summons come for us to meet him;
    He will stay,
  And darken our sun;
    He will stay
A desolate night, a weary day.
  Since in that shadow our work is done,
  And in that shadow our crowns are won,
Let us say still, while his bitter chalice
  Slowly into our hearts is poured,—
"Blessed is he that cometh
  In the name of the Lord!"

IV

Who is the Angel that cometh?
Death!
But do not shudder and do not fear;
Hold your breath,
For a kingly presence is drawing near.
Cold and bright
Is his flashing steel,
Cold and bright
The smile that comes like a starry light
To calm the terror and grief we feel;
He comes to help and to save and heal:
Then let us, baring our hearts and kneeling,
Sing, while we wait this Angel's sword,—
"Blessed is he that cometh
In the name of the Lord!"

Adelaide Anne Procter, 1825–1864

1408. BIGOT

Though you be scholarly, beware
The bigotry of doubt.
Some people take a strange delight
In blowing candles out.

Eleanor Slater, 1903–

1409. CONVENTIONALITY

Men wrap themselves in smug cocoons
Of dogmas they believe are wise,
And look askance at one who sees
In worms potential butterflies.

Eloise Hackett, contemporary American

1410. UNDERSTANDING

If I knew you and you knew me,
If both of us could clearly see,
And with an inner sight divine
The meaning of your heart and mine,
I'm sure that we would differ less,
And clasp our hands in friendliness;
Our thoughts would pleasantly agree
If I knew you and you knew me.

Nixon Waterman, 1859–1944

1411. IF WE KNEW

If we knew the cares and crosses
Crowding round our neighbor's way:
If we knew the little losses,
Sorely grievous day by day,
Would we then so often chide him
For the lack of thrift and gain—
Casting o'er his life a shadow,
Leaving on his heart a stain.

If we knew the silent story
Quivering through the heart of pain,
Would our womanhood dare doom them
Back to haunts of guilt again?
Life hath many a tangled crossing,
Joy hath many a break of woe,
And the cheeks tear-washed seem whitest,
This the blessed angels know.

Let us reach into our bosoms
For the key to other lives,
And with love to erring nature,
Cherish good that still survives;
So that when our disrobed spirits
Soar to realms of light again,
We may say, dear Father, judge us
As we judged our fellowmen.

Author unknown

1412. THE BLIND MEN AND THE ELEPHANT

A Hindoo Fable

It was six men of Indostan
To learning much inclined,
Who went to see the Elephant
(Though all of them were blind),
That each by observation
Might satisfy his mind.

The *First* approached the Elephant,
And happening to fall
Against his broad and sturdy side,
At once began to bawl:
"God bless me! but the Elephant
Is very like a wall!"

The *Second*, feeling of the tusk,
Cried, "Ho! what have we here
So very round and smooth and sharp?
To me 'tis mighty clear
This wonder of an Elephant
Is very like a spear!"

The *Third* approached the animal,
And happening to take
The squirming trunk within his hands,

Thus boldly up and spake:
"I see," quoth he, "the Elephant
Is very like a snake!"

The *Fourth* reached out an eager hand,
And felt about the knee.
"What most this wondrous beast is like
Is mighty plain," quoth he;
"'Tis clear enough the Elephant
Is very like a tree!"

The *Fifth*, who chanced to touch the ear,
Said: "E'en the blindest man
Can tell what this resembles most;
Deny the fact who can,
This marvel of an Elephant
Is very like a fan!"

The *Sixth* no sooner had begun
About the beast to grope,
Than, seizing on the swinging tail
That fell within his scope,
"I see," quoth he, "the Elephant
Is very like a rope!"

And so these men of Indostan
Disputed loud and long,
Each in his own opinion
Exceeding stiff and strong,
Though each was partly in the right,
And all were in the wrong!

MORAL

So oft in theologic wars,
The disputants, I ween,
Rail on in utter ignorance
Of what each other mean,
And prate about an Elephant
Not one of them has seen!

John Godfrey Saxe, 1816–1887

1413. UPON DISCOVERING ONE'S OWN INTOLERANCE

MY HEART and I were not so well acquent,
So intimate as I had thought, before
I saw, with curious enlightenment,
The frigid countenance her virtue wore.
Not that she consciously betrayed my trust,
She was unaltered, but my scales were shed.
I thought her gentle—she was hardly just;
I called her good—I found her smug, instead.

Now must I turn her from the swift disdain
Of all a stubborn conscience might believe
Falls short the mark one's personal creed sets
plain;
Teach her respect for that which may not bear
The known device; and help her to perceive
How cold a visage Righteousness may wear.

Sara Henderson Hay,
contemporary American

1414. INTOLERANCE

Across the way my neighbor's windows shine,
His roof-tree shields him from the storms that frown;
He toiled and saved to build it, staunch and brown.
And though my neighbor's house is not like mine,
I would not pull it down!

With patient care my neighbor, too, had built
A house of faith, wherein his soul might stay,
A haven from the winds that sweep life's way.
It differed from my own—I felt no guilt—
I burned it yesterday!

Molly Anderson Haley, 1888–

1415. HEM AND HAW

Hem and Haw were the sons of sin,
Created to shally and shirk;
Hem lay 'round and Haw looked on
While God did all the work.

Hem was a fogey, and Haw was a prig,
For both had the dull, dull mind;
And whenever they found a thing to do,
They yammered and went it blind.

Hem was the father of bigots and bores;
As the sands of the sea were they.
And Haw was the father of all the tribe
Who criticize today.

But God was an artist from the first,
And knew what he was about;
While over his shoulder sneered these two,
And advised him to rub it out.

They prophesied ruin ere man was made;
"Such folly must surely fail!"
And when he was done, "Do you think, my
Lord,
He's better without a tail?"

And still in the honest working world,
With posture and hint and smirk,
These sons of the devil are standing by
While man does all the work.

They balk endeavor and baffle reform,
In the sacred name of law;
And over the quavering voice of Hem
Is the droning voice of Haw.

Bliss Carman, 1861–1929

1416. From ADDRESS TO THE UNCO GUID

or The Rigidly Righteous

Then gently scan your brother man,
Still gentler sister woman;
Tho' they may gang a kennin wrang
To step aside is human:
One point must still be greatly dark,
The moving *why* they do it;
And just as lamely can ye mark
How far perhaps they rue it.

Who made the heart, 'tis He alone
Decidedly can try us:
He knows each chord, its various tone,
Each spring, its various bias:
Then at the balance let's be mute,
We never can adjust it;
What's done we partly may compute,
But know not what's resisted.

Robert Burns, 1759–1796

1417. YES AND NO

Oh would I were a politician,
Or else a person with a mission.
Heavens, how happy I could be
If only I were sure of me.

How would I strut, could I believe
That, out of all the sons of Eve,
God had granted this former youth
A binding option on His truth.

One side of the moon we've seen alone;
The other she has never shown.
What dreamless sleep, what sound digestion,
Were it the same with every question!

Sometimes with secret pride I sigh
To think how tolerant am I;
Then wonder which is really mine:
Tolerance, or a rubber spine?

Ogden Nash, 1902–

1418. I WILL TRUST

I am glad to think
I am not bound to make the world go right,
But only to discover and to do
With cheerful heart the work that God
appoints.

I will trust in him
That he can hold his own; and I will take
His will, above the work he sendeth me,
To be my chiefest good.

Jean Ingelow, 1820–1897

1419. TO-DAY

Build a little fence of trust
Around to-day;
Fill the space with loving deeds,
And therein stay.
Look not through the sheltering bars
Upon to-morrow;
God will help thee bear what comes
Of joy or sorrow.

Mary Frances Butts, 1836–1902

1420. IN THE HOSPITAL

Because on the branch that is tapping my pane
A sun-wakened, leaf-bud uncurled,
Is bursting its rusty brown sheathing in twain,
I know there is spring in the world.

Because through the sky-patch whose azure and white
My window frames all the day long,
A yellow bird dips for an instant of flight,
I know there is song.

Because even here, in this Mansion of Woe,
Where creep the dull hours, leaden-shod,
Compassion and tenderness aid me, I know
There is God.

Arthur Guiterman, 1871–1943

1421. LORD, IT BELONGS NOT TO MY CARE

Lord, it belongs not to my care,
Whether I die or live;
To love and serve Thee is my share,
And this Thy grace must give.

If life be long I will be glad,
That I may long obey;
If short—yet why should I be sad
To soar to endless day?

Christ leads me through no darker rooms
Than He went through before;
He that unto God's kingdom comes,
Must enter by this door.

Come, Lord, when grace has made me meet
Thy blessèd face to see;
For if Thy work on earth be sweet,
What will Thy glory be!

Then I shall end my sad complaints,
And weary, sinful days;
And join with the triumphant saints,
To sing Jehovah's praise.

My knowledge of that life is small,
The eye of faith is dim;
But 'tis enough that Christ knows all,
And I shall be with Him.

Richard Baxter, 1615–1691

1422. TRUTH

Truth, be more precious to me than eyes
Of happy love; burn hotter in my throat
Than passion, and possess me like my pride;
More sweet than freedom, more desired than joy,
More sacred than the pleasing of a friend.

Max Eastman, 1883–

1423. THE HIGHER GOOD

Father, I will not ask for wealth or fame,
Though once they would have joyed my carnal sense:
I shudder not to bear a hated name,
Wanting all wealth, myself my sole defense.
But give me, Lord, eyes to behold the truth;
A seeing sense that knows the eternal right;
A heart with pity filled, and gentlest ruth;
A manly faith that makes all darkness light:
Give me the power to labor for mankind;
Make me the mouth of such as cannot speak;
Eyes let me be to groping men and blind;
A conscience to the base; and to the weak
Let me be hands and feet; and to the foolish, mind,
And lead still further on such as thy kingdom seek.

Theodore Parker, 1810–1860

1424. TRUTH IS WITHIN

From "Paracelsus," Part I

Truth is within ourselves; it takes no rise
From outward things, whate'er you may believe.
There is an inmost centre in us all,
Where truth abides in fullness; and around,
Wall upon wall, the gross flesh hems it in,
This perfect, clear perception—which is truth.
A baffling and perverting carnal mesh
Binds it, and makes all error: and, to KNOW,
Rather consists in opening out a way
Whence the imprisoned splendour may escape,
Than in effecting entry for a light
Supposed to be without.

Robert Browning, 1812–1889

1425. TRUTH

Whether conditioned by God, or their neural structure, still
All men have this common creed, account for it as you will:—
The Truth is one and incapable of contradiction;
All knowledge that conflicts with itself is Poetic Fiction.

W. H. Auden, 1907–

1426. From WATCHERS OF THE SKY

Newton: Fools have said
That knowledge drives out wonder from the world;
They'll say it still, though all the dust's ablaze
With miracles at their feet; while Newton's laws
Foretell that knowledge one day shall be song,
And those whom Truth has taken to her heart
Find that it beats in music.

❖

"I know not how my work may seem to others—"
So wrote our mightiest mind—"but to myself
I seem a child that wandering all day long
Upon the sea-shore gathers here a shell,
And there a pebble, colored by the wave,
While the great ocean of truth, from sky to sky
Stretches before him, boundless, unexplored."

Alfred Noyes, 1880–

1427. BE TRUE

Thou must be true thyself
If thou the truth wouldst teach;
Thy soul must overflow if thou
Another's soul wouldst reach!
It needs the overflow of heart
To give the lips full speech.

Think truly, and thy thoughts
Shall the world's famine feed;
Speak truly, and each word of thine
Shall be a fruitful seed;
Live truly, and thy life shall be
A great and noble creed.

Horatius Bonar, 1808–1889

1428. From WATCHERS OF THE SKY, III

This music leads us far
From all our creeds, except that faith in law.
Your quest for knowledge—how it rests on that!
How sure the soul is that if truth destroy
The temple, in three days the truth will build
A nobler temple; and that order reigns
In all things. Even your atheist builds his doubt
On that strange faith; destroys his heaven and God
In absolute faith that his own thought is true
To law, God's lanthorn to our stumbling feet;
And so, despite himself, he worships God,
For where true souls are, there are God and heaven.

Alfred Noyes, 1880–

1429. HONEST DOUBT

I say unto you: Cherish your doubts,
For doubt is the handmaiden of truth.
Doubt is the servant of discovery;
She is the key unto the door of knowledge.
Let no man fear for the truth, that doubt may consume her;
Only he that would shut out his doubts denieth the truth.

Robert Weston

1430. TRUTH AND LOVE ABIDE

From "Elegy on The Death of Dr. Channing"

Truth needs no champions: in the infinite deep
  Of everlasting Soul her strength abides,
From Nature's heart her mighty pulses leap,
  Through Nature's veins her strength, undying tides.

Peace is more strong than war, and gentleness,
  Where force were vain, makes conquest o'er the wave;
And love lives on and hath a power to bless,
  When they who loved are hidden in the grave.

❖

No power can die that ever wrought for Truth;
  Thereby a law of Nature it became,
And lives unwithered in its sinewy youth,
  When he who called it forth is but a name.

James Russell Lowell, 1819–1891

1431. SUB PONDERE CRESCIT

The hope of Truth grows stronger, day by day;
I hear the soul of Man around me waking,
Like a great sea, its frozen fetters breaking,
And flinging up to heaven its sunlit spray,
Tossing huge continents in scornful play,
And crushing them, with din of grinding thunder,
That makes old emptinesses stare in wonder;
The memory of a glory passed away
Lingers in every heart, as, in the shell,
Resounds the bygone freedom of the sea,
And, every hour new signs of promise tell
That the great soul shall once again be free,
For high, and yet more high, the murmurs swell
Of inward strife for truth and liberty.

James Russell Lowell, 1819–1891

1432. MAGNA EST VERITAS

Here, in this little Bay,
Full of tumultuous life and great repose,
Where, twice a day,
The purposeless, glad ocean comes and goes
Under high cliffs, and far from the huge town,
I sit me down.
For want of me the world's course will not fail:
When all its work is done, the lie shall rot;
The truth is great, and shall prevail.
When none cares whether it prevail or not.

Coventry Patmore, 1823–1896

1433. From SACRIFICE

Though love repine, and reason chafe,
  There came a voice without reply,—
"'Tis man's perdition to be safe,
  When for the truth he ought to die."

Ralph Waldo Emerson, 1803–1882

1434. TRUTH

From "A Death In The Desert"

For life, with all it yields of joy and woe,
And hope and fear,—believe the aged friend,—
Is just our chance o' the prize of learning love,
How love might be, hath been indeed, and is;
And that we hold thenceforth to the uttermost
Such prize despite the envy of the world.
And, having gained truth, keep truth: that is all.

Robert Browning, 1812–1889

1435. From THE BATTLE-FIELD

Truth, crushed to earth shall rise again,—
The eternal years of God are hers;
But Error, wounded, writhes in pain,
And dies among his worshippers.

William Cullen Bryant, 1794–1878

1436. THERE ARE FOUR DOORS WHICH OPEN ON THE SKIES

There are four doors which open on the skies.
The first is truth, by which the living word
Goes forth to seek the spirit and be heard;
Lost in the universe, the spirit lies.
Then justice with her veiled and quiet eyes
Stands at the second portal; at the third,
Faith and her sparrow, the immortal bird;
And the last gate is love's, to paradise.
These are the doors by which the mighty pass.
Yet in the wall there is one wicket more,
With rusty hinges and a splintered floor,
A shattered sill half hidden in the grass.
Small is the gateway as the Scriptures tell;
Its name is pity, and God loves it well.

Robert Nathan, 1894–

1437. DYING MEN

From "King Richard II," Act II, sc. 1

The tongues of dying men
Enforce attention, like deep harmony:
When words are scarce, they're seldom spent in vain;
For they breathe truth that breathe their words in pain.

William Shakespeare, 1564–1616

1438. STEALING

In vain we call old notions fudge,
And bend our conscience to our dealing;
The Ten Commandments will not budge,
And stealing will continue stealing.[1]

James Russell Lowell, 1819–1891

[1] Motto of The American Copyright League (November 20, 1885).

1439. ON LOOKING BACKWARD

They bid us live each day afresh,
Trade last year's grief for a better morrow;
But happiness were flabby flesh
If it should lack the bones of sorrow.

Ernestine Mercer, contemporary American

1440. IN SPITE OF SORROW

In spite of sorrow, loss, and pain,
Our course be onward still;
We sow on Burmah's barren plain,
We reap on Zion's hill.

Adoniram Judson, 1788–1850

1441. SORROW

Count each affliction, whether light or grave,
God's messenger sent down to thee; do thou
With courtesy receive him; rise and bow;
And, ere his shadow pass thy threshold, crave
Permission first his heavenly feet to lave;
Then lay before him all thou hast; allow
No cloud of passion to usurp thy brow,
Or mar thy hospitality; no wave
Of mortal tumult to obliterate
Thy soul's marmoreal calmness. Grief should be
Like joy, majestic, equable, sedate;
Confirming, cleansing, raising, making free;
Strong to consume small troubles; to commend
Great thoughts, grave thoughts, thoughts lasting to the end.

Aubrey Thomas de Vere, 1814–1902

1442. THROUGH SORROW TO SERVICE

Because of one small low-laid head all crowned
With golden hair,
For evermore all fair young brows to me
A halo wear.
I kiss them reverently. Alas! I know
The pain I bear.

Because of little pallid lips which once
My name did call,
No childish voice in vain appeal upon
My ears doth fall.
I count it all my joy their joys to share,
And sorrows small.

Because of little death-cold feet, for earth's
Rough roads unmeet,
I'd journey leagues to save from sin and harm
Such little feet,
And count the lowliest service done for them,
So sacred sweet.

Author unknown

1443. SORROW TURNED INTO JOY

Sometimes at night when human-kind
And beasts and birds are sleeping,
It seems as if the woods and banks
And meadows have been weeping.
Wrapt in night's mantle, dews have drenched
The land with tears of sorrow,
But God will bathe it with His golden veil
Before the morrow,
Turning the tears of grief to tears of joy
Like glistening manna,
Until the hills and valleys laugh again
And sing *Hosanna.*

John Alexander Bouquet, 1875-

1444. SWEET ARE THE USES OF ADVERSITY

From "As You Like It," Act II, sc. 1

Sweet are the uses of adversity;
Which, like the toad, ugly and venomous,
Wears yet a precious jewel in his head;
And this our life, exempt from public haunt,
Finds tongues in trees, books in the running brooks,
Sermons in stones, and good in every thing.

William Shakespeare, 1564–1616

1445. PAIN[1]

The cry of man's anguish went up to God,
"Lord, take away pain!
The shadow that darkens the world Thou hast made;
The close coiling chain
That strangles the heart: the burden that weighs
On the wings that would soar—
Lord, take away pain from the world Thou hast made
That it love Thee the more!"

Then answered the Lord to the cry of the world,
"Shall I take away pain,
And with it the power of the soul to endure,
Made strong by the strain?
Shall I take away pity that knits heart to heart,
And sacrifice high?
Will ye lose all your heroes that lift from the fire
White brows to the sky?
Shall I take away love that redeems with a price,
And smiles with its loss?
Can ye spare from your lives that would cling unto mine
The Christ on his cross?"

Author unknown

[1] Found on a hospital wall.

1446. PLEASURE AND SORROW

I walked a mile with Pleasure,
She chattered all the way,
But left me none the wiser
For all she had to say.

I walked a mile with Sorrow,
And ne'er a word said she;
But, oh, the things I learned from her
When Sorrow walked with me!

Robert Browning Hamilton, 1880–

1447. FRIENDLY OBSTACLES

For every hill I've had to climb,
For every stone that bruised my feet,
For all the blood and sweat and grime,
For blinding storms and burning heat,
My heart sings but a grateful song—
These were the things that made me strong!

For all the heartaches and the tears,
For all the anguish and the pain,
For gloomy days and fruitless years,
And for the hopes that lived in vain,
I do give thanks, for now I know
These were the things that helped me grow!

'Tis not the softer things of life
Which stimulate man's will to strive;
But bleak adversity and strife
Do most to keep man's will alive.
O'er rose-strewn paths the weaklings creep,
But brave hearts dare to climb the steep.

Author unknown

1448. SORROWS HUMANIZE OUR RACE

Sorrows humanize our race;
Tears are the showers that fertilize this world:
And memory of things precious keepeth warm
The heart that once did hold them.

They are poor
That have lost nothing: they are poorer far
Who, losing, have forgotten: they most poor
Of all, who lose and wish they might forget.
For life is one, and in its warp and woof
There runs a thread of gold that glitters fair,
And sometimes in the pattern shows more sweet
Where there are sombre colors. It is true
That we have wept. But O, this thread of gold,
We would not have it tarnish: let us turn
Oft and look back upon the wondrous web,
And when it shineth sometimes we shall know
That memory is possession.

Jean Ingelow, 1820–1897

1449. SORROW

Who never broke with tears, his bread,
Who never watched through anguished hours
With weeping eyes, upon his bed,
He knows ye not, O heavenly Powers.

Johann Wolfgang von Goethe, 1749–1832; tr. by Gretchen Warren

1450. STIGMATA

He cannot heal who has not suffered much,
For only Sorrow sorrow understands;
They will not come for healing at our touch
Who have not seen the scars upon our hands.

Edwin McNeill Poteat, 1892–

1451. PRAYER FOR STRENGTH

Though I should be maligned by those
I trust, let not my spirit be
Broken and bowed, but may the throes
Of suffering set me free

From pettiness and that desire
Which goads one to retaliate;
With patience I would quench the fire
Of vengeance, ere it be too late.

And in defeat may I cast out
The moods of envy and despair,
And from my heart, Lord, I would rout
All bitterness. This is my prayer.

Margaret E. Bruner, contemporary American

1452. PRAYER IN AFFLICTION

Keep me from bitterness. It is so easy
To nurse sharp bitter thoughts each dull dark hour.
Against self-pity, Man of sorrows, defend me,

With Thy deep sweetness and Thy gentle
power.
And out of all this hurt of pain and
heartbreak
Help me to harvest a new sympathy
For suffering human kind, a wiser pity
For those who lift a heavier cross with Thee.

Violet Alleyn Storey

1453. A WARRIOR'S PRAYER

Long since, in sore distress, I heard one pray:
"Lord, who prevailest with resistless might,
Ever from war and strife keep me away;
My battles fight!"

I know not if I play the Pharisee,
And if my brother after all be right;
But mine shall be the warrior's plea to
Thee—
Strength for the fight.

I do not ask that Thou shalt front the fray,
And drive the warring foeman from my
sight;
I only ask, O Lord, by night, by day,
Strength for the fight.

When foes upon me press, let me not quail,
Nor think to turn me into coward flight.
I only ask, to make mine arms prevail,
Strength for the fight.

And when, at eventide, the fray is done,
My soul to Death's bed-chamber do Thou
light,
And grant me, be the field or lost or won,
Rest from the fight.

Paul Laurence Dunbar, 1872–1906

1454. PUT GRIEF AWAY

From "Tibetan Comforter"

When all is said and done, I urge again,
Put grief away. And think not of the past.
No! Hold the past and future both within
The compass of your faith and hope. You have
What should put all of bitter grief away,
And bring your heart to final blessed peace.

Robert K. Ekvall, contemporary
American missionary to Tibet

1455. THE SEA OF PEACE

I stand above a white-rimmed sea:
Its deeps are mine, its mirrored height;
Mine its low plaint of mystery;
All mine its glee-song of delight.

Mine its strong soul; its body mine;
I lave me in its kind embrace;
In dreams upon its buoyant brine
It gives me back a cherished face.

Mayhap it helps me understand
The language of infinity,
The secret of the shifting sand,
The testimony of the sea.

I am above all circumstance,
I am beyond all power to hurt;
No more I shrink from sorrow's lance,
So with all strength am I begirt.

I've tasted every bitter sup;
Earth's bulwarks all are proven frail;
Yet sweetened now is life's low cup,
All hallowed: 'tis my Holy Grail.

Above its wreck of ship and men
The placid ocean shows no scars;
Above my deeps where storms have been
My tranquil soul reflects the stars.

Ruth McEnery Stuart, 1849–1917

1456. PEACE AFTER SORROW

There is a peace which cometh after sorrow,
A peace of hope surrendered, not fulfilled;
A peace that looketh not upon the morrow
But backward, on the storm already stilled.
It is the peace in sacrifice secluded,
The peace that is from inward conflict free;
'Tis not the peace which over Eden brooded
But that which triumphed in Gethsemane.

Jessie Rose Gates

1457. PEACE AND JOY

From "The Suffering God"

Peace does not mean the end of all our
striving,
Joy does not mean the drying of our tears;
Peace is the power that comes to souls arriving
Up to the light where God Himself appears.

Joy is the wine that God is ever pouring
Into the hearts of those who strive with Him,
Light'ning their eyes to vision and adoring,
Strength'ning their arms to warfare glad and grim.

G. A. Studdert-Kennedy, 1883–1929

1458. INWARD PEACE

From "Lines Written In Kensington Gardens"

Calm soul of all things! make it mine
To feel, amid the city's jar,
That there abides a peace of thine,
Man did not make, and cannot mar!

The will to neither strive nor cry,
The power to feel with others give!
Calm, calm me more! nor let me die
Before I have begun to live.

Matthew Arnold, 1822–1888

1459. PEACE

With eager heart and will on fire,
I strove to win my great desire.
"Peace shall be mine," I said; but life
Grew bitter in the barren strife.

My soul was weary, and my pride
Was wounded deep; to Heaven I cried,
"God grant me peace or I must die;"
The dumb stars glittered no reply.

Broken at last, I bowed my head,
Forgetting all myself, and said,
"Whatever comes, His will be done;"
And in that moment peace was won.

Henry van Dyke, 1852–1933

1460. IN ACCEPTANCE LIETH PEACE

He said, "I will forget the dying faces;
The empty places,
They shall be filled again.
O voices moaning deep within me, cease."
But vain the word; vain, vain:
Not in forgetting lieth peace.

He said, "I will crowd action upon action,
The strife of faction
Shall stir me and sustain;
O tears that drown the fire of manhood cease."
But vain the word; vain, vain:
Not in endeavour lieth peace.

He said, "I will withdraw me and be quiet,
Why meddle in life's riot?
Shut be my door to pain.
Desire, thou dost befool me, thou shalt cease."
But vain the word; vain, vain:
Not in aloofness lieth peace.

He said, "I will submit; I am defeated.
God hath depleted
My life of its rich gain.
O futile murmurings, why will ye not cease?"
But vain the word; vain, vain:
Not in submission lieth peace.

He said, "I will accept the breaking sorrow
Which God to-morrow
Will to His son explain."
Then did the turmoil deep within him cease.
Not vain the word, not vain;
For in Acceptance lieth peace.

Amy Carmichael, contemporary English

1461. O GOD, IN RESTLESS LIVING

O God, in restless living
We lose our spirits' peace.
Calm our unwise confusion,
Bid Thou our clamor cease.
Let anxious hearts grow quiet
Like pools at evening still,
Till Thy reflected heavens
All our spirits fill.

Teach us, beyond our striving,
The rich rewards of rest.
Who does not live serenely
Is never deeply blest.
O tranquil, radiant Sunlight,
Bring Thou our lives to flower,
Less wearied with our effort,
More aware of power.

Receptive make our spirits,
Our need is to be still;

As dawn fades flickering candle
So dim our anxious will.
Reveal Thy radiance through us,
Thine ample strength release.
Not ours but Thine the triumph
In the power of peace.

We grow not wise by struggling,
We gain but things by strain.
We cease to water gardens,
When comes Thy plenteous rain.
O, beautify our spirits
In restfulness from strife;
Enrich our souls in secret
With abundant life.

Harry Emerson Fosdick, 1878–

1462. A LAST PRAYER

Father, I scarcely dare to pray,
So clear I see, now it is done,
That I have wasted half my day,
And left my work but just begun;

So clear I see that things I thought
Were right or harmless were a sin;
So clear I see that I have sought,
Unconscious, selfish aims to win;

So clear I see that I have hurt
The souls I might have helped to save;
That I have slothful been, inert,
Deaf to the calls thy leaders gave.

In outskirts of thy kingdoms vast,
Father, the humblest spot give me;
Set me the lowliest task thou hast;
Let me repentant work for thee!

Helen Hunt Jackson, 1830–1885

1463. LAUGHTER AND TEARS

When I no more as now can find
A joy in little common things;
When mirth which blesses humankind
No laughing mantle o'er me flings;
Veneered with mock solemnity,
Then pity me, O pity me!

When from my eyes no tears will flow,
But all those tender springs are dead;
When any tale or mortal woe
Still leaves unbowed a haughty head:
Aloof in self-complacency,
Then pity me, O weep for me!

When any cry of human wrong
Shall fail to draw me from my path;
Or evil fail to make me strong
With impulse of a righteous wrath:
Dead in my own sufficiency,
Then pity me, O grieve for me!

But while I weep with unfeigned tears,
Or mayhap laugh with simple mirth,
And spend the talents of the years
In love and labor on the earth;
Then God is my security,
Rejoice with me, O sing with me!

Tertius van Dyke, 1886–

1464. PRAYER FOR STRENGTH

Father, in Thy mysterious presence kneeling,
Fain would our souls feel all Thy kindling love;
For we are weak, and need some deep revealing
Of trust and strength and calmness from above.

Lord, we have wandered forth through doubt and sorrow,
And Thou hast made each step an onward one;
And we will ever trust each unknown morrow,—
Thou wilt sustain us till its work is done.

In the heart's depths a peace serene and holy
Abides; and when pain seems to have its will,
Or we despair, O may that peace rise slowly,
Stronger than agony, and we be still!

Now, Father, now, in Thy dear presence kneeling,
Our spirits yearn to feel Thy kindling love:
Now make us strong, we need Thy deep revealing
Of trust and strength and calmness from above.

Samuel Johnson, 1822–1882

1465. CONTENT

From "King Henry VI," Part III, Act III, sc. 1

My crown is in my heart, not on my head;
Not deck'd with diamonds and Indian stones,
Nor to be seen: my crown is call'd content;
A crown it is that seldom kings enjoy.

William Shakespeare, 1564–1616

1466. HAPPY THE MAN

From "Ode on Solitude"

Happy the man, whose wish and care
A few paternal acres bound,
Content to breathe his native air
In his own ground.

Whose herds with milk, whose fields with bread,
Whose flocks supply him with attire;
Whose trees in summer yield him shade,
In winter fire.

Blest, who can unconcernedly find
House, days, and years, slide soft away
In health of body, peace of mind;
Quiet by day.

Sound sleep by night; study and ease
Together mixed, sweet recreation,
And innocence, which most does please
With meditation.

Thus let me live, unseen, unknown;
Thus unlamented let me die;
Steal from the world, and not a stone
Tell where I lie.

Alexander Pope, 1688–1744

1467. CHARACTER OF A HAPPY LIFE

How happy is he born and taught
That serveth not another's will;
Whose armour is his honest thought
And simple truth his utmost skill!

Whose passions not his masters are,
Whose soul is still prepared for death,
Not tied unto the world with care
Of public fame, or private breath;

Who envies none that chance doth raise
Or vice; who never understood
How deepest wounds are given by praise;
Nor rules of state, but rules of good:

Who hath his life from rumours freed,
Whose conscience is his strong retreat;
Whose state can neither flatterers feed,
Nor ruin make accusers great;

Who God doth late and early pray
More of his grace than gifts to lend;
And entertains the harmless day
With a well-chosen book or friend;

—This man is freed from servile bands
Of hope to rise, or fear to fall;
Lord of himself, though not of lands;
And having nothing, yet hath all.

Sir Henry Wotton, 1568–1639

1468. OF A CONTENTED MIND

When all is done and said,
In the end this shall you find:
He most of all doth bathe in bliss
That hath a quiet mind;
And, clear from worldly cares,
To deem can be content
The sweetest time in all his life
In thinking to be spent.

The body subject is
To fickle Fortune's power,
And to a million of mishaps
Is casual every hour;
And death in time doth change
It to a clod of clay;
Whenas the mind, which is divine,
Runs never to decay.

Companion none is like
Unto the mind alone;
For many have been harmed by speech,
Through thinking, few, or none:
Fear oftentimes restraineth words,
But makes not thought to cease;
And he speaks best that hath the skill
When for to hold his peace.

Our wealth leaves us at death,
Our kinsmen at the grave;
But virtues of the mind unto
The heavens with us we have:
Wherefore, for Virtue's sake,
I can be well content
The sweetest time in all my life
To deem in thinking spent.

Sir Thomas Vaux, 1510–1556

1469. HAPPY THE MAN

From "Imitation of Horace"

Happy the man, and happy he alone,
He who can call to-day his own;
He who, secure within, can say,
"To-morrow, do thy worst, for I have liv'd
to-day.
Be fair or foul, or rain or shine,
The joys I have possessed, in spite of fate,
are mine.
Not heaven itself upon the past has power;
But what has been, has been, and I have had
my hour."

John Dryden, 1631–1700

1470. THE BEATITUDES OF JESUS

Matthew 5: 3–12

Blessed are the poor in spirit: for theirs is the kingdom of heaven.
Blessed are they that mourn: for they shall be comforted.
Blessed are the meek: for they shall inherit the earth.
Blessed are they which do hunger and thirst after righteousness: for they shall be filled.
Blessed are the merciful: for they shall obtain mercy.
Blessed are the pure in heart: for they shall see God.
Blessed are the peacemakers: for they shall be called the children of God.
Blessed are they which are persecuted for righteousness' sake: for theirs is the kingdom of heaven.
Blessed are ye, when men shall revile you, and persecute you, and shall say all manner of evil against you falsely, for my sake.
Rejoice, and be exceeding glad: for great is your reward in heaven: for so persecuted they the prophets which were before you.

King James Version, 1611

1471. MY PEACE I GIVE UNTO YOU

Blessed are the eyes that see
The things that you have seen,
Blessed are the feet that walk
The ways where you have been.

Blessed are the eyes that see
The Agony of God,
Blessed are the feet that tread
The paths His feet have trod.

Blessed are the souls that solve
The paradox of Pain,
And find the path that, piercing it,
Leads through to Peace again.

G. A. Studdert-Kennedy, 1883–1929

1472. SAINT FRANCIS OF ASSISI

You saved the golden seeds of holy mirth—
Light-hearted Little Brother To The Sun—
In laughter-famished furrows of the earth,
Singing Creation's praises one by one.
You knew no dismal tyranny of sin—
But simply, gaily—from all fear set free—
Water and wind and fire you claimed as kin,
And prayed upon the stars for rosary.

Husband to poverty and son to charity—
  Ragged and homeless—happy as a thrush—
You journeyed vestured in divine hilarity,
  And slept content beneath a wayside bush;
And though you preached to men in glowing words,
  You gave your best, I fancy, to the birds.

Joan Ramsay, 1902–

1473. CONTENT

I was too ambitous in my deed,
And thought to distance all men in success,
Till God came on me, marked the place, and said,
"Ill-doer, henceforth keep within this line,
Attempting less than others"—and I stand
And work among Christ's little ones, content.

Elizabeth Barrett Browning, 1806–1861

1474. MY MIND TO ME A KINGDOM IS

Excerpts

My mind to me a kingdom is;
  Such present joys therein I find,
That it excels all other bliss
  That earth affords or grows by kind;
Though much I want which most would have,
Yet still my mind forbids to crave.

I see how plenty surfeits oft,
  And hasty climbers soon do fall;
I see that those which are aloft
  Mishap doth threaten most of all,
They get with toil, they keep with fear;
Such cares my mind could never bear.

Content to live, this is my stay;
  I seek no more than may suffice;
I press to bear no haughty sway;
  Look, what I lack my mind supplies:
Lo, thus I triumph like a king,
Content with that my mind doth bring.

Some have too much, yet still do crave;
  I little have, and seek no more:
They are but poor, though much they have,
  And I am rich with little store:
They poor, I rich; they beg, I give;
They lack, I leave; they pine, I live.

I laugh not at another's loss;
  I grudge not at another's gain;
No worldly wave my mind can toss;
  My state at one doth still remain:
I fear no foe, nor fawn on friend;
I loathe not life, nor dread my end.

My wealth is health and perfect ease;
  My conscience clear my chief defence;
I never seek by bribes to please,
  Nor by desert to give offence.
Thus do I live, thus will I die;
Would all did so as well as I!

Edward Dyer, c. 1540–1607

1475. BLIND BUT HAPPY

O what a happy soul am I!
  Although I cannot see,
I am resolved that in this world
  Contented I will be;
How many blessings I enjoy
  That other people don't!
To weep and sigh because I'm blind,
  I cannot, and I won't.

Fanny Crosby,[1] *1820–1918*

1476. From APPARENT FAILURE

It's wiser being good than bad;
  It's safer being meek than fierce:
It's fitter being sane than mad.
  My own hope is, a sun will pierce
The thickest cloud earth ever stretched;
  That, after Last, returns the First,
Though a wide compass round be fetched;
  That what began best, can't end worst,
Nor what God blessed once, prove accurst.

Robert Browning, 1812–1889

1477. HOW GOD ANSWERS

He prayed for strength that he might achieve;
He was made weak that he might obey.
He prayed for wealth that he might do greater things;

[1] Written at the age of eight years.

He was given infirmity that he might do better things.
He prayed for riches that he might be happy;
He was given poverty that he might be wise.
He prayed for power that he might have the praise of men;
He was given infirmity that he might feel the need of God.
He prayed for all things that he might enjoy life;
He was given life that he might enjoy all things.
He had received nothing that he asked for—all that he hoped for;
His prayer was answered—he was most blessed.

Author unknown

1478. GRADATIM

Heaven is not reached at a single bound;
  But we build the ladder by which we rise
  From the lowly earth to the vaulted skies,
And we mount to its summit round by round.

I count this thing to be grandly true,
  That a noble deed is a step toward God,
  Lifting the soul from the common sod
To a purer air and a broader view.

We rise by things that are 'neath our feet;
  By what we have mastered of good and gain,
  By the pride deposed and the passion slain,
And the vanquished ills that we hourly meet.

We hope, we aspire, we resolve, we trust,
  When the morning calls us to life and light;
  But our hearts grow weary, and ere the night,
Our lives are trailing the sordid dust.

We hope, we resolve, we aspire, we pray,
  And we think that we mount the air on wings
  Beyond the recall of sensual things,
While our feet still cling to the heavy clay.

Wings for angels, but feet for men!
  We may borrow the wings to find the way;
  We may hope, and resolve, and aspire, and pray;
But our feet must rise, or we fall again.

Only in dreams is a ladder thrown
  From the weary earth to the sapphire walls,
  But the dreams depart, and the vision falls,
And the sleeper wakes on his pillow of stone.

Heaven is not reached at a single bound:
  But we build the ladder by which we rise
  From the lowly earth to the vaulted skies,
And we mount to its summit round by round.

Josiah Gilbert Holland, 1819–1881

1479. WHO LIVETH WELL

He liveth long who liveth well;
  All else is being flung away;
He liveth longest who can tell
  Of true things truly done each day.

Fill up each hour with what will last;
  Use well the moments as they go;
The life above, when this is past,
  Is the ripe fruit of life below.

Horatius Bonar, 1808–1889

1480. SURVIVAL

A thousand years from this tonight
  When Orion climbs the sky,
The same swift snow will still the roofs,
  The same mad stars run by.

And who will know of China's war,
  Or poison gas in Spain?
The dead . . . they'll be forgotten, lost,
  Whether they lose or gain.

Of all the brilliant strategies
  Of war-lords now alive,
Perhaps a Chinese iris vase
  Of porcelain, may survive . . .

Perhaps a prayer, perhaps a song,
  Fashioned of love and tears,
But only beauty . . . only truth
  Will last a thousand years.

Margaret Moore Meuttman,
contemporary American

1481. DEAF AND DUMB

Only the prism's obstruction shows aright
The secret of a sunbeam, breaks its light
Into the jewelled bow from blankest white;
  So may a glory from defeat arise;
Only by Deafness may the vexed Love wreak
Its insuppressive sense on brow and cheek,
Only by Dumbness adequately speak,
As favored mouth could never, through the
    eyes.

Robert Browning, 1812–1889

1482. THE UNDISCOURAGED GOD

The grass grows slowly up the hill
With faith the torrent cannot kill,
And rocks are rough, and still the clover
The stony fields will yet run over—
And I know nothing that the true,
The good, the gentle cannot do.

Woodlands that the winters sadden
The leaves of Spring again will gladden;
And so must life forever be—
The gentle hands work patiently
And yet accomplish more forever
Than these too strong or those too clever.

So toils an undiscouraged God
And covers barren fields with sod,
And so will hate and sin surrender
To faith still strong and love still tender—
And I know nothing that the true,
The good, the gentle cannot do.

Author unknown

Book V: THE KINGDOM OF GOD

1483. THE KINGDOM OF GOD[1]

"In No Strange Land"

O WORLD invisible, we view thee,
O world intangible, we touch thee,
O world unknowable, we know thee,
Inapprehensible, we clutch thee!

Does the fish soar to find the ocean,
The eagle plunge to find the air—
That we ask of the stars in motion
If they have rumour of thee there?

Not where the wheeling systems darken,
And our benumbed conceiving soars!—
The drift of pinions, would we hearken,
Beats at our own clay-shuttered doors.

The angels keep their ancient places;—
Turn but a stone and start a wing!
'Tis ye, 'tis your estrangèd faces,
That miss the many-splendoured thing.

But (when so sad thou canst not sadder)
Cry;—and upon thy so sore loss
Shall shine the traffic of Jacob's ladder
Pitched betwixt Heaven and Charing Cross.

Yea, in the night, my Soul, my daughter,
Cry,—clinging Heaven by the hems;
And lo, Christ walking on the water
Not of Gennesareth, but Thames!

Francis Thompson, 1859–1907

1484. "THY KINGDOM COME!" O LORD

"Thy kingdom come!" O Lord, we daily cry,
Weary and sad with earth's long strife and pain.
"How long, O Lord!" Thy suffering children sigh,
"Speed Thou the dawn, and o'er the nations reign."

Thy kingdom come! then all the din of war
Like some dark dream shall vanish with the night!
Peace, holy peace, her myriad gifts shall pour,
Resting secure from danger and affright.

[1] Found among the poet's unpublished poems after his death.

Thy kingdom come! no more shall deeds of shame
Brutish and base, destroy the soul divine;
Bright with Thy love's all-purifying flame
Thy human temples evermore shall shine.

Thy kingdom come! mad greed for wealth and power
No more shall grind the weaklings in the dust;
Then mind and strength shall share Thy ample dower,
Brothers in Thee, and one in equal trust.

Henry Warburton Hawkes, 1843–

1485. THY KINGDOM, LORD, WE LONG FOR

Thy Kingdom, Lord, we long for,
Where Love shall find its own;
And brotherhood triumphant
Our years of pride disown.
Thy captive people languish
In mill and mart and mine:
We lift to thee their anguish,
We wait thy promised Sign.

❖

If now perchance in tumult
The destined Sign appear—
The Rising of the People—
Dispel our coward fear!
Let comforts that we cherish,
Let old tradition die,
Our wealth, our wisdom perish,
If so thou mayst draw nigh.

Vida D. Scudder, 1861–

1486. O LORD OF LIFE, THY KINGDOM IS AT HAND

O Lord of life, Thy kingdom is at hand,
Blest reign of love and liberty and light;
Time long foretold by seers of every land;
The cherished dream of watchers through the night.

Lo! in our hearts shines forth the morning star,
Shedding its luster on our darkened way;
And we behold, as pilgrims from afar,
The holy dawning of Thy perfect day.

Now gleams at last upon our waiting eyes
The glory of the kingdom that shall be;
When truth in conquering grandeur shall arise,
And man shall rule the world with equity.

❖

Forward again we move at Thy command,
The flaming pillar leading on anew;
One in the faith of all Thy prophet band,
Onward we press to make the vision true.

Marion Franklin Ham, 1867–

1487. AN AFFIRMATION

How shall come the kingdom holy,
In which all the earth is blest,
That shall lift on high the lowly,
And to weary souls give rest?
Not with trumpet call of legions
Bursting through the upper sky,
Waking earth thro' all its regions
With their heav'n-descending cry.

Not with dash or sudden sally,
Swooping down with rushing wing;
But, as, creeping up a valley,
Come the grasses in the spring;
First one blade and then another,
Still advancing are they seen,
Rank on rank, each by its brother,
Till each inch of ground is green.

Thro' the weary days of sowing,
Burning sun and drenching show'r,
Day by day, so slowly growing,
Comes the waited harvest hour.
So the kingdom cometh ever,
Though it seems so far away;
Each high thought and true endeavor
Hastens on the blessed day.

Minot Judson Savage, 1841–1918

1488. DAY'S END

Day ends:
Breasting the North
My shoulders shiver
As I onward go.
And yet,
I utterly forget
The cruel cold,
Nor feel the dark,
Because my heart
Aches with the people's woe.

Oh, let me trust
That through my tears
God's Kingdom has
One little inch drawn near!
Then what is it to me
That my weak body be
Beaten to dust?
Midnight:
I crawl from my bed
Into the cold,
And gaze at the stars again,
Finding God there
To help me bear
My daily load
Of grief and care,
Sorrow and pain.

Deep in the night
Our spirits meet,
And prayer is sweet!

Toyohiko Kagawa, 1888–;
tr. by Lois J. Erickson

1489. SWINGING TOWARD THE LIGHT

"I do believe the world is swinging toward the light,"
So spoke a soul on fire with holy flame.
Amid the dark such faith pierced through the night,
The dreamers wrought, and living fruitage came.
To give of self, and not to count the cost,
To learn, to teach, to labor, and to pray,
To serve like Christ the least, the last, the lost—
These were the beacon fires that lit the way.

Our light grows dim; the air is thick with doom,
And everywhere men's souls are crushed with fears.
Yet high above the carnage and the gloom
The call resounds across the teeming years,
"Lift high Christ's cross! Serve God and trust His might!"
I do believe the world is swinging toward the light!

Georgia Harkness, 1891–

1490. ODE

We are the music-makers,
And we are the dreamers of dreams,
Wandering by lone sea-breakers,
And sitting by desolate streams;
World-losers and world-forsakers,
On whom the pale moon gleams:
Yet we are the movers and shakers
Of the world forever, it seems.

With wonderful deathless ditties
We build up the world's great cities,
And out of a fabulous story
We fashion an empire's glory:
One man with a dream, at pleasure,
Shall go forth and conquer a crown;
And three with a new song's measure
Can trample a kingdom down.

We, in the ages lying
In the buried past of the earth,
Built Nineveh with our sighing,
And Babel itself with our mirth;
And o'erthrew them with prophesying
To the old of the new world's worth;
For each age is a dream that is dying,
Or one that is coming to birth.

Arthur William O'Shaughnessy, 1844–1881

1491. From IN THE DAWN

We are standing in the great dawn of a day they did not know,
On a height they only dreamed of, toiling darkly far below;
But our gaze is toward a summit, loftier, airier, mist-encurled,
Soaring skyward through the twilight from the bases of the world.
Up and up, achieving, failing, weak in flesh but strong of soul.
We may never live to reach it—ah, but we have seen the goal!

Odell Shepard, 1884–

1492. THE WORLD

I saw Eternity the other night,
Like a great *Ring* of pure and endless light,
All calm, as it was bright,
And round beneath it, Time, in hours, days, years,
Driven by the spheres,
Like a vast shadow moved, in which the world
And all her train were hurled.
The doting lover, in his quaintest strain,
Did there complain;
Near him his lute, his fancy, and his flights,
Wit's sour delights;
With gloves, and knots, the silly snares of pleasure,
Yet his dear treasure,
All scattered lay, while he his eyes did pour
Upon a flower.

The darksome Statesman, hung with weights and woe,
Like a thick midnight fog, moved there so slow,
He did nor stay, nor go;
Condemning thoughts (like sad eclipses) scowl
Upon his soul,
And Clouds of crying witnesses without
Pursued him with one shout;
Yet digged the Mole, and, lest his ways be found,
Work'd under ground,
Where he did clutch his prey; but one did see
That policy;
Churches and altars fed him; perjuries
Were gnats and flies;
It rained about him blood and tears, but he
Drank them as free.

The fearful Miser, on a heap of rust
Sat pining all his life there; did scarce trust
His own hands with the dust;
Yet would not place one piece above, but lives
In fear of thieves:
Thousands there were as frantic as himself,
And hugged each one his pelf;
The downright Epicure placed heaven in sense,
And scorned pretence;
While others, slipt into a wide excess,
Said little less;
The weaker sort, slight, trivial wares enslave,
Who think them brave;
And poor, despisèd Truth sat counting by
Their victory.

Yet some, who all this while did weep and sing,
And sing, and weep, soared up into the *Ring;*
But most would use no wing.
"O fools," said I, "thus to prefer dark night
Before true light!
To live in grots, and caves, and hate the day
Because it shews the way,—
The way which, from this dead and dark abode,
Leads up to God;
A way where you might tread the sun and be
More bright than he!"
But, as I did their madness so discuss,
One whispered thus,—
"*This Ring the Bridegroom did for none provide,*
But for his Bride."

Henry Vaughan, 1622–1695

1493. IN HOC SIGNO

The Kingdoms of the Earth go by
In purple and in gold;
They rise, they triumph, and they die,
And all their tale is told.

One Kingdom only is divine,
  One banner triumphs still;
Its King a servant, and its sign
  A gibbet on a hill.

Godfrey Fox Bradby, 1863–

1494. WHERE IS HEAVEN?

From "Here and Now"

Where is Heaven? Is it not
Just a friendly garden plot,
Walled with stone and roofed with sun,
Where the days pass one by one
Not too fast and not too slow,
Looking backward as they go
At the beauties left behind
To transport the pensive mind.

❖

Does not Heaven begin that day
When the eager heart can say,
Surely God is in this place,
I have seen Him face to face
In the loveliness of flowers,
In the service of the showers,
And His voice has talked to me
In the sunlit apple tree.

Bliss Carman, 1861–1929

1495. GOD, THE OMNIPOTENT

God, the omnipotent! King, who ordainest
Great winds thy clarions, lightnings thy sword;
Show forth thy pity on high where thou reignest,
Give to us peace in our time, O Lord.

God the All-merciful! earth hath forsaken
Thy ways of blessedness, slighted Thy word;
Bid not Thy wrath in its terrors awaken:
Give to us peace in our time, O Lord!

God the All-righteous One! man hath defied Thee,
Yet to eternity standeth Thy word;
Falsehood and wrong shall not tarry beside Thee:
Give to us peace in our time, O Lord!

God the All-wise! by the fire of Thy chastening
Earth shall to freedom and truth be restored;
Through the thick darkness Thy kingdom is hastening:
Thou wilt give peace in Thy time, O Lord!

So shall Thy children with thankful devotion
Praise Him who saved them from peril and sword,
Singing in chorus from ocean to ocean,
Peace to the nations and praise to the Lord.

Henry F. Chorley, 1808–1872;
John Ellerton, 1826–1893

1496. LINES FOR THE HOUR

If what we fought for seems not worth the fighting,
  And if to win seems in the end to fail,
Know that the vision lives beyond all blighting
  And every struggle rends another veil.

The tired hack, the cynic politician,
Can dim but cannot make us lose the goal,
Time moves with measured step upon her mission,
Knowing the slow mutations of the soul.

Hamilton Fish Armstrong, 1893–

1497. RING OUT, WILD BELLS

From "In Memoriam," CVI

Ring out, wild bells, to the wild sky,
The flying cloud, the frosty light:
The year is dying in the night;
Ring out, wild bells, and let him die.

Ring out the old, ring in the new,
Ring, happy bells, across the snow:
The year is going, let him go;
Ring out the false, ring in the true.

Ring out the grief that saps the mind,
For those that here we see no more;
Ring out the feud of rich and poor,
Ring in redress to all mankind.

Ring out a slowly dying cause,
And ancient forms of party strife;
Ring in the nobler modes of life,
With sweeter manners, purer laws.

Ring out the want, the care, the sin,
The faithless coldness of the times;
Ring out, ring out my mournful rhymes,
But ring the fuller minstrel in.

Ring out false pride in place and blood,
The civic slander and the spite;
Ring in the love of truth and right,
Ring in the common love of good.

Ring out old shapes of foul disease;
Ring out the narrowing lust of gold;
Ring out the thousand wars of old,
Ring in the thousand years of peace.

Ring in the valiant man and free,
The larger heart, the kindlier hand;
Ring out the darkness of the land,
Ring in the Christ that is to be.

Alfred Tennyson, 1809–1892

1498. HYMN

O world of love and beauty,
O world of life and light,
O child of law and duty
Created out of night—

Roll ever onward, forward,
From chaos, slime, and clod
Through eons bearing upward
To the city of our God.

George Edward Hoffman, 1901–

1499. From THE GOD-MAKER, MAN

Yes, nothing seems changeless, but Change.
And yet, through the creed-wrecking years,
One story for ever appears;
The tale of a City Supernal—
The whisper of Something eternal—
A passion, a hope, and a vision
That peoples the silence with Powers;
A fable of meadows Elysian
Where Time enters not with his Hours;—
Manifold are the tale's variations,
Race and clime ever tinting the dreams,
Yet its essence, through endless mutations,
Immutable gleams.

Deathless, though godheads be dying,
Surviving the creeds that expire,

Illogical, reason-defying,
  Lives that passionate, primal desire;
Insistent, persistent, forever
Man cries to the silences, "*Never*
Shall Death reign the lord of the soul,
Shall the dust be the ultimate goal—
I will storm the black bastions of Night!
  I will tread where my vision has trod,
I will set in the darkness a light,
  In the vastness, a god!"

As the forehead of Man grows broader, so do his creeds;
And his gods they are shaped in his image, and mirror his needs;
And he clothes them with thunders and beauty, he clothes them
    with music and fire;
Seeing not, as he bows by their altars, that he worships his own
    desire;
And mixed with his trust there is terror, and mixed with his mad-
    ness is ruth,
And every man grovels in error, yet every man glimpses a truth.

For all of the creeds are false, and all of the creeds are true;
And low at the shrines where my brothers bow, there will I bow,
    too;
For no form of a god, and no fashion
Man has made in his desperate passion
But is worthy some worship of mine;—
Not too hot with a gross belief,
  Nor yet too cold with pride,
I will bow me down where my brothers bow,
  Humble—but open-eyed!

Don Marquis, 1878–1937

1500. THE SEEKERS

Friends and loves we have none, nor wealth nor blessed abode,
But the hope of the City of God at the other end of the road.

Not for us are content, and quiet, and peace of mind,
For we go seeking a city that we shall never find.

There is no solace on earth for us—for such as we—
Who search for a hidden city that we shall never see.

Only the road and the dawn, the sun, the wind, and the rain,
And the watch fire under stars, and sleep, and the road again.

We seek the City of God, and the haunt where beauty dwells,
And we find the noisy mart and the sound of burial bells.

Never the golden city, where radiant people meet,
But the dolorous town where mourners are going about the street.

We travel the dusty road till the light of the day is dim,
And sunset shows us spires away on the world's rim.

We travel from dawn to dusk, till the day is past and by,
Seeking the Holy City beyond the rim of the sky.

Friends and loves we have none, nor wealth nor blest abode,
But the hope of the City of God at the other end of the road.

John Masefield, 1875–

1501. From MILTON

And did those feet in ancient time
  Walk upon England's mountain green?
And was the holy Lamb of God
  On England's pleasant pastures seen?

And did the Countenance Divine
  Shine forth upon our clouded hills?
And was Jerusalem builded here
  Among these dark Satanic mills?

Bring me my bow of burning gold!
  Bring me my arrows of desire!
Bring me my spear! O clouds, unfold!
  Bring me my chariot of fire!

I will not cease from mental fight,
  Nor shall my sword sleep in my hand,
Till we have built Jerusalem
  In England's green and pleasant land.

William Blake, 1757–1827

1502. CIVITAS DEI

Walls cannot save the cities from their fate;
Fire, disease, the weight
Of arms, Babylon, Athens or Jerusalem—
London, New York will follow them.
Each city springs to its appointed hour,
Buds, blossoms like a flower,
But cannot stand or stay
When the dull autumn of decay
Arrives.

Only the city set upon a hill
Is tainted not with ill.
The gates of gold, the stairs of amethyst
Warp not with time, nor list
In any wind. The arches of untarnished glass
Tower above the centuries that pass,
Lay siege to all the stories made of stone;
The unbuilt city of our dream alone
Endures.

Love's perpendicular high wall
Becomes a rod by which the bastions fall
Which measure not, nor span,
The unguessed compass of the mind of man.
The river of life twists backward every
    street
That seeks to hold the feet
Of the star-wandering human race
That yet has found no final resting place
On earth.

Edith Lovejoy Pierce, 1904–

1503. CONTAGION OF COURAGE

From "Rugby Chapel"

At your voice,
Panic, despair, flee away.
Ye move through the ranks, recall
The stragglers, refresh the outworn,
Praise, reinspire the brave!
Order, courage, return.
Eyes rekindling, and prayers,
Follow your steps as ye go.
Ye fill up the gaps in our files,
Strengthen the wavering line,
'Stablish, continue our march,
On, to the bound of the waste,
On, to the city of God.

Matthew Arnold, 1822–1888

1504. THE CITY OF GOD

O God, Thy heavens, in the hush of night,
So awesome, with their galaxies alight,
Stir to their depths our silent, brooding souls,
As, all above, the wondrous scroll unrolls.

In tones more awesome than the scene we
    scan,
Thy Voice bespeaketh, in the heart of man,
A way of life comporting with Thine own,
Who hast not left us in the dark alone,

But Who, throughout our tragic night, art
nigh,
In deep compassion ever standing by,
Until, awakened, we shall seek Thy face,
Thou Lover of our sadly stricken race.

O Living Spirit, all our powers reclaim;
Let Thy compassion set our souls aflame;
Form Thou in us a purpose true and pure,
That what we build together may endure.

High on the mountain of Thy holiness
Above the fogs, where Thou canst own and
bless,
Help us the City of our God to build
Where all Thy plan for us may be fulfilled.

Then hither from the shadows yet shall
throng
The multitudes unblest, to join the song
Whose joyous note shall fill the earth again:
"To God be glory! Peace, good-will to men!"

Henry B. Robins, 1874–

1505. THE CITY OF GOD

Ἰδοὺ γάρ, ἡ βασιλεία τοῦ θεοῦ ἐντὸς ὑμῶν ἐστί.

O Thou not made with hands,
Not throned above the skies,
Nor wall'd with shining walls,
Nor framed with stones of price,
More bright than gold or gem,
God's own Jerusalem.

Where'er the gentle heart
Finds courage from above;
Where'er the heart forsook
Warms with the breath of love;
Where faith bids fear depart,
City of God! thou art.

Thou art where'er the proud
In humbleness melts down;
Where self itself yields up;
Where martyrs win their crown;
Where faithful souls possess
Themselves in perfect peace.

Where in life's common ways
With cheerful feet we go;
When in His steps we tread
Who trod the way of woe;
Where He is in the heart,
City of God! thou art.

Not throned above the skies,
Nor golden-wall'd afar,
But where Christ's two or three
In His name gather'd are,
Be in the midst of them,
God's own Jerusalem!

Francis Turner Palgrave, 1824–1897

1506. From THE NEW CITY

Have we seen her, The New City, O my brothers, where she stands,
The superb, supreme creation of unnumbered human hands:
The complete and sweet expression of unnumbered human souls,
Bound by love to work together while their love their work controls;
Built by brothers for their brothers, kept by sisters for their mates,
Garlanded by happy children playing free within the gates,
Brooded by such mighty mothers as are born to lift us up
Till we drink in full communion of God's wondrous "loving cup"?

❖

Have ye seen her, O my brothers, The New City, where each hour
Is a poet's revelation, or a hero's perfect power,
Or an artist's new creation, or a laborer's new strength,
Where a world of aspiration clings God by the feet, at length?
Have ye seen her, The New City, in her glory? Ah, not yet
Gilds the sun with actual splendor chimney top and minaret,
But her site is surely purchased and her pattern is designed,
And her blessed ways are visions for all striving human kind!

The New City, O my brothers, we ourselves shall never see—
She will gladden children's children into holy ecstasy—
Let our lives be in the building! We shall lay us in the sod
Happier, if our human travail builds their avenues to God!

Marguerite Wilkinson, 1883–1928

1507. CHRIST IN THE CITY

Where cross the crowded ways of life,
  Where sound the cries of race and clan,
Above the noise of selfish strife,
  We hear Thy voice, O Son of man.

In haunts of wretchedness and need,
  On shadowed thresholds dark with fears,
From paths where hide the lures of greed
  We catch the vision of Thy tears.

From tender childhood's helplessness,
  From woman's grief, man's burdened toil,
From famished souls, from sorrow's stress,
  Thy heart has never known recoil.

The cup of water given for Thee
  Still holds the freshness of Thy grace;
Yet long these multitudes to see
  The sweet compassion of Thy face.

O Master, from the mountain side,
  Make haste to heal these hearts of pain;
Among these restless throngs abide,
  O tread the city's streets again,

Till sons of men shall learn Thy love
  And follow where Thy feet have trod;
Till, glorious from Thy heaven above,
  Shall come the City of our God!

Frank Mason North, 1850–1935

1508. THY KINGDOM COME, O LORD

Thy kingdom come, O Lord,
  Wide-circling as the sun;
Fulfil of old thy word
  And make the nations one;—

One in the bond of peace,
  The service glad and free
Of truth and righteousness
  Of love and equity.

Speed, speed the longed-for time
  Foretold by raptured seers—
The prophecy sublime,
  The hope of all the years;—

Till rise at last, to span
  Its firm foundations broad,
The commonwealth of man,
  The city of our God.

Frederick L. Hosmer, 1840–1929

1509. CITY OF GOD

City of God, how broad and far
  Outspread thy walls sublime!
The true thy chartered freemen are,
  Of every age and clime.

One holy Church, one army strong,
  One steadfast, high intent;
One working band, one harvest-song,
  One King omnipotent.

How purely hath thy speech come down
  From man's primeval youth!
How grandly hath thine empire grown,
  Of freedom, love, and truth!

How gleam thy watch-fires through the night
  With never-fainting ray!
How rise thy towers, serene and bright,
  To meet the dawning day!

In vain the surge's angry shock,
  In vain the drifting sands:
Unharmed upon the eternal Rock
  The eternal City stands.

Samuel Johnson, 1822–1882

1510. THE HOLY CITY

O Holy City seen of John,
  Where Christ the Lamb doth reign,
Within whose foursquare walls shall come

No night, nor need, nor pain,
And where the tears are wiped from eyes
That shall not weep again!

Hark, how from men whose lives are held
More cheap than merchandise,
From women struggling sore for bread,
From little children's cries,
There swells the sobbing human plaint
That bids Thy walls arise!

Give us, O God, the strength to build
The City that hath stood
Too long a dream, whose laws are love,
Whose ways are brotherhood,
And where the sun that shineth is
God's grace for human good.

Already in the mind of God
That City riseth fair;
Lo, how its splendor challenges
The souls that greatly dare—
Yea, bids us seize the whole of life
And build its glory there!

W. Russell Bowie, 1882-

1511. THE CITY OF OUR HOPES

Hail the glorious Golden City,
  Pictured by the seers of old!
Everlasting light shines o'er it,
  Wondrous tales of it are told:
Only righteous men and women
  Dwell within its gleaming wall;
Wrong is banished from its borders,
  Justice reigns supreme o'er all.

We are builders of that city;
  All our joys and all our groans
Help to rear its shining ramparts;
  All our lives are building stones
Whether humble or exalted,
  All are called to task divine;
All must aid alike to carry
  Forward one sublime design.

And the work that we have builded,
  Oft with bleeding hands and tears,
Oft in error, oft in anguish,
  Will not perish with our years:
It will live and shine transfigured
  In the final reign of Right;
It will merge into the splendors
  Of the City of the Light.

Felix Adler, 1851–1933

1512. GLORIOUS THINGS OF THEE ARE SPOKEN

Glorious things of thee are spoken,
  Zion, city of our God;
He whose word cannot be broken
  Formed thee for His own abode.
On the Rock of Ages founded,
  What can shake thy sure repose?
With salvation's walls surrounded,
  Thou mayst smile at all thy foes.

See! the streams of living waters,
  Springing from eternal love,
Well supply thy sons and daughters,
  And all fear of want remove.
Who can faint when such a river
  Ever flows their thirst to assuage,—
Grace, which, like the Lord the Giver,
  Never fails from age to age?

Blest inhabitants of Zion,
  Washed in the Redeemer's blood,
Jesus, whom their souls rely on,
  Makes them kings and priests to God.
'Tis His love His people raises
  Over self to reign as kings;
And as priests, His solemn praises
  Each for a thankoffering brings.

Saviour, if of Zion's city
  I, through grace, a member am,
Let the world deride or pity,
  I will glory in Thy Name.
Fading is the worldling's pleasure,
  All his boasted pomp and show;
Solid joys and lasting treasure
  None but Zion's children know.

John Newton, 1725–1807

1513. JERUSALEM, THE GOLDEN

Jerusalem the Golden,
  With milk and honey blest,
Beneath thy contemplation,
  Sink heart and voice opprest;
I know not, O I know not,

What joys await us there,
What radiancy of glory,
What bliss beyond compare.

They stand, those walls of Zion,
All jubilant with song,
And bright with many an angel,
And all the martyr throng:
The Prince is ever in them
The daylight is serene;
The pastures of the blessed
Are decked in glorious sheen.

There is the throne of David;
And there, from care released,
The shout of them that triumph,
The song of them that feast;
And they, who with their Leader
Have conquered in the fight,
Forever and forever
Are clad in robes of white.

O sweet and blessed country,
The home of God's elect!
O sweet and blessed country
That eager hearts expect!
Jesus, in mercy bring us
To that dear land of rest;
Who art, with God the Father,
And Spirit, ever blest.

Bernard of Cluny, c. 1145;
tr. by John M. Neale, 1818–1866

1514. THE CITY OF GOD

Not in the wind-hushed isles and gardens Elysian,
Not on the snow-pure peaks, forever untrod,
Not with the timeless stars,—is the prophet-vision
Of the ultimate dwelling of God.

Lo, a City, a City,—behold in its center
Justice throned in light exceeding the sun;
Nothing unclean or that maketh a lie shall enter
The House of the Righteous One.

Only a nation of conquerors ever may win it;
Its streets shall be filled with the shouting of children at play
The peoples of earth shall gather their treasures within it
And laugh in the light of its day.

Age by age shall toil in the night, disclaiming
Peril and pain for hope of its distant gleam;
Life by life shall the laborers pay in attaining
The gray world's desperate dream,

Thus shall we build it,—the crown of His ended creations,
Stone by stone of our hunger and faith and love,—
A City of cities, a City of mighty nations,
And God the ruler thereof.

Anna Louise Strong, 1885–

1515. WHAT MAKES A CITY

What makes a city great and strong?
Not architecture's graceful strength,
Not factories' extended length,
But men who see the civic wrong,
And give their lives to make it right,
And turn its darkness into light.

What makes a city man can love?
Not things that charm the outward sense,
Not gross display of opulence,
But right that wrong cannot remove,
And truth, that faces civic fraud
And smites it, in the name of God.

This is a city that shall stand,
A light upon a nation's hill,
A voice that evil cannot still,
A source of blessing to the land;
Its strength not brick, nor stone, nor wood,
But Justice, Love and Brotherhood.

Author unknown

1516. THE CITY'S CROWN

What makes a city great? Huge piles of stone
Heaped heavenward? Vast multitudes who dwell
Within wide circling walls? Palace and throne
And riches past the count of man to tell,
And wide domain? Nay, these the empty husk!
True glory dwells where glorious deeds are done,
Where great men rise whose names athwart the dusk
Of misty centuries gleam like the sun!
In Athens, Sparta, Florence, 'twas the soul
That was the city's bright, immortal part,
The splendor of the spirit was their goal,
Their jewel the unconquerable heart!
So may the city that I love be great
Till every stone shall be articulate.

William Dudley Foulke, 1848–1935

1517. A NATION'S STRENGTH

What makes a nation's pillars high
And its foundations strong?
What makes it mighty to defy
The foes that round it throng?

It is not gold. Its kingdoms grand
Go down in battle shock;
Its shafts are laid on sinking sand,
Not on abiding rock.

Is it the sword? Ask the red dust
Of empires passed away;
The blood has turned their stones to rust,
Their glory to decay.

And is it pride? Ah, that bright crown
Has seemed to nations sweet;
But God has struck its luster down
In ashes at His feet.

Not gold but only men can make
A people great and strong;
Men who for truth and honor's sake
Stand fast and suffer long.

Brave men who work while others sleep,
Who dare while others fly—
They build a nation's pillars deep
And lift them to the sky.

Ralph Waldo Emerson, 1803–1882

1518. TURN BACK, O MAN[1]

Turn back, O man, forswear thy foolish ways.
Old now is Earth, and none may count her days,
Yet thou, her child, whose head is crowned with flame,
Still wilt not hear thine inner God proclaim—
"Turn back, O man, forswear thy foolish ways."

Earth might be fair and all men glad and wise.
Age after age their tragic empires rise,
Built while they dream, and in that dreaming weep:
Would man but wake from out his haunted sleep,
Earth might be fair and all men glad and wise.

Earth shall be fair, and all her people one:
Nor till that hour shall God's whole will be done.
Now, even now, once more from earth to sky,
Peals forth in joy man's old, undaunted cry—
"Earth shall be fair, and all her folk be one!"

Clifford Bax, 1886–1932

[1] Written after the first World War

1519. TO WIN THE WORLD

Would you win all the world for Christ?
One way there is and only one;
You must live Christ from day to day,
And see His will be done.

But who lives Christ must tread His way,
Leave self and all the world behind,
Press ever up and on, and serve
His kind with single mind.

No easy way,—rough—strewn with stones,
And wearisome, the path He trod.
But His way is the only way
That leads man back to God.

And lonesome oft, and often dark
With shame, and outcastry, and scorn,
And, at the end, perchance a cross,
And many a crown of thorn.

But His lone cross and crown of thorn
Endure when crowns and empires fall.
The might of His undying love
In dying conquered all.

Only by treading in His steps
The all-compelling ways of Love,
Shall earth be won, and man made one
With that Great Love above.

John Oxenham, 1852–1941

1520. BUILDERS

We would be building; temples still undone
O'er crumbling walls their crosses scarcely lift
Waiting till love can raise the broken stone,
And hearts creative bridge the human rift;
We would be building, Master, let Thy plan
Reveal the life that God would give to man.

Teach us to build; upon the solid rock
We set the dream that hardens into deed,
Ribbed with the steel that time and change doth mock,
Th' unfailing purpose of our noblest creed;
Teach us to build; O Master, lend us sight
To see the towers gleaming in the light.

O keep us building, Master; may our hands
Ne'er falter when the dream is in our hearts,
When to our ears there come divine commands
And all the pride of sinful will departs;
We build with Thee, O grant enduring worth
Until the heav'nly Kingdom comes on earth.

Purd E. Deitz, 1897–

1521. OF GREATNESS IN TEACHING

A PRAYER

God, save our land from that unblessed sedateness
Which arrogates unto itself a greatness
Built of the rubble leavings of the past!
Now that our star-lit banners stream at last
On land, and in the air and on the sea
Beyond the reach of doubt, how great are we?

Not that the mightiest armament is ours
Will make us great, nor pacts to balance powers,
Not the bright treasure guarded under ground,
Nor the plump grain with which our fields abound,
Not trade, nor vast domain securely barred
Against assault, not cities all unscarred,
Not the strong tramp of armies marching back
Exultant from victorious attack,
Not pride that we are safe, while hallowed lands
Must perish, or find succor at our hands,

Not the vain cry blown down the heedless wind
That we alone of peoples have not sinned,—
These are but perishables, crumbled stones
Of an old world for which a new atones.
Never in these will any searching find
The greatness of the nations of mankind.

O grant us, rather, vision of the state
Whose citizens in dream and soul are great,
Whose ordinances bend with reverent awe
Before the categoric moral law.
Triumphant in the bitter fight to live,
Exalt our spirits grandly to forgive.
With matchless power to shackle every foe,
Give us the heart of wisdom to forego.

And this above all else vouchsafe—that we,
In blood-bought peace, may set our children free
From ancient self-delusions, greeds and hates
Whereby the crash of dynasties and states
Has written red the chronicles of time.
O let our children scale those heights sublime
Whither our feet have faltered. Let them see
How beautiful a land may come to be
When brotherhood is more than word or thought,
Being the substance of our living, wrought
Into the noblest ends our souls may reach,
And flowing in the stream of all we teach.

Beyond all empire then our eyes may scan
The coming Kingdom of the Son of Man,
Built of a dream, abiding, undefiled—
The glory of its throne, a little child.

Leslie Pinckney Hill, 1880–

1522. INTERNATIONAL HYMN

Two empires by the sea,
Two nations great and free,
One anthem raise.
One race of ancient fame,
One tongue, one faith we claim,
One God whose glorious name
We love and praise.

What deeds our fathers wrought,
What battles we have fought,
Let fame record.
Now, vengeful passion, cease,
Come, victories of peace;
Nor hate nor pride's caprice,
Unsheath the sword.

Though deep the sea and wide,
'Twixt realm and realm, its tide
Binds strand to strand.
So be the gulf between
Gray coasts and islands green,
With bonds of peace serene,
And friendship spann'd.

Now may our God above
Guard the dear lands we love,
Both East and West.
Let love more fervent glow,
As peaceful ages go,
And strength yet stronger grow,
Blessing and blest.

George Huntington, 1835–1916

1523. PROLOGUE TO MORNING

Watchman, what of the night?
The night has no stars and the winds are rising.
Watchman, what of the sea?
The sea is wild, and the shores are strewn with ships.
Watchman—
I hear.
What of the hearts of men?
They are as the night, and as the sea.
Watchman, I am Everyman, and I am troubled.
Where is my hope?
Your hope is where it has *been.*
Watchman, your answer is dark.
To your mind, but not to your heart. Let the heart
Listen and it will hear,
Though the winds cry and the seas break.
My heart is open.
What does it hear?
Storm.
What else?
A crying, as of a child lost in the dark.
A crying?
A fury, as of a child destroying his toys.
No more?
A Voice.
A Voice?
A Voice that cries, Think!
What else?
A Voice that calls, Aspire!
What more?
A Voice that whispers, Believe!
Bow down, and hear!
A Voice that commands, Dare!
Lift up your eyes!
Watchman, what have I heard?
You have heard God speaking to Moses and to Socrates;
To Jesus in the lonely places,
To Isaiah and Amos and Micah,
And Peter and John and Paul and Francis and Joan.
You have heard God speaking to all His saints
Who have fought for the recognition of His glory,
And for liberation, and the expansion of the imprisoned, the dwarfed spirit.
You have heard God speaking
To the men who dared the seas to build a new nation,
To Franklin and Washington and Jefferson
And all the makers of the immortal Declaration
That utters the hunger for life, for liberty and the right of man to be free of the chain, the bars, and the whip.
You have heard God speaking to Abraham Lincoln—
And to you.
To me? What am I that the God Who spoke to these
Should speak to me?
What does the Voice say, the Voice in the heart?

The Voice says, You are of the great succession.
Men have torn down, men have broken, men have destroyed.
It is yours to build, says the Voice, yours to build.
Out of the disaster of hate to bring the miracle of love.
Out of the fury of destruction to bring a new creation.
By men has the world been brought low.
By men shall the world again be lifted up.
By men and the Voice of God.
The Voice of God is calling through the world!
It is calling to me.
I hear!
What does the Voice say, the Voice in the heart?
The Voice says, Everyman,
I have a burden for you and a splendor.
You are the end of things—
Or a new world.
Think!
Believe!
Aspire!
Dare!
What more?
The Voice says, Day and night, let your heart listen.
What is your answer, Everyman?
My heart is listening. . . .
Then the new world is born.

Hermann Hagedorn, 1882–

1524. A NEW EARTH

God grant us wisdom in these coming days,
And eyes unsealed, that we clear visions see
Of that new world that He would have us build.
To Life's ennoblement and His high ministry.

God give us sense,—God-sense of Life's new needs,
And souls aflame with new-born chivalries—
To cope with those black growths that foul the ways,—
To cleanse our poisoned founts with God-born energies.

To pledge our souls to nobler, loftier life,
To win the world to His fair sanctities,
To bind the nations in a Pact of Peace,
And free the Soul of Life for finer loyalties.

Not since Christ died upon His lonely cross
Has Time such prospect held of Life's new birth;
Not since the world of chaos first was born
Has man so clearly visaged hope of a new earth.

Not of our own might can we hope to rise
Above the ruts and soilures of the past,
But, with His help who did the first earth build,
With hearts courageous we may fairer build this last.

John Oxenham, 1852–1941

1525. THE FATHERLAND

Where is the true man's fatherland?
Is it where he by chance is born?
Doth not the yearning spirit scorn
In such scant borders to be spanned?
Oh, yes! his fatherland must be
As the blue heaven wide and free!

Is it alone where freedom is,
Where God is God and man is man?
Doth he not claim a broader span
For the soul's love of home than this?
Oh, yes! his fatherland must be
As the blue heaven wide and free!

Where'er a human heart doth wear
Joy's myrtle-wreath or sorrow's gyves,
Where'er a human spirit strives
After a life more true and fair,
There is the true man's birthplace grand,
His is a world-wide fatherland!

Where'er a single slave doth pine,
Where'er one man may help another,—
Thank God for such a birthright, brother,—
That spot of earth is thine and mine!
There is the true man's birthplace grand,
His is a world-wide fatherland!

James Russell Lowell, 1819–1891

1526. WRITTEN 1811

Jesus said, "Wouldst thou love one who never died
For thee, or ever die for one who had not died for thee?
And if God dieth not for Man and giveth not Himself
Eternally for Man, Man could not exist; for Man is Love
As God is Love: every kindness to another is a little death
In the Divine Image, nor can Man exist but by Brotherhood."
He who would see the Divinity must see Him in His Children.
One first, in friendship and love; then a Divine Family, and in the midst
Jesus will appear; and so he who wishes to see a Vision, a perfect Whole
Must see it in its Minute Particulars.

William Blake, 1757–1827

1527. A CREED

There is a destiny that makes us brothers;
None goes his way alone:
All that we send into the lives of others
Comes back into our own.

I care not what his temples or his creeds,
One thing holds firm and fast—
That into his fateful heap of days and deeds
The soul of man is cast.

Edwin Markham, 1852–1940

1528. O BROTHER MAN

O brother man, fold to thy heart thy brother;
Where pity dwells, the peace of God is there;
To worship rightly is to love each other,
Each smile a hymn, each kindly deed a
prayer.

Follow with reverent steps the great example
Of Him whose holy work was doing good:
So shall the wide earth seem our Father's
temple,
Each loving life a psalm of gratitude.

Then shall all shackles fall; the stormy clangor
Of wild war-music o'er the earth shall cease;
Love shall tread out the baleful fire of anger,
And in its ashes plant the tree of peace.

John Greenleaf Whittier, 1807–1892

1529. BROTHERHOOD

At length there dawns the glorious day
By prophets long foretold;
At length the chorus clearer grows
That shepherds heard of old.
The day of dawning Brotherhood
Breaks on our eager eyes,
And human hatreds flee before
The radiant eastern skies.

For what are sundering strains of blood,
Or ancient caste and creed?
One claim unites all men in God
To serve each human need.
Then here together, Brother men,
We pledge the Lord anew
Our loyal love, our stalwart faith,
Our service strong and true.

One common faith unites us all,
We seek one common goal,
One tender comfort broods upon
The struggling human soul.
To this clear call of Brotherhood
Our hearts responsive ring;
We join the glorious new crusade
Of our great Lord and King.

Ozora Stearns Davis, 1866–1931

1531. CREED AND DEED

What care I for caste or creed?
It is the deed, it is the deed;
What for class or what for clan?
It is the man, it is the man;
Heirs of love, and joy, and woe,
Who is high, and who is low?
Mountain, valley, sky, and sea,
Are for all humanity.

What care I for robe or stole?
It is the soul, it is the soul;
What for crown, or what for crest?
It is the heart within the breast;
It is the faith, it is the hope,
It is the struggle up the slope,
It is the brain and eye to see,
One God and one humanity.

Robert Loveman, 1864–1923

1530. BROTHERHOOD

The crest and crowning of all good,
Life's final star is Brotherhood;
For it will bring again to Earth
Her long-lost Poesy and Mirth,
Will send new light on every face,
A kingly power upon the race,
And till it comes, we men are slaves,
And travel downward to the dust of graves.

Come, clear the way then, clear the way:
Blind creeds and kings have had their day.
Break the dead branches from the path:
Our hope is in the aftermath—
Our hope is in heroic men,
Star-led to build the world again.
To this Event the ages ran:
Make way for Brotherhood—make way for
Man.

Edwin Markham, 1852–1940

1532. WHERE IS THY BROTHER?

Say not, "It matters not to me;
My brother's weal is his behoof."
For in this wondrous human web
If your life's warp, his life is woof.
Woven together are the threads,
And you and he are in one loom;
For good or ill, for glad or sad,
Your lives must share one common doom.

Man is dear to man: the poorest poor
Long for some moments in a weary life,
When they can feel and know that they have
been
Themselves the fathers and the dealers-out
Of some small blessings; have been kind to
such
As needed kindness, for the single cause
That we have all of us one common heart.

Author unknown

1533. WHO IS SO LOW

Who is so low that I am not his brother?
Who is so high that I've no path to him?
Who is so poor I may not feel his hunger?
Who is so rich I may not pity him?

Who is so hurt I may not know his heartache?
Who sings for joy my heart may never share?
Who in God's heaven has passed beyond my vision?
Who to hell's depths where I may never fare?

May none, then, call on me for understanding,
  May none, then, turn to me for help in pain,
And drain alone his bitter cup of sorrow,
  Or find he knocks upon my heart in vain.

S. Ralph Harlow, 1885–

1534. THY BROTHER

When thy heart, with joy o'erflowing
  Sings a thankful prayer,
In thy joy, O let thy brother
    With thee share.

When the harvest-sheaves ingathered
  Fill thy barns with store,
To thy God and to thy brother
    Give thee more.

If thy soul, with power uplifted,
  Yearn for glorious deed,
Give thy strength to serve thy brother
    In his need.

Hast thou borne a secret sorrow
  In thy lonely breast?
Take to thee thy sorrowing brother
    For a guest.

Share with him thy bread of blessing,
  Sorrow's burden share;
When thy heart enfolds a brother,
    God is there.

Theodore Chickering Williams, 1855–1915

1535. WOE TO HIM

Woe to him that has not known the woe of man,
Who has not felt within him burning all the want
Of desolated bosoms, since the world began;
Felt, as his own, the burden of the fears that daunt;
Who has not eaten failure's bitter bread, and been
Among those ghosts of hope that haunt the day, unseen.

Only when we are hurt with all the hurt untold,—
In us the thirst, the hunger, and ours the helpless hands,
The palsied effort vain, the darkness and the cold,—
Then, only then, the Spirit knows and understands,
And finds in every sigh breathed out beneath the sun
The human heart that makes us infinitely one.

Laurence Binyon, 1869–1943

1536. LOVE'S STRENGTH

Measure thy life by loss instead of gain,
Not by the wine drunk, but the wine poured forth;
For love's strength standeth in love's sacrifice,
And whoso suffers most hath most to give.
For labor, the common lot of man,
Is part of the kind Creator's plan;
And he is a king whose brow is wet
With the pearl-gemmed crown of honest sweat.
Some glorious day, this understood,
All toilers will be a brotherhood,
With brain or hand the purpose is one,
And the Master-workman, God's own Son.

Author unknown

1537. From BALLAD OF EAST AND WEST

Oh, East is East, and West is West, and never the twain shall meet,
Till Earth and Sky stand presently at God's great Judgment Seat.
But there is neither East nor West, Border, nor Breed, nor Birth,
When two strong men stand face to face, though they come from the ends of the earth!

Rudyard Kipling, 1865–1936

1538. GERMAN PRISONERS

When first I saw you in the curious street
Like some platoon of soldier ghosts in grey,
My mad impulse was all to smite and slay,
To spit upon you—tread you 'neath my feet.
But when I saw how each sad soul did greet
My gaze with no sign of defiant frown,
How from tired eyes looked spirits broken down,
How each face showed the pale flag of defeat,
And doubt, despair, and disillusionment,
And how were grievous wounds on many a head,
And on your garb red-faced was other red;
And how you stooped as men whose strength was spent,
I knew that we had suffered each as other,
And could have grasped your hand and cried, "My brother!"

Joseph Johnston Lee,[1] *contemporary English*

1539. From A NEW YORK SKYSCRAPER

O sprawling city! worlds in a world!
What means the Ghetto to Morningside?

❖

Why, the souls in one car where they hang on the straps,
Could send this city a-wing from the sod.
Each man is a tiny faucet that taps the infinite reservoir of God!
What if they turned the faucet full-stream?
What if our millions tonight were aware?
What if tomorrow they built in their dream the City of Brothers in laughter and prayer?

James Oppenheim, 1882–1932

1540. I DREAM'D IN A DREAM

I dream'd in a dream, I saw a city invincible to the attacks of the whole of the rest of the earth;
I dream'd that was the new City of Friends;
Nothing was greater there than the quality of robust love—it led the rest;
It was seen every hour in the actions of the men of that city,
And in all their looks and words.

Walt Whitman, 1819–1892

1541. ALL HAIL, THE PAGEANT OF THE YEARS

All hail, the pageant of the years
That endless come and go,
The brave procession of the spheres
In Time's resistless flow:
Arise, and crown your days with good,
In glad, exultant brotherhood!

Behind us fade the centuries
Of man at war with man,

[1] Served with British army; became prisoner of war in Germany.

The fierce and foul futilities
  Of battling tribe and clan—
Arise, and crown your days with good,
  In glad, exultant brotherhood!

Around us lies the heritage
  Of clashing sword and shield,
The want and waste, the hate and rage
  Of many a gloried field:
Arise, and crown your days with good,
  In glad, exultant brotherhood!

Behold, there looms the mystery
  Of love diviner far,
There speaks the stead-fast prophecy
  Of nations freed from war:
Arise, and crown your days with good,
  In glad, exultant brotherhood!

The aeons come, the aeons go,
  The stars nor pause nor cease;
On wings of silence, soft as snow,
  Shall come the boon of peace:
All hail, our days are crowned with good,
  In glad, exultant brotherhood!

John Haynes Holmes, 1879–

1542. O GOD OF LIGHT

O God of Light, break forth anew
Upon the darkness of the earth,
In the new glory of the day
When brotherhood shall come to birth;
Open our eyes that we may see
The coming of thy dawn afar,
And find the way of fellowship
The promise of thy morning star.

O God of Love, show us thy love
Forever seeking all mankind,
In eager questing of thy heart
To win and bless and heal and bind;
May thy rich mercy help us love
Our neighbour as we honour thee,
And seek his good as 'twere our own
In glad and deep fraternity.

O God of Peace, bring peace on earth
Where men and nations haste to war;
Restrain our passion and our pride
Ere thine inheritance we mar;
Spare us the guilt of brother's blood
That judgment be not our desert;
Teach us to build and not destroy,
Teach us to heal and not to hurt.

O God of Life, abundant, free,
Make known thyself to men today;
Kindle thy flame of life in us
And lead us in thy living way;
Make us the heralds of thy word,
And builders of thy city fair,
That all the sons of men may hear
The song of freedom in the air.

R. B. Y. Scott, contemporary Canadian

1543. GREAT HEART

Where are you going, Great-Heart?
  To fight a fight with all my might,
  For Truth and Justice, God and Right,
  To grace all Life with His fair light.
    Then God go with you, Great-Heart!

Where are you going, Great-Heart?
  To lift To-day above the Past;
  To make To-morrow sure and fast;
  To nail God's colors to the mast.
    Then God go with you, Great-Heart!

Where are you going, Great-Heart?
  To set all burdened peoples free;
  To win for all God's liberty;
  To 'stablish His Sweet Sovereignty.
    God goeth with you, Great-Heart!

John Oxenham, 1852–1941

1544. LIVE AND HELP LIVE

"Live and let live!" was the call of the Old—
The call of the world when the world was cold—
The call of men when they pulled apart—
The call of the race with a chill on the heart.

But "Live and help live!" is the cry of the New—
The cry of the world with the Dream shining through—
The cry of the Brother World rising to birth—
The cry of the Christ for a Comrade-like earth.

Edwin Markham, 1852–1940

1545. BROTHERS

I honor the land that gave me birth,
  I thrill with joy when the flag's unfurled,
But the gift she gives of supremest worth,
  Is the brother's heart for all the world;
So come, ye sons of the near and far,
  Teuton and Latin, Slav and Jew,
For brothers beloved of mine ye are—
  Blood of my blood in a world made new.

George E. Day, contemporary American

546. CHALLENGE

This is no time for fear, for doubts of good,
For broodings on the tragedies of fate.
It is a time for songs of brotherhood,
For hymns of joy, of man's divine estate.
Though echoes of old wars depress the heart,
Though greed and hate still curse men's
    nobler ways,
Though foul suspicion blasts our life apart,
It is a time for confidence and praise.
Let prophets prophesy, let poets sing,
Our dreams are not in vain. The night is past.
Together, as new hopes are wakening,
Let us proclaim, The Kingdom comes at last!
Our Babels crash. Let selfish flags be furled.
As brothers all, we build a Friendly World.

Thomas Curtis Clark, 1877–

1547. MY CHARGE

This is the charge I keep as mine,
The goal of every hope and plan—
To cancel the dividing line
Between me and my fellow man.

The atom shock, the radared moon,
Annihilated time and space—
What were the profit or the boon
If hate be in my brother's face!

More deadly than the blackest art,
More horror-fraught than shell or bomb,
Hate dims the mind, corrodes the heart
And strikes the voice of conscience dumb.

I dare not pass the lowliest waif
With scorn or condescending pride,
For never can my path be safe
Until his want is satisfied.

My *brothers* are they across the track,
In hall of state or jungle den—
Yellow or white or brown or black—
All are my kin for all are men.

And if but one shall lack of bread
Or bleed for justice still in vain,
The guilt is heavy on my head,
And of that blood I wear the stain.

And so for me all fear shall end
Save this—that I may fail to see
My neighbor as a needed friend,
Or sense my neighbor's need of me.

Though parliaments may rise and fall,
I hold to this eternal good,
This deathless truth—that men are all
One earth-encircling brotherhood.

Leslie Pinckney Hill, 1880–

1548. WHAT DOTH THE LORD REQUIRE OF THEE

What doth the Lord require of thee,
Friend of the friendless poor?
Put out thy hands upon thy cross,
And take the nails He bore!

What doth the Lord require of thee,
Son of the living God?
Challenge the whips that harry thee,
And break th' oppressor's rod!

What doth the Lord require of thee
If Justice be His name?
Let Mercy be the altar fire
To set thy soul aflame!

O Flame of God, O Son of Man,
Dare us to drink Thy blood,
To make our world of wrath and tears
A House of Brotherhood!

Allen Eastman Cross, 1864–1943

1549. A PRAYER FOR BROTHERHOOD

Christ,
Grant us this boon,
To look with Thine eyes of pity and love
On all men's need:
To feel from within, with Thee,

The bite of pain, of hunger, of wrong:
To live wholly beyond ourselves,
In deep and active desire of help for the
needy and weak.

Christ,
Conquer the selfish greed in our hearts,
And grant us power to act,
To struggle, to build,
For the coming of Thy full Kingdom,
Where no man is wronged, greed and
violence vanish away,
And in all God's world true brotherhood
reigns.

John S. Hoyland, 1887–

1550. A LOFTIER RACE

These things shall be,—a loftier race
Than ere the world hath known shall rise
With flame of freedom in their souls,
And light of knowledge in their eyes.

They shall be gentle, brave, and strong
To spill no drop of blood, but dare
All that may plant man's lordship firm
On earth, and fire, and sea, and air.

Nation with nation, land with land,
Unarmed shall live as comrades free;
In every heart and brain shall throb
The pulse of one fraternity.

❖

New arts shall bloom of loftier mould
And mightier music fill the skies,
And every life shall be a song,
When all the earth is paradise.

John Addington Symonds, 1840–1893

1551. MAN'S INHUMANITY TO MAN

From "Man Was Made To Mourn"

Many and sharp the num'rous ills
Inwoven with our frame!
More pointed still we make ourselves
Regret, remorse, and shame!
And Man, whose heav'n-erected face
The smiles of love adorn,—
Man's inhumanity to man
Makes countless thousands mourn!

Robert Burns, 1759–1796

1552. HOW CAN I SING?

I want to sing lyrics, lyrics
Mad as a brook in spring
I want to shout the music
Of flushed adventuring.

But how can I sing lyrics?
I who have seen to-day
The stoop of factory women,
The children kept from play.

And on an open hilltop,
Where the cloak of the sky is wide,
Have seen a tree of terror
Where a black man died.

I want to sing lyrics, lyrics
But these have hushed my song.
I am mute at the world's great sadness
And stark at the world's great wrong.

Author unknown

1553. I SIT AND LOOK OUT

From "Leaves or Grass"

I sit and look out upon all the sorrows of the world, and upon all oppression and shame;
I hear secret convulsive sobs from young men, at anguish with themselves, remorseful after
deeds done;
I see, in low life, the mother misused by her children, dying, neglected, gaunt, desperate;
I see the wife misused by her husband—I see the treacherous seducer of young women;
I mark the ranklings of jealousy and unrequited love, attempted to be hid—I see these sights
on the earth;
I see the workings of battle, pestilence, tyranny—I see martyrs and prisoners;

I observe a famine at sea—I observe the sailors casting lots who shall be kill'd, to preserve the lives of the rest;
I observe the slights and degradations cast by arrogant persons upon laborers, the poor, and upon negroes, and the like;
All these—all the meanness and agony without end, I sitting, look out upon,
See, hear, and am silent.

Walt Whitman, 1819–1892

1554. From THE PEOPLE, YES

Who can make a poem of the depths of weariness
bringing meaning to those never in the depths?
Those who order what they please
when they choose to have it—
can they understand the many down under
who come home to their wives and children at night
and night after night as yet too brave and unbroken
to say, "I ache all over"?
How can a poem deal with production cost
and leave out definite misery paying
a permanent price in shattered health and early old age?
When will the efficiency engineers and the poets
get together on a program?
Will that be a cold day? will that be a special hour?
Will somebody be coocoo then?
And if so, who?
And what does the Christian Bible say?
And the Mohammedan Koran and Confucius and the Shintoists
and the Encyclicals of the Popes?
Will somebody be coocoo then?
And if so, who??

Carl Sandburg, 1878–

1555. IN LONDON, SEPTEMBER, 1802

O Friend! I know not which way I must look
For comfort, being, as I am, opprest,
To think that now our life is only drest
For show; mean handy-work of craftsman, cook,
Or groom!—We must run glittering like a brook
In the open sunshine, or we are unblest:
The wealthiest man among us is the best:
No grandeur now in nature or in book
Delights us. Rapine, avarice, expense,
This is idolatry; and these we adore:
Plain living and high thinking are no more:
The homely beauty of the good old cause
Is gone; our peace, our fearful innocence,
And pure religion breathing household laws.

William Wordsworth, 1770–1850

1556. AUGURIES OF INNOCENCE

To see a World in a grain of sand
And a Heaven in a wild flower,
Hold Infinity in the palm of your hand
And Eternity in an hour.

A robin redbreast in a cage
Puts all Heaven in a rage.
A dove house filled with doves and pigeons
Shudders Hell through all its regions.
A dog starved at his master's gate
Predicts the ruin of the State.
A horse misused upon the road
Calls to Heaven for human blood.
Each outcry of the hunted hare
A fibre from the brain does tear.
A skylark wounded in the wing,
A cherubim does cease to sing.

The game cock clipped and armed for fight
Does the rising sun affright.

❖

The soldier, armed with sword and gun,
Palsied strikes the summer's sun.
The poor man's farthing is worth more
Than all the gold on Africa's shore.
One mite wrung from the lab'rour's hands
Shall buy and sell the miser's lands:
Or, if protected from on high,
Does that whole nation sell and buy.
He who mocks the infant's faith
Shall be mocked in Age and Death.
He who shall teach the child to doubt
The rotting grave shall ne'er get out.
He who respects the infant's faith
Triumphs over Hell and Death.

❖

He who doubts from what he sees
Will ne'er believe, do what you please.
If the Sun and Moon should doubt,
They'd immediately go out.
To be in a passion you good may do,
But no good if a passion is in you.
The whore and gambler, by the state
Licenced, build that nation's fate.
The harlot's cry from street to street
Shall weave old England's winding sheet.
The winner's shout, the loser's curse,
Dance before dead England's hearse.
Every night and every morn
Some to misery are born.
Every morn and every night
Some are born to sweet delight.
Some are born to sweet delight,
Some are born to endless night.
We are led to believe a lie
When we see not through the eye
Which was born in a night to perish in a night
When the soul slept in beams of light.
God appears and God is Light
To those poor souls who dwell in Night,
But does a human form display
To those who dwell in realms of Day.

William Blake, 1757–1827

1557. TO A PRINCE OF THE CHURCH

The vestments in your church, they say,
Are rich with dyes and stiff with gold;
A thousand miner's kids to-day
Hide in their shanties from the cold.
That chalice—gift of loving pride—
The gems blaze as you lift it up;
A thousand babies, solemn-eyed,
Click spoons within an empty cup.

So might I sling the sneering stone.
But God will judge both me and you;
You sin not, nor are judged, alone.
I had two coats; *I still have two.*

Kenneth W. Porter, 1905–

1558. GENTLEMEN OF THE HIGH COMMAND

From "Heil, Heilige Nacht!"

"Gentlemen of the High Command,
Who crucify the slums,
There was an earlier Golgotha;
The Third day comes."

Ogden Nash, 1902–

1559. CROSS MAKERS

Three workmen fashioning a cross
On which the fourth must die!
Yet none of any other asked
"And why? And why? And why?'

Said they: "This is our business.
Our living we must earn;
What happens to the other man
Is none of our concern!"

Clyde McGee, 1875–

1560. MUNITIONS EXPERT

From "On This Island," Poem XVIII

The expert designing the long-range gun
To exterminate everyone under the sun,
Would like to get out but can only mutter;—
"What can I do? It's my bread and butter."

W. H. Auden, 1907–

1561. "WHERE THERE IS NO VISION—"

From "Aurora Leigh," Second Book

The human race
To you, means such a child or such a man
You saw one morning waiting in the cold

Beside that gate, perhaps. . . .Why, I call you hard
To general suffering. . . .
Does one of you
Stand still from dancing, stop from stringing pearls
And pine and die because of the great sum
Of universal anguish? . . . You cannot count
That you should weep for this account; not you.
You weep for what you know. A red-haired child,
Sick in a fever, if you touch him once,
Though but so little as with a finger-tip,
Will set you weeping; but a million sick . . .
You could as soon weep for the rule of three
Or compound fractions. Therefore, this same world,
Uncomprehended by you, must remain
Uninfluenced by you. . . .
We get no Christ from you.

Elizabeth Barrett Browning, 1806–1861

1562. THE COMMON MAN

From "The Deserted Village"

Ill fares the land, to hastening ills a prey,
Where wealth accumulates, and men decay;
Princes and lords may flourish or may fade;
A breath can make them, as a breath has made;
But a bold peasantry, their country's pride,
When once destroy'd, can never be supplied.

Oliver Goldsmith, 1728–1774

1563. COMRADE JESUS

Thanks to St. Matthew, who had been
At mass-meetings in Palestine,
We knew whose side was spoken for
When Comrade Jesus had the floor.

"Where sore they toil and hard they lie,
Among the great unwashed, dwell I:—
The tramp, the convict, I am he;
Cold-shoulder him, cold-shoulder me."

By Dives' door, with thoughtful eye,
He did tomorrow prophesy:—
"The Kingdom's gate is low and small;
The rich can scarce wedge through at all."

"A dangerous man," said Caiaphas,
"An ignorant demagogue, alas!
Friend of low women, it is he
Slanders the upright Pharisee."

For law and order, it was plain,
For Holy Church, he must be slain.
The troops were there to awe the crowd:
And "violence" was not allowed.

Their clumsy force with force to foil
His strong, clean hands he would not soil.
He saw their childishness quite plain
Between the lightnings of his pain.

Between the twilights of his end
He made his fellow-felon friend:
With swollen tongue and blinding eyes,
Invited him to Paradise . . .

Sarah N. Cleghorn, 1876–1928

1564. A PARABLE

Said Christ our Lord, "I will go and see
How the men, my brethren, believe in me."
He passed not again through the gate of birth,
But made himself known to the children of earth.

Then said the chief priests, and rulers, and kings,
"Behold, now, the Giver of all good things;
Go to, let us welcome with pomp and state
Him who alone is mighty and great."

With carpets of gold the ground they spread
Wherever the Son of Man should tread,
And in palace-chambers lofty and rare
They lodged him, and served him with kingly fare.

Great organs surged through arches dim
Their jubilant floods in praise of him;
And in church, and palace, and judgment-hall,
He saw his image high over all.

But still, wherever his steps they led,
The Lord in sorrow bent down his head,
And from under the heavy foundation-stones,
The son of Mary heard bitter groans.

And in church, and palace, and judgment-
hall,
He marked great fissures that rent the wall,
And opened wider and yet more wide
As the living foundation heaved and sighed.

"Have ye founded your thrones and altars,
then,
On the bodies and souls of living men?
And think ye that building shall endure,
Which shelters the noble and crushes the
poor?

"With gates of silver and bars of gold
Ye have fenced my sheep from their Father's
fold;
I have heard the dropping of their tears
In heaven these eighteen hundred years."

"O Lord and Master, not ours the guilt,
We build but as our fathers built;
Behold thine images, how they stand,
Sovereign and sole, through all our land!"

❖

Then Christ sought out an artisan,
A low-browed, stunted, haggard man,
And a motherless girl, whose fingers thin
Pushed from her faintly want and sin.

These set he in the midst of them,
And as they drew back their garment-hem,
For fear of defilement, "Lo, here," said he,
"The images ye have made of me!"

James Russell Lowell, 1819–1891

1565. THE DEVIL'S MEDITATION

The cities are mine!
By all that's damned, He shall not have them.
I have not built these slums
To let Him raise His saints;
And darkened streets are not
To glow with Light.
He has the country,
Let Him sow His holiness out there.
He has the towns;
He said He loved Obscurity.
But now—
Until He chases me down every ill-lit street,
Until He razes every building, burns them
down,
Until He searches every wharf,
And every hospital and jail—
I still hold these, my cities.

Michael Sweany

1566. MOURN NOT THE DEAD

Mourn not the dead that in the cool earth lie—
Dust unto dust—
The calm sweet earth that mothers all who die
As all men must;

Mourn not your captive comrades who must
dwell—
Too strong to strive —
Each in his steel-bound coffin of a cell,
Buried alive;

But rather mourn the apathetic throng—
The cowed and the meek—
Who see the world's great anguish and its
wrong
And dare not speak!

Ralph Chaplin, 1880–

1567. THE SECOND COMING

The Saviour came. With trembling lips
He counted Europe's battleships.
"Yet millions lack their daily bread:
So much for Calvary!" He said.

Norman Gale, 1862–1942

1568. THE AGONY OF GOD

I listen to the agony of God—
I who am fed,
Who never yet went hungry for a day.
I see the dead—
The children starved for lack of bread—
I see, and try to pray.

I listen to the agony of God—
I who am warm,
Who never yet have lacked a sheltering
home.
In dull alarm
The dispossessed of hut and farm,
Aimless and "transient" roam.

I listen to the agony of God—
I who am strong,
With health, and love, and laughter in my soul.
I see a throng
Of stunted children reared in wrong,
And wish to make them whole.

I listen to the agony of God—
But know full well
That not until I share their bitter cry—
Earth's pain and hell—
Can God within my spirit dwell
To bring His kingdom nigh.

Georgia Harkness, 1891-

1569. THE MASKED BALL

The heralds of dawn are blowing at the last star;
When it goes out the masks will come off
And the dancers will lean homeward on their weariness.

All who dance at the Ball of Life are masked
Save the children and the poets and dreamers
And a few old men and women.

Sometimes a daring soul tugs at his mask;
And the smart young fellows chide him and he hesitates,
And the gay young ladies taunt him and he desists.

No man can see God through a mask;
No man can enter Heaven who is masked;
But God and Heaven are small things at the Masked Ball.

When the masks are tossed away I shall see
The lovely, grown hideous—the hideous, lovely.
O, the joy when I shall behold nakedness of soul!

Then shall I observe the courage of the coward
And the timidity of the brave man.
O, the joy when I shall behold nakedness of soul!

Then shall I discover the purity of harlots
And the lewdness of men at their morning prayers.
O, the joy when I shall behold nakedness of soul!

A mask is a hiding-place from truth,
From virtue, from honor:
It hates the nudity of love and the nakedness of kindness.

At the Masked Ball the false are the proudest
Of flesh, and their limbs are all beauty—
Their breasts are abundant, their fingers are tapered.

But when the masks are torn from their eyes
Their flesh will be foul and their limbs will be laggard,
And their breasts will be milkless and withered.

If Jesus should come to-day He would say:
"Tear off the masks."
And the Pharisees would lift another cross against the sky.

Masks, masks, masks!
How He hated them—this Man of the Desert
Who came once and danced with us at the Masked Ball.

Comrades, I warn you the Masked Ball is near an end—
The heralds of dawn are blowing at the last star;
When it goes out the masks will come off
And the dancers will lean homeward on their weariness.

Wilson MacDonald, 1880–

1570. COME LIVE WITH ME AND BE MY LOVE

Come, live with me and be my love,
And we will all the pleasures prove
Of peace and plenty, bed and board,
That chance employment may afford.

I'll handle dainties on the docks
And thou shalt read of summer frocks:
At evening by the sour canals
We'll hope to hear some madrigals.

Care on thy maiden brow shall put
A wreath of wrinkles, and thy foot
Be shod with pain: not silken dress
But toil shall tire thy loveliness.

Hunger shall make thy modest zone
And cheat fond death of all but bone—
If these delights thy mind may move,
Then live with me and be my love.

Cecil Day Lewis, 1904–

1571. THE MAN WITH THE HOE

Written after seeing Millet's world-famous painting of a brutalized toiler.

God made man in his own image
in the image of God made He him.—*Genesis.*

Bowed by the weight of centuries he leans
Upon his hoe and gazes on the ground,
The emptiness of ages in his face,
And on his back the burden of the world.
Who made him dead to rapture and despair,
A thing that grieves not and that never hopes,
Stolid and stunned, a brother to the ox?
Who loosened and let down this brutal jaw?
Whose was the hand that slanted back this brow?
Whose breath blew out the light within this brain?

Is this the Thing the Lord God made and gave
To have dominion over sea and land;
To trace the stars and search the heavens for power;
To feel the passion of Eternity?
Is this the dream He dreamed who shaped the suns
And marked their ways upon the ancient deep?
Down all the caverns of Hell to their last gulf
There is no shape more terrible than this—
More tongued with censure of the world's blind greed—
More filled with signs and portents for the soul—
More packed with danger to the universe.

What gulfs between him and the seraphim!
Slave of the wheel of labor, what to him
Are Plato and the swing of Pleiades?
What the long reaches of the peaks of song,
The rift of dawn, the reddening of the rose?
Through this dread shape the suffering ages look;
Time's tragedy is in that aching stoop;
Through this dread shape humanity betrayed,
Plundered, profaned and disinherited,
Cries protest to the Powers that made the world,
A protest that is also prophecy.

O masters, lords and rulers in all lands,
Is this the handiwork you give to God,
This monstrous thing distorted and soul-quenched?
How will you ever straighten up this shape;
Touch it again with immortality;
Give back the upward looking and the light;

Rebuild in it the music and the dream;
Make right the immemorial infamies,
Perfidious wrongs, immedicable woes?

O masters, lords and rulers in all lands,
How will the future reckon with this man?
How answer his brute question in that hour
When whirlwinds of rebellion shake all shores?
How will it be with kingdoms and with
kings—
With those who shaped him to the thing he
is—
When this dumb Terror shall rise to judge
the world,
After the silence of the centuries?

Edwin Markham, 1852–1940

1572. CALIBAN IN THE COAL MINES

God, we don't like to complain;
We know that the mine is no lark.
But—there's the pools from the rain;
But—there's the cold and the dark.

God, You don't know what it is—
You, in Your well-lighted sky—
Watch the meteors whizz;
Warm, with the sun always by.

God, if You had but the moon
Stuck in Your cap for a lamp,
Even You'd tire of it soon,
Down in the dark and the damp.

Nothing but blackness above
And nothing that moves but the cars—
God, if You wish for our love,
Fling us a handful of stars!

Louis Untermeyer, 1885–

1573. "WHEN I THINK OF THE HUNGRY PEOPLE"

I have a suit of new clothes in this happy new
year;
Hot rice cake soup is excellent to my taste;
But when I think of the hungry people in
this city,
I am ashamed of my fortune in the presence
of God.

O-Shi-O, Japanese scholar, 18th century

1574. BREATHLESS AWE

"Two things," said Kant, "fill me with
breathless awe:
The starry heaven and the moral law!"
But I know a thing more awful and obscure—
The long, long patience of the plundered poor.

Edwin Markham, 1852–1940

1575. THE JERICHO ROAD

I know the road to Jericho,
It's in a part of town
That's full of factories and filth.
I've seen the folk go down,

Small folk with roses in their cheeks
And starlight in their eyes,
And seen them fall among the thieves,
And heard their helpless cries

When toiling took their roses red
And robbed them of their stars
And left them pale and almost dead.
The while, in motor-cars

The priests and levites speeding by
Read of the latest crimes
In headlines spread in black or red
Across the "Evening Times."

How hard for those in limousines
To heal the hurt of man!
It was a slow-paced ass that bore
The Good Samaritan.

Edwin McNeill Poteat, 1892–

1576. NOT IN DUMB RESIGNATION

Not in dumb resignation
We lift our hands on high;
Not like the nerveless fatalist,
Content to do and die;
Our faith springs like the eagle,
That soars to meet the sun,
And cries exulting unto Thee,
"O Lord, Thy will be done!"

When tyrant feet are trampling
Upon the common weal,
Thou dost not bid us cringe and writhe
Beneath the iron heel;

In Thy name we assert our right,
  By sword and tongue and pen,
And ev'n the headsman's axe may flash
  Thy message unto men.

Thy will,—it bids the weak be strong,
  It bids the strong be just:
No hand to beg, no lip to fawn,
  No brow to kiss the dust;
Wherever man oppresses man
  Beneath the liberal sun,
O Lord, be there, Thine arm made bare,
  Thy righteous will be done!

John Hay, 1838–1905

1577. WHEN WILT THOU SAVE THE PEOPLE?

From "Corn Law Rhymes"

When wilt Thou save the people?
  O God of mercy, when?
Not kings and lords, but nations!
  Not thrones and crowns, but men!
Flowers of Thy heart, O God, are they;
Let them not pass, like weeds, away—
Their heritage, a sunless day.
  God save the people!

Shall crime bring crime forever,
  Strength aiding still the strong?
Is it Thy will, O Father,
  That man shall toil for wrong?
'No,' say Thy mountains; 'No,' Thy skies;
Man's clouded sun shall brightly rise,
And songs ascend, instead of sighs.
  God save the people!

When wilt Thou save the people?
  O God of mercy, when?
The people, Lord, the people,
  Not thrones and crowns, but men!
God save the people; Thine they are,
Thy children as Thine angels fair;
From vice, oppression, and despair,
  God save the people!

Ebenezer Elliott, 1781–1849

1578. From KING COTTON

The mills of Lancashire grind very small,
  The mills of Lancashire grind very great,
And small and great alike are passing poor,
  Too poor to read the writing of their fate.
It is a kingdom knows an awful rule,
  It is a kingdom of a direful plan,
Where old and young are thrown to the
    machine,
  And no man dreams machines were made
    for man.

Sir Leo Money

1579. SWEATED LABOR

From "The Song of the Shirt"

O Men, with sisters dear!
  O Men, with mothers and wives!
It is not linen you're wearing out,
  But human creatures' lives!
    Stitch—stitch—stitch,
  In poverty, hunger, and dirt,—
Sewing at once, with a double thread,
  A shroud as well as a shirt!

But why do I talk of death—
  That phantom of grisly bone?
I hardly fear his terrible shape,
  It seems so like my own,—
It seems so like my own
  Because of the fasts I keep;
O God! that bread should be so dear,
  And flesh and blood so cheap!

Thomas Hood, 1799–1845

1580. PRAYER OF AN UNEMPLOYED MAN

Here in the quiet of my room,
I come to Thee for friendship; to feel
That Someone is with me, though unseen.
All day I have seen a multitude of people,
But I am still lonely and hungry for human
    cheer.

No life has touched mine in understanding;
No hand has clasped mine in friendship;
My heart is empty and my hands are idle.
Help me to feel Thy presence,
So that the disappointment of this day
Shall not overwhelm me.

Keep me from becoming cynical and bitter;
Keep me warm and human, and set a new
    faith
Before my eyes—a new hope to live by

And a new spirit with which to overcome
discouragements.
Guide me to that very necessary thing
Of life—Work!
Abide with me and be my friend.

W. C. Ackerly, contemporary American

1581. PRAYER OF THE UNEMPLOYED[1]

Father in Heaven, give us bread;
(God, make us want to live, instead.)
May we be clothed by charity;
(Oh, give us back our faith in Thee)
For our sick bodies, give us care;
(God, save our souls from this despair)
Shelter us from the wind and rain;
(Oh, help us learn to smile again)
Grant that our babies may be fed;
(But what of hopes forever dead?)
Father in Heaven, give us bread—
(Oh, give us back our dreams instead!)

Author unknown

1582. HYMN OF THE UNEMPLOYED

O Saviour, when we have no work,
And cannot find it though we seek,
And like a lamp that burneth low
Our courage grows each day more weak:

When hope and strength are failing fast
And every door we try is barred;
Stand by us in the fading light
From doubt, despair and sin to guard.

In Salem's market-place Thy glance
Fell kindly on the man unhired
Who idle stood eleven hours;
Not losing heart, though faint and tired.

With Thee the will counts as the deed,
And labour sought is labour wrought;
"They also serve who stand and wait"
To labour, though the days bring nought.

Thomas Tiplady, 1882–

1583. QUATRAIN

The golf links lie so near the mill
That almost every day
The laboring children can look out
And see the men at play.

Sarah N. Cleghorn, 1876–1928

1584. FACTORY CHILDREN

Here toil the striplings, who should be a-swarm
In open, sun-kissed meadows; and each day,
Amid the monstrous murmur of the looms
That still their treble voices, they become
Tiny automata, mockeries of youth:
To her that suckled them, to him whose name
They bear, mere fellow-earners of life's bread:
No time for tenderness, no place for smiles,—
These be the world's wee workers, by your leave!

Naught is more piteous underneath the sky
Than at the scant noon hour to see them play,
Feebly, without abandon or delight,
At some poor game; so grave they seem and crushed.
The gong! And foulness sucks them in once more.

Yet still the message wonderful rings clear
Above all clang of commerce and of mart:
"Suffer the little children," and again,
"My Kingdom is made up of such as these."

Richard Burton, 1861–1940

[1] Written by a young woman who was referred to New York's Church Mission of Help.

1585. THE FACTORIES

I have shut my little sister in from life and light
(For a rose, for a ribbon, for a wreath across my hair),
I have made her restless feet still until the night,
Locked from sweets of summer and from wild spring air;
I who ranged the meadowlands, free from sun to sun,
Free to sing and pull the buds and watch the far wings fly,
I have bound my sister till her playing-time was done—
Oh, my little sister, was it I? Was it I?

I have robbed my sister of her day of maidenhood
(For a robe, for a feather, for a trinket's restless spark),
Shut from Love till dusk shall fall, how shall she know good,
How shall she go scatheless through the sin-lit dark?
I who could be innocent, I who could be gay,
I who could have love and mirth before the light went by,
I have put my sister in her mating-time away—
Sister, my young sister, was it I? Was it I?

I have robbed my sister of the lips against her breast,
(For a coin, for the weaving of *my* children's lace and lawn),
Feet that pace beside the loom, hands that cannot rest—
How can she know motherhood, whose strength is gone?
I who took no heed of her, starved and labor-worn,
I, against whose placid heart my sleepy gold-heads lie,
Round my path they cry to me, little souls unborn—
God of Life! Creator! It was I! It was I!

Margaret Widdemer, 1880–

1586. THE CRY OF THE CHILDREN

"The Cry of the Children," first published in *Blackwood's Magazine*, for August, 1843, was called forth by Mr. Horne's report as assistant Commissioner on the employment of children in mines and factories.

I

Do ye hear the children weeping, O my brothers,
Ere the sorrow comes with years?
They are leaning their young heads against their mothers,
And *that* cannot stop their tears.
The young lambs are bleating in the meadows,
The young birds are chirping in the nest,
The young fawns are playing with the shadows,
The young flowers are blowing toward the west—
But the young, young children, O my brothers,
They are weeping bitterly!
They are weeping in the playtime of the others
In the country of the free.

XII

And well may the children weep before you!
They are weary ere they run;
They have never seen the sunshine, nor the glory

Which is brighter than the sun.
They know the grief of man, without its wisdom;
They sink in man's despair, without its calm;
Are slaves, without the liberty in Christdom,
Are martyrs, by the pang without the palm:
Are worn as if with age, yet unretrievingly
The harvest of its memories cannot reap,—
Are orphans of the earthly love and heavenly.
Let them weep! let them weep!

XIII

They look up with their pale and sunken faces,
And their look is dread to see,
For they mind you of their angels in high places,
With eyes turned on Deity.
'How long,' they say, 'how long, O cruel nation,
Will you stand, to move the world, on a child's heart,—
Stifle down with a mailèd heel its palpitation,
And tread onward to your throne amid the mart?
Our blood splashes upward, O goldheaper,
And your purple shows your path!
But the child's sob in the silence curses deeper
Than the strong man in his wrath.'

Elizabeth Barrett Browning, 1806–1861

1587. THE LITTLE CHILDREN

Sadly through the factory doors
The little children pass,
They do not like to leave behind
The morning sky and grass.

All day the wheels will eat their joy
And turn it into gold,
And when they pass the doors again
The world will seem so old!

Irwin Granich

1588. LITANY OF THE DARK PEOPLE

Our flesh that was a battle-ground
Shows now the morning-break;
The ancient deities are drowned
For Thy eternal sake.
Now that the past is left behind,
Fling wide Thy garment's hem
To keep us one with Thee in mind,
Thou Christ of Bethlehem.

The thorny wreath may ridge our brow,
The spear may mar our side,
And on white wood from a scented bough
We may be crucified;
Yet no assault the old gods make
Upon our agony
Shall swerve our footsteps from the wake
Of Thine toward Calvary.

And if we hunger now and thirst,
Grant our withholders may,
When heaven's constellations burst
Upon Thy crowning day,
Be fed by us, and given to see
Thy mercy in our eyes,
When Bethlehem and Calvary
Are merged in Paradise.

Countee Cullen, 1903–1946

1589. A FREE NATION

And this freedom will be the freedom of all.
It will loosen both master and slave from the chain.
For, by a divine paradox,
Wherever there is one slave
There are two.
So in the wonderful reciprocities of being,
We can never reach the higher levels
Until all our fellows ascend with us.

There is no true liberty for the individual
Except as he finds it
In the liberty of all.
There is no true security for the individual
Except as he finds it
In the security of all.

Edwin Markham, 1852–1940

1590. A LADY I KNOW

She thinks that even up in heaven
Her class lies late and snores,
While poor black cherubs rise at seven
To do celestial chores.

Countee Cullen, 1903–1946

1591. THE CHURCH'S ONE FOUNDATION

The Church's one foundation
Is Jesus Christ her Lord;
She is His new creation
By water and the word;
From heaven He came and sought her
To be His holy bride;
With His own blood He bought her,
And for her life He died.

Elect from every nation,
Yet one o'er all the earth,
Her charter of salvation
One Lord, one faith, one birth;
One holy name she blesses,
Partakes one holy food,
And to one hope she presses,
With every grace endued.

'Mid toil and tribulation,
And tumult of her war,
She waits the consummation
Of peace for evermore;
Till with the vision glorious
Her longing eyes are blest,
And the great church victorious
Shall be the church at rest.

Yet she on earth hath union
With Father, Spirit, Son,
And mystic sweet communion
With those whose rest is won;
O happy ones and holy!
Lord, give us grace that we,
Like them, the meek and lowly,
On high may dwell with Thee.

Samuel J. Stone, 1839–1900

1592. CHURCH TRIUMPHANT

O Church of God triumphant, above the world's dark fears;
In thee our souls find refuge through all these earthly years,
Christ's steadfast holy purpose, illumined by the cross,
When hosts encamp against us, reveals their might but dross.

Her bells on Christmas morning have set our hearts aglow,
At Easter-time her carols with faith still over-flow;
Within her sacred portals our children learn God's truth,
While at her hallowed altars to Christ we pledge our youth.

Through manhood's sterner challenge, in womanhood's brave years,
The Church of Christ continues in gladness or in tears,
To guide our footsteps onward till sunset's lingering rays
Reveal God's Heavenly Country beyond our earthly days.

O Church of God triumphant, we pledge anew in prayer,
Our youth, our fuller manhood, for Christ's great cause to dare;
Till his redeeming purpose shall prove beyond defeat,
When gather all God's children around His mercy seat.

S. Ralph Harlow, 1885–

1593. THE CHURCH IN THE HEART

Who builds a church within his heart
And takes it with him everywhere
Is holier far than he whose church
Is but a one-day house of prayer.

Morris Abel Beer, 1887–

1594. COUNTRY CHURCH

He could not separate the thought
Of God from daisies white and hot
In blinding thousands by a road
Or dandelion disks that glowed
Like little suns upon the ground.
Holiness was like the sound
Of thousands of tumultuous bees
In full-blossomed apple trees,
Or it was smell of standing grain,
Or robins singing up a rain.

For the church he went to when
He was eight and nine and ten,
And good friends with the trees and sun,
Was a small white country one.
The caraway's lace parasols
Brushed the clapboards of its walls,
The grass flowed round it east and west,
And one blind had a robin's nest.
Before the sermon was half over,
It turned to fragrance of red clover.

May and June and other weather
And farmers' wives came in together,
At every window swung a bough,
Always, far off, someone's cow
Lowed and lowed at every pause.
The rhythms of the mighty laws
That keep men going, to their graves,
Were no holier than the waves
The wind made in the tasselled grass
A small boy saw through window glass.

Robert P. Tristram Coffin, 1892–

1595. THE PROBLEM

I like a church; I like a cowl;
I love a prophet of the soul;
And on my heart monastic aisles
Fall like sweet strains or pensive smiles:
Yet not for all his faith can see,
Would I that cowlèd churchman be.

Why should the vest on him allure,
Which I could not on me endure?
Not from a vain or shallow thought
His awful Jove young Phidias brought;
Never from lips of cunning fell
The thrilling Delphic oracle;
Out from the heart of nature rolled
The burdens of the Bible old;
The litanies of nations came,
Like the volcano's tongue of flame,
Up from the burning core below,—
The canticles of love and woe:
The hand that rounded Peter's dome,
And groined the aisles of Christian Rome,
Wrought in a sad sincerity;
Himself from God he could not free;
He builded better than he knew;—
The conscious stone to beauty grew.

Know'st thou what wove yon woodbird's nest
Of leaves, and feathers from her breast?
Or how the fish outbuilt her shell,
Painting with morn each annual cell?
Or how the sacred pine-tree adds
To her old leaves new myriads?
Such and so grew these holy piles,
Whilst love and terror laid the tiles.
Earth proudly wears the Parthenon,
As the best gem upon her zone,
And Morning opes with haste her lids,
To gaze upon the Pyramids;
O'er England's abbeys bends the sky,
As on its friends, with kindred eye;
For, out of Thought's interior sphere,
These wonders rose to upper air;
And Nature gladly gave them place,
Adopted them into her race,
And granted them an equal date
With Andes and with Ararat.

These temples grew as grows the grass;
Art might obey but not surpass.
The passive Master lent his hand,
To the vast soul that o'er him planned;
And the same power that reared the shrine
Bestrode the tribes that knelt within.
Ever the fiery Pentecost
Girds with one flame the countless host,
Trances the heart through chanting choirs,
And through the priest the mind inspires.
The word unto the prophet spoken
Was writ on tables yet unbroken;
The word by seers or sibyls told,

In groves of oak, or fanes of gold,
Still floats upon the morning wind,
Still whispers to the willing mind.
One accent of the Holy Ghost
The heedless world hath never lost.
I know what say the fathers wise,—
The Book itself before me lies,
Old *Chrysostom*, best Augustine,
And he who blent both in his line,
The younger *Golden Lips* or mines,
Taylor, the Shakespeare of divines.
His words are music in my ear,
I see his cowlèd portrait dear;
And yet, for all his faith could see,
I would not the good bishop be.

Ralph Waldo Emerson, 1803–1882

1596. HE PRAYETH BEST

From "The Rime of the Ancient Mariner," Part VII

O sweeter than the marriage-feast,
'Tis sweeter far to me,
To walk together to the kirk
With a goodly company!—

To walk together to the kirk,
And all together pray,
While each to his great Father bends,
Old men, and babes, and loving friends,
And youths and maidens gay!

Farewell, farewell! but this I tell
To thee, thou Wedding-Guest!
He prayeth well, who loveth well
Both man and bird and beast.

He prayeth best, who loveth best
All things both great and small;
For the dear God who loveth us,
He made and loveth all.

Samuel Taylor Coleridge, 1772–1834

1597. GOD'S ALTAR

There is in all the sons of men
A love that in the spirit dwells,
That panteth after things unseen,
And tidings of the future tells.

And God hath built his altar here
To keep this fire of faith alive,
And sent his priests in holy fear
To speak the truth—for truth to strive.

Ralph Waldo Emerson, 1803–1882

1598. ON WORSHIP

From "The Church Porch"

When once thy foot enters the Church, be bare;
God is more there than thou; for thou art there
Only by His permission: then beware,
And make thyself all reverence and fear.
  Kneeling ne'er spoiled silk stocking; quit thy state;
  All equal are within the Church's gate.

Resort to sermons, but to prayers most:
Praying's the end of preaching. O, be drest;
Stay not for the other pin! Why, thou hast lost
A joy for it worth worlds. Thus Hell doth jest
  Away thy blessings, and extremely flout thee,
  Thy clothes being fast, but thy soul loose about thee.

In time of service seal up both thine eyes,
And send them to thy heart; that, spying sin,
They may weep out the stains by them did rise:
Those doors being shut, all by the ear comes in.
  Who marks in church-time others' symmetry,
  Makes all their beauty his deformity.

Let vain or busy thoughts have there no part;
Bring not thy plough, thy plots, thy pleasures thither.
Christ purged His Temple; so must thou thy heart:
All worldly thoughts are but thieves met together
To cozen thee. Look to thy actions well;
For churches either are our Heaven or Hell.

Judge not the preacher, for he is thy judge;
If thou mislike him, thou conceiv'st him not.
God calleth preaching folly: do not grudge
To pick out treasures from an earthen pot.
The worst speak something good; if all want sense,
God takes a text, and preacheth patience.

❖

Sum up at night what thou hast done by day,
And in the morning what thou hast to do;
Dress and undress thy soul; mark the decay
And growth of it; if with thy watch that too
Be down, then wind up both: since we shall be
Most surely judged, make thy accounts agree.

In brief, acquit thee bravely, play the man;
Look not on pleasures as they come, but go;
Defer not the least virtue: life's poor span
Make not an ell by trifling in thy woe.
If thou do ill, the joy fades, not the pains;
If well, the pain doth fade, the joy remains.

George Herbert, 1593–1632

1599. MY CHURCH

On me nor Priest nor Presbyter nor Pope,
Bishop nor Dean may stamp a party name;
But Jesus, with his largely human scope,
The service of my human life may claim.
Let prideful priests do battle about creeds,
The church is mine that does most Christlike deeds.

Author unknown

1600. THE CHARTER OF SALVATION

Wait! Church of God! in quiet contemplation
Before His throne, where grace and truth hold sway.
Lift up your hearts in holy adoration,
As now to Him with heart and mind we pray.
Wait! Church of God! It is thy preparation
On earth to strive in faith to speed His Day.

❖

Speak! Church of God! His Gospel clear proclaiming
To hearts in grief and broken by the wrong.
Hold high His Cross, God's grace fore'er retaining,

God's answer true, to each and to the throng.
Speak! Church of God! nor cease thy witness, claiming
Each soul for Christ, till all to God belong.

Go! Church of God! thy Charter of Salvation
Take to all nations torn by war and hate.
Thy mission high is to all God's creation
Until God's peace shall rule each land and state.
Go! Church of God! and by thy consecration
God's blessing bring, and world-wide love create.

George Arthur Clarke, 1887–

1601. THE CHURCH UNIVERSAL

One holy Church of God appears
Through every age and race,
Unwasted by the lapse of years,
Unchanged by changing place.

From oldest time, on farthest shores,
Beneath the pine or palm,
One Unseen Presence she adores,
With silence or with psalm.

Her priests are all God's faithful sons,
To serve the world raised up;
The pure in heart her baptized ones;
Love, her communion-cup.

The truth is her prophetic gift,
The soul her sacred page;
And feet on mercy's errands swift
Do make her pilgrimage.

O living Church! thine errand speed;
Fulfil thy task sublime;
With bread of life earth's hunger feed;
Redeem the evil time!

Samuel Longfellow, 1819–1892

1602. WE LOVE THE VENERABLE HOUSE

We love the venerable house
Our fathers built to God;
In heaven are kept their grateful vows,
Their dust endears the sod.

Here holy thoughts a light have shed
From many a radiant face,
And prayers of humble virtue spread
The perfume of the place.

And anxious hearts have pondered here
The mystery of life,
And prayed th' Eternal Light to clear
Their doubts and aid their strife.

They live with God, their homes are dust;
Yet here their children pray,
And in this fleeting life-time trust
To find the narrow way.

Ralph Waldo Emerson, 1803–1882

1603. I LOVE THY KINGDOM, LORD

I love Thy Kingdom, Lord,
The house of Thine abode,
The Church our blest Redeemer saved
With His own precious blood.

I love Thy Church, O God:
Her walls before Thee stand,
Dear as the apple of Thine eye,
And graven on Thy hand.

For her my tears shall fall,
For her my prayers ascend;
To her my cares and toils be given,
Till toils and cares shall end.

Beyond my highest joy
I prize her heavenly ways,
Her sweet communion, solemn vows,
Her hymns of love and praise.

Jesus, Thou Friend divine,
Our Saviour, and our King!
Thy hand from every snare and foe
Shall great deliverance bring.

Sure as Thy truth shall last,
To Zion shall be given
The brightest glories earth can yield,
And brighter bliss of heaven.

Timothy Dwight, 1752–1817

1604. WITHIN THE GATES[1]

I love to step inside a church,
To rest, and think, and pray;
The quiet, calm, and holy place
Can drive all cares away.

❖

I feel that from these simple walls
There breathes a moving sound
Of sacred music, murmured prayers,
Caught in the endless round

Of bygone worship, from the store
The swinging seasons bring—
Gay Christmas pageant, Lenten tears,
And the sweet hallowing

Of all that makes our human life:
Birth, and the union blest
Of couples at the altar wed,
And loved ones laid to rest.

Into my soul this harmony
Has poured, and now is still;
The Lord's own benediction falls
Upon me, as I kneel.

Once more, with lifted head, I go
Out in the jarring mart,
The spring of gladness in my step,
God's peace about my heart.

David W. Foley, contemporary Canadian

1605. CHURCHES

Beautiful is the large church,
With stately arch and steeple;
Neighborly is the small church,
With groups of friendly people;
Reverent is the old church,
With centuries of grace;
And a wooden church or a stone church
Can hold an altar place.
And whether it be a rich church
Or a poor church anywhere,
Truly it is a great church
If God is worshipped there.

Author unknown

1606. AN ANGEL UNAWARES

If after kirk ye bide a wee,
There's some would like to speak to ye;
If after kirk ye rise and flee,
We'll all seem cold and stiff to ye.
The one that's in the seat wi' ye,
Is stranger here than you, may be;
All here hae got their fears and cares—
Add you your soul unto our prayers;
Be you our angel unawares.

Author unknown

1607. GOD OF GRACE AND GOD OF GLORY[2]

God of grace and God of glory,
On Thy people pour Thy power;
Crown Thine ancient church's story;
Bring her bud to glorious flower.
Grant us wisdom, Grant us courage,
For the facing of this hour.

Lo! the hosts of evil round us
Scorn Thy Christ, assail His ways!
From the fears that long have bound us
Free our hearts to faith and praise:
Grant us wisdom, Grant us courage,
For the living of these days.

Cure Thy children's warring madness,
Bend our pride to Thy control;
Shame our wanton, selfish gladness,
Rich in things and poor in soul.
Grant us wisdom, Grant us courage,
Lest we miss Thy kingdom's goal.

Set our feet on lofty places;
Gird our lives that they may be
Armored with all Christ-like graces
In the fight to set men free.
Grant us wisdom, Grant us courage,
That we fail not man nor Thee!

[1] Written in France, August 1944, while serving with the Canadian Army.
[2] Written for the dedication of the Riverside Church, New York, 1930.

Save us from weak resignation
To the evils we deplore;
Let the search for Thy salvation
Be our glory evermore.
Grant us wisdom, Grant us courage,
Serving Thee whom we adore.

Harry Emerson Fosdick, 1878–

1608. THE CORNERSTONE

Almighty Builder, bless, we pray,
The cornerstone that here we lay;
And fair above it may we see
A house to serve mankind and Thee!

In truth be these foundations laid,
Each ordered course in wisdom made,
That firm these rising walls may stand,
Thy witness in a waiting land.

So shall Thy people honor yet
The sure foundation Thou hast set,
In prophets and apostles known,
With Jesus Christ the Cornerstone.

Eternal One, to Thee we raise
This house of service and of praise;
Thy love and glory shall not fade
When all earth's temples low are laid.

Edward A. Church, 1844–1929

1609. THOU, WHOSE UNMEASURED TEMPLE STANDS

Thou, whose unmeasured temple stands,
Built over earth and sea,
Accept the walls that human hands
Have raised, O God, to Thee.

And let the Comforter and Friend,
Thy Holy Spirit, meet
With those who here in worship bend
Before Thy mercy seat.

May they who err be guided here
To find the better way;
And they who mourn, and they who fear,
Be strengthened as they pray.

May faith grow firm, and love grow warm,
And pure devotion rise,
While round these hallowed walls the storm
Of earth-born passion dies.

William Cullen Bryant, 1794–1878

1610. DEDICATION

We dedicate a church today.
Lord Christ, I pray
Within the sound of its great bell
There is no mother who must hold
Her baby close against the cold—
So only have we served Thee well;
The wind blows sharp, the snow lies deep.
If we shall keep
Thy hungry ones, and sore distressed,
From pain and hardship, then may we
Know we have builded unto Thee,
And that each spire and arch is blest.

Lord Christ, grant we may consecrate
To Thee this church we dedicate.

Ethel Arnold Tilden,
contemporary American

1611. YOUR SANCTUARY

I stand serene beside the struggling marts
  Of trade, and towering temples built to greed,
  Where dazzling gold rates more than human need—
And plumb the bitter depths of hungry hearts.
Where cruel, deadening strife for gain and power
  And self have made life cheap and things the goal,
  When self has stilled the music of the soul,
I lure you in to sit with God an hour.

I lure you in to lift your sense of worth,
  To give you vision, fill your soul with life,

Reveal the Christ-like God who walks the earth
  With anguish in His eyes from human strife.
I send you forth, in love, His truth to carry
With joyous hope. I am your Sanctuary.

Walter Lyman French, contemporary American

1612. ON ENTERING A CHAPEL

Love built this shrine; these hallowed walls uprose
To give seclusion from the hurrying throng,
From tumult of the street, complaint and wrong,
From rivalry and strife, from taunt of foes—
If foes thou hast. On silent feet come in,
Bow low in penitence. Whoe'er thou art
Thou, too, hast sinned. Uplift in prayer thy heart.
Thy Father's blessing waiteth. Read within
This holy place, in pictured light portrayed,
The characters of worthies who, from years
Long past, still speak the message here displayed
In universal language not to fade.
Leave then thy burden, all thy cares and fears;
Faith, hope, and love are thine, for thou hast prayed.

John Davidson, 1857–1909

1613. THE WAKING WORLD

O Master of the waking world,
  Who hast the nations in Thy heart—
The heart that bled and broke to send
  God's love to earth's remotest part—
Show us anew in Calvary
The wondrous power that makes men free.

On every side the walls are down,
  The gates swing wide to every land.
The restless tribes and races feel
  The pressure of Thy piercèd hand:
Thy way is in the sea and air,
Thy world is open everywhere.

We hear the throb of surging life,
  The clank of chains, the curse of greed,
The moan of pain, the futile cries
  Of superstition's cruel creed;
The peoples hunger for Thee, Lord,
The isles are waiting for Thy Word.

O Church of God, awake! Awake!
  The waking world is calling Thee.
Lift up thine eyes! Hear Thou once more
  The challenge of humanity.
O Christ, we come! our all we bring
To serve Thy world and Thee, our King.

Frank Mason North, 1850–1935

1614. MEDITATION

Here is a quiet room!
Pause for a little space;
And in the deepening gloom
With hands before thy face,
Pray for God's grace.

Let no unholy thought
Enter thy musing mind;
Things that the world hath wrought—
Unclean—untrue—unkind—
Leave these behind.

Pray for the strength of God,
Strength to obey His plan;
Rise from your knees less clod
Than when your prayer began,
More of a man.

Donald Cox, contemporary English

1615. IS THIS THE TIME TO HALT?

Is this the time, O Church of Christ! to sound
Retreat? To arm with weapons cheap and
blunt
The men and women who have borne the
brunt
Of truth's fierce strife, and nobly held their
ground?
Is this the time to halt, when all around
Horizons lift, new destinies confront,
Stern duties wait our nation, never wont
To play the laggard, when God's will was
found?

No! rather, strengthen stakes and lengthen
cords,
Enlarge thy plans and gifts, O thou elect,
And to thy kingdom come for such a time!
The earth with all its fullness is the Lord's.
Great things attempt for Him, great things
expect,
Whose love imperial is, whose power sublime.

Charles Sumner Hoyt

1616. O WORD OF GOD INCARNATE

O Word of God incarnate,
O Wisdom from on high,
O Truth unchanged, unchanging,
O Light of our dark sky,
We praise Thee for the radiance
That from the hallowed page,
A lantern to our footsteps,
Shines on from age to age.

The Church from her dear Master
Received the gift divine,
And still that light she lifteth
O'er all the earth to shine.
It is the golden casket,
Where gems of truth are stored;
It is the heaven-drawn picture
Of Christ, the living Word.

It floateth like a banner
Before God's host unfurled;
It shineth like a beacon
Above the darkling world;
It is the chart and compass
That o'er life's surging sea,
'Mid mists and rocks and quick-sands,
Still guides, O Christ, to Thee.

O make Thy Church, dear Saviour,
A lamp of purest gold,
To bear before the nations
Thy true light, as of old.
O teach Thy wandering pilgrims
By this their path to trace,
Till, clouds and darkness ended,
They see Thee face to face.

William Walsham How, 1823–1897

1617. THE CHURCH TODAY[1]

Outwardly splendid as of old—
Inwardly sparkless, void and cold—
Her force and fire all spent and gone—
Like the dead moon, she still shines on.

William Watson, 1858–1935

1618. O CHURCH OF GOD

O Church of God, our solitude forsaking,
We now unite with all who seek thy way—
With those who sing, with those whose hearts are breaking,
We lift our spirits as to God we pray;
O Church of God, our love for thee is waking,
We bring our alleluias to-day.

O Church of God, like bells at noon-day pealing,
Thy call has come to us that we may bring
Our strength to serve to all the Christ revealing
In deeds of love and when our hopes take wing;
O Church of God, where sin and pain find healing,
To thee our alleluias we sing.

[1]Written 1908.

Our Spirit's Home, with joy to thee returning
  Our voices join to sing our highest praise,
For hours of cheer where friendship's fires are burning,
  For strength and peace which gladden all our days;
O Church of God, for thee our hearts are yearning,
  To thee our alleluias we raise.

Rolland W. Schloerb, 1893–

1619. KNOWLEDGE WITHOUT WISDOM

From "The Rock," I

The Eagle soars in the summit of Heaven,
The Hunter with his dogs pursues his circuit.
O perpetual revolution of configured stars,
O perpetual recurrence of determined seasons,
O world of spring and autumn, birth and dying!
The endless cycle of idea and action,
Endless invention, endless experiment,
Brings knowledge of motion, but not of stillness;
Knowledge of speech, but not of silence;
Knowledge of words, and ignorance of the Word.
All our knowledge brings us nearer to our ignorance,
All our ignorance brings us nearer to death,
But nearness to death no nearer to God.
Where is the Life we have lost in living?
Where is the wisdom we have lost in knowledge?
Where is the knowledge we have lost in information?
The cycles of Heaven in twenty centuries
Bring us farther from God and nearer to the Dust.

I journeyed to London, to the timekept City,
Where the River flows, with foreign flotations.
There I was told: we have too many churches,
And too few chop-houses. There I was told
Let the vicars retire. Men do not need the Church
In the place where they work, but where they spend their Sundays.
In the City, we need no bells:
Let them waken the suburbs.
I journeyed to the suburbs, and there I was told:
We toil for six days, on the seventh we must motor
To Hindhead, or Maidenhead.
If the weather is foul we stay at home and read the papers,
In industrial districts, there I was told
Of economic laws.
In the pleasant countryside, there it seemed
That the country now is only fit for picnics.
And the church does not seem to be wanted
In country or in suburb; and in the town
Only for important weddings.

T. S. Eliot, 1888–

1620. WHEN THE CHURCH IS NO LONGER REGARDED

From "The Rock," VII

But it seems that something has happened that has never happened before: though we know not just when, or why, or how, or where.
Men have left GOD not for other gods, they say, but for no god; and this has never happened before
That men both deny gods and worship gods, professing first Reason,
And then Money, and Power, and what they call Life, or Race, or Dialectic.
The Church disowned, the tower overthrown, the bells upturned, what have we to do
But stand with empty hands and palms turned upwards
In an age which advances progressively backwards?

VOICE OF THE UNEMPLOYED (*afar off*):
In this land
There shall be one cigarette to two men,
To two women one half pint of bitter
Ale. . . .

CHORUS:
What does the world say, does the whole world stray in high-powered cars on a by-pass way?

VOICE OF THE UNEMPLOYED (*more faintly*):
In this land
No man has hired us. . . .

CHORUS:
Waste and void. Waste and void. And darkness on the face of the deep.
Has the Church failed mankind, or has mankind failed the Church?
When the Church is no longer regarded, not even opposed, and men have forgotten
All gods except Usury, Lust and Power.

T. S. Eliot, 1888–

1621. THERE SHALL ALWAYS BE THE CHURCH

There shall always be the Church and the World,
And the heart of man
Shivering and fluttering between them choosing and chosen,
Valiant, ignoble, dark, and full of light
Swinging between hell gate and heaven gate
And the gates of hell shall not prevail.

T. S. Eliot, 1888–

1622. ONWARD, CHRISTIAN SOLDIERS

Onward, Christian soldiers,
Marching as to war,
With the cross of Jesus
Going on before:
Christ the royal Master
Leads against the foe;
Forward into battle,
See His banners go:

At the sound of triumph
Satan's host doth flee;
On, then, Christian soldiers,
On to victory!
Hell's foundations quiver
At the shout of praise;
Brothers lift your voices,
Loud your anthems raise.

Like a mighty army
Moves the Church of God;
Brothers, we are treading
Where the saints have trod;

We are not divided,
  All one body, we,
One in hope and doctrine,
  One in charity.

Crowns and thrones may perish,
  Kingdoms rise and wane,
But the Church of Jesus
  Constant will remain;
Gates of hell can never
  'Gainst that Church prevail;
We have Christ's own promise,
  And that cannot fail.

Onward, then, ye people,
  Join our happy throng,
Blend with ours your voices
  In the triumph-song;
Glory, laud and honor
  Unto Christ the King;
This through countless ages
  Men and angels sing.

Sabine Baring-Gould, 1834–1924

1623. O WHERE ARE KINGS AND EMPIRES NOW

O where are kings and empires now
Of old that went and came?
But, Lord, Thy Church is praying yet,
A thousand years the same.

We mark her goodly battlements,
And her foundations strong;
We hear within the solemn voice
Of her unending song.

For not like kingdoms of the world,
Thy holy Church, O God;
Though earthquake shocks are
    threat'ning her,
And tempests are abroad.

Unshaken as eternal hills,
Immovable she stands,
A mountain that shall fill the earth,
A house not made by hands.

Arthur Cleveland Coxe, 1818–1896

1624. GOD'S WORD

I paused last eve beside the blacksmith's door,
  And heard the anvil ring, the vesper's chime,
And looking in I saw upon the floor
  Old hammers, worn with beating years of time.
"How many anvils have you had?" said I,
  "To wear and batter all these hammers so?"
"Just one," he answered. Then with twinkling eye:
  "The anvil wears the hammers out, you know."
And so, I thought, the anvil of God's Word
  For ages skeptics' blows have beat upon,
But though the noise of falling blows was heard
  The anvil is unchanged; the hammers gone.

John Clifford, 1836–1923

1625. A SOWER OF DISCORD

Proverbs 6: 16–19

There be six things which the LORD *hateth,*
Yea, seven which are an abomination unto him:
  Haughty eyes,
  A lying tongue,
  And hands that shed innocent blood;
  An heart that deviseth wicked imaginations,
  Feet that be swift in running to mischief,
  A false witness that uttereth lies;
And he that Soweth Discord among brethren.

Moulton: The Modern Reader's Bible, 1895

1626. CREEDS

How pitiful are little folk—
They seem so very small;
They look at stars, and think they are
Denominational.

Willard Wattles, 1888–

1627. THE GOAL

All roads that lead to God are good;
What matters it, your faith or mine;
Both center at the goal divine
Of love's eternal brotherhood.

A thousand creeds have come and gone;
But what is that to you or me?
Creeds are but branches of a tree,
The root of love lives on and on.

Though branch by branch proves withered wood,
The root is warm with precious wine;
Then keep your faith, and leave me mine;
All roads that lead to God are good.

Ella Wheeler Wilcox, 1855–1919

1628. ETERNAL GOD WHOSE SEARCHING EYE DOTH SCAN

A HYMN FOR THE ECUMENICAL MOVEMENT

Eternal God whose searching eye doth scan
Ages and climes no limits can confine,
Broaden Thy vistas in the eyes of man
'Till he shall share the vision that is Thine.

Help him to see the Kingdom of Thy Son
Wider than nation, deeper still than race;
Chasten his joy in meager vict'ries won,
Stablish his goings in a broader place.

Lengthen the Light that shines upon his day;
Gird with Thy love the weakness of his creeds;
Teach him to trust his fellows in the Way,
Give him the faith that conquers and concedes.

Strike from his soul the fetters of his fears,
Level the barriers of the narrow mind;
Forward Thy church throughout the coming years
Wide as the world and broad as humankind.

Edwin McNeill Poteat, 1892–

1629. RELIGIOUS UNITY

Yes, we do differ when we most agree,
For words are not the same to you and me,
And it may be our several spiritual needs
Are best supplied by seeming different creeds.
And, differing, we agree in one
Inseparable communion,
If the true life be in our hearts; the faith
Which not to want is death;
To want is penance; to desire
Is purgatorial fire;
To hope is paradise; and to believe
Is all of heaven that earth can e'er receive.

Hartley Coleridge, 1796–1849

1630. FORGIVE

Forgive, O Lord, our severing ways,
The separate altars that we raise,
The varying tongues that speak Thy praise!

Suffice it now. In time to be
Shall one great temple rise to Thee,
Thy church our broad humanity.

White flowers of love its walls shall climb,
Sweet bells of peace shall ring its chime,
Its days shall all be holy time.

Thy hymn, long sought, shall then be heard,
The music of the world's accord,
Confessing Christ, the inward word!

That song shall swell from shore to shore,
One faith, one love, one hope restore
The seamless garb that Jesus wore!

John Greenleaf Whittier, 1807–1892

1631. YOUR CHURCH AND MINE

You go to your church, and I'll go to mine,
But let's walk along together;
Our Father has built them side by side,
So let's walk along together.
The road is rough and the way is long,

But we'll help each other over;
You go to your church and I'll go to mine,
But let's walk along together.

You go to your church, and I'll go to mine,
But let's walk along together;
Our heavenly Father is the same,
So let's walk along together.
The chimes of your church ring loud and
clear,
They chime with the chimes of my church;
You go to your church, and I'll go to mine,
But let's walk along together.

You go to your church, and I'll go to mine,
But let's walk along together;
Our heavenly Father loves us all,
So let's walk along together.
The Lord will be at my church today,
But He'll be at your church also;
You go to your church, and I'll go to mine,
But let's walk along together.

Phillips H. Lord, 1902–

1632. BREAD

Be gentle
When you touch bread.
Let it not lie
Uncared for—unwanted.
So often bread
Is taken for granted.

There is so much beauty
In bread—
Beauty of sun and soil,
Beauty of patient toil.
Winds and rains have caressed it,
Christ often blessed it.
Be gentle
When you touch bread.

Author unknown

1633. BREAD OF THE WORLD

Bread of the world in mercy broken,
Wine of the soul in mercy shed,
By whom the words of life were spoken,
And in whose death our sins are dead:

Look on the heart by sorrow broken,
Look on the tears by sinners shed;
And be Thy feast to us the token
That by Thy grace our souls are fed.

Reginald Heber, 1783–1826

1634. BREAK THOU THE BREAD OF LIFE

Break Thou the bread of life,
Dear Lord, to me,
As Thou didst break the loaves
Beside the sea;
Beyond the sacred page
I seek Thee, Lord;
My spirit pants for Thee,
O living Word!

Bless Thou the truth, dear Lord,
To me, to me,
As Thou didst bless the bread
By Galilee;
Then shall all bondage cease,
All fetters fall;
And I shall find my peace,
My All in All.

Mary A. Lathbury, 1841–1913

1635. ACCORDING TO THY GRACIOUS WORD

According to Thy gracious word,
In meek humility,
This will I do, my dying Lord,
I will remember Thee.

Thy body, broken for my sake,
My bread from heaven shall be;
Thy testamental cup I take,
And thus remember Thee.

Remember Thee, and all Thy pains,
And all Thy love to me:
Yea, while a breath, a pulse remains,
Will I remember Thee.

And when these failing lips grow dumb,
And mind and memory flee,
When Thou shalt in Thy kingdom come,
Jesus, remember me.

James Montgomery, 1771–1854

1636. BENEATH THE FORMS OF OUTWARD RITE

Beneath the forms of outward rite
Thy supper, Lord, is spread
In every quiet upper room
Where fainting souls are fed.

The bread is always consecrate
Which men divide with men;
And every act of brotherhood
Repeats Thy feast again.

The blessed cup is only passed
True memory of Thee,
When life anew pours out its wine
With rich sufficiency.

O Master, through these symbols shared,
Thine own dear self impart,
That in our daily life may flame
The Passion of Thy heart.

James A. Blaisdell, 1867–

1637. COMMUNION HYMN

How sweet and silent is the place,
My God, alone, with Thee!
Awaiting here Thy touch of grace,
Thy heavenly mystery.

So many ways Thou hast, dear Lord,
My longing heart to fill:
Thy lovely world, Thy spoken word,
The doing Thy sweet will,

Giving Thy children living bread,
Leading Thy weak ones on,
The touch of dear hands on my head,
The thought of loved ones gone.

Lead me by many paths, dear Lord,
But always in Thy way;
And let me make my earth a heaven
Till next communion day.

Alice Freeman Palmer, 1855–1902

1638. ETERNAL GOD, WHOSE POWER UPHOLDS

Eternal God, whose power upholds
Both flower and flaming star,
To whom there is no here nor there,
No time, no near nor far,
No alien race, no foreign shore,
No child unsought, unknown,
O, send us forth, Thy prophets true,
To make all lands Thine own!

O God of love, whose spirit wakes
In every human breast,
Whom love, and love alone, can know,
In whom all hearts find rest,
Help us to spread Thy gracious reign
Till greed and hate shall cease,
And kindness dwell in human hearts,
And all the earth find peace!

O God of truth, whom science seeks
And reverent souls adore,
Who lightest every earnest mind
Of every clime and shore,
Dispel the gloom of error's night,
Of ignorance and fear,
Until true wisdom from above
Shall make life's pathway clear!

O God of beauty, oft revealed
In dreams of human art,
In speech that flows to melody,
In holiness of heart;
Teach us to ban all ugliness
That blinds our eyes to Thee,
Till all shall know the loveliness
Of lives made fair and free.

O God of righteousness and grace,
Seen in the Christ, Thy Son,
Whose life and death reveal Thy face,
By whom Thy will was done,
Inspire Thy heralds of good news
To live Thy life divine,
Till Christ is formed in all mankind
And every land is Thine!

Henry Hallam Tweedy, 1868–

1639. GOD OF THE PROPHETS

God of the prophets!
Bless the prophets' sons;
Elijah's mantle o'er Elisha cast;
Each age its solemn task may claim but once;
Make each one nobler, stronger than the last.

Anoint them prophets!
Make their ears attent

To Thy divinest speech; their hearts awake
To human need; their lips make eloquent
To gird the right and every evil break.

Anoint them priests!
Strong intercessors, Lord!
Anoint them with the Spirit of Thy Son;
Theirs not a jeweled crown, a blood-stained sword:
Theirs, by sweet love, for Christ a kingdom won.

Make them apostles!
Heralds of Thy cross,
Forth may they go to tell all realms Thy grace:
Inspired of Thee, may they count all but loss,
And stand at last with joy before Thy face.

Denis Wortman, 1835–1922

1640. SERVANTS OF THE GREAT ADVENTURE

Servants of the great adventure,
Patriots of God's fatherland,
Fir'd by one supreme ambition,
Ready for the call we stand.
Cleanse our minds, thou Love all-ruling,
Steel our wills, unbind our eyes
That we see a-right thy kingdom;
Make us daring, free and wise.

Millions lie in crying darkness,
Unredeemed, untam'd, untaught,
Women prone in seal'd oppression,
Men like cattle sold and bought;
Millions grope through out-worn systems;
Many a cruel ancient faith
Binds the earth; and many a rebel,
Dooms the Christ again to death.

Yet men ev'rywhere have found thee,
Christ, the crown of ev'ry creed;
All the faiths and all the systems,
To thy revelation lead;
Thou dost guide our human groping,
Who hast won the hearts of men;
Thou wilt fill the world with splendor,
In our hands the how and when.

All the world shall live in kindness,
Hate and war shall pass away,
When men grow from out their blindness,
Wake, and see the blaze of day:
Each but needs the truth to win him,
Shape the beauty of his soul,
Fan the fire of love within him,
Save from self and make him whole.

Praise God for the hidden leaven,
For the depths yet unexplored;
Praise him for the Realm of Heaven—
All ye peoples, praise the Lord!
Sing, the round world all together,
With one mind and heart and mouth;
Glorify the Lord All-Father,
East and West and North and South!

Percy Dearmer, 1867–1936

1641. TO A YOUNG PRIEST

Such old, illustrious tidings you proclaim,
With quiet incandescence in your face;
Until the altar candles do not flame
With any surer radiance and grace.
It is the fire that burned in Augustine;
The passion that is selfless and most white;
That made of Francis, gentle and serene,
A torch uplifted on a somber night.
Such still adventure, and such steep a stair!
And, yet, to travel with you I would toss
The trifling cargo of myself and share
Your braver burdens and more excellent cross;
And give my little dream to be imbued
With your grave joy and flaming certitude.

Anne Blackwell Payne

1642. WHO SEEKS TO PLEASE ALL MEN

Who seeks to please all men each way
And not himself offend,
He may begin his work today,
But God knows when he'll end.

Lord Holland

1643. From TO THE PREACHER

Preach about the old sins, Preacher!
And the old virtues, too:
You must not steal nor take man's life,
You must not covet your neighbor's wife,
And woman must cling at every cost

To her one virtue, or she is lost—
Preach about the old sins, Preacher!
Not about the new!

Preach about the other man, Preacher!
The man we all can see!
The man of oaths, the man of strife,
The man who drinks and beats his wife,
Who helps his mates to fret and shirk
When all they need is to keep at work—
Preach about the other man, Preacher!
Not about me!

Charlotte Perkins Gilman, 1860–1935

1644. TO PULPIT AND TRIBUNE

Speak holy words—too many blasphemies,
Too many insolent and strident cries
And jeers and taunts and maledictions rise.

Speak faithful words—too many tongues that please,
And idle vows, and disingenuous pleas,
And heartless and disheartening levities.

Speak quiet words—the constellations wait,
The mountains watch; the hour for man is late
Likewise to still his heart and supplicate.

Speak chastened words—for anguish is at hand,
Intolerable, that none can understand,
And writs of ill no mortal eye has scanned.

Speak gentle words—for fallen on the knives
These sentient hearts and these exceeded lives
Bleed till their pitying Advocate arrives.

Speak holy words—and O thou tarrying Lord,
Leave not thy cherished to the power of the sword;
Come with thy hosts and rout the opprobrious horde.

Amos N. Wilder, 1895–

1645. SCULPTOR OF THE SOUL

I fain would be a sculptor of the soul,
Making each strong line fine,
Each feature faultless.
Yet the sculptor cannot carve
In wood or stone
An image nobler than he sees
Within his own stout soul.

So, gazing at the tools within my hand,
I shudder! How escape from self—
Pitiable, limited—
That I may be indeed
God's carver?
Happy in this thought;
There is a Guide for me,
Who in His living flesh
Has given me the perfect image that I seek, of God!

Toyohiko Kagawa, 1888–

1646. PREACHERS: THE TRUE VS. THE INSINCERE

From "The Task"

Would I describe a preacher, such as Paul,
Were he on earth, would hear, approve, and own—
Paul should himself direct me. I would trace
His master-strokes, and draw from his design.
I would express him simple, grave, sincere;
In doctrine uncorrupt; in language plain,
And plain in manner; decent, solemn, chaste,
And natural in gesture; much impressed
Himself, as conscious of his awful charge,
And anxious mainly that the flock he feeds
May feel it too; affectionate in look,
And tender in address, as well becomes
A messenger of grace to guilty men.
Behold the picture!—Is it like?—Like whom?
The things that mount the rostrum with a skip,
And then skip down again; pronounce a text;
Cry—hem! and reading what they never wrote,
Just fifteen minutes, huddle up their work,
And with a well-bred whisper close the scene!

William Cowper, 1731–1800

1647. A POET-PREACHER'S PRAYER

From "Paradise Lost," Book I

O Spirit, that dost prefer
Before all temples the upright heart and pure,
Instruct me, for Thou know'st; . . .
What in me is dark

Illumine, what is low raise and support;
That, to the highth of this great argument,
I may assert Eternal Providence,
And justify the ways of God to men.

John Milton, 1608–1674

1648. THE PARSON'S PRAYER

I do not ask
That crowds may throng the temple,
That standing room be priced;
I only ask that as I voice the message
They may see Christ!

I do not ask
For churchly pomp or pageant,
Or music such as wealth alone can buy;
I only ask that as I voice the message
He may be nigh!

I do not ask
That men may sound my praises
Or headlines spread my name abroad;
I only pray that as I voice the message
Hearts may find God!

I do not ask
For earthly place or laurel,
Or of this world's distinctions any part;
I only ask, when I have voiced the message,
My Saviour's heart!

Ralph Spaulding Cushman, 1879–

1649. THINK IT NOT STRANGE

Think it not strange, if he who stedfast leaveth
All that he loveth for the love of Me,
Be as the prey of him who rendeth, rieveth,
Breaketh and bruiseth, woundeth sore and grieveth,
And carefully a spray of sharp thorn weaveth
To crown the man who chooseth Calvary.

Count it all joy, the blaming and the scorning,
Ye who confess love's pure transcendent power;
Stay not for speech, heed not the wise world's warning,
Thine is an incommunicable dower.
What will it be when sudden, in the morning,
From brown thorn buddeth purple Passion flower?

Amy Carmichael, contemporary English

1650. THE PREACHER'S PRAYER

If thou wouldst have me speak, Lord, give me speech.
So many cries are uttered now-a-days,
That scarce a song, however clear and true,
Will thread the jostling tumult safe, and reach
The ears of men buz-filled with poor denays:
Barb thou my words with light, make my song new,
And men will hear, or when I sing or preach.

George Macdonald, 1824–1905

1651. EAST LONDON

'Twas August, and the fierce sun overhead
Smote on the squalid streets of Bethnal Green,
And the pale weaver, through his windows seen
In Spitalfields, look'd thrice dispirited.

I met a preacher there I knew, and said:
"Ill and o'er-worked, how fare you in this scene?"
"Bravely!" said he; "for I of late have been
Much cheer'd by thoughts of Christ, *the living bread.*"

O human soul! so long as thou canst so
Set up a mark of everlasting light,
Above the howling senses' ebb and flow,
To cheer thee, and to right thee if thou roam—
Not with lost toil thou labourest through the night!
Thou mak'st the heaven thou hop'st indeed thy home.

Matthew Arnold, 1822–1888

1652. A PREACHER'S URGENCY

I preached as never sure to preach again,
And as a dying man to dying men.

Richard Baxter, 1615–1691

1653. SERMON WITHOUT WORDS

Saint Francis came to preach. With smiles he met
The friendless, fed the poor, freed a trapped bird,
Led home a child. Although he spoke no word,
His text, God's love, the town did not forget.

Elizabeth Patton Moss

1654. THE PREACHER'S MISTAKE

The parish priest
Of Austerity,
Climbed up in a high church steeple
To be nearer God,
So that he might hand
His word down to His people.

When the sun was high,
When the sun was low,
The good man sat unheeding
Sublunary things.
From transcendency
Was he forever reading.

And now and again
When he heard the creak
Of the weather vane a-turning,
He closed his eyes
And said, "Of a truth
From God I now am learning."

And in sermon script
He daily wrote
What he thought was sent from heaven,
And he dropped this down
On his people's heads
Two times one day in seven.

In his age God said,
"Come down and die!"
And he cried out from the steeple,
"Where art Thou, Lord?"
And the Lord replied,
"Down here among my people."

Brewer Mattocks, 1841–1934

1655. THE TRUE PREACHER

From "The Task"

The pulpit, therefore (and I name it filled
With solemn awe, that bids me well beware
With what intent I touch that holy thing)—
The pulpit (when the sat'rist has at last,
Strutting and vap'ring in an empty school,
Spent all his force, and made no proselyte)—
I say the pulpit (in the sober use
Of its legitimate, peculiar powers)
Must stand acknowledged, while the world shall stand,
The most important and effectual guard,
Support, and ornament of Virtue's cause.
There stands the messenger of truth: there stands
The legate of the skies!—His theme divine,
His office sacred, his credentials clear.
By him the violated law speaks out
Its thunders; and by him, in strains as sweet
As angels use, the Gospel whispers peace.
He 'stablishes the strong, restores the weak,
Reclaims the wand'rer, binds the broken heart,
And, armed himself in panoply complete
Of heavenly temper, furnishes with arms
Bright as his own, and trains, by ev'ry rule
Of holy discipline, to glorious war,
The sacramental host of God's elect!

William Cowper, 1731–1800

1656. THE GOOD PARSON

From "The Canterbury Tales:" Prologue

The parson of a country town was he
Who knew the straits of humble poverty;
But rich he was in holy thought and work,
Nor less in learning as became a clerk.

The word of Christ most truly did he preach,
And his parishioners devoutly teach.
Benign was he, in labours diligent,
And in adversity was still content—
As proved full oft. To all his flock a friend,
Averse was he to ban or to contend
When tithes were due. Much rather was he
fond,
Unto his poor parishioners around,
Of his own substance and his dues to give,
Content on little, for himself to live.
Wide was his parish, scattered far asunder,
Yet none did he neglect, in rain, or thunder.
Sorrow and sickness won his kindly care;
With staff in hand he travelled everywhere.
This good example to his sheep he brought
That first he wrought, and afterwards he
taught.
This parable he joined the Word unto—
That, "If gold rust, what shall iron do?"
For if a priest be foul in whom we trust,
No wonder if a common man should rust!
And shame it were, in those the flock who
keep
For shepherds to be foul yet clean the sheep.
Well ought a priest example fair to give,
By his own cleanness, how his sheep should
live.
He did not put his benefice to hire,
And leave his sheep encumbered in the mire,
Then haste to St. Paul's in London Town,
To seek a chantry where to settle down,
And there at least to sing the daily mass,
Or with a brotherhood his time to pass.
He dwelt at home, with watchful care to keep
From prowling wolves his well-protected
sheep.
Though holy in himself and virtuous
He still to sinful men was piteous,
Not sparing of his speech, in vain conceit,
But in his teaching kindly and discreet.
To draw his flock to heaven with noble art,
By good example, was his holy art.
Nor less did he rebuke the obstinate,
Whether they were of high or low estate.
For pomp and worldly show he did not
care;
No morbid conscience made his rule severe.
The lore of Christ and his apostles twelve
He taught, but first he followed it himself.

Geoffrey Chaucer, 1340–1400;
tr., by H. C. Leonard

1657. THE VILLAGE PREACHER

From "The Deserted Village"

Near yonder copse, where once the garden smiled,
And still where many a garden-flower grows wild;
There, where a few torn shrubs the place disclose,
The village preacher's modest mansion rose.
A man he was to all the country dear,
And passing rich with forty pounds a year;
Remote from towns he ran his godly race,
Nor e'er had changed, nor wished to change, his place;
Unpractised he to fawn, or seek for power,
By doctrines fashioned to the varying hour;
Far other aims his heart had learned to prize,
More skilled to raise the wretched than to rise.
His house was known to all the vagrant train;
He chid their wanderings, but relieved their pain;
The long-remembered beggar was his guest,
Whose beard descending swept his aged breast;
The ruined spendthrift, now no longer proud,
Claimed kindred there, and had his claims allowed;
The broken soldier, kindly bade to stay,
Sat by his fire and talked the night away,
Wept o'er his wounds, or, tales of sorrow done,

Shouldered his crutch and showed how fields were won.
Pleased with his guests, the good man learned to glow,
And quite forgot their vices in their woe;
Careless their merits or their faults to scan,
His pity gave ere charity began.
  Thus to relieve the wretched was his pride.
And e'en his failings lean'd to Virtue's side;
But in his duty prompt at every call,
He watched and wept, he prayed and felt for all;
And, as a bird each fond endearment tries
To tempt its new-fledg'd offspring to the skies,
He tried each art, reprov'd each dull delay,
Allur'd to brighter worlds, and led the way.
  Beside the bed where parting life was laid,
And sorrow, guilt and pain by turns dismayed,
The reverend champion stood. At his control
Despair and anguish fled the struggling soul;
Comfort came down the trembling wretch to raise,
And his last faltering accents whispered praise.
  At church, with meek and unaffected grace,
His looks adorned the venerable place:
Truth from his lips prevailed with double sway,
And fools, who came to scoff, remain'd to pray.
The service past, around the pious man,
With steady zeal, each honest rustic ran;
Even children follow'd with endearing wile,
And pluck'd his gown, to share the good man's smile
His ready smile a parent's warmth expressed;
Their welfare pleased him and their cares distrest:
To them his heart, his love, his griefs were given,
But all his serious thoughts had rest in heaven.
As some tall cliff, that lifts its awful form,
Swells from the vale, and midway leaves the storm,
Though round its breast the rolling clouds are spread,
Eternal sunshine settles on its head.
In arguing too, the parson own'd his skill,
For e'en though vanquished, he could argue still;
While words of learned length and thundering sound
Amaz'd the gazing rustics rang'd around,
And still they gaz'd, and still the wonder grew,
That one small head could carry all he knew.

Oliver Goldsmith, 1728–1774

1658. GENERAL WILLIAM BOOTH ENTERS INTO HEAVEN

(To be sung to the tune of "The Blood of the Lamb" with indicated instrument)

I

(*Bass drum beaten loudly.*)
Booth led boldly with his big bass drum—
(Are you washed in the blood of the Lamb?)

The Saints smiled gravely and they said: "He's come."
(Are you washed in the blood of the Lamb?)
Walking lepers followed, rank on rank,
Lurching bravos from the ditches dank,
Drabs from the alleyways and drug fiends pale—
Minds still passion-ridden, soul-powers frail:—
Vermin-eaten saints with moldy breath,
Unwashed legions with the ways of Death—
(Are you washed in the blood of the Lamb?)

(*Banjos.*)
Every slum had sent its half-a-score
The round world over. (Booth had groaned for more.)
Every banner that the wide world flies
Bloomed with glory and transcendent dyes.
Big-voiced lasses made their banjos bang,
Tranced, fanatical they shrieked and sang:—
"Are you washed in the blood of the Lamb?"
Hallelujah! It was queer to see
Bull-necked convicts with that land make free.
Loons with trumpets blowed a blare, blare, blare
On, on upward thro' the golden air!
(Are you washed in the blood of the Lamb?)

II

(*Bass drum slower and softer.*)
Booth died blind and still by faith he trod,
Eyes still dazzled by the ways of God.
Booth led boldly, and he looked the chief,
Eagle countenance in sharp relief,
Beard a-flying, air of high command
Unabated in that holy land.

(*Sweet flute music.*)
Jesus came from out the court-house door,
Stretched his hands above the passing poor.
Booth saw not, but led his queer ones there
Round and round the mighty court-house square.
Then, in an instant all that blear review
Marched on spotless, clad in raiment new.
The lame were straightened, withered limbs uncurled
And blind eyes opened on a new, sweet world.

(*Bass drum louder.*)
Drabs and vixens in a flash made whole!
Gone was the weasel-head, the snout, the jowl!
Sages and sibyls now, and athletes clean,
Rulers of empires, and of forests green!

(*Grand chorus of all instruments. Tambourines to the foreground.*)
The hosts were sandalled, and their wings were fire!
(Are you washed in the blood of the Lamb?)
But their noise played havoc with the angel-choir.

(Are you washed in the blood of the Lamb?)
Oh, shout Salvation! It was good to see
Kings and Princes by the Lamb set free.
The banjos rattled and the tambourines
Jing-jing-jingled in the hands of Queens.

(*Reverently sung, no instruments.*)
And when Booth halted by the curb for prayer
He saw his Master thro' the flag-filled air.
Christ came gently with a robe and crown
For Booth the soldier, while the throng knelt down.
He saw King Jesus. They were face to face,
And he knelt a-weeping in that holy place.
Are you washed in the blood of the Lamb?

Vachel Lindsay, 1879–1931

1659. THE WAGES

Who storms the moss-grown walls of eld
And beats some falsehood down
Shall pass the pallid gates of death
Sans laurel, love, or crown;
For him who fain would teach the world
The world holds hate in fee—
For Socrates, the hemlock cup;
For Christ, Gethsemane.

Don Marquis, 1878–1937

1660. THE REFORMERS

O pure reformers! not in vain
Your trust in human kind;
The good which bloodshed could not gain,
Your peaceful zeal shall find.

The truths ye urge are borne abroad
By every wind and tide;
The voice of nature and of God
Speaks out upon your side.

The weapons which your hands have found
Are those which heaven hath wrought,
Light, truth, and love; your battleground,
The free, broad field of thought.

O may no selfish purpose break
The beauty of your plan,
No lie from throne or altar shake
Your steady faith in man.

Press on! and, if we may not share
The glory of your fight,
We'll ask at least, in earnest prayer,
God's blessing on the right.

John Greenleaf Whittier, 1807–1892

1661. THE BUILDER

A builder builded a temple,
He wrought it with grace and skill;
Pillars and groins and arches
All fashioned to work his will.
Men said, as they saw its beauty,
"It shall never know decay;
Great is thy skill, O Builder!
Thy fame shall endure for aye."

A Teacher builded a temple
With loving and infinite care,
Planning each arch with patience,
Laying each stone with prayer.
None praised her unceasing efforts,
None knew of her wondrous plan,
For the temple the Teacher builded
Was unseen by the eyes of man.

Gone is the Builder's temple,
Crumpled into the dust;
Low lies each stately pillar,
Food for consuming rust.
But the temple the Teacher builded
Will last while the ages roll,
For that beautiful unseen temple
Was a child's immortal soul.

Author unknown

1662. SCULPTURE

I took a piece of plastic clay
And idly fashioned it one day.
And as my fingers pressed it, still
It moved and yielded to my will.

I came again when days were past:
The bit of clay was hard at last.
The form I gave it still it bore,
And I could fashion it no more!

I took a piece of living clay,
And gently pressed it day by day,
And moulded with my power and art
A young child's soft and yielding heart.

I came again when years had gone:
It was a man I looked upon.
He still that early impress bore,
And I could fashion it no more!

Author unknown

1663. EDUCATION

Mark Hopkins sat on one end of a log
And a farm boy sat on the other.
Mark Hopkins came as a pedagogue
And taught as an elder brother.
I don't care what Mark Hopkins taught,
If his Latin was small and his Greek was naught,
For the farm boy he thought, thought he,
All through the lecture time and quiz,
"The kind of a man I mean to be
Is the kind of a man Mark Hopkins is."

Theology, languages, medicine, law,
Are peacock feathers to deck a daw
If the boys who come from your splendid schools
Are well-trained sharpers or flippant fools,
You may boast of your age and your ivied walls,
Your great endowments, your marble halls,
And all your modern features,
Your vast curriculum's scope and reach
And the multifarious things you teach—
But how about your teachers?
Are they men who can stand in a father's place,
Who are paid, best paid, by the ardent face
When boyhood gives, as boyhood can,
Its love and faith to a fine, true man?

No printed word nor spoken plea
Can teach young hearts what men should be,
Not all the books on all the shelves,
But what the teachers are, themselves.
For Education is, Making Men;
So is it now, so was it when
Mark Hopkins sat on one end of a log
And James Garfield sat on the other.

Arthur Guiterman, 1871–1943

1664. THE TEACHER

Lord, who am I to teach the way
To little children day by day,
So prone myself to go astray?

I teach them KNOWLEDGE, but I know
How faint they flicker and how low
The candles of my knowledge glow.

I teach them POWER to will and do,
But only now to learn anew
My own great weakness through and through.

I teach them LOVE for all mankind
And all God's creatures, but I find
My love comes lagging far behind.

Lord, if their guide I still must be,
Oh, let the little children see
The teacher leaning hard on Thee.

Leslie Pinckney Hill, 1880–

1665. THE TEACHER'S PRAYER

Lord, thou who didst teach, forgive me for teaching,
And for presuming to carry the name of teacher,
A name that thou didst carry while on earth.
Give me a single-hearted love for my school,
So that not even the blazing whirl of beauty could steal from me my tenderness
At all times.

Teacher, make my fervor everlasting and my despondency a passing phase.
Snatch from me this impure desire for justice that still troubles me—
This protest that arises within me when I am grieved.
Grant that when my pupils neglect me, I may not be forlorn
Nor be pained when they misunderstand me.
Make me more of a mother than all the mothers,
In order that I may love and defend, with like devotion,
Those who are not flesh of my flesh.
Grant that I may be successful in moulding one of my pupils
Into my perfect poem,
And in weaving her into my most haunting melody,
Against the day when the song of my lips shall be silent.
Show me how thy Gospel is possible in this day and age,
So that I may never renounce the good fight of faith.
In my democratic school let thy radiance
Rest upon the circle of barefoot boys.
Make me strong even in my position—
That of a poor and despised woman.
Help me to scorn all power that is not pure
And all force that is not in harmony with thy flaming will.
Friend, stand by my side, sustain me.
Many times I shall have no one but thee at my side.
When my doctrine is purer and my truth is glowing,
I shall be alone, but thou shalt press me to thy heart,
Thou who wert lonely and forsaken.
I shall seek approbation only in thy look.
Give me simplicity and give me depth.
Free me from the temptation of being vainglorious
Or commonplace in my teaching.
Permit me to lift my eyes from my wounded breast each morning
As I enter my school.
Grant that I may never carry to my desk my petty cares,
My trifling disappointments.
May my hand be light in punishment and smooth in caresses.
Help me to reprove with pain
That I may be sure that while I am correcting I yet love the child.
Grant that my school may not be built of bricks but of spirit.
May the splendor of my enthusiasm be reflected from the bare walls
And fill the classroom.
Let my heart be a sustaining bulwark and my good will be a brighter gold
Than all the gold and all the pillars in the halls of the wealthy.
Let this be my supreme lesson, inspired by the pallid beauty of Velazquez' "Crucifixion"—
To teach and love with fervor on this earth
Means to enter, finally, with the spear-thrust of Longinus, the Roman centurion,
Into the throbbing, cosmic heart of Love.

Gabriela Mistral,[1] *1889–*
tr. from the Spanish by James H. McLean

1666. CHRIST IN INTROSPECT

I—who have the healing creed,
The faith benign of Mary's Son,
Shall I behold my brother's need,
And, selfishly, to aid him shun?
I—who upon my mother's knee,
In childhood, read Christ's written word,
Received His legacy of peace,

[1] Gabriela Mistral, a Chilean, is one of the five women of the world to be awarded the Nobel Prize, in Literature.

His holy rule of action heard;
I—in whose heart the sacred sense
Of Jesus' love was early felt;
Of His pure, full benevolence,
His pitying tenderness for guilt;
His shepherd-care for wandering sheep,
For all weak, sorrowing, trembling things,
His mercy vast, His passion deep,
Of anguish for man's sufferings;
I—schooled from childhood in such lore—
Dared I draw back or hesitate
When called to heal the sickness sore
Of those far off and desolate?

Charlotte Brontë, 1816–1855

1667. FOREIGN MISSIONS IN BATTLE ARRAY

An endless line of splendor,
These troops with heaven for home,
With creeds they go from Scotland,
With incense go from Rome.
These, in the name of Jesus,
Against the dark gods stand,
They gird the earth with valor,
They heed their King's command.

Onward the line advances,
Shaking the hills with power,
Slaying the hidden demons,
The lions that devour.
No bloodshed in the wrestling,—
But souls new-born arise—
The nations growing kinder,
The child-hearts growing wise.

What is the final ending?
The issue, can we know?
Will Christ outlive Mohammed?
Will Kali's altar go?
This is our faith tremendous,—
Our wild hope, who shall scorn,—
That in the name of Jesus
The world shall be reborn!

Vachel Lindsay, 1879–193

1668. OUR MISSIONARIES

Forget them not, O Christ, who stand
Thy vanguard in the distant land!

In flood, in flame, in dark, in dread,
Sustain, we pray, each lifted head!

Be Thou in every faithful breast,
Be peace and happiness and rest!

Exalt them over every fear;
In peril, come Thyself more near!

Let heaven above their pathway pour
A radiance from its open door!

Turn Thou the hostile weapons, Lord,
Rebuke each wrathful alien horde!

Thine are the loved for whom we crave
That Thou wouldst keep them strong and brave.

Thine is the work they strive to do;
Their foes so many, they so few.

Yet Thou art with them and Thy Name
Forever lives, is aye the same.

Thy conquering Name, O Lord, we pray,
Quench not its light in blood today!

Be with Thine own, Thy loved, who stand
Christ's vanguard in the storm-swept land!

Margaret E. Sangster, 1838–1912

1669. DAVID LIVINGSTONE

He knew not that the trumpet he had blown
Out of the darkness of that dismal land
Had reached and roused an army of its own
To strike the chains from the slave's fettered hand.

Open the Abbey doors and bear him in
To sleep with kings and statesmen, chief and sage,
The missionary come of weaver-kin,
But great by work that brooks no lower wage.

He needs no epitaph to guard a name
Which men shall prize while worthy work is known;
He lived and died for good—be that his fame:
Let marble crumble, this is Living-stone.

Author unknown—Lines from "Punch" on the burial of Dr. Livingstone in Westminster Abbey, 1873

Book VI: THE NATION AND THE NATIONS

1670. BREATHES THERE THE MAN

From "The Lay of the Last Minstrel," Canto VI

Breathes there the man, with soul so dead,
Who never to himself hath said,
This is my own, my native land!
Whose heart hath ne'er within him burn'd,
As home his footsteps he hath turn'd
From wandering on a foreign strand?
If such there breathe, go, mark him well;
For him no minstrel raptures swell;
High though his titles, proud his name,
Boundless his wealth as wish can claim,—
Despite those titles, power, and pelf,
The wretch, concentred all in self,
Living, shall forfeit fair renown,
And, doubly dying, shall go down
To the vile dust from whence he sprung,
Unwept, unhonor'd, and unsung.

Sir Walter Scott, 1771–1832

1671. PRAYER FOR MY NATIVE LAND

From "The Cotter's Saturday Night"

O Scotia! my dear, my native soil!
For whom my warmest wish to Heaven is sent!
Long may thy hardy sons of rustic toil
Be blest with health, and peace, and sweet content!
And O! may Heaven their simple lives prevent
From Luxury's contagion, weak and vile!
Then, howe'er crowns and coronets be rent,
A virtuous populace may rise the while,
And stand a wall of fire around their much-lov'd Isle.

O THOU! who pour'd the patriotic tide,
That stream'd thro' Wallace's undaunted heart,
Who dar'd to nobly stem tyrannic pride,
Or nobly die, the second glorious part:
(The patriot's God, peculiarly Thou art,
His friend, inspirer, guardian, and reward!)
O never, never Scotia's realm desert;
But still the patriot, and the patriot-bard
In bright succession raise, her ornament and guard!

Robert Burns, 1759–1796

1672. RECESSIONAL[1]

God of our fathers, known of old—
  Lord of our far-flung battle line—
Beneath Whose awful hand we hold
  Dominion over palm and pine—
Lord God of Hosts, be with us yet,
  Lest we forget—lest we forget!

The tumult and the shouting dies;
  The captains and the kings depart—
Still stands Thine ancient Sacrifice,
  An humble and a contrite heart.
Lord God of Hosts, be with us yet,
  Lest we forget—lest we forget!

Far-called, our navies melt away;
  On dune and headland sinks the fire—
Lo, all our pomp of yesterday
  Is one with Nineveh and Tyre!
Judge of the Nations, spare us yet,
  Lest we forget—lest we forget!

If, drunk with sight of power, we loose
  Wild tongues that have not Thee in awe—
Such boasting as the Gentiles use
  Or lesser breeds without the Law—
Lord God of Hosts, be with us yet,
  Lest we forget—lest we forget!

For heathen heart that puts her trust
  In reeking tube and iron shard—
All valiant dust that builds on dust,
  And guarding, calls not Thee to guard—
For frantic boast and foolish word,
  Thy mercy on Thy people, Lord!
Amen.

Rudyard Kipling, 1865–1936

1673. LAND OF OUR BIRTH

"The Children's Song"

Land of our Birth, we pledge to thee
Our love and toil in the years to be;
When we are grown and take our place,
As men and women with our race.

Father in heaven, who lovest all,
O help Thy children when they call;
That they may build from age to age,
An undefilèd heritage.

Teach us to bear the yoke in youth,
With steadfastness and careful truth;
That, in our time, Thy grace may give
The truth whereby the nations live.

Teach us to rule ourselves alway,
Controlled and cleanly night and day;
That we may bring, if need arise,
No maimed or worthless sacrifice.

Teach us to look, in all our ends,
On Thee for Judge, and not our friends;
That we, with Thee, may walk uncowed
By fear or favour of the crowd.

Teach us the strength that cannot seek,
By deed or thought, to hurt the weak;
That, under Thee, we may possess
Man's strength to succour man's distress.

Teach us delight in simple things,
And mirth that has no bitter springs;
Forgiveness free of evil done,
And love to all men 'neath the sun!

Land of our Birth, our faith, our pride,
For whose dear sake our fathers died;
O Motherland, we pledge to thee,
Head, heart, and hand through the years to be!

Rudyard Kipling, 1865–1936

1674. IT IS NOT TO BE THOUGHT OF

It is not to be thought of that the Flood
Of British freedom, which, to the open sea
Of the world's praise, from dark antiquity
Hath flowed, "with pomp of waters, unwithstood,"
Roused though it be full often to a mood
Which spurns the check of salutary bands,
That this most famous Stream in bogs and sands
Should perish; and to evil and to good
Be lost for ever. In our halls is hung
Armoury of the invincible Knights of old:
We must be free or die, who speak the tongue
That Shakespeare spake; the faith and morals hold
Which Milton held.—In everything we are sprung
Of Earth's first blood, have titles manifold.

William Wordsworth, 1770–1850

[1] Written on the occasion of Queen Victoria's Diamond Jubilee, June 1897.

1675. FREEDOM

Of old sat Freedom on the heights,
The thunders breaking at her feet;
Above her shook the starry lights;
She heard the torrents meet.

There in her place she did rejoice,
Self-gather'd in her prophet-mind,
But fragments of her mighty voice
Came rolling on the wind.

Then stept she down thro' town and field
To mingle with the human race,
And part by part to men reveal'd
The fullness of her face—

Grave mother of majestic works,
From her isle-altar gazing down,
Who, Godlike, grasps the triple forks,
And, king-like, wears the crown.

Her open eyes desire the truth.
The wisdom of a thousand years
Is in them. May perpetual youth
Keep dry their light from tears;

That her fair form may stand and shine,
Make bright our days and light our dreams,
Turning to scorn with lips divine
The falsehood of extremes!

Alfred Tennyson, 1809–1892

1676. GIVE US MEN!

Give us Men!
Men—from every rank,
Fresh and free and frank;
Men of thought and reading,
Men of light and leading,
Men of loyal breeding,
The nation's welfare speeding;
Men of faith and not of fiction,
Men of lofty aim in action;
Give us Men—I say again,
Give us Men!

Give us Men!
Strong and stalwart ones;
Men whom highest hope inspires,
Men whom purest honor fires,
Men who trample self beneath them,
Men who make their country wreathe
them
As her noble sons,
Worthy of their sires;
Men who never shame their mothers,
Men who never fail their brothers,
True, however false are others:
Give us Men—I say again,
Give us Men!

Give us Men!
Men who, when the tempest gathers,
Grasp the standard of their fathers
In the thickest fight;
Men who strike for home and altar,
(Let the coward cringe and falter),
God defend the right!
True as truth the lorn and lonely,
Tender, as the brave are only;
Men who tread where saints have trod,
Men for Country, Home—and God:
Give us Men! I say again—again—
Give us Men!

Edward Henry Bickersteth, 1825–1906

1677. GOD SEND US MEN

God send us men whose aim 'twill be,
Not to defend some outworn creed,
But to live out the laws of Christ
In every thought and word and deed.

God send us men alert and quick
His lofty precepts to translate,
Until the laws of Christ become
The laws and habits of the state.

God send us men of steadfast will,
Patient, courageous, strong and true;
With vision clear and mind equipped
His will to learn, His work to do.

God send us men with hearts ablaze,
All truth to love, all wrong to hate;
These are the patriots nations need,
These are the bulwarks of the state.

Frederick J. Gillman, 1866–

1678. FOUR THINGS

Four things in any land must dwell,
If it endures and prospers well:
One is manhood true and good;
One is noble womanhood;
One is child life, clean and bright;
And one an altar kept alight.

Author unknown

1679. GOD SAVE THE KING

BRITISH NATIONAL ANTHEM

God save our gracious King,
Long live our noble King,
  God save the King:
Send him victorious,
Happy and glorious,
Long to reign over us;
  God save the King.

Nor on this land alone[1]—
But be God's mercies known,
  From shore to shore.
Lord make the nations see
That men should brothers be
And form one family
  The wide world o'er.

Thy choicest gifts in store
On him be pleased to pour;
  Long may he reign:
May he defend our laws,
And ever give us cause
To sing with heart and voice,
  God save the King.

1680. THE STAR-SPANGLED BANNER

THE AMERICAN NATIONAL ANTHEM

Oh, say, can you see, by the dawn's early light,
  What so proudly we hailed at the twilight's last gleaming?
Whose broad stripes and bright stars, thro' the perilous fight,
  O'er the ramparts we watched, were so gallantly streaming.
And the rockets' red glare, the bombs bursting in air,
Gave proof through the night that our flag was still there.
  Oh, say, does that star-spangled banner yet wave
  O'er the land of the free and the home of the brave?

On the shore dimly seen, thro' the mists of the deep,
  Where the foe's haughty host in dread silence reposes,
What is that which the breeze, o'er the towering steep,
  As it fitfully blows, half conceals, half discloses?
Now it catches the gleam of the morning's first beam,
In full glory reflected, now shines on the stream;
  'Tis the star-spangled banner; oh, long may it wave
  O'er the land of the free and the home of the brave.

❖

Oh, thus be it ever when freemen shall stand,
  Between their loved homes and the war's desolation;
Blest with vict'ry and peace, may the heav'n-rescued land
  Praise the Power that has made and preserved us a nation.

[1]The second stanza, written in 1836 by William E. Hickson (1803-1870), was inserted following the second World War. With the approval of and in the presence of King George VI the revised National Anthem was first sung officially in a United Nations service of intercession in St. Paul's Cathedral in 1946. This stanza is the third stanza of the hymn, "God Bless Our Native Land," an exalted petition for America, sung to the same tune as the British National Anthem and found in many American hymnals, especially after the first World War. The first and third stanzas of the British National Anthem are of unknown authorship. They were first sung officially in 1745. The original anthem contained, as its second stanza, the following lines:

O Lord our God arise,
Scatter our enemies
  And make them fall.
Confound their politics,
Frustrate their knavish tricks;
On Thee our hopes we fix,
  God save us all.

Then conquer we must, when our cause it is just,
And this be our motto: "In God is our trust";
And the star-spangled banner in triumph shall wave
O'er the land of the free and the home of the brave.

Francis Scott Key, 1779–1843

1681. AMERICA

I

My country, 'tis of thee,
Sweet land of liberty,
Of thee I sing;
Land where my fathers died,
Land of the pilgrims' pride,
From every mountain side
Let freedom ring!

II

My native country, thee,
Land of the noble free,
Thy name I love;
I love thy rocks and rills,
Thy woods and templed hills;
My heart with rapture thrills,
Like that above.

III

Let music swell the breeze,
And ring from all the trees
Sweet freedom's song;
Let mortal tongues awake;
Let all that breathe partake;
Let rocks their silence break,
The sound prolong.

IV

Our fathers' God, to Thee,
Author of liberty,
To Thee we sing;
Long may our land be bright
With freedom's holy light;
Protect us by Thy might,
Great God, our King.

Samuel F. Smith, 1808–1895

Lord, let war's tempest cease,
Fold the whole world in peace
Under Thy wings.
Make all the nations one,
All hearts beneath the sun,
Till Thou shalt reign alone,
Great King of Kings.

Written for "America" by
Henry Wadsworth Longfellow, 1807–1882

1682. AMERICA THE BEAUTIFUL

O beautiful for spacious skies,
For amber waves of grain,
For purple mountain majesties
Above the fruited plain!
America! America!
God shed His grace on thee
And crown thy good with brotherhood
From sea to shining sea!

O beautiful for pilgrim feet,
Whose stern, impassioned stress
A thoroughfare for freedom beat
Across the wilderness!
America! America!
God mend thine every flaw,
Confirm thy soul in self-control,
Thy liberty in law!

O beautiful for heroes proved
In liberating strife,
Who more than self their country loved,
And mercy more than life!
America! America!
May God thy gold refine,
Till all success be nobleness
And every gain divine!

O beautiful for patriot dream
That sees beyond the years
Thine alabaster cities gleam
Undimmed by human tears!
America! America!
God shed His grace on thee
And crown thy good with brotherhood
From sea to shining sea!

Katharine Lee Bates, 1859–1929

1683. O BEAUTIFUL, MY COUNTRY

O Beautiful, my Country!
Be thine a nobler care
Than all thy wealth of commerce,
Thy harvests waving fair;

Be it thy pride to lift up
The manhood of the poor;
Be thou to the oppressed
Fair freedom's open door!

For thee our fathers suffered;
For thee they toiled and prayed;
Upon thy holy altar
Their willing lives they laid.
Thou hast no common birthright,
Grand memories on thee shine;
The blood of pilgrim nations
Commingled flows in thine.

O beautiful, our country!
Round thee in love we draw;
Thine is the grace of freedom,
The majesty of law.
Be righteousness thy scepter,
Justice thy diadem;
And on thy shining forehead
Be peace the crowning gem!

Frederick L. Hosmer, 1840–1928

1684. I AM AN AMERICAN

I am an American.
My father belongs to the Sons of the Revolution;
My mother, to the Colonial Dames.
One of my ancestors pitched tea overboard in Boston Harbor;
Another stood his ground with Warren;
Another hungered with Washington at Valley Forge.
My forefathers were America in the making:
They spoke in her council halls;
They died on her battle-fields;
They commanded her ships;
They cleared her forests.
Dawns reddened and paled.
Stanch hearts of mine beat fast at each new star
In the nation's flag.
Keen eyes of mine foresaw her greater glory:
The sweep of her seas,
The plenty of her plains,
The man-hives in her billion-wired cities.
Every drop of blood in me holds a heritage of patriotism.
I am proud of my past.
I AM AN AMERICAN.

I am an American.
My father was an atom of dust,
My mother a straw in the wind,
To his serene majesty.
One of my ancestors died in the mines of Siberia;
Another was crippled for life by twenty blows of the knout.
Another was killed defending his home during the massacres.
The history of my ancestors is a trail of blood
To the palace-gate of the Great White Czar.
But then the dream came—
The dream of America.
In the light of the Liberty torch
The atom of dust became a man
And the straw in the wind became a woman
For the first time.
"See," said my father, pointing to the flag that fluttered near,

"That flag of stars and stripes is yours;
It is the emblem of the promised land.
It means, my son, the hope of humanity.
Live for it—die for it!"
Under the open sky of my new country I swore to do so;
And every drop of blood in me will keep that vow.
I am proud of my future.
I AM AN AMERICAN.

Elias Lieberman, 1883–

1685. AMERICA FIRST

America first, not only in things material,
But in things of the spirit.
Not merely in science, invention, motors, skyscrapers,
But also in ideals, principles, character.
Not merely in the calm assertion of rights,
But in the glad assumption of duties.

Not flouting her strength as a giant,
But bending in helpfulness over a sick and wounded world like a Good Samaritan.
Not in splendid isolation,
But in courageous cooperation.

Not in pride, arrogance, and disdain of other races and peoples,
But in sympathy, love, and understanding.
Not in treading again the old, worn, bloody pathway which ends inevitably in chaos and disaster,
But blazing a new trail along which, please God, other nations will follow into the new Jerusalem where wars shall be no more.

Some day, some nation must take that path—unless we are to lapse into utter barbarism—and that honor I covet for my beloved America.
And so in that spirit and with these hopes, I say with all my heart and soul, "America First."

G. Ashton Oldham, 1877–

1686. THE NEW COLOSSUS

As inscribed in bronze on the Statue of Liberty, Bedloe Island, New York Harbor

Not like the brazen giant of Greek fame,
With conquering limbs astride from land to land;
Here at our sea-washed, sunset gates shall stand
A mighty woman with a torch, whose flame
Is the imprisoned lightning, and her name
Mother of Exiles. From her beacon-hand
Glows world-wide welcome; her mild eyes command
The air-bridged harbor that twin cities frame.
"Keep, ancient lands, your storied pomp!" cries she
With silent lips. "Give me your tired, your poor,
Your huddled masses yearning to breathe free,

The wretched refuse of your teeming shore,
Send these, the homeless, tempest-tost to me,
I lift my lamp beside the golden door."

Emma Lazarus, 1848–1887

1687. From AMERICA FOR ME

I know that Europe's wonderful, yet something seems to lack:
The Past is too much with her, and the people looking back.
But the glory of the Present is to make the Future free,—
We love our land for what she is and what she is to be.

Oh, it's home again, and home again, America for me!
I want a ship that's westward bound to plough the rolling sea,
To the blessed Land of Room Enough beyond the ocean bars,
Where the air is full of sunlight and the flag is full of stars.

Henry van Dyke, 1852–1933

1688. OUR COUNTRY

To all who hope for Freedom's gleam
Across the warring years,
Who offer life to build a dream
In laughter or in tears,
To all who toil, unmarked, unknown,
By city, field or sea,
I give my heart, I reach my hand,
A common hope, a common land
Is made of you and me.

For we have loved her summer dawns
Beyond the misty hill,
And we have shared her toil, her fruit
Of farm and shop and mill.
Our weaknesses have made her shame,
Our strength has built her powers,
And we have hoped and we have striven
That to her children might be given
A fairer world than ours.

We dreamed to hold her safe, apart
From strife; the dream was vain.
Her heart is now earth's bleeding heart,
She shares the whole earth's pain.
To men oppressed in all the lands
One flashing hope has gone,
One vision wide as earth appears,
We seek, across the warring years,
The gray world's golden dawn.

Anna Louise Strong, 1885–

1689. AMERICA'S GOSPEL

Our country hath a gospel of her own
To preach and practice before all the world—
The freedom and divinity of man,
The glorious claims of human brotherhood,
And the soul's fealty to none but God.

James Russell Lowell, 1819–1891

1690. UNMANIFEST DESTINY[1]

To what new fates, my country, far
And unforeseen of foe or friend,
Beneath what unexpected star
Compelled to what unchosen end,

Across the sea that knows no beach,
The Admiral of Nations guides
Thy blind obedient keels to reach
The harbor where thy future rides!

The guns that spoke at Lexington
Knew not that God was planning then
The trumpet word of Jefferson
To bugle forth the rights of men.

To them that wept and cursed Bull Run,
What was it but despair and shame?
Who saw behind the cloud the sun?
Who knew that God was in the flame?

[1] The phrase "manifest destiny," which came into usage during the Spanish-American War, was meant to indicate America's paternal (or, as the opposing faction claimed, imperialistic) mission.

Had not defeat upon defeat,
  Disaster on disaster come,
The slave's emancipated feet
  Had never marched behind the drum.

There is a Hand that bends our deeds
  To mightier issues than we planned;
Each son that triumphs, each that bleeds,
  My country, serves Its dark command.

I do not know beneath what sky
  Nor on what seas shall be thy fate;
I only know it shall be high,
  I only know it shall be great.

Richard Hovey, 1864–1900

1691. THE AMERICAN FLAG

When Freedom from her mountain-height
  Unfurled her standard to the air,
She tore the azure robe of night,
  And set the stars of glory there.
She mingled with its gorgeous dyes
The milky baldric of the skies,
And striped its pure, celestial white
With streakings of the morning light.

❖

Flag of the free heart's hope and home!
  By angel hands to valor given;
Thy stars have lit the welkin dome,
  And all thy hues were born in heaven.
Forever float that standard sheet!
  Where breathes the foe but falls before us,
With Freedom's soil beneath our feet,
  And Freedom's banner streaming o'er us!

Joseph Rodman Drake, 1795–1820

1692. THE SHIP OF STATE

Thou, too, sail on, O Ship of State!
Sail on, O Union! strong and great!
Humanity with all its fears,
With all the hopes of future years,
Is hanging breathless on thy fate!
We know what Master laid thy keel,
What Workmen wrought thy ribs of steel,
Who made each mast, and sail, and rope,
What anvils rang, what hammers beat,
In what a forge and what a heat
Were shaped the anchors of thy hope!
Fear not each sudden sound and shock,
'Tis of the wave, and not the rock;
'Tis but the flapping of the sail,
And not a rent made by the gale!
In spite of rock and tempest's roar,
In spite of false lights on the shore,
Sail on, nor fear to breast the sea!
Our hearts, our hopes, are all with thee,
Our hearts, our hopes, our prayers, our tears,
Our faith, triumphant o'er our fears,
Are all with thee,—are all with thee!

Henry Wadsworth Longfellow, 1807–1882

1693. CONCORD HYMN

Sung at the Dedication of the Battle Monument,
July 4, 1837

By the rude bridge that arched the flood,
  Their flag to April's breeze unfurled,
Here once the embattled farmers stood,
  And fired the shot heard round the world.

The foe long since in silence slept;
  Alike the conqueror silent sleeps;
And Time the ruined bridge has swept
  Down the dark stream which seaward
    creeps.

On this green bank, by this soft stream,
  We set to-day a votive stone;
That memory may their deed redeem,
  When, like our sires, our sons are gone.

Spirit, that made those heroes dare
  To die, and leave their children free,
Bid Time and Nature gently spare
  The shaft we raise to them and thee.

Ralph Waldo Emerson, 1803–1882

1694. BATTLE-HYMN OF THE REPUBLIC

Mine eyes have seen the glory of the coming of the Lord;
He is trampling out the vintage where the grapes of wrath are stored;
He hath loosed the fateful lightning of His terrible, swift sword;
  His truth is marching on.

I have seen Him in the watch-fires of a hundred circling camps;
They have builded Him an altar in the evening dews and damps;
I can read His righteous sentence by the dim and flaring lamps:
His day is marching on.

I have read a fiery gospel, writ in burnished rows of steel:
"As ye deal with my contemners, so with you my grace shall deal;
Let the Hero, born of woman, crush the serpent with his heel,
Since God is marching on."

He has sounded forth the trumpet that shall never call retreat;
He is sifting out the hearts of men before His judgment-seat:
O, be swift, my soul, to answer Him! be jubilant, my feet!
Our God is marching on.

In the beauty of the lilies Christ was born across the sea,
With a glory in His bosom that transfigures you and me;
As He died to make men holy, let us die to make men free,
While God is marching on.

He is coming like the glory of the morning on the wave,
He is wisdom to the mighty, He is honor to the brave,
So the world shall be His footstool, and the soul of wrong his slave,
Our God is marching on!

Julia Ward Howe, 1819–1910

1695. INVOCATION

O Thou whose equal purpose runs
In drops of rain or streams of suns,
And with a soft compulsion rolls
The green earth on her snowy poles;
O Thou who keepest in Thy ken
The times of flowers, the dooms of men,
Stretch out a mighty wing above—
Be tender to the land we love!

If all the huddlers from the storm
Have found her hearthstone wide and warm;
If she has made men free and glad,
Sharing, with all, the good she had;
If she has blown the very dust
From her bright balance to be just,
Oh, spread a mighty wing above—
Be tender to the land we love.

When in the dark eternal tower
The star-clock strikes her trial hour,
And for her help no more avail
Her sea-blue shield, her mountain mail,
But sweeping wide, from Gulf to Lakes,
The battle on her forehead breaks,
Throw Thou a thunderous wing above—
Be lightning for the land we love!

Wendell Phillips Stafford, 1861–

1696. GOD BLESS OUR NATIVE LAND

God bless our native land;
Firm may she ever stand
Through storm and night:
When the wild tempests rave,
Ruler of wind and wave,
Thou who art strong to save,
Be Thou her might!

For her our prayer shall be,
Our fathers' God, to Thee,
On Whom we wait:
Be her walls, holiness,
Her rulers, righteousness,
In all her homes be peace,
God save the State!

Not for this land alone,
But be God's mercies shown
From shore to shore;
And may the nations see
That men should brothers be,
And form one family
The wide world o'er.

Siegfried A. Mahlmann, 1771–1826;
William E. Hickson, 1803–1870

1697. LORD, WHILE FOR ALL MANKIND WE PRAY

Lord, while for all mankind we pray,
Of every clime and coast,
O hear us for our native land,
The land we love the most.

O guard our shores from every foe;
With peace our borders bless;
With prosp'rous times our cities crown,
Our fields with plenteousness.

Unite us in the sacred love
Of knowledge, truth, and Thee,
And let our hills and valleys shout
The songs of liberty.

Lord of the nations, thus to Thee
Our country we commend;
Be Thou her refuge and her trust,
Her everlasting friend.

John R. Wreford, 1800–1881

1698. O GOD, HEAR THOU THE NATION'S PRAYER

O God, hear Thou the nation's prayer,
We lift our cause to Thee;
We wage the holy war of Christ;
We fight to make men free.

Give us to build our cities pure,
Salvation throned above,
To shelter lowly homes from ill,
And tune our mills with love.

Give us to guide the alien feet,
To teach the brother's way,
To save our motherhood from need;
To guard our children's play.

May visions call and faith enflame,
And banish lust and greed;
Make Thou America to be
A land of soulful deed.

Irving Maurer, 1879–1942

1699. GOD OF A UNIVERSE WITHIN WHOSE BOUNDS

God of a universe within whose bounds
Thy vast creation moves in ordered space;
Sons of a nation born of faith and wounds,
We seek from Thee our true appointed place.

Within Thy purpose, through the ages' span,
We would discern our country's destined role:
In all our councils, man with brother man,
We would obey the law of love's control.

By all the grief man's strife with man entails,
By all the woe that stalks oppression's train,
By Thy great sacrifice which still prevails,
Free us from lust for all unworthy gain.

So shall we deal in justice like to Thine;
So shall the love of mercy light our land,
Marking the footprints of the Love Divine,
Where we walk humbly, guided by Thy hand.

Lead us into the light that shines from Thee
For all mankind; for ne'er shall it fulfill
Its pure effulgence till all men are free,
Free through the truth which is th' eternal will.

Katharine L. Aller, contemporary American

1700. From THE COMING AMERICAN

Bring me men to match my mountains,
Bring me men to match my plains—
Men with empires in their purpose
And new eras in their brains.
Bring me men to match my prairies,
Men to match my inland seas,
Men whose thought shall prove a highway
Up to ampler destinies,
Pioneers to clear thought's marshlands
And to cleanse old error's fen;
Bring me men to match my mountains—
Bring me men!

Bring me men to match my forests,
Strong to fight the storm and blast,
Branching toward the skyey future,
Rooted in the fertile past.
Bring me men to match my valleys,
Tolerant of sun and snow,
Men within whose fruitful purpose
Time's consummate blooms shall grow,

Men to tame the tigerish instincts
  Of the lair and cave and den,
Cleanse the dragon slime of nature—
  Bring me men!

Bring me men to match my rivers,
  Continent cleavers, flowing free,
Drawn by the eternal madness
  To be mingled with the sea;

Men of oceanic impulse,
  Men whose moral currents sweep
Towards the wide-infolding ocean
  Of an undiscovered deep;
Men who feel the strong pulsation
  Of the Central Sea, and then
Time their currents to its earth throb—
  Bring me men!

Sam Walter Foss, 1858–1911

1701. THE PRESENT CRISIS

When a deed is done for Freedom, through the broad earth's aching breast
Runs a thrill of joy prophetic, trembling on from east to west,
And the slave, where'er he cowers, feels the soul within him climb
To the awful verge of manhood, as the energy sublime
Of a century bursts full-blossomed on the thorny stem of Time.

Through the walls of hut and palace shoots the instantaneous throe,
When the travail of the Ages wrings earth's systems to and fro;
At the birth of each new Era, with a recognizing start,
Nation wildly looks at nation, standing with mute lips apart,
And glad Truth's yet mightier man-child leaps beneath the Future's heart.

So the Evil's triumph sendeth, with a terror and a chill,
Under continent to continent, the sense of coming ill,
And the slave, where'er he cowers, feels his sympathies with God
In hot tear-drops ebbing earthward, to be drunk up by the sod,
Till a corpse crawls round unburied, delving in the nobler clod.

For mankind are one in spirit, and an instinct bears along,
Round the earth's electric circle, the swift flash of right or wrong;
Whether conscious or unconscious, yet Humanity's vast frame
Through its ocean-sundered fibres feels the gush of joy or shame;—
In the gain or loss of one race all the rest have equal claim.

Once to every man and nation comes the moment to decide;
In the strife of Truth with Falsehood, for the good or evil side;
Some great cause, God's new Messiah, offering each the bloom or blight,
Parts the goats upon the left hand and the sheep upon the right,
And the choice goes by forever 'twixt that darkness and that light.

Hast thou chosen, O my people, on whose party thou shalt stand,
Ere the Doom from its worn sandals shakes the dust against our land?
Though the cause of Evil prosper, yet 'tis Truth alone is strong,
And, albeit she wander outcast now, I see around her throng
Troops of beautiful, tall angels, to enshield her from all wrong.

Backward look across the ages and the beacon-moments see,
That, like peaks of some sunk continent, jut through Oblivion's sea;
Not an ear in court or market for the low foreboding cry
Of those Crises, God's stern winnowers, from whose feet earth's chaff must fly;
Never shows the choice momentous till the judgment hath passed by.

Careless seems the great Avenger; history's pages but record
One death-grapple in the darkness 'twixt old systems and the Word;
Truth forever on the scaffold, Wrong forever on the throne,—
Yet that scaffold sways the future, and, behind the dim unknown,
Standeth God within the shadow, keeping watch above his own.

We see dimly in the Present what is small and what is great,
Slow of faith how weak an arm may turn the iron helm of fate,
But the soul is still oracular; amid the market's din,
List the ominous stern whisper from the Delphic cave within,—
"They enslave their children's children who make compromise with sin."

Slavery, the earth-born Cyclops, fellest of the giant brood,
Sons of brutish Force and Darkness, who have drenched the earth with blood,
Famished in his self-made desert, blinded by our purer day,
Gropes in yet unblasted regions for his miserable prey;—
Shall we guide his gory fingers where our helpless children play?

Then to side with Truth is noble when we share her wretched crust,
Ere her cause bring fame and profit, and 'tis prosperous to be just;
Then it is the brave man chooses, while the coward stands aside,
Doubting in his abject spirit, till his Lord is crucified,
And the multitude make virtue of the faith they had denied.

Count me o'er earth's chosen heroes,—they were souls that stood alone,
While the men they agonized for hurled the contumelious stone,
Stood serene, and down the future saw the golden beam incline
To the side of perfect justice, mastered by their faith divine,
By one man's plain truth to manhood and to God's supreme design.

By the light of burning heretics Christ's bleeding feet I track,
Toiling up new Calvaries ever with the cross that turns not back,
And these mounts of anguish number how each generation learned
One new word of that grand *Credo* which in prophet-hearts hath burned
Since the first man stood God-conquered with his face to heaven upturned.

For humanity sweeps onward: where to-day the martyr stands,
On the morrow crouches Judas with the silver in his hands;
Far in front the cross stands ready and the crackling fagots burn,
While the hooting mob of yesterday in silent awe return
To glean up the scattered ashes into History's golden urn.

'Tis as easy to be heroes as to sit the idle slaves
Of a legendary virtue carved upon our fathers' graves,
Worshippers of light ancestral make the present light a crime;—
Was the Mayflower launched by cowards, steered by men behind their time?
Turn those tracks toward Past or Future, that make Plymouth Rock sublime?

They were men of present valor, stalwart old iconoclasts,
Unconvinced by axe or gibbet that all virtue was the Past's;
But we make their truth our falsehood thinking that hath made us free,
Hoarding it in mouldy parchments, while our tender spirits flee
The rude grasp of that great Impulse which drove them across the sea.

They have rights who dare maintain them; we are traitors to our sires,
Smothering in their holy ashes Freedom's new-lit altar-fires;
Shall we make their creed our jailer? Shall we, in our haste to slay,
From the tombs of the old prophets steal the funeral lamps away
To light up the martyr-fagots round the prophets of to-day?

New occasions teach new duties; Time makes ancient good uncouth;
They must upward still, and onward, who would keep abreast of Truth:
Lo, before us gleam her camp-fires! we ourselves must Pilgrims be,
Launch our Mayflower, and steer boldly through the desperate winter sea,
Nor attempt the Future's portal with the Past's blood-rusted key.

James Russell Lowell, 1819–1891

1702. WASHINGTON

From The "Commemoration Ode"
World's Exposition, Chicago, 1892

When dreaming kings, at odds with swift-paced time,
Would strike that banner down,
A nobler knight than ever writ or rhyme
With fame's bright wreath did crown
Through armed hosts bore it till it floated high
Beyond the clouds, a light that cannot die!
Ah, hero of our younger race!
Great builder of a temple new!
Ruler, who sought no lordly place!
Warrior, who sheathed the sword he drew!
Lover of men, who saw afar
A world unmarred by want or war,
Who knew the path, and yet forbore
To tread, till all men should implore;
Who saw the light, and led the way
Where the gray world might greet the day;
Father and leader, prophet sure,
Whose will in vast works shall endure,
How shall we praise him on this day of days,
Great son of fame who has no need of praise?

How shall we praise him? Open wide the doors
Of the fair temple whose broad base he laid.
Through its white halls a shadowy cavalcade
Of heroes moves o'er unresounding floors—
Men whose brawned arms upraised these columns high,
And reared the towers that vanish in the sky,—
The strong who, having wrought, can never die.

Harriet Monroe, 1861–1936

1703. GEORGE WASHINGTON

Washington, the brave, the wise, the good.
Supreme in war, in council, and in peace.
Valiant without ambition, discreet without fear, confident without presumption.
In disaster, calm; in success, moderate; in all, himself.
The hero, the patriot, the Christian.

The father of nations, the friend of mankind,
Who, when he had won all, renounced all, and sought in the bosom of his family and of nature, retirement, and in the hope of religion, immortality.

Inscription at Mount Vernon

1704. From LINCOLN, THE MAN OF THE PEOPLE[1]

The color of the ground was in him, the red earth;
The smack and tang of elemental things:
The rectitude and patience of the cliff;
The good-will of the rain that loves all leaves;
The friendly welcome of the wayside well;
The courage of the bird that dares the sea;
The gladness of the wind that shakes the corn;
The pity of the snow that hides all scars;
The secrecy of streams that make their way
Under the mountain to the rifted rock;
The tolerance and equity of light
That gives as freely to the shrinking flower
As to the great oak flaring to the wind—
To the grave's low hill as to the Matterhorn
That shoulders out the sky.

❖

So came the Captain with the mighty heart.
And when the judgment thunders split the house,
Wrenching the rafters from their ancient rest,
He held the ridgepole up, and spiked again
The rafters of the Home. He held his place—
Held the long purpose like a growing tree—
Held on through blame and faltered not at praise—
Towering in calm rough-hewn sublimity.
And when he fell in whirlwind, he went down
As when a lordly cedar, green with boughs,
Goes down with a great shout upon the hills,
And leaves a lonesome place against the sky.

Edwin Markham, 1852–1940

1705. ABRAHAM LINCOLN WALKS AT MIDNIGHT[2]

(In Springfield, Illinois)

It is portentous, and a thing of state
That here at midnight, in our little town
A mourning figure walks, and will not rest,
Near the old court-house pacing up and down.

Or by his homestead, or in shadowed yards,
He lingers where his children used to play,
Or through the market, on the well-worn stones
He stalks until the dawn-stars burn away.

A bronzed, lank man! His suit of ancient black,
A famous high top-hat and plain worn shawl
Make him the quaint great figure that men love,
The prairie-lawyer, master of us all.

He cannot sleep upon his hillside now.
He is among us:—as in times before!
And we who toss and lie awake for long
Breathe deep, and start, to see him pass the door.

His head is bowed. He thinks on men and kings.
Yea, when the sick world cries, how can he sleep?
Too many peasants fight, they know not why,
Too many homesteads in black terror weep.

The sins of all the war-lords burn his heart.
He sees the dreadnaughts scouring every main.
He carries on his shawl-wrapped shoulders now
The bitterness, the folly and the pain.

He cannot rest until a spirit-dawn
Shall come; the shining hope of Europe free;
The league of sober folk, the Workers' Earth,
Bringing long peace to Cornland, Alp and Sea.

It breaks his heart that kings must murder still,
That all his hours of travail here for men
Seem yet in vain. And who will bring white peace
That he may sleep upon his hill again?

Vachel Lindsay, 1879–1931

[1] Selected from more than two hundred tributes to the martyr-President and read at the dedication ceremonies of the Lincoln Memorial at Washington, D. C., May 30, 1922.
[2] Written during World War I.

1706. O CAPTAIN! MY CAPTAIN!

IN MEMORY OF ABRAHAM LINCOLN

O Captain! my Captain! our fearful trip is done;
The ship has weathered every rack, the prize we sought is won;
The port is near, the bells I hear, the people all exulting,
While follow eyes the steady keel, the vessel grim and daring:
    But O heart! heart! heart!
      O the bleeding drops of red,
    Where on the deck my Captain lies,
      Fallen cold and dead.

O Captain! my Captain! rise up and hear the bells;
Rise up—for you the flag is flung—for you the bugle trills;
For you bouquets and ribbon'd wreaths—for you the shores a-crowding;
For you they call, the swaying mass, their eager faces turning;
    Here Captain! dear father!
      This arm beneath your head;
        It is some dream that on the deck,
          You've fallen cold and dead.

My Captain does not answer, his lips are pale and still;
My father does not feel my arm, he has no pulse nor will;
The ship is anchor'd safe and sound, its voyage closed and done;
From fearful trip, the victor ship, comes in with object won:
    Exult, O shores, and ring, O bells!
      But I, with mournful tread,
    Walk the deck my Captain lies,
      Fallen cold and dead.

Walt Whitman, 1819–1892

1707. THE GETTYSBURG ADDRESS

At the Dedication of the National Cemetery, November 19, 1863

Fourscore and seven years ago, our fathers brought forth upon this continent a new nation,
Conceived in liberty, and dedicated to the proposition that all men are created equal.

Now we are engaged in a great civil war, testing whether that nation, or any nation, so conceived and so dedicated, can long endure.
We are met on a great battlefield of that war.
We have come to dedicate a portion of that field as a final resting place for those who here gave their lives that that nation might live.
It is altogether fitting and proper that we should do this.

But in a larger sense we cannot dedicate, we cannot consecrate, we cannot hallow this ground.
The brave men, living and dead, who struggled here, have consecrated it far above our poor power to add or to detract.
The world will little note nor long remember what we say here,
But it can never forget what they did here.

It is for us, the living, rather, to be dedicated here to the unfinished work which they who fought here have thus far so nobly advanced.
It is rather for us to be here dedicated to the great task remaining before us;
That from these honored dead we take increased devotion to that cause for which they gave the last full measure of devotion;
That we here highly resolve that these dead shall not have died in vain;
That this nation, under God, shall have a new birth of freedom;
And that government of the people, by the people, and for the people,
Shall not perish from the earth.

Abraham Lincoln, 1809–1865

1708. LINCOLN

A martyred Saint, he lies upon his bier,
While, with one heart, the kneeling nation weeps,
Until across the world the knowledge sweeps
That every sad and sacrificial tear
Waters the seed, to patriot mourners dear,
That flowers in love of Country. He who reaps
The gift of martyrdom forever keeps
His soul in love of man, and God's own fear.
Great Prototype benign of Brotherhood—
Incarnate of the One who walked the shore
Of lonely lakes in distant Galilee;
With patient purpose undismayed he stood,
Steadfast and unafraid, and calmly bore
A Nation's Cross to a new Calvary!

Corinne Roosevelt Robinson, 1861–1933

1709. WITH MALICE TOWARD NONE

From the Second Inaugural Address, March 4, 1865

With malice toward none;
With charity for all;
With firmness in the right, as God gives us to see the right,
Let us strive on to finish the work we are in;
To bind up the nation's wounds;
To care for him who shall have borne the battle,
And for his widow,
And his orphan—
To do all which may achieve and cherish a just and lasting peace among ourselves,
And with all nations.

Abraham Lincoln, 1809–1865

1710. THE BULWARK OF LIBERTY

What constitutes the bulwark of our own liberty and independence?
It is not our frowning battlements, our bristling seacoast, our army and our navy.
Our reliance is in the love of liberty which God has planted in us.

Our defense is in the spirit which prizes liberty as the heritage of all men in all lands everywhere.
Destroy this spirit, and we have planted the seeds of despotism at our own doors.

Abraham Lincoln, 1809–1865

1711. From LINCOLN PORTRAIT

"Fellow citizens, we cannot escape history."
That is what he said,
That is what Abraham Lincoln said:
"Fellow citizens, we cannot escape history.
"We of this Congress and this administration will be remembered
in spite of ourselves. No personal significance or insignificance
can spare one or another of us.
"The fiery trial through which we pass will light us down,
in honor or dishonor, to the latest generation.
We—even here—hold the power and bear the responsibility."

He was born in Kentucky, raised in Indiana, and lived in Illinois.
This is what he said:
This is what Abe Lincoln said:
"The dogmas of the quiet past are inadequate to the stormy present.
The occasion is piled high with difficulty,
and we must rise with the occasion.
As our cause is new, so we must think anew and act anew.
We must disenthrall ourselves, and then we shall save our country."

When standing erect he was six feet four inches tall.
And this is what he said: he said:
"It is the eternal struggle between two principles—
right and wrong throughout the world. . . .
It is the same spirit that says:
'You toil and work and earn bread and I'll eat it.'
No matter in what shape it comes,
whether from the mouth of a king who seeks
to bestride the people in his own nation and live
by the fruit of their labor, or from one race of men
as an apology for enslaving another race,
it is the same tyrannical principle."
Lincoln was a quiet man.

Abe Lincoln was a quiet and a melancholy man.
But when he spoke of democracy,
This is what he said: he said:
"As I would not be a slave, so I would not be a master.
This expresses my idea of democracy.
Whatever differs from this, to the extent of the difference,
is no democracy."

Abraham Lincoln, sixteenth President of these United States,
is everlasting in the memory of his countrymen,
for on the battleground at Gettysburg, this is what he said:
This is what Abe Lincoln said:

"That from these honored dead we take increased devotion
to that cause for which they gave the last full
measure of devotion:
that we here highly resolve that these dead
shall not have died in vain: that this nation, under God,
shall have a new birth of freedom;
and that the government of the people, by the people,
for the people, shall not perish from the earth."

Material assembled by Aaron Copland, 1900–

1712. TRUE WORK IS WORSHIP

From "The Angelus"

For each true deed is worship; it is prayer,
And carries its own answer unaware.
Yes, they whose feet upon good errands run
Are friends of God, with Michael of the sun;
Yes, each accomplished service of the day
Paves for the feet of God a lordlier way.
The souls that love and labor through all wrong,
They clasp His hand and make the Circle strong;
They lay the deep foundation stone by stone,
And build into Eternity God's throne!

Edwin Markham, 1852–1940

1713. GLORY TO THEM

Glory to them, the toilers of the earth,
Who wrought with knotted hands, in wood and stone,
Dreams their unlettered minds could not give birth
And symmetries their souls had never known.
Glory to them, the artisans, who spread
Cathedrals like brown lace before the sun,
Who could not build a rhyme, but reared instead
The Doric grandeur of the Parthenon.

I never cross a marble portico,
Or lift my eyes where stained glass windows steal
From virgin sunlight moods of deeper glow,
Or walk dream-peopled streets, except to feel
A hush of reverence for that vast dead
Who gave us beauty for a crust of bread.

Anderson M. Scruggs, 1897–

1714. From GITANJALI

10

Here is thy footstool and there rest thy feet where live the poorest, and lowliest, and lost.

When I try to bow to thee, my obeisance cannot reach down to the depth where thy feet rest among the poorest, and lowliest, and lost.

Pride can never approach to where thou walkest in the clothes of the humble among the poorest, and lowliest, and lost.
My heart can never find its way to where thou keepest company with the companionless among the poorest, the lowliest, and the lost.

II

Leave this chanting and singing and telling of beads!
Whom dost thou worship in this dark corner of a temple with doors all shut?
Open thine eyes and see thy God is not before thee!
He is there where the tiller is tilling the hard ground and where the path-maker is breaking stones. He is with them in sun and in shower, and his garment is covered with dust. Put off thy holy mantle and even like him come down on the dusty soil!
Deliverance? Where is this deliverance to be found? Our master himself has joyfully taken upon him the bonds of creation; he is bound with us all forever.

Come out of thy meditations and leave aside thy flowers and incense! What harm is there if thy clothes become tattered and stained? Meet him and stand by him in toil and in the sweat of thy brow.

Rabindranath Tagore, 1861–1941

1715. LABOR

From "A Glance Behind The Curtain"

No man is born into the world whose work
Is not born with him; there is always work,
And tools to work withal, for those who will;
And blessèd are the horny hands of toil!

James Russell Lowell, 1819–189-

1716. THE SACRAMENT OF WORK

Upon thy bended knees, thank God for work,—
Work—once man's penance, now his high reward!
For work to do, and strength to do the work,
We thank Thee, Lord!

Since outcast Adam toiled to make a home,
The primal curse a blessing has become,
Man in his toil finds recompense for loss,
A workless world had known nor Christ nor Cross.

Some toil for love, and some for simple greed,
Some reap a harvest past their utmost need,
More, in their less find truer happiness,
And all, in work, relief from bitterness.

Upon thy bended knees, thank God for work!
In workless days all ills and evils lurk.
For work to do, and strength to do the work,
We thank Thee, Lord!

John Oxenham, 1852–1941

1717. WHEN THROUGH THE WHIRL OF WHEELS

When through the whirl of wheels, and engines humming,
Patiently powerful for the sons of men,
Peals like a trumpet promise of His coming,
Who in the clouds is pledged to come again;

When through the night the furnace fires a-flaring,
Shooting out tongues of flame like leaping blood,
Speak to the heart of Love, alive and daring,
Sing of the boundless energy of God;

When in the depths the patient miner striving,
Feels in his arms the vigor of the Lord,
Strikes for a kingdom and his King's arriving,
Holding his pick more splendid than the sword;

When on the sweat of labor and its sorrow,
Toiling in twilight flickering and dim,
Flames out the sunshine of the great tomorrow,
When all the world looks up because of Him—

Then will He come with meekness for His glory,
God in a workman's jacket as before,
Living again th' eternal gospel story,
Sweeping the shavings from His work-shop floor.

G. A. Studdert-Kennedy, 1883–1929

1718. WORK

From "The Three Best Things"

Let me but do my work from day to day
  In field or forest, at the desk or loom,
  In roaring market-place or tranquil room;
Let me but find it in my heart to say,
When vagrant wishes beckon me astray,
  "This is my work; my blessing, not my doom;
  Of all who live, I am the one by whom
This work can best be done in the right way."

Then shall I see it not too great, nor small,
  To suit my spirit and to prove my powers;
  Then shall I cheerful greet the labouring hours,
And cheerful turn, when the long shadows fall
At eventide, to play and love and rest,
Because I know for me my work is best.

Henry van Dyke, 1852–1933

1719. THANKSGIVING DAY

  We give Thee thanks, O Lord!
Not for the armed legions, marching in their might,
Not for the glory of the well-earned fight

Where brave men slay their brothers also brave;
But for the millions of Thy sons who work—
And do Thy task with joy,—and never shirk,
And deem the idle man a burdened slave:
For these, O Lord, our thanks!

We give Thee thanks, O Lord!
Not for the turrets of our men-of-war—
The monstrous guns, and deadly steel they pour
To crush our foes and make them bow the knee;
But for the homely sailors of Thy deep,
The tireless fisher-folk who banish sleep
And lure a living from the miser sea:
For these, O Lord, our thanks!

We give Thee thanks, O Lord!
Not for the mighty men who pile up gold,
Not for the phantom millions, bought and sold,
And all the arrogance of pomp and greed;
But for the pioneers who plow the field,
Make deserts blossom, and the mountain yield
Its hidden treasures for man's daily need:
For these, O Lord, our thanks!

We give Thee thanks, O Lord!
Not for the palaces that wealth has grown,
Where ease is worshipped—duty dimly known,
And pleasure leads her dance the flowery way;
But for the quiet homes where love is queen
And life is more than baubles, touched and seen,
And old folks bless us, and dear children play:
For these, O Lord, our thanks!

Robert Bridges, 1844–1930

1720. HARVEST HOME

Come, ye thankful people, come,
Raise the song of harvest home:
All is safely gathered in,
Ere the winter storms begin;
God, our Maker, doth provide
For our wants to be supplied:
Come to God's own temple, come,
Raise the song of harvest home.

All the world is God's own field,
Fruit unto His praise to yield;
Wheat and tares together sown,
Unto joy or sorrow grown;
First the blade, and then the ear,
Then the full corn shall appear:
Lord of harvest, grant that we
Wholesome grain and pure may be.

For the Lord our God shall come,
And shall take His harvest home;
From His field shall in that day
All offenses purge away;
Give His angels charge at last
In the fire the tares to cast;
But the fruitful ears to store
In His garner evermore.

Even so, Lord, quickly come
To Thy final harvest home;
Gather Thou Thy people in,
Free from sorrow, free from sin;
There, for ever purified,
In Thy presence to abide:
Come, with all Thine angels, come,
Raise the glorious harvest home.

Henry Alford, 1810–1871

1721. THE PEOPLE'S THANKSGIVING

Not alone for mighty empire,
 Stretching far o'er land and sea,
Not alone for bounteous harvests,
 Lift we up our hearts to Thee:
Standing in the living present,
 Memory and hope between,
Lord, we would with deep thanksgiving
 Praise Thee more for things unseen.

Not for battle-ship and fortress,
 Not for conquests of the sword,
But for conquests of the spirit
 Give we thanks to Thee, O Lord;
For the heritage of freedom,
 For the home, the church, the school,
For the open door to manhood
 In a land the people rule.

For the armies of the faithful,
 Lives that passed and left no name;
For the glory that illumines
 Patriot souls of deathless fame;
For the people's prophet-leaders,
 Loyal to Thy living word,—
For all heroes of the spirit,
 Give we thanks to Thee, O Lord.

God of justice, save the people
 From the war of race and creed,
From the strife of class and faction,—
 Make our nation free indeed;
Keep her faith in simple manhood
 Strong as when her life began,
Till it find its full fruition
 In the brotherhood of man!

William Pierson Merrill, 1867-

1722. MORE LIGHT SHALL BREAK FROM OUT THY WORD[1]

"The Lord hath more truth and light yet to break forth out of His Holy Word."—Pastor Robinson's farewell to the Mayflower Pilgrims.

More light shall break from out Thy Word
 For Pilgrim followers of the Gleam,
Till, led by Thy free spirit, Lord,
 We see and share the Pilgrim dream!

What mighty hopes are in our care,
 What holy dreams of Brotherhood:
God of our Fathers, help us dare
 Their passion for the Common Good.

Wild roars the blast, the storm is high;
 Above the storm are shining still
The lights by which we live and die;
 Our peace is ever in Thy Will.

The ancient stars, the ancient faith,
 Defend us till our voyage is done;
Across the floods of fear and death
 The Mayflower still is sailing on.

Allen Eastman Cross, 1864–1943

[1] Written for the Pilgrim Tercentenary, 1920.

1723. THE PILGRIM FATHERS

O God, beneath Thy guiding hand
 Our exiled fathers crossed the sea;
And when they trod the wintry strand,
 With prayer and psalm they worshipped Thee.

Thou heard'st, well pleased, the song, the prayer:
 Thy blessing came; and still its power
Shall onward through all ages bear
 The memory of that holy hour.

Laws, freedom, truth, and faith in God
 Came with those exiles o'er the waves;
And where their pilgrim feet have trod,
 The God they trusted guards their graves.

And here Thy name, O, God of love,
 Their children's children shall adore,
Till these eternal hills remove,
 And spring adorns the earth no more.

Leonard Bacon, 1802–1881

1724. LANDING OF THE PILGRIM FATHERS

The breaking waves dashed high
 On a stern and rockbound coast,
And the woods against a stormy sky
 Their giant branches tossed;

And the heavy night hung dark
 The hills and waters o'er,
When a band of exiles moored their bark
 On the wild New England shore.

Not as the conqueror comes,
  They, the truehearted, came;
Not with roll of stirring drums,
  And the trumpet that sings of fame;

Not as the flying come,
  In silence and in fear—
They shook the depths of the desert's gloom
  With their hymns of lofty cheer. . . .

❖

What sought they thus afar?
  Bright jewels of the mine?
The wealth of seas? the spoils of war?
  They sought a faith's pure shrine!

Aye, call it holy ground,
  The soil where first they trod:
They have left unstained what there they found—
  Freedom to worship God!

Felicia Hemans, 1793–1835

1725. MEMORIAL DAY

From out our crowded calendar
  One day we pluck to give;
It is the day the Dying pause
  To honor those who live.

McLandburgh Wilson

1726. PRAISE OF FAMOUS MEN

Ecclesiasticus 44: 1–10, 14

Let us now praise famous men,
And our fathers that begat us.

The Lord manifested in them great glory,
Even his mighty power from the beginning.

Such as did bear rule in their kingdoms,
And were men renowned for their power,

Giving counsel by their understanding,
Such as have brought tidings in prophecies:

Leaders of the people by their counsels,
And by their understanding men of learning for the people;
Wise were their words in their instruction:

Such as sought out musical tunes,
And set forth verses in writing:

Rich men, furnished with ability,
Living peaceably in their habitations:

All these were honoured in their generations,
And were a glory in their day.

There be of them, that have left a name behind them,
To declare their praises.

And some there be, which have no memorial;
Who are perished as though they had not been born;
And their children after them.

But these were men of mercy,
Whose righteous deeds have not been forgotten. . . .
Their bodies were buried in peace,
And their name liveth to all generations.

From the Hebrew, 1st century B.C.

1727. MEMORIAL DAY

Is it enough to think to-day
Of all our brave, then put away
The thought until a year has sped?
Is this full honor for our dead?

Is it enough to sing a song
And deck a grave; and all year long
Forget the brave who died that we
Might keep our great land proud and free?

Full service needs a greater toll—
That we who live give heart and soul
To keep the land they died to save,
And be ourselves, in turn, the brave!

Annette Wynne, contemporary American

1728. FLOWER-STREWN GRAVES

Breathe balmy airs, ye fragrant flowers,
O'er every silent sleeper's head;
Ye crystal dews and summer showers,
Dress in fresh green each lowly bed.

Strew loving offerings o'er the brave,
Their country's joy, their country's pride;
For us their precious lives they gave,
For Freedom's sacred cause they died.

Long, where on glory's fields they fell,
May Freedom's spotless banner wave,
And fragrant tributes grateful tell
Where live the free, where sleep the brave.

Samuel F. Smith, 1808–1895

1729. MEMORIAL DAY

"Dulce et decorum est"

The bugle echoes shrill and sweet,
  But not of war it sings to-day.
The road is rhythmic with the feet
  Of men-at-arms who come to pray.

The roses blossom white and red
  On tombs where weary soldiers lie;
Flags wave above the honored dead
  And martial music cleaves the sky.

Above their wreath-strewn graves we kneel,
  They kept the faith and fought the fight.
Through flying lead and crimson steel
  They plunged for Freedom and the Right.

May we, their grateful children, learn
  Their strength, who lie beneath this sod,
Who went through fire and death to earn
  At last the accolade of God.

In shining rank on rank arrayed
  They march, the legions of the Lord;
He is their Captain unafraid,
  The Prince of Peace . . . Who brought a sword.

Joyce Kilmer,[1] *1886–1918*

1730. MEMORIAL DAY

I heard a cry in the night from a far-flung host,
From a host that sleeps through the years the last long sleep,
By the Meuse, by the Marne, in the Argonne's shattered wood,
In a thousand rose-thronged churchyards through our land.
Sleeps! Do they sleep! I know I heard their cry,
Shrilling along the night like a trumpet blast:
"We died," they cried, "for a dream. Have ye forgot?
We dreamed of a world reborn whence wars had fled,
Where swords were broken in pieces and guns were rust,
Where the poor man dwelt in quiet, the rich in peace,
And children played in the streets, joyous and free.
We thought we could sleep content in a task well done;
But the rumble of guns rolls over us, iron upon iron
Sounds from the forge where are fashioned guns anew;

"New fleets spring up in new seas, and under the wave
Stealthy new terrors swarm, with emboweled death.
Fresh cries of hate ring out loud from the demagogue's throat,
While greed reaches out afresh to grasp new lands.
Have we died in vain? Is our dream denied?
You men who live on the earth we bought with our woe,
Will ye stand idly by while they shape new wars,
Or will ye rise, who are strong, to fulfill our dream,
To silence the demagogue's voice, to crush the fools
Who play with blood-stained toys that crowd new graves?
We call, we call in the night, will ye hear and heed?"

In the name of our dead will we hear? Will we grant them sleep?

William E. Brooks, 1875–

[1] Killed serving with American Army, World War I

1731. NINETEEN TWENTY-SIX

How shall we keep it—
This power we have gained?
"With steel-lipped guns
And with men well trained,
With wave-smashing battleships,
With wind-smashing aircraft,
Red rum on our hips,
Battle-songs on our lips:
That's the way we'll keep it,"
The War Men laughed.

But the world is heavy
With a dead, cold host
Who died sword-weary,
Who died gun-weary,
Who died ere their time
To the deep, dull rhyme
Of the War Man's boast

These did not keep it—
The power they had gained
With full-throated gun-song,
Blood-spouting bayonets
And men well trained:
These did not keep it—
The power they had gained.

And here we stand,
NINETEEN TWENTY-SIX.
Hemmed in with steel guns
And full of the old tricks;
Holding here a hand-grenade,
Holding there a crucifix.

Wilson MacDonald, 1880–

1732. WORD TO A DICTATOR

So by your edict Christ once more lies slain
And buried in a tortured people's brain.
But you remember only Calvary;
Doubt not that Easter, too, will come again.

Adelaide Love, contemporary American

1733. AFTER BATTLE

From "The Bhagavad-Gîtâ"

Better to live on beggar's bread
With those we love alive,
Than taste their blood in rich feasts spread,
And guiltily survive!
Ah! were it worst—who knows?—to be
Victor or vanquished here,
When those confront us angrily
Whose death leaves living drear?

From the Sanskrit;
tr. by Edwin Arnold, 1832–1904

1734. THE PEACEMAKER[1]

Upon his will he binds a radiant chain,
For Freedom's sake he is no longer free.
It is his task, the slave of Liberty,
With his own blood to wipe away a stain.
That pain may cease, he yields his flesh to pain.
To banish war, he must a warrior be,
He dwells in Night, eternal Dawn to see,
And gladly dies, abundant life to gain.

What matters Death, if Freedom be not dead?
No flags are fair, if Freedom's flag be furled.
Who fights for Freedom, goes with joyful tread
To meet the fires of Hell against him hurled,
And had for Captain Him whose thorn-wreathed head
Smiles from the Cross upon a conquered world.

Joyce Kilmer, 1886–1918

1735. "ICI REPOSE"

A little cross of weather-silvered wood,
Hung with a garish wreath of tinselled wire,
And on it carved a legend—thus it runs:
"*Ici repose*—" Add what name you will,
And multiply by thousands: in the fields,
Along the roads, beneath the trees—one here,
A dozen there, to each its simple tale
Of one more jewel threaded star-like on
The sacrificial rosary of France.

And as I read and read again those words,
Those simple words, they took a mystic sense;
And from the glamour of an alien tongue
They wove insistent music in my brain,
Which, in a twilight hour, when all the guns
Were silent, shaped itself to song.

[1] His last poem, written on the battlefield in France shortly before his death.

O happy dead! who sleep embalmed in glory,
Safe from corruption, purified by fire,—
Ask you our pity?—ours, mud-grimed and gory,
Who still must grimly strive, grimly desire?

You have outrun the reach of our endeavour,
Have flown beyond our most exalted quest,—
Who prate of Faith and Freedom, knowing ever
That all we really fight for's just—a rest,

The rest that only Victory can bring us—
Or Death, which throws us brother-like by you—
The civil commonplace in which 'twill fling us
To neutralize our then too martial hue.

But you have rest from every tribulation
Even in the midst of war; you sleep serene,
Pinnacled on the sorrow of a nation,
In cerements of sacrificial sheen.

Oblivion cannot claim you: our heroic
War-lustred moment, as our youth, will pass
To swell the dusty hoard of Time the Stoic,
That gathers cobwebs in the nether glass.

We shall grow old, and tainted with the rotten
Effluvia of the peace we fought to win,
The bright deeds of our youth will be forgotten,
Effaced by later failure, sloth, or sin;

But you have conquered Time, and sleep forever,
Like gods, with a white halo on your brows—
Your souls our lode-stars, your death-crowned endeavour
The spur that holds the nations to their vows.

Bernard Freeman Trotter,[1] 1890–1917

1736. FOR THE FALLEN

With proud thanksgiving, a mother for her children,
England mourns for her dead across the sea.
Flesh of her flesh they were, spirit of her spirit,
Fallen in the cause of the free.

Solemn the drums thrill: Death august and royal
Sings sorrow up into immortal spheres.
There is music in the midst of desolation
And a glory that shines upon our tears.

They went with songs to the battle, they were young,
Straight of limb, true of eye, steady and aglow.
They were staunch to the end against odds uncounted,
They fell with their faces to the foe.

They shall grow not old, as we that are left grow old:
Age shall not weary them, nor the years condemn.
At the going down of the sun and in the morning
We will remember them.

They mingle not with their laughing comrades again;
They sit no more at familiar tables of home;
They have no lot in our labour of the day-time:
They sleep beyond England's foam.

But where our desires are and our hopes profound,
Felt as a well-spring that is hidden from sight,

[1] His last poem, the manuscript of which reached his parents the day after he was killed in France.

To the innermost heart of their own land they are known
As the stars are known to the Night;

As the stars that shall be bright when we are dust
Moving in marches upon the heavenly plain,
As the stars that are starry in the time of our darkness,
To the end, to the end, they remain.

Laurence Binyon, 1869–1943

1737. THE SPIRES OF OXFORD

I saw the spires of Oxford
As I was passing by,
The gray spires of Oxford
Against the pearl-gray sky.
My heart was with the Oxford men
Who went abroad to die.

The years go fast in Oxford,
The golden years and gay,
The hoary Colleges look down
On careless boys at play.
But when the bugles sounded war
They put their games away.

They left the peaceful river,
The cricket-field, the quad,
The shaven lawns of Oxford,
To seek a bloody sod—
They gave their merry youth away
For country and for God.

God rest you happy, gentlemen,
Who laid your good lives down,
Who took the khaki and the gun
Instead of cap and gown.
God bring you to a fairer place
Than even Oxford town.

Winifred Mary Letts, 1882–

1738. ANTHEM FOR DOOMED YOUTH

What passing-bells for these who die as cattle?
Only the monstrous anger of the guns.
Only the stuttering rifles' rapid rattle
Can patter out their hasty orisons.
No mockeries for them; no prayers nor bells,
Nor any voice of mourning save the choirs,—
The shrill, demented choirs of wailing shells;
And bugles calling for them from sad shires.
What candles may be held to speed them all?
Not in the hands of boys, but in their eyes
Shall shine the holy glimmers of goodbyes.
The pallor of girls' brows shall be their pall;
Their flowers the tenderness of patient minds,
And each slow dusk a drawing-down of blinds.

Wilfred Owen,[1] *1893–1918*

[1] English soldier, killed in World War I.

1739. THERMOPYLAE AND GOLGOTHA

Men lied to them and so they went to die.
Some fell, unknowing that they were deceived,
And some escaped, and bitterly bereaved,
Beheld the truth they loved shrink to a lie
And those there were that never had believed,
But from afar had read the gathering sky,
And darkly wrapt in that dread prophecy
Died trusting that their truth might be retrieved.

It matters not. For life deals thus with Man;
To die alone deceived or with the mass,
Or disillusioned to complete his span.
Thermopylae or Golgotha, all one—
The young dead legions in the narrow pass;
The stark black cross against the setting sun.

Robert Hillyer, 1895–

1740. APPARITIONS

Who goes there, in the night,
Across the storm-swept plain?
We are the ghosts of a valiant war—
A million murdered men!

Who goes there, at the dawn,
Across the sun-swept plain?
We are the hosts of those who swear:
It shall not be again!

Thomas Curtis Clark, 1877–

1741. GRASS[1]

Pile the bodies high at Austerlitz and
Waterloo.
Shovel them under and let me work—
I am the grass; I cover all.

And pile them high at Gettysburg
And pile them high at Ypres and Verdun.
Shovel them under and let me work.
Two years, ten years, and passengers ask the
conductor:
What place is this?
Where are we now?

I am the grass.
Let me work.

Carl Sandburg, 1878–

1742. HALLOWED GROUND

What's hallowed ground? Has earth a clod
Its Maker meant not should be trod
By man, the image of his God,
Erect and free,
Unscourged by Superstition's rod
To bow the knee?

❖

What hallows ground where heroes sleep?
'Tis not the sculptured piles you heap!
In dews that heavens far distant weep
Their turf may bloom;
Or Genii twine beneath the deep
Their coral tomb.

But strew his ashes to the wind
Whose sword or voice has served mankind,—
And is he dead, whose glorious mind
Lifts thine on high?—
To live in hearts we leave behind
Is not to die.

❖

What's hallowed ground? 'Tis what gives
birth
To sacred thoughts in souls of worth!—
Peace! Independence! Truth! go forth
Earth's compass round;
And your high-priesthood shall make earth
All hallowed ground.

Thomas Campbell, 1777–1844

1743. IN FLANDERS FIELDS

In Flanders fields the poppies blow
Between the crosses, row on row,
That mark our place; and in the sky
The larks, still bravely singing, fly,
Scarce heard amid the guns below.

We are the Dead. Short days ago
We lived, felt dawn, saw sunset glow,
Loved and were loved, and now we lie
In Flanders fields.[2]

Take up our quarrel with the foe:
To you from falling hands we throw
The torch; be yours to hold it high!
If ye break faith with us who die
We shall not sleep, though poppies grow
In Flanders fields.

John McCrae, 1872–1918

1744. IN FLANDERS NOW

Written at the close of World War I, in answer to Colonel McCrae's well-known poem. "In Flanders Now" was used at the unveiling of the tomb of the Unknown Soldier in Washington. Printed on a card with the Belgium National Anthem and sold by the Federation of Women's Clubs, a million dollars were raised and used for the restoration of the Louvain Library. As we read the poem now in the aftermath of another world war, it awakens many conflicting emotions that search our hearts.

We have kept faith, ye Flanders' dead,
Sleep well beneath those poppies red
That mark your place.
The torch your dying hands did throw,
We've held it high before the foe,
And answered bitter blow for blow,
In Flanders fields.

And where your heroes' blood was spilled,
The guns are now forever stilled
And silent grown.
There is no moaning of the slain,
There is no cry of tortured pain,
And blood will never flow again,
In Flanders fields.

Forever holy in our sight
Shall be those crosses gleaming white,

[1] Published 1918.

[2] Lieut. Colonel McCrae died in France, serving with the Canadian Medical Corps, and is buried in the Wimereux Communal Cemetery.

That guard your sleep.
Rest you in peace, the task is done,
The fight you left us we have won,
And Peace on Earth has just begun,
In Flanders now.

Edna Jaques, contemporary Canadian

1745. GOD PRAYS

Last night I tossed and could not sleep.
When sodden heavens weep and weep,
As they have wept for many a day,
One lies awake to fear and pray,
One thinks of bodies blown like hail
Across the sky where angels quail;
One's sickened pulses leap and hark
To hear the horror in the dark.

"What is Thy will for the people, God?
Thy will for the people, tell it me!
For war is swallowing up the sod
And still no help from Thee.
Thou, who art mighty, hast forgot;
And art Thou God, or art Thou not?
When wilt Thou come to save the earth
Where death has conquered birth?"

And the Lord God whispered and said to me,
"These things shall be, these things shall be,
Nor help shall come from the scarlet skies,
Till the people rise!
Till the people rise, my arm is weak;
I cannot speak till the people speak;
When men are dumb, my voice is dumb—
I cannot come till my people come."

And the Lord God's presence was white, so white,
Like a pillar of stars against the night.
"Millions on millions pray to me
Yet hearken not to hear me pray;
Nor comes there any to set me free
Of all who plead from night to day.
So God is mute and Heaven is still
While the nations kill."

"Thy people have travailed much," I cried,
"I travail even as they," God sighed.
"I have cradled their woe since the stars were young—
My infant planets were scarcely hung
When I dreamed the dream of my liberty
And planned a people to utter me.
I am the pang of their discontent,
The passion of their long lament;
I am the purpose of their pain,
I writhe beneath their chain."

"But Thou art mighty, and need'st no aid.
Can God, the Infinite, be afraid?"
"They, too, are God, yet know it not.
'Tis they, not I, who have forgot.
And war is drinking the living sod,"
Said God.

"Thy people are fettered by iron laws
And each must follow a country's cause
And all are sworn to avenge their dead—
How may the people rise?" I said.
And then God's face! It was white, so white,
With the grief that sorroweth day and night.

"Think you I planted my image there
That men should trample it to despair?
Who fears the throe that rebellion brings
Hath bartered God for the will of kings."

"Help them stand, O Christ!" I prayed.
"Thy people are feeble and sore afraid."
"My people are strong," God whispered me,
"Broad as the land, great as the sea;
They will tower tall as the tallest skies
Up to the level of my eyes,
When they dare to rise.
Yea, all my people everywhere!
Not in one land of black despair
But over the flaming earth and sea
Wherever wrong and oppression be
The shout of my people must come to me.
Not till their spirit break the curse
May I claim my own in the universe;
And this the reason of war and blood
That men may come to their angelhood.
If the people rise, if the people rise,
I will answer them from the swarming skies
Where Herculean hosts of might
Shall spring to splendor over night.
Blazing systems of sun and star
Are not so great as my people are,
Nor chanting angels so sweet to hear
As the voice of nations, freed from fear.
They are my mouth, my breath, my soul!
I wait their summons to make me whole."

All night long I toss and cannot sleep;
When shattered heavens weep and weep,
As they have wept for many days.
I know at last 'tis God who prays.

Angela Morgan, contemporary American

1746. THE NIGHTINGALES OF SURREY

The nightingales of Surrey
They hear the planes go by,
Yet fling upon the evening air
Their sharp, ecstatic cry.

God gave the creatures joy of life,
Joy of the perfect law,
While man reverts to jungle days
Of tooth and claw.

Jessie B. Rittenhouse, contemporary American

1747. THE CONSCRIPT

Indifferent, flippant, earnest, but all bored,
The doctors sit in the glare of electric light
Watching the endless stream of naked white
Bodies of men for whom their hasty award
Means life or death maybe or the living death
Of mangled limbs, blind eyes or a darkened brain:
And the chairman as his monocle falls again
Pronounces each doom with easy indifferent breath.

Then suddenly I shudder as I see
A young man move before them wearily,
Cadaverous as one already dead:
But still they stare untroubled as he stands
With arms outstretched and drooping thorn-crowned head,
The nail-marks glowing in his feet and hands.

Wilfrid W. Gibson,[1] *1878?–*

1748. BACK

They ask me where I've been,
And what I've done and seen.
But what can I reply
Who know it wasn't I,
But someone just like me,
Who went across the sea
And with my head and hands
Killed men in foreign lands . . .
Though I must bear the blame
Because he bore my name.

Wilfrid W. Gibson, 1878?–

1749. A WAR-TIME PRAYER

Though the hands be raised to kill,
Though the body be beguiled
Into combat fierce and wild,
Holy Spirit keep the will,
Keep us from our subtlest foes
Hope of gain or fear of ill,
Keep our purpose undefiled,
Fruitful amid all our woes,
Let not Europe's bitter throes
Bring forth a still-born child.

Anna Bunston de Bary, contemporary English

1750. ONE CROWDED HOUR

From "Old Mortality"

Sound, sound the clarion, fill the fife!
To all the sensual world proclaim,
One crowded hour of glorious strife
Is worth an age without a name.

Sir Walter Scott, 1771–1832

1751. BETWEEN MIDNIGHT AND MORNING

You that have faith to look with fearless eyes
Beyond the tragedy of a world at strife,
And trust that out of night and death shall rise
The dawn of ampler life;
Rejoice, whatever anguish rend your heart,
That God has given you, for a priceless dower,
To live in these great times and have your part
In Freedom's crowning hour;
That you may tell your sons who see the light
High in the heaven—their heritage to take—
"I saw the powers of darkness put to flight!
I saw the morning break!"

Owen Seaman,[2] *1861–1936*

1752. THE UNPARDONABLE SIN[3]

This is the sin against the Holy Ghost:—
To speak of bloody power as right divine,
And call on God to guard each vile chief's house,

[1] English soldier, World War I.
[2] English soldier, World War I.
[3] Written at the beginning of World War I.

And for such chiefs, turn men to wolves and
swine:—

To go forth killing in White Mercy's name,
Making the trenches stink with spattered
brains,
Tearing the nerves and arteries apart,
Sowing with flesh the unreaped golden plains.

In any Church's name, to sack fair towns,
And turn each home into a screaming sty,
To make the little children fugitive,
And have their mothers for a quick death
cry,—

This is the sin against the Holy Ghost:
This is the sin no purging can atone:—
To send forth rapine in the name of Christ:—
To set the face, and make the heart a stone.

Vachel Lindsay, 1879–1931

1753. VICTORY

I . . . . . What a fine statue!
Myself . . . . . It is Victory.
I . . . . . Proud figure!
Myself . . . . . We won the war.
I . . . . . Why, there's a tear in her eye!
Myself . . . . . I know. We did not win the
enemy.

Arthur B. Rhinow,
contemporary American

1754. WORLD-RUIN

(Suggested by world events of 1940–1941)

Ah, what if Time forgot to light the stars,
Weary of viewing our long, senseless plight
Of greed and blundering death, and dawnless
night
Sealed with a frozen doom our gaping scars!
Fantastic ice-crags loomed. Colossal spars
Stood fixed in writhing grandeur! Still and
white,
A tortured phantom-sea where sound nor
sight
Disturbed the avenging dark's unfathomed
bars.

And some lone Being lost from outer-space
Should aeons hence feel wonder to behold,
Written with chasmal runes, that a proud race
Could so have fallen; and deep in the mold
Of Conquest's ruined dreams and shattered
gold
Find, wrought in stone, an anguished, thorn-
crowned face!

Hugh Wilgus Ramsaur,
contemporary American

1755. WEAPONS OF EVIL

From "The Tao Teh King"

Soldiers are weapons of evil.
They are not the weapons of the gentleman.
When the use of soldiers cannot be helped,
The best policy is calm restraint.

Even in victory, there is no beauty,
And who calls it beautiful
Is one who delights in slaughter.
He who delights in slaughter
Will not succeed in his ambition to rule the
world. . . .

The slaying of multitudes should be mourned
with sorrow.
A victory should be celebrated with the
Funeral Rite.

From the Chinese; tr. by Lin Yutang, 1895–

1756. THE DIPLOMATS

Each was honest after his way,
Lukewarm in faith, and old;
And blood, to them, was only a word,
And the point of a phrase their only sword,
And the cost of war, they reckoned it
In little disks of gold.

Alfred Noyes, 1880–

1757. SCAPEGOATS

The young men die in battle,
The old men sleep in bed.
The tortured earth of Europe
Is furrowed deep with red.

The old men sat conferring
With smile and scheme and lie.
The old men made the blunders,
Today the young men die.

Eleanor D. Breed, contemporary American

1758. MARCHING SONG[1]

We, wandering to death,
By earthly fate bound,
For the end prepared,
We victims uncrown'd,

We born of a mother,
Herself unfulfill'd,
We without will, and
By agony still'd,

We tears of the women,
We night without light,
We, the orphans of earth,
March dumb to the fight.

Ernst Toller, 1893–1939

1759. FIVE SOULS

FIRST SOUL

I was a peasant of the Polish plain;
I left my plough because the message ran:
Russia, in danger, needed every man
To save her from the Teuton; and was slain.
I gave my life for freedom—This I know;
For those who bade me fight had told me so.

SECOND SOUL

I was a Tyrolese, a mountaineer;
I gladly left my mountain home to fight
Against the brutal treacherous Muscovite;
And died in Poland on a Cossack spear.
I gave my life for freedom—This I know;
For those who bade me fight had told me so.

THIRD SOUL

I worked at Lyons, at my weavers' loom
When suddenly the Prussian despot hurled
His felon blow at France and at the world;
Then went I forth to Belgium and my doom.
I gave my life for freedom—This I know;
For those who bade me fight had told me so.

FOURTH SOUL

I owned a vineyard by the wooded Main,
Until the Fatherland, begirt by foes
Lusting her downfall, called me, and I rose,
Swift to the call, and died in fair Lorraine.
I gave my life for freedom—This I know;
For those who bade me fight had told me so.

FIFTH SOUL

I worked in a great shipyard by the Clyde.
There came a sudden word of wars declared,
Of Belgium peaceful, helpless, unprepared,
Asking our aid: I joined the ranks, and died.
I gave my life for freedom—This I know;
For those who bade me fight had told me so.

W. N. Ewer

1760. MAKE THEM FORGET

I saw the Prince of Darkness, with his Staff,
Standing bare-headed by the Cenotaph:
Unostentatious and respectful, there
He stood, and offered up the following prayer
"Make them forget, O Lord, what this Memorial
Means; their discredited ideas revive;
Breed new belief that War is purgatorial
Proof of the pride and power of being alive;
Men's biologic urge to readjust
The Map of Europe, Lord of Hosts, increase;
Lift up their hearts in large destructive lust;
And crown their heads with blind vindictive Peace!"
The Prince of Darkness to the Cenotaph
Bowed. As he walked away I heard him laugh.

Siegfried Sassoon,[2] 1886–

[1] This protest against war was written by a brilliant young Jewish poet who served in the German army in World War I, and who ended his life as Hitler began World War II.
[2] English soldier, World War I.

1761. LINES FOR AN INTERMENT[1]

Now it is fifteen years you have lain in the meadow:
The boards at your face have gone through: the earth is
Packed down and the sound of the rain is fainter:
The roots of the first grass are dead:

It's a long time to lie in the earth with your honor:
The world, Soldier, the world has been moving on:

The girls wouldn't look at you twice in the cloth cap:
Six years old they were when it happened:

It bores them even in books: "Soissons besieged!"
As for the gents they have joined the American Legion:

Belts and a brass band and the ladies' auxiliaries:
The Californians march in the OD silk:

We are all acting again like civilized beings:
People mention it at tea. . .

The Facts of Life we have learned are Economic:
You were deceived by the detonations of bombs:

You thought of courage and death when you thought of warfare:
Hadn't they taught you the fine words were unfortunate?

Now that we understand we judge without bias:
We feel of course for those who had to die:

Women have written us novels of great passion
Proving the useless death of the dead was a tragedy:

Nevertheless it is foolish to chew gall:
The foremost writers on both sides have apologized:

The Germans are back in the Midi with cropped hair:
The English are drinking the better beer in Bavaria:

You can rest now in the rain in the Belgian meadow—
Now that it's all explained away and forgotten:
Now that the earth is hard and the wood rots:

Now you are dead . . .

Archibald MacLeish, 1892–

1762. AFTER BATTLE

When after many battles past,
Both, tired with blows, make peace at last,
What is it, after all, the people get?
Why, taxes, widows, wooden legs, and debt.

Author unknown

[1] Written 1933. The soldier was the poet's brother.

1763. WAR

War
I abhor,
And yet how sweet
The sound along the marching street
Of drum and fife; and I forget

Wet eyes of widows, and forget
Broken old mothers, and the whole
Dark butchery without a soul.

Without a soul—save this bright drink
Of heady music, sweet as hell;
And even my peace-abiding feet
Go marching with the marching street,
For yonder goes the fife,
And what care I for human life!

The tears fill my astonished eyes
And my full heart is like to break,
And yet 'tis all embannered lies,
A dream those little drummers make.

Oh, it is wickedness to clothe
Yon hideous, grinning thing that stalks
Hidden in music, like a queen
That in a garden of glory walks,
Till good men love the thing they loathe.

Art, thou hast many infamies,
But not an infamy like this—
Oh, snap the fife and still the drum,
And show the monster as she is.

Richard Le Gallienne, 1866–1947

1764. SATAN ON WAR

From "Paradise Lost"

O shame to men! Devil with devil damned
Firm concord holds; men only disagree
Of creatures rational, though under hope
Of heavenly grace, and, God proclaiming
peace,
Yet live in hatred, enmity, and strife
Among themselves, and levy cruel wars
Wasting the earth, each other to destroy:
As if (which might induce us to accord)
Man had not hellish foes enow besides,
That day and night for his destruction wait!

John Milton, 1608–1674

1765. SOLDIER, WHAT DID YOU SEE?

What did you see, Soldier? What did you see at war?
I saw such glory and horror as I've never seen before.
I saw men's hearts burned naked in red crucibles of pain.
I saw such godlike courage as I'll never see again.

What did you hear, Soldier? What did you hear at war?
I heard the prayers on lips of men who had never prayed before.
I heard men tell their very souls, confessing each dark stain.
I heard men speak the sacred things they will not speak again.

What did you eat, Soldier? What did you eat at war?
I ate the sour bread of fear, the acrid salt of gore.
My lips were burned with wine of hate, the scalding drink of Cain.
My tongue has known a bitter taste I would not taste again.

What did you think, Soldier? What did you think at war?
I thought, how strange we have not learned from wars that raged before,
Except new ways of killing, new multiples of pain.
Is all the blood that men have shed but blood shed all in vain?

What did you learn, Soldier? What did you learn at war?
I learned that we must learn sometime what was not learned before,
That victories won on battlefields are victories won in vain
Unless in peace we kill the germs that breed new wars again.

What did you pray, Soldier? What did you pray at war?
I prayed that we might do the thing we have not done before;
That we might mobilize for peace . . . nor mobilize in vain.
Lest Christ and man be forced to climb stark Calvary again.

Don Blanding,[1] *1894–*

[1] American soldier in World Wars I and II.

1766. CASUALTY

Our neighbor, Mrs. Waters' only son,
After Pearl Harbor, left her and enlisted.
He chose the Navy, since, as he insisted,
This was a war most likely to be won
At sea. He liked the danger; called it fun.

For months she had a weekly word from Sam
And Easter Sunday got a radiogram
Sent from a cruiser steaming toward the sun.

Last night she stepped outside the cottage
door
To get the evening paper off the floor.
The headline said: "Round One of Naval
Fight
In Coral Sea Is Ours. The Foe in Flight."

She raised her face and smiled; and saw a lad
Bringing a message in an envelope.
The color was familiar; and a hope
Stirred as she opened it, uncertain, glad.
Army and Navy Building, Washington:
"I have the duty to report your son
Missing in action in the Coral Sea.
Your loss is honored by our victory."

She did not weep, but thanked the boy and
then
Fumbled a moment with the News again.
She did not see the line that mocked her
plight
And said: "Our losses relatively light."

Edwin McNeill Poteat, 1892–

1767. POEM FOR COMBATANTS

It is not death so much we dread
as maiming and disfigurement,
the crucifixion of the heart by bitterness,
the mind made gibberish,
for some survive and others die,
and both perhaps are fortunate.

The cruellest ravishments of war are these—

the violinist's hands,
that loved the gliding bow and singing
strings,
made fingerless by a grenade,
the artist's eyes,
that drank the coloured rivers forming
beauty,
now made blind and lustreless,
no more conveying genius to the brush,
the athlete's limbs,
that leapt so lithely on the track and over
hurdle,
changed to metal or misshapen,
and the poet's tongue,
that could recite so lyrically,
now mumbling with a mad delirium as muse
of cells and birds and woodchopping.

There is consumed the highest sacrifice of
man,
the undeliberate loss that plants
the deepest suffering.

Alan White[1]

[1] English soldier, World War II, killed in Italy.

1768. BROKEN BODIES

Not for the broken bodies,
When the War is over and done,
For the miserable eyes that never
Again shall see the sun;
Not for the broken bodies
Crawling over the land,
The patchwork limbs, the shoddies,
Not for the broken bodies
Dear Lord, we crave Your hand.

Not for the broken bodies,
We pray Your dearest aid,
When the ghost of War for ever
Is levelled at last and laid;
Not for the broken bodies
That wrought their sorrowful parts
Our chiefest need of God is,
Not for the broken bodies,
Dear Lord—the broken hearts!

Louis Golding, 1895–

1769. WAR POEM

Don't stand at night by the gate, love,
He will not come again,
And there are eyes that laugh to see
The flowering of a pain.

Do not lay him a place, dear,
For you will eat alone;

Nor put you on that pretty dress,
 The need for that is gone.

Just go into your room, lass,
And make yourself a prayer,
For that will be your strength now,
This many and many a year.

Henry Treece, 1912–

1770. THE WAR FILMS

O living pictures of the dead,
 O songs without a sound,
O fellowship whose phantom tread
 Hallows a phantom ground—
How in a gleam have these revealed
 The faith we had not found.

We have sought God in a cloudy Heaven,
 We have passed by God on earth:
His seven sins and his sorrows seven,
 His wayworn mood and mirth,
Like a ragged cloak have hid from us
 The secret of his birth.

Brother of men, when now I see
 The lads go forth in line,
Thou knowest my heart is hungry in me
 As for thy bread and wine:
Thou knowest my heart is bowed in me
 To take their death for mine.

Henry Newbolt, 1862–1938

1771. WAR

Ez fer war, I call it murder,—
 There you hev it plain an' flat;
I don't want to go no furder
 Than my Testyment fer that;
God hez said so plump an' fairly,
 It's ez long ez it is broad,
An' you've gut to git up airly
 Ef you want to take in God.

James Russell Lowell, 1819–1891

1772. CRUSHED FENDER

It happened in Milan one summer night,
 While we were driving down a narrow street.
A fender crashed—the brakes froze to a stop
 Beneath the pressure of the driver's feet.
I hurled my ire against the guilty one:
 "You should be taught to signal as you turn!
At least put out your arm!" I cried at him.
 "You could have caused our car to overturn!"
At first the man was silent, then he spoke:
 "Sorry," he said, "to cause you such alarm.
You did not see it, for the night is dark,
 But as I turned, I did put out my arm.
Please take my license number and my name—
 I hope you will forgive and understand.
I was a soldier once, somewhere in France. . . .
 My left arm is a stub. I have no hand."

I could not speak. The words choked in my throat—
 I did not take his number, nor his name—
I turned the car against the dull black night,
 My face averted to conceal my shame.

Rosa Zagnoni Marinoni, 1891–

1773. "THEY"

The Bishop tells us: "When the boys come back
They will not be the same; for they'll have fought
In a just cause: they led the last attack

On Anti-Christ; their comrade's blood has bought
New right to breed an honorable race.
They have challenged Death and dared him face to face."

"We're none of us the same!" the boys reply.
"For George lost both his legs; and Bill's stone blind;
Poor Jim's shot through the lungs and like to die;
And Bert's gone syphilitic: you'll not find
A chap who's served that hasn't found *some* change."
And the bishop said: "The ways of God are strange!"

Siegfried Sassoon, 1886-

1774. ULTIMA RATIO REGUM

The guns spell money's ultimate reason
In letters of lead on the spring hillside.
But the boy lying dead under the olive trees
Was too young and too silly
To have been notable to their important eye.
He was a better target for a kiss.

When he lived, tall factory hooters never summoned him.
Nor did restaurant plate-glass doors revolve to wave him in.
His name never appeared in the papers.
The world maintained its traditional wall
Round the dead with their gold sunk deep as a well,
Whilst his life, intangible as a Stock Exchange rumour, drifted outside.

O too lightly he threw down his cap
One day when the breeze threw petals from the trees.
The unflowering wall sprouted with guns,
Machine-gun anger quickly scythed the grasses;
Flags and leaves fell from hands and branches;
The tweed cap rotted in the nettles.

Consider his life which was valueless
In terms of employment, hotel ledgers, news files.
Consider. One bullet in ten thousand kills a man.
Ask. Was so much expenditure justified
On the death of one so young and so silly
Lying under the olive trees, O world, O death?

Stephen Spender, 1909-

1775. THE DEAD[1]

The dead are silent. Passionless and still
They lie in dreamless slumber, robed in peace.
They will not stir though raging armies fill
The air with frightful clamor. The sweet release
Of death has soothed their anguish. They have found
Within that timeless land the secrets men

[1] Written in a German prison camp in the spring of 1945.

Have sought since time began. They are not bound
  By fetters forged of race or creed . . . and when
The frantic living join the quiet dead
  We, too, shall learn that in that gentle dust
All flesh is kin; within that narrow bed
  There is no room for hate or fear or lust. . . .

The living plague the gods with selfish cries:
The dead are silent—the dead are wise!

Robert J. Crot,[1] *contemporary American*

1776. THE SOLDIER

If I should die, think only this of me:
  That there's some corner of a foreign field
That is for ever England. There shall be
  In that rich earth a richer dust concealed;
A dust whom England bore, shaped, made aware,
  Gave, once, her flowers to love, her ways to roam,
A body of England's, breathing English air,
  Washed by the rivers, blest by suns of home.

And think, this heart, all evil shed away,
  A pulse in the eternal mind, no less
    Gives somewhere back the thoughts by England given;
Her sights and sounds; dreams happy as her day;
  And laughter, learnt of friends; and gentleness,
    In hearts at peace, under an English heaven.

Rupert Brooke,[2] *1887–1915*

1777. PEACE

Now, God be thanked, Who has matched us with His hour,
  And caught our youth, and wakened us from sleeping,
With hand made sure, clear eye and sharpened power,
  To turn, as swimmers into cleanness leaping,
Glad from a world grown old and cold and weary,
  Leave the sick hearts that honour could not move,
And half-men and their dirty songs and dreary,
  And all the little emptiness of love!
Oh! We who have known shame, we have found release there
  Where there's no ill, no grief, but sleep has mending,
  Naught broken save this body, lost but breath;
Nothing to shake the laughing heart's long peace there
  But only agony, and that has ending;
  And the worst friend and enemy is but Death.

Rupert Brooke, 1887–1915

[1] American soldier, World War II.

[2] English soldier in World War I; died in the Aegean on his way to the Dardanelles; buried at Skyros, an island off the coast of Greece.

1778. BEFORE ACTION

By all the glories of the day
And the cool evening's benison,
By that last sunset touch that lay
Upon the hills when day was done,
By beauty lavishly outpoured
And blessings carelessly received,
By all the days that I have lived,
Make me a soldier, Lord.

By all of all man's hopes and fears,
And all the wonders poets sing,
The laughter of unclouded years,
And every sad and lovely thing;
By the romantic ages stored
With high endeavour that was his,
By all his mad catastrophes
Make me a man, O Lord.

I, that on my familiar hill
Saw with uncomprehending eyes
A hundred of Thy sunsets spill
Their fresh and sanguine sacrifice,
Ere the sun swings his noonday sword
Must say good-by to all of this;—
By all delights that I shall miss,
Help me to die, O Lord.

William Noel Hodgson,[1] *1893–1916*

1779. I HAVE A RENDEZVOUS WITH DEATH

I have a rendezvous with Death
At some disputed barricade,
When Spring comes back with rustling shade
And apple blossoms fill the air—
I have a rendezvous with Death
When Spring brings back blue days and fair.

It may be he shall take my hand,
And lead me into his dark land,
And close my eyes and quench my breath—
It may be I shall pass him still.
I have a rendezvous with Death
On some scarred slope of battered hill,
When Spring comes round again this year
And the first meadow flowers appear.

God knows 'twere better to be deep
Pillowed in silk and scented down,
Where Love throbs out in blissful sleep,
Pulse nigh to pulse, and breath to breath,
Where hushed awakenings are dear . . .
But I've a rendezvous with Death
At midnight in some flaming town,
When Spring trips north again this year;
And I to my pledged word am true,
I shall not fail that rendezvous.

Alan Seeger,[2] *1888–1916*

1780. AN AIRMAN'S PRAYER

Almighty and all present Power,
Short is the prayer I make to Thee,
I do not ask in battle hour
For any shield to cover me.

The vast unalterable way,
From which the stars do not depart
May not be turned aside to stay
The bullet flying to my heart.

I ask no help to strike my foe
I seek no petty victory here,
The enemy I hate, I know
To Thee is also dear.

But this I pray, be at my side
When death is drawing through the sky.
Almighty God who also died
Teach me the way that I should die.

Hugh R. Brodie,[3] *1912–1942*

1781. O GOD OF FIELD AND CITY

O God of field and city,
O Lord of shore and sea,
Behold us in Thy pity
Lift naked hands to Thee.
Our swords and spears are shattered,
Our walls of stone down-thrust,
Our reeking altars scattered
And trodden in the dust.

O God of law unbroken,
O Lord of justice done,
Thine awful word is spoken
From sun to flaming sun:
We hate and we are hated,

[1] English soldier, killed in France.
[2] American volunteer, killed in France, serving with the French Foreign Legion.
[3] Sergeant-observer with the Royal Australian Air Force, killed in his plane over Europe in World War II.

We slay, and lo, are slain;
We feed and still unsated
We hunt our prey again.

O God of mercy tender,
O Lord of love most free,
Forgive as we surrender
Our wayward wills to Thee.
Absolve our fell allegiance
To captain and to king;
Receive in full obedience
The chastened hearts we bring.

John Haynes Holmes, 1879–

1782. THE OFFERING

How have we fallen from our high estate,
O Lord! plunged down from heaven!
In wanton pride, in lust for empires great,
For riches have we striven.
Are these not dust and ashes in thy sight,
Swept by the wind and lost?
Have we not sinned against the Spirit's might,
Blasphemed the Holy Ghost?

What dost thou ask from all the sons of men?
Atonement for this wrong?
Behold, we lay upon thine altar, then,
A host twelve million strong:
Twelve million dead; they stand before thy face,
An offering for sin;
Their cry goes forth into the bounds of space;
They crowd thy courts within.

Our dead they are,—friend, foe, alike,—our dead;
On sodden battlefield
They laid them down; for us their blood was shed;
By their stripes were we healed;
For our transgressions were we smitten sore;
Slaughtered with shot and shell;
For us the chastisement of peace they bore,
Descending into hell.

Not theirs alone the atoning sacrifice:
Wives, mothers, at the call,
In unity of sorrow paid the price,
Gave of their best, their all:
One was the heartache, one the darkened home,
And one the company
Of living dead, who wait to see God come:
A mighty company.

Olive Cecilia Jacks, 1868–1945

1783. A SONG OF THE OLD DAYS

Givenchy village lies a wreck, Givenchy church is bare—
No more the peasant maidens come to say their vespers there,
The altar rails are wrenched apart, with rubble littered o'er,
The sacred sanctuary lamp lies smashed upon the floor,
And mute upon the crucifix He looks upon it all—
The great white Christ, the shrapnel-scourged upon the war-scarred wall:

He sees the churchyard delved by shells, the tombstones flung about,
And dead men's skulls and lean white bones the shells have shovelled out—
The trenches running line by line through meadow fields of green,
Thy bayonets on the parapets, the wasting flesh between—
Around Givenchy's ruined church the levels, poppy-red,
Are set apart for silent hosts, the legions of the dead.

And when at night on sentry-go with danger keeping tryst,
I see upon the crucifix the blood-stained form of Christ
Defiled and maimed, the Merciful on vigil all the time,
Pitying His children's wrath, their passion and their crime.
Mute, mute He hangs upon His cross, the Symbol of His pain,
And as men scourged Him years ago they scourge Him once again—
There in the lonely warlit night to Christ the Lord, I call:
"Forgive all those who work Thee harm! O Lord, forgive us all."

Patrick MacGill,[1] *1890–*

[1] British soldier in France, World War I.

1784. RECONCILIATION

Word over all, beautiful as the sky!
Beautiful that war, and all its deeds of carnage, must in time be utterly lost;
That the hands of the sisters Death and Night, incessantly softly wash again, and ever again, this soil'd world:
. . . For my enemy is dead—a man divine as myself is dead;
I look where he lies, white-faced and still, in the coffin—I draw near;
I bend down, and touch lightly with my lips the white face in the coffin.

Walt Whitman, 1819–1892

1785. PRAYER FOR PEACE

O God, whose will is life and peace
For all the sons of men,
Let not our human hates release
The sword's dread power again.
Forgive our narrowness of mind;
Destroy false pride, we plead:
Deliver us and all mankind
From selfishness and greed.

O God, whose ways shall lead to peace,
Enlighten us, we pray;
Dispel our darkness and increase
The light along our way.
Illumine those who lead the lands
That they may make at length
The laws of right to guide the hands
That wield the nations' strength.

O God, who callest us to peace,
We join with everyone
Who does his part that wars may cease
And justice may be done.
Enable us to take the way
The Prince of Peace hath trod;
Create the will to build each day
The family of God.

Rolland W. Schloerb, 1893–

1786. IS IT A DREAM?

Is it a dream, and nothing more—this faith
That nerves our brains to thought, our hands to work
For that great day when wars shall cease, and men
Shall live as brothers in a unity
Of love—live in a world made splendid?
Is it a dream—this faith of ours that pleads
And pulses in our hearts, and bids us look,
Through mists of tears and time, to that great day
When wars shall cease upon the earth, and men,
As brothers bound by love of man and God,
Shall build a world as gloriously fair
As sunset skies, or mountains when they catch
The farewell kiss of evening on their heights?

In our hearts this question, in our minds
The haunting echoes of the song of war;
When will the nations cure the itching palm?
Change curse of pride to love of peace?
How long before such peace can pass our lips,
Can claim our minds and drive out all distrust?
When shall our fingers dare to drop the sword,
While with unquestioning eyes we reach two hands
In open comradeship to all the world?

G. A. Studdert-Kennedy,[1] *1883–1929*

1787. THE PROPHECY[2]

There's a voice on the wind of the world
speaking dreams from the ancient books:
they shall beat their swords into plowshares,
and their spears into pruninghooks.

Have you heard the voice in the darkness,
coming up from the foggy past?
Do you hear, you winged warriors,
over the cyclonic blast
of motors, and the shriek of the bombs as they fall?
Did you hear it, you beautiful sons,

[1] Chaplain with the British Forces in France, World War I, and Chaplain to King George V.
[2] Written 1945.

you dead of Caen and Tarawa,
as you fell in the flash of the guns?

You can hear it, earth, you can hear it
in the crackle of cities that burn,
in the lancing cry of the children,
in the silence of those who will never return.

There's a voice on the wind of the world,
beating loud on the uttermost shore:
nation shall not lift up sword against nation,
neither shall they learn war any more.

There's a voice on the wind of the world,
the voice long-crushed.
Woe to the waters, the dust and the cloud,
if the voice be hushed!

Lon Woodrum, contemporary American

1788. THE DAWN OF PEACE

From "The Wine Press:" Epilogue

Yes—"on our brows we feel the breath
Of dawn," though in the night we wait!
An arrow is in the heart of Death,
A God is at the doors of Fate!
The Spirit that moved upon the Deep
Is moving through the minds of men:
The nations feel it in their sleep,
A change has touched their dreams again.

❖

Dreams are they? But ye cannot stay them,
Or thrust the dawn back for one hour!
Truth, Love, and Justice, if ye slay them,
Return with more than earthly power:
Strive, if ye will, to seal the fountains
That send the Spring thro' leaf and spray:
Drive back the sun from the Eastern
mountains,
Then—bid this mightier movement stay.

It is the Dawn! The Dawn! The nations
From East to West have heard a cry,—
Though all earth's blood-red generations
By hate and slaughter climbed thus high,
Here—on this height—still to aspire,
One only path remains untrod,
One path of love and peace climbs higher.
Make straight that highway for our God.

Alfred Noyes, 1880–

1789. LET US HAVE PEACE

The earth is weary of our foolish wars.
Her hills and shores were shaped for lovely
things,
Yet all our years are spent in bickerings
Beneath the astonished stars.

April by April laden with beauty comes,
Autumn by Autumn turns our toil to gain,
But hand at sword hilt, still we start and
strain
To catch the beat of drums.

Knowledge to knowledge adding, skill to skill,
We strive for others' good as for our own—
And then, like cavemen snarling with a bone,
We turn and rend and kill. . . .

With life so fair, and all too short a lease
Upon our special star! Nay, love and trust,
Not blood and thunder shall redeem our dust.
Let us have peace!

Nancy Byrd Turner, 1880–

1790. THE PRINCE OF PEACE

The Prince of Peace His banner spreads,
His wayward folk to lead
From war's embattled hates and dreads,
Its bulwarked ire and greed.
O marshal us, the sons of sires
Who braved the cannon's roar,
To venture all that peace requires
As they dared death for war.

Lead on, O Christ! That haunting song
No centuries can dim,
Which long ago the heavenly throng
Sang over Bethlehem.
Cast down our rancor, fear, and pride,
Exalt goodwill again!
Our worship doth Thy name deride,
Bring we not peace to men.

Thy pardon, Lord, for war's dark shame,
Its death-strewn, bloody fields!
Yet thanks to Thee for souls aflame
Who dared with swords and shields;
O Christ, who died to give men life,
Bring that victorious hour,
When man shall use for peace, not strife,
His valor, skill, and power.

Cleanse all our hearts from our disgrace—
We love not world, but clan!
Make clear our eyes to see our race
One family of man.
Rend Thou our little temple veils
That cloak the truth divine,
Until Thy mighty word prevails,
That cries, "All souls are mine."

Harry Emerson Fosdick, 1878–

1791. A HYMN OF PEACE

The Son of God goes forth for Peace,
Our Father's love to show;
From war and woe He brings release,
O, who with Him will go?
He strikes the fetters from the slave,
Man's mind and heart makes free;
And sends His messengers to save
O'er every land and sea!

The Son of God goes forth for Peace,
That men like brothers live,
And all desire the other's good,
And other's sin forgive.
He turns our spears to pruning hooks,
Our swords to ploughshares warm,
And war no more its death-blast brings
Nor men their brothers harm!

The Son of God goes forth for Peace,
Nor lands nor pow'r to gain;
He seeks to serve, to love, to lift,—
Who follows in His train?
A glorious band, in every age.
In spite of scorn and pain,
True sons of God, His peace have made;
Who follows in their train?

Now let the world to Peace be won,
And every hatred slain;
Let force and greed be overcome
And love supreme remain!
Let justice rule in all the earth,
And mercy while we live,
Lest we—forgiven much—forget
Our brother to forgive!

We send our love to every land—
True neighbors would we be;
And pray God's Peace to reign in them,
Where'er their homeland be!
O God, to us may grace be given,
Who bear the dear Christ's name,
To live at peace with every man,
And thus our Christ acclaim!

Ernest Bourner Allen, 1868–1931

1792. GOD OF THE NATIONS

God of the nations, near and far,
Ruler of all mankind,
Bless Thou Thy peoples as they strive
The paths of peace to find.

The clash of arms still shakes the sky,
King battles still with king;
Wild through the frighted air of night
The bloody tocsins ring.

But clearer far the friendly speech
Of scientists and seers,
The wise debate of statesmen, and
The shouts of pioneers.

And stronger far the claspèd hands
Of labor's teeming throngs,
Who in a hundred tongues repeat
Their common creeds and songs.

From shore to shore the peoples call
In loud and sweet acclaim;
The gloom of land and sea is lit
With pentecostal flame.

O Father, from the curse of war
We pray Thee give release;
And speed, O speed Thy blessèd day
Of justice, love, and peace.

John Haynes Holmes, 1879–

1793. WHEN WAR SHALL BE NO MORE

From "The Arsenal at Springfield"

Were half the power that fills the world with terror,
  Were half the wealth bestowed on camps and courts,
Given to redeem the human mind from error,
  There were no need of arsenals and forts.

The warrior's name would be a name abhorrèd!
  And every nation, that should lift again
Its hand against a brother, on its forehead
  Would wear forevermore the curse of Cain!

Down the dark future, through long generations,
  The echoing sounds grow fainter and then cease;
And like a bell, with solemn, sweet vibrations,
  I hear once more the voice of Christ say, "Peace!"

Peace! and no longer from its brazen portals
  The blast of war's great organ shakes the skies!
But beautiful as songs of the immortals,
  The holy melodies of Love arise.

Henry Wadsworth Longfellow, 1807–1882

1794. PEACE IN THE WORLD

(Message for the Livre d'Or de la Paix, Geneva)

God send us wit to banish far
The incense and the reeking breath,
The lances and the fame of war,
And all the devilments of death.
Let there be wisdom and increase,
The harvest reconcilement brings,
So shall we see the eyes of Peace,
And feel the wafting of Her wings.

John Galsworthy, 1867–1933

1795. CREATE GREAT PEACE

From "1914—and After"

Would you end war?
Create great Peace. . . .
The peace that demands all of a man,
His love, his life, his veriest self;
Plunge him into the smelting fires of a work that becomes his child. . . .

Give him a hard Peace: a Peace of discipline and justice . . .
Kindle him with vision, invite him to joy and adventure:
Set him to work, not to create *things*
But to create *men*:
Yea, himself.

Go search your heart, America. . . .
Turn from the machine to man,
Build, while there is yet time, a creative Peace . . .
While there is yet time! . . .
For if you reject great Peace,
As surely as vile living brings disease,
So surely will your selfishness bring war.

James Oppenheim, 1882–1932

1796. STRANGER AT THE PEACE TABLE

There is a stranger in the council hall
  Where nations meet to plan the peace again.
He sits unnoticed by the farther wall,

His eyes upon the leaders among men.
His ears attend their clearly laid designs
For living in tomorrow's homes and marts,
As though beneath their spoken words and lines
He hears the inner voices of their hearts.

But when the delegates of all the world
Have cried their million wants, and lists are long,
And after blueprints, charts, and plans are hurled
In varied protest at the core of wrong,
He is our hope; He is the peace we seek.
O listen, world, and let the Stranger speak!

Esther Baldwin York, 1911–

1797. IN OUR TIME

No holy pointer, no unchanging Light
Where Evil wars with Virtue, foul with fair,
Dusk with the dawn—a world of black and white
Mixing itself into a grey despair?

When shall this strife between the Nations cease? . . .
During our pilgrimage this side the tomb
Life shall be storm, the world shall know not peace
Until within all hearts Christ finds a home!

Huw Menai, contemporary Welsh miner

1798. From ARRAIGNMENT[1]

What did you do with the world that you bade us to bow to anew?
With the strength and the beauty of life, and its valor, what things did you do?
Did you lead out of bondage the captives, or fetter Mankind for the few?
Did you shine for example, till all men declared for the right and the true?
Did you plant on the mountains, for Youth to aspire to, a fire and a star?
Did you lift a great song for a chant on the march to the feet going far?
Did you kindle our pride in a wide smiling country where under the sun
There was scorn for the liar and scorn for the cruel, and justice was done?

❖

By the horrors we have faced, by the carnage and pain . . . we cry . . .
Our shuddering, urgent, ultimate desire:
Build in the spirit again—create, create—
Lest, at the last, it prove too late, too late.

William Rose Benét, 1886–

1799. THE BATTLE OF PEACE

The windmills of Holland are turning again;
The brown hands of Denmark are churning again;
The red hearths of England are burning again;
And Russians no longer must die.

[1] Written toward the close of the second World War.

The birds of the air are home-winging again;
The legions of China are singing again;
The church bells in Poland are ringing again:
And Scotch lasses laugh in the rye.

Toronto and Melbourne are joyous again;
The Mothers are glad from Seattle to Maine;
For fire, from the skies, falls no longer like rain;
And war, like a dream, has passed by.

Beneath the command of a Carpenter's Son
The battle of peace must be fought now, and won;
A battle that hears not the cry of a gun
In the land or the sea or the sky.

Wilson MacDonald, 1880–

1800. THE YOUNG DEAD SOLDIERS[1]

The young dead soldiers do not speak.
Nevertheless they are heard in the still houses.
(Who has not heard them?)

They have a silence that speaks for them at night
And when the clock counts.

They say,
We were young. We have died. Remember us.

They say,
We have done what we could
But until it is finished it is not done.

They say,
We have given our lives
But until it is finished no one can know what our lives gave.

They say,
Our deaths are not ours,
They are yours,
They will mean what you make them.

They say,
Whether our lives and our deaths were for peace and a new hope
Or for nothing
We cannot say.
It is you who must say this.

They say,
We leave you our deaths,
Give them their meaning,
Give them an end to the war and a true peace,
Give them a victory that ends the war and a peace afterwards,
Give them their meaning.

We were young, they say.
We have died.
Remember us.

Archibald MacLeish, 1892–

[1] Written at the end of World War II.

1801. THE PACT

They have no pact to sign—our peaceful dead;
Pacts are for trembling hands and heads grown gray.
Ten million graves record what youth has said,
And cannot now un-say.

They have no pact to sign—our quiet dead
Whose eyes in that eternal peace are drowned.
Age doubts and wakes, and asks if night be fled;
But youth sleeps sound.

They have no pact to sign—our faithful dead.
Theirs was a deeper pledge, unseen, unheard,
Sealed in the dark; not written; sealed with red;
And they will keep their word.

They have no pact to sign—our happy dead.
But if, O God, if WE should sign in vain,
With dreadful eyes, out of each narrow bed,
Our dead will rise again.

Alfred Noyes, 1880–

1802. VALLEY OF THE SHADOW

God, I am travelling out to death's sea,
I, who exulted in sunshine and laughter,
Dreamed not of dying—death is such waste of me!—
Grant me one prayer: Doom not the hereafter
Of mankind to war, as though I had died not—
I, who in battle, my comrade's arm linking,
Shouted and sang, life in my pulses hot
Throbbing and dancing! Let not my sinking
In dark be for naught, my death a vain thing!
God, let me know it the end of man's fever!
Make my last breath a bugle call, carrying
Peace o'er the valleys and cold hills for ever!

John Galsworthy, 1867–1933

1803. DOXOLOGY FOR PEACE

Praise God, ye peoples of the earth,
Praise Him, ye heavens, with august mirth,
Praise Him who rules the nations still
And bends them to His peaceful will.

Praise God, the Father of us all,
Peoples and nations, great and small,
Praise Love that maketh wars to cease
And leads men in the paths of peace.

R. B. Y. Scott,[1] *contemporary Canadian*

1804. TO A JAPANESE GIRL

GRIEVED OVER THE WAR ON CHINA

Dear Cherry Blossom,
Torn between love of country
And suffering Christ,
Men shall turn to your fruitage
Of love, when hate grows bitter.

Belle Chapman Morrill,
contemporary American

1805. AFTERMATH

Have you forgotten yet? . . .
For the world's events have rumbled on since those gagged days,
Like traffic checked awhile at the crossing of city ways:
And the haunted gap in your mind has filled with thoughts that flow
Like clouds in the lit heavens of life; and you're a man reprieved to go,
Taking your peaceful share of time, with joy to spare.
But the past is just the same—and War's a bloody game. . . .
Have you forgotten yet? . . .
Look down, and swear by the slain of the War that you'll never forget.

Do you remember the dark months you held the sector at Mametz—
The nights you watched and wired and dug and piled sandbags on parapets?

Do you remember the rats; and the stench
Of corpses rotting in front of the front-line trench—
And dawn coming, dirty-white, and chill with a hopeless rain?
Do you ever stop and ask, "Is it all going to happen again?"

Do you remember that hour of din before the attack—
And the anger, the blind compassion that seized and shook you then
As you peered at the doomed and haggard faces of your men?
Do you remember the stretcher-cases lurching back

[1] Chaplain, Royal Canadian Air Force, World War II.

With dying eyes and lolling heads—those ashen-gray
Masks of the lads who once were keen and kind and gay?

Have you forgotten yet? . . .
Look up, and swear by the green of the Spring that you'll never forget.

Siegfried Sassoon,[1] 1886–

1806. TO ONE WHO DENIES THE POSSIBILITY OF A PERMANENT PEACE

Old friend, I greet you! you are still the same:
You poisoned Socrates, you crucified
Christ, you have persecuted, mocked, denied,
Rejected God and cursed Him—in God's name.
You gave monotonously to the flame
All those (whom now you honor) when the new
Truth stung their lips—for fear it might be true;
Then reaped where they had sown and felt no shame.
Familiar voice, old adversary—hail!
Yesterday's fools are now your gods. Behold!
The generations pass and we can wait.
You slandered Shelley, Florence Nightingale;
Now a new splendor quivers in the cold
Gray shadows overhead; *still* you are late.

Margaret Sackville, 1881–

1807. GOD OF THE NATIONS

God of the nations, who from dawn of days,
Hast led thy people in their widening ways,
Through whose deep purpose stranger thousands stand
Here in the borders of our promised land.

Thine ancient might rebuked the Pharaoh's boast.
Thou wast the shield for Israel's marching host,
And, all the ages through, past crumbling throne
And broken fetter, thou hast brought thine own.

Thy hand has led across the hungry sea
The eager peoples flocking to be free,
And, from the breeds of earth, thy silent sway
Fashions the nation of the broadening day.

Then, for thy grace to grow in brotherhood,
For hearts aflame to serve thy destined good,
For faith, and will to win what faith shall see,
God of thy people, hear us cry to thee.

W. Russell Bowie, 1882–

[1] English soldier, World War I.

1808. GOD OF THE STRONG, GOD OF THE WEAK

God of the strong, God of the weak,
Lord of all lands, and our own land;
Light of our souls, from Thee we seek
Light from Thy light, strength from Thy
hand.

In suffering Thou hast made us one,
In mighty burdens one are we;
Teach us that lowliest duty done
Is highest service unto Thee.

Teach us, great Teacher of mankind,
The sacrifice that brings Thy balm;
The love, the work that bless and bind;
Teach us Thy majesty, Thy calm.

Teach Thou, and we shall know, indeed,
The truth divine that maketh free;
And knowing, we may sow the seed
That blossoms through eternity.

Richard Watson Gilder, 1844–1909

1809. A WORLD-NATION

God of the glowing love, making men
brothers,
Burn out the dross of belief in the sword;
Fashion one vision more golden than others:
Peace evermore through thy mercy, Lord.

Then shall thy spirit-sons, purged of all
hatred,
Spurning all envy and martial reward,
Stand a world-nation, united and sacred,
Pledging eternal goodwill, O Lord.

Earl B. Marlatt, 1892–

1810. WORLD-BROTHERHOOD

My country is the world;
My flag with stars impearled,
Fills all the skies;
All the round earth I claim,
Peoples of every name;
And all inspiring fame,
My heart would prize.

Mine are all lands and seas,
All flowers, shrubs and trees,
All life's design,
My heart within me thrills,
For all uplifted hills,
And for all streams and rills;
The world is mine.

And all men are my kin,
Since every man has been,
Blood of my blood;
I glory in the grace
And strength of every race,
And joy in every trace
Of brotherhood.

Author unknown

1811. From THE KINDLY NEIGHBOR

I have a kindly neighbor, one who stands
Beside my gate and chats with me awhile,
Gives me the glory of his radiant smile
And comes at times to help with willing
hands.
No station high or rank this man commands;
He, too, must trudge, as I, the long day's
mile;
And yet, devoid of pomp or gaudy style,
He has a worth exceeding stocks or lands.

To him I go when sorrow's at my door;
On him I lean when burdens come my way;
Together oft we talk our trials o'er,
And there is warmth in each good-night we
say.
A kindly neighbor! Wars and strife shall end
When man has made the man next door his
friend.

Edgar A. Guest, 1881–

1812. NO NATION LIVETH UNTO ITSELF

Voices are crying from the dust of Tyre,
From Baalbec and the stones of Babylon:
"We raised our pillars upon self-desire,
And perished from the large gaze of the sun."

Eternity was on the pyramid,
And immortality on Greece and Rome;
But in them all the ancient traitor hid,
And so they tottered like unstable foam.

There was no substance in their soaring hopes;
The voice of Thebes is now a desert cry;

A spider bars the road with filmy ropes
Where once the feet of Carthage thundered
by.

A bittern booms where once fair Helen
laughed;
A thistle nods where once the Forum poured;
A lizard lifts and listens on a shaft,
Where once of old the Colosseum roared.

No house can stand, no kingdom can endure
Built on the crumbling rock of self-desire;
Nothing is living stone, nothing is sure,
That is not whitened in the social fire.

Author unknown

1813. OF ONE BLOOD HATH GOD CREATED

Of one blood hath God created
Every kindred, tribe and tongue;
His is every fane and altar,
Though man's empire be far-flung;
Even though some flout the others,
Underneath are they blood-brothers;
And shall learn, some crucial day,
How to walk a common way.

God of all the warring peoples,
Still art Thou the God of Peace;
Love art Thou, but Love in Sorrow,
Wounded until wars shall cease;
Until Right shall win, our burden
Thou, too, bearest; 'tis the guerdon
Of that dauntless Saviour-hood
Which shall rear the common good.

Keep before us, clear, the vision
Of Thy Holy common-wealth;
Guide us, Thou, in each decision;
Save us from the subtle stealth
Which would fill our souls this hour
With race-hatred, lust of power,
Alienate our life from Thee
And Thy Kingdom, yet to be.

May we, with the Man of Sorrows,
Tread the dangerous path of duty;
Seeking not our own, but serving,
May we grasp, O Lord, the beauty
Of Thy Holiness, wherever
Flames a Love that faileth never,
Burning out the waste and dross,
Saving men from shame and loss.

Grant to us a sense of presence:
Make us all aware of Thee;
May Thy Holy Love unite us
In the bond that sets men free—
Free to understand each other,
Free to claim each as his brother,
Free to build in unity,
Free, O God, yet bound to Thee.

Henry B. Robins, 1874

1814. THE WORLD IS ONE

The world is one; we cannot live apart,
To earth's remotest races we are kin;
God made the generations of one blood;
Man's separation is a sign of sin.

What though we solve the secret of the stars,
Or from the vibrant ether pluck a song,
Can this for all man's tyranny atone
While Mercy weeps and waits and suffers
long?

Put up the sword, its day of anguish past;
Disarm the forts, and then, the war-flags
furled,
Forever keep the air without frontiers,
The great, free, friendly highway of the
world.

So that at last to rapture men may come,
And hear again the music of the spheres,
And stand erect, illumined, radiant, free,
The travail and the triumph of the years.

Hinton White, 20th century American

1815. "ONE WORLD"

The war lords perish with the millions slain,
The glass is broken and the iron chain,
The madness passes and the fever dies;
The storms of passion and the lightning lies
That rent the mountains cease upon the plain,
The world we knew lies shattered in the dawn,
And all our sacrifice is one with Babylon!

Six widowed continents tomorrow
Must build One World out of the heart of
sorrow:
Europe, Africa, Russia, India, Asia,
America!—
Segments and continents aerially linked—
Selah!

Through crime and punishment, these six—
no more—
In balanced equity must vanquish war,
Or perish under hurricane of fire
From ruthless skies in total ruin dire!

The House of Europe, once united, whole,
A many-chambered mansion of the soul,
Must rise, redeemed from violent tears,
Resplendent over dead, demonic years;
The Dream of Europe, ordered, nobly
planned,
In freedom opens, luminous and grand
Above the dead—star-spangled in the dawn
Of peace that desperate eyes now gaze upon.
And East and West, once wide apart,
Must meet in truth—or crush the heart.
God's challenge with satanic bolts is hurled;
Man perishes—or welds his world!

Brent Dow Allinson,
contemporary American

1816. THE NEW AGE

When navies are forgotten
And fleets are useless things,
When the dove shall warm her bosom
Beneath the eagle's wings;

When the memory of battles
At last is strange and old,
When nations have one banner
And creeds have found one fold;

When the Hand that sprinkles midnight
With its dust of powdered suns
Has hushed this tiny tumult
Of sects, and swords, and guns,

Then hate's last note of discord
In all God's world shall cease
In the conquest which is service,
In the victory which is peace!

Frederick Lawrence Knowles, 1869–1905

1817. YEARS OF THE MODERN

Years of the modern! years of the unperform'd!
Your horizon rises—I see it parting away for more august dramas;
I see not America only—I see not only Liberty's nation, but other nations preparing;
I see tremendous entrances and exits—I see new combinations—I see the solidarity of races;
I see that force advancing with irresistible power on the world's stage;
(Have the old forces, the old wars, played their parts? are the acts suitable to them closed?)
I see Freedom, completely arm'd, and victorious, and very haughty, with Law on one side,
and Peace on the other,
A stupendous Trio, all issuing forth against the idea of caste;
—What historic denouements are these we so rapidly approach?
I see men marching and countermarching by swift millions;
I see the frontiers and boundaries of the old aristocracies broken;
I see the landmarks of European kings removed;
I see this day the People beginning their landmarks, (all others give way;)
—Never were such sharp questions ask'd as this day;
Never was average man, his soul, more energetic, more like a God;
Lo! how he urges and urges, leaving the masses no rest;
His daring foot is on land and sea everywhere—he colonizes the Pacific, the archipelagoes;
With the steam-ship, the electric telegraph, the newspaper, the wholesale engines of war,
With these, and the world-spreading factories, he interlinks all geography, all lands;
—What whispers are these, O lands, running ahead of you, passing under the seas?
Are all nations communing? is there going to be but one heart to the globe?
Is humanity forming, en-masse?—for lo! tyrants tremble, crowns grow dim;
The earth, restive, confronts a new era, perhaps a general divine war;
No one knows what will happen next—such portents fill the days and nights;
Years prophetical! the space ahead as I walk, as I vainly try to pierce it, is full of phantoms;
Unborn deeds, things soon to be, project their shapes around me;
This incredible rush and heat—this strange extatic fever of dreams, O years!

Your dreams, O years, how they penetrate through me! (I know not whether I sleep or wake!)
The perform'd America and Europe grow dim, retiring in shadow behind me,
The unperform'd, more gigantic than ever, advance, advance upon me.

Walt Whitman, 1819–1892

1818. THE FEDERATION OF THE WORLD

From "Locksley Hall"

Men, my brothers, men the workers, ever reaping something new;
That which they have done but earnest of the things that they shall do.

For I dipt into the future, far as human eye could see,
Saw the Vision of the world, and all the wonder that would be;

Saw the heavens fill with commerce, argosies of magic sails,
Pilots of the purple twilight, dropping down with costly bales;

Heard the heavens fill with shouting, and there rain'd a ghastly dew
From the nations' airy navies grappling in the central blue;

Far along the world-wide whisper of the south-wind rushing warm,
With the standards of the peoples plunging thro' the thunder-storm;

Till the war-drum throbb'd no longer, and the battle-flags were furl'd
In the Parliament of man, the Federation of the world.

There the common sense of most shall hold a fretful realm in awe,
And the kindly earth shall slumber, lapt in universal law.

❖

Yet I doubt not thro' the ages one increasing purpose runs,
And the thoughts of men are widen'd with the process of the suns.

❖

Not in vain the distance beacons. Forward, forward let us range,
Let the great world spin for ever down the ringing grooves of change.

Thro' the shadow of the globe we sweep into the younger day;
Better fifty years of Europe than a cycle of Cathay.

Alfred Tennyson, 1809–1892

1819. REPUBLIC OF THE WORLD

Upon the skyline glows i' the dark
The Sun that now is but a spark;
But soon will be unfurled—
The glorious banner of us all,
The flag that rises ne'er to fall,
Republic of the World!

Victor Hugo,[1] *1802–1895*

[1]On the wall of the room in which Hugo died, Place des Vosges, Paris, is the following prophecy in autograph:

I represent a party which does not yet exist:
the party of revolution, civilization.
This party will make the twentieth century.
There will issue from it first
the United States of Europe, then
the United States of the World.

Book VII: DEATH AND IMMORTALITY

1820. NATURE

As a fond mother, when the day is o'er,
Leads by the hand her little child to bed,
Half willing, half reluctant to be led,
And leave his broken playthings on the floor,
Still gazing at them through the open door,
Nor wholly reassured and comforted
By promises of others in their stead,
Which, though more splendid, may not please him more;
So Nature deals with us, and takes away
Our playthings one by one, and by the hand
Leads us to rest so gently, that we go
Scarce knowing if we wish to go or stay,
Being too full of sleep to understand
How far the unknown transcends the what we know.

Henry Wadsworth Longfellow, 1807–1882

1821. LIFE[1]

Life! I know not what thou art,
But know that thou and I must part;
And when, or how, or where we met
I own to me's a secret yet.

❖

Life! we've been long together,
Through pleasant and through cloudy weather;
'Tis hard to part when friends are dear—
Perhaps 'twill cost a sigh, a tear;
Then steal away, give little warning,
Choose thine own time;
Say not Good Night,—but in some brighter clime
Bid me Good Morning.

Anna Letitia Barbauld, 1743–1825

1822. YOU ARE THE FUTURE

You are the future, the great sunrise red
above the broad plains of eternity.
You are the cock-crow when time's night has fled,
You are the dew, the matins, and the maid,
the stranger and the mother, you are death.

You are the changeful shape that out of Fate
rears up in everlasting solitude,
The unlamented and the unacclaimed,
beyond describing as some savage wood.

You are the deep epitome of things
that keeps its being's secret with locked lip,
and shows itself to others otherwise:
to the ship, a haven—to the land, a ship.

Rainer Maria Rilke, 1875–1926; tr. from the German by Babette Deutsch, 1941

1823. THOUGHT

As I sit with others, at a great feast, suddenly, while the music is playing,
To my mind, (whence it comes I know not,) spectral, in mist, of a wreck at sea;
Of certain ships—how they sail from port with flying streamers, and wafted kisses—and that is the last of them!
Of the solemn and murky mystery about the fate of the President;

[1] Written c. 1813; published posthumously, 1825.

Of the flower of the marine science of fifty generations, founder'd off the Northeast coast,
and going down—Of the steamship Arctic going down,
Of the veil'd tableau—Women gather'd together on deck, pale, heroic, waiting the moment
that draws so close—O the moment!
A huge sob—A few bubbles—the white foam spirting up—And then the women gone,
Sinking there, while the passionless wet flows on—And I now pondering, Are those women
indeed gone?
Are Souls drown'd and destroy'd so?
Is only matter triumphant?

Walt Whitman, 1819–1892

1824. THE LAST INVOCATION

At the last, tenderly,
From the walls of the powerful, fortress'd house,
From the clasp of the knitted locks—from the keep of the well-closed doors,
Let me be wafted.

Let me glide noiselessly forth;
With the key of softness unlock the locks—with a whisper,
Set ope the doors, O Soul!

Tenderly! be not impatient!
(Strong is your hold, O mortal flesh!
Strong is your hold, O love.)

Walt Whitman, 1819–1892

1825. HAMLET CONTEMPLATES DEATH

From "Hamlet," Act III, sc. 1

To be, or not to be: that is the question:
Whether 'tis nobler in the mind to suffer
The slings and arrows of outrageous fortune,
Or to take arms against a sea of troubles,
And by opposing end them? To die: to sleep;
No more; and, by a sleep to say we end
The heart-ache and the thousand natural shocks
That flesh is heir to, 'tis a consummation
Devoutly to be wish'd. To die, to sleep;
To sleep: perchance to dream: ay, there's the rub;
For in that sleep of death what dreams may come
When we have shuffled off this mortal coil,
Must give us pause. There's the respect
That makes calamity of so long life;
For who would bear the whips and scorns of time,
The oppressor's wrong, the proud man's contumely,
The pangs of dispriz'd love, the law's delay,
The insolence of office, and the spurns
That patient merit of the unworthy takes,
When he himself might his quietus make
With a bare bodkin? who would fardels bear,

To grunt and sweat under a weary life,
But that the dread of something after death,
The undiscover'd country from whose bourn
No traveler returns, puzzles the will,
And makes us rather bear those ills we have
Than fly to others that we know not of?
Thus conscience doth make cowards of us all;
And thus the native hue of resolution
Is sicklied o'er with the pale cast of thought,
And enterprises of great pith and moment
With this regard their currents turn awry,
And lose the name of action.

William Shakespeare, 1564–1616

1826. DEATH

As the production of the metal proveth the work of the alchemist, so is death the test of our lives, the assay which sheweth the standard of all our actions.

He hath not spent his life ill, who knoweth to die well; neither can he have lost all his time, who employeth the last portion of it to his honor.

Avoid not death, for it is a weakness; fear it not, for thou understandest not what it is; all that thou certainly knowest is, that it putteth an end to thy sorrows.

Think not the longest life the happiest; that which is best employed, doth man the most honor. . . .

From an Indian manuscript

1827. THE TWO MYSTERIES

We know not what it is, dear, this sleep so deep and still;
The folded hands, the awful calm, the cheek so pale and chill;
The lids that will not lift again, though we may call and call;
The strange white solitude of peace that settles over all.

We know not what it means, dear, this desolate heart pain;
This dread to take our daily way, and walk in it again;
We know not to what other sphere the loved who leave us go,
Nor why we're left to wonder still, nor why we do not know.

But this we know: our loved and dead, if they should come this day,—
Should come and ask us, "What is Life?"—not one of us could say.
Life is a mystery, as deep as ever death can be;
Yet, oh, how dear it is to us, this life we live and see!

Then might they say—these vanished ones—and blessed is the thought,
"So death is sweet to us, beloved! though we may show you naught;
We may not to the quick reveal the mystery of death—
Ye cannot tell us, if ye would, the mystery of breath!"

The child who enters life comes not with knowledge or intent,
So those who enter death must go as little children sent.
Nothing is known. But I believe that God is overhead;
And as life is to the living, so death is to the dead.

Mary Mapes Dodge, 1838–1905

1828. WHO ARE THE DEAD?

Who knows if in the world beneath the ground,
Life is accounted death, death life? who knows?

Euripides, 484–406 B.C., tr. by James Adam

1829. THE OUTER AND THE INNER MAN

Sonnet CXLVI

Poor Soul, the centre of my sinful earth,
Fail'd by those rebel powers that thee array,
Why dost thou pine within and suffer dearth,
Painting thy outward walls so costly gay?
Why so large cost, having so short a lease,
Dost thou upon thy fading mansion spend?
Shall worms, inheritors of this excess,
Eat up thy charge? Is this thy body's end?
Then, Soul, live thou upon thy servant's loss,
And let that pine to aggravate thy store;
Buy terms divine in selling hours of dross;
Within be fed, without be rich no more;
So shalt thou feed on Death, that feeds on men;
And Death once dead, there's no more dying then.

William Shakespeare, 1564–1616

1830. DEATH THE LEVELER

From "The Contention of Ajax and Ulysses," Sc. 3

The glories of our blood and state
Are shadows, not substantial things;
There is no armor against fate;
Death lays his icy hand on kings:
Scepter and Crown
Must tumble down,
And in the dust be equal made
With the poor crooked scythe and spade.

Some men with swords may reap the field,
And plant fresh laurels where they kill:
But their strong nerves at last must yield;
They tame but one another still:
Early or late
They stoop to fate,
And must give up their murmuring breath
When they, pale captives, creep to death.

The garlands wither on your brow;
Then boast no more your mighty deeds;
Upon Death's purple altar now
See where the victor-victim bleeds;
Your heads must come
To the cold tomb;
Only the actions of the just
Smell sweet, and blossom in their dust.

James Shirley, 1596–1666

1831. LINES ON THE TOMBS IN WESTMINSTER

Mortality, behold and fear!
What a change of flesh is here!
Think how many royal bones
Sleep within this heap of stones;
Here they lie had realms and lands,
Who now want strength to stir their hands;
Where from their pulpits sealed with dust
They preach, 'In greatness is no trust.'
Here's an acre sown indeed
With the richest royal'st seed
That the earth did e'er suck in,
Since the first man died for sin;
Here the bones of birth have cried,
'Though gods they were, as men they died.'
Here are sands, ignoble things,
Dropt from the ruined sides of kings.
Here's a world of pomp and state,
Buried in dust, once dead by fate.

Francis Beaumont, 1584–1616

1832. ON DEATH—A SONNET

Ecclesiasticus 41

O Death,
How bitter is the remembrance of thee
To a man that is at peace in his possessions,
Unto the man that hath nothing to distract him,
And hath prosperity in all things,
And that still hath strength to receive meat!

O Death,
Acceptable is thy sentence
Unto a man that is needy, and that faileth in strength,
That is in extreme old age,
And is distracted about all things,
And is perverse, and hath lost patience!

Fear not the sentence of Death;
Remember them that have been before thee,
And that come after.
This is the sentence from the LORD over all flesh:
And why dost thou refuse,
When it is the good pleasure of the Most High?
Whether it be ten, or a hundred,
Or a thousand years,
There is no inquisition of life in the grave.

Moulton: The Modern Reader's Bible, 1895

1833. FORGIVENESS

My heart was heavy, for its trust had been
Abused, its kindness answered with foul wrong;
So, turning gloomily from my fellow-men
One summer Sabbath day I strolled among
The green mounds of the village burial-place;
Where, pondering how all human love and hate
Find one sad level; and how, soon or late,
Wronged and wrongdoer, each with meekened face,
And cold hands folded over a still heart,
Pass the green threshold of our common grave,
Whither all footsteps tend, whence none depart,
Awed for myself, and pitying my race,
Our common sorrow, like a mighty wave,
Swept all my pride away, and trembling I forgave!

John Greenleaf Whittier, 1807–1892

1834. MEN WHO TURN FROM GOD

From "The Rock," III

O weariness of men who turn from GOD
To the grandeur of your mind and the glory of your action,
To arts and inventions and daring enterprises,
To schemes of human greatness thoroughly discredited,
Binding the earth and the water to your service,
Exploiting the seas and developing the mountains,
Dividing the stars into common and preferred,
Engaged in devising the perfect refrigerator,
Engaged in working out a rational morality,
Engaged in printing as many books as possible,
Plotting of happiness and flinging empty bottles,
Turning from your vacancy to fevered enthusiasm
For nation or race or what you call humanity;
Though you forget the way to the Temple,
There is one who remembers the way to your door:
Life you may evade, but Death you shall not.
You shall not deny the Stranger.

T. S. Eliot, 1888–

1835. THE HOMELAND

I vow to thee, my country, all earthly things above
Entire and whole and perfect, the service of my love.
The love that asks no questions; the love that stands the test,
That lays upon the altar the dearest and the best;
The love that never falters, the love that pays the price;
The love that makes undaunted the final sacrifice.

And there's another country I've heard of long ago,
Most dear to them that love her, most great to them that know
We may not count her armies, we may not see her King;
Her fortress is a faithful heart, her pride is suffering.
And soul by soul and silently her shining bounds increase,
And her ways are ways of gentleness and all her paths are peace. Amen.

Sir Cecil Spring-Rice,[1] *1859–1918*

1836. BE NOT AFRAID

From "The Song of the Open Road"

We too take ship, O soul
Joyous we too launch out on trackless seas . . .
Caroling free, singing our song of God,
Chanting our chant of pleasant exploration . . .
Sail forth—steer for the deep waters only,
Reckless, O soul, exploring, I with thee, and thou with me,
For we are bound where the mariner has not yet dared to go,
And we will risk the ship, ourselves and all.

O my brave soul!
O farther, farther sail!
O daring joy but safe! are they not all the seas of God?
O farther, farther, farther sail.

Walt Whitman, 1819–1892

1837. DEATH

From "Continuation of Lucan"

The wisest men are glad to die; no fear
Of death can touch a true philosopher.
Death sets the soul at liberty to fly.

Thomas May, 1594–1650

1838. WHEN I HAVE FEARS

When I have fears that I may cease to be
Before my pen has glean'd my teeming brain,
Before high-pilèd books, in charact'ry
Hold like rich garners the full-ripen'd grain;
When I behold, upon the night's starr'd face,
Huge cloudy symbols of a high romance,
And think that I may never live to trace
Their shadows, with the magic hand of
chance;
And when I feel, fair Creature of an hour!
That I shall never look upon thee more,
Never have relish in the fairy power
Of unreflecting love—then on the shore
Of the wide world I stand alone, and think
Till Love and Fame to nothingness do sink.

John Keats, 1795–1821

[1] Written the night he completed his term as British Ambassador to the United States. The next day, fatally ill, he sailed for England.

1839. PROSPICE

FEAR death?—to feel the fog in my throat,
  The mist in my face,
When the snows begin, and the blasts denote
  I am nearing the place,
The power of the night, the press of the storm,
  The post of the foe;
Where he stands, the Arch Fear in a visible form,
  Yet the strong man must go:
For the journey is done and the summit attained,
  And the barriers fall,
Though a battle's to fight ere the guerdon be gained,
  The reward of it all.
I was ever a fighter, so—one fight more,
  The best and the last!
I would hate that death bandaged my eyes, and forbore,
  And bade me creep past.
No! let me taste the whole of it, fare like my peers
  The heroes of old,
Bear the brunt, in a minute pay glad life's arrears
  Of pain, darkness, and cold.
For sudden the worst turns the best to the brave,
  The black minute's at end,
And the elements' rage, the fiend-voices that rave,
  Shall dwindle, shall blend,
Shall change, shall become first a peace out of pain,
  Then a light, then thy breast,
O thou soul of my soul! I shall clasp thee again,
  And with God be the rest!

Robert Browning,[1] *1812–1889*

1840. DEATH

Why be afraid of death, as though your life were breath?
Death but anoints your eyes with clay. O glad surprise!

Why should you be forlorn? Death only husks the corn.
Why should you fear to meet the thresher of the wheat?

Is sleep a thing to dread? Yet sleeping you are dead
Till you awake and rise, here, or beyond the skies.

Why should it be a wrench to leave your wooden bench?
Why not, with happy shout, run home when school is out?

The dear ones left behind? Oh, foolish one and blind!
A day and you will meet—a night and you will greet.

[1] When Robert Browning's father lay dying—he was past eighty at the time—his cheerfulness alarmed the attending physician. "Does the old gentleman know he is dying?", the doctor inquired of his daughter in a low voice. The father overheard him and smiled, "Death is no enemy in my eyes." The poet-son seems to have shared his father's Christian optimism with regard to death as is evidenced by the above poem written shortly after the death of his wife, Elizabeth Barrett Browning.

This is the death of death, to breathe away a breath
And know the end of strife, and taste the deathless life,

And joy without a fear, and smile without a tear;
And work, nor care to rest, and find the last the best.

Maltbie D. Babcock, 1858–1901

1841. DEATH STANDS ABOVE ME

Death stands above me, whispering low
I know not what into my ear:
Of his strange language all I know
Is, there is not a word of fear.

Walter Savage Landor, 1775–1864

1842. DEATH

What if some little paine the passage haue,
That makes fraile flesh to feare the bitter waue?
Is not short paine well borne, that brings long ease,
And layes the soule to sleepe in quiet graue?
Sleepe after toyle, port after stormie seas,
Ease after warre, death after life does greatly please.

Edmund Spenser, 1552?–1599

1843. MY SOUL AND I

As treading some long corridor,
My soul and I together go;
Each day unlocks another door
To a new room we did not know.

And every night the darkness hides
My soul from me awhile—but then
No fear nor loneliness abides;
Hand clasped in hand, we wake again

So when my soul and I, at last,
Shall find but one dim portal more,
Shall we, remembering all the past,
Yet fear to try that other door?

Charles Buxton Going, 1863–

1844. TO DEATH

But for your Terror
Where would be Valour?
What is Love for
But to stand in your way?
Taker and Giver,
For all your endeavour
You leave us with more
Than you touch with decay!

Oliver St. John Gogarty, 1878–

1845. DAREST THOU NOW, O SOUL

From "Whispers of Heavenly Death"

Darest thou now, O Soul,
Walk out with me toward the Unknown Region,
Where neither ground is for the feet, nor any path to follow?

No map, there, nor guide,
Nor voice sounding, nor touch of human hand,
Nor face with blooming flesh, nor lips, nor eyes, are in that land.

I know it not, O Soul;
Nor dost thou—all is a blank before us;
All waits, undream'd of, in that region—that inaccessible land.

Till, when the ties loosen,
All but the ties eternal, Time and Space,
Nor darkness, gravitation, sense, nor any bounds, bound us.

Then we burst forth—we float,
In Time and Space, O Soul—prepared for them;
Equal, equipt at last—(O Joy! O fruit of all!) them to fulfil, O Soul.

Walt Whitman, 1819–1892

1846. THE DYING CHRISTIAN TO HIS SOUL

Vital spark of heavenly flame!
Quit, O quit this mortal frame!
Trembling, hoping, lingering, flying,
O the pain, the bliss of dying!
Cease, fond Nature, cease thy strife,
And let me languish into life!

Hark! they whisper; angels say:—
"Sister Spirit, come away!"
What is this absorbs me quite?
Steals my senses, shuts my sight,
Drowns my spirit, draws my breath?
Tell me, my soul, can this be death?

The world recedes; it disappears!
Heaven opens on my eyes! my ears
With sounds seraphic ring!
Lend, lend your wings! I mount! I fly!
O Grave! where is thy victory?
O Death! where is thy sting?

Alexander Pope, 1688–1744

1847. LAST LINES

No coward soul is mine,
No trembler in the world's storm-troubled sphere:
I see Heaven's glories shine,
And faith shines equal, arming me from fear.

O God within my breast,
Almighty, ever-present Deity!
Life—that in me has rest,
As I—undying Life—have power in Thee.

Vain are the thousand creeds
That move men's hearts: unutterably vain;
Worthless as wither'd weeds,
Or idlest froth amid the boundless main,

To waken doubt in one
Holding so fast by thine infinity;
So surely anchored on
The steadfast rock of immortality.

With wide-embracing love
Thy spirit animates eternal years,
Pervades and broods above,
Changes, sustains, dissolves, creates, and rears.

Though earth and man were gone,
And suns and universes ceased to be,
And Thou were left alone,
Every existence would exist in Thee.

There is not room for Death,
Nor atom that his might could render void:
Thou—THOU art Being and Breath,
And what Thou art may never be destroyed.

Emily Brontë, 1818–1848

1848. INVICTUS

In Memoriam R. T. Hamilton Bruce

Out of the night that covers me,
Black as the Pit from pole to pole,
I thank whatever gods may be
For my unconquerable soul.

In the fell clutch of circumstance
I have not winced nor cried aloud.
Under the bludgeonings of chance
My head is bloody, but unbowed.

Beyond this place of wrath and tears
Looms but the Horror of the shade,
And yet the menace of the years
Finds, and shall find me unafraid.

It matters not how strait the gate,
How charged with punishments the scroll,
I am the master of my fate;
I am the captain of my soul.

William Ernest Henley, 1849–1003

1849. THE JOURNEY

When Death, the angel of our higher dreams,
Shall come, far ranging from the hills of light
He will not catch me unaware; for I
Shall be as now communing with the dawn.
For I shall make all haste to follow him
Along the valley, up the misty slope
Where life lets go and Life at last is born.
There I shall find the dreams that I have lost
On toilsome earth, and they will guide me on,
Beyond the mists unto the farthest height.
I shall not grieve except to pity those
Who cannot hear the songs that I shall hear!

Thomas Curtis Clark, 1877–

1850. THE TRYST

O the way sometimes is low,
And the waters dark and deep,
And I stumble as I go.

But I have a tryst to keep:
It was plighted long ago
With some who lie asleep.

And though days go dragging slow,
And the sad hours gravewards creep,
And the world is hush'd with woe,

I neither wail nor weep,
For He would not have it so:
And I have a tryst to keep.

Lauchlan MacLean Watt, 1867–

1851. BE YE ALSO READY

From "Thanatopsis"

So live, that when thy summons comes to join
The innumerable caravan, which moves
To that mysterious realm, where each shall take
His chamber in the silent halls of death,
Thou go not, like the quarry-slave at night,
Scourged to his dungeon, but, sustained and soothed
By an unfaltering trust, approach thy grave,
Like one who wraps the drapery of his couch
About him, and lies down to pleasant dreams.

William Cullen Bryant, 1794–1878

1852. LET ME DIE WORKING

Let me die, working.
Still tackling plans unfinished, tasks undone!
Clean to its end, swift may my race be run.
No laggard steps, no faltering, no shirking;
Let me die, working!

Let me die, thinking.
Let me fare forth still with an open mind,
Fresh secrets to unfold, new truths to find,
My soul undimmed, alert, no question blinking;
Let me die, thinking!

Let me die, laughing.
No sighing o'er past sins; they are forgiven.
Spilled on this earth are all the joys of Heaven;
The wine of life, the cup of mirth quaffing.
Let me die, laughing!

S. Hall Young, 1847–1927

1853. AFTER WORK

Lord, when Thou seest that my work is done,
Let me not linger on,
With failing powers,
Adown the weary hours,—
A workless worker in a world of work.
But, with a word,
Just bid me home,
And I will come
Right gladly,—
Yea, right gladly
Will I come.

John Oxenham, 1852–1941

1854. FROM DARK TO LIGHT

I know the night is drawing near,
The mists lie low on hill and bay,
The autumn sheaves are dewless, dry,
But I have had the day.

Yes, I have had, dear Lord, the day.
When at Thy call I have the night,
Brief be the twilight as I pass
From light to dark, from dark to light.

S. Weir Mitchell, 1829–1914

1855. IN THE HOSPITAL[1]

I lay me down to sleep,
With little thought or care
Whether my waking find
Me here or there.

A bowing, burdened head,
That only asks to rest,
Unquestioning, upon
A loving breast.

My good right hand forgets
Its cunning now.
To march the weary march
I know not how.

I am not eager, bold,
Nor strong—all that is past;
I am ready not to do
At last, at last.

My half day's work is done,
And this is all my part;
I give a patient God
My patient heart,

And grasp His banner still,
Though all its blue be dim;
These stripes, no less than stars,
Lead after Him.

M. W. Howland, 1832–1864

1856. SO BE MY PASSING

"In Memoriam Margaritæ Sorori"

A late lark twitters from the quiet skies:
And from the west,
Where the sun, his day's work ended,
Lingers as in content,
There falls on the old, gray city
An influence luminous and serene,
A shining peace.
The smoke ascends
In a rosy-and-golden haze. The spires
Shine, and are changed. In the valley
Shadows rise. The lark sings on. The sun,
Closing his benediction,
Sinks, and the darkening air
Thrills with a sense of the triumphing night—
Night with her train of stars
And her great gift of sleep.

So be my passing!
My task accomplish'd and the long day done,
My wages taken, and in my heart
Some late lark singing,
Let me be gather'd to the quiet west,
The sundown splendid and serene,
Death.

William Ernest Henley, 1849–1903

1857. ON HIS SEVENTY-FIFTH BIRTHDAY

I strove with none; for none was worth my strife,
Nature I loved, and next to Nature, Art;
I warmed both hands before the fire of life,
It sinks, and I am ready to depart.

Walter Savage Landor, 1775–1864

1858. L'ENVOI

Seek not for me within a tomb;
You shall not find me in the clay!
I pierce a little wall of gloom
To mingle with the Day!

I brothered with the things that pass,
Poor giddy Joy and puckered Grief;
I go to brother with the Grass
And with the sunning Leaf.

Not Death can sheathe me in a shroud;
A joy-sword whetted keen with pain,
I join the armies of the Cloud,
The Lightning and the Rain.

O subtle in the sap athrill,
Athletic in the glad uplift,
A portion of the Cosmic Will,
I pierce the planet-drift.

[1] Said to have been found under the pillow of a soldier who died in hospital, Port Royal, S. Carolina, 1864.

My God and I shall interknit
As rain and Ocean, breath and Air;
And O, the luring thought of it
Is prayer!

John G. Neihardt, 1881–

1859. PRAYER BEFORE EXECUTION

O merciful Father, my hope is in thee!
O Gracious Redeemer, deliver thou me!
My bondage bemoaning, with sorrowful
groaning,
I long to be free;
Lamenting, relenting, and humbly repenting,
O Jesu, my Saviour, I languish for thee!

Mary Queen of Scots, 1542–1587

1860. DIES IRAE

That day of wrath, that dreadful day,
When heaven and earth shall pass away,
What power shall be the sinner's stay?
How shall he meet that dreadful day?

When, shrivelling like a parchèd scroll,
The flaming heavens together roll;
When louder yet, and yet more dread,
Swells the high trump that wakes the dead:

Oh, on that day, that wrathful day,
When man to judgment wakes from clay,
Be Thou the trembling sinner's stay,
Tho' heaven and earth shall pass away.

Sir Walter Scott, 1771–1832

1861. HOPE IN HIM WHILE THOU LIVEST

O Friend, hope in Him while thou livest,
Know Him while thou livest,
For in life is thy release.
If thy bonds be not broken when thou livest,
What hope of deliverance in death?

It is but an empty dream that the soul must
pass into union with Him,
Because it hath passed from the body.

If He is found now, He is found then:
If not, we go but to dwell in the city of Death.

If thou hast union now, thou shalt have it
hereafter.

Kabir, (India), 1450–1518

1862. A PRAYER IN THE PROSPECT OF DEATH

O Thou unknown, Almighty Cause
Of all my hope and fear!
In whose dread presence, ere an hour,
Perhaps I must appear!

If I have wander'd in those paths
Of life I ought to shun—
As something, loudly, in my breast,
Remonstrates I have done—

Thou know'st that Thou hast formèd me
With passions wild and strong;
And list'ning to their witching voice
Has often led me wrong.

Where human weakness has come short,
Or frailty stept aside,
Do thou, All-Good—for such Thou art—
In shades of darkness hide.

Where with intention I have err'd,
No other plea I have,
But, Thou art good; and Goodness still
Delighteth to forgive.

Robert Burns, 1759–1796

1863. EPILOGUE

From "Asolando"[1]

At the midnight in the silence of the sleep-time,
When you set your fancies free,
Will they pass to where—by death, fools think, imprisoned—

[1] First published the day of Browning's death.

Low he lies who once so loved you, whom you loved so,
—Pity me?

Oh to love so, be so loved, yet so mistaken!
What had I on earth to do
With the slothful, with the mawkish, the unmanly?
Like the aimless, helpless, hopeless, did I drivel
—Being—who?

One who never turned his back but marched breast forward,
Never doubted clouds would break,
Never dreamed, though right were worsted, wrong would triumph,
Held we fall to rise, are baffled to fight better,
Sleep to wake.

No, at noonday in the bustle of man's work-time
Greet the unseen with a cheer!
Bid him forward, breast and back as either should be,
"Strive and thrive!" cry "Speed,—fight on, fare ever
There as here!"

Robert Browning, 1812–1889

1864. O COME QUICKLY!

Never weather-beaten sail more willing bent to shore,
Never tired Pilgrim's limbs affected slumber more,
Than my wearied sprite now longs to fly out of my troubled breast.
O come quickly, sweetest Lord, and take my soul to rest.

Ever-blooming are the joys of heav'n's high paradise,
Cold age deafs not there our ears, nor vapour dims our eyes:
Glory there the sun outshines, whose beams the blessèd only see;
O come quickly, glorious Lord, and raise my sprite to thee.

Thomas Campion, 1567–1620

1865. MY SUN SETS TO RISE AGAIN

From "At the Mermaid"

Have you found your life distasteful?
My life did, and does, smack sweet.
Was your youth of pleasure wasteful?
Mine I saved, and hold complete.
Do your joys with age diminish?
When mine fail me, I'll complain.
Must in death your daylight finish?
My sun sets to rise again.

Robert Browning, 1812–1889

1866. From THE FROGS

Let us hasten—let us fly—
Where the lovely meadows lie;
Where the living waters flow;
Where the roses bloom and blow.
Heirs of immortality,
Segregated, safe and pure,
Easy, sorrowless, secure;
Since our earthly course is run,
We behold a brighter sun.
Holy lives—a holy vow—
Such rewards await us now.

From the Greek of
Aristophanes, 455–375 B.C.

1867. From THE LAST PORTAGE

As the stars go out so let me go
With a quick leap and a clear light
And a joyous understanding—
My form erect in the driving snow
And the winds that over the borders blow,

Whether by day or by drear night
I make my lonely landing.
You shall not know
That I am old
By word of woe
Or hands grown cold;
But swift and bold, as when a boy,
I'll make the Last Portage with joy—
And I'll find there
White-robed and fair
The Lord of Life commanding.

Wilson MacDonald, 1880–

1868. TO PATHS UNKNOWN

When on my day of life the night is falling,
And, in the winds from unsunned spaces blown,
I hear far voices out of darkness calling
My feet to paths unknown,

Thou, who hast made my home of life so pleasant,
Leave not its tenant when its walls decay:
O Love Divine, O Helper ever present,
Be Thou my strength and stay!

Be near me when all else is from me drifting:
Earth, sky, home's pictures, days of shade and shine,
And kindly faces to my own uplifting
The love which answers mine.

I have but Thee, my Father! let Thy Spirit
Be with me then to comfort and uphold;
No gate of pearl, no branch of palm I merit
Nor street of shining gold.

Suffice it if—my good and ill unreckoned,
And both forgiven through Thy abounding grace—
I find myself by hands familiar beckoned
Unto my fitting place.

Some humble door among Thy many mansions,
Some sheltering shade where sin and striving cease,
And flows forever through heaven's green expansions
The river of Thy peace.

There, from the music round about me stealing,
I fain would learn the new and holy song,
And find at last, beneath Thy trees of healing,
The life for which I long.

John Greenleaf Whittier, 1807–1892

1869. THE TWO SHIPS

As I stand by the cross on the lone mountain's crest,
Looking over the ultimate sea,
In the gloom of the mountain a ship lies at rest,
And one sails away from the lea:
One spreads its white wings on a far-reaching track,
With pennant and sheet flowing free;
One hides in the shadow with sails laid aback,—
The ship that is waiting for me!

But lo! in the distance the clouds break away,
The Gate's glowing portals I see;
And I hear from the outgoing ship in the bay
The song of the sailors in glee.
So I think of the luminous footprints that bore
The comfort o'er dark Galilee,
And wait for the signal to go to the shore,
To the ship that is waiting for me.

Bret Harte, 1836–1902

1870. JOURNEY'S END

"The spirit shall return unto God who gave it"

We go from God to God—then though
The way be long,
We shall return to Heaven our home
At evensong.

We go from God to God—so let
The space between
Be filled with beauty, conquering
Things base and mean.

We go from God to God—lo! what
Transcendent bliss,
To know the journey's end will hold
Such joy as this!

Evelyn H. Healey

1871. DEATH IS BEFORE ME TO-DAY[1]

Death is before me to-day
Like the recovery of a sick man,
Like going forth into a garden after sickness.

Death is before me to-day
Like the odor of myrrh,
Like sitting under the sail on a windy day. . . .

Death is before me to-day
Like the course of the freshet,
Like the return of a man from the war-galley
to his house.

Death is before me to-day
Like the clearing of the sky,
Like a man fowling therein toward that which
he knew not.

Death is before me to-day
As a man longs to see his house
When he has spent years in captivity.

From the Egyptian, 2500–1600 B.C.

1872. WELL DONE

Servant of God, well done!
Rest from thy loved employ:
The battle fought, the victory won,
Enter thy Master's joy.

The pains of death are past,
Labour and sorrow cease,
And Life's long warfare closed at last,
Thy soul is found in peace.

James Montgomery, 1771–1854

1873. THE HILLS OF REST

Beyond the last horizon's rim,
Beyond adventure's farthest quest,
Somewhere they rise, serene and dim,
The happy, happy, Hills of Rest.

Upon their sunlit slopes uplift
The castles we have built in Spain—
While fair amid the summer drift
Our faded gardens flower again.

Sweet hours we did not live go by
To soothing note, on scented wing;
In golden-lettered volumes lie
The songs we tried in vain to sing.

They all are there; the days of dream
That build the inner lives of men;
The silent, sacred years we deem
The might be and the might have been.

Some evening when the sky is gold
I'll follow day into the west;
Nor pause, nor heed, till I behold
The happy, happy Hills of Rest.

Albert Bigelow Paine, 1861–1937

1874. TEARS

When I consider Life and its few years—
A wisp of fog betwixt us and the sun;
A call to battle, and the battle done
Ere the last echo dies within our ears;
A rose choked in the grass; an hour of fears;
The gusts that past a darkening shore do beat;
The burst of music down an unlistening
street,—
I wonder at the idleness of tears.

Ye old, old dead, and ye of yesternight,
Chieftains, and bards, and keepers of the
sheep,
By every cup of sorrow that you had,
Loose me from tears, and make me see aright

[1] Mr. Walter de la Mare speaks of this as "the most ancient poem I know."

How each hath back what once he stayed to
weep:
Homer his sight, David his little lad!

Lizette Woodworth Reese, 1856–1935

1875. SWING LOW, SWEET CHARIOT

Swing low, sweet chariot,
Comin' for to carry me home,
Swing low, sweet chariot,
Comin' for to carry me home.

I look'd over Jordan,
An' what did I see,
Comin' for to carry me home?
A band of angels comin' after me,
Comin' for to carry me home.

If you get-a dere befo' I do,
Comin' for to carry me home,
Tell all my friends I'm comin' too,
Comin' for to carry me home.

O swing low, sweet chariot,
Comin' for to carry me home,
Swing low, sweet chariot,
Comin' for to carry me home.

Negro Spiritual

1876. WHEN DEATH SHALL COME

When death shall come to summon us at last,
Some will remember children and the sound
Of little footsteps hallowing the past,
As driven snowflakes hallow oft the ground;
Some will remember sunlight on a fence;
And some the breath of blossoms in the
rain;
Some will glimpse stars. And all the going
hence
Of these will be a wishing to remain.
But some will think of One who said, "And I,
If I be lifted up will draw to me
All men." And when these latter come to die,
With faces lifted to Eternity
They shall go forth with calm, untroubled
eyes,
Like children hasting to a glad surprise.

Helen Frazee-Bower,
contemporary American

1877. DEATH CAROL

From "President Lincoln's Burial Hymn: When Lilacs Last in the Dooryard Bloom'd," 16

Come, lovely and soothing Death,
Undulate round the world, serenely arriving, arriving,
In the day, in the night, to all, to each,
Sooner or later, delicate Death.

Prais'd be the fathomless universe,
For life and joy, and for objects and knowledge curious,
And for love, sweet love—but praise! praise! praise!
For the sure-enwinding arms of cool-enfolding Death.

Dark Mother, always gliding near, with soft feet,
Have none chanted for thee a chant of fullest welcome?
Then I chant it for thee—I glorify thee above all;
I bring thee a song that when thou must indeed come, come unfalteringly.

Approach, strong deliveress;
When it is so—when thou hast taken them, I joyously sing the dead,
Lost in the loving, floating ocean of thee,
Laved in the flood of thy bliss, O Death.

From me to thee glad serenades,
Dances for thee I propose saluting thee—adornments and feastings for thee;

And the sights of the open landscape, and the high-spread sky, are fitting,
And life and the fields, and the huge and thoughtful night.

The night, in silence, under many a star;
The ocean shore, and the husky whispering wave, whose voice I know;
And the soul turning to thee, O vast and well-veil'd Death,
And the body gratefully nestling close to thee.
Over the tree-tops I float thee a song;
Over the rising and sinking waves—over the myriad fields, and the prairies wide;
Over the dense-pack'd cities all, and the teeming wharves and ways,
I float this carol with joy, with joy to thee, O Death!

Walt Whitman, 1819–1892

1878. THE OLD ENEMY

Rebellion against death, the old rebellion,
Is over; I have nothing left to fight;
Battles have always had their meed of music,
But peace is quiet as a windless night.

Therefore I make no songs—I have grown certain,
Save when he comes too late, death is a friend,
A shepherd leading home his flock serenely
Under the planet at the evening's end.

Sara Teasdale, 1884–1933

1879. EARLY DEATH

She passed away, like morning dew,
Before the sun was high;
So brief her time, she scarcely knew
The meaning of a sigh.

As round the rose its soft perfume,
Sweet love around her floated;
Admired she grew—while mortal doom
Crept on, unfeared, unnoted.

Love was her guardian Angel here,
But love to death resigned her;
Tho' love was kind, why should we fear,
But holy death is kinder?

Hartley Coleridge, 1796–1849

1880. THE DEATH-BED

We watch'd her breathing thro' the night,
Her breathing soft and low,
As in her breast the wave of life
Kept heaving to and fro.

So silently we seem'd to speak,
So slowly moved about,
As we had lent her half our powers
To eke her living out.

Our very hopes belied our fears,
Our fears our hopes belied—
We thought her dying when she slept,
And sleeping when she died.

For when the morn came dim and sad
And chill with early showers,
Her quiet eyelids closed—she had
Another morn than ours.

Thomas Hood, 1799–1845

1881. THE SILENT VOICES

When the dumb Hour, clothed in black,
Brings the Dreams about my bed,
Call me not so often back,
Silent Voices of the dead,
Toward the lowland ways behind me,
And the sunlight that is gone!
Call me rather, silent voices,
Forward to the starry track
Glimmering up the heights beyond me
On, and always on!

Alfred Tennyson,[1] 1809–1892

1882. A JOURNEY ENDS

I have seen death too often to believe in death.
It is not an ending . . . but a withdrawal,
As one who finishes a long journey,
Stills the motor,
Turns off the lights,

[1] Written shortly before his death.

Steps from his car
And walks up the path
To the home that awaits him.

Don Blanding, 1894–

1883. BEYOND THE HORIZON

When men go down to the sea in ships,
'Tis not to the sea they go;
Some isle or pole the mariners' goal,
And thither they sail through calm and gale,
When down to the sea they go.

When souls go down to the sea by ship,
And the dark ship's name is Death,
Why mourn and wail at the vanishing sail?
Though outward bound, God's world is
round,
And only a ship is Death.

When I go down to the sea by ship,
And Death unfurls her sail,
Weep not for me, for there will be
A living host on another coast
To beckon and cry, "All hail!"

Robert Freeman, 1878–1940

1884. À DIEU! AND AU REVOIR

As you love me, let there be
No mourning when I go,—
No tearful eyes,
No hopeless sighs,
No woe,—nor even sadness!
Indeed I would not have you sad,
For I myself shall be full glad,
With the high triumphant gladness
Of a soul made free
Of God's sweet liberty.
—No windows darkened;
For my own
Will be flung wide, as ne'er before,
To catch the radiant inpour
Of Love that shall in full atone
For all the ills that I have done;
And the good things left undone;
—No voices hushed;
My own, full-flushed
With an immortal hope, will rise
In ecstasies of new-born bliss
And joyful melodies.

Rather, of your sweet courtesy,
Rejoice with me
At my soul's loosing from captivity.
Wish me "Bon Voyage!"
As you do a friend
Whose joyous visit finds its happy end.
And bid me both "à Dieu!"
And "au revoir!"
Since, though I come no more,
I shall be waiting there to greet you,
At His Door.

And, as the feet of The Bearers tread
The ways I trod,
Think not of me as dead,
But rather—
"Happy, thrice happy, he whose course
is sped!
He has gone home—to God,
His Father!"

John Oxenham, 1852–1941

1885. TO NIGHT

Mysterious Night! when our first parent knew
Thee from report divine, and heard thy name,
Did he not tremble for this lovely frame,
This glorious canopy of light and blue?

Yet 'neath a curtain of translucent dew,
Bathed in the rays of the great setting flame,
Hesperus with the host of heaven came,
And lo! Creation widened in man's view.

Who could have thought such darkness lay concealed
Within thy beams, O Sun! or who could find,
Whilst flower and leaf and insect stood revealed,

That to such countless orbs thou madst us blind!
Why do we then shun Death with anxious strife?
If Light can thus deceive, wherefore not Life?

Joseph Blanco White, 1775–1841

1886. From DREAMS AND REALITIES

Sometimes, I think, the things we see
Are shadows of the things to be;
That what we plan we build;
That every hope that hath been crossed,
And every dream we thought was lost,
In heaven shall be fulfilled;

That even the children of the brain
Have not been born and died in vain,
Though here unclothed and dumb;
But on some brighter, better shore
They live, embodied evermore,
And wait for us to come.

And when on that last day we rise,
Caught up between the earth and skies,
Then shall we hear our Lord
Say, Thou hast done with doubt and death,
Henceforth, according to thy faith,
Shall be thy faith's reward.

Phoebe Cary, 1824–1871

1887. From THERE IS NO DEATH

There is no death! The stars go down
To rise upon some other shore,
And bright in heaven's jeweled crown
They shine for evermore.

There is no death! the dust we tread
Shall change beneath the summer showers
To golden grain, or mellow fruit,
Or rainbow-tinted flowers.

There is no death! An angel form
Walks o'er the earth with silent tread;
He bears our best loved ones away,
And then we call them "dead."

Born unto that undying life,
They leave us but to come again;
With joy we welcome them—the same
Except in sin and pain.

And ever near us, though unseen,
The dear immortal spirits tread;
For all the boundless universe
Is life—there are no dead!

John Luckey McCreery, 1835–1906

1888. AWAY

I cannot say, and I will not say
That he is dead. He is just away.

With a cheery smile, and a wave of the hand,
He has wandered into an unknown land.

And left us dreaming how very fair
It needs must be since he lingers there.

And you—O you, who the wildest yearn
For the old-time step and the glad return—

Think of him faring on, as dear
In the love of there as the love of here;

Think of him still as the same, I say;
He is not dead—he is just away!

James Whitcomb Riley, 1849–1916

1889. FOREVER

Those we love truly never die,
Though year by year the sad memorial
wreath,
A ring and flowers, types of life and death,
Are laid upon their graves.

For death the pure life saves,
And life all pure is love; and love can reach
From heaven to earth, and nobler lessons
teach
Than those by mortals read.

Well blest is he who has a dear one dead;
A friend he has whose face will never change—
A dear communion that will not grow strange;
The anchor of a love is death.

John Boyle O'Reilly, 1844–1890

1890. ON THE DEATH OF AN AGED FRIEND

You are not dead—Life has but set you free!
Your years of life were like a lovely song,
The last sweet poignant notes of which, held long,
Passed into silence while we listened, we
Who loved you listened still expectantly!
And we about you whom you moved among
Would feel that grief for you were surely wrong—
You have but passed beyond where we can see.

For us who knew you, dread of age is past:
You took life, tiptoe, to the very last;
It never lost for you its lovely look;
You kept your interest in its thrilling book;
To you Death came no conqueror; in the end—
You merely smiled to greet another friend!

Roselle Mercier Montgomery, 1874–1933

1891. THEY SOFTLY WALK

They are not gone who pass
Beyond the clasp of hand,
Out from the strong embrace.
They are but come so close
We need not grope with hands,
Nor look to see, nor try
To catch the sound of feet.
They have put off their shoes
Softly to walk by day
Within our thoughts, to tread
At night our dream-led paths
Of sleep.

They are not lost who find
The sunset gate, the goal
Of all their faithful years.
Not lost are they who reach
The summit of their climb,
The peak above the clouds
And storms. They are not lost
Who find the light of sun
And stars and God.
They are not dead who live
In hearts they leave behind.
In those whom they have blessed
They live a life again,
And shall live through the years
Eternal life, and grow
Each day more beautiful
As time declares their good,
Forgets the rest, and proves
Their immortality.

Hugh Robert Orr, 1887–

1892. IMMORTAL

How living are the dead!
Enshrined, but not apart,
How safe within the heart
We hold them still—our dead,
Whatever else be fled!

Our constancy is deep
Toward those who lie asleep
Forgetful of the strain and mortal strife
That are so large a part of this, our earthly life.

They are our very own—
From them—from them alone
Nothing can us estrange,
Nor blight autumnal, no, nor wintry change.

The midnight moments keep a place for them
And though we wake to weep
They are beside us still in joy, in pain—
In every crucial hour, they come again
Angelic from above—
Bearing the gifts of blessing and of love
Until the shadowy path, they lonely trod
Becomes for us a bridge,
That upwards leads to God.

Florence Earle Coates, 1850–1927

1893. From HE IS RISEN

He is not dead,
Your son, your dear beloved son,
Your golden one,
With his blond touseled head,
The shining and excited words he said!
Ah no! Be comforted.
For him the world will never
Grow flat and tired and dull;
He is a part of all swift things forever,
All joyous things that run
Or fly,
Familiar to the wind and cloud and sky,
Forever beautiful!

Joseph Auslander, 1897–

1894. MEMORY

Music, when soft voices die,
Vibrates in the memory—
Odours, when sweet violets sicken,
Live within the sense they quicken.

Rose leaves, when the rose is dead,
Are heap'd for the beloved's bed;
And so thy thoughts, when thou art gone,
Love itself shall slumber on.

Percy Bysshe Shelley, 1792–1822

1895. RESURGENCE

Though he that, ever kind and true,
Kept stoutly step by step with you
Your whole long gusty lifetime through
  Be gone awhile before,
Be now a moment gone before,
Yet, doubt not, soon the seasons shall restore
    your friend to you.

He has but turned a corner—still
He pushes on with right goodwill,
Thro' mire and marsh, by heugh and hill
  That self-same arduous way,—
That self-same upland hopeful way,
That you and he through many a doubtful
    day attempted still.

He is not dead, this friend—not dead
But, in the path we mortals tread,
Got some few, trifling steps ahead
  And nearer to the end,
So that you, too, once past the bend,
Shall meet again, as face to face, this friend
    you fancy dead.

Push gaily on, strong heart! The while
You travel forward mile by mile,
He loiters with a backward smile
  Till you can overtake,
And strains his eyes, to search his wake,
Or whistling, as he sees you through the
    brake, waits on a stile.

Robert Louis Stevenson, 1850–1894

1896. FOR ALL THE SAINTS

For all the saints who from their labors rest,
Who Thee by faith before the world confessed,
Thy Name, O Jesus, be forever blessed,
    Alleluia!

Thou wast their Rock, their Fortress and
    their Might:
Thou, Lord, their Captain in the well-fought
    fight;
Thou in the darkness drear, the one true
    Light.
    Alleluia!

O may Thy soldiers, faithful, true and bold,
Fight as the saints who nobly fought of old,
And win, with them, the victor's crown of
    gold.
    Alleluia!

O blest communion, fellowship divine!
We feebly struggle; they in glory shine,
Yet all are one in Thee, for all are Thine.
    Alleluia!

And when the strife is fierce, the warfare long,
Steals on the ear the distant triumph song,
And hearts are brave again, and arms are
    strong.
    Alleluia!

The golden evening brightens in the west;
Soon, to faithful warriors cometh rest;
Sweet is the calm of paradise the blest.
    Alleluia!

But lo! there breaks a yet more glorious day;
The saints triumphant rise in bright array;
The King of glory passes on His way.
    Alleluia!

From earth's wide bounds, from ocean's
    farthest coast,
Through gates of pearl streams in the
    countless host,
Singing to Father, Son, and Holy Ghost,
    "Alleluia! Alleluia!"

William Walsham How, 1823–1897

1897. SELFISHNESS

Death takes our loved ones—
We are bowed in grief. For whom?
Are we not selfish?
A mourner weeps for himself,
The dead know nought of sorrow.

Margaret E. Bruner,
contemporary American

1898. SHED NOT TOO MANY TEARS

Shed not too many tears when I shall leave;
Be brave enough to smile.
It will not shorten, howsoe'er you grieve,
Your loneliness the while.
I would not have you sorrowful and sad,
But joyfully recall
The glorious companionship we've had,
And thank God for it all.
Don't let your face grow tear-streaked, pale and wan:
Have heart for mirth and song—
Rejoice, though for a little while I've gone,
That I was here so long.
For if I thought your faith would fail you so,
And leave you so distressed,
That sobbing to my body's grave you'd go,
My spirit could not rest.

Author unknown

1899. TURN AGAIN TO LIFE

If I should die and leave you here a while,
Be not like others, sore undone, who keep
Long vigil by the silent dust and weep.
For my sake turn again to life and smile,
Nerving thy heart and trembling hand to do
That which will comfort other souls than thine;
Complete these dear unfinished tasks of mine,
And I, perchance, may therein comfort you.

Mary Lee Hall

1900. NO FUNERAL GLOOM

No funeral gloom, my dears, when I am gone,
Corpse-gazings, tears, black raiment, graveyard grimness.
Think of me as withdrawn into the dimness,
Yours still, you mine.
Remember all the best of our past moments and forget the rest,
And so to where I wait come gently on.

Ellen Terry, 1847–1928

1901. REMEMBER

Remember me when I am gone away,
Gone far away into the silent land;
When you can no more hold me by the hand,
Nor I half turn to go, yet turning stay.
Remember me when no more day by day
You tell me of our future that you plann'd:
Only remember me; you understand
It will be late to counsel then or pray.
Yet if you should forget me for a while
And afterwards remember, do not grieve:
For if the darkness and corruption leave
A vestige of the thoughts that once I had,
Better by far you should forget and smile
Than that you should remember and be sad.

Christina G. Rossetti, 1830–1894

1902. RESIGNATION

There is no death! What seems so is transition.
This life of mortal breath
Is but a suburb of the life elysian,
Whose portal we call Death.

She is not dead,—the child of our affection,
But gone unto that school
Where she no longer needs our poor protection,
And Christ himself doth rule.

In that great cloister's stillness and seclusion,
By guardian angels led,
Safe from temptation, safe from sin's pollution,
She lives, whom we call dead.

Day after day we think what she is doing
In those bright realms of air;
Year after year her tender steps pursuing,
Behold her grown more fair.

Thus do we walk with her, and keep unbroken
The bond which nature gives,
Thinking that our remembrance, though unspoken,
May reach her where she lives.

Not as a child shall we again behold her;
For when with raptures wild
In our embraces we again enfold her,
She will not be a child;

But a fair maiden, in her Father's mansion,
Clothed with celestial grace;
And beautiful with all the soul's expansion
Shall we behold her face.

Henry Wadsworth Longfellow, 1807–1882

1903. AZRAEL

The angels in high places
  Who minister to us,
Reflect God's smile, their faces
  Are luminous;
Save one, whose face is hidden,
  (The Prophet saith).
The unwelcome, the unbidden.
  Azrael, Angel of Death.
And yet that veilèd face, I know
  Is lit with pitying eyes,
Like those faint stars, the first to glow
  Through cloudy winter skies.

That they may never tire,
  Angels, by God's decree,
Bear wings of snow and fire—
  Passion and purity;
Save one, all unavailing,
  (The Prophet saith),
His wings are gray and trailing,
  Azrael, Angel of Death.
And yet the souls that Azrael brings
  Across the dark and cold,
Look up beneath those folded wings,
  And find them lined with gold.

Robert Gilbert Walsh, 1784–1859

1904. AFTER SUNSET

I have an understanding with the hills
At evening when the slanted radiance fills
Their hollows, and the great winds let them be,
And they are quiet and look down at me.
Oh, then I see the patience in their eyes
Out of the centuries that made them wise.
They lend me hoarded memory and I learn
Their thoughts of granite and their whims of fern,
And why a dream of forests must endure
Though every tree be slain: and how the pure
Invisible beauty has a word so brief,
A flower can say it or a shaken leaf,
But few may ever snare it in a song,
Though for the quest a life is not too long.
When the blue hills grow tender, when they pull
The twilight close with gesture beautiful,
And shadows are their garments, and the air
Deepens, and the wild veery is at prayer,
Their arms are strong around me; and I know
That somehow I shall follow when you go
To the still land beyond the evening star,
Where everlasting hills and valleys are,
And silence may not hurt us any more,
And terror shall be past, and grief, and war.

Grace Hazard Conkling,
contemporary American

1905. BE COMFORTED

From "The Death of the Duke of Clarence and Avondale"

  Be comforted; . . .
The face of Death is toward the Sun of Life,
His shadow darkens earth: his truer name
Is "Onward," no discordance in the roll
And march of that Eternal Harmony
Whereto the worlds beat time, tho' faintly heard
Until the great Hereafter. Mourn in hope!

Alfred Tennyson, 1809–1892

1906. THE SLEEP

"He giveth his beloved sleep."—Psalm 127: 2

Of all the thoughts of God that are
Borne inward unto souls afar,
Along the Psalmist's music deep,
Now tell me if that any is,
For gift or grace, surpassing this:
"He giveth his belovèd—sleep?"

What would we give to our beloved?
The hero's heart to be unmoved,
The poet's star-tuned harp to sweep,
The patriot's voice to teach and rouse,
The monarch's crown to light the brows?
He giveth his belovèd—sleep.

What do we give to our beloved?
A little faith all undisproved,
A little dust to overweep,
And bitter memories to make
The whole earth blasted for our sake:
He giveth his belovèd—sleep.

"Sleep soft, beloved!" we sometimes say,
Who have no tune to charm away
Sad dreams that through the eyelids creep:
But never doleful dream again
Shall break the happy slumber when
He giveth his belovèd—sleep.

O earth, so full of dreary noises!
O men, with wailing in your voices!
O delvèd gold, the wailers heap!
O strife, O curse, that o'er it fall!
God strikes a silence through you all,
And giveth his belovèd—sleep.

His dews drop mutely on the hill,
His cloud above it saileth still,
Though on its slope men sow and reap:
More softly than the dew is shed,
Or cloud is floated overhead,
He giveth his belovèd—sleep.

Aye, men may wonder while they scan
A living, thinking, feeling man
Confirmed in such a rest to keep;
But angels say,—and through the word
I think their happy smile is *heard*—
"He giveth his belovèd—sleep."

For me, my heart that erst did go
Most like a tired child at a show,
That sees through tears the mummers leap,
Would now its wearied vision close,
Would childlike on his love repose
Who giveth his belovèd—sleep.

And friends, dear friends, when it shall be
That this low breath is gone from me,
And round my bier ye come to weep,
Let One, most loving of you all,
Say "Not a tear must o'er her fall!
He giveth his belovèd—sleep."

Elizabeth Barrett Browning, 1806–1861

1907. From ON THE DEATH OF A FRIEND'S CHILD

'Tis sorrow builds the shining ladder up,
Whose golden rounds are our calamities,
Whereon our firm feet planting, nearer God
The spirit climbs, and hath its eyes unsealed.

True is it that Death's face seems stern and cold,
When he is sent to summon those we love,
But all God's angels come to us disguised;
Sorrow and sickness, poverty and death,
One after other lift their frowning masks,
And we behold the seraph's face beneath,
All radiant with the glory and the calm
Of having looked upon the front of God.
With every anguish of our earthly part
The spirit's sight grows clearer; this was meant
When Jesus touched the blind man's lids with clay.
Life is the jailer; Death the angel sent
To draw the unwilling bolts and set us free.

James Russell Lowell, 1819–1891

1908. BEREAVED

Let me come in where you sit weeping,—aye,
Let me, who have not any child to die,
Weep with you for the little one whose love
I have known nothing of.

The little arms that slowly, slowly loosed
Their pressure round your neck; the hands you used
To kiss.—Such arms—such hands I never knew.
May I not weep with you?

Fain would I be of service—say some thing,
Between the tears, that would be comforting,—
But ah! so sadder than yourselves am I,
Who have no child to die.

James Whitcomb Riley, 1849–1916

1909. THE RESURRECTION AND THE LIFE

O little friend, I wait on you with praise,
Seeking to celebrate your early days
Of bugle, drum and gallant rocking-horse
Without complaint of tears, without remorse.

For why should man regret the silver dawn,
Now that the sun has set and from the lawn
Slow mist arises as of quiet tears
Shed for the swift futility of years.

At first when you were gone I turned my face
From life and sat upon a lonely place
Apart from men, bewailed but nursed my sorrow
And, loving yesterday, I loathed tomorrow.

Then suddenly you said, "O foolish one,
Awake, there are no dead—I *am* your son!"
And then above my sorrow and my strife
I found the Resurrection and the Life.

Robert Norwood,[1] *1874–1932*

[1] On the death of his only son.

1910. OF SUCH IS THE KINGDOM

My darling boy, so early snatched away
  From arms still seeking thee in empty air,
That thou shouldst come to me I do not pray,
  Lest, by thy coming, heaven should be less
    fair.

Stay, rather, in perennial flower of youth,
  Such as the Master, looking on, must love;
And send to me the spirit of the truth,
  To teach me of the wisdom from above.

Beckon to guide my thoughts, as stumblingly
  They seek the kingdom of the undefiled;
And meet me at its gateway with thy key,
  The unstained spirit of a little child.

Francis Greenwood Peabody, 1847–1936

1911. MATER DOLOROSA

I'd a dream to-night
  As I fell asleep,
O! the touching sight
  Makes me still to weep:
Of my little lad,
Gone to leave me sad,
Ay, the child I had,
  But was not to keep.

As in heaven high,
  I my child did seek,
There in train came by
  Children fair and meek,
Each in lily white,
With a lamp alight;
Each was clear to sight,
  But they did not speak.

Then, a little sad,
  Came my child in turn,
But the lamp he had,
  O it did not burn!
He, to clear my doubt,
Said, half turn'd about,
"Your tears put it out;
  Mother, never mourn."

William Barnes, 1801–1886

1912. AULD LANG SYNE

It singeth low in every heart,
  We hear it each and all,—
A song of those who answer not,
  However we may call:
They throng the silence of the breast,
  We see them as of yore,—
The kind, the brave, the true, the sweet,
  Who walk with us no more.

'T is hard to take the burden up,
  When these have laid it down;
They brightened all the joy of life,
  They softened every frown;
But oh, 'tis good to think of them,
  When we are troubled sore!
Thanks be to God that such have been,
  Though they are here no more.

More homelike seems the vast unknown,
  Since they have entered there;
To follow them were not so hard,
  Wherever they may fare;
They cannot be where God is not,
  On any sea or shore;
Whate'er betides, Thy love abides,
  Our God, for evermore.

John White Chadwick, 1840–1904

1913. BE STILL

Be still, my soul: the Lord is on thy side;
  Bear patiently the cross of grief or pain;
Leave to thy God to order and provide;
  In every change he faithful will remain.
Be still, my soul: thy best, thy heavenly
    Friend
Through thorny ways leads to a joyful end.

Be still, my soul: thy God doth undertake
  To guide the future as he has the past.
Thy hope, thy confidence let nothing shake;
  All now mysterious shall be bright at last.
Be still, my soul: the waves and winds still
    know
His voice who ruled them while he dwelt
    below.

Be still, my soul: the hour is hastening on
  When we shall be forever with the Lord,
When disappointment, grief, and fear are
    gone,
  Sorrow forgot, love's purest joys restored.
Be still, my soul: when change and tears are
    past,
All safe and blessed we shall meet at last.

Katharina von Schlegel, b. 1697;
tr. by Jane L. Borthwick

1914. CHRISTUS CONSOLATOR

Beside the dead I knelt for prayer,
And felt a presence as I prayed.
Lo! it was Jesus standing there.
He smiled: "Be not afraid!"

"Lord, thou hast conquered death, we know;
Restore again to life," I said,
"This one who died an hour ago."
He smiled: "She is not dead!"

"Asleep then, as thyself didst say;
Yet thou canst lift the lids that keep
Her prisoned eyes from ours away."
He smiled: "She doth not sleep!"

"Nay, then, tho' haply she doth wake
And look upon some fairer dawn,
Restore her to our hearts that ache."
He smiled: "She is not gone!"

"Alas! too well we know our loss,
Nor hope again our joy to touch,
Until the stream of death we cross."
He smiled: "There is no such!"

"Yet our beloved seem so far,
The while we yearn to feel them near,
Albeit with thee we trust they are."
He smiled: "And I am here!"

"Dear Lord, how shall we know that they
Still walk unseen with us and thee,
Nor sleep, nor wander far away?"
He smiled: "Abide in me!"

Rossiter W. Raymond, 1840–1918

1915. From THE FRIEND'S BURIAL

For all her quiet life flowed on
As meadow streamlets flow,
Where fresher green reveals alone
The noiseless ways they go.

❖

Her path shall brighten more and more
Unto the perfect day;
She cannot fail of peace who bore
Such peace with her away.

O sweet, calm face that seemed to wear
The look of sins forgiven!
O voice of prayer that seemed to bear
Our own hands up to heaven!

How reverent in our midst she stood,
Or knelt in grateful praise!
What grace of Christian womanhood
Was in her household ways!

For still her holy living meant
No duty left undone;
The heavenly and the human blent
Their kindred loves in one.

❖

She kept her line of rectitude
With love's unconscious ease;
Her kindly instincts understood
All gentle courtesies.

❖

The dear Lord's best interpreters
Are humble human souls;
The Gospel of a life like hers
Is more than books or scrolls.

John Greenleaf Whittier, 1807–1892

1916. O HAPPY SOUL

O happy soul, be thankful now, and rest!
Heaven is a goodly land;
And God is love; and those he loves are blest;
Now thou dost understand
The least thou hast is better than the best
That thou didst hope for; now upon thine eyes
The new life opens fair;
Before thy feet the blessed journey lies
Through homelands everywhere;
And heaven to thee is all a sweet surprise.

Washington Gladden, 1836–1918

1917. GO DOWN, DEATH

(A FUNERAL SERMON)

Weep not, weep not,
She is not dead;
She's resting in the bosom of Jesus.
Heart-broken husband—weep no more;

Grief-stricken son—weep no more;
Left-lonesome daughter—weep no more;
She's only just gone home.

Day before yesterday morning,
God was looking down from his great, high heaven,
Looking down on all his children,
And his eye fell on Sister Caroline,
Tossing on her bed of pain.
And God's big heart was touched with pity,
With the everlasting pity.

And God sat back on his throne,
And he commanded that tall, bright angel standing at his right hand:
Call me Death!
And that tall, bright angel cried in a voice
That broke like a clap of thunder:
Call Death!—Call Death!
And the echo sounded down the streets of heaven
Till it reached away back to that shadowy place,
Where Death waits with his pale, white horses.

And Death heard the summons,
And he leaped on his fastest horse,
Pale as a sheet in the moonlight.
Up the golden street Death galloped,
And the hoofs of his horse struck fire from the gold,
But they didn't make no sound.
Up Death rode to the Great White Throne,
And waited for God's command.

And God said: Go down, Death, go down,
Go down to Savannah, Georgia,
Down in Yamacraw,
And find Sister Caroline.
She's borne the burden and heat of the day,
She's labored long in my vineyard,
And she's tired—
She's weary—
Go down, Death, and bring her to me.

And Death didn't say a word,
But he loosed the reins on his pale, white horse,
And he clamped the spurs to his bloodless sides,
And out and down he rode,
Through heaven's pearly gates
Past suns and moons and stars;
On Death rode,
And the foam from his horse was like a comet in the sky;
On Death rode,
Leaving the lightning's flash behind;
Straight on down he came.

While we were watching round her bed,
She turned her eyes and looked away,
She saw what we couldn't see;
She saw Old Death. She saw Old Death,
Coming like a falling star.
But Death didn't frighten Sister Caroline;
He looked to her like a welcome friend.
And she whispered to us: I'm going home,
And she smiled and closed her eyes.

And Death took her up like a baby,
And she lay in his icy arms,
But she didn't feel no chill.
And Death began to ride again—
Up beyond the evening star,
Out beyond the morning star,
Into the glittering light of glory,
On to the Great White Throne.
And there he laid Sister Caroline
On the loving breast of Jesus.

And Jesus took his own hand and wiped away her tears,
And he smoothed the furrows from her face,
And the angels sang a little song,
And Jesus rocked her in his arms,
And kept a-saying: Take your rest
Take your rest, take your rest.

Weep not—weep not,
She is not dead;
She's resting in the bosom of Jesus.

James Weldon Johnson, 1871–1938

1918. EASTER EUCHARIST

Lord, where Thou art our holy dead must be,
Unpierced, as yet, the Sacramental mist;
But we are nearest them and nearest Thee
At solemn Eucharist.

O Lord, we crave for those gone home to Thee,
For those who made the earthly home so fair;
How little we may know, how little see,
Only—that Thou art there.

Dear hands unclasped from ours are clasping
Thee;
Thou holdest us forever in Thy Heart;
So close the One Communion—are we
In very truth, apart?

Lord, where Thou art our happy dead must
be;
And if with Thee, what then their boundless
bliss!
Till faith be sight; and Hope, reality;
Love's Anchorage is this.

Author unknown

1919. THE LONG LAST MILE

Carry me over the long last mile,
Man of Nazareth, Christ for me!
Weary I wait by Death's dark stile,
In the wild and the waste, where the wind
blows free;
And the shadows and sorrows come out of my
past,
Look clean through my heart,
And will not depart,
Now that my poor world has come to its last.

Lord, is it long that my spirit must wait?
Man of Nazareth, Christ for me!
Deep is the stream, and the night is late,
And grief blinds my soul that I cannot see.
Speak to me out of the silences, Lord,
That my spirit may know
As forward I go,
Thy pierc'd hands are lifting me over the
ford.

Lauchlan MacLean Watt, 1867–

1920. A THOUGHT FOR A LONELY DEATH-BED

If God compel thee to this destiny,
To die alone, with none beside thy bed
To ruffle round with sobs thy last word said,
And mark with tears the pulses ebb from
thee,—
Pray then alone, "O Christ, come tenderly!
By thy forsaken Sonship in the red
Drear wine-press,—by the wilderness
outspread,—
And the lone garden where thine agony
Fell bloody from thy brow,—by all of those
Permitted desolations, comfort mine!
No earthly friend being near me, interpose
No deathly angel 'twixt my face and thine,
But stoop thyself to gather my life's rose,
And smile away my mortal to Divine!"

Elizabeth Barrett Browning, 1806–1861

1921. ABIDE WITH ME

Abide with me! fast falls the eventide;
The darkness deepens: Lord, with me abide!
When other helpers fail, and comforts flee,
Help of the helpless, O abide with me!

Swift to its close ebbs out life's little day;
Earth's joys grow dim, its glories pass away;
Change and decay in all around I see:
O Thou who changest not, abide with me!

I need Thy presence every passing hour:
What but Thy grace can foil the tempter's
power?
Who like Thyself my guide and stay can be?
Through cloud and sunshine, O abide with
me!

I fear no foe, with Thee at hand to bless:
Ills have no weight, and tears no bitterness:
Where is death's sting? where, grave, thy
victory?
I triumph still, if Thou abide with me!

Hold Thou Thy cross before my closing eyes;
Shine through the gloom and point me to the
skies;
Heaven's morning breaks, and earth's vain
shadows flee
In life, in death, O Lord, abide with me!

Henry Francis Lyte, 1793–1847

1922. ONE LOVE

"Stricken to earth, the sword snapped in his
hand,
Shield cast away, down-beaten to the knee,
He sees the foes he made above him stand—
Now he has only Me.

The towers are fallen; at his feet they lie
Wrecks of the hopes that now he will not
see,
Naked unto the blast, Death drawing nigh—
Now he has only Me.

But he has Me. The last illusions fade,
The trumpet sounds no more, and man, set free
From tyranny of dreams his pride has made,
At last has only Me.

For many loves he now has only one,
His many gods before the tempest flee,
His light is dying, and his day is done,
But he at last has Me."

Edward Shillito, 1872–1948

1923. From PRAYER OF COLUMBUS

My terminus near,
The clouds already closing in upon me,
The voyage balk'd—the course disputed, lost,
I yield my ships to Thee. . . .

My hands, my limbs grow nerveless;
My brain feels rack'd, bewildered;
Let the old timbers part—I will not part!
I will cling fast to Thee, O God, though the waves buffet me;
Thee, Thee, at least, I know.

Walt Whitman, 1819–1892

1924. DOMINUS ILLUMINATIO MEA

In the hour of death, after this life's whim,
When the heart beats low, and the eyes grow dim,
And pain has exhausted every limb—
The lover of the Lord shall trust in Him.

When the will has forgotten the life-long aim,
And the mind can only disgrace its fame,
And a man is uncertain of his own name,
The power of the Lord shall fill this frame.

When the last sigh is heaved and the last tear shed,
And the coffin is waiting beside the bed,
And the widow and child forsake the dead,
The angel of the Lord shall lift this head.

For even the purest delight may pall,
The power must fail, and the pride must fall,
And the love of the dearest friends grow small—
But the glory of the Lord is all in all.

Richard D. Blackmore, 1825–1900

1925. TO POETS ALL

We shall not wholly die.
Perhaps some truth
That we have sung
Shall linger on,
And from some tongue
More eloquent
Shall hail the dawn
That we have glimpsed.
Though we be spent,
We shall be well content.

Thomas Curtis Clark, 1877–

1926. TRIUMPH OF THE DEFEATED

They never fail who die
In a great cause. The block may soak their gore;
Their heads may sodden in the sun; their limbs
Be strung to city gates and castle walls;
But still their spirit walks abroad.
Though years
Elapse and others share as dark a doom,
They but augment the deep and sweeping thoughts
Which overpower all others and conduct
The world, at last, to freedom.

George Gordon, Lord Byron, 1788–1824

1927. O MAY I JOIN THE CHOIR INVISIBLE

O, may I join the choir invisible
Of those immortal dead who live again
In minds made better by their presence: live
In pulses stirred to generosity,
In deeds of daring rectitude, in scorn
For miserable aims that end with self,
In thoughts sublime that pierce the night like stars,
And with their mild persistence urge man's search
To vaster issues.

So to live is heaven:
To make undying music in the world,
Breathing as beauteous order that controls
With growing sway the growing life of man.
So we inherit that sweet purity
For which we struggled, failed and agonized
With widening retrospect that bred despair.

Rebellious flesh that would not be subdued,
A vicious parent shaming still its child,—
Poor anxious penitence,—is quick dissolved;
Its discords, quenched by meeting harmonies,
Die in the large and charitable air;
And all our rarer, better, truer self,
That sobbed religiously in yearning song,
That watched to ease the burthen of the
world,
Laboriously tracing what must be,
And what may yet be better,—saw within
A worthier image for the sanctuary,
And shaped it forth before the multitude,
Divinely human, raising worship so
To higher reverence more mixed with love,—
That better self shall live till human Time
Shall fold its eyelids, and the human sky
Be gathered like a scroll within the tomb,
Unread forever.

This is life to come,
Which martyred men have made more
glorious
For us who strive to follow. May I reach
That purest heaven; be to other souls
The cup of strength in some great agony,
Enkindle generous ardor, feed pure love;
Beget the smiles that have no cruelty,
Be the sweet presence of a good diffused,
And in diffusion ever more intense!
So shall I join the choir invisible
Whose music is the gladness of the world.

George Eliot, 1819–1880

1928. OUR ECHOES ROLL FROM SOUL TO SOUL

From "The Princess," Part III

The splendor falls on castle walls
And snowy summits old in story;
The long light shakes across the lakes,
And the wild cataract leaps in glory.
Blow, bugle, blow, set the wild echoes flying,
Blow, bugle; answer, echoes, dying, dying,
dying.

O, hark, O, hear! how thin and clear,
And thinner, clearer, farther going!
O, sweet and far from cliff and scar
The horns of Elfland faintly blowing!
Blow, let us hear the purple glens replying,
Blow, bugle; answer, echoes, dying, dying,
dying.

O love, they die in yon rich sky,
They faint on hill or field or river;
Our echoes roll from soul to soul,
And grow for ever and for ever.
Blow, bugle, blow, set the wild echoes flying,
And answer, echoes, answer, dying, dying,
dying.

Alfred Tennyson, 1809–1892

1929. From SNOW-BOUND

And yet, dear heart! remembering thee,
Am I not richer than of old?
Safe in thy immortality,
What change can reach the wealth I hold?
What chance can mar the pearl and gold
Thy love hath left in trust for me?

And while in life's long afternoon,
Where cool and long the shadows grow,
I walk to meet the night that soon
Shall shape and shadow overflow,
I cannot feel that thou art far,
Since near at need the angels are;

And when the sunset gates unbar,
Shall I not see thee waiting stand,
And, white against the evening star,
The welcome of thy beckoning hand?

John Greenleaf Whittier, 1807–1892

1930. PROMOTION[1]

Great Heart is dead, they say—
What is death to such a one as Great Heart?
One sigh, perchance, for work unfinished
here—
Then a swift passing to a mightier sphere,
New joys, perfected powers, the vision clear,
And all the amplitude of heaven to work
The work he held so dear.
A soul so fiery sweet can never die
But lives and loves to all eternity.

John Oxenham, 1852–1941

1931. THE IMMORTAL RESIDUE

Wouldst thou find my ashes? Look
In the pages of my book;
And, as these thy hand doth turn,
Know here is my funeral urn.

Adelaide Crapsey, 1878–1914

[1] From "Tamate," written in memory of James Chalmers, Scottish missionary, martyred in New Guinea in 1901

1932. A CROSS OF SNOW[1]

In the long, sleepless watches of the night,
A gentle face—the face of one long dead—
Looks at me from the wall, where round its head
The night-lamp casts a halo of pale light.
Here in this room she died; and soul more white
Never through martyrdom of fire was led
To its repose; nor can in books be read
The legend of a life more benedight.
There is a mountain in the distant West
That, sun-defying, in its deep ravines
Displays a cross of snow upon its side.
Such is the cross I wear upon my breast
These eighteen years, through all the changing scenes
And seasons, changeless since the day she died.

Henry Wadsworth Longfellow, 1807–1882

1933. INSIDE OF KING'S COLLEGE CHAPEL, CAMBRIDGE

Tax not the royal saint with vain expense,
With ill-matched aims the Architect who planned,
Albeit labouring for a scanty band
Of white-robed scholars only, this immense
And glorious Work of fine intelligence!
Give all thou canst; high Heaven rejects the lore
Of nicely-calculated less or more;
So deemed the man who fashioned for the sense
These lofty pillars, spread that branching roof
Self-poised, and scooped into ten thousand cells,
Where light and shade repose, where music dwells
Lingering—and wandering on as loath to die;
Like thoughts whose very sweetness yieldeth proof
That they were born for immortality.

William Wordsworth, 1770–1850

1934. ON THE DEATH OF JOSEPH RODMAN DRAKE

Green be the turf above thee,
Friend of my better days!
None knew thee but to love thee,
Nor named thee but to praise.

Tears fell when thou wert dying,
From eyes unused to weep,
And long, where thou art lying,
Will tears the cold turf steep.

When hearts, whose truth was proven,
Like thine, are laid in earth,
There should a wreath be woven
To tell the world their worth;

And I who woke each morrow
To clasp thy hand in mine,
Who shared thy joy and sorrow,
Whose weal and woe were thine;

It should be mine to braid it
Around thy faded brow,
But I've in vain essayed it,
And feel I cannot now.

While memory bids me weep thee,
Nor thoughts nor words are free,—
The grief is fixed too deeply
That mourns a man like thee.

Fitz-Greene Halleck, 1790–1867

1935. IF MY BARK SINK

If my bark sink
'Tis to another sea.
Mortality's ground floor
Is immortality.

Emily Dickinson, 1830–1886

1936. MYSTERY

What is this mystery that men call death?
My friend before me lies; in all save breath
He seems the same as yesterday. His face
So like to life, so calm, bears not a trace
Of that great change which all of us so dread.
I gaze on him and say: He is not dead,
But sleeps; and soon he will arise and take
Me by the hand. I know he will awake
And smile on me as he did yesterday;
And he will have some gentle word to say,
Some kindly deed to do; for loving thought

[1] Written in 1879, eighteen years after the death of his wife, and found in his portfolio after his death.

Was warp and woof of which his life was
wrought.
He is not dead. Such souls forever live
In boundless measure of the love they give.

Jerome B. Bell

1937. LEGACIES

Unto my friends I give my thoughts,
Unto my God my soul,
Unto my foe I leave my love—
These are of life the whole.

Nay, there is something—a trifle—left;
Who shall receive this dower?
See, Earth Mother, a handful of dust—
Turn it into a flower.

Ethelwyn Wetherald, 1857–1940

1938. IN AFTER DAYS

In after days when grasses high
O'er-top the stone where I shall lie,
Though ill or well the world adjust
My slender claim to honoured dust,
I shall not question nor reply.

I shall not see the morning sky;
I shall not hear the night-wind sigh;
I shall be mute, as all men must,
In after days.

But yet, now living, fain were I
That some one then should testify,
Saying—"He held his pen in trust
To Art, not serving shame or lust."
Will none?—Then let my memory die
In after days!

Austin Dobson, 1840–1921

1939. THE SINGING SAVIORS

"Dead men tell no tales!" they chuckled,
As the singing saviors died,
A few serene, and many shackled,
Scourged, tortured, crucified.

Dead men tell no tales. . . . Is Shelley
Dust blown dumbly over the ground?
Are Keats and Burns silenced wholly?
Do Milton's stiff lips give no sound?

Is Shakespeare voiceless, Dante tongueless?
And, in this black, protesting year
Is the dead Jesus wordless, songless?
Listen! . . . They are all that you can hear!

Clement Wood, 1888–

1940. "MY DAYS AMONG THE DEAD"

My days among the Dead are past;
Around me I behold,
Where'er these casual eyes are cast,
The mighty minds of old:
My never-failing friends are they,
With whom I converse day by day.

With them I take delight in weal
And seek relief in woe;
And while I understand and feel
How much to them I owe,
My cheeks have often been bedewed
With tears of thoughtful gratitude.

My thoughts are with the Dead; with
them
I live in long-past years,
Their virtues love, their faults condemn,
Partake their hopes and fears;
And from their lessons seek and find
Instruction with an humble mind.

My hopes are with the Dead; anon
My place with them will be,
And I with them shall travel on
Through all Futurity;
Yet leaving here a name, I trust,
That will not perish in the dust.

Robert Southey, 1774–1843

1941. 'AND THE LIFE EVERLASTING'

It will not meet us where the shadows fall
Beside the sea that bounds the Evening Land;
It will not greet us with its first clear call
When Death has borne us to the farther strand.

It is not something yet to be revealed—
The everlasting life—'tis here and now;
Passing unseen because our eyes are sealed
With blindness for the pride upon our brow.

It calls us 'mid the traffic of the street,
And calls in vain, because our ears are lent
To these poor babblements of praise that cheat
The soul of heaven's truth, with earth's content

It dwells not in innumerable years;
It is the breath of God in timeless things—
The strong, divine persistence that inheres
In love's red pulses and in faith's white wings.

It is the power whereby low lives aspire
Unto the doing of a selfless deed,
Unto the slaying of a soft desire,
In service of the high, unworldly creed.

It is the treasure that is ours to hold
Secure, while all things else are turned to dust;
That priceless and imperishable gold
Beyond the scathe of robber and of rust.

It is a clarion when the sun is high,
The touch of greatness in the toil for bread,
The nameless comfort of the Western sky,
The healing silence where we lay our dead.

And if we feel it not amid our strife,
In all our toiling and in all our pain—
This rhythmic pulsing of immortal life—
Then do we work and suffer here in vain.

Percy Clough Ainsworth, 1873–1909

1942. THE VILLAGE ATHEIST

Ye young debaters over the doctrine
Of the soul's immortality,
I who lie here was the village atheist,
Talkative, contentious, versed in the arguments
Of the infidels.
But through a long sickness
Coughing myself to death
I read the *Upanishads* and the poetry of Jesus.
And they lighted a torch of hope and intuition
And desire which the Shadow,
Leading me swiftly through the caverns of darkness,
Could not extinguish.
Listen to me, ye who live in the senses
And think through the senses only:

Immortality is not a gift,
Immortality is an achievement;
And only those who strive mightily
Shall possess it.

Edgar Lee Masters, 1869–

1943. DEPARTED FRIENDS

They are all gone into the world of light!
And I alone sit ling'ring here;
Their very memory is fair and bright,
And my sad thoughts doth clear:

It glows and glitters in my cloudy breast
Like stars upon some gloomy grove,
Or those faint beams in which this hill is dress'd,
After the sun's remove.

I see them walking in an air of glory,
Whose light doth trample on my days:
My days which are at best but dull and hoary,
Mere glimmering and decays.

O holy Hope! And high Humility,
High as the heavens above!
These are your walks, and you have show'd them me
To kindle my cold love.

Dear, beauteous Death! the jewel of the just,
Shining nowhere but in the dark!
What mysteries do lie beyond thy dust,
Could man outlook that mark!

He that hath found some fledg'd bird's nest may know
At first sight if the bird be flown;
But what fair grove or dell he sings in now,
That is to him unknown.

And yet, as angels in some brighter dreams
Call to the soul, when man doth sleep,
So some strange thoughts transcend our wonted themes,
And into glory peep.

If a star were confin'd into a tomb,
The captive flames must needs burn there;
But when the hand that lock'd her up, gives room,
She'll shine through all the sphere.

O Father of eternal life, and all
Created glories under Thee!
Resume Thy spirit from this world of thrall
Into true liberty.

Either disperse these mists, which blot and fill
My perspective still as they pass;
Or else remove me hence unto that hill,
Where I shall need no glass.

Henry Vaughan, 1622–1695

1944. From ELEGY ON THE DEATH OF DR. CHANNING

Therefore I cannot think thee wholly gone;
The better part of thee is with us still;
Thy soul its hampering clay aside hath thrown,
And only freer wrestles with the Ill.

Thou art not idle: in thy higher sphere
Thy spirit bends itself to loving tasks,
And strength, to perfect what it dreamed of here
Is all the crown and glory that it asks.

For sure, in Heaven's wide chambers, there is room
For love and pity, and for helpful deeds,
Else were our summons thither but a doom
To life more vain than this in clayey weeds.

James Russell Lowell, 1819–1891

1945. From HELEN

The soul of the deceased, although it live
Indeed no longer, yet doth it still retain
A consciousness which lasts for ever, lodged
In the eternal scene of its abode,
The liquid ether.

Euripides, 484–406 B.C.

1946. IMMORTALITY

Foiled by our fellow-men, depressed,
outworn,
We leave the brutal world to take its way,
And, *Patience! in another life*, we say,
*The world shall be thrust down, and we
up-borne.*

And will not, then, the immortal armies scorn
The world's poor, routed leavings? or will
they,
Who failed under the heat of this life's day,
Support the fervours of the heavenly morn?

No, no! the energy of life may be
Kept on after the grave, but not begun;
And he who flagged not in the earthly strife,
From strength to strength advancing—only
he,
His soul well-knit, and all his battles won,
Mounts, and that hardly, to eternal life.

Matthew Arnold, 1822–1888

1947. THE LAND O' THE LEAL

I'm wearing awa', Jean,
Like snaw when it's thaw, Jean,
I'm wearing awa'
To the land o' the leal.
There's nae sorrow there, Jean,
There's neither cauld nor care, Jean,
The day is aye fair
In the land o' the leal.

Ye were aye leal and true, Jean,
Your task's ended noo, Jean,
And I'll welcome you
To the land o' the leal.
Our bonnie bairn's there, Jean,
She was baith guid and fair, Jean;
O we grudged her right sair
To the land o' the leal!

Then dry that tearfu' e'e, Jean,
My soul langs to be free, Jean,
And angels wait on me
To the land o' the leal.
Now fare ye weel, my ain Jean,
This warld's care is vain, Jean;
We'll meet and aye be fain
In the land o' the leal.

Carolina Oliphant, Lady Nairne, 1766–1845

1948. ONE WITH NATURE

From "Adonais"[1]

41

He lives, he wakes—'tis Death is dead, not he;
Mourn not for Adonais.—Thou young Dawn.
Turn all thy dew to splendour, for from thee
The spirit thou lamentest is not gone;
Ye caverns and ye forests, cease to moan!
Cease, ye faint flowers and fountains, and thou Air,
Which like a mourning veil thy scarf hadst thrown
O'er the abandoned Earth, now leave it bare
Even to the joyous stars which smile on its despair!

42

He is made one with Nature: there is heard
His voice in all her music, from the moan
Of thunder, to the song of night's sweet bird;
He is a presence to be felt and known
In darkness and in light, from herb and stone,
Spreading itself where'er that Power may move
Which has withdrawn his being to its own;
Which wields the world with never wearied love,
Sustains it from beneath, and kindles it above.

[1] An elegy on the death of John Keats, in Rome, in his twenty-sixth year.

43

He is a portion of the loveliness
Which once he made more lovely: he doth bear
His part, while the one Spirit's plastic stress
Sweeps through the dull dense world, compelling there
All new successions to the forms they wear;
Torturing th' unwilling dross that checks its flight
To its own likeness, as each mass may bear;
And bursting in its beauty and its might
From trees and beasts and men into the Heaven's light.

44

The splendours of the firmament of time
May be eclipsed, but are extinguished not;
Like stars to their appointed height they climb
And death is a low mist which cannot blot
The brightness it may veil. When lofty thought
Lifts a young heart above its mortal lair,
And love and life contend in it, for what
Shall be its earthly doom, the dead live there
And move like winds of light on dark and stormy air.

Percy Bysshe Shelley, 1792–1822

1949. L'ENVOI

When Earth's last picture is painted, and the tubes are twisted and dried,
When the oldest colors have faded, and the youngest critic has died,
We shall rest, and, faith, we shall need it—lie down for an aeon or two,
Till the Master of All Good Workmen shall put us to work anew.

And those that were good shall be happy: they shall sit in a golden chair;
They shall splash at a ten-league canvas with brushes of comets' hair;
They shall find real saints to draw from—Magdalene, Peter, and Paul;
They shall work for an age at a sitting, and never be tired at all!

And only the Master shall praise us, and only the Master shall blame;
And no one shall work for money, and no one shall work for fame;
But each for the joy of the working, and each, in his separate star,
Shall draw the Thing as he sees It for the God of Things as They Are!

Rudyard Kipling, 1865–1936

1950. IMMORTAL LIVING

There is immortal living now and here,
A way of life beyond the bounds of space,
A spirit life transcending death's frontier,
Where man and God meet hourly face to face.
No Euclid's mind can demonstrate the sums
Proving the problems sprung from death and birth—
Faith in immortal living only comes
To those who live immortally on earth.
First life and then belief—as flowers blow
Before the ordered science of research;
First life and faith before mankind may know
The pillared structure of a living church.
I know that spirits pass the body's tomb
Freely from life—into God's other room.

Harold T. Pulsifer, 1886–1948

1951. HEAVEN

Some seek a heaven for rest,
And some an ample shore
For doing work they cannot do
While they are prisoned here.

Some seek a heaven of song,
And others fain would rise
From an articulate utterance
To silent ecstasies.

Some seek a home in heaven,
And some would pray to be
Alone with God, beyond the reach
Of other company.

But in God's perfect heaven
All aspirations meet,
Each separate longing is fulfilled
Each separate soul complete.

Edwin Hatch, 1835–1889

1952. THE EARTH IS FULL OF GOD'S GOODNESS

If God hath made this world so fair,
Where sin and death abound,
How beautiful, beyond compare,
Will paradise be found!

James Montgomery, 1771–1854

1953. From THE BHAGAVAD-GÎTÂ

or Song Celestial

Never the spirit was born; the spirit shall cease to be never;
Never was time when it was not; End and Beginning are dreams!
Birthless and deathless and changeless remaineth the spirit for ever;
Death hath not touched it at all, dead though the house of it seems!

From the Sanskrit; tr. by Edwin Arnold, 1832–1904

1954. SURE

Father of the bare boughs, and the leaves that die,
Father of the beaten grass, where dead flowers lie,
Father of the pale fields where the snow has lain,
Are you always very sure
Spring will come again?

Father of the gray world, sick for spring's return,
Father of the dank damp, where the willows yearn,
Father of the cold wind and the haunting rain,
Are you sure that after March,
April comes again?

Father of the bare heart and the dreams that yearn,
Father of the gray soul and the thoughts that burn,
Father of the beaten hopes and the haunting pain,
Are you sure that after death
Life comes again?

Ted Robinson, contemporary American

1955. LIVING UNTO THEE

God of the living, in whose eyes
Unveiled thy whole creation lies!
All souls are thine; we must not say
That those are dead who pass away;
From this our world of flesh set free,—
We know them living unto thee.

Released from earthly toil and strife,
With thee is hidden still their life;
Thine are their thoughts, their words, their powers,
All thine, and yet most truly ours:
For well we know, where'er they be,
Our dead are living unto thee.

❖

O Breather into man of breath!
O Holder of the keys of death!
O Giver of the Life within!
Save us from death, the death of sin;
That body, soul, and spirit be
Forever living unto thee!

John Ellerton, 1826–1893

1956. BREATHE ON ME, BREATH OF GOD

Breathe on me, Breath of God;
Fill me with life anew,
That I may love what Thou dost love,
And do what Thou wouldst do.

Breathe on me, Breath of God,
Until my heart is pure,
Until with Thee I will one will,
To do and to endure.

Breathe on me, Breath of God,
Till I am wholly Thine,
Until this earthly part of me
Glows with Thy fire divine.

Breathe on me, Breath of God;
So shall I never die,
But live with Thee the perfect life
Of Thine eternity.

Edwin Hatch, 1835–1889

1957. IF A MAN DIE SHALL HE LIVE AGAIN?

From "A Blue Wave Breaking"

I will repudiate the lie
Men tell of life:
How it will pass
As fragile flower, or butterfly,
Whose dust shall nourish
April grass.

Since One, for love, died on a tree
And in the stony
Tomb has lain,
Behold I show a mystery:
All sepulchres
Are sealed in vain!

John Richard Moreland, 1880–1947

1958. THE PARADOX

Our death implicit in our birth,
We cease, or cannot be;
And know when we are laid in earth
We perish utterly.

And equally the spirit knows
The indomitable sense
Of immortality, which goes
Against all evidence.

See faith alone, whose hand unlocks
All mystery at a touch,
Embrace the awful Paradox
Nor wonder overmuch.

Ruth Pitter, contemporary English

1959. From ANDREA DEL SARTO

Ah, but a man's reach should exceed his grasp,
Or what's a heaven for?

Robert Browning, 1812–1889

1960. UPHILL

Does the road wind uphill all the way?
Yes, to the very end.
Will the day's journey take the whole long day?
From morn to night, my friend.

But is there for the night a resting-place?
A roof for when the slow dark hours begin.
May not the darkness hide it from my face?
You cannot miss the inn.

Shall I meet other wayfarers at night?
Those who have gone before.
Then must I knock or call when just in sight?
They will not keep you standing at the door.

Shall I find comfort, travel-sore and weak?
Of labor you shall find the sum.
Will there be beds for me and all who seek?
Yes, beds for all who come.

Christina G. Rossetti, 1830–1894

1961. DEAR NIGHT, THIS WORLD'S DEFEAT

Dear Night, this world's defeat,
The stop to busie fools, Care's check and curb,
The Day of Spirits, my Soul's calm retreat

Which none disturb;
Christ's progress, and his prayer time;
The hours to which high Heaven doth chime;

God's silent searching flight,
When my Lord's head is fill'd with dew, and all
His locks are wet with the clear drops of night;
His still, soft call;
His knocking time; the Soul's dumb watch
When Spirits their fair kindred catch:

Were all my loud, evil days
Calm and unhaunted as is thy dark Tent,
Whose peace but by some Angel's wing or voice,
Is seldom rent;
Then I in Heaven all the long year
Would keep, and never wander here.

There is in God, some say,
A deep but dazzling darkness: as men here
Say it is late and dusky, because they
See not all clear.
O for that Night, where I in him
Might live invisible and dim!

Henry Vaughan, 1622–1695

1962. YET LOVE WILL DREAM

Yet Love will dream, and Faith will trust,
(Since he who knows our need is just)
That somehow, somewhere, meet we must.
Alas for him who never sees
The stars shine through his cypress trees!
Who, hopeless, lays his dead away,
Nor looks to see the breaking day
Across the mournful marble play!
Who hath not learned, in hours of faith,
The truth to flesh and sense unknown,
That Life is ever Lord of Death,
And Love can never lose its own!

John Greenleaf Whittier, 1807–1892

1963. From SONG OF THE UNIVERSAL

5

All, all for Immortality!
Love, like the light, silently wrapping all!
Nature's amelioration blessing all!
The blossoms, fruits of ages—orchards divine and certain;
Forms, objects, growths, humanities, to spiritual Images ripening.

Give me, O God, to sing that thought!
Give me—give him or her I love, this quenchless faith
In Thy ensemble. Whatever else withheld, withhold not from us,
Belief in plan of Thee enclosed in Time and Space;
Health, peace, salvation universal.

Is it a dream?
Nay, but the lack of it the dream,
And, failing it, life's lore and wealth a dream,
And all the world a dream.

Walt Whitman, 1819–1892

1964. A HOPE

And, oh! there lives within my heart
A hope, long nursed by me;
(And should its cheering ray depart
How dark my soul would be!)

That as in Adam all have died,
In Christ shall all men live;
And ever round His throne abide,
Eternal praise to give.

That even the wicked shall at last
  Be fitted for the skies;
And when their dreadful doom is past
  To life and light arise.

I ask not how remote the day,
  Nor what the sinners' woe,
Before their dross is purged away;
  Enough for me to know—

That when the cup of wrath is drained,
  The metal purified,
They'll cling to what they once dis-
    dained,
  And live by Him that died.

Anne Brontë, 1820–1849

1965. From AFTER DEATH IN ARABIA

Farewell, friends! yet not farewell;
Where I am, ye too shall dwell.
I am gone before your face,
A moment's time, a little space.
When ye come where I have stepped,
Ye will wonder why ye wept;
Ye will know, by wise love taught
That here is all, and there is naught.
Weep a while, if ye are fain,—
Sunshine still must follow rain;
Only not at death,—for death,
Now I know, is that first breath
Which our souls draw when we enter
Life, which is of all life center.

Edwin Arnold, 1832–1904

1966. HE IS NOT DEAD

From "Adonais"

39

Peace, peace! he is not dead, he doth not sleep—
He hath awakened from the dream of life—
'Tis we who, lost in stormy visions, keep
With phantoms an unprofitable strife. . . .

40

He has outsoared the shadow of our night;[1]
Envy and calumny, and hate and pain,
And that unrest which men miscall delight,
Can touch him not, and torture not again. . . .

42

The One remains, the many change and pass;
Heaven's light forever shines, Earth's shadows fly;
Life, like a dome of many-colored glass,
Stains the white radiance of Eternity.

Percy Bysshe Shelley, 1792–1822

1967. IMMORTALITY

From "Lycidas"

Weep no more, woful Shepherds, weep no more,
For *Lycidas* your sorrow is not dead,
Sunk though he be beneath the watery floor.
So sinks the day-star in the Ocean bed,

[1] This line was inscribed by Theodore Roosevelt over the grave of his son, Quentin, killed in his plane in France in World War I.

And yet anon repairs his drooping head,
And tricks his beams, and with new spangled Ore,
Flames in the forehead of the morning sky:
So *Lycidas* sunk low, but mounted high,
Through the dear might of him that walk'd the waves
Where, other groves, and other streams along,
With *Nectar* pure his oozy Locks he laves,
And hears the unexpressive nuptial Song,
In the blest Kingdoms meek of joy and love.
There entertain him all the Saints above,
In solemn troops, and sweet Societies
That sing, and singing in their glory move,
And wipe the tears for ever from his eyes.
Now *Lycidas* the Shepherds weep no more;
Henceforth thou art the Genius of the shore,
In thy large recompense, and shalt be good
To all that wander in the perilous flood.

John Milton, 1608–1674

1968. FRIENDS BEYOND

I cannot think of them as dead,
Who walk with me no more;
Along the path of life I tread—
They have but gone before.

The Father's House is mansioned fair,
Beyond my vision dim;
All souls are His, and here or there
Are living unto Him.

And still their silent ministry
Within my heart hath place,
As when on earth they walked with me,
And met me face to face.

Their lives are made forever mine;
What they to me have been
Hath left henceforth its seal and sign
Engraven deep within.

Mine are they by an ownership
Nor time nor death can free;
For God hath given to love to keep
Its own eternally.

Frederick L. Hosmer, 1840–1929

1969. A GRAMMARIAN'S FUNERAL

SHORTLY AFTER THE REVIVAL OF LEARNING IN EUROPE

Let us begin and carry up this corpse,
Singing together.
Leave we the common crofts, the vulgar thorpes
Each in its tether
Sleeping safe on the bosom of the plain,
Cared-for till cock-crow:
Look out if yonder be not day again
Rimming the rock-row!
That's the appropriate country; there, man's thought,
Rarer, intenser,
Self-gathered for an outbreak, as it ought,
Chafes in the censer.

❖

Till lo, the little touch, and youth was gone!
  Cramped and diminished,
Moaned he, "New measures, other feet anon!
  My dance is finished"?
No, that's the world's way: (keep the mountainside,
  Make for the city!)
He knew the signal, and stepped on with pride
  Over men's pity;
Left play for work, and grappled with the world
  Bent on escaping:
"What's in the scroll," quoth he, "thou keepest furled?
  Show me their shaping,
Theirs who most studied man, the bard and sage,—
  Give!"—So, he gowned him,
Straight got by heart that book to its last page:
  Learned, we found him.
Yea, but we found him bald too, eyes like lead,
  Accents uncertain:
"Time to taste life," another would have said,
  "Up with the curtain!"
This man said rather, "Actual life comes next?
  Patience a moment!
Grant I have mastered learning's crabbed text,
  Still there's the comment.
Let me know all! Prate not of most or least,
  Painful or easy!
Even to the crumbs I'd fain eat up the feast,
  Ay, nor feel queasy."
Oh, such a life as he resolved to live,
  When he had learned it,
When he had gathered all books had to give!
  Sooner, he spurned it.
Image the whole, then execute the parts—
  Fancy the fabric
Quite, ere you build, ere steel strike fire from quartz,
  Ere mortar dab brick!

(Here's the town-gate reached: there's the market-place
  Gaping before us.)
Yea, this in him was the peculiar grace
  (Hearten our chorus!)
That before living he'd learn how to live—
  No end to learning:
Earn the means first—God surely will contrive
  Use for our earning.
Others mistrust and say, "But time escapes:
  Live now or never!"
He said, "What's time? Leave Now for dogs and apes!
  Man has Forever."
Back to his book then: deeper drooped his head:
  Calculus racked him:
Leaden before, his eyes grew dross of lead:
  Tussis attacked him.
"Now, master, take a little rest!"—not he!

(Caution redoubled,
Step two abreast, the way winds narrowly!)
Not a whit troubled,
Back to his studies, fresher than at first,
Fierce as a dragon
He (soul-hydroptic with a sacred thirst)
Sucked at the flagon.
Oh, if we draw a circle premature,
Heedless of far gain,
Greedy for quick returns of profit, sure
Bad is our bargain!
Was it not great? did not he throw on God,
(He loves the burthen)—
God's task to make the heavenly period
Perfect the earthen?
Did not he magnify the mind, show clear
Just what it all meant?
He would not discount life, as fools do here,
Paid by instalment.
He ventured neck or nothing—heaven's success
Found, or earth's failure:
"Wilt thou trust death or not?" He answered "Yes!
Hence with life's pale lure!"
That low man seeks a little thing to do,
Sees it and does it:
This high man, with a great thing to pursue,
Dies ere he knows it.
That low man goes on adding one to one,
His hundred's soon hit:
This high man, aiming at a million,
Misses an unit.
That, has the world here—should he need the next,
Let the world mind him!
This, throws himself on God, and unperplexed
Seeking shall find him.
So, with the throttling hands of death at strife,
Ground he at grammar;
Still, thro' the rattle, parts of speech were rife:
While he could stammer
He settled *Hoti's* business—let it be!—
Properly based *Oun*—
Gave us the doctrine of the enclitic *De*,
Dead from the waist down.
Well, here's the platform, here's the proper place:
Hail to your purlieus,
All ye highfliers of the feathered race,
Swallows and curlews!
Here's the top-peak; the multitude below
Live, for they can, there:
This man decided not to Live but Know—
Bury this man there?
Here—here's his place, where meteors shoot, clouds form,
Lightnings are loosened,
Stars come and go! Let joy break with the storm,

Peace let the dew send!
Lofty designs must close in like effects:
Loftily lying,
Leave him—still loftier than the world suspects,
Living and dying.

Robert Browning, 1812–1889

1970. CATO'S SOLILOQUY

From "Cato," Act V, sc. 1

It must be so—Plato, thou reason'st well—
Else whence this pleasing hope, this fond desire,
This longing after immortality?
Or whence this secret dread, and inward horror
Of falling into nought? Why shrinks the Soul
Back on herself, and startles at destruction?
'Tis the Divinity, that stirs within us;
'Tis Heav'n itself, that points out a hereafter,
And intimates eternity to man.
Eternity! thou pleasing, dreadful thought!
Through what variety of untried being,
Through what new scenes and changes must we pass!
The wide, th' unbounded prospect lies before me;
But shadows, clouds, and darkness rest upon it.
Here will I hold. If there's a power above us,
(And that there is, all Nature cries aloud
Through all her works,) He must delight in virtue;
And that which He delights in must be happy.
But when or where?—This world was made for Caesar.
I'm weary of conjectures—this must end 'em.
Thus am I doubly arm'd—My death and life,
My bane and antidote are both before me.
This in a moment brings me to an end;
But this informs me I shall never die.
The Soul, secured in her existence, smiles
At the drawn dagger, and defies its point;
The stars shall fade away, the Sun himself
Grow dim with age, and Nature sink in years;
But thou shalt flourish in immortal youth,
Unhurt amidst the war of elements,
The wreck of matter and the crash of worlds.

Joseph Addison, 1672–1719

1971. EVENING HYMN

The night is come like to the day,
Depart not Thou, great God, away;
Let not my sins, black as the night,
Eclipse the lustre of Thy light.
Keep still in my horizon, for to me
The sun makes not the day, but Thee.
Thou whose nature cannot sleep,
On my temples sentry keep;
Guard me 'gainst those watchful foes,
Whose eyes are open while mine close.
Let no dreams my head infest,
But such as Jacob's temples blest.
While I do rest, my soul advance,

Make my sleep a holy trance:
That I may, my rest being wrought,
Awake into some holy thought.
And with as active vigour run
My course, as doth the nimble sun.
Sleep is a death, O make me try
By sleeping what it is to die.
And as gently lay my head
On my grave, as now my bed.
Now ere I rest, great God, let me
Awake again at last with Thee.
And thus assured, behold I lie
Securely, or to wake or die.
These are my drowsy days, in vain
I do now wake to sleep again.
O come that hour, when I shall never
Sleep again, but wake for ever!

Thomas Browne, 1605–1682

1972. HEART'S HAVEN

It matters not, when I am dead,
Where this dull clay shall lie,
Nor what the dogmas, creeds and rites
Decree to us who die.

I only know that I shall tread
The paths my dead have trod,
And where the hearts I love have gone,
There I shall find my God.

Kendall Banning, 1879–1944

1973. BEYOND

It is an old belief
That on some solemn shore,
Beyond the sphere of grief
Dear friends shall meet once more.

Beyond the sphere of Time
And sin and Fate's control,
Serene in changeless prime
Of body and of soul.

That creed I fain would keep,
That hope I'll ne'er forego;
Eternal be the sleep
If not to waken so.

John Gibson Lockhart, 1794–1854

1974. From THE OARSMEN

We have known sins and evils every day and death we have known;
They pass over our world like clouds mocking us with their transient lightning laughter.
Suddenly they have stopped, become a prodigy,
And men must stand before them saying:
"We do not fear you, O Monster! for we have lived every day by conquering you,
"And we die with the faith that Peace is true, and Good is true, and true is the eternal One!"

If the Deathless dwell not in the heart of death,
If glad wisdom bloom not bursting the sheath of sorrow,
If sin do not die of its own revealment,
If pride break not under its load of decorations,
Then whence comes the hope that drives these men from their homes like stars rushing to their death in the morning light?
Shall the value of the martyrs' blood and mothers' tears be utterly lost in the dust of the earth, not buying Heaven with their price?
And when Man bursts his mortal bounds, is not the Boundless revealed that moment?

Rabindranath Tagore, 1861–1941

1975. THE CHARIOT

Because I could not stop for Death,
He kindly stopped for me;
The carriage held but just ourselves
And Immortality.

Emily Dickinson, 1830–1886

1976. WHEN ALL IS DONE

When all is done, and my last word is said,
And ye who loved me murmur, "He is dead,"
Let no one weep, for fear that I should know,
And sorrow too that ye should sorrow so.

When all is done and in the oozing clay,
Ye lay this cast-off hull of mine away,
Pray not for me, for, after long despair,
The quiet of the grave will be a prayer.

For I have suffered loss and grievous pain,
The hurts of hatred and the world's disdain,
And wounds so deep that love, well-tried and pure,
Had not the power to ease them or to cure.

When all is done, say not my day is o'er,
And that through night I seek a dimmer shore;
Say rather that my morn has just begun,—
I greet the dawn and not a setting sun,
When all is done.

Paul Laurence Dunbar, 1872–1906

1977. SIR WALTER RALEIGH'S VERSES, FOUND IN HIS BIBLE IN THE GATE-HOUSE AT WESTMINSTER

Even such is time, that takes in trust
Our youth, our joys, our all we have,
And pays us but with age and dust;
Who in the dark and silent grave,
When we have wandered all our ways,
Shuts up the story of our days.
But from this earth, this grave, this dust,
My God shall raise me up, I trust!

Walter Raleigh,[1] *1552–1618*

1978. THE BEYOND

It seemeth such a little way to me,
Across to that strange country, the Beyond;
And yet, not strange, for it has grown to be
The home of those of whom I am so fond;
They make it seem familiar and most dear,
As journeying friends bring distant countries near.

❖

And so for me there is no sting to death,
And so the grave has lost its victory;
It is but crossing with abated breath
And white, set face, a little strip of sea,
To find the loved ones waiting on the shore,
More beautiful, more precious than before.

Ella Wheeler Wilcox, 1855–1919

[1] Said to have been written the night before his execution.

1979. HE LIVES AT LAST

I would not that immortal soul reclaim,
To lift again his burden of the earth.
It is God's recognition of his worth
That sends him forth to be a living flame
Of liberated life. No transient fame,
Or wealth, or circumstance of birth,
No high adventure, or glad days of mirth
And comradeship could hold him. In the name
Of all I reverence in him, of all I love,
Forth now I speed him, armed with faith, assured
That all the glory of his mortal past,
Spread wide, will light the way, like stars above,
For those who cherish him. I have endured
His loss, triumphant that he lives at last!

Lucile Lippitt

1980. LIFE SHALL LIVE FOR EVERMORE

From "In Memoriam"

XXXIV

My own dim life should teach me this,
 That life shall live for evermore,
 Else earth is darkness at the core,
And dust and ashes all that is;

This round of green, this orb of flame,
 Fantastic beauty; such as lurks
 In some wild poet, when he works
Without a conscience or an aim.

What then were God to such as I?
 'Twere hardly worth my while to choose
 Of things all mortal; or to use
A little patience ere I die;

'Twere best at once to sink to peace,
 Like birds the charming serpent draws,
 To drop head-foremost in the jaws
Of vacant darkness and to cease.

Alfred Tennyson, 1809–1892

1981. WHY SHOULD WE WEEP FOR THOSE WHO DIE

Why should we weep for those who die?
 They fall—their dust returns to dust;
Their souls shall live eternally
 Within the mansions of the just.

They die to live—they sink to rise,
  They leave this wretched mortal shore;
But brighter suns and bluer skies
  Shall smile on them for evermore.

Why should we sorrow for the dead?
  Our life on earth is but a span;
They tread the path that all must tread,
  They die the common death of man.

The noblest songster of the gale
  Must cease, when Winter's frowns appear;
The reddest rose is wan and pale,
  When Autumn tints the changing year.

The fairest flower on earth must fade,
  The brightest hopes on earth must die:
Why should we mourn that man was made
  To droop on earth, but dwell on high?

The soul, th' eternal soul, must reign
  In worlds devoid of pain and strife;
Then why should mortal man complain
  Of death, which leads to happier life?

Charles Tennyson-Turner, 1808–1879

1982. JERUSALEM, MY HAPPY HOME

Jerusalem, my happy home,
  When shall I come to thee?
When shall my sorrows have an end?
  Thy joys when shall I see?

O happy harbor of the saints!
  O sweet and pleasant soil!
In thee no sorrow may be found,
  No grief, no care, no toil.

In thee no sickness may be seen,
  No hurt, no ache, no sore;
In thee there is no dread of death,
  But life for evermore.

Our sweet is mixed with bitter gall,
  Our pleasure is but pain,
Our joys scarce last the looking on,
  Our sorrows still remain.

But there they live in such delight,
  Such pleasure and such play,
As that to them a thousand years
  Doth seem as yesterday.

Jerusalem, my happy home,
  Would God I were in thee!
Would God my woes were at an end,
  Thy joys that I might see!

F. B. P., c. 1580. Based on St. Augustine

1983. From THE OLD ASTRONOMER

Though my soul may set in darkness, it will rise in perfect light,
I have loved the stars too fondly to be fearful of the night.

Sarah Williams, 1841–1868

1984. THE UNBELIEVABLE

Impossible, you say, that man survives
The grave—that there are other lives?
More strange, O friend, that we should ever rise
Out of the dark to walk below these skies.
Once having risen into life and light,
We need not wonder at our deathless flight.

Life is the unbelievable; but now
That this Incredible has taught us how,
We can believe the all-imagining Power
That breathed the Cosmos forth as a golden flower,
Had potence in his breath
To plan us new surprises beyond death—
New spaces and new goals
For the adventure of ascending souls.

Be brave, O heart, be brave:
It is not strange that man survives the grave:
'Twould be a stranger thing were he destroyed
Than that he ever vaulted from the void.

Edwin Markham, 1852–1940

1985. EVOLUTION

Out of the dusk a shadow,
  Then a spark;
Out of the cloud a silence,
  Then a lark;

Out of the heart a rapture,
  Then a pain;
Out of the dead, cold ashes,
  Life again.

John Banister Tabb, 1845–1909

1986. "YE WHO FEAR DEATH REMEMBER APRIL"

Ye who fear death, remember April,
With swords of jade on a thousand hills
And the warm, south wind that whispers
Of cornel and of purple squills.

Ye who fear death, remember April,
With moon-white trees, the new turned sod,
And the bare brown branch that quickens
Like a sudden thought of God.

Ye who fear death, remember April,
Earth holds the seed until that hour
Of miracle when out of clay
Comes forth at last the flame-like flower!

John Richard Moreland, 1880–1947

1987. PRAYER IN APRIL

God grant that I may never be
A scoffer at Eternity—
As long as every April brings
The sweet rebirth of growing things;
As long as grass is green anew,
I shall believe that God looks down
Upon his wide earth, cold and brown,
To bless its unborn mystery
Of leaf, and bud, and flower to be;
To smile on it from tender skies—
How could I think it otherwise?
Had I been dust for many a year,
I still would know when Spring was near,
For the good earth that pillowed me
Would whisper immortality,
And I, in part, would rise and sing
Amid the grasses murmuring.
When looking on the mother sod,
Can I doubt that this be God?
Or when a primrose smiles at me,
Can I distrust Eternity?

Sara Henderson Hay, contemporary American

1988. THE BUTTERFLY

I hold you at last in my hand,
  Exquisite child of the air.
Can I ever understand
  How you grew to be so fair?

You came to my linden tree
  To taste its delicious sweet,
I sitting here in the shadow and shine
  Playing around its feet.

Now I hold you fast in my hand,
  You marvelous butterfly,
Till you help me to understand
  The eternal mystery.

From that creeping thing in the dust
  To this shining bliss in the blue!
God give me courage to trust
  I can break my chrysalis too!

Alice Freeman Palmer, 1855–1902

1989. SEA SHELL

Out from this fluted shell the muffled roar
Murmurs monotonously to the ear—
Seas that have dashed on some Achaean shore
Now whisper to a hollow hemisphere;

And even we, who have so lately come
Upon the sands of an eternal sea,
Hold echoes of a past millennium
Sounding the drift of immortality.

Elizabeth Stanton Hardy, contemporary American

1990. WHEN I SAIL AWAY

Sometime at eve when the tide is low,
  I shall slip my mooring and sail away,
With no response to the friendly hail
  Of kindred craft in the busy bay;
In the silent hush of the twilight pale,
  When the night stoops down to embrace the day
And the voices call o'er the waters flow—
  Sometime at evening when the tide is low
I shall slip my moorings and sail away.

Through the purple shadows that darkly trail
  O'er the ebbing tide of the Unknown Sea,
I shall fare me away, with a dip of sail
  And a ripple of waters to tell the tale
Of a lonely voyager sailing away
  To Mystic Isles where at anchor lay
The crafts of those who have sailed before
  O'er the Unknown Sea to the Unknown Shore.

A few who have watched me sail away
  Will miss my craft from the busy bay;
Some friendly barks that were anchored near,
  Some loving hearts that my heart held dear,
In silent sorrow will drop a tear.
  But I shall have peacefully furled my sail
In moorings sheltered from storm or gale,
  And greeted the friends who have sailed before
O'er the Unknown Sea to the Unseen Shore.

Lizzie Clark Hardy

1991. CROSSING THE BAR

Sunset and evening star,
  And one clear call for me!
And may there be no moaning of the bar,
  When I put out to sea,

But such a tide as moving seems asleep,
  Too full for sound and foam,
When that which drew from out the boundless deep
  Turns again home.

Twilight and evening bell,
  And after that the dark!
And may there be no sadness of farewell,
  When I embark;

For tho' from out our bourne of Time and Place
  The flood may bear me far,
I hope to see my Pilot face to face
  When I have crost the bar.

Alfred Tennyson, 1809–1892

1992. 'TIS LIFE BEYOND

I watched a sail until it dropped from sight
Over the rounding sea—a gleam of light,
A last, far-flashed farewell, and, like a thought
Slipt out of mind, it vanished and was not.

Yet, to the helmsman standing at the wheel,
Broad seas still swept beneath the gliding keel;
Disaster? Change? He left no slightest sign,
Nor dreamed he of that dim horizon line.
So may it be, perchance, when down the tide
Our dear ones vanish. Peacefully they glide
On level seas, nor mark the unknown bound.
We call it death—to them 'tis life beyond.

Author unknown

1993. IF A MAN DIE

When I am dead, ah, shall I then remember,
  All the dear beauty of the fields of home,
  These winding ways where I now love to roam,
Know the enchanting June, the chill November—
See the red sumach, glowing like an ember
  On my warm hearth? And shall I also hear
  The wild winds sounding in my listening ear?
Or is the grave the end, the last December?

Shall I remember or shall I forget?
  Into the brown earth shall I then be thrust
Feel no more joy or sorrow, calm or fret,
  Be only dust returned to mother dust?
Be only soil for grass and tree wind-shaken?
Oh, *do* the dead remember and awaken?

Florence Hamilton, 1878–

1994. THE SOUL ETERNAL

If in the material world
  No atom ever perished—though
In multitudinous changes hurl'd
  Upwards and downwards, to and fro;
And all that in the present orb'd
  From silent growth and sudden storms,
Is but a former past absorb'd
  In ever-shifting frames and forms,—

If He who made the worlds that were,
  And makes the worlds that are to be,
Has with all-wise, all-potent care
  Preserved the smallest entity
Imperishable—though it pass
  From shape to shape, by heat or cold
Dispersed, attracted, monad, mass—
  A wind-blown sand, a solid mass,—

Shall He not save those nobler things,
  Those elements of mind and thought,
Whose marvellous imaginings
  Have the great deeds of progress wrought?

Those instincts, be they what they may,
  Of which the soul of man is made,
By which he works his wondrous way
  Up to the light's very fountain head? . . .

If in the cycle of the earth
  No atom of that earth can die—
The soul, which is of nobler birth,
  Must live,—and live eternally.

John Bowring, 1792–1872

1995. THE UNDYING SOUL

Yet howsoever changed or tost,
Not even a wreath of mist is lost,
No atom can itself exhaust.

So shall the soul's superior force
Live on and run its endless course
In God's unlimited universe.

John Greenleaf Whittier, 1807–1892

1996. ALTARS

Ye barren peaks, so mightily outlined
  In naked rock against the viewless sky,
Your rugged grandeur mocks my human pride,
  And rouses it to passionate reply.

Ye scorn the foot that treads your pathless ways,
  The voice that breaks your primal solitudes,
Yea, e'en the eye that views your serried heights,
  The ear that hears your canyon interludes.

Yet know that when your music-making brooks
  Have buried you beneath the conquering sea,
And mingled heart of stone with oozy mud,
  The topmost summit with the level lea,

This ear shall hear the deathless song of Life,
  This eye shall see beyond the outmost skies,
This voice shall sing soul-music, and this foot
  Shall tread the love-lit paths of Paradise.

Should I, then, born immortal, bow to you,
  Who are but transient mounds of earthy clod?—
O glorious heights!—I kneel in humble awe
  To worship at the altars of my God.

Bernard Freeman Trotter, 1890–1917

At Montecito, 1908.

1997. NOW THE LABORER'S TASK IS O'ER

Now the laborer's task is o'er;
  Now the battle day is past;
Now upon the farther shore
  Lands the voyager at last.
Father, in Thy gracious keeping
Leave we now Thy servant sleeping.

There the tears of earth are dried;
  There its hidden things are clear;
There the work of life is tried
  By a juster Judge than here.
Father, in Thy gracious keeping
Leave we now Thy servant sleeping.

❖

"Earth to earth, and dust to dust,"
  Calmly now the words we say;
Left behind, we wait in trust
  For the resurrection day.
Father, in Thy gracious keeping
Leave we now Thy servant sleeping.

John Ellerton, 1826–1893

1998. AT A BURIAL

Lord of all Light and Darkness,
  Lord of all Life and Death,
Behold, we lay in earth to-day
  The flesh that perisheth.
Take to Thyself whatever may
  Be not as dust and breath—
Lord of all Light and Darkness,
  Lord of all Life and Death.

William Watson, 1858–1935

1999. THE ENQUIRING SOUL

This busy, vast enquiring Soul
  Brooks no Controul,
  No limits will endure,
Nor any Rest: it will all see,
Not Time alone, but ev'n Eternity.
  What is it? Endless, sure.

Thomas Traherne, 1637?–1674

2000. DEATH

From "The Bhagavad-Gîtâ"

As when one layeth
His worn-out robes away,
And, taking new ones, sayeth,
  "These will I wear to-day!"
So putteth by the spirit
  Lightly its garb of flesh,
And passeth to inherit
  A residence afresh.

From the Sanskrit;
tr. by Edwin Arnold, 1832–1904

2001. WHEN LIFE'S DAY CLOSES

When on my day the evening shadows fall,
  I will go down to where a quiet river flows
Into a sea from whence no man returns;
  And there embark for lands where life
    immortal grows.

Thomas Tiplady, 1882–

2002. DEATH

From "Holy Sonnets"

10

Death, be not proud, though some have called thee
Mighty and dreadful, for thou art not so:
For those whom thou think'st thou dost overthrow
Die not, poor Death; nor yet canst thou kill me.
From rest and sleep, which but thy picture be,
Much pleasure; then from thee much more must flow;
And soonest our best men with thee do go—
Rest of their bones and souls' delivery!
Thou'rt slave to fate, chance, kings, and desperate men,
And dost with poison, war, and sickness dwell;
And poppy or charms can make us sleep as well
And better than thy stroke. Why swell'st thou then?
  One short sleep past, we wake eternally,
  And Death shall be no more: Death, thou shalt die!

John Donne, 1573–1631

2003. ON HIS BAPTISMAL BIRTHDAY

God's child in Christ adopted—Christ my all—
What that earth boasts were not lost cheaply rather
Than forfeit that blessed name, by which I call
The Holy One, the Almighty God, my Father?
Father! in Christ we live, and Christ in Thee,

Eternal Thou, and everlasting we.
The heir of heaven, henceforth I fear not death;
In Christ I live! in Christ I draw the breath
Of the true life! Let then, earth, sea, and sky
Make war against me; on my front I show
Their mighty Master's seal. In vain they try
To end my life, that can but end its woe.
Is that a deathbed where a Christian lies?
Yes, but not his—'Tis Death itself there dies.

Samuel Taylor Coleridge, 1772–1834

2004. EVEN THIS SHALL PASS AWAY

Once in Persia reigned a King,
Who upon his signet ring
'Graved a maxim true and wise,
Which, if held before the eyes,
Gave him counsel at a glance,
Fit for every change and chance.
Solemn words, and these are they:
"Even this shall pass away."

Trains of camels through the sand
Brought him gems from Samarcand;
Fleets of galleys through the seas
Brought him pearls to match with these.
But he counted not his gain
Treasures of the mine or main;
"What is wealth?" the King would say;
"Even this shall pass away."

In the revels of his court
At the zenith of the sport,
When the palms of all his guests
Burned with clapping at his jests,
He, amid his figs and wine,
Cried, "Oh, loving friends of mine!
Pleasure comes, but not to stay;
Even this shall pass away."

❖

Fighting on a furious field,
Once a javelin pierced his shield;
Soldiers with a loud lament
Bore him bleeding to his tent;
Groaning from his tortured side,
"Pain is hard to bear," he cried,
"But with patience, day by day—
Even this shall pass away."

Towering in the public square,
Twenty cubits in the air,
Rose his statue, carved in stone.
Then the King, disguised, unknown,
Stood before his sculptured name,
Musing meekly, "What is fame?
Fame is but a slow decay—
Even this shall pass away."

Struck with palsy, sere and old,
Waiting at the gates of gold,
Said he, with his dying breath:
"Life is done, but what is death?"
Then, in answer to the King,
Fell a sunbeam on his ring,
Showing by a heavenly ray—
"Even this shall pass away."

Theodore Tilton, 1835–1907

2005. "FROM GOD TO GOD"

Then since from God those lesser lives began,
And the eager Spirits entered into man,
To God again the enfranchised Soul must
tend,
He is her home, her Author is her End.
No death is hers; when earthly eyes grow dim
Starlike she soars and Godlike melts in Him.

Virgil, 70 B.C.,
tr. by F. W. H. Myers, 1843–1901

2006. AT THE DAWN

Rudyard Kipling's mother, Alice Macdonald, was not only, as her son said, "the wittiest woman in India," but a poet in her own right. One day when her brother, the Reverend F. W. Macdonald, visited her she handed him without comment these lines which she had written early that morning after a wakeful night.

As from my window at first glimpse of dawn
I watch the rising mist that heralds day,
And see by God's strong hand the curtain
drawn

That through the night has hid the world away;
So I, through windows of my soul shall see
One day Death's fingers with resistless might
Draw back the curtained gloom that shadows life,
And on the darkness of Time's deepest night,
Let in the perfect Day—Eternity.

Alice Macdonald Kipling, d. 1910

2007. AND SO AT LAST

And so at last, it may be you and I
In some far realm of blue Infinity
Shall find together some enchanted shore
Where Life and Death shall be no more,
Leaving Love only and Eternity.
When each concession Time from Life has wrung,
Like outworn garments from the Soul be flung,
And it shall stand erect, no longer bent,
Slave to the lash of Life's environment,
Even this great world of ours may shrink at last
To some bare Isla Blanca of the past—
A rock unnoticed in the mighty sea
Whose solemn pulse-beat marks Eternity.

David Starr Jordan, 1851–1931

EPITAPHS

2008. AN EPITAPH

Let us not think of our departed dead
As caught and cumbered in these graves of earth;
But think of death as of another birth,
As a new freedom for the wings outspread,
A new adventure waiting on ahead,
As a new joy of more ethereal mirth,
As a new world with friends of nobler worth,
Where all may taste a more immortal bread.

So, comrades, if you pass my grave sometime,
Pause long enough to breath this little rhyme:
"Here now the dust of Edwin Markham lies,
But lo, he is not here: he is afar
On life's great errands under brighter skies,
And pressing on toward some melodious star."

Edwin Markham, 1852–1940

2009. EPITAPH ON A FRIEND

An honest man here lies at rest,
As e'er God with His image blest:
The friend of man, the friend of truth,
The friend of age, and guide of youth:
Few hearts like his—with virtue warm'd,
Few heads with knowledge so inform'd:
If there's another world, he lives in bliss;
If there is none, he made the best of this.

Robert Burns, 1759–1796

2010. EPITAPH

Here lie I, Martin Elginbrodde;
Ha'e mercy o' my soul, Lord God;
As I wad do, were I Lord God,
An' ye were Martin Elginbrodde.

Quoted by George Macdonald, from a tombstone in Aberdeen Churchyard

2011. MY EPITAPH

Below lies one whose name was traced in sand:
He died, not knowing what it was to live:
Died, while the first sweet consciousness of manhood
To maiden thoughts electrified his soul,
Faint heatings in the calyx of the rose.
Bewildered reader, pass without a sigh
In a proud sorrow! There is life with God
In other kingdom of a sweeter air.
In Eden every flower is blown: Amen.

David Gray, 1838–1861

2012. EPITAPH

Upon a child that died

Here she lies, a pretty bud,
Lately made of flesh and blood:
Who as soon fell fast asleep
As her little eyes did peep.
Give her strewings, but not stir
The earth that lightly covers her.

Robert Herrick, 1591–1674

2013. EPITAPH ON MY FATHER

O ye, whose cheek the tear of pity stains,
Draw near with pious rev'rence, and attend!
Here lie the loving husband's dear remains,
The tender father, and the gen'rous friend.

The pitying heart that felt for human woe,
  The dauntless heart that fear'd no human pride.
The friend of man—to vice alone a foe;
  For 'ev'n his failings lean'd to virtue's side.'

Robert Burns, 1759–1796

2014. AN EPITAPH UPON HUSBAND AND WIFE, WHICH DIED, AND WERE BURIED TOGETHER

To these, whom death again did wed,
This grave's the second marriage-bed.
For though the hand of fate could force
'Twixt soul and body a divorce,
It could not sunder man and wife,
Because they both lived but one life.
Peace, good reader. Do not weep.
Peace, the lovers are asleep.
They, sweet turtles, folded lie
In the last knot love could tie.
And though they lie as they were dead,
Their pillow stone, their sheets of lead
(Pillow hard, and sheets not warm),
Love made the bed; they'll take no harm.
Let them sleep: let them sleep on,
Till this stormy night be gone,
Till the eternal morrow dawn.
Then the curtains will be drawn
And they wake into a light
Whose day shall never die in night.

Richard Crashaw, 1613?–1649

2015. EPITAPH ON HIMSELF

Stop, Christian passer-by!—Stop, child of God,
And read with gentle breast. Beneath this sod
A poet lies, or that which once seem'd he.
O, lift one thought in prayer for S. T. C.;
That he who many a year with toil of breath
Found death in life, may here find life in death!
Mercy for praise—to be forgiven for fame
He ask'd, and hoped, through Christ. Do thou the same!

Samuel Taylor Coleridge, 1772–1834

2016. REQUIEM

Under the wide and starry sky,
Dig the grave and let me lie.
Glad did I live and gladly die,
  And I laid me down with a will.

This be the verse you grave for me:
Here he lies where he longed to be;
Home is the sailor, home from sea,
  And the hunter home from the hill.

Robert Louis Stevenson,[1] 1850–1894

2017. OUR REVELS NOW ARE ENDED[2]

From "The Tempest," Act IV, sc. 1

The cloud-capp'd towers, the gorgeous palaces,
The solemn temples, the great globe itself,
Yea, all which it inherit, shall dissolve;
And, like this insubstantial pageant faded,
Leave not a wrack behind.

William Shakespeare, 1564–1616

2018. ON THE TOMB OF BLISS CARMAN

1861–1929

Have little care that life is brief
And less that art is long.
Success is in the silences,
Though fame is in the song.

From his "Songs from Vagabondia"

2019. EPITAPH PLACED ON HIS DAUGHTER'S TOMB BY MARK TWAIN

Warm summer sun,
Shine kindly here.
Warm southern wind,
Blow softly here.

Green sod above,
Lie light, lie light.
Good night, dear heart,
Good night, good night.

Adapted from
Robert Richardson, 1835–1910

[1] In keeping with the poet's request the above words were inscribed on his grave on the peak of Vaea, Samoa.
[2] Inscribed on the scroll held by the marble figure of Shakespeare in Westminster Abbey.

2020. THE EPITAPH

When from this good world I depart,
I fain would leave behind
Some record of a grateful heart
To God and all mankind—
For love of blessed home and friends,
For health and work and prayer,
For all good gifts our Father sends,
For kindness everywhere.
The broken word, neglected task
Hid talent, I confess.
But more than all, I pardon ask
For all heart heaviness.
If I have failed to give God praise
May my dumb lips be shriven—
Prepare me, Lord, some lowly place
To sing Thy praise in Heaven.

John Alexander Bouquet, 1875–
Canterbury, 1947.

BENEDICTION

From the conclusion of "The Canterbury Tales"

And fare now well, my tale is at an end.
Now Jesus Christ, that of His might may send
Joy after woe, govern us in His grace,
And keep us alle that be in this place.

Geoffrey Chaucer, 1340?–1400

INDEXES

INDEX OF AUTHORS

The birth year or life span is indicated in parentheses. The reference numbers following the biographical data are to the poems.

INDEX OF TITLES

The references are to the numbers of the poems.
(S) indicates subtitle in this volume.

INDEX OF FIRST LINES

The references are to the numbers of the poems

TOPICAL INDEX

The references are to the numbers of the poems; the topics and references set in italics embrace a subdivision in the anthology. For the convenience of ministers, teachers, and others the Topical Index follows, in general, the main subjects of Harper's Topical Concordance *compiled by Charles R. Joy.*

ACKNOWLEDGMENTS

Acknowledgment is made on the copyright pages in the front of this volume to publishers and others for permission to reproduce in this anthology poems covered by copyright. Acknowledgment is also made to the following magazines and newspapers for permission to use the poems indicated:

AMERICA for "Quo Vadis?" by Myles E. Connolly; "Prodigal" by Ellen Gilbert.

THE CHAUTAUQUA PRESS for "Song Of Hope," "Break Thou the Bread of Life" by Mary A. Lathbury.

CHICAGO TRIBUNE for "The Back of God," by J. R. Perkins.

CHRISTENDOM and the author for "Jesus of Nazareth" by Ernest Cadman Colwell.

THE CHRISTIAN CENTURY and the poets indicated for "Loyalty Hymn," "Sons of Failure" by Edith Lovejoy Pierce; "God Is Here" by Madelaine Aaron; "Strength" by Jessie W. Murton; "The Hills Keep Holy Ground" by Hellene Seaman; "We Would See Jesus" by W. J. Suckow; "Scapegoats" by Eleanor Breed; "Reflections" by Edna Becker; "Through a Fog of Stars" by John Nixon, Jr.; "One World" by Dow Brent Allinson; "World Conqueror" by Laura Simmons; "Meditation" by Antoinette Goetschius; "The Poem I Should Like to Write" by Margaret A. Windes; "These Times" by Gertrude Ryder Bennett; "Holy Places" by Herbert D. Gallaudet.

DETROIT FREE PRESS for "Unbelief" by Elizabeth York Case.

GOOD HOUSEKEEPING and the poets indicated for "Let Us Keep Christmas" by Grace Noll Crowell; "The Poet Considers Perfection" by Virginia Raplee; "Only Heaven Is Given Away" by Rose Darrough; "The Reward" by Grace Bostwick; "By Night" by Philip Jerome Cleveland (also by permission of L. Victor Cleveland).

THE NEW YORK EVENING POST, INC. for "Lines for the Hour" by Hamilton Fish Armstrong, copyright New York Evening Post, Inc.

NEW YORK HERALD TRIBUNE for "High Flight" by James G. Magee, Jr.

THE NEW YORK TIMES and the poets indicated for "Small Song" by Daniel Whitehead Hicky; "Conventionality" by Eloise Hackett.

PRESBYTERIAN TRIBUNE for "Life" by W. M. Vories; "Apprehension" by James A. Fraser.

THE PROPRIETORS OF PUNCH for "Between Midnight and Morning" by Sir Owen Seaman; "In Flanders Fields" by John McCrae.

In addition to the acknowledgments made on the copyright pages in the front of this volume, special appreciation is due the following poets or their representatives for the privilege of including poems selected from their works:

A. D. PETERS & W. N. ROUGHHEAD for "Turn Back, O Man" by Clifford Bax.

N. V. ADAM for the translation of "The Hymn of Cleanthes" from *The Vitality of Platonism and Other Essays* by James Adam.

HORACE L. FRIES for "The City of Our Hopes" by Felix Adler.

CHARLES C. ALBERTSON for "The Holy Child."

MRS. ERNEST B. ALLEN for "The Son of God Goes Forth for Peace" by Ernest B. Allen.

MRS. EVERARD J. APPLETON for "The One" from *The Quiet Courage* by Everard J. Appleton.

NORMAL AULT for "Without and Within" from his anthology *The Poet's Life of Christ*, published by the Oxford University Press.

JOSEPH AUSLANDER for "A Blackbird Suddenly" from *Sunrise Trumpets*, published by Harper & Brothers; for "Gifts without Season."

MRS. JOHN KENDRICK BANGS for "A Thanksgiving," "Blind," "I Never Knew A Night So Black" by John Kendrick Bangs.

MRS. KENDALL BANNING for "Heart's Haven" by Kendall Banning.

MRS. HENRY H. BARSTOW for "If Easter Be Not True" by Henry H. Barstow.

THE ESTATE OF KATHARINE LEE BATES for "America the Beautiful," "The Kings of the East," "Alone into the Mountain" by Katharine Lee Bates.

ELIZABETH D. R. BELLINGER for "Christus Consolator" by Rossiter W. Raymond.

MRS. ROBERT F. JEFFERYS for "Dedication," "Songs of Jesus," "The Light of God Is Falling," "O Thou Whose Feet Have Climbed Life's Hill," and the translation of "Near the Cross Her Vigil Keeping" by Louis F. Benson.

CANON JOHN ALEXANDER BOUQUET for "Sorrow Turned into Joy," "The Epitaph."

W. RUSSELL BOWIE for "The Empty Soul" from *Christianity and Crisis;* "The Continuing Christ."

THE EXECUTORS OF THE ESTATE OF WILLIAM CHARLES BRAITHWAITE for "Christ Our Contemporary" by William Charles Braithwaite.

KATHARINE BRÉGY for "Gethsemane's Gift" from *Ladders and Bridges*, published by David McKay Company.

CANON G. W. BRIGGS for "I Knew Thee Not."

WILLIAM E. BROOKS for "Memorial Day," from *Survey Graphic.*

ALICE BROWN for "Hora Christi," "Cloistered."

JOHN GILLAND BRUNINI for "Resurrection."

VINCENT G. BURNS for "Sonnet for Christmas."

MAXWELL STRUTHERS BURT for "The Hill-Born."

HILDA BURTON for "Pass It On," "A Light upon the Mountains" by Henry Burton.

AMY CARMICHAEL for "Toward Jerusalem," "In Acceptance Lieth Peace," "Think It Not Strange," "The Last Defile" from *Toward Jerusalem.*

MRS. WILLIAM HERBERT CARRUTH for "Each in His Own Tongue," "Dreamers of Dreams" from *Each in His Own Tongue and Other Poems* by William Herbert Carruth.

ALLAN KNIGHT CHALMERS for "Oh, Haunting Spirit of the Ever True" from *The Commonplace Prodigal.*

RALPH CHAPLIN for "Mourn Not the Dead."

THE GOVERNING BODY OF CHRIST CHURCH, OXFORD for "The Guest" from an early Christ Church manuscript.

THOMAS CURTIS CLARK for "The Search" from *Love off to the War and Other Poems*, and for other selections.

LESLIE SAVAGE CLARK for "The Hands of Christ."

GEORGE A. CLARKE for "The Charter of Salvation."

SARAH KENT for "Quatrain" by Sarah Cleghorn.

THE ESTATE OF FLORENCE EARLE COATES for "Immortal" by Florence Bates Coates.

E. V. COOK for "How Did You Die" by Edmund Vance Cook.

MRS. CALVIN COOLIDGE for "The Open Door."

LILIAN EDITH COX for "Never Night Again."

E. H. DANIELL for "The Silent Stars."

CAROLYN DAVIS for "Leading."

ANNA BUNSTON DE BARY for "Thou Shall Purge Me with Hysop," "A Primrose by the Wayside," "A

Wartime Prayer," "Close to the Sod," "In the Heart" from *Collected Poems of Anna Bunston de Bary*, published by the Mitre Press, London.
THE ESTATE OF MARGARET DELAND for "Life" from *From the Old Garden* by Margaret Deland.
MRS. EDWARD DOWDEN for "Communion," "Seeking God," by Edward Dowden.
LUCY G. KENDALL for "The Bridge Builder" by Will Allen Dromgoole.
MAX EASTMAN for "Truth."
MARY S. EDGAR for "The Upward Road."
MRS. MAX EHRMANN for "A Prayer" by Max Ehrmann.
MRS. H. W. FARRINGTON for "Our Christ," "The Airmen's Hymn," "Dear Lord, Who Sought at Dawn of Day" by Harry Webb Farrington.
PHIL J. FISHER for "I Die Daily."
SIR NEWMAN FLOWER for "A Creed in a Garden."
DAVID W. FOLEY for "Within the Gates."
HARRY EMERSON FOSDICK for "God of Grace and God of Glory," "The Prince of Peace," "O God in Restless Living."
FLORENCE KIPER FRANK for "The Jew to Jesus."
HELEN FRAZEE-BOWER for "This Is the Tragedy," "Who Goeth Hence" from *Inner Pilgrim*.
MRS. ROBERT FREEMAN for "God Bless Our Home," "Beyond The Horizon," "Prayer" by Robert Freeman.
WINIFRED E. GARRISON for "Thy Sea So Great."
STRICKLAND GILLILAN for "As I Go on My Way," "Folks Need a lot of Loving."
OLIVER ST. JOHN GOGARTY for "To Death."
EDWIN S. GORHAM, INC. for "Via Lucis" from *The Living Church*.
HILDA M. A. HANKEY for "Lord of Us All" by Donald Hankey.
ELIZABETH STANTON HARDY for "Sea Shell" from *Time in the Turning*.
RUTH GUTHRIE HARDING for "On a Fly-Leaf of Schopenhauer's 'Immortality'" from *The Music Makers*.
S. RALPH HARLOW for "O Young and Fearless Prophet," "Church Triumphant," "Who Is So Low."
DANIEL M. HENDERSON for "The Lilies of the Field," "Hymn for a Household."
LESLIE PINCKNEY HILL for "My Charge," and other poems.
WILLIAM HURD HILLYER for "My Master's Face."
GEORGE E. HOFFMAN for "O World of Love and Beauty."
SARA HENDERSON HAY HOLDEN for "Upon Discovering One's Own Intolerance," "The Search," "Prayer in April."
SIR MAURICE G. HOLMES for "Immanence," by Edmond G. A. Holmes.
JOHN HAYNES HOLMES for "All Hail, the Pageant of the Years," "O God of Field and City," "God of the Nations Near and Far," "Hymn of Atonement," "O Father, Thou Who Givest All," "The Voice of God Is Calling," "O God, Whose Love Is over All," "The God of Sea and Shore."
SCHARMEL IRIS for "After the Martyrdom."
CHRISTOPHER ISHERWOOD and SWAMI PRABHAVANANDA for the translation of "Give Me Your Whole Heart" from the Bhagavad-Gîtâ.
L. P. JACKS for "The Offering" by Olive Cecilia Jacks.
F. C. VAUGHAN JENKINS for "O God of Love, to Thee We Bow" by William V. Jenkins.
JOSEPHINE JOHNSON for "In This Stern Hour," from *Harper's Magazine*.
W. S. HANDLEY JONES for "He Is Not Risen" from *The Unveiling and Other Poems*.
TOYOHIKO KAGAWA for "Meditation."
HELEN KELLER for "In the Garden of the Lord."
HARRY KEMP for "The Conquerors," "The Voice of Christmas," "God, the Architect," "Joses the Brother of Jesus," and selection from "A Prayer."
HUGH THOMSON KERR for "God of Our Life," "Thy Will Be Done."
KENTON KILMER and CHRISTOPHER KILMER for "Victory" from *Selected Poems* by Aline Kilmer.
WATSON KIRKCONNELL for "The Road to Bethlehem."
GRENVILLE KLEISER for "My Daily Prayer," and selection from "The Bridge You'll Never Cross."
GLADYS LATCHAW for "My Yoke Is Easy."
MRS. HARRY LEE for "Madness," "My Master Was So Very Poor" by Harry Lee.
ELIAS LIEBERMAN for "I Am an American" from *Paved Streets;* for "It Is Time to Build" from *Man in the Shadows*.
THERESE LINDSEY for "The Man Christ."
PHILLIPS H. LORD for "Your Church and Mine" from *The Seth Parker Hymnal*, published by Carl Fischer Inc.
LILITH LORRAINE for "If He Should Come," "When Planes Outsoar the Spirit" from *Let the Patterns Break*.
ONA FREEMAN LOTHROP for "A Mother's Reward," from *American Voices 1939*.
REV. JOHN G. MAGEE for "High Flight" by John G. Magee, Jr.
MRS. G. A. MCCULLOUGH for "Thought for Easter," "Presence" by Mary Eleanor McCullough.
THE EXECUTORS OF THE ESTATE OF GEORGE MACDONALD for selections by George Macdonald.
ARTHUR R. MACDOUGALL, JR. for "The Captains of the Years" from *Far Enough for All the Years*.
CLYDE MCGEE for "Mary at the Cross," "Cross Makers."
ARCHIBALD MACLEISH for "The Young Dead Soldiers" from *Selected Poems*.
JAMES H. MCLEAN for translations of "Hymn for the Day," "The Teacher's Prayer" by Gabriela Mistral, made for this volume, courtesy Gabriela Mistral.
MRS. DOUGLAS MALLOCH for "My Son," "The Things of the Spirit" by Douglas Malloch.
ROSA ZAGNONI MARINONI for "Crushed Fender."
VIRGIL MARKHAM for "A Prayer," and selection from "Anchored to the Infinite," "The Unbelievable," "Victory in Defeat," "Revelation," "A Creed," "Brotherhood," "Outwitted," "The Man with the Hoe," "True Work Is Worship," "Breathless Awe," "The Pilgrim," "The Place of Peace," "A Free Nation," "Man-Making," "An Epitaph," "Live and Help Live," "Quatrain," "Man-Test," "The Nail-Torn God," "Earth Is Enough," and selection from "Lincoln the Man of the People" by Edwin Markham.
EARL B. MARLATT for "A World-Nation."
ANNE MARRIOTT for "Search" from *Christian Advocate.*
EDGAR LEE MASTERS for selection from "Supplication," "The Village Atheist" from *Spoon River Anthology*.
HUW MENAI for "In Our Time," "Paradox" from *The Simple Vision* published by Chapman & Hall Ltd., London.
WILLIAM P. MERRILL for "Rise Up, O Men of God," "The People's Thanksgiving."
MADELINE SWEENY MILLER for "How Far Is It to Bethlehem Town."
J. LEWIS MILLIGAN for "Where Is Thy God?"
ALAN A. MILNE for "London, 1940."
WEIR MITCHELL for "Vesperal," "Good-Night" by Dr. S. Weir Mitchell.
JOHN J. MOMENT for "How Burn the Stars Unchanging."
JOHN R. MORELAND for "Kings," "Ye Who Fear Death Remember April," "His Hands" from *Shadows at My Heel;* "To One Who Worshipped Gods of Gold," "Christ Is Crucified Anew," "The Coins of Love."
ANGELA MORGAN for "God Prays," "Song of the New

World," "Stand Forth," "The Housewife's Hymn," "Hymn to Labor," "Today."
Christopher Morley for "Private Enterprise," "The Power-House."
Elizabeth Morrow for "Wall," from *Harper's Magazine.*
David Morton for "Adoration" from *Earth's Processional;* "Symbol" from *Ships In Harbor*, published by G. P. Putnam's Sons; "Chorus for Easter," from *Saturday Review of Literature.*
Mrs. S. A. Nagel for "God and Man" by S. A. Nagel.
Captain Francis Newbolt for "Vitai Lampada," "The War Films" from *Poems New and Old* by Henry Newbolt, published by John Murray.
Joseph Fort Newton for "The White Presence."
Eric M. North for "Christ in the City," "The Waking World" by Frank Mason North.
Bishop G. Ashton Oldham for "America First" from *World Call.*
Wade Oliver for "Christ Speaks."
Arthur B. Spingarn for "The Slave" by James Oppenheim.
Hugh Robert Orr for "They Softly Walk" from *Harp of My Heart and Other Poems.*
Miss Erica Oxenham for "A Dieu! And Au Revoir," "After Work," "A New Earth," "Credo," "Dies Irae-Dies Pacis," "Great Heart," "Faith," "Follow Me," "Hearts Courageous," "How-When-Where," "Promotion," "The Coming Day," "The Cross at the Crossways," "The Sacrament of Work," "To Win the World," "Your Place," and selections from "The Vision of the Splendid" and "Pageant of Darkness and Light" by John Oxenham.
Charles Nelson Pace for "A Prayer for Today."
The Family of Albert Bigelow Paine for "The Superman," "The Little Child," "Hills of Rest" by Albert Bigelow Paine.
J. Edgar Park for "We Would See Jesus."
Edith Lovejoy Pierce for "Dirge" reprinted from *Wings.*
K. W. Porter for "To a Prince of the Church" from *Christ in the Breadline.*
Edwin McNeill Poteat for "Stigmata" published in this volume for the first time.
Alice M. Pullen for "The Quest Eternal" from *Thoughts of God for Boys and Girls*, published by the Pilgrim Press.
Hugh Wilgus Ramsaur for "World-Ruin," "Epitaph Found Somewhere in Space."
E. F. Rawnsley for "Father, Whose Will Is Life and Good" by Hardwick D. Rawnsley.
Joan Ramsey for "St. Francis of Assisi," "Green Branches."
L. L. Rice for "The Mystic" by Cale Young Rice.
Mrs. Norman E. Richardson for "A Prayer for Aviators" by Norman E. Richardson.
Jessie B. Rittenhouse for "Bethlehem," "Petition," "The Great Voice," "Sanctuary," "The High Hill" by Clinton Scollard; for "The Nightingales of Surrey" by Jessie Rittenhouse.
Henry B. Robins for "Better a Day of Faith," "Eternal Spirit Evermore Creating," "Life of Our Life," "Of One Blood Hath God Created," "The City of God," "A One Hundred Fifty-first Psalm."
Ted Robinson for "Sure," "Ditty," "Unfaith."
Mrs. John Jerome Rooney for "The Woodland Singer" by John Jerome Rooney, published by Dodd, Mead & Company, Inc.
Lady Margaret Sackville for "To One Who Denies the Possibility of a Permanent Peace."
Siegfried Sassoon for "Make Them Forget," "They," "Aftermath."
Rolland Schloerb for "O Church of God," "Thou Light of Ages," "Prayer for Peace."
R. B. Y. Scott for "Doxology for Peace," "O Voice That Calls to Me."
Odell Shepard for selection from "In the Dawn."
Edward Shillito for "Jesus of the Scars," "One Love," "Prayer of a Modern Thomas," "Ave Crux, Spes Unica!"
Lee Shippey for "A Battle Cry."
Upton Sinclair for "On a Steamship."
John R. Slater for "An Easter Reveille."
Charles Anderson Kelly for "Sometime," "The Tree-Top Road" by May Riley Smith.
A. J. M. Smith for "Good Friday" from *News of the Phoenix* (also permission of Ryerson Press, Toronto).
Hilda W. Smith for "The Carpenter of Galilee."
Dr. Solomon Solis-Cohen for "Spiritual Vision."
Eleanor B. Stock for "The Prayer of the Spirit."
Arthur Stringer for "The Final Lesson," "The Keeper" from *The Woman in The Rain and Other Poems*, published by Little, Brown & Company.
Hildegarde Hoyt Swift for "The Teacher."
Miriam Teichner for "Awareness."
Afton Thacker for "I Found God."
Mary Dixon Thayer for "Prayer."
Charles Hanson Towne for "Silence," "A Song at Easter," "An Easter Canticle."
Reginald Trotter for "Altars," "The Songs We Need," "Ici Repose" from *A Canadian Twilight and Other Poems* by Bernard Freeman Trotter, published by McClelland and Stewart, Ltd.
Nancy Byrd Turner for "Let Us Have Peace," "Prayer on Christmas Eve," "The Christmas Star."
Henry Hallam Tweedy for "Christmas at Babbitt's," "Eternal God Whose Power Upholds."
John Curtis Underwood for "The Strong."
Consuela Valencia for "After Christmas."
Blanche Shoemaker Wagstaff for "Pilgrimage."
Laughlan MacLean Watt for "I Bind My Heart," "The Tryst," "The Long Last Mile."
Thomas Wearing for "New Year" from *The Tower and Other Verse.*
Horace Westwood for "A Psalm of Confidence."
Mary Brent Whiteside for "Who Has Known Heights."
Mr. Vyoyan Beresford Holland, Executor, for "E. Tenebris;" selections from "The Ballad of Reading Gaol" by Oscar Wilde.
Clement Wood for "The Singing Saviors."

PERSONAL INDEX